Births, Deaths and Marriages

on

California's Mendocino Coast

FORT BRAGG

MENDOCINO

UKIAH

Volume Two

1910–1919

Mendocino Coast
Genealogical Society

Heritage Books
2024

HERITAGE BOOKS
AN IMPRINT OF HERITAGE BOOKS, INC.

Books, CDs, and more—Worldwide

For our listing of thousands of titles see our website
at
www.HeritageBooks.com

Published 2024 by
HERITAGE BOOKS, INC.
Publishing Division
5810 Ruatan Street
Berwyn Heights, MD 20740

Heritage Books by MCGS:

Births, Deaths and Marriages on California's Mendocino Coast: Volume 1, 1889–1909

Births, Deaths and Marriages on California's Mendocino Coast: Volume 2, 1910–1919

Births, Deaths and Marriages on California's Mendocino Coast: Volume 3, 1920–1929

Births, Deaths and Marriages on California's Mendocino Coast: Volume 4, 1930–1939

Births, Deaths and Marriages on California's Mendocino Coast: Volume 5, 1940–1949

Births, Deaths and Marriages on California's Mendocino Coast: Volume 6, 1950–1959

Births, Deaths and Marriages on California's Mendocino Coast: Volume 7, 1960–1969

Births, Deaths and Marriages on California's Mendocino Coast: Volume 8, 1970–1979

Births, Deaths and Marriages on California's Mendocino Coast: Volume 9, 1980–1989

Births, Deaths and Marriages on California's Mendocino Coast: Volume 10, 1990–1999
Items from the Fort Bragg Advocate-News

CD: *Births, Deaths and Marriages on California's Mendocino Coast, Volumes 1–4*

International Standard Book Number
Paperbound: 978-0-7884-0609-6

INTRODUCTION

THIS VOLUME

This volume is the second in a series chronicling the births, deaths and marriages in one of California's more remote and beautiful counties from 1910 through 1919.

Mendocino County occupies over ninety miles of California's rugged North Pacific Coast. Unpopulated by other than native peoples until 1851, the region's immense stands of giant redwoods attracted several waves of immigration from the rest of the United States, Canada and Europe to work in the woods, sawmills, railroads, ranches and harbors. Many of their activities and achievments were reported by the local newspapers from 1877. The first volume of this series recorded information originally published in the *Fort Bragg Advocate* from its inception in 1889 through 1909. This second volume continues the record through 1919.

THE DECADE

The period covered by this volume probably represents the greatest change in the coastal county's life. The rough and tumble aspect of pioneer life was moderated by the advent of electricity, extension of the telephone network and completion of the railroad that connected (1912) the coast with the rest of the Nation's system. Improvement of education, medical services (the hospital opened 1915), establishment of civic organizations such as a chamber of commerce in Fort Bragg (1915), slow improvement of roads for the growing numbers of automobiles and extension of agriculture were notable. While over 600 sawmills have been identified in Mendocino County from 1852 to the present, logging of the redwoods reached a peak in this period. The greatest impact on the County's history, however, was the World War which called a substantial number of young men to service outside the county and stimulated many others to migrate to the San Francisco Bay area to work in war-related industries.

THE NEWSPAPER

The newspaper accounts collected for this volume came from the *Fort Bragg Advocate* established May 29, 1889 and published continously to date. The publisher, Charles J.Cavanagh, acquired the paper in 1893 and ran it until his death in 1925. A typical country paper of four to six pages, copy was hand set so that birth, death and marriage notices tended to be brief. In the early part of the decade the paper acquired a Linotype machine. That purchase along with low cost newsprint resulted (1912) in an 8 page newspaper with a corresponding expansion of coverage. Birth, death and marriage notices along with news, reports of social events, legal notices, court proceedings, filings with the county recorder, advertising plus items from other local and regional papers expanded to fill the space available. The resulting volume of information included in this publication for a ten year span equaled the previous twenty year period.

THE PEOPLE

The first non-native arrivals to Mendocino County were primarily white Americans who came to California either across the great plains by wagon, horse or on foot or sailed to San Francisco with a land crossing at Panama. The first groups of foreign peoples came first from Canada and then from northern Europe attracted by the lumberjobs in the woods. Finns were a major element before the turn of the century followed by a wave of Portuguese mostly from the Azores. Many of the latter first worked in the Hawaii cane fields before coming to Mendocino County. In the first decade of the twentieth century the principal origin of new immigrants was Italy, primarily from the northern sections. In 1921 the Federal census reported 20% of the county were foreign born with 35 countries represented, Italy and Finland being the largest contributors.

The War

This volume contains a special section listing the names of Mendocino County men serving in World War I. These are listings of Selective Service registrations, calls to physical examinations, results thereof, draft numbers, reported delinquincies, calls to active duty, service performed, *etc.* as reported in the newspaper. A 1927 Roll of the Dead is shown on the final page.

THE DATA AND STYLE

This volume of births, deaths and marriages for the years 1910 through 1919 is similar to Volume One. Some of the news items were edited to provide a normal presentation of information; minor extraneous material was deleted.

As in the earlier work children and women's names are often lacking. Birth announcements usually mention the father's name, rarely the mother's and seldom the child's. The death of a child, especially before the age of twelve, was announced as the child of the father. Women's death notices rarely mentioned the deceased's maiden name; only their married name was reported, *i.e.* Mrs.A.B.Smith, wife of A.B.Smith, or, sometimes, Mrs.Anna Smith. Fortunately, marriage records often gave the bride's maiden surname. Yet, a change is to seen in this decade. As the reportage expanded, death notices began to include names of survivors, their residences, circumstances of death, some personal attributes, place of burial, and officiating clergy. The marriage notices also expanded to include parents' names, relatives, location and date of ceremony and officiating judge or clergy.

The spelling of names are generally shown as printed with obvious errors corrected. Many immigrants anglicized their names on arrival in the United States or, if retaining their native spellings, came up with a great variety of different combinations. Children often changed their names when first attending school as foreign spellings and strange vowel combinations sometimes complicated their acceptance. The publisher of the newspaper set down a wide range of strange name spellings in his newspaper and little attempt has been made to correct or change his product.

THE MENDOCINO COAST GENEALOGICAL SOCIETY

The Mendocino Coast Genealogical Society, founded in 1976, has supported and sponsored the production of this book as a community project to record the local history of Fort Bragg's pioneer settlers and their descendants. The assistance and enthusiasm of the publisher and staff of the *Fort Bragg Advocate-News*, successor to the *Fort Bragg Advocate*, is gratefully acknowledged and deeply appreciated by the Society's researchers.

Eugene M.Lewis
Editor and Compiler
August 7, 1996

TABLE OF CONTENTS

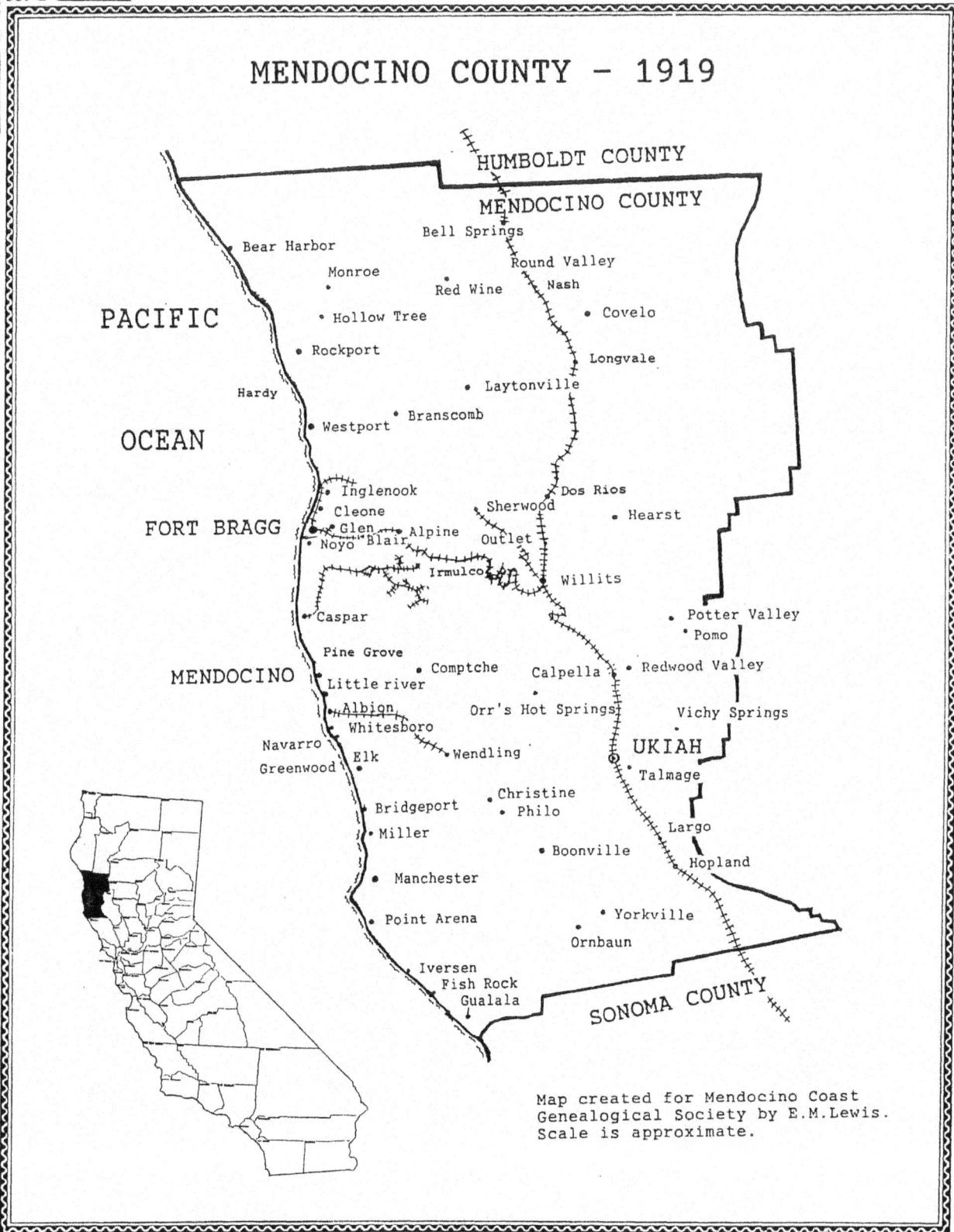

MENDOCINO COUNTY – 1919

HUMBOLDT COUNTY

MENDOCINO COUNTY

PACIFIC

OCEAN

FORT BRAGG

MENDOCINO

Bell Springs

Bear Harbor

Monroe

Red Wine

Round Valley

Nash

Covelo

Hollow Tree

Rockport

Longvale

Hardy

Laytonville

Westport

Branscomb

Inglenook

Dos Rios

Cleone

Sherwood

Hearst

Glen

Alpine

Noyo

Blair

Outlet

Irmulco

Willits

Caspar

Potter Valley

Pomo

Pine Grove

Comptche

Calpella

Redwood Valley

Little river

Orr's Hot Springs

Vichy Springs

Albion

Whitesboro

Navarro

Elk

Wendling

UKIAH

Greenwood

Talmage

Christine

Philo

Largo

Bridgeport

Miller

Boonville

Hopland

Manchester

Point Arena

Yorkville

Ornbaun

Iversen

Fish Rock

Gualala

SONOMA COUNTY

Map created for Mendocino Coast
Genealogical Society by E.M.Lewis.
Scale is approximate.

Births Reported	Issue Date
A son was born to the wife of I.J.Abbott in Fort Bragg July 30, 1918.	Jul 31, 1918
A daughter was born to the wife of Andrew Abramson of Elk in Fort Bragg April 21, 1919.	Apr 23, 1919
A daughter was born to the wife of August Ackaman at Albion February 19, 1910.	Mar 2, 1910
A son was born to the wife of J.R.Adama at Pine Grove May 19, 1915.	May 26, 1915
A son was born to the wife of Ah Hee at Mendocino June 2, 1913.	Jun 11, 1913
A daughter was born to the wife of Ah Sing at Mendocino September 15, 1913.	Sep 17, 1913
A son was born to the wife of P.Aime at Greenwood May 10, 1911.	May 24, 1911
A son was born to the wife of W.J.Ainsworth at Willits April 29, 1913.	May 7, 1913
A daughter was born to the wife of Gus Akins at Willits August 2, 1914.	Aug 12, 1914
A son was born to the wife of Guy Akins at Willits October 11, 1915.	Oct 20, 1915
A son was born to the wife of Frank Albrecht at Inglenook January 5, 1917.	Jan 10, 1917
A son was born to the wife of Charles Alexander at Mendocino March 13, 1916.	Mar 15, 1916
A son was born to the wife of W.H.Alfred at Ukiah July 24, 1914.	Jul 29, 1914
A daughter was born to the wife of Albert A.Anderson at Albion May 12, 1913.	May 21, 1913
A daughter was born to the wife of Ed Anderson at Mitchell Creek August 14, 1911.	Aug 16, 1911
A daughter was born to the wife of Harry Anderson near Iversen Landing December 29, 1918.	Jan 8, 1919
A son was born to the wife of Andrew Andrea at Fort Bragg December 16, 1918.	Dec 18, 1918
A son was born to the wife of L.Andreani of Fort Bragg "last week".	Nov 27, 1912
A daughter was born to Louise Andreani in Fort Bragg June 25, 1914.	Jul 1, 1914
A son was born to the wife of Andrew Andreas in Fort Bragg August 15, 1917.	Aug 22, 1917
A daughter was born to the wife of Florine Anker in Ukiah October 15, 1916.	Oct 18, 1916
A son was born to the wife of H.Atwood at Mendocino February 5, 1916.	Feb 9, 1916
A son was born to the wife of H.A.Atwood at Mendocino January 5, 1917.	Jan 10, 1917

A son was born to the wife of Fred <u>Aulin</u> at Fort Bragg   Jul 30, 1913
July 26, 1913.

A daughter was born to the wife of J.L.<u>Austin</u>   Oct 19, 1910
October 13, 1910.

A daughter was born to the wife of Fred <u>Avers</u> of Talmage   Feb 5, 1913
January 20, 1913.

A daughter was born to the wife of George <u>Azbil</u> at Covelo Sep 7, 1910
August 25, 1910.

A daughter was born to the wife of Fred <u>Babbit</u> at Fort Bragg May 15, 1918
May 11, 1918.

A daughter was born to the wife of J.H.<u>Babcock</u> at Largo   Jul 19, 1911
July 5, 1911.

A daughter was born to the wife of Dr.Raymond <u>Babcock</u> at   Nov 8, 1916
Willits October 29, 1916.

A son was born to the wife of Peter <u>Back</u> in Fort Bragg   Jun 14, 1916
June 8, 1916.

A son was born to the wife of Fred <u>Backlund</u> at Fort Bragg Feb 24, 1915
"last week".

A daughter was born to the wife of Gordon <u>Baechtel</u> at   Jul 11, 1917
Willits July 3, 1917.

A son was born to the wife of Luther <u>Baechtel</u> in Willits   Nov 5, 1913
"last week".

A son was born to the wife of Alfred <u>Bainbridge</u> in Fort   Sep 4, 1918
Bragg September 2, 1918.

A ten pound son was born to the wife of Harold <u>Bainbridge</u> at Dec 10, 1919
Fort Bragg December 4, 1919.

A daughter was born to the wife of R.P.<u>Baker</u> at Fort Bragg Mar 17, 1915
March 3, 1915.

A daughter was born to the wife of Ned <u>Ball</u>, *nee* Addie   Jun 16, 1915
Scott, at Fort Bragg June 9, 1915.

A daughter was born to the wife of Ned <u>Ball</u> at Ten Mile   Aug 15, 1917
[no date reported]

A nine pound son was born to the wife of Ned <u>Ball</u> at Ten   Nov 27, 1918
Mile November 25, 1918.

A son was born to the wife of Walter <u>Ball</u> at Camp 7 in the Oct 4, 1911
Noyo woods September 30, 1911.

A daughter was born to the wife of Jack <u>Barlow</u> at Monroe   Mar 12, 1919
February 23, 1919.

A son was born to the wife of Harold <u>Barnard</u> at Westport   Aug 23, 1916
"this week".

A daughter was born to the wife of Harold <u>Barnard</u>   Dec 4, 1918
"last week" at Westport.

A son was born to the wife of Al <u>Barnes</u> of Albion   Jul 9, 1919
[no date reported].

A daughter was born to the wife of George <u>Barnes</u> at   Nov 25, 1914
Littleriver November 16, 1914.

A son was born to the wife of W.<u>Barnes</u> at Navarro   Mar 24, 1915
[no date reported].

2

A 10½ pound son was born to the wife of Earl <u>Barnett</u>, son of George Barnett formerly of Fort Bragg, in Continental, Arizona, January 7, 1918.	Jan 23, 1918
A nine pound son was born to the wife of Allen <u>Barns</u> at Albion December 23, 1917.	Dec 26, 1917
A daughter was born to the wife of G.E.<u>Barquist</u> in Fort Bragg August 5, 1915.	Aug 11, 1915
A daughter was born to the wife of Frank <u>Barto</u> at Willits May 30, 1913.	Jun 11, 1913
A daughter was born to the wife of Henry <u>Bartow</u> at Willits February 21, 1910.	Feb 23, 1910
A son was born to the wife of John <u>Bauer</u> at Willits January 25, 1917.	Feb 7, 1917
A ten pound daughter was born to the wife of Dr <u>Baxter</u> at Gonzales July 18, 1917.	Jul 25, 1917
A daughter was born to the wife of Luther <u>Bean</u> at Willits May 29, 1915.	Jun 9, 1915
A daughter was born to the wife of Walter <u>Beane</u> in Fort Bragg March 18, 1914.	Mar 25, 1914
A daughter was born to the wife of Ira <u>Beasley</u> of Northwestern at Willits October 2, 1916.	Oct 11, 1916
A daughter was born to the wife of Carl <u>Beattie</u> at Willits September 10, 1914.	Sep 23, 1914
A daughter was born to the wife of F.L.<u>Bechtol</u> at Ukiah April 6, 1917.	Apr 11, 1917
An eight pound son was born to the wife of Ed <u>Beck</u> in Fort Bragg April 5, 1919.	Apr 9, 1919
A daughter was born to the wife of T.<u>Beebe</u> at Fish Rock September 2, 1914.	Sep 9, 1914
A daughter was born to the wife of William <u>Beebe</u> at Schooner Gulch December 10, 1910.	Dec 21, 1910
A son was born to the wife of C.<u>Beef</u> at Talmage February 2, 1911.	Feb 15, 1911
A son was born to the wife of Harry <u>Bell</u>, nee Vera Smith of Mendocino, in San Francisco January 27, 1917.	Jan 31, 1917
Twins, a boy and a girl, were born to the wife of <u>Bendetti</u> at Fort Bragg August 16, 1914.	Aug 19, 1914
A son was born to the wife of A.<u>Bendetti</u> of Fort Bragg November 23, 1912.	Nov 27, 1912
A son was born to the wife of A.<u>Bendetti</u> at Fort Bragg December 20, 1917.	Dec 26, 1917
A son was born to the wife of P.<u>Bendetti</u> at Fort Bragg July 15, 1916.	Jul 19, 1916
A son was born to the wife of Mr.<u>Benedetti</u> at Noyo February 5, 1914.	Feb 11, 1914
A son was born to the wife of J.L.<u>Benoit</u> at Ukiah January 1, 1910.	Jan 12, 1910

A daughter was born to the wife of C.B.Benton at Ukiah September 5, 1911.	Sep 13, 1911
A daughter was born to the wife of Mr.Benz at Willits February 1, 1912.	Feb 7, 1912
A son was born to the wife of W.F.Benz at Willits October 19, 1914.	Oct 28, 1914
A daughter was born to the wife of P.Berringer at Fort Bragg January 30, 1913.	Feb 5, 1913
A son was born to the wife of Perley Berringer at Fort Bragg February 11, 1914.	Feb 11, 1914
A nine pound daughter was born to the wife of J.C.Berry at Fort Bragg April 27, 1911.	May 3, 1911
A daughter, the 13th child, was born to the wife of George Berryhill at Fort Bragg January 12, 1917.	Jan 17, 1917
A daughter was born to the wife of Otto Bertini at Irmulco August 29, 1919.	Sep 3, 1919
A son was born to the wife of James Biaggi Jr. at Point Arena January 7, 1919.	Jan 15, 1919
A son was born to the wife of G.A.Bigelow in Berkeley August 5, 1914. The mother was the former Edith McCornack.	Aug 19, 1914
A son was born to the wife of J.W.Bills in Fort Bragg November 11, 1916.	Nov 15, 1916
A son was born to the wife of A.Bishop of Point Arena in Fort Bragg May 23, 1919.	May 28, 1919
A ten pound son was born to the wife of Austin Bishop at Point Arena January 14, 1918.	Jan 23, 1918
A daughter was born to the wife of C.Bishop at Point Arena July 15, 1917.	Jul 25, 1917
A son was born to the wife of Chester E.Bishop of Point Arena September 11, 1918. The baby died September 20th.	Sep 18, 1918 Sep 25, 1918
A son was born to the wife of E.Bishop at Point Arena August 4, 1914.	Aug 12, 1914
A seven pound daughter was born to the wife of Ed Bishop at Fort Bragg December 6, 1919.	Dec 10, 1919
A son was born to the wife of Fred Bishop of Manchester in San Francisco September 5, 1919.	Sep 17, 1919
A son was born to the wife of Herbert Bishop at Point Arena May 16, 1913.	May 28, 1913
A daughter was born to the wife of Herbert Bishop of Point Arena February 20, 1916.	Mar 1, 1916
A daughter was born to the wife of Perry Bishop at Point Arena November 9, 1918.	Nov 20, 1918
A son was born to the wife of Mr.Bither July 12, 1918.	Jul 17, 1918
A daughter was born to the wife of Dwain Bittenbender at Northwestern February 17, 1915.	Feb 24, 1915
A son was born to the wife of Carl Bjorkas at Fort Bragg November 20, 1915.	Dec 1, 1915

Births Reported	Issue Date
A daughter, 6½ pounds was born to the wife of Mr.Blackledge, nee Esther Rasmussen of Fort Bragg, in Oakland "last week".	Jun 2, 1915
A son was born to the wife of Freeman Blakely of Fort Bragg September 14, 1913.	Sep 17, 1913
A son was born to the wife of Roy Blosser in Santa Rosa "last week".	Dec 29, 1915
A daughter was born to the wife of T.R.Bolden in Fort Bragg March 14, 1913.	Mar 19, 1913
A son was born to the wife of Ben Boni at Fort Bragg February 20, 1915.	Feb 24, 1915
A daughter was born to the wife of O.Bonini at Willits April 21, 1913.	Apr 30, 1913
Anastasia Bortolomei born in Fort Bragg about November 1918, the daughter of Roberto Bortolomei, was adopted at the age of 5 months by city attorney Leonard and Helen Stone. The child's name was changed to Elizabeth "Betty" Stone. The mother, N.Bortolomei, died January 22, 1919.	Jan 29, 1919
A son was born to the wife of Chester Bourne of Mendocino March 3, 1912.	Mar 13, 1912
A son was born to the wife of Edwin Bower at Noyo December 12, 1915.	Dec 15, 1915
A daughter was born to the wife of Fred Bradley at Willits [no date reported].	Aug 13, 1919
A son was born to the wife of Paul Bradley at Willits February 24, 1915.	Mar 3, 1915
A nine pound son was born to the wife of Leo Brandon at Fort Bragg December 29, 1919.	Dec 31, 1919
A son was born to the wife of L.Brandt at Covelo February 2, 1912.	Feb 14, 1912
A son was born to the wife of Arthur Branscomb at Laytonville April 19, 1910.	Apr 27, 1910
A 9½ pound son was born to the wife of Albert Brien at Mendocino February 23, 1918.	Feb 27, 1918
A son was born to the wife of Chester Briggs at Albion July 23, 1916.	Aug 2, 1916
A son was born to the wife of Atley Bowles at Point Arena December 26, 1909.	Jan 19, 1910
A son was born to the wife of Atley Bowles at Point Arena August 10, 1911.	Aug 16, 1911 Aug 30, 1911
A daughter was born to the wife of Atley Bowles of Point Arena January 11, 1913.	Jan 22, 1913
A daughter was born to the wife of Atley Bowles at Point Arena November 24, 1914.	Dec 2, 1914
A daughter was born to the wife of B.Bowman at Willits May 15, 1910.	May 25, 1910
A daughter was born to the wife of James Bowman of Mendocino December 9, 1912.	Dec 18, 1912
A daughter was born to the wife of James Bowman at Mendocino July 20, 1917.	Jul 25, 1917

A daughter was born to the wife of Antone Bozani of Fort Bragg February 14, 1914. — Feb 18, 1914

A daughter was born to the wife of C. Brink at Fort Bragg May 12, 1914. — May 13, 1914

A son was born to the wife of Clarence Broback at Fort Bragg June 26, 1911. — Jun 28, 1911

A daughter was born to the wife of Henry Brock of Fort Bragg December 2, 1915. — Dec 8, 1915

A son was born to the wife of A.C. Brooks of Caspar at the Mendocino State Hospital May 12, 1912. — May 22, 1912

A daughter was born to the wife of Clyde Brooks at Willits [no date reported]. — Aug 13, 1919

A son was born to the wife of A.M. Brown at Covelo January 14, 1912. — Jan 31, 1912

A daughter was born to the wife of Charles Brown at Fort Bragg February 14, 1917. — Feb 21, 1917

A son was born to the wife of Charles Brown in Fort Bragg August 9, 1917. — Aug 15, 1917

A son was born to the wife of Herbert Brown at Willits December 16, 1916. — Dec 27, 1916

A son was born to the wife of Howard Brown at Camp Curry in Yosemite Valley Park August 21, 1917. — Aug 29, 1917

A daughter was born to the wife of J. McAllen Brown November 19, 1915. — Nov 24, 1915

A daughter was born to the wife of James Brown at Willits [no date reported]. — Aug 13, 1919

A son was born to the wife of R.L. Brown at Albion June 7, 1914. — Jun 17, 1914

A daughter was born to the wife of Mr. Bruckridge at Point Arena November 10, 1917. — Dec 12, 1917

A daughter was born to the wife of Bert Bruckridge at Point Arena April 1, 1913. — Apr 9, 1913

A son was born to the wife of Den Brush at Round Valley "last week". — Mar 5, 1913

A daughter was born to the wife of Henry Brush at Covelo January 20, 1913. — Feb 5, 1913

A daughter was born to the wife of I. Brush at Covelo February 7, 1912. — Feb 21, 1912

A daughter was born to the wife of Victor Buccheoni at Fort Bragg August 21, 1916. — Aug 23, 1916

A son was born to the wife of H. Bucknell at Covelo May 2, 1911. — May 10, 1911

A son was born to the wife of F.C. Bull at Ukiah April 30, 1913. — May 7, 1913

A daughter was born to the wife of J.W. Bullis at Fort Bragg August 8, 1919. — Aug 13, 1919

A son was born to the wife of W.A. Burke at Willits January 25, 1913. — Jan 29, 1913

A son was born to the wife of W.C.Burke in the Ukiah Valley June 25, 1919.

Jul 2, 1919

A daughter was born to the wife of William Burke May 15, 1914.

May 20, 1914

A son was born to the wife of J.O.Burnges at Point Arena "yesterday".

May 7, 1913

A son was born to the wife of Mr.Burns, ticket agent of the Northwestern Pacific Railroad, at Willits August 11, 1915.

Aug 25, 1915

A daughter was born to the wife of Chris Burns at Ukiah September 17, 1911.

Oct 4, 1911

A stillborn child was born to Mrs.J.L.Burr at Fort Bragg March 16, 1911.

Mar 22, 1911

A daughter was born to the wife of J.L.Burr of Noyo August 6, 1917.

Aug 8, 1917

An eleven pound son was born to the wife of L.Burr at their home between Noyo and Caspar June 19, 1919.

Jul 2, 1919

A daughter was born to the wife of John Burton at Willits June 8, 1911.

Jun 14, 1911

A daughter was born to the wife of Ed Busch,, nee Marie Brown of Mendocino, in Portland, Oregon, "last week".

Dec 24, 1919

Daughter was born to the wife of David Bush, nee Aila Holm, in Oakland February 25, 1919. The mother was the daughter of Mrs.Dora Holm and a former schoolteacher in Mendocino.

Mar 5, 1919

An eleven pound son was born to the wife of W.M.Butts August 28, 1916.

Sep 27, 1916

A daughter was born to the wife of Harry Byers at Point Arena October 18, 1911.

Nov 1, 1911

A ten pound son was born to the wife of Chester Byrne of Mendocino "last week".

Feb 12, 1913

A son was born to the wife of G.Byrne at Gualala January 6, 1917.

Jan 10, 1917

A son, Philip, was born to the wife of Jack Byrnes in San Francisco February 7, 1914. She was the former Mamie Jefferson of Fort Bragg.

Feb 11, 1914
Feb 9, 1921

A daughter was born to the wife of John Byrnes [no date reported].

May 15, 1912

A son was born to the wife of Sheriff Ralph Byrnes in Ukiah February 5, 1914.

Feb 11, 1914

A son was born to the wife of Mr.Cable at Fort Bragg August 14, 1911.

Aug 16, 1911

A daughter was born to the wife of Richard Caldwell at Ten Mile October 25, 1913.

Oct 29, 1913

A son was born to the wife of Richard Caldwell July 9, 1918.

Jul 17, 1918

A daughter was born to the wife of J.Calli at Bridgeport March 24, 1915.

Mar 31, 1915

A son was born to the wife of A.Cameron at Comptche June 4, 1911.

Jun 14, 1911

A daughter was born to the wife of Archie Cameron Jr. at Fort Bragg January 9, 1915.

Jan 13, 1915

A son was born to the wife of Archie Cameron at Fort Bragg October 2, 1919. — Oct 8, 1919

A son was born to the wife of Rod Cameron at Manchester March 9, 1915. — Mar 17, 1915

A son was born to the wife of Rod Cameron at Mendocino August 6, 1918. — Aug 7, 1918

A son was born to the wife of Mr.Campbell at Noyo February 8, 1914. — Feb 11, 1914

A daughter was born to the wife of Dr.F.McLain Campbell of Fort Bragg September 15, 1915. — Sep 22, 1915

A son was born to the wife of Fred Campbell at Noyo December 13, 1914. — Dec 16, 1914

A son was born to the wife of S.B.Campbell at Ukiah December 9, 1910. — Dec 21, 1910

A daughter was born to the wife of Maurice R.Carey in San Francisco "last week". — Apr 6, 1910

A son was born to the wife of S.F.Carey in Fort Bragg December 13, 1910. — Dec 14, 1910

A son was born to the wife of S.F.Carey at Fort Bragg October 25, 1912. — Oct 30, 1912

A daughter was born to the wife of R.Carlson at Albion February 24, 1915. — Mar 3, 1915

A son was born to the wife of William Carlson at Caspar May 16, 1915. — May 19, 1915

A son was born to the wife of William Carlson near Caspar September 26, 1916. — Oct 4, 1916

A son was born to the wife of Bert Carmichael at Albion July 27, 1915. — Aug 4, 1915

A daughter was born to the wife of Thomas Carmichael at Mendocino May 27, 1912. — Jun 5, 1912

A daughter was born to the wife of Tom Carmichael in Fort Bragg March 8, 1916. — Mar 15, 1916

A son was born to the wife of B.Carner at Covelo March 24, 1913. — Apr 2, 1913

A daughter was born to the wife of Elmer Carner at Willits March 14, 1914. — Mar 25, 1914

A son was born to the wife of W.A.Carpenter at Caspar October 15, 1915. — Oct 20, 1915

A daughter was born to the wife of Herbert Carr of Manchester April 21, 1913. — Apr 23, 1913

A daughter was born to the wife of Herbert Carr at Manchester September 16, 1915. — Sep 29, 1915

A son was born to the wife of Buck Carter in Ukiah August 15, 1910. — Aug 31, 1910

A son was born to the wife of R.H.Carter of Ukiah May 1, 1917. — May 9, 1917

A daughter was born to the wife of William Carter of Longvale October 4, 1916. — Oct 11, 1916

A daughter was born to the wife of Matt Casey at East Mendocino September 25, 1914. — Sep 30, 1914

A son was born to the wife of Ed Cavanagh in Fort Bragg April 24, 1911. — Apr 26, 1911

A daughter was born to the wife of J.A. Cedarquist at Willits January 19, 1915. — Jan 27, 1915

A daughter was born to the wife of E.W. Chalmers at Point Arena June 30, 1916. — Jul 5, 1916

A 9½ pound daughter was born to the wife of E.W. Chalmers at Point Arena April 29, 1918. — May 1, 1918

A son was born to the wife of Hadley Chambers at Mendocino May 2, 1912. — May 8, 1912

An eight pound son was born to the wife of Francis Chandler at Fort Bragg February 6, 1917. — Feb 7, 1917

A daughter was born to the wife of Rev. H.D. Chandler, a former pastor of the Point Arena Presbyterian church, in Berkeley "recently". — Aug 13, 1919

A son was born to the wife of W.R. Chandler at Willits July 17, 1913. — Jul 30, 1913

A daughter was born to the wife of H.C. Chapin in San Francisco March 23, 1918. Chapin formerly ran the Grand Hotel in Fort Bragg. — Apr 3, 1918

A son was born to the wife of Samuel Chase at Willits December 24, 1919. — Dec 31, 1919

A daughter, the second child, was born to the wife of T.A. Cheal in Burlingame April 30, 1918. — May 1, 1918

A daughter was born to the wife of Theodore Chester, formerly of Fort Bragg, at Fruitvale on May 29, 1910. — Jun 15, 1910

A son was born to the wife of Mike Christiani at Northspur [no date reported]. — Jul 28, 1915

A ten pound son was born to the wife of Mike Christiani at Alpine "this week". — Dec 6, 1916

A daughter was born to the wife of M.A. Christy of the Ukiah valley September 1, 1916. — Sep 6, 1916

A son was born to the wife of V. Church at Ukiah August 12, 1915. — Aug 18, 1915

A daughter was born to the wife of Charles Ciancio in Ukiah January 6, 1916. — Jan 12, 1916

A son was born to the wife of Mr. Cittoni at Covelo January 6, 1913. — Feb 5, 1913

A ten pound son was born to the wife of the Rev. A.H. Clark at Point Arena January 27, 1913. — Feb 5, 1913

A daughter was born to the wife of Frank Clark of Laytonville at Berkeley October 16, 1916. [date may be November 16th]. — Nov 22, 1916

A daughter was born to the wife of L.S. Clark at Albion September 17, 1917. — Sep 26, 1917

A daughter was born to the wife of Scott Clark at Albion March 15, 1915. — Mar 17, 1915

A son was born to the wife of W.H.Clark at Willits May 2, 1912.	May 22, 1912
A son was born to the wife of W.M.Clark at Willits April 21, 1913.	Apr 30, 1913
A daughter was born to the wife of W.A.Clow, nee Stella Bever, in San Francisco August 27, 1916.	Sep 6, 1916
A son was born to the wife of Lester Clyma at Ukiah May 2, 1916.	May 17, 1916
A son was born to the wife of Dr.W.A.Colburn, formerly of Fort Bragg, in San Francisco February 21, 1912.	Feb 28, 1912
A son was born to the wife of P.Colby at Caspar August 5, 1914.	Aug 12, 1914
A daughter was born to the wife of Percy Colby in Caspar September 19, 1913.	Sep 24, 1913
A son was born to the wife of Percy Colby at Caspar February 6, 1916.	Feb 9, 1916
A nine pound son was born to the wife of Cyrus J.Cole at Fort Bragg September 2, 1916.	Sep 20, 1916
Twin daughters were born to the wife of J.Colli in Willits "last week".	May 26, 1915
A son was born to the wife of E.S.Compton at Willits July 3, 1915.	Jul 14, 1915
A son was born to the wife of W.Conkey at Mendocino August 19, 1917.	Aug 22, 1917
A son was born to the wife of W.R.Conner at Covelo May 1, 1912.	May 22, 1912
A son, eleven pounds, was born to the wife of P.J.Conway at Ukiah "last week".	Jun 23, 1915
A daughter was born to the wife of C.E.Cook at Wendling December 4, 1917.	Dec 19, 1917
A son was born to Vera Cook at Point Arena "last week".	Feb 17, 1915
A son was born to the wife of W.B.Coombs in San Francisco April 6, 1911.	Apr 12, 1911
A son was born to the wife of Mr.Cooney at Irmulco August 6, 1912.	Aug 14, 1912
A daughter was born to the wife of John Cooney in Richmond "last week".	Jun 25, 1919
A daughter was born to Mrs.Cooper nee Lita Olds formerly of Fort Bragg, in Fruitvale June 7, 1911.	Jun 14, 1911
A son was born to the wife of A.Copland at Fort Bragg October 2, 1918.	Oct 9, 1918
A daughter was born to the wife of Nat Copeland at Caspar July 24, 1914.	Jul 29, 1914
A daughter was born to the wife of Nat Copeland at Caspar February 15, 1916.	Feb 16, 1916
A son was born to the wife of B.Corbet Jr. at Willits April 18, 1915.	Apr 28, 1915

A son was born to the wife of Ed Corbett at Willits
May 20, 1913.   May 28, 1913

A daughter was born to the wife of Charles Corda at Willits   Apr 2, 1913
March 23, 1913.

A son was born to the wife of R.Corville at Cleone   Nov 8, 1911
November 3, 1911.

A daughter, 10 pounds, was born to the wife of   May 14, 1919
R.Corville in Fort Bragg May 9, 1919.

A son was born to the wife of M.Coska at Albion   Jun 5, 1912
May 23, 1912.

A son was born to the wife of J.G.Court at Willits   Nov 15, 1911
November 7, 1911.

A son was born to the wife of W.S.Cowles at Fort Bragg May 22, 1918
May 19, 1918.

A son was born to the wife of Elbert Cox in Ukiah   Jun 2, 1915
May 27, 1915.

A son was born to the wife of J.F.Cox in Fort Bragg   Jun 4, 1913
"last week".

A ten pound daughter was born to the wife of W.A.Cox,   May 10, 1916
a salesman for the firm of Baker and Hamilton.
[no other details].

A daughter was born to the wife of Pearl Crawford   Sep 30, 1914
in the Ukiah valley September 22, 1914.

A daughter was born to the wife of George Cremonini of Mar 18, 1914
of Manchester March 6, 1914.

A son was born to the wife of C.J.Cretser at Fort Bragg Dec 3, 1913
November 26, 1913.

A son was born to the wife of Charles Cretser at Fort   Jan 12, 1916
Bragg January 2, 1916.

A daughter was born to the wife of Charles Crispin at   May 4, 1910
Point Arena April 17, 1910.

A son was born to the wife of E.W.Crocker of Fort Bragg Oct 26, 1910
October 25, 1910.

A daughter was born to the wife of Al Culver of Caspar Dec 31, 1919
December 28, 1919.

A daughter was born to the wife of Dr.Cureton at Fort Bragg   Jan 14, 1914
January 12, 1914.

A son was born to the wife of C.Cureton at Point Arena Oct 12, 1910
October 7, 1910.

An eight pound son was born to the wife of C.A.Curtis in Jun 26, 1918
San Francisco June 19, 1918.

A son was born to the wife of Ernest Cuthbertson at   Jul 26, 1916
Manchester July 18, 1916.

A ten pound son was born to the wife of Aner Dahl in   Apr 9, 1919
Los Gatos April 2, 1919.

A daughter was born to the wife of Erich Dahl at   Oct 1, 1919
Manchester September 20, 1919.

A son was born to the wife of John Dahl at Fort Bragg   Apr 12, 1916
April 6, 1916.

A daughter was born to the wife of G.Dahlberg at Fort Bragg August 16, 1914.	Aug 19, 1914
A daughter was born to the wife of W.H.Dahle at Willits March 13, 1911.	Mar 22, 1911
A son was born to the wife of John Dalin at Westport April 23, 1915.	Apr 28, 1915
A daughter was born to the wife of P.L.Daniels at Mendocino September 29, 1910.	Oct 5, 1910
A daughter was born to the wife of J.E.Danska in Fort Bragg "last week".	May 14, 1919
A daughter was born to the wife of G.Daubensek at Albion April 13, 1910.	Apr 27, 1910
A son was born to the wife of Louis Daum at Bridgeport November 23, 1911.	Dec 20, 1911
A son was born to the wife of M.Davidson at Willits February 22, 1911.	Mar 1, 1911
Twin sons were born to the wife of W.F.Davis of Albion in Lakeport September 25, 1915.	Sep 29, 1915
A son was born to the wife of A.S.Day at Ukiah August 15, 1911.	Aug 30, 1911
A son was born to the wife of Leslie Day of Philo November 14, 1914.	Nov 18, 1914
A son was born to the wife of Harry Deal at Covelo July 14, 1917.	Jul 25, 1917
A son was born to the wife of H.G.Dean at Point Arena May 2, 1910.	May 4, 1910
A daughter was born to the wife of Joe Dean at Long Beach August 28, 1918.	Sep 11, 1918
A daughter was born to the wife of Lester Deane at Ukiah May 23, 1910.	Jun 1, 1910
Twin daughters were born to the wife of T.DeBernardi in San Francisco December 18, 1911. He owned land on the Noyo and operated the Fremont House Hotel in San Francisco.	Jan 3, 1912
A son was born to the wife of Peter Della Bosca of Ten Mile November 13, 1917.	Nov 21, 1917
A son was born to the wife of H.J.Dellett of Fort Bragg August 2, 1910.	Aug 10, 1910
A daughter was born to the wife of J.Del Rauolls of Fort Bragg "last week".	Jul 15, 1914
A son was born to the wife of James Dempsey at Fort Bragg December 6, 1914.	Dec 9, 1914
A son, the fourth child, was born to the wife of James Dempsey in Fort Bragg November 22, 1919.	Nov 26, 1919
A son was born to the wife of Ardie Dennan at Point Arena July 4, 1910.	Jul 6, 1910
A daughter was born to the wife of R.L.Dennen of Point Arena in San Francisco March 1, 1919.	Mar 5, 1919
A daughter was born to the wife of Joseph Dias at Mendocino March 17, 1913.	Mar 26, 1913

A daughter was born to the wife of Mr.Dietsche at Albion October 7, 1917. — Oct 17, 1917

A daughter was born to the wife of Albert Dilling at Point Arena July 19, 1910. — Aug 10, 1910

A daughter was born to the wife of Frank Dilling in Elk May 3, 1911. — May 24, 1911

A son was born to Mr.Dini at Glen Blair August 28, 1912. — Sep 4, 1912

A daughter was born to the wife of Pete Dixon at Fort Bragg March 15, 1914. — Mar 25, 1914

An 11 pound son was born to the wife of Fred Dodge December 31, 1910. — Jan 11, 1911

A son was born to the wife of H.Dodge at Fort Bragg April 29, 1913. — Apr 30, 1913

A son was born to the wife of James Doig at Caspar February 2, 1915. — Feb 10, 1915

A daughter was born to the wife of James Doig at Caspar November 10, 1916. — Nov 15, 1916

A daughter was born to the wife of Thomas Dollard October 27, 1914. — Nov 4, 1914

A daughter was born to the wife of M.Domenigoni of Fort Bragg June 29, 1914. — Jul 1, 1914

A son was born to the wife of Mr.Dominogini at Fort Bragg January 21, 1919. — Feb 26, 1919

A son was born to the wife of Robert Donaldson at Fern Grove May 6, 1910. — May 18, 1910

A daughter was born to the wife of Martin Donohoe at Ukiah May 5, 1910. — May 11, 1910

A son was born to the wife of P.R.Donohoe at Mendocino October 20, 1913. — Oct 29, 1913

A daughter was born to the wife of Marvin Dooley at Hopland April 7, 1917. — Apr 11, 1917

A nine pound son was born to the wife of Thomas Dornan [no date reported], *nee* Flossie Woodward. — Jan 17, 1912

A daughter was born to the wife of F.Dougherty at Point Arena February 25, 1911. — Mar 15, 1911

A daughter was born to the wife of Mr.Drake near Gualala June 21, 1914. — Jun 24, 1914

A son was born to the wife of Fay Dryden at Fort Bragg September 19, 1916. — Sep 20, 1916

A daughter was born to the wife of Ralph Duncan of Willits in Ukiah October 28, 1913. — Nov 5, 1913

A son was born to the wife of Roy Dunlap at Covelo December 12, 1911. — Dec 27, 1911

A son was born to the wife of Theodore Dunlap at Covelo August 19, 1915. — Sep 1, 1915

A daughter was born to the wife of Mr.Dunwal in Fort Bragg "last week". — Apr 14, 1915

A daughter was born to the wife of Albert H.Dusick   Jun 16, 1915
June 9, 1915.

A daughter was born to the wife of Jesse Dwinelle at   Sep 20, 1911
Mendocino September 4, 1911.

A daughter was born to the wife of Ed Dyer of Sherwood at   Nov 11, 1914
Willits November 1, 1914.

A daughter was born to the wife of Raymond Dyer at Westport Oct 30, 1912
[no date reported].

A daughter was born to the wife of Bert Eagle at Caspar   Oct 8, 1913
September 28, 1913.

A son was born to the wife of W.Taylor Eddie August 30, 1915 Sep 8, 1995
in Potter Valley.

A daughter was born to the wife of Mr.Edwards at Ukiah   Oct 6, 1915
September 28, 1915.

A son was born to the wife of Fred Eisenhauer at Potter   Apr 11, 1917
Valley April 6, 1917.

A son was born to the wife of J.Elliott at Willits   May 22, 1912
May 4, 1912.

A daughter was born to the wife of Jack Elliott at Willits Nov 18, 1914
November 8, 1914.

A son was born to the wife of C.Ellison at Fort Bragg   Jun 26, 1918
June 21, 1918.

A daughter was born to the wife of Larry Ellison at   May 22, 1918
Mendocino May 17, 1918.

A five pound daughter was born to the wife of W.A.Elmslie   Jun 16, 1915
of Caspar in Fort Bragg June 9, 1915.

A son was born to the wife of W.English at Covelo   Apr 2, 1913
March 19, 1913.

A son was born to the wife of Ed Enright at Inglenook   Jan 9, 1918
December 26, 1917. The baby died January 4, 1918.

A son was born to the wife of Ed Enright of Ten Mile   Apr 9, 1919
"last week".

A child was born to Mrs.Erickson on the South Fork   Jun 11, 1919
of the Noyo June 6, 1919. [sex unspecified.]

A daughter was born to the wife of Eric Erickson   Mar 22, 1916
at Gualala March 16, 1916.

A son was born to the wife of E[rnest].H.Escher of San Mateo Mar 10, 1915
March 4, 1915. Mrs.Escher was the daughter of George Taylor
of Fort Bragg.

A son was born to the wife of Ernest H.Escher, *nee* Hazel   Mar 22, 1916
Taylor, the daughter of George Taylor of Fort Bragg, in
Mill Valley March 15, 1916.

A son was born to the wife of Ernest H.Escher, *nee* Hazel   Jul 24, 1918
Taylor of Fort Bragg, in Mill Valley "this week".

A son was born to the wife of Andrew Escola at Wendling   Mar 20, 1918
March 11, 1918. Escola was a locomotive engineer.

John Leslie Escola, son of John and Nannie (*nee* Flood)   May 5, 1915
Escola, was born at Fort Bragg, April 30, 1915, dying   May 12, 1915
five days later on May 2nd.

A son was born to the wife of William Evans at Irmulco   Aug 10, 1910
July 31, 1910.

An eleven pound son was born to the wife of E.Everson at   Feb 17, 1915
Noyo February 11, 1915.

A son was born to the wife of E.Everson at Noyo   Aug 15, 1917
July 23, 1917.

A son was born to the wife of C.M.Ewing, *nee* Bessie   May 9, 1917
Petersen, at Gualala April 28, 1917.

A son was born to the wife of Otto Faber at Ukiah   May 17, 1911
May 7, 1911.

A nine pound son was born to the wife of J.D.Fair at   Apr 24, 1918
Fort Bragg April 17, 1918.

A son was born to the wife of C.M.Faulkner at Point Arena   Nov 22, 1916
November 18, 1916.

A son was born to the wife of Charles Fay at Caspar   Sep 30, 1914
September 27, 1914.

Jacqueline Fayal, a daughter, was born to Herman and Amelia Dec 7, 1995
Fayal in Mendocino March 5, 1917.

A 12 pound daughter was born to the wife of Ed Fee at   Mar 25, 1914
Westport "last week".

A daughter was born to the wife of Ed Fee April 23, 1919.   Apr 30, 1919

A son was born to the wife of Jack Fee at Westport   Mar 20, 1918
March 16, 1918.

A ten pound son was born to the wife of Jack Fee at   Sep 24, 1919
Westport September 17, 1919.

A daughter was born to the wife of J.H.Felton in Little   Feb 23, 1910
Lake Valley February 15, 1910.

A daughter was born to the wife of C.Fernandez at Fort   Feb 26, 1919
Bragg January 20, 1919.

A son was born to the wife of Manuel Fernandez in   May 9, 1917
Fort Bragg May 8, 1917.

A daughter was born to the wife of Mr.Figone Jr. at Willits Apr 30, 1913
April 18, 1913.

A 9½ pound daughter was born to the wife of Lawrence   Oct 18, 1911
Filosi of Newport October 16, 1911.

A daughter was born to the wife of Rev.J.M.Fisher at   May 25, 1910
Mendocino May 19, 1910.

A son was born to the wife of Rev.J.M.Fisher at Mendocino   Feb 3, 1915
January 29, 1915.

A son was born to the wife of William Fisher at Fort Bragg Oct 30, 1918
October 23, 1918.

A son was born to the wife of Peter Fistolera at Manchester Nov 26, 1919
November 17, 1919.

A son was born to the wife of Henry Ford at Willits   Dec 31, 1919
December 26, 1919.

A daughter was born to the wife of J.A.Ford of Redwood   Apr 9, 1919
Valley "this week".

A son was born to the wife of James Ford at Willits
"last week".   Apr 2, 1919

A daughter was born to the wife of Roy Ford in Redwood
Valley November 15, 1913.   Nov 19, 1913

A son was born to the wife of Roy Ford of Redwood Valley
November 10, 1918.   Nov 20, 1918

A daughter was born to the wife of William Ford,
nee Margaret Van Dyke, at Ukiah November 27, 1919.   Dec 3, 1919

A son was born to the wife of Mr.Forster at Fort Bragg
May 26, 1918.   May 29, 1918

A son was born to the wife of L.H.Foster at Ukiah
August 21, 1913.   Sep 3, 1913

A son was born to the wife of W.A.S.Foster at Northwestern
May 8, 1911.   May 24, 1911

A son [John] was born to the wife of W.A.S.Foster at   Jul 23, 1913
Northwestern July 14, 1913. The mother, Marion Burness   Jul 30, 1913
Foster, died July 20, 1913.

A son was born to the wife of W.Fox in Ukiah
June 26, 1919.   Jul 2, 1919

A daughter was born to the wife of W.L.Frasier in Potter
Valley January 8, 1911.   Feb 1, 1911

A son was born to the wife of Ed Freathy in Greenwood
"last week".   Mar 5, 1919

A son was born to the wife of Mr.Fredson at Fort Bragg
December 11, 1914.   Dec 23, 1914

A daughter was born to the wife of Charles Fredson at
Fort Bragg November 26, 1913.   Dec 3, 1913

A ten pound son was born to the wife of J.Fredson at
Fort Bragg September 5, 1916.   Sep 13, 1916

A son was born to the wife of G.E.Freeman at Ukiah
July 17, 1914.   Jul 22, 1914

A son was born to the wife of Joaquin Freitas at
Mendocino October 3, 1914.   Oct 7, 1914

A daughter was born to the wife of Carl Fritzsche
at South Bend, Washington, May 15, 1911.   May 17, 1911

A son was born to the wife of T.C.Fulton at Willits
February 4, 1915.   Feb 10, 1915

A son was born to the wife of Louis Funke at Willits
July 22, 1914.   Jul 29, 1914

A son was born to the wife of J.N.Gall at Willits
March 31, 1913.   Apr 9, 1913

A son was born to the wife of Charles Galletti
at Point Arena September 15, 1916.   Sep 20, 1916

A son was born to the wife of Charles Galletti
at Point Arena March 20, 1919.   Apr 9, 1919

A daughter was born to the wife of August Gamberg
in Fort Bragg April 1, 1918.   Apr 3, 1918

A daughter was born to the wife of Ed Gamberg at
Fort Bragg "last week".   Apr 14, 1915

Births Reported	Issue Date
A daughter was born to the wife of F[ranz] Gamberg in Fort Bragg January 20, 1918.	Jan 30, 1918
A son was born to the wife of George Gamble at Fort Bragg December 1, 1918.	Dec 4, 1918
A daughter was born to the wife of Henry Gamble of Greenwood June 24, 1911.	Jun 28, 1911
A son was born to the wife of Al Ganter at Ukiah November 16, 1915.	Nov 24, 1915
Dean Gardner, a ten pound boy, was born to the wife of Dr.Robert Gardner at Long Beach October 2, 1915.	Oct 13, 1915
A daughter was born to the wife of Rev.J.C.Garth at Fort Bragg March 3, 1913.	Mar 5, 1913
A son was born to the wife of C.Gaspar at Mendocino February 13, 1915.	Feb 17, 1915
A daughter was born to the wife of Cecil M.Gaspar at Point Arena October 21, 1916.	Oct 25, 1916
A daughter was born to the wife of A.S.Gelsten, nee Myrtle Gray of Fort Bragg, in Los Angeles December 13, 1913.	Jan 28, 1914
A son was born to the wife of Arthur Gelston, nee Myrtle Gray of Mendocino, at Walnut Creek February 7, 1917.	Feb 14, 1917
A son was born to the wife of G.Gennosses at Willits February 18, 1910.	Mar 2, 1910
A son was born to the wife of L.A.German at Ukiah April 27, 1917.	May 9, 1917
A daughter was born to the wife of Antonio Ghiose "this week".	Feb 20, 1918
A 13½ pound son was born to the wife of V.Gianini at Wendling [no date reported].	Jan 17, 1917
A son was born to the wife of George Gibney at Caspar November 4, 1914.	Nov 18, 1914
A son was born to the wife of Peter Gibney at Mendocino February 16, 1913.	Feb 25, 1914
A son was born to the wife of Pete Gibney at Caspar November 19, 1915.	Dec 1, 1915
A son was born to the wife of Frank Gibson at Potter Valley. July 28, 1916.	Aug 9, 1916
A daughter was born to the wife of Roy C.Gibson at Ukiah April 9, 1917.	Apr 11, 1917
A son was born to the wife of Sam Gibson at Ukiah January 8, 1912.	Jan 17, 1912
A daughter was born to the wife of Sam Gibson in Ukiah April 3, 1915.	Apr 14, 1915
A son was born to the wife of C.Gignoux, nee Daisy Hill, in Berkeley December 29, 1918.	Jan 15, 1919
A son was born to the wife of H.C.Giles at Ukiah January 25, 1915.	Feb 3, 1915
A son was born to the wife of John Gilliland at Ukiah February 13, 1912.	Feb 21, 1912

An eleven pound daughter was born to the wife of   Feb 27, 1918
O.Gillmore at Point Arena February 25, 1918.

A son was born to the wife of John Gilman at Covelo   May 3, 1911
April 7, 1911.

A son was born to the wife of Victor Giusti at Fort Bragg   Jan 9, 1918
January 2, 1918.

A daughter was born to Meta Glass, an unmarried girl of 20,   Nov 10, 1915
in Fort Bragg November 9, 1915. She had abandoned the baby
under a house where it was found and saved.

A daughter was born to the wife of Matt Gleason at Wendling   Apr 25, 1917
April 21, 1917.

A daughter was born to the wife of A.J.Goetz, nee Mabel   Nov 1, 1916
Silverthorne, in San Francisco October 23, 1916.

A son was born to the wife of Mr.Golden at Fort Bragg   Sep 13, 1916
September 8, 1916.

A daughter was born to the wife of Allen Golden at Fort   Apr 5, 1916
Bragg March 29, 1916.

A daughter [Maria doRosario] was born to the wife of Antone   Oct 10, 1917
Gomes at Mendocino October 4, 1917.

A daughter was born to the A.L.Gonsalves at Melburne   Jan 27, 1915
January 17, 1915.

A daughter was born to the wife of B.Good at Willits   Jul 11, 1917
July 2, 1917.

A daughter was born to the wife of Roy Good in Willits   Sep 5, 1917
September 1, 1917.

A daughter was born to the wife of Roy Good, the school   Apr 23, 1919
superintendent, at Ukiah "this week".

A daughter was born to the wife of Arthur Goranson at   Jun 6, 1917
Wendling May 6, 1917.

A son was born to the wife of Arthur Goranson at Wendling   Jul 28, 1915
"last week".

A daughter was born to Arthur Goranson at Hardy   Aug 30, 1911
August 25, 1911.

A daughter was born to the wife of F.Goranson at Willits   Feb 12, 1913
February 9, 1913. [The girl's name was "Vernona". Her father was
Fred Goranson; her mother was Anna Maria nee Bishop, changed by her
mother, Mary, from "Biskop". Vernona was born in Fort Bragg
February 11, 1913 according to her personal account published
in Fort Bragg Remembered, 1976.]

A son was born to the wife of Fred Goranson at Alpine   Oct 12, 1910
October 4, 1910.

A son was born to the wife of George Gordon at Westport   Dec 5, 1917
November 30, 1917.

A son was born to the wife of William D.Gorman, nee Irene   Jan 21, 1914
McLeod of Mendocino, in Oakland "last week".

A daughter was born to the wife of Louis Gotari of the   Dec 17, 1919
Caspar woods "this week".

A daughter was born to the wife of E.Gould at Ukiah   Sep 6, 1911
August 28, 1911.

A son was born to the wife of Hiram Gowan at Ukiah   Jan 24, 1917
January 20, 1917.

A daughter was born to the wife of Mr. Gowen at Philo November 26, 1917.	Dec 5, 1917
A daughter was born to the wife of E.A. Grant near Manchester July 27, 1911.	Aug 16, 1911
A nine pound daughter was born to the wife of Ed Grant at Point Arena November 20, 1918.	Nov 27, 1918
A daughter was born to the wife of Theodore Grant at Point Arena July 12, 1917.	Jul 25, 1917
A daughter was born to Mrs. Grass at Westport [no date reported].	Oct 19, 1910
A son, was born to the wife of Arthur J. Gray at Berkeley November 19, 1914.	Nov 25, 1914
A son was born to the wife of Dana Gray at Ukiah January 16, 1910.	Jan 26, 1910
An eight pound son was born to the wife of Dana Gray at Fort Bragg June 4, 1913.	Jun 11, 1913
A son was born to the wife of Harold Gray in Mendocino February 27, 1911.	Mar 1, 1911
A son was born to the wife of L. Gray at Fort Bragg August 15, 1915.	Aug 18, 1915
Arden H. Gray, a son, was born to the wife of Howard Gray May 4, 1910.	May 11, 1910 May 9, 1923
Donald Cameron Gray, the son of Arthur J. Gray, was born at Fort Bragg July 18, 1917.	Jul 18, 1917
A son was born to the wife of E.A. Green of Ukiah April 29, 1917.	May 9, 1917
A nine pound son was born to the wife of F.H. Greenough at Fort Bragg August 10, 1911.	Aug 23, 1911
A daughter was born to the wife of F.A. Griffiths at Ukiah January 20, 1911.	Feb 1, 1911
A 10½ pound daughter was born to Mrs. A. Grosz of Caspar "this week". [also given as "Grosse"].	Dec 13, 1916
A daughter was born to the wife of Franz Grothe of Bell Springs September 28, 1919.	Oct 8, 1919
A daughter was born to the wife of Leon L. Grover of Potter Valley at Ukiah August 25, 1916.	Aug 30, 1916
A son was born to the wife of Joe Guenza October 25, 1914.	Nov 4, 1914
A son was born to the wife of J. Hackabout at Willits June 2, 1915.	Jun 9, 1915
A daughter was born to the wife of Edwin Hackley in San Francisco July 12, 1913.	Jul 23, 1913
A daughter was born to the wife of Mr. Hale in the San Francisco Bay area "last week". In 1917 Mr. Hale drove the laundry wagon in Fort Bragg.	Jun 4, 1919
A daughter was born to the wife of J.M. Hale at Willits June 16, 1912.	Jun 26, 1912
Twin boys were born to the wife of Henry J. Halliday at Point Arena August 8, 1911.	Aug 30, 1911

A daughter was born to the wife of J.C.Halliday at Point Arena September 10, 1914.   Sep 23, 1914

A daughter was born to the wife of J.H.Halliday at Point Arena May 9, 1917.   May 16, 1917

A son was born to the wife of J.H.Halliday at Point Arena November 3, 1918.   Nov 13, 1918

A son was born to the wife of O.A.Hamblin in East Mendocino April 12, 1918.   Apr 17, 1918

A son was born to the wife of L.Hamilton at Point Arena May 9, 1917.   May 16, 1917

A son was born to the wife of Captain Hammer at Berkeley March 6, 1910.   Mar 16, 1910

A son was born to the wife of Levi Hammock at Willits December 3, 1919.   Dec 10, 1919

A daughter was born to the wife of Emil Handelin at Mendocino July 19, 1910.   Jul 27, 1910

A 10½ pound son was born to the wife of Arthur Hansen January 15, 1916.   Jan 19, 1916

A son was born to the wife of L.Hansen at Willits September 21, 1916.   Sep 27, 1916

A daughter was born to the wife of Albert Hanson, *nee* Gwen McCallum of Mendocino, in Berkeley last week".   Aug 28, 1918

A daughter was born to the wife of Dewey Hanson, *nee* Verda Cromwell, at Westport "last week".   Jun 18, 1919

A daughter was born to the wife of H.Hanson at Ukiah February 24, 1911.   Mar 8, 1911

A son was born to the wife of P.O.Hardell at Fort Bragg January 16, 1916.   Jan 19, 1916

A daughter was born to the wife of Henry Harms at Willits January 12, 1917.   Jan 24, 1917

A daughter was born to the wife of George Harris, *nee* Effie Gamberg, in San Francisco December 20, 1919.   Dec 24, 1919

A son was born to the wife of Tom Harris at Inglenook December 5, 1918.   Dec 11, 1918 / Dec 18, 1918

A daughter was born to the wife of J.D.Harrison at Muir's Mill May 16, 1910.   May 25, 1910

A daughter was born to the wife of Jesse Harrison at Irmulco April 18, 1913.   Apr 30, 1913

A 9½ pound daughter was born to the wife of F.Hartman of Fort Bragg October 28, 1912.   Oct 30, 1912

A son was born to the wife of Frank Hartman at Fort Bragg March 28, 1911.   Apr 12, 1911

A son was born to the wife of Charles Hasch in the Caspar woods June 1, 1913.   Jun 4, 1913

A daughter was born to the wife of Max Haskett at Willits April 18, 1917.   Apr 25, 1917

A son was born to the wife of Max Haskett at Willits April 12, 1919.   Apr 16, 1919

A son was born to the wife of A.J.Haun of Branscomb
"recently".   Jun 13, 1917

A daughter was born to the wife of Ernest Hawn at Ukiah
December 6, 1914.   Dec 16, 1914

A daughter was born to the wife of J.E.Hayter at
Fort Bragg April 2, 1913.   Apr 9, 1913

An eight pound son was born to the wife of James Hayter
at Fort Bragg April 15, 1911.   Apr 19, 1911

Twins, a boy and a girl, were born to the wife of   Oct 27, 1915
James Hayter, nee Olga Gamberg, at Albion October 16, 1915.   Dec 1, 1915
The girl died November 29, 1915 and was buried at Little-   Mar 22, 1916
river November 30th. The boy died March 15, 1916.

A son was born to the wife of James Hayter at Greenwood
April 11, 1917.   Apr 18, 1917

A son was born to the wife of Roy Hayter at Albion
June 17, 1915.   Jun 30, 1915

A daughter was born to the wife of W.Hayward near Ukiah   Jul 20, 1910
July 25, 1910. [date error, perhaps June 25th].   Jul 27, 1910

A daughter was born to the wife of Mr.Hazelschwartz
at Willits November 14, 1919.   Nov 19, 1919

A son was born to the wife of Stacy Heathcock at Fort Bragg
December 18, 1917.   Dec 19, 1917

An 11½ pound son was born to the wife of Dan Hebron   Feb 19, 1913
in Fort Bragg February 18, 1913.   Feb 26, 1913

A son was born to the wife of Donald Hedden at Manchester
"last week".   Nov 7, 1917

A son was born to the wife of W.D.L.Held of Ukiah
at Willows December 25, 1909.   Jan 5, 1910

A son was born to the wife of John Helela at Cleone
July 16, 1915.   Jul 21, 1915

A son was born to the wife of John Helela in Fort Bragg
May 18, 1917.   May 23, 1917

A daughter was born to the wife of John Helela at
Fort Bragg June 3, 1919.   Jun 4, 1919

A son was born to the wife of John Helland of Long Valley
February 13, 1917. He was the game warden.   Feb 21, 1917

A daughter was born to the wife of Henry Helm of Longvale,
nee Julia Bohn of Fort Bragg, in Fort   May 2, 1917
Bragg April 29, 1917.

A daughter was born to the wife of Gilbert Henderson in
Fort Bragg May 11, 1915.   May 19, 1915

A son was born to the wife of Gilbert Henderson at Mendocino
November 2, 1916.   Nov 8, 1916

A daughter was born to the wife of K.N.Hengeveld at Ukiah
June 5, 1919.   Jun 18, 1919

A son was born to the wife of Albert Henningsen of Carlotta,
Humboldt County, on May 7, 1910. Mr.Henningsen was formerly   Jun 1, 1910
a resident of Fort Bragg and Caspar.

A daughter was born to the wife of Albert Henningsen at
Carlotta April 3, 1911.   Apr 26, 1911

A son was born to the wife of Mr. Hennsen at Mitchell Creek "recently".

Jul 14, 1915

A son was born to the wife of C.L. Hensley at Fort Bragg "last week".

Sep 18, 1918

A son was born to the wife of Bert Henton at Redwood Valley December 31, 1911.

Jan 17, 1912

A son was born to the wife of Frank Heryford at Willits September 1, 1919.

Sep 3, 1919

A daughter was born to the wife of I. Hickman at Point Arena December 27, 1912.

Jan 8, 1913

A son was born to the wife of E. Higgins at Point Arena October 5, 1910.

Oct 12, 1910

A son was born to the wife of Walter Higgins of Caspar in San Francisco [December 1916]. The child died at Caspar Caspar April 8, 1917. The funeral was held there with burial in Fort Bragg. Rev. W.A. Chapman presided.

Dec 13, 1916
Apr 11, 1917

A daughter was born to the wife of Victor Hildreth in Ukiah in Ukiah April 4, 1915.

Apr 14, 1915

A daughter was born to the wife of Walter Hildreth in Ukiah May 24, 1915.

Jun 2, 1915

A daughter was born to the wife of A.W. Hill August 21, 1913.

Sep 3, 1913

A daughter was born to the wife of Chester Hill, nee [Annie] Raudio, at Fort Bragg February 3, 1918.

Feb 6, 1918

A daughter was born to the wife of F. Hillard at Ukiah August 28, 1913.

Sep 3, 1913

A son was born to the wife of Tom Ho at Albion September 19, 1910.

Sep 28, 1910

A daughter was born to the wife of Tom Ho at Albion November 11, 1914.

Nov 18, 1914

A daughter was born to the wife of Tom Hoe, Chinese, at Albion. [no date reported].

Feb 26, 1913

A son was born to the wife of H.J. Hoff at Willits January 26, 1915.

Feb 3, 1915

A daughter was born to the wife of Emil Hoglund in Fort Bragg August 27, 1919.

Aug 27, 1919

A daughter was born to the wife of Andrew Holberg [perhaps "Kolberg"] of Wages Creek October 5, 1918.

Oct 9, 1918
Oct 16, 1918

A son was born to the wife of Harold Holliday in Ukiah January 9, 1916.

Jan 19, 1916

A daughter was born to the wife of Oscar Hollingsworth at Willits December 11, 1913.

Dec 24, 1913

A son was born to the wife of Harry Holmes of Noyo "last week".

Aug 6, 1913

A 12½ pound son was born to the wife of Harry Holmes at Noyo October 2, 1916.

Oct 4, 1916

A 14 pound son was born to the wife of Charles Holquist at Caspar January 15, 1914.

Jan 21, 1914

A son was born to the wife of H. Holquist in Fort Bragg November 9, 1918.

Nov 13, 1918

A daughter was born to the wife of L.J.Holzhauser at Ukiah August 17, 1911.	Aug 30, 1911
A son was born to the wife of F.E.Hopkins at Potter Valley May 17, 1912.	May 29, 1912
A daughter was born to the wife of Bert Hopper in Willits December 12, 1913.	Dec 17, 1913
A daughter was born to the wife of C.Hopper at Covelo February 7, 1911.	Mar 1, 1911
A son was born to the wife of Ed Hopper at Albion March 4, 1914.	Mar 11, 1914
A 13 pound son was born to the wife of Ed Hopper of Navarro ridge "last week".	Jul 24, 1918
A daughter was born to the wife of Henry Hopper at Fort Bragg June 30, 1919.	Jul 9, 1919
Twin boys were born to the wife of L.C.Hopper at Willits "this week".	Apr 25, 1917
A daughter was born to the wife of Winifred Hopper at Willits April 2, 1919.	Apr 9, 1919
A son was born to the wife of Mr.Horton of the Coast Guard September 28, 1916.	Oct 11, 1916
An 8 pound son was born to the wife of Lloyd Hotz at Mendocino March 21, 1915.	Mar 31, 1915
An 8 pound daughter was born to the wife of Carl Howard of Caspar June 29, 1919.	Jul 9, 1919
A son was born to Mrs.Mabel Howard at Ukiah February 13, 1917.	Feb 21, 1917
A nine pound son was born to the wife of William Howard at DeHaven October 28, 1916.	Nov 1, 1916
A daughter was born to the wife of C.F.Howe at Hopland April 28, 1912.	May 8, 1912
A daughter was born to the wife of A.S.Howell at Ukiah March 17, 1911.	Apr 5, 1911
A son was born to the wife of M.C.Hoxie at Covelo March 1, 1912.	Mar 20, 1912
A daughter was born to the wife of Frank Hubbard of Inglenook at Ten Mile "this week".	Jun 11, 1919
A six pound son was born to the wife of Claire Hufft at at Fort Bragg July 24, 1915.	Jul 28, 1915
A son was born to the wife of Claire Hufft at Ukiah June 4, 1917.	Jun 6, 1917
A son was born to the wife of Nilas Hughes at Ukiah January 25, 1915.	Feb 3, 1915
A daughter was born to the wife of Quin Hughes at Redwood Valley April 16, 1913.	Apr 23, 1913
Twin sons were born to the wife of Mr.Hull at Fort Bragg March 14, 1916.	Mar 15, 1916
A daughter was born to the wife of Amos Hull at Point Arena April 3, 1910.	Apr 6, 1910

A son was born to the wife of B.Hull at Caspar "last week".   Jan 19, 1910

A daughter was born to the wife of Milton Hunt, formerly   Jan 3, 1917
of Ukiah, at Petaluma December 26, 1916.

A daughter was born to the wife of Charles Hunter at   Apr 6, 1910
Point Arena April 1, 1910.

A daughter was born to the wife of Harold Hunter at   Feb 5, 1919
Point Arena January 28, 1919.

A son was born to the wife of L.G.Huntting in Fort Bragg   Oct 8, 1919
October 3, 1919.

A son was born to the wife of Judge J.C.Hurley at Ukiah   Aug 8, 1917
August 2, 1917.

A nine pound son was born to the wife of Oscar Hurling at   Mar 1, 1916
Elk February 21, 1916.

A daughter was born to the wife of Bert Hutson at Ukiah   Mar 29, 1916
March 23, 1916.

A son was born to the wife of Nels Hutton at Point Arena   Mar 23, 1910
March 18, 1910.

A son was born to the wife of Frank Hyman at Fort Bragg   Nov 4, 1914
October 24, 1914.

A 7½ pound son was born to the wife of Frank Hyman of   Nov 8, 1916
Cleone October 31, 1916.

A son was born to the wife of Joe Ielmoni at Point Arena   Feb 16, 1916
February 10, 1916.

A son was born to the wife of John Inman at Manchester   Jan 7, 1914
December 20, 1913.

A son was born to Mrs.Garfield (Daisy) Iversen at Point   Apr 12, 1916
Arena April 2, 1916.

A daughter was born to the wife of Henry Iversen at   Aug 4, 1915
Point Arena July 29, 1915.

A son was born to the wife of Isaac Jaackala at Comptche   Sep 22, 1915
September 12, 1915.

A son was born to the wife of J.A.Jackson at Fort Bragg   Sep 3, 1913
August 28, 1913.

An eleven pound son was born to the wife of Joe Jackson   Feb 1, 1911
in Fort Bragg. [no date reported].

A daughter was born to the wife of Thomas Jackson   Oct 28, 1914
at Point Arena October 19, 1914.

A son was born to the wife of G.R.Jahnigen in Fort Bragg   Dec 14, 1910
December 9, 1910.

A son was born to the wife of J.R.Jahnigen at Manchester   Oct 15, 1913
October 10, 1913.

A daughter was born to the wife of A.Jaldini in the Hardy   Nov 29, 1911
Creek woods [no date reported].

A son was born to the wife of Frank Jameson in Redwood   Aug 5, 1914
Valley July 20, 1914.

A son was born to the wife of Tom Jameson May 12, 1914.   May 20, 1914

A daughter was born to the wife of Earl Jamison at Willits   Sep 1, 1915
August 23, 1915.

A daughter was born to the wife of August <u>Jarf</u> of Westport   Oct 17, 1917
at Fort Bragg October 10, 1917.

A son was born to the wife of Dan <u>Jensen</u> at Point Arena   Mar 26, 1913
March 22, 1913.

A son was born to the wife of C.<u>Jeremias</u> in Fort Bragg   Jan 30, 1918
January 23, 1918.

A son was born to the wife of A.R.<u>Johnson</u> at Boonville   Aug 5, 1914
July 22, 1914.

A son was born to the wife of C.D.<u>Johnson</u> at Albion   Sep 11, 1912
September 6, 1912.

A nine pound son was born to the wife of C.D.<u>Johnson</u> at   Nov 24, 1915
Albion November 18, 1915.

A son was born to the wife of C.F.<u>Johnson</u> in Fort Bragg   Nov 1, 1916
October 25, 1916.

A nine pound son was born to the wife of Charles <u>Johnson</u>,   May 12, 1915
nee Anna Olsen, Mendocino May 10, 1915.

Twin sons were born to the wife of Charles <u>Johnson</u> at   May 3, 1916
Caspar April 25, 1916.

A son was born to the wife of Emery <u>Johnson</u> at   May 21, 1919
Point Arena May 12, 1919.

A daughter was born to the wife of Emil <u>Johnson</u> of Caspar   Jul 20, 1910
"recently".

A son was born to the wife of Frank <u>Johnson</u> at Fort Bragg   Jan 12, 1916
January 2, 1916.

A daughter was born to the wife of Fred <u>Johnson</u> of   Nov 5, 1913
Northwestern October 30, 1913.

A son was born to the wife of H.E.<u>Johnson</u> at Fort Bragg   Nov 5, 1913
October 30, 1913.

Mary Elizabeth Johnson was born to the wife of H.G.<u>Johnson</u>   Feb 5, 1919
at Oakland "last week".

A daughter was born to the wife of H.Glen <u>Johnson</u> at   Sep 10, 1913
Fort Bragg September 8, 1913.

A daughter was born to the wife of L.<u>Johnson</u> at Albion   May 3, 1911
April 16, 1911.

A son was born to the wife of L.M.<u>Johnson</u> of Fort Bragg at   Jun 14, 1911
Eureka June 6, 1911. The infant died June 9th.

A daughter was born to the wife of O.E.<u>Johnson</u> at Willits   Feb 14, 1912
February 8, 1912.

A daughter was born to the wife of O.E.<u>Johnson</u>, a sawyer   Apr 9, 1913
at the Irmulco mill, in Willits April 2, 1913.

A son was born to the wife of O.R.<u>Johnson</u> in San   Apr 2, 1913
Francisco March 29, 1913.

A son was born to the wife of T.D.<u>Johnson</u> at Richmond   May 27, 1914
May 10, 1914.

A son was born to the wife of A.E.<u>Johnston</u> at   Jun 26, 1912
Fort Bragg June 20, 1912.

A son was born to the wife of William <u>Johnston</u>   Apr 16. 1913
at Point Arena April 8, 1913.

A son was born to the wife of E.T.Jones at Hardy January 24, 1911.	Feb 15, 1911
A daughter was born to the wife of R.Jones at Ukiah February 5, 1910.	Feb 16, 1910
A son was born to the wife of Ben Joseph in Kings County, California, February 27, 1917.	Mar 7, 1917
A ten pound daughter was born to the wife of M.Jussel at Ukiah "the first of the week".	Sep 15, 1915
A daughter was born to the wife of Mr.Kaarto at Irmulco September 9, 1919.	Sep 17, 1919
A daughter was born to the wife of John Kaarto in Little Valley October 18, 1916.	Oct 25, 1916
A daughter was born to the wife of Mr.Kajamaki August 30, 1911.	Sep 6, 1911
A son, the 14th child, was born to the wife of August Kanaanen on Sherwood Road east of Fort Bragg January 3, 1913.	Jan 8, 1913
A son was born to the wife of Herman Karvonen at Fort Bragg February 12, 1918.	Feb 20, 1918
A daughter was born to the wife of N.Kaufman at Westport October 30, 1911.	Nov 1, 1911
A daughter was born to the wife of Thomas Kearns of Littleriver July 11, 1916.	Jul 19, 1916
Son was born to the wife of Ed Kehoe at Ukiah June 9, 1919.	Jun 18, 1919
John Keller Jr.was born at Willits June 20, 1913.	Jun 25, 1913
A son was born to the wife of J.W.Kelly at Covelo August 25, 1910.	Sep 7, 1910
A son was born to the wife of Fred Kemppe at Fort Bragg June 13, 1918.	Jun 19, 1918
A son was born to the wife of Alfred Kendall at Manchester July 27, 1910.	Aug 10, 1910
A son was born to the wife of Alfred Kendall at Point Arena August 16, 1914.	Aug 26, 1914
A son was born to the wife of Lee King at Mendocino September 12, 1910.	Sep 28, 1910
A daughter was born to the wife of Percy King at Fort Bragg January 10, 1919.	Jan 15, 1919
A son was born to the wife of Oliver Kinyon at Willits December 5, 1919.	Dec 10, 1919
A ten pound son was born to the wife of William Kirkland at Point Arena May 23, 1917.	May 30, 1917
A son was born to the wife of C.R.Kjeldsen at Fort Bragg August 28, 1912.	Sep 4, 1912
A 12 pound daughter was born to the wife of Frank Knacke at Mendocino January 24, 1914.	Jan 28, 1914
A son was born to the wife of Gus Koeffe at Ukiah December 30, 1916.	Jan 3, 1917

A son was born to the wife of Abraham Koski at Fort Bragg   Sep 18, 1918
September 12, 1918.

A son was born to the wife of Guy Kraft January 16, 1911,   Jan 18, 1911
but it died at birth.

A daughter was born to the wife of L.E.Kramer at Willits   Mar 22, 1911
March 5, 1911.

A daughter was born to the wife of Frank Lagreen at Elk   Sep 20, 1911
September 7, 1911.

A daughter was born to the wife of Joe Lamb at Fort Bragg   Sep 17, 1913
September 14, 1913.

A daughter was born to the wife of Attorney Lambert in   Dec 16, 1914
Santa Rosa December 1, 1914.

A daughter was born to the wife of Edward Lampkins   Oct 1, 1913
at Albion September 24, 1913.

A son was born to the wife of Bert Lane at Willits   May 14, 1913
May 1, 1913.

A son was born to the wife of Michael Lang at Ukiah   Apr 21, 1915
April 8, 1915.

A son was born to the wife of Henry Langeley in   Dec 1, 1915
Fort Bragg November 23, 1915.

A child was born to Nellie Langley, the wife of William   Mar 29, 1911
Langley, in Fort Bragg March 18, 1911. The baby died at
birth. Mrs.Langley died of puerperal septicemia
March 24, 1911. Born and raised in Fort Bragg, Nellie
was 20 years old. Catholic rites were conducted by Father
Brennan March 25th.

A son was born to the wife of William Langley of   Oct 15, 1913
Fort Bragg October 12, 1913.

A daughter was born to the wife of Frank Larry at Navarro   Aug 23, 1916
August 18, 1916.

A daughter was born to the wife of Elerth Larson, nee   Apr 30, 1919
Alma Wikstrom of Fort Bragg, at Oakland April 27, 1919.

A daughter was born to the wife of Walter Larson in   Aug 28, 1918
Fort Bragg August 25, 1918.

A daughter was born to the wife of Ed LaSelle in Fort Bragg   Dec 16, 1914
December 9, 1914. [Name is probably LaSalle].

A son was born to the wife of H.Laughlin, nee Ella Britton   Sep 28, 1910
of Fort Bragg, in San Jose September 17, 1910.

A son was born to the wife of Robert Law at Mendocino   Jun 5, 1918
June 2, 1918.

A son was born to the wife of Frank Lawrence at Ukiah   Dec 9, 1914
"last week".

A daughter was born to the wife of Frank Ledford at Ornbaun   May 5, 1915
April 29, 1915.

A daughter was born to the wife of Guy Ledger at Fort Bragg   Oct 7, 1914
September 29, 1914.

A son was born to Mrs.Lee at Westport March 3, 1919.   Mar 12, 1919

An eight pound son was born to the wife of L[oyal] A.   Oct 4, 1916
Lemmon at Noyo September 27, 1916.

A son was born to Mrs.L[oyal] A.Lemmon of Noyo at Fort Bragg   Nov 7, 1917
November 4, 1917.

A daughter was born to the wife of L[oyal] A.Lemmon   Dec 10, 1919
of Mitchell Creek in Fort Bragg December 6, 1919.

A son was born to the wife of Antone Lemos at Mendocino   Jan 4, 1911
December 25, 1910.

A daughter was born to the wife of Antone Lemos at   Nov 20, 1918
Mendocino November 14, 1918.

A daughter was born to the wife of C.Lemos at Mendocino   Jul 27, 1910
July 19, 1910.

A son was born to the wife of George Lewis of Westport   Dec 15, 1915
in Fort Bragg December 12, 1915. [Mr.Lewis operated the cannery at
at Westport].

A son was born to the wife of George Lewis at Westport   Feb 21, 1917
February 15, 1917.

A son was born to the wife of M.Lewis, nee Mamie Mendosa,   Feb 9, 1916
January 31, 1916.

A son was born to the wife of V.Lewis at Willits   Aug 12, 1914
August 1, 1914.

A son was born to the wife of Verne Lewis at Willits   Aug 6, 1913
August 1, 1913.

A son was born to the wife of Mr.Lincoln at Westport   Feb 19, 1919
"last week".

A son was born to the wife of John Lind of Willits   Mar 26, 1913
March 16, 1913.

A nine pound son was born to the wife of Emil Lindberg at   Jan 15, 1919
Fort Bragg January 12, 1919.

A son was born to the wife of Emil Lindquist in   Sep 26, 1917
Fort Bragg September 21, 1917.

A son was born to the wife of Henry Lindstrom at Del Mar   Aug 16, 1911
July 25, 1911.

A son was born to the wife of Henry Lindstrom at   Jul 30, 1913
Point Arena July 26, 1913.

A son was born to the wife of Chester Lineburger at   Nov 17, 1915
Fort Bragg November 12, 1915.

A daughter was born to the wife of E.P.Livingston at   Nov 18, 1914
Willits November 11, 1914.

A nine pound son was born to the wife of John V.Long in   Sep 1, 1915
Fort Bragg August 26, 1915.

A daughter was born to the wife of C.H.Lovell at Covelo   Mar 22, 1911
February 27, 1911.

A son was born to the wife of E.Lovell at Sherwood   Mar 29, 1916
March 18, 1916.

A son was born to the wife of Mr.Lowe in San Francisco   Feb 3, 1915
January 28, 1915. The mother was the former Emily Johnson,
daughter of C.R.Johnson of Fort Bragg.

A son was born to the wife of A.Lubreni at Ukiah   Dec 31, 1913
December 15, 1913.

A ten pound daughter was born to the wife of R.D.Lucas   May 14, 1913
May 9, 1913.

A son was born to the wife of C.Luiz at Mendocino December 6, 1914.	Dec 23, 1914
A daughter was born to the wife of Charles Luiz at Mendocino June 16, 1912.	Jun 26, 1912
A son was born to the wife of V.Lundstrum at Willits May 25, 1913.	Jun 4, 1913
A son was born to the wife of Jack Luoma at Fort Bragg February 5, 1914.	Feb 11, 1914
A daughter was born to the wife of Mr.Lydick at Westport [no date reported].	Sep 10, 1913 Sep 17, 1913
A nine pound daughter was born to the wife of D.O.Lydick at Fort Bragg April 8. 1919.	Apr 9, 1919
A son was born to the wife of Harry Lynch at Westport December 23, 1916.	Dec 27, 1916
A daughter was born to the wife of Grover Lyons at Ukiah August 30, 1915.	Sep 8, 1915
A daughter was born to the wife of Russell MacKerricher in Oakland March 5, 1911.	Mar 15, 1911
A son was born to the wife of Russell MacKerricher in Fruitvale August 2, 1915.	Aug 11, 1915
A daughter was born to the wife of Charles MacPherson, *nee* Mae Werner of Fort Bragg, in San Francisco "last week".	Oct 31, 1917
A daughter was born to the wife of G.E.Maddox at Bridgeport March 30, 1917.	Apr 11, 1917
A son was born to the wife of George Maddox at Albion February 7, 1916.	Feb 23, 1916
A child was born to the wife of the late George Maddox of Elk who died December 4, 1918, "on the day his father was buried".	Dec 11, 1918 Dec 18, 1918
A daughter was born to the wife of Joseph Madeira in Mendocino September 10, 1913.	Sep 24, 1913
Lillian Bernhardine Madison, the infant daughter of Robert Madison, was christened in Santa Rosa November 19, 1916 by Father Crook of Ukiah. The mother was the former Genevieve White of Santa Rosa.	Nov 22, 1916
A daughter was born to the wife of Henry Madsen in Greenwood September 11, 1913.	Sep 24, 1913
A daughter was born to the wife of Henry Madsen at Fort Bragg February 22, 1919.	Feb 26, 1919
A son was born to the wife of Angelo Maffini at Fort Bragg "last week".	Oct 29, 1913
A son was born to the wife of Frank Maffini in Fort Bragg September 1, 1912.	Sep 4, 1912
A daughter was born to the wife of Mr.Mahler [no date].	Jul 21, 1915
Hellen Wright Mahler was born in San Francisco to the wife of Oscar Mahler July 26, 1919.	Aug 6, 1919
A twelve pound son was born to the wife of Amos Mahurin at the Caspar Lumber Company's ranch June 22, 1918.	Jun 26, 1918

A son was born to the wife of Rupert Mahurin at Ukiah January 31, 1917. — Feb 7, 1917

A daughter was born to the wife of Jack Majors at Cleone August 6, 1915. — Aug 11, 1915

A daughter was born to the wife of Jack Majors at Cleone April 30, 1917. — May 2, 1917

A son was born to the wife of Jack Male at Fort Bragg May 17, 1915. — May 19, 1915

A daughter was born to the wife of Cecil Mallory at Mendocino July 23, 1917. — Jul 25, 1917

A daughter was born to the wife of T.J.Maloney of Noyo December 17, 1918. — Dec 18, 1918

A daughter was born to the wife of Lewis Manchester at Fort Bragg December 13, 1915. — Dec 15, 1915

A daughter was born to the wife of Luke Manchester in Fort Bragg January 27, 1918. — Jan 30, 1918

A daughter was born to the wife of Louis Mann near Ukiah September 5, 1911. — Sep 13, 1911

A daughter was born to the wife of C.M.Mannon at Ukiah October 9, 1915. — Oct 20, 1915

A daughter was born to the wife of Charles M.Mannon at Ukiah December 20, 1913. — Dec 31, 1913

A son was born to the wife of J.W.Mantelli at Fort Bragg July 21, 1918. — Jul 24, 1918

A daughter was born to the wife of Ed March in Potter Valley March 14, 1919. — Mar 26, 1919

A daughter was born to the wife of John Mariaui at Mendocino April 1, 1913. — Apr 16, 1913

Twins, a boy and a girl, were born to the wife of Matt Markkula October 16, 1910. — Oct 19, 1910

A nine pound son was born to the wife of Matt Markkula at Fort Bragg December 11, 1911. — Jan 17, 1912

A ten pound daughter was born to the wife of A.I.Marks in Ukiah September 26, 1916. — Oct 4, 1916

A son was born to the wife of C.H.Marshall at Wendling May 5, 1912. — May 22, 1912

A son was born to the wife of Pete Martelle at Fort Bragg March 16, 1918. — Mar 20, 1918

A son was born to the wife of Pete Martelle at Fort Bragg July 26, 1919. — Jul 30, 1919

Twin daughters were born to the wife of Charles Martin at Fort Bragg March 29, 1916. One of the girls died at birth. — Apr 5, 1916

A daughter was born to the wife of John Martins in Fort Bragg December 9, 1917. — Dec 12, 1917

Twin daughters were born to the wife of M.Martonovich, the the steward on the steamer Brunswick, in San Francisco "last week". — Jun 11, 1913

A son was born to the wife if B.D.Mason at Outlet April 30, 1915. — May 5, 1915

An eleven pound son was born to the wife of Mr.Mathews at Westport [no date reported].	Apr 19, 1911
A son was born to the wife of George Mathews in Westport "last week".	Dec 10, 1913
A daughter was born to the wife of J.Mathews November 10, 1910.	Nov 16, 1910
A daughter was born to the wife of George Mathison at Sherwood March 30, 1911.	Apr 12, 1911
A daughter was born to H.Mattson at Fort Bragg August 7, 1915.	Aug 11, 1915
A daughter was born to the wife of P.Maxwell at Mendocino February 5, 1912.	Feb 21, 1912
A son was born to the wife of Jarvcis Mazzetta at Point Arena [no date reported].	Jan 29, 1913
A son was born to the wife of John McCallum at Point Arena October 16, 1916.	Oct 25, 1916
A son was born to the wife of Ed McCanse at Mendocino March 4, 1912. The baby died.	Mar 13, 1912
A daughter was born to Mrs.J.G.McClelland at McCloud, Siskiyou County, June 27, 1910 - the mother died.	Jun 29, 1910
A daughter was born to the wife of B.S.McClintock of Calpella February 28, 1915.	Mar 10, 1915
A son was born to the wife of A.A.McDonald of Northspur in Fort Bragg September 26, 1919.	Oct 1, 1919
A daughter was born to the wife of A.J.McDonald at Manilla, Humboldt County, April 29, 1914. The mother was the former Mollie Randolph.	May 13, 1914
A daughter was born to the wife of Ed McDonald February 24, 1913.	Feb 26, 1913
A daughter was born to the wife of Ed McDonald at Littleriver "last week".	Dec 29, 1915
A daughter was born to the wife of Glen McDonald of Northspur June 9, 1915.	Jun 16, 1915
A 9½ pound son was born to Mrs.John McDonald at Fort Bragg April 30, 1917.	May 2, 1917
A daughter was born to the wife of James McFarland at Ukiah November 28, 1911.	Nov 29, 1911
A twelve pound son was born to the wife of Ed McFaul of Union Landing January 4, 1914.	Jan 14, 1914
A son was born to the wife of Taylor McGarvey in Ukiah November 23, 1915.	Dec 1, 1915
A daughter was born to the wife of Taylor McGarvey in Ukiah July 30, 1918.	Aug 7, 1918
A daughter was born to the wife of J.W.McKinley at Northwestern July 26, 1910.	Aug 3, 1910
A daughter was born to the wife of Dan McLean at Willits February 1, 1915.	Feb 10, 1915
A son was born to the wife of J.McManus in Fort Bragg June 14, 1915.	Jun 16, 1915

Births Reported	Issue Date

A daughter was born to the wife of A.L.McMillen in Point Arena January 19, 1914. — Jan 28, 1914

A daughter was born to the wife of C.A.McMillen at Point Arena December 24, 1915. — Jan 5, 1916

A daughter was born to the wife of Dr.[Robert] McMurchy at Noyo December 8, 1915. — Dec 15, 1915

A son was born to the wife of Robert McMurchy at Noyo December 20, 1917. — Dec 26, 1917

A son was born to the wife of Pat McPhillips at Willits January 25, 1919. — Jan 29, 1919

A son was born to the wife of F.Mellon in Fort Bragg July 31, 1918. — Aug 7, 1918

A daughter was born to the wife of William Melville at Willits February 20, 1910. — Mar 9, 1910

A son was born to the wife of W.A.Menefee at Willits December 1, 1910. — Dec 7, 1910

A daughter was born to the wife of V.Menefel at Caspar March 22, 1910. — Mar 30, 1910

A son was born to the wife of Howard Merritt, nee Loretto of Fort Bragg, in Massachusetts May 13, 1917. — May 23, 1917

A son was born to the wife of Dr.Middleton at Fort Bragg October 12, 1913. — Oct 15, 1913

A son was born to the wife of Mr.Miller at Fort Bragg August 10, 1915. — Aug 11, 1915

A son was born to the wife of J.J.Miller at Fort Bragg January 11, 1914. — Jan 14, 1914

An 8½ pound son was born to the wife of J.J.Miller of Pittsburg, Contra Costa County, December 24, 1915. — Jan 5, 1916

A son was born to the wife of R.A.Miller at Northwestern February 10, 1910. — Feb 16, 1910

A son was born to the wife of Wallace Miller at Caspar November 4, 1915. — Nov 10, 1915

A daughter was born to the wife if Leland Milliken at Fort Bragg December 13, 1915. — Dec 15, 1915

An 8½ pound daughter was born to the wife of M.Milrick at Ukiah March 29, 1913. — Apr 9, 1913

A daughter was born to the wife of Dan Minnehan at Caspar "this week". — Jun 9, 1915

A daughter was born to the wife of J.W.Minton Jr.of Sherwood November 2, 1914. — Nov 11, 1914

A daughter was born to the wife of Fred Mitchell at Union [Landing] "last week". — Dec 27, 1911

A daughter was born to the wife of Albert Moe of Elk February 11, 1919. — Feb 19, 1919

An eleven pound son was born to the wife of Matt Moilnen of Littleriver April 4, 1917. — Apr 11, 1917

A daughter was born to the wife of A.Montedonico at Albion March 9, 1912. — Mar 20, 1912

32

A son was born to the wife of C.C.Montgomery at Fort Bragg "this week".   Feb 23, 1916

A son was born to the wife of James Montgomery at Ukiah November 16, 1915.   Nov 24, 1915

A daughter was born to the wife of C.Montini at Fort Bragg July 7, 1916.   Jul 19, 1916

A daughter was born to the wife of C.E.Moore at Sherwood December 8, 1913.   Dec 17, 1913

A daughter was born to the wife of Thomas Moore at Ukiah June 6, 1915.   Jun 16, 1915

A son was born to the wife of G.Morani at Fort Bragg "last week".   Dec 18, 1918

A daughter was born to the wife of A.Moretta at Mendocino May 18, 1910.   May 25, 1910

Bert Morley, the son of H.W.Morley of Fort Bragg, celebrated his 18th birthday September 29, 1919.   Oct 8, 1919

A nine pound daughter was born to the wife of H.W.Morley in Fort Bragg November 18, 1916.   Nov 22, 1916

A son was born to the wife of Mike Moroni at Wendling February 8, 1917.   Feb 14, 1917

An 8½ pound son was born to the wife of Mike Morrone at Northspur "last week".   Jan 3, 1917

A 9½ pound son was born to the wife of Jessie Morton at Fort Bragg November 8, 1915.   Nov 10, 1915

A son was born to the wife of F.M.Mosier at Westport November 9, 1910.   Nov 30, 1910

A daughter was born to the wife of Milton Moyles at Point Arena December 13, 1917.   Dec 19, 1917

A son was born to the wife of L.P.Murray at Willits July 23, 1910.   Aug 3, 1910

A daughter was born to the wife of Julius Nealy at Ukiah November 1, 1913.   Nov 12, 1913

A daughter was born to the wife of Mr.Needham of Calpella at Ukiah February 14, 1916.   Feb 23, 1916

A daughter was born to the wife of A.T.Nelson at Albion November 24, 1910.   Dec 14, 1910

A son was born to the wife of Arvid Nelson in Fort Bragg in "the middle of last week".   Nov 29, 1916

A son was born to the wife of Samuel Nesbitt July 5, 1915.   Jul 14, 1915

A son was born to the wife of Sam Nesbitt at Willits August 15, 1918.   Aug 28, 1918

Twin daughters were born to the wife of J.R.Neto at Point Arena May 3, 1910.   May 11, 1910

A daughter was born to the wife of J.Newgard at Albion March 1, 1916.   Mar 8, 1916

A 10½ pound daughter was born to the wife of William Newton at Caspar. [No date reported].   Nov 29, 1916

A daughter was born to the wife of Herbert Nichols in
Los Angeles December 28, 1919.   Jan 7, 1920

A son was born to the wife of J.H.Nichols at Mendocino
March 26, 1910.   Apr 6, 1910

A son was born to the wife of Joseph Nichols at Mendocino
May 28, 1912.   May 29, 1912

A twelve pound daughter was born to the wife of Joseph
Nichols at Mendocino August 26, 1914.   Sep 2, 1914

A son was born to the wife of Alfred Nicholson of Mendocino
[no date reported].   Jul 9, 1919

A nine pound daughter was born to the wife of Elmer Nielsen,
nee Gladys Gray, December 3, 1917.   Dec 5, 1917

A nine pound son was born to the wife of Elmer Nielsen at
Fort Bragg April 5, 1919.   Apr 9, 1919

A daughter was born to the wife of Julius Niely at Ukiah
November 21, 1914.   Nov 25, 1914

A son was born to the Olaf Noilanders in Caspar "this week".   Jun 19, 1918

A son was born to the wife of L.Noncentelli at Comptche
March 31, 1915.   Apr 14, 1915

A son was born to the wife of Chris Norgard at Ukiah
November 21, 1914.   Dec 9, 1914

A daughter was born to the wife of Carl Nystrom at
Mendocino May 18, 1913.   May 21, 1913

A son was born to the wife of C.P.O'Brien at Point Arena
May 9, 1912.   May 15, 1912

A daughter was born to the wife of J.O'Donnell at Wendling
"this week".   May 1, 1918

A daughter was born to the wife of James O'Donnell of
Mendocino in San Francisco "last week".   May 21, 1919

A daughter was born to the wife of A.O'Neil at Potter
Valley October 5, 1911.   Oct 25, 1911

A daughter was born to the wife of Niels Offerson at
Willits April 10, 1919.   Apr 16, 1919

A daughter was born to the wife of Emil Ohlson in
Fort Bragg April 3, 1911.   Apr 12, 1911

Twins were born to the wife of J.Olsen of Fort Bragg
November 27, 1918 and died the next day.   Dec 4, 1918

A daughter was born to the wife of O.Olsen at Albion
April 10, 1916.   Apr 19, 1916

A daughter was born to the wife of Charles Olson at Caspar
July 12, 1919.   Jul 16, 1919

A 9¼ pound son was born to the wife of Frank Olson at
Fort Bragg April 26, 1916.   Apr 26, 1916

A daughter was born to the wife of S.Onomiya at Ukiah
August 11, 1914.   Aug 19, 1914

A daughter was born to the wife of William Oppenlander at
Comptche August 27, 1914.   Sep 2, 1914

A daughter was born to the wife of Mr.Ordway at Fort Bragg
[no date reported].   Aug 5, 1914

A daughter was born to the wife of Ira Ordway at Willits October 17, 1911.	Nov 1, 1911
A daughter was born to the wife of A.N.Orr at Albion July 3, 1910.	Jul 20, 1910
A daughter was born to the wife of Barney Orr at Wendling February 1, 1918.	Feb 13, 1918
A daughter was born to the wife of R.H.Orr at Fort Bragg March 27, 1910.	Mar 30, 1910
A child was born to the wife of Robert Orr in Fort Bragg October 18, 1911.	Nov 1, 1911
A daughter was born to the wife of Joaquin Osborn of Mendocino January 19, 1914.	Jan 28, 1914
A son was born to the wife of Charles Ostfeld, nee Irene Wright, in Fort Bragg May 25, 1919.	May 28, 1919
A daughter was born to the wife of Rosso Oteno in Willits August 5, 1910.	Aug 17, 1910
A daughter was born to the wife of G.Ottoson at Littleriver July 14, 1915.	Jul 21, 1915
A son was born to the wife of Edward Owens at Fort Bragg August 7, 1915.	Aug 11, 1915
A daughter was born to the wife of Frank Pacini at Ukiah March 11, 1912.	Mar 20, 1912
A son was born to the wife of Ernest Page at Willits January 21, 1915.	Jan 27, 1915
A daughter was born to the wife of Ernest Pages at Willits January 23, 1917.	Jan 31, 1917
A daughter was born to the wife of F.Palmer at Albion [no date reported].	Apr 14, 1915
A daughter was born to the wife of A.Pamelli at Glen Blair February 2, 1912.	Feb 7, 1912
A daughter was born to the wife of O.Paoli at Mendocino July 13, 1910.	Jul 20, 1910
Twins, a boy and a girl, were born to the wife of O.Paoli at Mendocino July 23, 1914.	Jul 29, 1914
A son was born to the wife of R.Paoli at Mendocino August 9, 1911.	Aug 16, 1911
A son was born to the wife of Ira Parrish at Mitchell Creek September 22, 1910.	Oct 19, 1910
A daughter was born to Ira Parrish at Fort Bragg November 1, 1912.	Nov 6, 1912
A son was born to the wife of Mark Parrish at Noyo April 12, 1915.	Apr 14, 1915
A daughter was born to the wife of Mark Parrish at Mitchell Creek [no date reported].	Aug 16, 1916
A nine pound son was born to the wife of Walter L.Parrish June 1, 1912.	Jun 5, 1912
A son was born to the wife of George Partin at Willits December 24, 1910.	Jan 4, 1911

A son was born to the wife of C.L.Patten, nee Martha Barton
formerly of Albion, in Eureka January 11, 1917.   Jan 17, 1917

A son was born to the wife of O.Patton at Muir's old mill
March 13, 1910.   Mar 23, 1910

A daughter was born to Mrs.J.E.Paul Jr., nee Kreiger,
"recently".   Sep 11, 1918

A son was born to the wife of Dr.Harper Peddicord at
Fort Bragg January 10, 1918.   Jan 9, 1918

A daughter was born to Mrs.Joe Pedro at Ukiah
March 7, 1917.   Mar 14, 1917

A 6½ pound daughter was born to the wife of Ray Pedrotti
at Fort Bragg September 16, 1913.   Sep 17, 1913

A ten pound son was born to the wife of Ray Pedrotti at
Fort Bragg July 16, 1916.   Jul 19, 1916

A daughter was born to the wife of Ray Pedrotti in Fort
Bragg May 25, 1919. It was their third child.   May 28, 1919

A daughter was born to the wife of Albert Peers at Willits
August 21, 1914.   Sep 2, 1914

A daughter was born to the wife of O.F.Pendleton at Hardy
October 9, 1911.   Oct 25, 1911

An 8½ daughter was born to the wife of Charles Roy Perkins
at Fort Bragg January 29, 1918.   Jan 30, 1918

A daughter was born to the wife of Antone Perry
August 31, 1911.   Sep 6, 1911

A son was born to the wife of Walter B.Perry at Covelo
March 11, 1911.   Mar 29, 1911

A daughter was born to the wife of Mr.Pesseri at Wendling
December 27, 1917.   Jan 2, 1918

A daughter was born to the wife of C.J.Peters at Point Arena
July 13, 1915.   Jul 21, 1915

A son was born to the wife of August Peterson at Fort Bragg
August 8, 1915.   Aug 11, 1915

A son was born to the wife of C.Peterson at Littleriver
September 4, 1916.   Sep 13, 1916

A daughter was born to the wife of Carl Peterson in San
Francisco March 8, 1913. Mrs.Peterson was the former Kate
Stauer of Mendocino.   Mar 26, 1913

A son was born to Mrs.L.Petit at Ukiah January 23, 1915. Feb 3, 1915

A son was born to the wife of S.Phelan of Fort Bragg
"last week".   Feb 26, 1913

A daughter was born to the wife of M.Philbert at Gualala
July 29, 1911.   Aug 16, 1911

A daughter was born to the wife of M.Philbert at
Point Arena June 11, 1914.   Jun 17, 1914

A daughter was born to the wife of John Philbrick at
Comptche September 25, 1914.   Sep 30, 1914

A daughter was born to the wife of John C.Philbrick at
Berkeley May 4, 1916.   May 10, 1916

A son was born to the wife of William Phillips at
Fort Bragg June 19, 1916.   Jun 21, 1916

A son was born to the wife of G. Philo at Ukiah
April 22, 1911.   May 3, 1911

A son was born to the wife of F.W. Pickerell at
Point Arena "last week".   Apr 26, 1916

An 8¼ pound daughter was born to the wife of John Pimental   May 24, 1916
at Fort Bragg May 23, 1916.

A daughter was born to the wife of John Pimental at
Fort Bragg September 12, 1918.   Sep 18, 1918

A son was born to the wife of Matt Piper at Albion ridge
August 21, 1911.   Sep 6, 1911

A daughter was born to the wife of Matt Piper at Albion
August 18, 1915.   Sep 1, 1915

A son was born to the wife of O.E. Pitzer at Covelo
August 18, 1911.   Sep 6, 1911

A nine pound son was born to the wife of George Plowman,   Jun 11, 1918
late of Caspar, in San Francisco "last week".

A son was born to the wife of Charlie Plummer at Talmage
May 21, 1911.   May 31, 1911

An 8 pound daughter was born to the wife of H. Plummer,   Jul 12, 1916
formerly of Fort Bragg, in Los Angeles July 8, 1916.

A son was born to the wife of Jim Poe August 27, 1914.   Sep 9, 1914

A son was born to the wife of Mr. Poroti at Wendling
April 28, 1917.   May 2, 1917

A son was born to the wife of Rex Porter of Ukiah valley
September 29, 1919.   Oct 8, 1919

A son was born to the wife of George Porterfield at Ukiah   Jul 16, 1913
July 12, 1913.

A daughter was born to the wife of A(?) Pozzi at
Point Arena February 8, 1912.   Feb 14, 1912

A daughter was born to the wife of Hale Prather at Ukiah   Oct 1, 1913
"last week".

A son was born to the wife of the County Clerk, Hale   Mar 10, 1915
Prather, at Ukiah "last week".

A son was born to the wife of C.A. Pratt at Willits
July 11, 1914.   Jul 29, 1914

A son was born to the wife of T.L. Prenton at Mendocino
July 9, 1910.   Jul 20, 1910

A daughter was born to the wife of Claude Presley in Ukiah   Mar 3, 1915
February 22, 1915.

A son was born to the wife of Vernon Presley of Boonville   Sep 10, 1919
at Ukiah August 31, 1919.

A daughter was born to the wife of Mr. Prest at Point Arena   May 23, 1917
May 11, 1917.

A daughter was born to the wife of George W. Preston, nee   Sep 28, 1910
Kathleen Mero of Napa whose parents once lived in Fort
Bragg, in Fairbanks, Alaska, September 22, 1910.

A son was born to the former Kathleen Mero, the wife of George W.Preston at Fairbanks, Alaska, March 29, 1913.	Apr 2, 1913
A daughter was born to the wife of H.P.Preston at Oakland "this week".	Aug 23, 1916
A daughter was born to the wife of Gilbert Price at Ukiah November 16, 1915.	Nov 24, 1915
A daughter was born to the wife of J.C.Pruitt of Fort Bragg September 25, 1917.	Sep 26, 1917
A daughter was born to the wife of Robert Pruitt October 20, 1914.	Oct 28, 1914
A daughter was born to the wife of Elmer Purdy at Ukiah March 21, 1914.	Apr 1, 1914
A son was born to the wife of Arthur Quaill February 15, 1917.	Feb 21, 1917
A son was born to the wife of Joe Quaill at Mendocino May 27, 1919.	Jun 4, 1919
A son was born to the wife of Paul Racine in Fort Bragg April 2, 1910. [Father's Christian name was Napoleon.]	Apr 13, 1910
A daughter was born to the wife of Frank Radnick of Comptche April 25, 1913. The child died soon after birth.	May 7, 1913
An eight pound son was born to the wife of C.Rafter in Weed, Siskiyou County, California, August 21, 1912.	Aug 28, 1912
A daughter was born to the wife of Bolivar Raines at Ukiah November 24, 1914.	Dec 2, 1914
A son was born to the wife of C.H.Raines at Talmage January 14, 1912.	Jan 24, 1912
A son was born to the wife of J.T.Ramus at Mendocino December 23, 1909.	Jan 5, 1910
A son was born to the wife of W.Randell at Caspar July 22, 1911.	Aug 2, 1911
A son was born to the wife of J.E.Randis November 14, 1910.	Nov 16, 1910
A daughter was born to the wife of Charles Raudio at Fort Bragg October 26, 1918. The father died two days later of influenza.	Oct 30, 1918
A son was born to the wife of J.L.Ray at Ukiah March 26, 1916.	Apr 5, 1916
Twins, a boy and a girl, were born to the wife of Paul Ray at Willits February 14, 1914.	Feb 18, 1914
A son was born to the wife of S.Rea at Ukiah January 20, 1912. January 20, 1912.	Jan 31, 1912
A son was born to the wife of Otis Redemeyer in Ukiah May 30, 1917.	Jun 6, 1917
A daughter was born to the wife of Joe Reilly, nee Winnie Atkinson, in Ukiah July 26, 1915.	Aug 4, 1915
An eleven pound son was born to the wife of G.Reinke at September 3, 1911.	Sep 6, 1911
A son was born to the wife of Fred Remsted at Albion ridge August 16, 1914.	Aug 26, 1914

A daughter was born to the wife of R.Remstedt at Point Arena August 1, 1911.	Aug 16, 1911
A daughter was born to the wife of Sam Remstedt at Point Arena June 28, 1916.	Jul 5, 1916
A son was born to the wife of Abe Requa of Laytonville October 39 [sic], 1916.	Nov 8, 1916
A son was born to the wife of Theodore Reuck at Noyo January 26, 1916.	Feb 2, 1916
A son was born to the wife of A.Rianolda at Point Arena June 1, 1912.	Jun 5, 1912
A son was born to the wife of Charles Rice at Willits January 22, 1913.	Jan 29, 1913
A son was born to the wife of J.C.Rice of Mendocino. [No date reported].	Jul 9, 1919
A daughter was born to the wife of James C.Rice at Fort Bragg September 11, 1916.	Sep 13, 1916
A daughter was born to the wife of George Richards at Fort Bragg August 23, 1917.	Aug 29, 1917
A son was born to the wife of L.Richetti at Ukiah September 6, 1911.	Sep 20, 1911
A son was born to the wife of Isaac Richie at Ukiah May 6, 1910.	May 11, 1910
A son was born to the wife of Mr.Ridley at Westport [No date reported].	Feb 9, 1910
A son was born to the wife of E.Ridley at Wendling June 9, 1915.	Jun 16, 1915
A son was born to the wife of Lester Rieff at Ukiah March 3, 1917.	Mar 14, 1917
A son was born to the wife of W.H.Ries, nee Elizabeth Helela of Fort Bragg, in Oakland May 12, 1917.	May 16, 1917
A son was born to the wife of L.L.Riffe at Talmage [No date reported].	Aug 12, 1914
A daughter was born to the wife of M.M.Riggs at Willits February 16, 1913.	Feb 19, 1913
A son was born to the wife of Andrew Rinaldi at Point Arena May 3, 1916.	May 17, 1916
A son was born to the wife of Andrew Rinaldo at Point Arena March 19, 1915.	Mar 31, 1915
A ten pound son was born to the wife of John Rizzi at Alpine [no date reported].	Mar 29, 1916
An eleven pound daughter was born to the wife of John Rizzi at Ten Mile [no date reported].	Nov 28, 1917
A 13 pound son was born to the wife of G.M.Roach at Westport "last week".	Nov 19, 1919
A son was born to the wife of George Roach at Westport [no date reported].	Feb 14, 1912
A son was born to the wife of Judge George Roach at Westport September 23, 1917.	Sep 26, 1917

Twin daughters was born to the wife of E.P.Robbins at   Jun 29, 1910
Talmage June 24, 1910.   Jul 13, 1910

A daughter was born to the wife of John Roberts at   Mar 8, 1916
Ten Mile February 25, 1916.

A ten pound daughter was born to the wife of John Roberts   Apr 30, 1919
at Inglenook [no date reported].

A daughter was born to the wife of C.F.Rodenberg   Dec 6, 1916
November 24, 1916.

A son was born to the wife of Pascal Roderigez north of   Nov 17, 1915
Pudding Creek November 15, 1915.

A son was born to the wife of J.S.Rodgers at Mendocino   Oct 18, 1911
October 7, 1911.

A son was born to the wife of John Rodgers of Mendocino   Apr 11, 1917
"this week".

A son was born to the wife of Walter Roesman at Annapolis,   Jun 4, 1913
Sonoma County, May 24, 1913.

A son was born to the wife of E.J.Rogers at Willits   Apr 30, 1913
April 24, 1913.

A son was born to the wife of Otto M.Rosenblatt of   Jan 6, 1915
Del Mar at Point Arena December 24, 1914.

A son was born to the wife of Mr.Ross, the daughter of   Jul 3, 1918
Mrs.P.W.Smith, at Fort Bragg July 1, 1918.

Robert Ralston Ross was born March 28, 1919 at the Sand   Apr 2, 1919
Dunes Ranch north of Cleone, the son of Robert Ross.

A daughter was born to the wife of Mr.Rossi in Inglenook   May 19, 1915
"last week".

A son was born to the wife of D[elbert].S.Rossiter at   Oct 22, 1919
Point Arena "this week".

A son was born to the wife of Mr.Roth of Albion in   Jan 17, 1917
San Francisco January 8, 1917.

A daughter was born to the wife of J.W.Roux at Ukiah   Sep 20, 1916
September 10, 1916.

A son was born to the wife of B.G.Rowe, nee Alice Johnson   Mar 26, 1919
of Ukiah, in San Francisco March 10, 1919.

A son was born to the wife of Frank Rowe at Albion   Apr 30, 1913
April 27, 1913.

A daughter was born to the wife of Frank Rowe at Albion   Aug 4, 1915
July 28, 1915.

A daughter was born to the wife of George Rowe at   May 23, 1917
Point Arena May 15, 1917.

A daughter was born to the wife of Gus Rowe at Albion   Mar 20, 1912
March 4, 1912.

A daughter was born to the wife of Gus Rowe at Albion   Dec 31, 1913
December 29, 1913.

A daughter was born to the wife of Gus Rowe of Albion   Feb 26, 1919
in Fort Bragg February 22, 1919.

A daughter was born to the wife of R.Royster, nee Mabel   Jan 26, 1916
Sweeney, in San Francisco [no date reported].

A son was born to the wife of Earl Rucker at Willits   Jan 3, 1917
December 25, 1916.

A son was born to the wife of W.E.Rucker at   Jul 22, 1914
Willits July 11, 1914.

A daughter was born to the wife of Paul Rudd in Comptche   Dec 10, 1913
"last week".

A daughter was born to the wife of J.Ruonavaara in Cleone   May 9, 1917
May 7, 1917.

A son was born to the wife of John Ruonavaara in Fort Bragg Oct 8, 1919
October 5, 1919.

A son was born to the wife of Matt Ruonavaara at   Dec 12, 1917
Inglenook December 10, 1917.

A daughter was born to the wife of Dave Russell at Comptche Dec 27, 1911
December 1, 1911.

A son was born to the wife of Dave Russell at Comptche   Nov 10, 1915
November 4, 1915.

A son was born to the wife of R.D.Russell at Comptche   Jan 19, 1910
January 8, 1910.

A son was born to the wife of Robert Russell at San Rafael Feb 5, 1919
January 29, 1919. The Russells were former residents of
Point Arena.

A daughter was born to the wife of Matt Ruuska in Fort Bragg Nov 21, 1917
November 21, 1917.

A daughter was born to the wife of Ed Ryan at Willits   Nov 18, 1914
November 1, 1914.

A ten pound son was born to the wife of Mr.Rynearson at   Jun 7, 1911
Fort Bragg June 6, 1911.

A son was born to the wife of Richard St.Claire at Willits Jan 26, 1910
December 20, 1909.

A son was born to the wife of Mr.Salanave, nee Ethel Allen Dec 5, 1917
of Fort Bragg, in San Francisco "this week".

A son was born to the wife of F.Salines at Fort Bragg   Apr 19, 1911
April 18, 1911.

A son was born to Mrs.Sallinen at Mitchell Creek   Oct 27, 1915
"this week".

A son was born to the wife of Ed Sallinen at Mitchell Creek Oct 19, 1910
October 6, 1910.

A son was born to the wife of Ed Sallinen of Noyo "this week". Oct 30, 1918

A son was born to the wife of F.Sallinen at Noyo   Jan 24, 1917
January 16, 1917.

A daughter was born to the wife of Frank Sallinen of Noyo   Sep 25, 1918
in Fort Bragg September 25, 1918.

A daughter was born to the wife of Mr.Salmela at Wendling   Jun 12, 1918
June 8, 1918.

A daughter was born to the wife of Charles Salvador at   Feb 2, 1916
Fort Bragg January 28, 1916.

A daughter was born to the wife of Charles Salvador at   Feb 26, 1919
Fort Bragg "this week".

A nine pound son was born to the wife of John Salvador,   Sep 23, 1914
nee Sine Packard, at Mendocino September 18, 1914.

A son was born to the wife of John Salvador at Mendocino   Jun 21, 1916
June 12, 1916.

A daughter was born to the wife of Gus M.Sampson, nee   Jun 16, 1915
Nellie Cameron, the sister of Mrs.Arthur Gray of Northspur,
at Buhl on June 10, 1915.

A daughter [Nadine] was born to the wife of Gus M.Sampson,   Jul 18, 1917
nee Nellie Cameron, at Berkeley July 15, 1917.   Jun 5, 1918

A daughter was born to the wife of "Chief" Sanford at   Mar 29, 1916
Ukiah March 24, 1916.

A daughter was born to the wife of E.J.Sanford in Ukiah   Feb 26, 1919
"last week".

An eight pound son was born to the wife of J.B.Sanford at   May 24, 1916
Ukiah May 15, 1916.

A son was born to the wife of Matt Sankovich at Fort Bragg   Feb 7, 1917
February 5, 1917.

A son was born to the wife of Matt Sankovitch   Jan 30, 1918
January 29, 1918.

A daughter was born to the wife of A.Sapp at Ukiah   Sep 6, 1911
August 31, 1911.

A son was born to the wife of J.Sargentine May 11, 1914.   May 20, 1914

A son was born to the wife of Carl Sauers at Albion   Aug 2, 1916
July 23, 1916. [see "saver, C.W.]

A son was born to the wife of C.Saunders of Covelo   Apr 23, 1913
April 18, 1913.

A son was born to the wife of D.H.Saunders of Elk at   Nov 14, 1917
Fort Bragg November 7, 1917.

A son was born to the wife of T.R.Saunders of Little Valley   Oct 29, 1919
October 22, 1919.

A nine pound son was born to the wife of Walter Saunders   Apr 3, 1918
at Fort Bragg March 30, 1918.

A son was born to the wife of C.W.Saver at Albion   Aug 2, 1916
July 23, 1916. [see "Sauers, Carl"].

A son was born to the wife of M.L.Sawyers at Willits   Jan 18, 1911
January 15, 1911. [In fact, a daughter, Goldie to Millie (Bahn) and
Murvin Lee Sawyers.]

A daughter was born to the wife of P.F.Scammon at Ukiah   Dec 9, 1914
"last week".

A son was born to the wife of Domingo Scarona at Manchester   May 28, 1913
May 18, 1913.

A son was born to the wife of John Schaaf at Manchester   Jun 29, 1910
June 12, 1910.

A daughter was born to the wife of Ed Schroeder at Willits   Jun 15, 1910
June 1, 1910.

A son was born to the wife of G.W.Schultz at Fort Bragg   Jul 29, 1914
July 11, 1914.

A ten pound daughter was born to the wife of William   Aug 4, 1915
Schwandt, nee Carrie Jensen, at Glenn, California,
July 26, 1915.

A son was born to the wife of Mr.Scott at Boonville March 21, 1918.	Mar 27, 1918
A son was born to the wife of Abbe P.Scott in South San Francisco May 25, 1912.	May 29, 1912
A son was born to the wife of Chester Scott September 13, 1910.	Sep 14, 1910
A son was born to the wife of Chester Scott at Fort Bragg January 8, 1914.	Jan 14, 1914
A daughter was born to the wife of Frank O.Scott at Ukiah September 3, 1911.	Sep 13, 1911
A son was born to the wife of Joe Scott of Fort Bragg August 6, 1910.	Aug 10, 1910
A daughter was born to the wife of Otto Scott of Fort Bragg January 16, 1915.	Jan 20, 1915
A son was born to the wife of Saxon Scott in San Francisco December 21, 1913.	Dec 24, 1913
A daughter was born to the wife of William Scott at Glen Blair November 15, 1919.	Nov 19, 1919
A son was born to the wife of Otto Seaholm in Fort Bragg February 11, 1911.	Feb 15, 1911
Twin daughters were born to the wife of W.Senders in Ukiah "last week".	May 26, 1915
A son was born to the wife of Clee Shaffer at Fort Bragg May 15, 1915. The baby died October 19, 1915 and was buried the next day.	May 19, 1915 Oct 20, 1915
A son was born to the wife of Harry Shafsky in Fort Bragg December 18, 1916.	Dec 20, 1916
A daughter was born to the wife of Harry Shafsky in Fort Bragg December 26, 1918.	Jan 1, 1919
A son was born to the wife of A.Shandry at Mendocino October 28, 1916.	Nov 1, 1916
A son was born to the wife of Will Shattuck at Ukiah August 21, 1913.	Sep 3, 1913
A son was born to the wife of Ed Shean in San Francisco August 25, 1914.	Sep 2, 1914
A daughter was born to the wife of C.Shelton at Wages Creek "last week".	Feb 19, 1913
A daughter was born to the wife of Charles Shelton at Westport "last week".	Jan 27, 1915
A daughter was born to the wife of Eugene Shelton in Willits September 30, 1913.	Oct 8, 1913
A son was born to the wife of Eugene Shelton at Willits January 18, 1915.	Jan 27, 1915
A son was born to the wife of Eugene Shelton at Willits October 31, 1916.	Nov 15, 1916
A daughter was born to the wife of Jerry Shelton at Willits December 29, 1914.	Jan 13, 1915
A son was born to the wife of K.J.Sherborn at Covelo May 19, 1911.	May 31, 1911

A son was born to the wife of C.Sherrick at Gualala   Aug 12, 1914
July 24, 1914.

A son was born to the wife of Charles E.Sherwood at   Aug 10, 1910
Fort Bragg August 9, 1910.

A son was born to the wife of L.A.Shibley in San Francisco   Nov 8, 1916
"this week". Mr.Shibley was the son of J.H.Shibley of Fort
Bragg, the proprietor of the Baldwin Hotel in San Francisco.

A son was born to the wife of B.Shimmin of Willit   Feb 26, 1913
February 23, 1913.

A son was born to the wife of C.L.Shuster at Willits   Sep 3, 1913
August 23, 1913.

A son was born to Maria Silva, the wife of Joe King Silva,   Oct 24, 1917
at Fort Bragg October 18, 1917. The mother died October 20th.

A daughter was born to the wife of Antone V.Silveria at   May 21, 1913
at Mendocino "last week".

A daughter was born to the wife of Milo Silverthrone at   Oct 11, 1916
Willits "this week".

A daughter was born to the wife of Frank O.Simmerly   Jan 24, 1912
at Redwine January 11, 1912.

A daughter was born to the wife of O.M.Simonson at   Sep 23, 1914
Willits September 15, 1914.

A son was born to the wife of Henry Simpson at Hardy   Jun 14, 1911
May 11, 1911.

A son was born to the wife of Henry Simpson at Northspur   Sep 4, 1912
August 29, 1912.

A son was born to the wife of Thomas Simpson, *nee* Wanda   Dec 25, 1918
Lawson, at Crockett December 1, 1918. She formerly taught
school at Albion.

A son was born to the wife of William Simpson of   Feb 5, 1913
Fort Bragg January 31, 1913.

A daughter, Louise Lee, was born to the wife of Lee Sing   Oct 21, 1914
in Fort Bragg October 18, 1914.

An eight pound son was born to the wife of Lee Sing in   Nov 15, 1916
Fort Bragg November 8, 1916.

A daughter was born to the wife of Lee Sing of Boyle's   Sep 24, 1919
Camp in Fort Bragg "this week".

Twin daughters, seven pounds each, were born to the wife of Oct 11, 1916
William E.Skirk at Willits September 28, 1916.

A daughter was born to the wife of John J.Slattery   Sep 27, 1916
September 21, 1916.

Twins, a boy and a girl were born to the wife of John J.   Dec 4, 1918
Slattery at Bridgeport November 26, 1918. This was the third
set of twins making 12 children in the family.

A son was born to the wife of George Sloan at Mitchell   Dec 11, 1912
Creek [no date reported].

A daughter was born to the wife of Mr.Smith at Navarro   Nov 18, 1914
"last week".

A son was born to Mrs.Smith, a Covelo Indian, in Ukiah   Oct 15, 1919
October 6, 1919.

A son was born to the wife of A. Smith at Willits
February 25, 1910.   Mar   9, 1910

A daughter was born to the wife of C.A. Smith at Fort Bragg   Oct 31, 1917
October 28, 1917.

A son was born to the wife of E.L. Smith at Willits
February 25, 1910.   Mar   9, 1910

An eleven pound daughter was born to the wife of Fred   Nov 24, 1915
Smith, nee Mable Johnson of Albion, at McCloud, Siskiyou
County, November 14, 1915.

A daughter was born to the wife of J.C. Smith at Fort Bragg   May 14, 1913
May 7, 1913.

A daughter was born to the wife of J.C. Smith at Fort Bragg   Jul   1, 1914
June 25, 1914.

A daughter was born to the wife of J.C. Smith at Caspar   Jun 16, 1915
June 9, 1915.

A son was born to the wife of J.M. Smith of Noyo   Feb 26, 1913
February 20, 1913.

A daughter was born to the wife of J.P. Smith at Ukiah   Jun 16, 1915
June 9, 1915.

A ten pound son was born to the wife of R.E. Smith   Sep 16, 1914
in San Francisco September 14, 1914. The mother
was the former Mollie Wright of Fort Bragg.

A son was born to the wife of Roy Smith at Northwestern   Apr 30, 1913
April 10, 1913.

A daughter was born to the wife of J. Snider at Westport   May 18, 1910
May 1, 1910.

A daughter was born to the wife of L.M. Snook in Fort Bragg   Jan 30, 1918
January 11, 1918.

A daughter was born to the wife of J.L. Soanes, nee Vera   Oct   2, 1918
Stokes of Fort Bragg, in Alameda September 26, 1918.

A daughter was born to the wife of Joe Soldani at   Jan   6, 1915
Point Arena December 23, 1914.

A son was born to the wife of J. Sousa in Fort Bragg   Dec   4, 1918
November 30, 1918.

A son was born to the wife of L.D. Spenser in Potter   Aug   2, 1911
Valley July 17, 1911.

A son was born to the wife of George Spittler in Longvale   Nov   1, 1911
October 13, 1911.

A son was born to the wife of J. Spradley at Albion   Dec 15, 1915
December 9, 1915.

A son was born to the wife of Ed Spear in Ukiah   Aug   9, 1916
[date indeterminate].

A daughter was born to the wife of J. Stahl in   Jul   8, 1914
Los Angeles June 28, 1914.

A son was born to the wife of J. Stanley at Hardy Creek   Feb 19, 1913
"last week".

Twins, a boy and a girl, were born to the wife of   Dec 21, 1910
Jack Standley at Westport. [No date reported].

A son was born to the wife of H.Stauer of Mendocino
at Arcata "last week".   Dec 24, 1919

A son was born to the wife of [P.] Alex Stenberg in   Oct 31, 1917
Oakland October 23, 1917.

An eight pound son was born to the wife of Edward J.Stevens   May 26, 1915
at Fort Bragg May 24, 1915.

A ten pound daughter was born to the wife of Charles   Jun 21, 1911
Stevenson at Westport June 19, 1911.

A daughter was born to the wife of Joe Stevenson   Jan 20, 1915
January 11, 1915.

A son, the fifth child, was born to the wife of Calvin   Apr 10, 1918
Stewart Jr.of Petrolia "recently".

A daughter was born to the wife of A.B.Stipp at Ukiah   Jan 18, 1911
January 8, 1911.

Edward Stoddard was born to the wife of Ed Stoddard   Jan 19, 1916
at Fort Bragg January 15, 1916.   Jan 19, 1921

A son was born to the wife of A.Stornetta at Point Arena   Apr 12, 1916
"last week".

A son was born to the wife of J.O.Stornetta at Point Arena   Dec 22, 1915
December 12, 1915. The baby died December 28th.   Jan 5, 1916

A daughter was born to the wife of Phillip Stornetta at   Apr 11, 1917
Point Arena March 30, 1917.

A daughter was born to the wife of F.Straight at Potter   Jan 17, 1917
Valley January 9, 1917.

A daughter was born to the wife of George Strong   Jun 16, 1915
at Hopland June 3, 1915.

A daughter was born to the wife of Carl Struby,   Sep 3, 1919
nee Bonnie Gaine, at Concord "last week".

A daughter was born to the wife of T.Sutherland at   Feb 5, 1913
Navarro ridge "last week".

A daughter was born to the wife of Joe Sverko at Fort Bragg   Feb 7, 1917
February 1, 1917. The baby died August 12, 1917 and was   Aug 15, 1917
buried on August 14th.

A son was born to the wife of R.D.Swales of Fort Bragg   Oct 26, 1910
in San Francisco October 18, 1910.

William Wallace Swan was the son of Mrs.Georgia Swan,   Jan 9, 1918
nee Shaver.

A daughter was born to the wife of Carl Swanson   Oct 3, 1917
at Mendocino September 30, 1917.

A daughter was born to the wife of Henry Swanson   Jul 26, 1916
at Mendocino July 20, 1916.

A daughter was born to the wife of T.Swanson at Elk   Jul 19, 1911
July 1, 1911.

A son was born to the wife of A.J.Switzer,   Jun 23, 1915
nee Lottie Ryan of Fort Bragg. [No date reported].

A daughter was born to the wife of Bud Switzer   Oct 25, 1911
at Petaluma October 19, 1911.

A son was born to the wife of George Switzer at Mendocino   Jul 3, 1918
July 1, 1918.

A daughter was born to the wife of Charles <u>Talkington</u> at Sherwood January 16, 1913.   Jan 29, 1913

A daughter was born to the wife of Charles <u>Talkington</u> at Longvale September 4, 1919.   Sep 10, 1919

A son was born to the wife of J.J.<u>Tallman</u> in Fort Bragg July 28, 1918.   Jul 31, 1918

A son was born to the wife of Ernest <u>Taylor</u> at Northwestern April 2, 1916.   Apr 5, 1916

A daughter was born to the wife of J.T.<u>Taylor</u>, *nee* Della Fuller of Fort Bragg, at Reno, Nevada, January 30, 1915.   Feb 10, 1915

A son was born to the wife of Lee <u>Taylor</u> in Ukiah March 11, 1912.   Mar 20, 1912

A son was born to the wife of Max <u>Thelen</u>, the daughter of H.B.Muir of Willits, at Berkeley September 20, 1916.   Sep 27, 1916

A daughter was born to the wife of C.R.<u>Thomas</u> in Redwood Valley February 2, 1910.   Feb 23, 1910

A son was born to the wife of T.F.<u>Thomas</u> at Fort Bragg July 13, 1916.   Jul 19, 1916

A son was born to the wife of Mr.<u>Thompson</u> at Laughlin Laughlin February 6, 1912.   Feb 7, 1912

A daughter was born to the wife of A.D.<u>Thompson</u> October 7, 1910.   Oct 19, 1910

A daughter was born to the wife of August <u>Thompson</u> in Fort Bragg February 25, 1915.   Mar 3, 1915

A son was born to the wife of L.F.<u>Thompson</u> in Fort Bragg July 2, 1910.   Jul 20, 1910

A daughter was born to the wife of W.<u>Thompson</u> in the Ukiah valley December 16, 1911.   Dec 27, 1911

A son was born to the wife of D.E.<u>Thomson</u> at Covelo August 2, 1911.   Sep 13, 1911

A daughter was born to the wife of Albert <u>Thornton</u> at Caspar June 27, 1918.   Jul 3, 1918

A son was born to the wife of H.A.<u>Thurman</u>[?] at Fort Bragg August 13, 1916. [data uncertain account damaged original].   Aug 16, 1916

A daughter, the second, was born to the wife of John <u>Thurman</u> March 17, 1913.   Mar 19, 1913

A daughter was born to the wife of C.A.<u>Thurrow</u> of Calpella at Ukiah April 28, 1917.   May 9, 1917

A son was born to the wife of Bert <u>Thurston</u> at Ukiah November 28, 1914.   Dec 9, 1914

A daughter was born to the wife of Mr.E.P.<u>Thurston</u>, editor of *The Ukiah Dispatch* in February, 1915 [date lost].   Feb 17, 1915

A son was born to the wife of Frederick Horace <u>Tibbetts</u> in Berkeley June 3, 1911. Mrs.Tibbetts was the former [Edith] MacKerricher.   Jun 28, 1911

A son was born to the wife of O.B.<u>Tilbben</u> at Potter Valley July 14, 1911.   Aug 2, 1911

A daughter was born to the wife of E.<u>Titus</u> "last week".   Jun 15, 1910

A son, the ninth child, was born to the wife of Ernest   May 7, 1913
Titus near Manchester April 19, 1913.

A son was born to Mrs.Ernest Titus at Point Arena   Apr 17, 1918
April 12, 1918.

A daughter was born to the wife of P.H.Tock at Fish Rock   Jan 5, 1910
January 4, 1910.

A son was born to the wife of James Todd at Caspar   Oct 27, 1915
October 24, 1915.

A son was born to the wife of Adolph Tofallini at Willits   Apr 9, 1913
March 25, 1913.

A son was born to the wife of Alvin S.Tolman of Northspur   Sep 4, 1912
at Fort Bragg August 30, 1912.

A daughter was born to the wife of J.Torstrom at   Dec 17, 1913
Fort Bragg December 16, 1913.

A daughter was born to the wife of W.F.Totten of Noyo   Dec 17, 1919
"this week".

A son was born to the wife of W.Tracy of Westport   Nov 21, 1917
November 19, 1917.

A twelve pound son was born to the wife of Walter Tracy   Jun 21, 1911
at Westport June 17, 1911.

A son was born to the wife of H.Tregoning near Caspar   Nov 19, 1913
"last week".

A son was born to the wife of Mr.Trumbull in Fort Bragg   May 5, 1915
May 2, 1915.

A son was born to the wife of H.C.Tulener at Point Arena   Jan 5, 1910
December 29, 1909.

A daughter was born to the wife of A.Turner at Willits   Oct 20, 1915
October 8, 1915.

A son was born to the wife of Archie Tyson of Inglenook   Jan 16, 1918
at Fort Bragg January 14, 1918.

A daughter was born to the wife of Archie Tyson of   Jul 2, 1919
Inglenook in Fort Bragg June 29, 1919.

A 12 pound daughter was born to the wife of Bert Tyson   Dec 27, 1911
at Mendocino December 24, 1911.

Twin daughters were born to the wife of Robert Tyson at   Jun 4, 1913
Mendocino May 25, 1913.

A son was born to the wife of Sam Tyson at Fort Bragg   Sep 1, 1915
August 30, 1915.

An 8½ pound daughter was born to the wife of William   May 26, 1915
Tyson "this week".

A son was born to the wife of Adolph Urbon at   Jan 31, 1912
Point Arena January 13, 1912.

A son was born to the wife of Antone Urquidi at Mitchell   Jun 2, 1915
Creek "this week".

A son was born to the wife of H.C.Usinger in   Apr 18, 1917
San Anselmo "this week".

A son was born to the wife of M.Valadoa at Mendocino   Oct 7, 1914
October 4, 1914.

A daughter was born to the wife of Edward <u>Valanti</u>
at Elk March 12, 1911.   Mar 29, 1911

A son was born to the wife of G[aspar] <u>Valena</u> near
Mendocino May 15, 1910.   May 25, 1910

A daughter was born to the wife of Gaspar <u>Valena</u> at
Mendocino July 25, 1911.   Aug 16, 1911

A son was born to the wife of Gaspar <u>Valena</u> of Mendocino.
[No date reported].   Jul 9, 1919

A son was born to the wife of W.<u>Valeni</u> at Mendocino
September 7, 1911.   Sep 20, 1911

A son was born to R.C.<u>Valentine</u> in East Mendocino
August 26, 1918.   Sep 4, 1918

A daughter was born to the wife of Harry <u>Van Bebber</u>
at Willits March 13, 1919.   Mar 19, 1919

A daughter was born to the wife of Charles <u>Van Bibber</u> in
Willits December 31, 1915.   Jan 12, 1916

A son was born to the wife of C.<u>Van Dyke</u>, nee Miss
B.Steele of Fort Bragg, Stockton December 22, 1918.   Jan 1, 1919

A son was born to the wife of W.<u>Van Dyke</u> at Covelo
January 20, 1912.   Jan 31, 1912

An eleven pound son was born to the wife of Ernest <u>Vann</u>
at Westport September 28, 1911.   Oct 4, 1911

A daughter was born to the wife of Lester <u>Vann</u> at Ukiah
November 29, 1916.   Dec 6, 1916

A son was born to the wife of J.<u>Vassar</u> at Long Valley
July 16, 1914.   Jul 29, 1914

A daughter was born to the wife of James <u>Van Winkle</u> at
Willits January 6, 1914.   Jan 14, 1914

A son was born to the wife of J.M.<u>Vinton</u> at Laytonville
December 26, 1911.   Jan 17, 1912

A daughter was born to the wife of H.<u>Von Emmel</u> in
Fort Bragg September 5, 1914.   Sep 9, 1914

A daughter was born to the wife of Otto <u>Von Herman</u>
at Poonkinney March 6, 1911.   Mar 22, 1911

A daughter was born to the wife of Henry <u>Voss</u> at
Fort Bragg March 18, 1914.   Mar 25, 1914

The daughter of Miss Lena <u>Wages</u> of Ukiah died during child-   May 19, 1915
birth May 10, 1915. The father was Frank Engler, employed by   May 26, 1915
the Northwestern Pacific Railroad. The mother, 22, from the
Wages Creek area, was held by authorities until death of the
infant was found to have been from natural causes.

A daughter was born to the wife of Walter <u>Waldo</u> at
Fort Bragg February 19, 1916.   Feb 23, 1916

A son was born to the wife of E.L.<u>Waldteufel</u> at Ukiah
April 6, 1917.   Apr 11, 1917

A daughter was born to the wife of Charles <u>Walker</u>,
nee Ella Fairbanks, at Mendocino April 23, 1917.   Apr 25, 1917
She was the sister of Mrs.Carl Nystrom.

A son was born to the wife of Mr.Charles <u>Walker</u>,
nee Ella Fairbanks, formerly of Mendocino, in Washington.   Dec 24, 1919

A daughter was born to the wife of William Walker at Manchester December 18, 1919.	Dec 24, 1919
A son was born to the wife of E.J.Wallace at Laytonville April 12(?), 1915.	Apr 14, 1915
A son was born to the wife of Elmer Wallace of Manchester December 15, 1915.	Dec 22, 1915
An eight pound son was born to the wife of Tom Wallace at Wendling September 24, 1916.	Sep 27, 1916
A daughter was born to the wife of Thomas Wallace at Wendling February 22, 1918.	Feb 27, 1918
A daughter was born to the wife of Thomas Wallace at Wendling March 1, 1919.	Mar 12, 1919
A twelve pound son was born to the wife of William Wallace, nee Ethel Hicks of Fort Bragg, at Willits "recently".	May 5, 1915
A daughter was born to the wife of Charles Wallach at Bell Valley May 3, 1915.	May 12, 1915
A daughter was born to the wife of E.W.Wallen in Ukiah January 15, 1917.	Jan 24, 1917
An 8½ pound daughter was born to the wife of Ray Waller at Fort Bragg March 17, 1915.	Mar 24, 1915
A daughter was born to the wife of George Ward at Ukiah August 24, 1916.	Aug 30, 1916
A daughter was born to the wife of Walter Ward at Manchester July 22, 1910.	Aug 3, 1910
A daughter [Juanita] was born to the wife of William W.Ware in Fort Bragg February 4, 1911.	Feb 8, 1911
A daughter was born to the wife of George E.Warner at Willits December 13, 1911.	Dec 20, 1911
A daughter was born to the wife of John Warren at Willits August 20, 1913.	Aug 27, 1913
A daughter was born to the wife of Mack Washburn at Willits October 15, 1911.	Nov 1, 1911
A son was born to the wife of Elmer Waugh in the Ukiah valley September 22, 1915.	Sep 29, 1915
A daughter was born to the wife of Fred Waugh in the Ukiah valley September 15, 1914.	Sep 23, 1914
A son was born to the wife of Frank Wegar at Ukiah "last week".	Oct 27, 1915
A daughter was born to the wife of F.J.Wegner at Ukiah December 19, 1913.	Dec 31, 1913
A son was born to the wife of John Weisse of Fort Bragg August 16, 1918.	Aug 21, 1918
A 7½ pound son was born to the wife of Horace A.Weller Jr. at Ukiah September 7, 1911.	Sep 13, 1911
A daughter was born to the wife of O.P.Wells at Redwood Valley February 12, 1917.	Feb 21, 1917
A daughter was born to the wife of Erick West of Albion [no date reported].	Apr 30, 1913

A son was born to the wife of Victor Westerlund at
Mendocino October 14, 1916.   Oct 25, 1916

A son was born to the wife of W.Westfall at Albion
July 22, 1913.   Jul 30, 1913

A son was born to the wife of Joseph Westphalen at Willits
December 30, 1916.   Jan 3, 1917

A daughter was born to the wife of Jack Wetherby at Elk
Praire August 1, 1911.   Aug 16, 1911

A son was born to the wife of J.L.Wheeler at Fort Bragg
"this week".   Jul 3, 1918

Henry William Whipple Jr., 11 pounds, was born at Fort Bragg
January 24, 1917.   Jan 31, 1917

A son was born to the wife of Roscius Whipple in Oakland
May 15, 1911. He was formerly of Fort Bragg.   May 17, 1911

A son was born to the wife of George Whitcomb of the
Caspar woods in Fort Bragg May 22, 1918.   May 29, 1918

A son was born to the wife of Judge J.Q.White at Ukiah
"this week".   Dec 6, 1916

A son was born to the wife of Walter White at
Point Arena December 26, 1912.   Jan 1, 1913

A son was born to the wife of Postmaster Fred Whited at
Willits October 1, 1916.   Oct 11, 1916

A son was born to the wife of Fred Whited at Willits
July 6, 1919.   Jul 16, 1919

A son was born to the wife of O.Whitley at Monroe
July 2, 1911.   Jul 19, 1911

A daughter was born to the wife of Ed Whitney at Willits
April 20, 1915.   Apr 28, 1915

A daughter was born to the wife of Frank Whitney at Willits
December 9, 1918. He was in service with the U.S.Navy. Dec 11, 1918

A daughter was born to the wife of Roy Wilcox at
Point Arena November 15, 1913.   Nov 26, 1913

A son was born to the wife of C.R.Wiles at Fort Bragg
January 21, 1915.   Jan 27, 1915

A daughter was born to the wife of Charles R.Wiles in
Caspar March 6, 1918.   Mar 6, 1918

A son was born to the wife of Bert Williams in Albion
June 6, 1918.   Jun 19, 1918

A son was born to the wife of Elmer Williams at
Hammondton, California, August 9, 1919.   Sep 3, 1919

A 12 pound daughter was born to the wife of Frank Williams
at Ukiah August 26, 1916.   Aug 30, 1916

Mrs.J.M.Williams of Willits gave birth to her twentieth   Sep 7, 1910
child "recently". [Fred Williams, born August 23, 1910, killed in a   Jun 2, 1937
logging accident May 31, 1937].

A son was born to the wife of Jasper Williams Jr.
at Willits April 10, 1913.   Apr 16, 1913

A daughter was born to the wife of Merrill Williams at
Willits November 8, 1919. The father was the postmaster Nov 12, 1919
at Laytonville.

A son was born to the wife of William Williams of Caspar November 7, 1918.

Nov 13, 1918

A daughter was born to the wife of William W. Williams at Caspar January 25, 1916.

Jan 26, 1916

An 8½ pound boy was born to the wife of Williard Williams at Nordhoff, Ventura County, December 8, 1912. The mother was the former Eleanor Kelly, daughter of Frank Kelly.

Dec 18, 1912

A son was born to the wife of Charles Williford in San Francisco March 22, 1919.

Apr 9, 1919

A nine pound daughter was born to the wife of Mr. Willis, nee Dena Hansen, at Weed, Siskiyou County, April 18, 1917.

Apr 25, 1917

A ten pound son was born to the wife of Ensign William Willis at Fort Bragg June 6, 1918.

Jun 12, 1918

Margaret Eleanor Willoughby, 7½ pounds, was born at Santa Rosa March 15, 1919, the daughter of Arthur Willoughby.

Mar 19, 1919

A son was born to the wife of Bud Wilsey at Littleriver November 7, 1915.

Nov 17, 1915

An 11½ pound daughter was born to the wife of Bud Wilsey Littleriver "last week".

Jun 4, 1919

A daughter was born to the wife of D. Wilson at Manchester April 10, 1911.

May 3, 1911

A daughter was born to the wife of Devoe Wilson at Manchester December 13, 1913.

Dec 24, 1913

A daughter was born to the wife of F.E. Wilson at Covelo March 17, 1913.

Mar 26, 1913

A nine pound daughter was born to the wife of Kelly K. Wilson "across Pudding Creek" north of Fort Bragg September 2, 1916.

Sep 6, 1916

A nine pound son was born to the wife of Fred Windlinx Jr. in Fort Bragg September 25, 1915.

Sep 29, 1915

Margaret Windlinx, a nine pound daughter, was born to the wife of Fred Windlinx Jr. in Fort Bragg July 17, 1918.

Jul 24, 1918
Jul 22, 1925

A daughter was born to the wife of Abe Wineroth of Willits in San Francisco "last week".

Dec 17, 1913

Elizabeth Emma Winkler was born to the wife of Frank Winkler at Fort Bragg January 25, 1914. She died at age 11 following an appendix operation April 29, 1925. The funeral was held May 3rd with interment at Fort Bragg.

Feb 11, 1914
Apr 29, 1925
May 6, 1925

Charles Wintzer was born September 24, 1826. He celebrated his 85th birthday in 1911.

Sep 20, 1911

A son was born to the wife of Charles Wiss at Willits "last week".

Apr 2, 1919

A son was born to the wife of Gustave Wolfe at Ukiah January 14, 1911.

Jan 25, 1911

A son, the third, was born to the wife of Gustave Wolfe at Ukiah November 2, 1913.

Nov 12, 1913

A daughter was born to the wife of Gustave Wolfe at Ukiah November 20, 1914.

Nov 25, 1914

A daughter was born to the wife of E.E. Wonacott at Willits July 22, 1913.

Jul 30, 1913

A daughter was born to the wife of E.E.Wonacott at Willits   Oct 27, 1915
October 16, 1915.

A daughter was born to the wife of H.H.Wonacott May 6, 1913.   May 14, 1913

A son was born to the wife of H.H.Wonacott at Willits   Feb 3, 1915
January 26, 1915.

A son was born to the wife of K.N.Wonacott at Willits   Feb 3, 1915
January 27, 1915.

A son was born to the wife of K.N.Wonacott at Willits   Jan 17, 1917
January 5, 1917.

A 9½ pound son was born to the wife of F.E.Wood at   Aug 6, 1913
Fort Bragg August 3, 1913.

A son was born to G.C.Wood at Potter Valley March 11, 1911.   Mar 22, 1911

A daughter was born to the wife of Rev.I.H.Wood in Fort   May 19, 1915
Bragg "last week".

An eleven pound son was born to the wife of Rev.Wooduff   Nov 22, 1916
of Hopland in Ukiah November 12, 1916.

A daughter was born to the wife of Roy Woodward   Dec 25, 1918
at Green Acres, Washington, December 21, 1918.

A son was born to the wife of C.Workover at Two Rocks,   Jan 10, 1912
Sonoma County, January 3, 1912.

A son was born to the wife of Mr.Worse of Hop Flat   May 8, 1918
April 27, 1918.

A son was born to the wife of George Yeary at   Jun 20, 1917
Garberville June 13, 1917.

A son was born to the wife of C[larence] Ylitalo at Noyo   Jul 31, 1918
July 18, 1918.

An eight pound daughter was born to the wife of   Jan 17, 1917
Frank Young at Elk January 14, 1917.

A son was born to the wife of Tony Zappa May 7, 1913.   May 14, 1913

A daughter was born to the wife of H.P.Zill at Mendocino   Oct 19, 1910
September 30, 1910.

A daughter was born to the wife of Antone Zmak   Sep 6, 1911
September 3, 1911.

A 3¼ pound daughter was born to the wife of   Apr 5, 1916
Antone Zmak at Fort Bragg March 31, 1916.

A son was born to the wife of J.F.Zumino at Gualala   Jul 19, 1916
July 10, 1916.

Deaths Reported	Issue Date

Mrs.Mary Abarr, a former Laytonville resident, was a suicide at the State Hospital February 24, 1915. She tore a sheet into strips and hanged herself from a window. Her husband and seven children survived.

Mar 3, 1915

Abram Abramson hung himself at Fort Bragg October 21, 1916. A native of Finland, he was 59 years old. The funeral was held in Fort Bragg October 24th led by Rev.J.J.Hillberg.

Oct 25, 1916

C.A.Adams, former Fort Bragg resident, died at Ukiah August 19, 1912. The funeral was held on August 20th.

Aug 21, 1912

Mrs.Edward F.Adams, 73, the wife of a veteran editorial writer for the *San Francisco Chronicle* and an early settler on the north coast, died in San Francisco February 3, 1918. Born in Ohio, she came to California in 1879 living at Kibesillah until 1881. Her sisters were the late Mrs.H.A. Weller of Fort Bragg and Mrs.C.C.Stewart of Petrolia. Six children survived: Edward Adams of New York, Mrs.E.A.Spozia of San Francisco, Mrs.John S.Hicks of Cuervo, New Mexico, William Adams of Oakland, Frank Adams of Piedmont and Marion Adams of San Francisco. Her funeral was in San Francisco.

Feb 6, 1918

Mrs.Mary Ann Adams, 82, died at Point Arena December 25, 1915. She settled on the coast in 1859 and was the mother of ten children.

Jan 5, 1916

Isadore W.Adge died at Fort Bragg following an appendix operation. Born at Iowa Hill in Placer County September 15, 1876, he came to Fort Bragg about 1912. Masonic rites were held in Fort Bragg. His father and stepmother of Newcastle, daughter, Gladys Adge of Marysville, and two brothers, L.P. Adge and E.V.Adge of San Francisco, survived.

May 8, 1918

John Agnew, brother of W.F.Agnew of Fort Bragg, died at Elk May 7, 1912.

May 15, 1912

Mrs.Katheryn Agnew, 71, died in San Francisco July 10, 1916. A native of Vermont, she came to the coast in 1870, settling first at Cuffey's Cove and later, at Greenwood. Her son, William Agnew, survived.

Jul 12, 1916

Matt Aho, who died March 16, 1916, was buried at Fort Bragg the same day.

May 17, 1916

Mrs.Helen Ainslie, 81, died April 17, 1917 and was buried at Point Arena on April 21st. A native of Ontario, Canada, she came to California in 1867 with her late husband, Joseph Ainslie. They first lived one year at Manchester, then 19 at Gualala before locating in Point Arena in 1887. Eight of children survived, four daughters: Mrs T.Collins of Everett, Washington, Mrs.Mary Albee of Seattle, Mrs.Elizabeth Antrim and Mrs Eva Hunter of Point Arena; and four sons: Charles, George Ainslie of Seattle, Washington, Isaac and S.W.Ainslie of Point Arena.

Apr 25, 1917

Joseph Ainslie, 56, died at Boonville January 13, 1916 of acute asthma. A native of Canada, he came to Gualala in 1867. A widow, five sisters and four brothers survived.

Jan 19, 1916

Mrs.Sam Ainslie, a pioneer settler of Point Arena, died October 26, 1918 of influenza. Her husband and daughter survived.

Oct 30, 1918

Miss Aline Aja, 32, was buried in Fort Bragg April 1, 1917. A native of Finland, she lived at the Ranch on Noyo River.

Apr 4, 1917

Miss Allie Akins and her sister, Mrs.Lily Gillmore died at   Mar 11, 1914
Windsor March 3, 1914. Miss Akins was 30 and Mrs.Gillmore,
26. The former died of heart failure. Their joint funeral
was held at Point Arena March 7, 1914.

John Alander, a former resident of the Point Arena district,   Aug 27, 1919
died at the County Farm near Ukiah "recently".

Mrs.Fred D.Albee died in Palo Alto February 6, 1916. Born in   Feb 16, 1916
Ontario, Canada, she came to the coast with her parents. She
was married June 1882 in Gualala to Fred Albee. At her death
she was 52 years old.

Dominico Albergo, a native of Italy aged 21, drowned in the   Jul 16, 1913
Eel River about 25 miles below Dos Rios on July 4, 1913.

Botto Alberto and Gust Wesala were killed in a black powder   Apr 28, 1915
explosion while widening a cut on the California Western
Railroad near Camp 3 April 25, 1915. The funerals were held
April 29th.

Frank H.Alberts, a cousin of Dave Albert, was killed in a   Mar 12, 1913
mill accident at Eureka March 10, 1913.

The infant daughter of Mr.Alexander died at Mendocino   Sep 20, 1911
September 11, 1911.

George L.Alexander, manager of the American Type Foundry in   Aug 27, 1913
San Francisco, died "last week".

L.Alexander, formerly of Fort Bragg, died at the County   Nov 1, 1916
Hospital October 22, 1916 at the age of 63. He was buried
at Healdsburg.

Mrs.Minnie Drury Alexander died near Littleriver April 26,   May 3, 1916
1916. Born in Kingston, Ontario, she had lived at Mendocino,
Albion and Littleriver. Her husband, E.F.Alexander, and
four children survived. The funeral was held at Littleriver
April 28th.

The gasoline schooner *Alliance* sank after striking rocks in   Oct 20, 1915
a fog at Point Arena October 18, 1915. Eight drowned. The   Nov 3, 1915
ship was enroute to Mexico from Victoria, British Columbia.
The owner, Jean Albia, expected to get a mining concession
sion from Mexican president Carranza. The dead included Lena
Miller, about 25, the daughter of a rancher near Brittania
Mines, B.C.; Mr.Baillie of Victoria, Captain William
Delouchery; chief engineer F.E.Harrington; second engineer
J.A.Walsh, cook A.Allan; the owner, Jean Albia and Mrs.Albia.
Allan's body was discovered at Point Arena October 27, 1915
and buried there.

August Allen, a former resident of Point Arena, died at   Jan 12, 1910
Ukiah January 4, 1910 at the age of 88.   Jan 19, 1910

Dave Allen, formerly of Ukiah, died at Woodland "last week".   Nov 30, 1910
His wife was the former Hattie McPeak of Ukiah.

Samuel Allen, a former sheriff of Sonoma County and JP at   Jan 22, 1913
Sebastopol, died near there January 19, 1913.

Mrs.Clara L.Allyn died at Ukiah March 3, 1912.   Mar 13, 1912

Mrs.Susan Alsanson died at Ukiah November 7, 1912. As a   Nov 13, 1912
child she crossed the plains with her family in 1849.
She resided in Ukiah for 6 years. A daughter, Mrs.Lucy
Smith, and a son, S.C.Cornell, survived. Interment was
in Merced.

John <u>Alves</u>, a former Mendocino resident, was fatally   Dec 9, 1914
crushed by a log at Greenwood December 1, 1914. A native
of the Azores, he was 24. Two brothers, Frank of Greenwood
and Manuel of San Francisco, survived. The funeral was held
at Mendocino December 4th.

The daughter of Joseph <u>Ambrow</u> died at Mendocino   Mar 24, 1915
March 16, 1915.

Mrs.Joseph <u>Ambrow</u> died in Fort Bragg January 2, 1919 from Jan 8, 1919
pneumonia. Catholic rites were performed January 5th. Her
husband and three small children survived.

Mrs.E.S.<u>Ames</u> died at Ukiah April 10, 1915. Born in Iowa   Apr 21, 1915
February 3, 1850, she came to California with her parents in
1863. In 1871 at Sacramento she married Mr.Ames. Her husband,
three children and mother, Mrs.Chaplin, survived.

The infant daughter of Albert <u>Anderson</u> died at Albion   Feb 21, 1912
February 7, 1912.

One of 3½ year old twin sons of P.<u>Anderson</u> of Albion   Aug 25, 1915
died August 23, 1915.

Alie <u>Anderson</u>, the oldest son of of N.P.Anderson of   Feb 26, 1913
Mendocino, died February 21, 1913. He was about 20.
The funeral was held in Mendocino February 23rd.

Andrew <u>Anderson</u>, an old fisherman at Noyo, died   Jun 25, 1913
June 25, 1913.

Andrew <u>Anderson</u> fell into a coma on Thanksgiving Day,   Dec 24, 1919
November 27, 1919, and died in the Albion hospital
December 20, 1919. He worked for the Albion Lumber Company
about 20 years. His funeral was held December 21st followed
by burial at Littleriver.

Anna L.<u>Anderson</u> died at Ukiah November 20, 1910.   Nov 30 ,1910
She was 25 years 4 months and 26 years old.

Antone <u>Anderson</u>, 40, died at Fort Bragg September 11, 1918. Sep 18, 1918
He has recently released from San Quentin where he had been
incarcerated for shooting William McKelve [McKilva] at Noyo
on May 6, 1915.

Mrs.Chris <u>Anderson</u>, one of the first settlers at Caspar,   Apr 2, 1919
died there March 27, 1919 at the age of 79 years 5 months
and 12 days. Born in Sweden in 1839, she came to the U.S.
in 1872. Married in Sweden to Chris Anderson in 1859 (he
died about 20 years ago), they had five children: three
sons, Charles, Eddie and Ernest Anderson, and two daughters,
Mrs.Charles Nystrom and Mrs.Phil Arthur. She was buried at
Fort Bragg March 30th.

Fred <u>Anderson</u>, the son of Nicholas Anderson of Albion,   Sep 3, 1919
died following an appendix operation. Born and raised in
Albion, he was 28 years old. The funeral was held at
Littleriver August 31, 1919.

Gabriel Andrew <u>Anderson</u>, 27, died at Fort Bragg of influenza Nov 20, 1918
November 17, 1918. Born August 24, 1891 in Finland, he had Nov 27, 1918
been a resident for 8 years. He was buried at Fort Bragg
November 20th.

Gus <u>Anderson</u> was killed at Greenwood by a falling tree the Aug 14, 1912
"first of the week".

J.R.<u>Anderson</u> died at Fort Bragg April 1, 1912. The funeral Apr 3, 1912
was held on the 3rd. in Fort Bragg.

Mrs.P.Anderson died near Littleriver August 16, 1918. Two   Aug 21, 1918
sons and a daughter, Mrs.Al Johnston, survived. Burial was
at Littleriver August 18th.

Peter Anderson, a pioneer of Littleriver, died   Jan 31, 1912
January 24, 1912.

Robert Anderson was found dead in bed at Camp 10 near   Jan 29, 1913
Comptche January 20, 1913. From Sweden, he was a woodsman
about 40 years old and had been on the coast about 15 years.
He was known as a heavy drinker. Burial was at Mendocino
January 23rd.

William S.Anderson was severly injured in an accident at   Mar 18, 1914
the Greenwood mill March 16, 1914 and subsequently died at   Mar 25, 1914
Elk on March 17th. He was 40 years old and left a wife and
three children. His funeral was held at the Fort Bragg
Presbyterian church March 22nd.

William T.Anderson, a former soldier, died at Mendocino   Aug 27, 1919
August 19, 1919 of TB. He served in France with the 20th
Engineers as a tie maker. Born and raised in Littleriver,
his brother L.C.Anderson and sister, Mrs.A.R.Johnson,
survived. The funeral was held at Littleriver August 23rd.

Mrs.Bozdlina Andre died in Fort Bragg November 12, 1918.   Nov 13, 1918
She had given birth the previous day but the infant died.

Gertrude Ruschetti Andreani, the adopted ten year old   Oct 18, 1916
daughter of L.J.Andreani, died at St.Mary's Academy in San
Leandro of diptheria. Her father was the vice-president of
the First Savings Bank of Eureka. The funeral was held in
Fort Bragg October 14, 1916.

Jim Ankle, a.k.a.Old Jim, died at Pinolville September 27,   Oct 7, 1914
1914 at the age of 107.

Nick Anthon, a native of Greece, fell off a handcar near   Jul 14, 1915
Willits and died of his injuries [no date reported].

Luigi Antonelli, 29, was killed by a falling limb in the   Aug 30, 1916
woods at Comptche August 23, 1916. A native of Italy, he
was an 11 year resident. The funeral was August 27th.

David L.Antrim died at Sunnyvale "last week" He came to   May 28, 1919
the coast in 1865 and lived on Alder Creek until 1917
when he moved to Sunnyvale.

C.F.Apfel, 55, died at Ukiah August 3, 1914.   Aug 5, 1914

George Arfstein, about 60, died at the County Hospital in   Mar 27, 1918
Ukiah March 22, 1918. He was an early settler of the area.

John Aridson, 40, died at Willits July 3, 1912. A native of   Jul 10, 1912
Sweden, he was a railroad worker.

L.R.Arnold, a long time resident of the County, died at the   Dec 7, 1910
County hospital in Ukiah "last week". He was the stepfather
of Archibald Yell and Charles Tindall.

David Arnott, a visitor from Missouri, died suddenly at   Jun 23, 1915
Fort Bragg June 20, 1915. His son, D.W.Arnott of Fort Bragg   Jun 30, 1915
survived. His funeral was held June 27th in Fort Bragg.

Mrs.Sarah Arnott, 62 and a native of England, died in Grass   May 16, 1917
Valley May 11, 1917. Her son, David Arnott of Fort Bragg,
survived. She was buried at Fort Bragg May 14, 1917.

G.A.Assies, a native of Holland, died at Saratoga at age 71.   Oct 10, 1914
[Date of death indeterminate].

John Atkins, 82, died December 26, 1917 "across Pudding   Jan 2, 1918
Creek" north of Fort Bragg. A native of Pennsylvania, he had
been a 16 year resident while working as a carpenter. The
funeral was held from the Presbyterian church December 28th
with Rev.W.M.Sutherland officiating. Two daughters, Mrs.J.C.
Harper of Washington, Mrs.R.Hersey of New Mexico, and three
sons, W.H. Atkins of Stockton, A.E. and W.J.Atkins of New
Mexico survived.

Bernhardt Aulin , age 21, was buried in Fort Bragg by   May 11, 1910
Rev.W.A.Chapman [no date reported]. He was survived by his
mother and two brothers.

Mrs.Matilda Aulin, the mother of Fred and Ed Aulin, died   Sep 7, 1910
[September 6, 1910] at the age of 52. A native of Norway,
she was the widow of Charles Aulin. The funeral was held at
the Finn Hall September 8, 1910 with Rev.Hillberg conducting
the ceremony in Swedish and Rev.W.A.Chapman in English.

Harry Auser, formerly of Fort Bragg, died in San Francisco Apr 16, 1919
April 12, 1919 following an operation. The oldest son of
Frank Auser of Littleriver, he was born in Mendocino 25 years
ago. Married about 5 years earlier, he left a wife, parents,
two brothers, Jack and Seth Auser, and a sister, Frances
Auser. The funeral was held at Littleriver April 17, 1919
with Rev.W.A.Chapman officiating.

Lloyd Austin died at Largo November 16, 1910. His wife and Nov 23, 1910
baby survived.

Captain Ayles, formerly of Littleriver, died at Mendocino   Nov 14, 1917
November 11, 1917 at the age of 88. Two daughters, Miss
Blanche Ayles and Miss Gresham of Los Angeles, survived. The
funeral was held at Littleriver November 12th.

Mrs.Agnes May Ayres, 49, died September 22, 1917 from   Sep 26, 1917
ptomaine poisoning gotten from old sausage. Four of her sons
served in the U.S.Army.

Horace E.Babbitt, a resident of coast more than 25 years,   Jul 8, 1914
died at age 68 July 6, 1914. He was a native of Kansas.

David Babcock of Boonville, 86, died April 8, 1917 in Fort Apr 11, 1917
Bragg. Burial was in Boonville. A widow and 3 sons survived.

L.W.Babcock, 63, died suddenly December 1, 1919 at El Monte, Dec 10, 1919
Los Angeles County. A native of New York, he came to
Mendocino in 1882, taught school at Littleriver and, in 1885,
at Ukiah, serving as principal of the highschool until 1906
when he was elected County School Superintendent. He was
serving as principal at the El Monte highschool when he died.
He married Anna Pullen of Littleriver. His widow and sons
survived. The funeral was December 4th; burial, at Whittier.

Richard Babcock, aged 72, died at Willits November 1, 1910. Nov 9, 1910

W.A.Babcock, a Long Valley rancher, 45, was found dead   Dec 31, 1913
December 25, 1913. Born and raised near Cahto, he suffered
from heart disease.

Fred E.Backman died near Noyo Hill January 18, 1917 from a Jan 24, 1917
heart attack. A native of Finland, he left a widow, son,
Fred Backman, and a daughter, Mrs.D.O.Newton. The funeral
was held at Fort Bragg January 21st.

Harry Baechtel, 38, a rancher in Little Lake valley, died in Feb 11, 1914
Willits February 5, 1914 at the age of 88.

Samuel S.Baechtel died June 18, 1915. Born in Hagerstown,   Jun 23, 1915
Maryland, September 26, 1826, he came to California via
Panama and settled in Marin County where he operated a
sawmill with his brother Henry. He was the first elected

Samuel S.Baechtel (*continued*)
sheriff in Marin County. In 1855 Henry and Sam drove a herd
of cattle to Little Lake Valley where they were the first
white settlers. Their brother, Martin, later joined them in
the ranch business. They were the original incorporators of
the Irvine and Muir Lumber Company. In 1861 Samuel married
Harriet Henry. Four children were born: Gordon, William,
Miss Lizzie and Luther Baechtel.

Nancy Bahn, aged 58, died at Willits September 13, 1911.   Oct 4, 1911

Mrs.Minnie Bailey, wife of Eugene Bailey of Mendocino, died   Dec 23, 1914
at Fort Bragg December 22, 1914. The daughter of Isaac   Dec 30, 1914
Wainwright, she was born at Salmon Creek March 15, 1879. A
teacher at the Spring Grove school, she married Eugene Bailey
in 1911. Her funeral was held December 27th. Among those left
were her parents in Newman, brothers, Harry, of Navarro,
Edward of Skaggs Springs, Samuel of Newman, and sisters, Mrs.
D.Daniels of Mendocino and Mrs.Rose Pegg of Oakland.

Mrs.Sarah Ann Bailey, the wife of James Bailey, died at   May 24, 1916
Willits May 12, 1916. She was 90 years 7 months and 1 day
old. Born in Missouri, she settled in Willits in 1868.

Joseph Bainbridge, 74, dropped dead in Fort Bragg   Nov 8, 1916
November 6, 1916. A native of Quebec, he came to the coast   Nov 15, 1916
in 1890 living for four years at Usal and then at Cleone
where he ranched. His wife survived him. Catholic rites
were performed November 8th by Father Blanderfield.

Mrs.Olive Bainbridge, the wife of the late Joseph Bainbridge   Mar 6, 1918
of Cleone, died in San Francisco [no date reported] at age
72. She had settled at Usal in 1891 and Cleone in 1897.
Catholic rites were held March 7, 1918. Her daughter, Mrs.
E.Materne of San Francisco, survived.

Bessie Baker, aged 16, drowned in the Noyo River July 28,   Aug 3, 1910
1910 while on an outing with the Adulphus Jamison family.
Services were held at the Episcopal church, Rev.John Barrett
presided. A mother and brothers survived.

William Baker, 40, engineer on the steamer *Arctic*, was   Nov 7, 1917
believed to have drowned in the Fort Bragg harbor
October 27, 1917. His wife and two children in San
Francisco survived. The body was not recovered.

Claire Lyle Ball was found dead at the bottom of a bluff near   Oct 22, 1919
Point Arena "last week" and was buried October 17, 1919.

Dreame Life Ball of Albion died July 4, 1917. Born in Boon-   Jun 27, 1917
ville October 9, 1873, he became a school teacher. He wed   Jul 11, 1917
Louise "Dolly" Rice Handley at Ukiah July 4, 1897. His
widow, brother and three sisters survived: E.B.Ball of
Ukiah, Mrs.J.B.Hunt of Bakersfield, Mrs.J.J.Smiley of
Cloverdale, Mrs.G.M.Miller of Boonville. Burial was at
Littleriver with Rev.W.A.Chapman officiating.

J.D.Ball died at Point Arena August 3, 1915. Born near   Aug 18, 1915
Boonville March 4, 1863, he later married Lola Ledford.
His widow and five childen survived: Mrs.G.Philbert,
Raymond, Hazel, Clair and Clyde Ball of Point Arena. Two
brothers, E.B.Ball of Ukiah and D[reame L[ife] Ball of
Albion as well as two sisters, Mrs.J.B.Hunt and Mrs.G.
Miller, also survived.

Raymond Ball, 18, a U.S.Coast Guard member, was killed in   Mar 12, 1919
San Francisco by a streetcar "last week". He was a nephew
of Billy Phillips and had often visited in Fort Bragg.

William Ball, an Indian, died near Point Arena   Dec 11, 1918
December 7, 1918.

Mrs.Catherine Ballentine, 85, died in San Francisco
September 29, 1912. A former resident of Greenwood and
Cuffey's Cove, she was buried at Greenwood October 3rd.

Oct 9, 1912

Bud Banker, 23, of Ukiah, died in San Francisco
January 13, 1917 from pneumonia. The funeral was held in
Ukiah on January 15th.

Jan 17, 1917

Mrs.Charles Banker, a Mendocino pioneer, died there
November 4, 1917 of Bright's disease. Her husband and
daughter, Minnie Hayter, survived. The funeral was held
November 6th with Rev.H.P.Ingram officiating followed by
burial at Littleriver.

Nov 7, 1917

Daniel R.Bannerman, 69, an old coast pioneer, died at
Comptche August 27, 1917. Three daughters survived: Mrs.
Louis Anderson of Caspar, Mrs.Dolly Hodghead of Mendocino
and Mrs.Robert Linn of Navarro Ridge.

Aug 29, 1917

Frank Baptist died at Branscomb December 25, 1916.

Dec 27, 1916

James F.Barbee, a former Fort Bragg resident and Superintendent of schools for 8 years, died December 31, 1911 at
the age of 44. Born in Missouri, he came to Ukiah with his
family as a child. A wife, two sons and a daughter survived.

Jan 3, 1912

Leonard Bargqvist, 9, the son of Gus Bargqvist, died
January 16, 1919 from influenza. Rev.J.J.Hillberg led the
the funeral in Fort Bragg January 18, 1919.

Jan 22, 1919

Marion L.Barnett, 32, assistant cashier of the Bank of
Willits, died December 4, 1916 following an appendix
operation. He was a three year resident.

Dec 13, 1916

Thomas Barrett, 56,died at the State Hospital in
Talmage "last week".

Nov 10, 1915

Mrs.J.H.Barter died in San Francisco August 31, 1912
following an appendix operation. The funeral was held in the
Christian church at Ukiah with Rev.Moore presiding.

Sep 4, 1912

J.Bartlett, 87, died at Ukiah February 3, 1916. A native of
Tennessee, he came to Ukiah in the 1850s.

Feb 9, 1916

Robert Bartlett, a resident of the Ukiah Valley, died at
Berkeley May 3, 1910 and was buried in Ukiah.

May 4, 1910

Willie Bartley, about nine years old, died at Fort Bragg of
diptheria November 1, 1913.

Nov 5, 1913

Mrs.S.Barton, wife of Homer Barton, died at Littleriver
December 17, 1910. A daughter, Mrs.Will Coombs of Little-
river, survived. Rev.Fisher officiated at the funeral
December 19, 1910.

Dec 21, 1910

Frank Bartow, 32, leaped off a 75 foot bluff to his death
in the Wheelbarrow Valley sometime between April 12 and
15, 1919. He was thought to have been insane.

Apr 23, 1919

John Baskerville, an old Mendocino resident, died
February 6, 1910. A native of England born in 1845, he came
to Mendocino in 1876 and worked in the woods.

Feb 16, 1910

Mrs.A.Bateman died at Covelo May 2, 1912. Her son, George
Conrad, of Covelo survived.

May 8, 1912

M.M.Bates, died at Westport November 6, 1911. He was
69 years 9 months and 10 days old. He had been a resident of
California for 50 years, 30 of which were at Westport where
he had served as postmaster. A wife, two sons and a daughter
survived. His funeral was held November 8, 1911.

Nov 8, 1911

George <u>Batt</u>, 63, was buried at Point Arena September 21, 1918. September 21, 1918. A native of Wales, he left a widow and twelve living children-two had died earlier.

Helen A.<u>Baum</u>, 13, the daughter of Herman R.Baum of Fort Bragg, died December 30, 1911 of diabetes. She was born in Fort Bragg in 1898. The funeral was led January 3, 1912 by Rev.W.A.Chapman.

Jan 3, 1912

Mrs.Frank W.<u>Beach</u>, a former Mendocino resident, died in Portland, Oregon, "last week". Her husband, two sons, two daughters and a brother, Perry Stanley, survived.

Oct 2, 1912

Mrs.J.H.<u>Beal</u> of Caspar died in a San Francisco hospital November 30, 1919 at the age of 51 years 4 months and 4 days. A native of Maine, she lived in Caspar where the family ran a hotel. Her husband and seven children survived: Mrs.Nicey Brochier, Mrs.Amy Meister, Edward, Charles, Harold, Albert and Leslie Beal. On December 2nd Rev.T.W.Harris of Caspar led her funeral.

Dec 3, 1919

George <u>Bean</u>, 36, died in Tulare December 5, 1915. A former A former Cleone and Fort Bragg resident, he was the son of Mrs.William Nicholson and brother of Carl Bean of Fort Bragg. Mr.Bean was employed as a drayman and left a wife and three children.

Dec 8, 1915

Mrs.Louisa Maye <u>Bean</u>, the daughter of Dave LeBallister, a former resident of the coast, died in San Francisco September 26, 1913. She was 32 years 8 months and 7 days old.

Oct 1, 1913

Allen F.<u>Beard</u> died January 11, 1912 of TB. His mother and brothers survived. The funeral was held at the Baptist church January 14th with Rev.Garth officiating.

Jan 17, 1912

Mrs.Ida <u>Beard</u>, the wife of H.H.Beard of Dos Rios, died at Ukiah August 15, 1919 following an operation. *Nee* Ida Simonson, she was born at Willits February 22, 1872 and grew up there, teaching school 1892-1906. In 1907 she married Mr.Beard, a stockman. She left a husband and five small children.

Aug 20, 1919

E.H.<u>Beattie</u> of Ukiah died of stroke "last week".

Oct 5, 1910

Edward <u>Beattie</u> of Willits, aged 32, was killed by a falling tree near Sherwood June 29, 1911.

Jul 5, 1911

Karl S.<u>Beattie</u>, a Willits rancher, died May 13, 1915 at the age of 26. The son of S.P.Beattie, he left a wife and 8 month old daughter.

May 19, 1915

Thomas F.<u>Beattie</u> died in the Ukiah Valley August 20, 1911. Born in Virginia 1830, he came to Sonoma County in the early days.

Aug 23, 1911

Mrs.T[homas] F.<u>Beatie</u>, 77, died at Ukiah June 16, 1913. The funeral was held on the 18th.

Jun 25, 1913

Mr.and Mrs.<u>Beck</u> of Willits and two children were killed in a snow slide near Everett, Washington. [No date reported].

Mar 23, 1910

Chris <u>Beck</u>, 62, died in a San Francisco hospital of cancer December 5, 1915. A native of Germany, he came to the coast about 1882 after a shipwreck. Seven children survived. The funeral was held at Fort Bragg December 9, 1915.

Dec 8, 1915

Christopher <u>Beck</u> Jr., the son of Chris Beck, died Glendale, Los Angeles County, October 19, 1910. He was born in Fort Bragg in 1887. The body was shipped to Fort Bragg on the steamer *Arctic* for burial November 3, 1910.

Oct 26, 1910
Nov 2, 1910

Miss Emma Beck was killed in an automobile accident south of   Aug 21, 1918
Fort Bragg August 15, 1918. A telephone operator at Fort
Bragg, she was 26 years 6 months and 1 day old. The funeral
was held August 19th with Rev.W.A.Chapman officiating.

Mrs.Henry Beck, about 39, died at Sheldon, Iowa,   Nov 21, 1917
November 15, 1917. She had been a five year resident of Fort
Bragg coming from southern California.

Napoleon Beebe, a former Point Arena resident, died in   May 24, 1916
Humboldt County "in early May" [1916] at the age of 76. He
built the first hotel in Point Arena. His daughter, Mrs.H.
Eagan of Wendling, and a son in Humboldt County, survived.

Thomas H.Beggs died at Mendocino October 16, 1914. The   Oct 21, 1914
funeral was held there October 18th.

E.S.Belknap, 45, was a suicide by gunshot January 23, 1917.   Jan 24, 1917
Originally from Michigan, he operated a cigar shop in Fort
Bragg. A wife, two daughters and two sons survived. The
funeral was held in Fort Bragg January 25th.

Roy Stanley Belknap, aged 13, drowned in the Sand Hill lake   Jan 25, 1911
north of Cleone January 23, 1911. Standing in a canoe with a   Feb 1, 1911
companion who fired at a duck, he fell into the lake when
the boat capsized. His family had lived in the area for
about three years. The funeral was held January 26th.

Mrs.Nancy Ann Bellah, 86, died at Willits June 14, 1919. A   Jun 18, 1919
California resident for 65 years, she was the mother of
Mrs.F.W.Steele, who survived.

Pete Beltranni died of a fractured skull in a fight with   Aug 24, 1910
Emanuel Ballistessa August 24, 1910.

Joe Bennett, an old Covelo resident, died in Ukiah   Jun 4, 1913
May 27, 1913 and was buried there.

William Bennett was found dead in his cabin September 23,   Oct 4, 1916
1916 south of Fort Bragg. He had once been in charge of the
Union Lumber Company's powerhouse. He carved a 'family' of
wood which had became a local curiosity before he burned it.

Mrs.Hattie Berger, former Potter Valley resident, died in   Aug 23, 1911
Santa Rosa August 20, 1911.

William Bergerson, 28, the son of Louis Bergerson of Willits,   Oct 30, 1918
died at Ukiah October 23, 1918 from influenza. He left a
wife and two children.

Mrs.Hattie Noble Berke, wife of Edward Berke, died near   Jun 18, 1913
Galloway of pneumonia June 6, 1913.

Herman Berkovits dropped dead on a hunting trip August 27,   Sep 3, 1913
1913. A native of Finland, he was 51 years 1 month and
16 days old and a 25 year resident of Fort Bragg. The
funeral was held in Fort Bragg August 31, 1913.

John Berkyaca, 48, died October 24, 1915 in a San Fran-   Nov 3, 1915
cisco hospital following an appendix operation. A Croat,
he was a resident of Fort Bragg for seven years. The
funeral was held in Fort Bragg October 31st. His wife,
three daughters and two sons survived as well as his
two brothers. The oldest of his two sons served in the
Austrian army in Europe during World War I.

Mrs.Ida Bernstein died in San Francisco March 30, 1912. The   Apr 3, 1912
daughter of W.S.Saunders of Fort Bragg, she was 31 years
years old. The funeral was held in Fort Bragg April 2nd led
by Rev.R.C.Grace.

Simon <u>Berringer</u> died at Fort Bragg June 30, 1915. A native   Jul 7, 1915
of Canada, he was 63½ years old. He came to Caliornia in
1862 and lived near Fort Bragg for 25 years. A wife and son
survived. The funeral was held July 2nd in Fort Bragg.

The infant son of Mr.<u>Berry</u> of Boonville died March 15, 1915   Mar 24, 1915
at Philo. Burial was at Boonville March 17th.

Grandma <u>Berry</u>, mother of J.E.Berry proprietor of the Boon-   Nov 30, 1910
ville Hotel, died November 19, 1910 at 91.

Mrs.Frank D.<u>Berryhill</u>,42, died at Geyserville [no date   May 9, 1917
reported]. Her brother-in-law was George Berryhill of
Fort Bragg.

George H.<u>Berryhill</u> died in an Oakland hospital July 11, 1919   Jul 16, 1919
from a brain tumor. Born in Iowa, he was 61 years old. His
wife and 12 children survived: Melvin, Archie T., Elmer M.,
Pearl O., Myrtle A., Ruth M., Hazel E., Gladys H., Margerite
T.Berryhill, Mrs.C.F.Rafter, Mrs.W.F.Loescher and Mrs.P.G.
Pettier. The funeral was held July 17th at Fort Bragg with
Rev.A.J.Sturtevant and Dr.Bryan presiding.

Joseph T.<u>Berryhill</u>, father of George Berryhill of Fort   Oct 28, 1914
Bragg, died in Potter Valley October 22, 1914 at the age of
91 years 4 months and 7 days. Born in Greene County, Ohio,
June 16, 1823, he moved to Indiana in 1840, to Iowa in 1842
working as a carpenter until 1867 when he moved to Missouri
taking up farming and carpentry. In 1875 he came to California and lived at Caspar and in the Ukiah valley. In 1844
he married Jane Butler, who died July 4, 1867 after bearing
ten children. He remarried in 1868, to Mrs.Cynthia Faulken-
berry, who died about 1885. Joseph's funeral was held at
Ukiah October 26, 1914.

B.<u>Bersten</u>, a sailor of the steamer *Frank D.Stout*, died in   Jul 31, 1918
the Fort Bragg hospital from a fractured skull received when
he fell in a drunken stupor in San Francisco as the ship was
sailing. Brought ashore at Point Arena, he was carried by
automobile to Fort Bragg where he died.

Ulissme <u>Bertini</u> was killed when a pile of lumber fell on him   Jul 5, 1911
June 29, 1911. A native of Italy, he was 35 years old.
Catholic rites were performed July 2, 1911.

Mrs.Angelina <u>Bertola</u> of Manchester died November 11, 1918   Nov 13, 1918
from influenza. A native of Italy and 36 years old, she
left a husband and five children.

Harry <u>Betts</u> of Covelo was killed in action in France   Jan 15, 1919
September 8, 1918. He was survived by his parents, brothers
and sisters: Ross and Edward Betts of Laytonville, Mrs.
Hazne of Covelo, Minnie and May Betts of Covelo, Mrs.E.
McClure and Mrs.Frank Wilson of Fort Bragg and Mrs.Ethel
Downing of Santa Rosa.

I.<u>Betz</u>, 85, a former Fort Bragg resident for 19 years,   Sep 23, 1914
died at Sacramento September 16, 1914. His son, Fred Betz
of Sacramento, survived. Burial was in Ukiah.

Mrs.Mary <u>Bever</u> died at Mendocino January 29, 1917. Her   Jan 31, 1917
husband, Ben Bever, survived. The funeral February 1, 1917.

Napoleon B.<u>Bever</u> died at Mendocino January 4, 1913. Born in   Jan 15, 1913
Bates County, Missouri, February 13, 1841, he came overland
to California in 1860. He married Delia Handrahan January 4,
1864. (She died May 18, 1899). Four brothers, Samuel,
Benjamin, Robert of Mendocino and Thomas of Visalia survived
as did one sister, Mrs.Ellen Linscott of Point Arena. There
were four children: Mrs.Anna Mead of Ukiah, Mrs.Ida Sherwood,
Samuel and Charles Bever of Mendocino. The funeral was led by
Rev.J.M.Fisher at the Presbyterian church January 6, 1913.

Samuel <u>Bever</u>, 73, died December 27, 1919. A 58 year resident
of Mendocino, he arrived in 1861 and worked as a sawyer at
the mill until 1878 when he went into the hotel business.
About 1901 he retired and sold the hotel to John Silvia. Two
brothers, Ben and Robert Bever, a sister, Mrs.Lonscott
[Linscott?] Point Arena, survived. The funeral was held at
Mendocino December 30th.

Dec 31, 1919

David <u>Bickford</u>, age 10, was killed by his insane father,
George Bickford, in Potter Valley May 30, 1914. The father
later committed suicide at the State Hospital.

Jun 3, 1914

Mrs.Pauline <u>Bieber</u> died in San Francisco "this week" and was
buried in Fort Bragg August 7, 1918. She was well known on
the coast as a piano salesperson. Father Lawrence officiated.

Aug 7, 1918

William James <u>Biggar</u> died at Covelo April 16, 1916. He was
78 years 8 months and 10 days old. Born in Ireland, he came
to California in 1860, settling at Navarro where he farmed
until moving to Round Valley. Three sons survived: Arthur W.
Biggar was a contractor in Oakland, William J.Biggar, an
attorney in Bellingham, Washington, and George Milton Biggar,
a merchant in Covelo.

Apr 26, 1916

Charles <u>Biggers</u>, the brother of A.W.Biggers of Fort Bragg,
died in Bellingham, Washington, March 11, 1911.

Mar 29, 1911

Mrs.W.J.<u>Biggers</u> died at Covelo February 6, 1915. A native
of Canada, she had come to California in the early 1870s.
At death she was 66 years old and had lived at Navarro for
some time. Her son, A.W.Biggers, was a former Fort Bragg
resident, but had moved to Berkeley. The funeral was held at
Covelo February 9th.

Feb 17, 1915

Charles <u>Biggs</u> died at the County Hospital in Talmage
April 28, 1914 from injuries received when thrown from a
horse. Two sisters survived: Mrs.Della Albertson and Mrs.
D.Parnell, both of Oakland.

May 6, 1914

Arthur B.<u>Biglow</u>, 39, a former Covelo resident, died at
Fort Bragg September 28, 1914 of pneumonia.

Sep 30, 1914

Mrs.Polly <u>Billings</u>, 63, died at Noyo October 3, 1914. Two
sons, Edward Billings and William Brown, survived. She was
buried at Inglenook Octobr 5th.

Oct 7, 1914

Louis <u>Billodeau</u>, 70, died at Willits May 13, 1919. He first
ranched near Westport in 1870. About 1890 in partnership with
Albert Switzer, he ranched in Sherwood Valley selling out in
1901 and moving to Willits. He was buried with Masonic rites.

May 21, 1919

Fred <u>Binkley</u>, 75, a veteran of the Civil War and a coast
resident for 12 years, died in Fort Bragg June 3, 1919.

Jun 4, 1919

Charles <u>Bishop</u> died at Point Arena September 4, 1912. He
owned a ranch on the Garcia River.

Sep 11, 1912

Harry <u>Bishop</u> was killed in an automobile accident at
Gualala April 27, 1915. Born in Nova Scotia, he came to
California in 1884 locating at Manchester where he was in
the general merchandising business the last five years. A
widow and seven children survived. The funeral was held at
Manchester April 29th led by Rev.A.H.Clark.

May 5, 1915

John <u>Bishop</u>, 50, died suddenly in Fort Bragg March 21, 1919.
A native of Finland, he had been a 35 year resident of Point
Arena, Greenwood and, after 1917, Fort Bragg. His funeral
was held at Fort Bragg March 23rd under Father Grant.

Mar 26, 1919

L.H.<u>Bither</u>, a former Mendocino resident, died in San Francisco June 19, 1917. His wife and daughter, Mrs.Clara
Isabell, survived.

Jun 27, 1917

Daniel Blackman died from diptheria about 6 miles east of   Apr 19, 1911
Noyo April 18, 1911. The funeral was held the next day.

Austin Blair, 17, the son of Rufus C.Blair of DeHaven, died   Jan 17, 1917
at Fort Bragg January 16, 1917 following an operation in
which his arm was removed. The funeral was held at Fort
Bragg on January 18th.

Mrs.Samuel Blair died in San Francisco "this week".   Apr 28, 1915
She was an early settler on the coast in the 1850s.

William J.Blair, a pioneer settler in Mendocino 50 years   Oct 29, 1919
ago, died in Indio, Riverside County, October 26, 1919.
He ranched here until 1907. Born in Vermont August 21, 1846,
he was the last living member of the Cahto IOOF Lodge.
Burial was in Laytonville.

William S.Blair, 54, died in San Francisco June 25, 1916.   Jun 28, 1916
He was the only son of Capt.Samuel Blair and brother of
Jennie M.Blair. The funeral was in San Francisco June 28th.

Mrs.Martha Blake died at Mendocino March 5, 1919. Three   Mar 12, 1919
daughters survived: Mrs.Parker Gowell, Mrs.Kate Anderson and
Mrs.A.Linn. The funeral was held at Mendocino March 7th.

Clarence Blakely, the 4 month old son of Freeman Blakely,   Jan 28, 1914
died in Fort Bragg January 24, 1914.   Feb 4, 1914

The infant son of Charles Blakesley died at Sanger, Fresno   Oct 9, 1912
County "last week". The mother was the former Crystal
Sturtevant.

Z.V.Blalock died at the County Hospital September 14, 1914.   Sep 23, 1914
The funeral was held on September 16th.

Miss Edith T.Blank died June 30, 1911 of a ruptured appendix.   Jul 5, 1911
A native of Finland, she was 23 years 11 months and 7 days old.
She came to California with her parents in 1896. The funeral
was at the Presbyterian church in Fort Bragg July 2, 1911.

The infant son of Henry Block died at Westport   Feb 3, 1915
January 28, 1915. The funeral was held there.

George Block [later report "George Ward"] was shot and killed   Dec 10, 1913
by Mrs.Fabian Reyes [later report "Flora Reyes"] northwest of   Dec 17, 1913
Covelo December 2, 1913.

Mrs.J.T.Blosser, the mother of Walter Saunders of Fort Bragg,   Nov 1, 1916
died in San Francisco October 25, 1916. Born in Sonoma County
December 3, 1865, she came to Willits in the same year.

John Adam Blosser died at Santa Maria June 11, 1915. Born   Jun 23, 1915
in Jefferson County, Iowa, September 6, 1849, he crossed the
plains with his family in 1850 and lived near Stockton until
1858 when they moved to Little Lake Valley where they settled
in 1860. A rancher all his life, he married Ora Morgan in
1888. Two children survived: Miss Hazel Blosser, a teacher
in the Ukiah grammar school, and Roy Blosser, a professor of
manual training at Santa Rosa.

Nicholas J.Blosser, 85, died April 1, 1919 at Willits where   Apr 9, 1919
he had settled in 1860. He built the first sawmill there.
His son, Fred Blosser, six brothers, one of whom was Tobias
Blosser, survived.

John Blunck, a Fort Bragg businessman, died in San Francisco   Oct 24, 1917
following an operation. A native of Germany, he was 51 years
old and had lived on the coast for 16 years. His funeral was
held in Fort Bragg October 21st.

Mrs.Emma Bodine, sister of Mrs.Garsey and E.S.Ames, died at   Nov 13, 1912
Ukiah November 6, 1912.

Mrs.Aileen Bohn, a former Fort Bragg resident, died in an   Nov 28, 1917
Oakland hospital following an operation "last week". She was
the daughter of Mr.Corwin, an early coast resident and sister
of Mrs.H.G.Johnson.

Mrs.E.E.Boles, 56, was killed in a runaway accident near   Nov 22, 1916
Willits November 21, 1916. She was a local music teacher.

D.Caselli shot four people at the Maffini Hotel in Fort   Aug 16, 1916
Bragg August 13, 1916 in a crazed attack fatally wounding   Sep 6, 1916
two, John Bolson and A.Maffini, before turning the gun on
himself. Bolson was buried with Catholic rites at Fort Bragg
August 17, 1916.

Mrs.M.Bonamici died at Fort Bragg October 22, 1913.   Oct 29, 1913
Father Edwards held Catholic rites October 26th.

Elmer G.Bonee died at Oakland October 23, 1918. The son of   Oct 30, 1918
William Bonee, who operated a ranch near Greenwood about
1888, he was born and raised on the south coast. His sister,
Mrs.Della Grist, a former resident of Fort Bragg, survived.

Q.A.Bonesteel, 91, died at Fort Bragg May 28, 1917. A native   May 30, 1917
of Springfield, Illinois, he came to Fort Bragg in 1911. The
funeral was held there May 31st.

Mario Bonomini died at Fort Bragg of pneumonia   Jan 3, 1912
December 29, 1911. A native of Italy, he was 31 years old.
The funeral was held on December 31st.

Eugenio Bonzani, 34, died at Fort Bragg of influenza   Nov 6, 1918
November 2, 1918. A native of Italy, he had been a resident
for 6 years. He left a family in Italy and was buried in
Fort Bragg November 5th.

Victor Boos, formerly of Fort Bragg, died at Santa Maria   Dec 4, 1918
November 30, 1918 of pneumonia. His brother was Simon Boos
of Fort Bragg.

The two month old infant daughter of Gugilo Borelk died in   Oct 26, 1910
Fort Bragg October 21, 1910. The funeral was October 22nd.

Ernest Borgna, the three year old son of Joseph Borgna of   Nov 15, 1911
Mendocino, died November 11, 1911 in Fort Bragg. The funeral
was held the next day.

Joe Borgna, a former resident of Mendocino, was killed in   Sep 25, 1918
Sacramento when struck by a train [no date reported]. His
wife and three children in Mendocino survived.

Mrs.A.Borneman, nee Jane Eagle, died at Caspar September 28,   Oct 4, 1916
1916. A native of Caspar, she was 26 years old. Her husband,
father and mother (Joe Eagle of Caspar), two sisters and
two brothers survived. The funeral was held September 30th.

Mrs.N.Bortolomei died January 22, 1919 in Fort Bragg from   Jan 29, 1919
influenza. Her husband, Roberto, and three young children
survived. Catholic rites were led by Father Lawrence. One
daughter, Anastasia, 5 months old, was adopted by city
attorney Leonard and Helen Stone. The child's name was
changed to Elizabeth "Betty" Stone.

Emico Boscacci, 7, the son of E.Boscacci of Fort Bragg, died   Dec 4, 1918
there November 28, 1918 and was buried November 30th.

Lillie S.Bowen, the daughter of William M. and Minnie Bowen,   Feb 9, 1910
died January 24, 1910 at De Haven of consumption. Born in
Ukiah September 11, 1893, she was 16 years 4 months and
11 days old. The funeral was held at Westport.

The nine year old son of W.Bowen died at Westport of   Apr 26, 1911
convulsions "last week".

John P.<u>Bowers</u>, aged 84, died at Willits December 19, 1910.   Dec 28, 1910

Mrs.G.R.<u>Bowles</u> died at Ukiah March 12, 1911. She was a   Mar 15, 1911
resident from 1898.

E.B.<u>Bowman</u>, father of F.M.Bowman of Fort Bragg, died at   Jan 22, 1919
Covelo January 8, 1919 at the age of 86. A daughter also
survived, Mrs.L.B.Tuttle of Covelo.

Alexander William <u>Boyd</u> died in Fort Bragg April 19, 1913 at   Apr 23, 1913
the age of 83 years 10 months and 5 days. A resident of
California over fifty years, he settled with the Switzer
brothers at Westport in 1871 and, later, was in the livery
business with George Switzer at Mendocino. Born in 1829 in
Lanark, Ontario, Canada, he lived with the Switzers for
42 years. The funeral was April 22nd led by Rev.R.C.Grace.
A nephew, George Boyd, survived.

George "Sharkey" <u>Boyd</u>, a woodsman, killed himself with a   Jun 4, 1919
rifle shot at Comptche "last week".

Mrs.George <u>Boyd</u> died at Mendocino April 25, 1914. She was   Apr 29, 1914
buried at Fort Bragg April 30th.   May 6, 1914

Antoine <u>Boziadh</u> [also "Boziah"] died at Albion March 28, 1911   Mar 29, 1911
in a blasting accident. A Croat, his funeral was March 30th.   Apr 5, 1911

W.A.<u>Brace</u>, an old resident of San Francisco and an uncle of   Feb 20, 1918
H.W.Little of Fort Bragg, died in San Francisco
February 17, 1918.

Mrs.Harry <u>Braden</u>, 23, died in Fort Bragg November 28, 1916   Nov 29, 1916
following an appendix operation. Nellie was the daughter of
Gus Nelson, born and raised in Fort Bragg. She married Harry
Braden March 2, 1915 and lived at Northspur. The funeral was
at the Presbyterian church in Fort Bragg December 1, 1916.

J.H.<u>Braden</u>, a former Laytonville resident, died near Ukiah   Aug 7, 1912
July 30, 1912. He was 80 years old.

Mrs.Bertram <u>Bradley</u>, 39, died at Fort Bragg January 10, 1916   Jan 12, 1916
of TB. A native of Tennessee, she had come to the coast just
three months earlier. The funeral was held in Fort Bragg led
by Rev.Grant.

Filix <u>Brady</u>, an old pioneer of the area, died at Elk   Nov 1, 1916
October 30, 1916 of heart failure.

Levi <u>Brady</u> of Caspar died June 7, 1917. Born in Pennsylvania   Jun 13, 1917
November 13, 1831, he came to California in 1849, returning
to Pennsylvania in 1851 and then back again in 1888 settling
at Caspar in 1890. A wife, four sons and two daughters
survived: Leonard C., Roy A., Stanly T. and Walter G.Brady,
Mrs.Emily Montgomery and Mrs.Clara B.Crawford.

Michael <u>Brady</u>, 57, died at Oakland "last week". A native of   Jan 26, 1916
Ireland, he was a former coast resident.

Mrs.G.W.<u>Brandt</u>, 70, died at Point Arena December 3, 1917 of   Dec 12, 1917
pneumonia. Residents of Fish Rock since 1867, the couple had
celebrated their 50th wedding anniversary recently. Her
husband and six children, W.M., C.B., R.P., A.E.Brandt, Mrs.
P.H.Tock and Mrs.B.C.Brayton, survived.

Henry <u>Brandt</u>, 27, died December 3, 1919 of pneumonia. A long   Dec 10, 1919
time resident of Fish Rock, he was buried by Henry Shaw at
Fort Bragg.

The infant son of Mr.& Mrs.Arthur <u>Branscomb</u> died at   Dec 14, 1910
Laytonville December 8, 1910.

Mrs.Jane <u>Branscomb</u>, the wife of Benjamin Branscomb for whom the settlement of Branscomb was named, died at Ukiah April 9, 1919. She was the mother of 10 children.

Apr 16, 1919

William <u>Braudwell</u>, the son of Mrs.W.S.Saunders, died at Fort Bragg May 23, 1914. Born at Ten Mile, he lived most of his life in Fort Bragg. He was 32 years 9 months and 7 days old. Catholic rites were held by Father Edwards May 25th.

May 27, 1914

Patrick <u>Breen</u>, a Melburne rancher, died at age 57 in San Francisco "last week".

Nov 26, 1913

Herbert <u>Brenden</u> , a visitor in Fort Bragg the last summer, died in Vancouver [no date reported].

Feb 12, 1919

Tom <u>Brenner</u> of Inglenook died November 14, 1911 of pneumonia and heart disease. About 49 years old he left a son, Charles.

Nov 22, 1911

Mrs.C.<u>Brewer</u>, 70, a resident of Ukiah 28 years, died there December 3, 1913. The funeral was held December 5th.

Dec 10, 1913

S.<u>Brewer</u>, father of constable C.C.Brewer of Ukiah, Mrs.Hal F.Sawyers of Ukiah and Mrs.Ida Pryor, died at Fort Bragg January 1, 1915. The funeral was held January 2nd led by Rev.A.V.Dahl of the Baptist church.

Jan 6, 1915

Mrs.W.E.<u>Brewer</u> died at Northwestern April 4, 1912. Just 26 years old, she left three small children.

Apr 3, 1912

John <u>Brien</u> died at Mendocino March 23, 1917. Born in New Brunswick April 10, 1844, he came to California at 19 and worked for the Mendocino Lumber Company 50 years. His wife, two sons, John and Albert Brien, and two daughters, Mrs. Albert Henningsen and Mrs.Jerome Rafter of Fort Bragg survived. Catholic rites were held in Mendocino March 25th.

Mar 28, 1917

Mrs.Elizabeth Potter <u>Briggs</u>, the mother of County Auditor J.J.Mathews, died January 4, 1919 at Potter Valley. Born in Missouri, she was about 80 years old. Her parents, the Potters, settled in Potter Valley in the early 1850s. Four children, Mrs.Mathews, Mrs.Newnie Boulon, Mrs.Bell Elston and Kit Briggs survived.

Jan 8, 1919

Peter C.<u>Briggs</u>, a pioneer rancher in the Albion area, died "last week".

Dec 11, 1918

Mrs.Margaret J.<u>Brinzing</u> died February 13, 1914. A native of Canada, she was 48 years 11 months and 11 days old and had been a resident on the coast for 35 years. The funeral was held in Fort Bragg February 16th led by Rev.Hargreaves. A daughter was the late Mrs.M.Nolan and a sister was the late Mrs.McDonald.

Feb 18, 1914

Joseph J.<u>Britton</u>, an old resident of the coast, died October 3, 1910. Two of his children: Mrs.H.F.Milliken and Mrs.Greenough were present when he died.

Oct 5, 1910

Mrs.Charles W.<u>Broback</u> of Ukiah died there October 24, 1913. Born Frances A.Haigh in Missouri January 9, 1840, she crossed the plains in 1853 and settled in Santa Clara county. In 1856 the family moved to Healdsburg. She married Charles Broback December 25, 1860 and moved with him to Sacramento and Oregon returning to California in 1884 settling first at Hopland in 1886 and, finally, in Ukiah in 1890. Six children survived: Clarence of Fort Bragg, F.W. of Ukiah, Walter of San Francisco, Charles of Santa Rosa, Mrs.R.H.Douglass of Los Angeles, and Mrs.Bert Miller of Ukiah. The funeral was held in Ukiah October 27th.

Oct 29, 1913
Nov 5, 1913

G.W.<u>Broback</u>, 77, died at Ukiah August 27, 1912. He had been a 22 year resident of that place. A son, Clarence Broback, survived.

Aug 28, 1912

Alden Brochier of Caspar, one year old, died October 4, 1916.   Oct 11, 1916

Twin daughters of Henry Brock died at Hardy February 17,   Feb 25, 1914
1914 and were buried at Westport.

Mrs.William Brock, who lived between Noyo and Caspar, died   Aug 8, 1917
at her home August 8, 1917. Born in Marysville, she was
59 years 4 months and 16 days old. Her funeral was at Fort
Bragg August 11th.

A.Broderick was killed by a Northwestern Pacific train at   Feb 25, 1914
Asti, Sonoma County, February 18, 1913 when he slipped
while trying to board a moving train.

Henry Bronkini was killed at Greenwood June 11, 1915 when a   Jun 16, 1915
tree fell on him. The funeral was held June 13th.

Mrs.Lettie Wilson Bronnenberg died in Indiana "a few days   Apr 16, 1919
ago" from influenza. She taught school at Fish Rock in 1906
and in Manchester in 1907 until her marriage in February
1907 to Ernest Bronnenberg in Indiana.

A six year old child of Mrs.Brooks was fatally injured when   May 8, 1912
struck by a thrown piece of stove wood - at Caspar May 1,
1912. The child had been the victim of continued abuse by
the mother who was taken to the State Asylum at Talmage.

John S.Brooks, 76, a resident of Mitchell Creek, died   Mar 20, 1912
March 16, 1912. He was a California resident for 65 years.

Vergilio Brovelli, about 23 and a native of Italy, was   Dec 6, 1911
severly injured at Camp 4 in the Noyo woods and died in the
Fort Bragg hospital December 4, 1911. Catholic rites were
held December 6th.

Hirschel Brower, about 20 and the son of Con Brower, died on   Apr 16, 1919
April 12, 1919 from injuries received in an automobile
accident near Ukiah April 11th.

Austin H.Brown of Willits died in San Francisco   Feb 19, 1913
February 17, 1913.

Blevins M.Brown, 44, was killed January 3, 1917 by a falling   Jan 10, 1917
tree about three miles north of Sherwood. He left a wife and
eight children.

The 1½ year old daughter of Charles Brown of Fort Bragg   Dec 30, 1914
died December 24, 1914 of pneumonia. The funeral was held
on December 26th with Rev.M.Burt officiating.

Dan Brown died at the Hotel Windsor in Fort Bragg April 18,   Apr 20, 1910
1910. A native of Ireland, he was about 52 years old.

Mrs.Ella Bartlett Brown, a former Mendocino resident, died   Jul 15, 1914
at Healdsburg "last week".

Mrs.Ellen Brown, 72, died at her home east of Fort Bragg   Sep 20, 1916
September 14, 1916 of heart failure. Born in Pennsylvania,
she came to California in 1891 and settled in Fort Bragg in
1895. Her husband and 7 children survived: Jennie E.Kinman
of Carthage, Missouri; Joseph E.Brown of Phoenix, Arizona;
Arthur and Frank Brown of Synavep, Washington; Elsie Eagle
of Scotia and May I.Smith of Los Angeles. The funeral was
held in Fort Bragg September 19th led by Rev.Sutherland.

Hubert F.Brown, a real estate salesman on the coast   May 14, 1919
15 years earlier, died in San Francisco "this week".

James Brown, a tramp, was found dead near Calpella   Nov 8, 1911
November 5, 1911. He was 81 years old.

James Brown, 50, died in Fort Bragg November 5, 1916 of   Nov 8, 1916
pneumonia. A 25 year resident of the coast, he was a native   Nov 15, 1916
of Canada. A brother, Richard Brown of Tuolumne, and a
sister in the East survived. The funeral was held in
Mendocino November 9th led by Rev.Henry Shaw.

John Brown of Mendocino, 34, died October 23, 1918 of   Oct 30, 1918
influenza. A native of Mendocino, he was a tallyman at the
sawmill. His mother, Mrs.J.Q.Brown, four sisters, Mrs.A.G.
Stone, Mrs.Antone Lemos, Mrs.Carrie Redmayne amd Miss Mayme
Brown, survived. The funeral was held October 27th followed
by burial in the Catholic cemetery at Mendocino.

Lew Brown, a Mendocino coast woodsman, died in San Francisco   Mar 6, 1918
February 28, 1918 at the age of 74.

Mrs.Susan Agnes Brown, 84, died in Ukiah September 3, 1915.   Sep 8, 1915
She came to Ukiah in 1880.

Susan Jane Brown died at Willits January 5, 1917. She was a   Jan 17, 1917
Little Lake Valley resident for 43 years. Two sons, F.Davis
of Willits and P.B.Westerman of Amador County, survived.

William M.Brown died in Los Angeles March 1, 1917. He had   Mar 5, 1917
been a resident of Fort Bragg until three months ago. A
native of Pennsylvania, he was 82. Burial was in Fort Bragg
on March 5th with Rev.W.H.Sutherland officiating. His wife,
Mrs.Ellen Brown, died September 14, 1916. A daughter,
Mrs.Mary Smith of Los Angeles, survived as did other,
unnamed, children.

A.E."Brownie" Brownell, a brakeman on the Northwestern   Feb 5, 1919
Pacific Railroad, was killed when he fell from a freight car
and was run over at South Bay near Eureka February 3, 1919.
His wife and a six month old baby survived.

Henry Bruehl, 41, died at Fort Bragg December 4, 1912. The   Dec 11, 1912
The funeral was led by Rev.W.A.Chapman December 7th.

Victor Bruman died at Salmon Creek December 6, 1911. He was   Dec 13, 1911
36 years 5 months and 12 days old. The funeral was held at
Mendocino December 9th with Rev.Coates officiating. Two
brothers, Henry of Fort Bragg and Erick, in Finland, survived.

Mrs.Helena Schneider Brunges, the wife of John Brunges, Sr.,   Jun 18, 1913
died June 11, 1913 at Point Arena. She was the mother of   Jun 25, 1913
E.A.Zimmerman. The funeral was held at Point Arena June 15th.

John Brunges died at Point Arena January 29, 1916. Born in   Feb 2, 1916
Germany in 1828, he came to California in 1844 and lived at
Point Arena for 44 years.

Mrs.Nelson Brush, 77, died near Covelo "last week".   Jan 16, 1916

Edward Buchanan, 28, died in San Francisco July 18, 1913.   Jul 23, 1913
Born and raised on the coast, he operated a livery business
at Greenwood. He was buried at Point Arena.
[The son of Colin J.and Mary McMaster Buchanan.]

Mrs.Frank Buchanan, nee Emma Biaggi the daughter of James   Apr 9, 1919
Biaggi of Manchester, died at Elk April 5, 1919. Her funeral
was held at Greenwood April 7th with burial at Point Arena.
She was married in September 1918.

Willie Buchanan was crushed by a log when unloading from a   May 12, 1915
railroad car at the millpond in Greenwood May 8, 1915. He
was about 19 years old. The funeral was held May 10th at
Greenwood. A brother, Donald, and a younger sister, Frances
Buchanan, survived.

Alex Bucholtz, a former Fort Bragg resident, drowned on the   Jul 12, 1916
Sacramento River while working on a dredger "a short time ago".

F.Oscar Bucholtz died suddenly at Fort Bragg July 28, 1915.   Aug 4, 1915
Born in Norway, he was 34 years 8 months and 25 days old.
An 8 year resident, he operated an automobile livery service
in Fort Bragg. His mother, three sisters and two brothers
survived. The funeral was held in Fort Bragg.

D.J.Buckley, a coast resident, died at the County Hospital   Nov 20, 1918
in Ukiah November 17, 1918.

Dennis Buckley, an old resident of Fort Bragg and Greenwood,   Mar 28, 1917
died at Ukiah March 27, 1917. A native of Ireland, he was 82.

J.R.Buckman died at McDowell Valley June 26, 1910.   Jun 29, 1910

John Buckman of Littleriver died March 4, 1918. An old time   Mar 6, 1918
woodsman from Maine, his funeral was held at Littleriver.

Mrs.Nellie Bucknell died at Ukiah May 11, 1913 of TB.   May 14, 1913

Mrs.Tom Bullard, nee Winnie Knapp of Littleriver, died at   Jun 5, 1918
Prescott, Arizona, May 27, 1918 of TB. Just 18 years old
she was the daughter of Mrs.John Eglin.

Andrew Burbeck of Mendocino drowned in Big River   Feb 7, 1912
trying to break a log jam on February 2, 1912.

Mrs.Burger, the daughter of Mrs.Oleva Clark of Fort Bragg,   Jul 15, 1914
died in Ukiah July 7, 1914.

Dr.C.F.Burgess, a former Mendocino resident, died in   Feb 23, 1910
San Francisco February 6, 1910.

Mrs.John Burgess died near Hemlock September 19, 1914.   Sep 23, 1914

Neil Burk died at Mark West October 30, 1919. Born in   Nov 5, 1919
in Missouri in 1850, he came to the Ukiah Valley at an
early age with his parents. The funeral was held in
Ukiah November 8th.

Mrs.A.M.Burke, until recently a resident of Ukiah, died in   Dec 7, 1910
Oakland December 6, 1910.

Jack Burke died at Willits January 9, 1910 of pneumonia.   Jan 12, 1910

Mrs.Alvina Burkhardt died at Boonville January 8, 1914. She   Jan 21, 1914
was 73 years 1 month and 22 days old. Her son, M.V.Burkhardt
of Boonville, survived.

Homer S.Burlingame, a local San Jose businessman, died   Feb 26, 1913
February 23, 1913. He had lived at Kibesillah and Fort Bragg
working in the lumber trade at Glen Blair, Caspar, Scotia,
Tuolumne and Sanger.

F.C.Burmeister died at Northwestern of pneumonia   Nov 8, 1911
November 4, 1911.

Ed Burnett, who lived on the coast about 50 years, died at   Jan 31, 1912
Noyo January 27, 1912 at the age of 81. Catholic rites were
held in Mendocino January 29th.

Joseph Burnham, over 80, an old pioneer of Fort Bragg known   Dec 18, 1912
as "Uncle Joe" died December 9, 1912 in Fruitvale. He served
in the Federal army as a corporal, Co.E 69th.New York Volunteers, during the Civil War. He was buried in Oakland.

A child of Mr.Burnie died in San Francisco "recently". The   Jan 27, 1915
mother was the former Nettie Allen.

Joseph Burnman, a pioneer settler of the Ukiah valley, died   Mar 19, 1919
at Ukiah "last week".

Carrie B.Burns died at Redwood Valley November 14, 1915. A   Nov 24, 1915
native of Missouri, she was 48 years old.

Chris Burns, a resident of Ukiah for 20 years, died there   Feb 16, 1916
February 11, 1916. Two sons and a daughter survived. The
funeral was held February 14th.

Mrs.Mary A.Burroughs, 87, died at Point Arena January 29,   Feb 6, 1918
1918. Her funeral was January 31st.

Rev.J.A.Burt died in Seattle of influenza [no date reported].   Dec 11, 1918
He formerly lived at Fort Bragg where his daughter, Miss
Anna Burt, taught in the local highschool.

Andrew Burton, 67, died at Covelo June 11, 1913.   Jun 18, 1913

J.G.Busch died in Potter Valley June 26, 1910.   Jun 29, 1910

Mrs.Mary Buzdon, 22, died in childbirth in Fort Bragg   Mar 25, 1914
March 19, 1914. She came to Fort Bragg from Italy four
months earlier. Catholic rites were held March 22nd.

Mrs.Fred Byrne died at Gualala October 5, 1910.   Oct 12, 1910

James Byrne, 77, died in Gualala October 14, 1913.   Oct 22, 1913
The funeral was held there.

Moore Byrne, 9, the son of J.F.Byrne of Albion, died when   Nov 27, 1918
he fell from a chair and struck his head "last week".

Lt.Walter Byrner, formerly of Willits, was killed an air-   Apr 9, 1919
plane crash at an aviation training field in San Antonio,
Texas, when the engine of his machine failed "last week".

John Byrnes was shot by his brother, R.R.Byrnes, in a   Oct 21, 1914
hunting accident October 17, 1914. He died of the wound   Oct 28, 1914
October 19th. He was 38 years old. His wife, the former
Mamie Jefferson, a son, M.J.Byrnes of Fort Bragg, and a
daughter survived. The funeral was held at Fort Bragg
October 21st with Revs.J.S.Ross and Burt in attendance.

Mrs.Alice Byron died August 9, 1916. Born July 14, 1853 in   Aug 16, 1916
Sonoma County, she lived most of her life in Mendocino
County. She was the daughter of A.C.McDonald who came to
California in 1847 and served in the Mexican War. Two of
her sons survived: J.H.Byron and C.A.Byron of Cloverdale.
Brothers and sisters included: George H.McDonald of
Pendleton, Oregon; Mrs.Mary H.Peck of Santa Rosa; Richard
and James McDonald of Cloverdale; Mrs.Lillian White
(formerly of Fort Bragg); Mrs.Flora Cooper, Mrs.Anna Cooper
of Lovelock, Nevada. The funeral was held at Hopland
August 12th with Father Crook of Ukiah officiating.

David F.Cain, 83, died at Point Arena June 4, 1919. Born in   Jun 11, 1919
Hingham, Plymouth County, Massachusetts, March 12, 1837, he
came to California in 1869 settling on a farm near Manchester
and living there until 1914 when he sold up and moved to
Point Arena. On September 12, 1857 he married Betsy Perkins
Maxin. His widow and four children survived.

Derunda Call, 64, died at Fort Bragg September 17, 1917. A   Sep 19, 1917
native of Haverstraw, New York, he had been a five year
resident. His widow and son, Melville Call, survived. The
funeral was conducted by Rev.Sutherland in Fort Bragg
September 19th.

Patrick Callahan, an inmate at the State Hospital near   Jan 25, 1911
Ukiah died January 16, 1911 at age 64. The remains were
shipped to Salinas for interment.

Duncan Cameron, 74, died at Comptche June 18, 1918.   Jun 19, 1918
A native of Scotland, he had lived at Comptche since 1885.
Two brothers, Alex Cameron of Fort Bragg, and Archie
Cameron, Sr. of Ten Mile, survived. His funeral was at
Mendocino June 20th.

Edwin H.Cameron was found dead in bed in Eureka   Jan 8, 1919
January 4, 1919 from heart failure. A native of Ottawa,
Canada, he was about 70 years old. He came to Mendocino in
1868 and worked as a telegraph operator on the Petaluma-
Eureka line. Later he went into the lumber trade, served as
deputy county assessor for 8 years and went to Eureka in
1899 as a bookkeeper and salesman in the mills. A wife and
four children survived: Guy O.Cameron of the Northwestern
Pacific RR, Agnes Carlson and Verda Hess of Eureka, and
Edwin F.Cameron with the Southern Pacific RR in Berkeley.

Mrs.Margaret Cameron, the wife of George Cameron a pioneer   Jan 16, 1918
rancher at Navarro, died January 12, 1918. Born in London,
England, October 31, 1858, the daughter of William Wells,
she came to California with her parents and was raised at
Mendocino. Her husband, mother, Mrs.William Wells, and five
children, Mrs.James Carmichael of Ukiah, Mrs.C.F.Johnson
of Fort Bragg, Miss Lillie Wells of Navarro, Archie Cameron
of Albion and Roderick Cameron of Mendocino survived. Five
brothers and sisters were also left: Mrs.Martin of Oakland,
Miss Rose Wells of San Francisco, Mrs.Minnie Jones, Mrs.
Richard Bohn and John Cameron of Fort Bragg. The funeral
was at Fort Bragg January 15th led by Rev.W.M.Sutherland.

C.W.Campbell, 85, a resident of Point Arena, died at Ukiah   Feb 9, 1916
January 30, 1916.

Flora Campbell, 15, an Indian girl, died at Noyo from   Jul 5, 1916
peritonitis July 2, 1916. The funeral was held on July 4th.

Joseph G.Campbell of Rockland, California, died of pneumonia May 28, 1913
May 21, 1913. He had lived in the Point Arena area for 60   Jun 4, 1913
years as a rancher and was buried there. His wife, three
sons and a daughter survived. One son was Sam Campbell.

An infant child of W.C.Canada of Caspar died November 15,   Nov 22, 1911
1911 and was buried on the 17th.

Estell Capell, the son of Charles Capell aged 14, was   Sep 20, 1911
accidentally shot and killed by a .22 calibre rifle fired   Oct 4, 1911
by Marion Field at Laytonville September 9, 1911.

James Caraway, formerly of Willits, died at Napa "recently". Apr 9, 1919

Mrs.Mary D.Carey, wife of the late John Carey, died   Nov 11, 1914
November 5, 1914 in Los Angeles following a serious
operation. She worked as a nurse in that city and was
30 years old. The funeral held in Fort Bragg November 8th.

John Carleson hung himself at Willits February 10, 1915. He Feb 17, 1915
once had worked at Fort Bragg.

Alex Carlson, a pioneer jeweler on the coast, died in Fort   Jul 9, 1919
Bragg July 2, 1919. Born in Oland, Sweden, he came to the
U.S. 35 years ago and located at Greenwood until 1907 when
he moved to Fort Bragg. He was 57. His wife, Lucy Carlson,
four sons: Lucien, Glenn, Ray, and Edward, survived. Father
Grant conducted the funeral at Fort Bragg July 6th.

Mrs.Emil Carlson, the daughter of H.C.Olsen of Fort Bragg,   Nov 27, 1918
died there November 20, 1918 from influenza. Born in Nevada,
she was 28 years old. Her husband, parents, two sisters and
a brother survived. Rev.Shaw officiated at her funeral in
Fort Bragg on November 25th.

Fred Carlson, the son of Alex Carlson, died in San Francisco
June 18, 1919 from pneumonia. Born in Albion, he was 26 years
11 months and 20 days old. Some time ago the family moved
from Greenwood to Fort Bragg. The funeral was held June 22nd
in Fort Bragg.

Jun 18, 1919
Jun 25, 1919

John Edward Carlson died at work in the woods near Alpine
February 22, 1919 of heart failure. Born at Pine Grove, he
was raised in that area and in Caspar. He was 41 years and
8 months old.

Feb 26, 1919

John Erick Carlson, 46. died in Fort Bragg January 17, 1914
of pneumonia. He had been injured in a woods accident
recently. His wife and four children survived.The funeral
was held January 20th.

Jan 21, 1914

Victor Carlson died July 15, 1916 in the Fort Bragg hospital
of self-inflicted wounds with a razor at Camp 5 in the
Caspar woods July 13th. A native of Finland, he was 41.

Jul 19, 1916

Victor Carlson, 23, died at Elk November 22, 1916 of
pneumonia. He was born and raised in Greenwood.

Nov 22, 1916

William Carlson, 64, dropped dead in a field near Caspar
February 19, 1913. Born February 2, 1849 in Helsingfors,
Finland, he went to sea as a youth serving until 1872 when
he came to Gualala and later, to Caspar. On June 13, 1875
he married Annie O'Brien. They had three daughters and five
sons. The funeral was at Caspar February 25th.

Feb 26, 1913
Mar 5, 1913

Ethel Carmichael, 8 years and 6 months old, died of typhoid
October 17, 1911. Her funeral was held in the Episcopal
church October 19th with services led by Rev.J.Barrett.

Oct 18, 1911
Oct 25, 1911

James Carner, a pioneer of the Potter Valley, was found dead
at home November 27, 1919 apparently of heart failure.

Dec 3, 1919

T.L.Carothers, an attorney at Ukiah, died at Santa Rosa
November 30, 1915. Born in Illinois September 26, 1842, he
crossed the plains in 1850 and settled at Placerville.
Admitted to the bar in 1863, he located in Ukiah in 1866
and served as the first elected mayor. His wife survived.

Dec 8, 1915

The infant child of Mr.Carpenter of Caspar died
September 5, 1915; funeral was held the next day.

Sep 8, 1915

A.O.Carpenter, 82, died February 7, 1919 at Ukiah where he
had settled in 1859. He founded the *Ukiah Herald* in 1860
with E.R.Budd and in 1879 purchased the *Ukiah Press* with
Charles S.Paine. He was a well known author of a history of
Mendocino County. In 1856 he married Helen McCowen, sister
of Hale and George McCowen.

Feb 12, 1919

Mrs.B.L.Carpenter died at Hopland January 16, 1912 as the
result of a fall.

Jan 24, 1912

Mrs.Helen M.Carpenter died at Ukiah February 13, 1917. Born
in Mason County, Ohio, April 21, 1831, she was married in
December 1856 to Aurelius Carpenter and came across the
plains that year. They arrived in California in 1857 and
located in Potter Valley in 1859. She taught in the first
public school. They moved to Ukiah in 1869.

Feb 21, 1917

Lupie Carranza, a boxer, died at Watsonville "last week".

Mar 15, 1911

William Carrick, 40, died at San Francisco April 14, 1915.
He had been the purser of the steamer *Sea Foam*. He left a
wife and two children.

Apr 21, 1915

Leonardo Carreto, 29 and a native of Italy, died suddenly
at the State Hospital at Talmage August 23, 1913.

Sep 10, 1913

Mrs.Alberta Ozetta Carter died at Ukiah May 16, 1912.   May 22, 1912

Mrs.Tolman E.Cary, 65, died at Northwestern March 21, 1916.   Mar 29, 1916

Dr.E.G.Case, the father of Mrs.H.P.Preston and Miss Mar-   Sep 20, 1916
garet Case, died in Oakland "last week". A dentist at Ukiah
for many years, he was 58 years 9 months and 11 days old.

James Case died at age 90 at Willits March 14, 1911. He was   Mar 22, 1911
born in Kentucky in 1820.

D.Caselli shot four people at the Maffini Hotel in Fort   Aug 16, 1916
Bragg August 13, 1916 in a crazed attack, fatally wounding   Sep 6, 1916
two, John Bolson and A.Maffini, before turning the gun on
himself. Caselli had come from Greenwood in July, seemingly
a stable and sober individual. As no one claimed the body,
it was finally buried in September by W.A.Chapman.

C.L.Casey dropped dead at Oakland February 1, 1917. He had   Feb 14, 1917
worked for two years at Point Arena.

Frank Cask of Fort Bragg died July 5, 1910.   Jul 6, 1910

L.Cassade died one mile south of Ukiah September 17, 1912.   Sep 18, 1912
He had lived in Long Valley for more than 20 years.

Peter Cassidy died at Mendocino July 10, 1917 of pneumonia.   Jul 18, 1917

Charlie Caughey drowned at Boyd, Oregon, February 19, 1916.   Mar 1, 1916
The youngest son of Robert and Annie Caughey, he was a
native of Point Arena, and 19 years old.

Dot Caughey, the daughter of Frank Caughey, died at Ukiah   Aug 31, 1910
August 24, 1910.

Mrs.Ellen Caughey of Manchester died in San Francisco   Sep 24, 1919
September 21, 1919. A son, F.L.Caughey, and two daughters,
Mrs.J.C.Roberts, and Mrs.E.F.Tabor of San Francisco,
survived. The funeral was held in Manchester September 24th.

William Caughey, formerly of Manchester, died in Oakland   Nov 1, 1916
October 16, 1916 at age 57 years 8 months and 10 days. He
was the brother of Robert and Lavinia Caughey of Manchester.

Edward Cavanagh was severely injured in a woods accident   May 8, 1912
April 16, 1912 when a log rolled over him. He died   May 15, 1912
May 13, 1912. A native of Mendocino, he was 40 years
8 months and 4 days old. His widow and five children:
three boys and two girls, survived; the oldest 12, the
youngest 1 year old. His aged mother, two brothers and two
sisters also survived. Catholic rites were held in Mendocino
May 15, 1912. Father Brennen officiated.

Mrs.Elizabeth Cavanagh, died at Mendocino July 23, 1912.   Jul 24, 1912
Born in Dublin, Ireland, she was about 75. Two sons and   Jul 31, 1912
two daughters survived. Catholic rites were held by Father
Michael Smith July 25th.

Mrs.Ellen Cavanagh, a former resident of Cuffey's Cove and   Dec 25, 1912
Mendocino, died in Oakland December 5, 1912. A daughter,
Mrs.Mary McIntyre, survived.

Mrs.Sarah Cavanagh, 53, died January 21, 1919 in Fort Bragg   Jan 22, 1919
from heart failure and dropsy. A native of Michigan, she
left a husband and three children.

Thomas E.Cavanagh, a miner on the Klamath River, burned to   Apr 13, 1910
death April 2, 1910. He was about 52 years old.   Apr 27, 1910
                                                                   May 4, 1910
Albert Cave [also reported as "McCabe"] was shot and killed at   May 17, 1911
Williams, Colusa County, May 10, 1911. He formerly lived
in Potter Valley. A second report stated he was a suicide.

Silva Celeri dropped dead August 12, 1910 at the Glen Blair mill. The funeral was held in Fort Bragg August 14th.

Aug 17, 1910

Mrs.John A.Chambers of Mendocino died July 14, 1919 of a stroke. About 50 years old, she was a 20 year resident. Her husband, and son, Hadley Chambers, and two daughters, Gladys and Laing, survived. The funeral was July 18, 1919.

Jul 16, 1919

Mrs.William R.Chandler, 43, died at Willits July 16, 1914.

Jul 29, 1914

Mrs.J.T.Chapman, mother of Rev.W.A.Chapman of Fort Bragg, died in Wisbech, England November 14, 1913 at the age of 76.

Dec 3, 1913

Mrs.Mary Chapman died near Willits February 18, 1910.

Feb 23, 1910

Oliver L.Chapman died at Fort Bragg August 15, 1912. He was a steward on the coastal steamer Brunswick. Born in San Francisco in 1870, he left a wife in Oakland. Burial was in San Francisco.

Aug 21, 1912

Mrs.W.A.Chapman, the wife of Rev.W.A.Chapman, died in Fort Bragg of heart failure October 20, 1913. Born in Boston, England, November 6, 1871, she married Chapman in 1894. They came to California and served in the ministry until 1911 living in Westport and Fort Bragg. The husband and three sons survived. The funeral was held October 21st in Fort Bragg with Rev.Hargreaves officiating.

Oct 22, 1913

George Chapralis, a Greek, drowned when swimming in the Outlet Creek July 4, 1910.

Jul 6, 1910

Mrs.Thomas Charlton died in Ukiah in October 1915 [exact date lost]. Born May 1, 1843, she was a resident from 1872. She was married February 29, 1872.

Oct 27, 1915

Theodore Chester, 65, died in Fruitvale October 16, 1919. A native of New York, he worked in the coastal woods and later ran a saloon in Fort Bragg with Albert Saunders. His widow and four children survived.

Oct 22, 1919

Nathan B.Childers, an old resident of the north county, died at Santa Rosa of heart failure [no date reported]. He was born in Illinois March 5, 1837. A widow and five daughters survived, one of whom was Mrs.L.A.Moody of Moody.

Nov 15, 1911

Mrs.O.A.Chillson, 52, died at Ukiah April 4, 1917. She had been a twenty year resident. A son, D.W.Chillson of Ukiah, three sisters, Mrs.J.W.Rose of Richmond, Mrs.W.H.Lewis of Tracy, Mrs.Cora Ricks of Northspur, and two brothers, M.M.Grover of Byron and L.E.Grover of Boonville, survived.

Apr 11, 1917

Lee Chin, a Chinese cook at Albion, was buried at Mendocino November 20, 1915.

Nov 24, 1915

Charles Christensen, a former Fort Bragg resident, died at Crescent City March 2, 1916 following an appendix operation.

Mar 8, 1916

Mrs.Lydia A.Chute, 75, died at Caspar January 28, 1912. She had come there 18 months previously to live with her sister, Mrs.A.Fokes. The body was shipped to Halifax, Nova Scotia, for interment.

Feb 7, 1912

Pietro Ciambelli, proprietor of the Toscan Hotel at Wendling, was a suicide January 30, 1912.

Feb 14, 1912

John Cinches, the operator of the electric crane at Union Lumber Company, somehow got caught in the machinery August 3, 1915 and was killed. He was about 30 years old and a resident for 8 years.

Aug 4, 1915

Chief Engineer Clark from the steamer Noyo drowned at Cleone November 17, 1915.

Nov 17, 1915

Charles B.Clark, of Littleriver, died May 14, 1914. The   May 20, 1914
funeral was held May 15th at Littleriver led by the   Feb 5, 1936
Rev.J.H.Hargreaves.
[widow, Elizabeth Reed Clark, died January 27, 1936.]

J.J.Clark, a newcomer to Ukiah, died January 30, 1910.   Feb 2, 1910

William Clark died at Ukiah February 9, 1912. The funeral   Feb 14, 1912
was held in Long Valley.

Henry Clay was a suicide by hanging in String Valley about   May 28, 1919
four miles east of Willits on May 25, 1919. Born in Ukiah
January 12, 1890, he lived on a ranch south of town until
drafted for war service. He was sent to Camp Lewis, but
rejected for service and sent home.

George Clayton of Lewiston (Trinity County) died July 19,   Jul 22, 1914
1914 at age 81. He came to California in 1849.

Mrs.H.J.Clelland died at Ukiah January 14, 1911.   Jan 25, 1911

Mrs.C.J.Clement, 80, died at Hopland February 17, 1913.   Feb 26, 1913

George Clement, 19, died "last week" at Oakland from   Oct 23, 1918
Spanish influenza. Born in Mendocino, the family moved
to Oakland in 1915.

Mrs.Ann Howard Cleveland, 78, died November 1, 1916 in the   Nov 8, 1916
Ukiah Valley where she had resided 58 years. She raised ten
children, two orphans and a grandchild.

Oliver Cleveland, 48, died at Ukiah January 15, 1914. He had Jan 21, 1914
been a farmer.

Edward Clifton, 39, Round Valley, died in Ukiah May 3, 1910. May 11, 1910

Michael Clinton was struck by a piece of tree root thrown   Jul 5, 1916
from a blast June 22, 1916 and died June 29th at Elk
without regaining consciousness.

Mrs.Coates, nee Maggie Brett daughter of former superinten-   Dec 14, 1910
ent Brett of Fort Bragg, was buried December 12, 1910 at
Littleriver. The circumstances of her death were not revealed.

John Cobb, a ranch hand, died about four miles west of   Apr 9, 1919
Dos Rios April 4, 1919.

J.W.Coffer, an old resident of Calpella, died at Ukiah   Jan 25, 1911
January 13, 1911. [Another item reported his death at Calpella
January 19, 1911]. A native of Iowa, he was 76.

Hugh M.Coke was struck by lightning and killed at Covelo   Sep 6, 1916
September 3, 1916.

Burger Nathaniel "Bill" Colberg, 51, was a suicide at Fort   Sep 18, 1918
Bragg September 14, 1918. A native of Sweden , he lived on
the coast for 30 years. His wife, three sons, a daughter
and three brothers survived. The funeral was held at Fort
Bragg September 17, 1918.

Captain J.F.Colburn died at Caspar July 26, 1910. He was 88. Jul 27, 1910
Rev.Boyington conducted the funeral with interment in the
Fort Bragg cemetery. Four sons, W.A. of Napa, Joe and
Horations "up north", S.B. of Caspar, two daughters, Mrs.
Harris of Folsom and Mrs.Bailey of Caspar, survived.

Mrs.W.A.Colburn, 65 and a former resident of Mendocino, died Mar 29, 1916
at Calistoga March 17, 1916. She came to the coast when ten   Apr 5, 1916
years old and moved away in 1900. Her husband, daughter,
Mrs.Alice M.Byron of Oakland, and sons, Charles A.Carroll of
Calistoga and former Mendocino Beacon employee, Dr.W.A.
Colburn and R.L.Colburn of San Francisco, survived.

W.T.Cole died suddenly at Hopland March 28, 1913.   Apr 2, 1913

Mrs.Coli died in Ukiah June 7, 1910.   Jun 8, 1910

Mrs.M.Collbrough, a former Ukiah resident, died at Santa   Jun 13, 1917
Rosa June 12, 1917 of pneumonia. She was taken ill while
nursing her brother, Thomas Hornbuckle, who died June 1917.
Her sister was Mrs.C.R.Enders.

Howard Collier was shot and killed by J.J.Pulse in a   Aug 28, 1918
hunting accident near Laughlin August 25, 1918.

Dave Conkey drowned at Moro, San Luis Obispo County, while   Apr 28, 1915
fishing. He was a former Albion resident. [No date reported].

Michael Connaughton, 90, died at Oakland July 30, 1918. A   Aug 7, 1918
native of New Brunswick, he had been a seafarer and mill-
worker on the coast.

Tom Conoly, a guard at Folsom prison, was killed in a   Jul 11, 1917
hunting accident at Blue Rock by S.L.Meyers "last week".

"Grandma" Conrad, an early pioneer of the Anderson Valley,   Jul 22, 1914
died at Ukiah July 14, 1914.

Mrs.Jane Conway died at Greenwood November 9, 1916. A 50   Nov 15, 1916
year resident of the coast, she was born in Miramichi,
New Brunswick, April 5, 1844. At five she moved with her
family to Oldtown, Maine, and then to California in 1864.
In August 1864 she was married to John Conway, also from
Maine, and settled with him in Mendocino City in 1866. He
ran a tailor shop there for four years before moving to
Cuffey's Cove and, later, operated a store at Greenwood
when that place was founded. Her husband and three sons,
Edward of Fort Bragg, John of Greenwood and Joseph of Butte,
Montana, survived. Two brothers, John Brien of Mendocino and
Charles of Santa Monica, as well as two sisters, Mamie Ross
of Fort Bragg and Elizabeth of Greenwood, also survived.
The funeral was held on November 9th [probably the 11th]
at Greenwood with burial in Cuffey's Cove.

John Conway, Sr., died at Greenwood November 23, 1918 at the Nov 27, 1918
age of 82 years and 7 months. A native of Ireland, he came
to Maine as a young man and later to California, settling at
Mendocino in 1866. He worked as a tailor for 4 years, ran a
store at Cuffey's Cove and moved to Greenwood when that
place was settled. His wife died November 9, 1916. Five
children survived: John and Miss Lizzie Conway of Elk,
Mrs.J.O.Ross and Ed Conway of Fort Bragg, and Joe Conway of
Butte, Montana.

Clarence Cook died of throat trouble in Fort Bragg   Apr 19, 1911
April 14, 1911. Just 17 years old, he had worked at Glen
Blair. The funeral was held in Fort Bragg April 16, 1911.

Mrs.Edith Cook, the sister of L.J.Scoofy, died in San   May 28, 1919
Francisco "last week". She had lived on the upper Noyo
some years ago.

Leroy D.Cook, 65, a local rancher, died February 6, 1919   Feb 12, 1919
"across Pudding Creek" north of Fort Bragg, of stomach cancer.
A native of Missouri, he was a 25 year California resident.

Tom Cook died in the Anderson Valley "last week". Also known Jan 8, 1913
as "Boonville", he was a fruit peddler.

Weldon B.Cooke, 30, was killed in an airplane crash at   Sep 23, 1914
Pueblo, Colorado. He had flown his machine at Fort Bragg on
July 4, 1914 in an exhibition.

E.A.Cooley, about 50, shot himself on his parents' graves at Jul 25, 1917
Cloverdale July 16, 1917.

Lois Vadalia <u>Coombs</u>, the infant daughter of Mr.& Mrs.Silas Coombs, died at Littleriver April 10, 1910.

Apr 20, 1910

Mrs.Marcissa P.<u>Coombs</u>, wife of the late Richard R.Coombs, died at Fort Bragg February 8, 1916. A native of Bangor, Maine, she was 74 and lived in Littleriver for 40 years until moving in February 1911 to Fort Bragg. A son, Richard Coombs of San Francisco, and a daughter, Miss Callie Coombs of Fort Bragg, survived. The funeral was held February 11th at Littleriver led by Rev.W.A.Chapman.

Feb 9, 1916

Richard <u>Coombs</u> died July 16, 1910 as the result of a stage accident. Born in Whitefield, Massachusetts, May 19, 1835, he was 75. Coombs came to California in 1857 with a nephew, William White, and joined brother Silas Coombs and brother-in-law Ruel Stickney in logging at Albion. In 1861 he brought his sister Caroline Coombs and Mrs.Stevens to California. He and six family members made their homes in Littleriver. Richard Coombs married Narcissa Evans in San Francisco. Rev. J.S.Ross conducted the funeral at Littleriver July 18th. His wife, Narcissa, son and daughter, Callie M. Coombs, survived as did two sisters, Mrs.Stickney and Mrs.Pullen.

Jul 20, 1910
Aug 3, 1910

An infant child of Mr.& Mrs.<u>Cooney</u>, aged nine months, died in Fort Bragg February 14, 1910 of pneumonia and was buried on the 15th.

Feb 16, 1910

Miss Elizabeth <u>Cooney</u>, 19, died of typhoid at Greenwood January 19, 1914.

Jan 21, 1914

The badly burned body of Joe <u>Cooper</u> of Ornbaun Valley was found January 7, 1911. He had been missing since November 2, 1910. He was 65 years old. Pete Gianoli was thought to have killed him, but was adjudged not guilty by the inquest jury.

Jan 11, 1911
Mar 15, 1911

Mrs.Newton Sidney <u>Cooper</u> died at Sacramento "last week". She was the mother of Mrs.Ellen Knox formerly a Mendocino music teacher and organist at the Presbyterian church.

Jun 4, 1913

Nathaniel <u>Copeland</u>, 62, died at Fort Bragg September 15, 1915. A native of Canada, he had been a four year resident of Fort Bragg. His wife and two sons, Nat Copeland of Caspar and Tom Copeland of Oakland survived. The funeral was held at Fort Bragg September 19th.

Sep 22, 1915

Giovanni <u>Cornale</u>, 49, died at the County Hospital in Ukiah December 26, 1914 of TB and was buried with Catholic rites December 28th.

Jan 13, 1915

Eugene P.<u>Correll</u> died in Eureka November 9, 1917 following an appendix operation. A native of Germany, he was 47 years old. He came to Fort Bragg about 1902 and married Maud Dixon. He then ran a drugstore in Eureka for 14 years. His wife and son, 10, survived. The funeral was in Eureka November 12th.

Nov 14, 1917

Mrs.Emma Harris <u>Corrigan</u>, 66, died in San Diego July 3, 1917. Her husband once ran a business in Littleriver and Albion.

Jul 11, 1917

J.S.<u>Corrigan</u> died in San Diego March 30, 1913. A long time coast resident, he moved to Albion in 1895 and ran a drugstore at Littleriver until 1909. He married Emma Harris who survived him along with two daughters and a son.

Apr 2, 1913

Antonio <u>Cortez</u>, a.k.a George Cortez, a pioneer of Mendocino County, died February 6, 1911. Born in Malaga, Spain, in 1845, he came here in 1864 after serving in the Federal army from August 21, 1861 to 1863 as a seaman on the warships *Ohio* and *Kingfisher*. He also was on the posse that chased the Mendocino bandits in October 1879 and, later, was deputy marshal. The funeral was February 9, 1911 at the Presbyterian church led by John Barret. His son, George, and daughter, Mrs.George Gibbs, survived. Death was caused by typhoid fever.

Feb 8, 1911
Feb 15, 1911

The youngest son of Manuel <u>Costa</u> of Mendocino died October 28, 1918 of influenza.

Oct 30, 1918

Sidney <u>Covington</u> died at Peterson's tie camp east of Fish Rock August 8, 1915. Born in Noyo, he was about 50. Burial was at Fish Rock August 10th.

Aug 18, 1915

Mrs.M.E.<u>Cowling</u>, 85, died in San Jose December 25, 1916. A 30 year California resident, she was born in Pittsburgh, Pennsylvania. A daughter, Mrs.George Eldredge of Fort Bragg, survived.

Jan 10, 1917

Amy <u>Cox</u>, 13 and the daughter of W.M.Cox, died at Ukiah September 14, 1911.

Sep 20, 1911

Hugh <u>Cox</u>, a rancher in the Ukiah valley, died April 5, 1919. A major hop grower, his funeral was held April 7th.

Apr 9, 1919

Joseph <u>Cox</u> died at Ukiah December 15, 1910.

Dec 21, 1910

Robert William <u>Craft</u>, 73, was killed in a runaway accident November 11, 1916 in Fort Bragg. Born in Lancashire, England, he went to Australia where he lost his first wife and five children in two diptheria epidemics. The funeral was held at the Episcopal church in Fort Bragg by Rev.Grant November 14th.

Nov 15, 1916

J.<u>Craig</u>, *a.k.a.*Little Doc, was dead in Fort Bragg March 16, 1917. He was about 45 years old and died of pneumonia.

Mar 21, 1917

Mrs.Augusta Lorentz <u>Craighan</u> died December 7, 1917. Born in Lyons, New York, in 1844, she was educated at the Mount Holyoke Seminary in Massachusetts and came to California in 1865 settling in Mariposa County. She was a Fort Bragg resident from 1906. Her husband, J.D.Craighan, and six children, Miss L.A.Craighan of San Francisco, Mrs.E.A.Marris of Healdsburg, Miss N.L.Craighan of San Francisco, Mrs.C.R. Weller of Fort Bragg, J.F.Craighan of Sacramento, and Mrs. C.L.Kocher of Merced, survived. The funeral was held in Fort Bragg December 9th.

Dec 12, 1917

Mrs.Jennie O'Dell <u>Crawford</u>, formerly of Ukiah, died in San Francisco April 4, 1917.

Apr 11, 1917

Mrs.Omar R.<u>Crester</u>, *nee* Clara Talbot of Albion, died October 12, 1917 at Manchester of TB. Born September 23, 1896 at Manchester, she was married to Mr.Crester January 28, 1916. Her husband, mother, Mrs.A.Hepworth, and a brother survived.

Oct 24, 1917

Louise <u>Cringer</u> died at Wages Creek April 10, 1918 of pneumonia.

Apr 17, 1918

G.W.<u>Critchfield</u>, 87, died suddenly at Ukiah February 1, 1918. A 50 year resident, he had served as a justice of the peace and postmaster.

Feb 6, 1918

G.H.<u>Crocker</u>, a Mendocino County pioneer, died at the State Hospital in Talmage August 18, 1913.

Aug 27, 1913

Mrs.D.C.<u>Crockett</u>, 86, died in Ukiah May 27, 1919. She was a resident for more than 50 years. Her late husband was the sheriff of the county in 1872. Her son, D.C.Crockett of Albion, survived.

Jun 4, 1919

Isaac Patterson <u>Crockett</u>, a 37 year resident of Fort Bragg, died July 9, 1918. Born October 29, 1849 at Westvale, Nova Scotia, he came to California in 1875. In August 1877 he married Margaret Williams Quinliven of Calpella and moved to Fort Bragg. His wife, five daughters and a son survived. The funeral was led by Rev.W.A.Chapman on July 11th.

Jul 10, 1918

A young boy named <u>Cross</u> died in Redwood Valley of influenza   Oct 23, 1918
October 18, 1918.

Mrs.John <u>Cummings</u> died at Fort Bragg February 22, 1919   Feb 26, 1919
A native of Canada, she was 68 years 4 months and 14 days
old. She settled in Caspar about 1870 and was a resident of
Fort Bragg for 33 years. She was one of the first three
white women to settle on this part of the coast - the
others being Mrs.Dave Ross and Mrs.C.R.Johnson. Her
husband and four children survived: Mrs.Walter Hayter,
Mrs.C.W.Broback, Mrs.Chester Balfour and Jack Cummings.
Her funeral was February 26th led by Rev.W.A.Chapman.

T.<u>Cummings</u>, the trainmaster at Willits, died there   Feb 7, 1912
February 2, 1912.

Major W.W.<u>Cunningham</u>, an old resident of the county died   Feb 9, 1910
January 28, 1910 at the age of 88.

Mrs.W.W.<u>Cunningham</u> died at Ukiah May 27, 1910.   Jun 1, 1910

Mrs.Charles <u>Cureton</u> of Point Arena died in a San Francisco   Nov 26, 1913
hospital following an appendix operation November 21, 1913.
She was 23 years old. The funeral was held at the Presbyterian church in Fort Bragg November 25th.

The eight year old daughter of O.<u>Cureton</u> died at Cahto   Jul 24, 1912
July 16, 1912. Burial was in the Anderson Valley.

Tom <u>Cureton</u>, an old resident of Point Arena, was fatally   Nov 1, 1911
injured in San Francisco when he fell from a streetcar
October 29, 1911. He had settled in the Point Arena area
in 1857.

Paul <u>Curles</u>, 41, the son-in-law of J.F.Allen of Fort Bragg,   Aug 7, 1912
died in Mendocino August 2, 1912 of pneumonia. He left a
wife and six children.

Allen <u>Curless</u>, formerly of Mendocino, died at San Jose   Dec 17, 1913
[no date reported] and was buried at Mendocino
December 11, 1913.

C.M.<u>Curley</u>, a long time resident of Point Arena, died   Feb 28, 1912
February 18, 1912. Born in Canada August 28, 1843, he came
to the coast in 1868 to farm. A widow and son survived.

F.W.<u>Curry</u> drowned in the Glen Blair millpond February 24,   Mar 1, 1911
1911. He was 23 years old. The body was shipped to Boston.

John David <u>Curry</u>, a book keeper for the California Western   Mar 8, 1911
Railroad died March 2, 1911 of tuberculosis. Born in
Mendocino County, he was 31 years old. His wife survived.
Catholic rites were held in Fort Bragg March 6, 1911.

Mrs.<u>Curtis</u>, an old time resident of Ukiah, died there   Jun 25, 1913
June 18, 1913. She was 63 years old.

R.H.<u>Cuthbertson</u>, a pioneer settler of the Manchester area,   Oct 22, 1919
died at Palo Alto "recently" at 78. His widow survived him.

Dan <u>Cyphers</u>, a former resident of Andersonia, died at   Aug 9, 1911
Garberville July 27, 1911.

Edwin <u>Daggett</u>, a youth, died at Point Arena April 19, 1914   Apr 29, 1914
of diabetes.

The 18 month old son of P.<u>Dagnula</u> died at Westport March 5,   Mar 8, 1911
1911. The funeral was held in Fort Bragg on March 6th.

The four year old son of Mr.and Mrs.John <u>Dahl</u> died in Fort   Dec 7, 1910
Bragg December 7, 1910. The funeral was held the next day.   Dec 14, 1910

Mrs.Aner Dahl, nee Gladys Dean, died in San Francisco   Jul 9, 1919
July 7, 1919 at age 16 years 8 months and 27 days. The
oldest daughter of Ed Dean, she was born and raised at Union
Landing and grew up in Fort Bragg.Her husband and young
child survived. The funeral was at Fort Bragg July 10th.

Matt Dahl was murdered at Low Gap tie camp March 22, 1916 by   Mar 29, 1916
Harry Brinks in a drunken brawl.

Charles Dalin, a blacksmith at Littleriver, died in Fort   Mar 13, 1918
Bragg March 11, 1918. A 15 year resident, he was 55. The
funeral was held March 14th.

Mrs.Jess Darnell died at San Jose. Her husband was the   Jun 18, 1919
editor of the Willits News.

Jesse Darr, the 15 year old son of Wert Darr and Mrs.Hall,   Jan 25, 1911
died of tuberculosis January 21, 1911.

Jesse Darr, 39, son the Robert Darr of Fort Bragg, died   Feb 21, 1912
February 19, 1912. The funeral was held February 22nd.

Mrs.Nancy Darr, a Pitt River Indian about 70 years old, died Dec 5, 1917
December 2, 1917. She was raised by Charles Hargrave and married
Fred Heldt in 1892. At his death - said to have been by poisoned
whiskey - she inherited the Bald Hill ranch where he was buried.

L.E.Davidson, a former Willits resident, died at   Aug 12, 1914
Imperial Junction of heat stroke. He was 27.

Marshall Davidson, 30, the son of Allen Davidson of Willits, Jun 20, 1917
shot and killed himself June 15, 1917. He had wrecked his
father's automobile and was worried about the accident. His
wife survived.

D.D.Davis, 86, died at the County Hospital November 27, 1916. Nov 29, 1916

Mrs.D.R.Davis, nee Berneice E.Brown, the daughter of Henry   Dec 17, 1919
Brown of Mendocino, died at Fort Bragg December 15, 1919.
Born and raised in Mendocino, she was 26 years old. She
married D.R.Davis in 1914. Her funeral was December 17th
with Rev.H.P.Ingram officiating.

Harry Davis was killed at Muir's mill [no date reported],   Aug 24, 1910
the body being sent to Mansfield, Missouri, for burial.

Katherine Davis died at Blue Rock August 1, 1914   Aug 5, 1914
A native of Kansas, she was 34 years old.

M.J.Davis, 75, died at Covelo May 8, 1912. He was a native   May 22, 1912
of West Virginia.

William Davis, in military service at Camp Lewis,   Jan 9, 1918
Washington, died of pneumonia early January 1918.

Mrs.Mary Daw died at Hopland March 11[?], 1913.   Mar 19, 1913

Jacob Dawson, about 76, died at Fort Bragg July 7, 1915. He   Jul 14, 1915
had come from Redlands two months earlier. Two daughters and
two sons survived.

Mrs.Ben W.Day, formerly of Ukiah, died in San Francisco   Oct 26, 1910
"last week".

Mrs.Dearborn of Melburne was killed in an automobile wreck   Oct 2. 1912
near Mendocino October 2, 1912.   Oct 16, 1912

Peter DeCarli was killed at Manchester in a team runaway   Oct 19, 1910
accident October 17, 1910.

Andria DeGenni died at the Fort Bragg hospital November 18,   Nov 20, 1918
1918 from influenza. He had worked in the local mill.

Guiseppe <u>Deghi</u> of Camp 8, Duffey in Mendocino County, was   Apr 12, 1911
found a suicide in April, 1911. He had murdered John
Lafranchi and Augustine Albertoni at Ignacio in Marin County
March 11, 1911.

John B. <u>Del Curto</u>, 26, drowned while swimming after a big   Aug 13, 1913
meal August 6, 1913 in the Caspar woods. Catholic rites were
held in Mendocino August 8th.

Mrs. Rosina <u>Della Maggiori</u> died in Fort Bragg August 25, 1911   Aug 30, 1911
Bright's disease. A native of Italy, she was 31 years old
and had lived in California for two years. Her husband
survived. Catholic rites were conducted August 27th by
Father Edwards.

George H. <u>Dempsey</u>, a ten year employee of the Irvine and Muir   Jan 1, 1919
Lumber Company of Willits, was killed by a train at Davis
"last week".

Mrs. Susan <u>Dempsey</u>, the widow of George H. Dempsey killed two   Jan 22, 1919
weeks earlier in a railroad accident at Davis, died at Santa
Rosa of pneumonia January 18, 1919. A native of Missouri,
she was 41 years old and left four children.

John <u>Denecky</u>, a pioneer woodsman, died in Fort Bragg   Sep 5, 1917
September 3, 1917 at the age of 70.

John Nelson <u>Dennen</u> died at Fort Bragg March 19, 1915. Born   Mar 24, 1915
in Augusta, <u>Maine</u>, September 14, 1846, he enlisted in
Company C, 31st Maine Volunteer Infantry and served through-
out the Civil War. He came to California in March 1877
settling in Littleriver. In 1892 he moved to Fort Bragg
where he worked as a carpenter. His wife, Dora, daughter
Mrs. Lulu Gignac of Fort Bragg, and son, R.L. Dennen of Point
Arena, survived.

John <u>Devereux</u>, 36, died suddenly in Honolulu, Hawaii,   Mar 14, 1917
March 11, 1917. Born in Cuffey's Cove the son of John
Devereux of Cleone, he lived on the coast for 17 years
until going to sea as a master marine engineer on the
steamer *Maunaloa*. Three brothers, William of Honolulu,
Clarence, and Edward Devereux as well as a sister, Grace
Devereux, all of California, survived.

Andrew J. <u>Devilbiss</u> died February 19, 1911 in Los Angeles.   Feb 22, 1911
He had been shot three years earlier on a railroad
construction job in Mexico. Born in Kibesillah, he was
36 years old.

Mrs. Julia Lowell <u>Devilbiss</u>, the wife of H.A. Devilbiss, died   Apr 17, 1918
at Los Angeles April 13, 1918. Her husband, two sons, John
and Edgar, three daughters, Irene, Hattie and Ethel
Devilbiss, and two brothers, J.W. and A.J. Lowell, survived.

Mrs. Frank <u>Deyoe</u> died in Ukiah September 3, 1910.   Sep 7, 1910

Mrs. Maria <u>Dias</u> died at Mendocino February 4, 1918. Her   Feb 6, 1918
brothers, Joseph Lawrence of Mendocino and Manuel Lawrence
of Watsonville, and her son, Joseph Dias, survived.

William <u>Dibble</u>, a former Point Arena resident, died in   Feb 12, 1913
Alaska "a few weeks ago". He was 68 years old and left a
widow in San Francisco.

Alonzo <u>Dickinson</u> died in Vine Hill near Martinez   Dec 13, 1911
December 5, 1911 at the age of 69 years and 16 days. A
native of New Hampshire, he owned a ranch at Ten Mile. A
son, Alonzo S. Dickinson survived.

Grace <u>Diggles</u>, who taught at Mendocino highschool in 1909,   Jun 3, 1914
died at Morgan Hill, Santa Clara County, "recently".

The two year old daughter of Mrs.C.I.Dightman died at
Wendling "this week" from TB.   Oct 17, 1917

Giacomo Digoncelli was killed on the Greenwood railroad   Jan 26, 1916
extension January 20, 1916 when a steam shovel turned over
in soft ground and crushed him and Alfredo Rivetti.

John M.Dill, 70, died at Laytonville September 22, 1918 of   Oct 2, 1918
pneumonia. He had been a 50 year resident.

Albert Dilling died in San Francisco February 6, 1918 after   Feb 13, 1918
an operation. Born at Bridgeport October 6, 1876, he was a
long time coast resident. The funeral was held at Mendocino
February 10th followed by interment at Littleriver. His
wife, two daughters, Verona and Mabel, mother, Mrs.I.B.
Dilling of Noyo, five brothers, Harry of Wendling, Frank of
Miller, Ed of Eureka, Oscar of Noyo and Jim of Portland,
Oregon, three sisters, Mrs.J.Gordon of Littleriver, Mrs.
Ed Mowrey of Lodi and Mrs.Hesel of Oregon, survived.

Harry Dilling, 52, died at Elk January 14, 1919 from   Jan 15, 1919
influenza. He had been a long time resident.

Mrs.Mary Dilling, a Fort Bragg resident until five months   Oct 6, 1915
ago, died at Portland, Oregon, September 30, 1915. She was   Oct 13, 1915
53 years and 7 months of age and the mother of Charles
Gardner, the local druggist, Laura Gardner and Cecile
Dilling. Her husband, James Dilling, also survived.

Mrs.George Dillon died near Ukiah April 27, 1911.   May 3, 1911

Marshal John Dixon was shot and killed at Point Arena by   Sep 29, 1915
William S.Harvey September 23, 1915. Harvey was drunk and   Nov 17, 1915
shot Dixon as he entered the bar to enforce order. Dixon
was born in Utah June 6, 1871 and lived in Point Arena
from 1874. On October 29, 1901 he married Mary Reilly.
Harvey got 40 years for the murder.

The five month old son of P.H.Dixon died February 1, 1912   Feb 7, 1912
and was buried the next day.

Mrs.Pete Dixon, 36, died of cancer September 20, 1916.   Sep 20, 1916
Born in Lake View, Quebec, [as Mary Colkhoun], she married   Sep 27, 1916
Mr.Dixon in San Francisco in [October] 1910. Her funeral
was at Fort Bragg September 22nd.

The 18 month old son of Charles Dodge died in Fort Bragg   Jan 15, 1919
January 7, 1919.

Mr.Dodge, formerly a Fort Bragg resident, died in Santa Rosa   Jun 8, 1910
June 5, 1910. The funeral was held in Fort Bragg June 8th.   Jun 15, 1910
His wife and sons, Bud, Dave, Fred, Arthur and Charlie, and
daughter, Mrs.William Burke, survived.

Mrs.Harry Dodge, 37, died October 17, 1915 of cancer in Fort   Oct 20, 1915
Bragg. A native Californian, she was buried in San Jose
after her funeral in Fort Bragg October 18th.

Rebecca Plato Dodge died in Santa Rosa April 21, 1915. Born   Apr 28, 1915
in New York September 28, 1845, she came to San Francisco as
a child. In January 1862 she married G.O.Dodge and moved to
Mendocino County. The survivors included her daughter, Mrs.
William Burke of Santa Rosa (whose husband died in 1910) and
six sons: W.J.H., David L., Charles P., Arthur Dodge of
Mendocino, P.W. of Stockton and F.A.Dodge of Fort Bragg. She
was buried at Fort Bragg April 23rd with Rev.I.H.Wood
officiating.

Mrs.James Doig, 23, died in Caspar November 23, 1918, She   Nov 27, 1918
was a two month resident. The funeral was held at Caspar
November 26th with Rev.T.Harris officiating.

The two year old son of Thomas Dollard fell into a well and drowned at Comptche July 19, 1912. The funeral was held July 21st at Mandocino with Rev.J.M.Fisher officiating.

Jul 24, 1912

Harry Donaldson was buried in Fort Bragg August 23, 1919. He was 12 years and several months old and had been ill for nine years. Born in Fort Bragg, the family moved early in 1919 to Alameda where he died.

Aug 27, 1919

Robert Donaldson was killed when painting the electric loading crane at the Fort Bragg mill and getting caught in the machinery November 14, 1913. Born in Scotland about 40 years ago, he came to California in 1897. He married Lizzie Rodger in 1899. His widow and three children survived. The funeral was held at the Presbyterian church in Fort Bragg with Rev.R.C.Grace presiding.

Nov 19, 1913

Jim Donalvitch, [also "Donaldvitch"] drowned in the ocean at the mouth of Pudding Creek while swimming in the surf. A native of Finland and a four year resident, he was about 25 years old.

Mar 17, 1915
Mar 24, 1915

Dan Donegan was killed in action with Canadian troops in France in September 1917 during his first action. When a Fort Bragg resident, he was a barman in the Windsor Hotel until 1911 when he went to Oakland to work in the cigar business.

Nov 14, 1917

Milton Donnadieu was fatally stabbed by Henry Stepany during a quarrel at L.D.Wade's bark camp on Ten Mile, June 24, 1919.

Jul 2, 1919

Mrs.Ellen Donohoe died May 7, 1914 and was buried the next day at Ukiah. She was the mother of Emmett, Ves, Fred, Martin Donohoe, and Mrs.Eva Melton of Ukiah, Mrs.Alice McAbee of Nevada and Mrs.Margaret Dollar of Idaho. Born Ellen Nunn October 18, 1846 in Wellsville, Tennessee, she came to California with her family in 1852. On June 25, 1861 she married J.H.Donohoe in the Anderson Valley. (He died in 1902.)

May 13, 1914

Mrs.Michael Donohue, 93, died September 28, 1919 at Greenwood. A native of Ireland, she settled at Greenwood over 50 years ago. Her husband, Michael, who was 96 on September 29th, and five daughters, Mrs.Hugh Buchanan, Mrs.Andrew Cooney, Mrs.Charles McMaster, and Mrs.Kate Dougherty - all of Greenwood, survived. The Rev.Shaw of Fort Bragg officiated at the funeral October 1st.

Oct 1, 1919
Jul 18, 1923

Arthur W.Dooley, aged 30, died in Ukiah January 16, 1911.

Jan 25, 1911

Andrew Dornan, 79, died at the County Hospital at Talmage October 6, 1916.

Oct 11, 1916

Mrs.G.Dougherty was buried at Albion May 9, 1911.

May 17, 1911

John Dougherty died November 29, 1911 at the age of 88. A native of Ireland, he came to the coast in 1855. A daughter, Mrs. Albert Gregory survived. His funeral was held December 1st.

Dec 6, 1911

William Dougherty, about 45, died near Greenwood November 17, 1916 of pneumonia. Born and raised at Cuffey's Cove, he married Katheryn Donohoe of Greenwood. The wife and mother, Mrs.William Dougherty, Sr. of Greenwood survived. Four sisters, Mrs.Dave Brandon and Mrs.Jack A. Nelson of Fort Bragg, Mrs.Jack Furlong of Caspar and Mrs. Ellis Castner of Fresno also survived as well as a brother, John Dougherty of Greenwood. Catholic rites were held November 20th and Cuffey's Cove.

Nov 22, 1916

Jesse Dixon Dowd, the 7 year old daughter of J.E.Dowd, died at Covelo June 7, 1913.

Jun 18, 1913

Mrs.Emily Dowlen, 79, died at Ukiah July 19, 1915.   Jul 28, 1915

The son of Mrs.J.R.Dowling of Laytonville died at Longvale   Jan 13, 1915
station of the Northwestern Pacific Railroad January 10,
1915. He was being taken to the hospital at Willits for
treatment, but the train was delayed by a landslide.

Jack Downey, 46, died in San Francisco October 29, 1918   Nov 6, 1918
from influenza. A former resident of Fort Bragg, he moved
to San Francisco in 1916. He was buried there. His wife
and son survived.

John Doyle, a native of Ireland, died near Caspar   Nov 9, 1910
October 27, 1910. A fifty year resident of Caspar, his wife
nee Elizabeth McManus, and four children preceded him in
death. Seven living children survived: Mrs.J.P.McManus of
Caspar, Mrs.N.P.Rasmussen of Fort Bragg, William Doyle of
Eureka, John Doyle of Fort Bragg, Tom Doyle of Mendocino,
Dan Doyle of Santa Cruz, and Mrs.Nellie Smyrle of Finch,
Canada. The funeral was at the old homeplace with burial
in the Catholic cemetery in Mendocino October 28, 1910.

Valve Doyle, the oldest son of Dan Doyle, died October 29,   Oct 30, 1918
1918 of influenza. Born at Navarro, he was 33.

Walter Doyle, born at Caspar October 21, 1872, died there   Dec 4, 1918
"last week" of TB.

F.Duarte died at Hopland June 27, 1915.   Jul 14, 1915

A.D.Duffey died in Fort Bragg June 24, 1919. A native of   Jun 25, 1919
Canada, he was 76 years and six months old. He came to   Jul 2, 1919
California about 1902, built and operated a sawmill at
Alpine on the Noyo, and went to Howard Creek in 1911 to run
the mill there for two years. Two sons, Fred and Albert
Duffey, a daughter, Miss Almyra Duffey, survived. The
funeral with masonic rites was held June 27th with burial
at Fort Bragg.

Mrs.Annie S.Duffey, the wife of A.D.Duffey, died at Fort   Feb 27, 1918
Bragg February 22, 1918. She was born at Santa Cruz in
January 1858 and was a resident of Fort Bragg for 10 years.
Father Grant officiated at the funeral February 24th. Her
husband, two sons, Fred and Albert Duffey, and a daughter,
Almyra Duffey, survived.

Joe Dunati, 7 years and 5 months old, died in Fort Bragg   Oct 18, 1916
October 12, 1916 following an operation on his appendix.
The funeral was held on October 15th with Father Blander-
field serving.

Mrs.Fannie Holliday Duncan, the widow of the late Samuel M.   Sep 24, 1919
Duncan of Duncan's Mills, died in Berkeley September 11,
1919. She was the mother of Mrs.C.Queen, A.W., J.J. and
Anne J.Duncan.

Frank Duncan, 36, died at Hopland July 1, 1911.   Jul 12, 1911

George W.Duncan, an old resident and merchant of Round   Dec 24, 1919
Valley, died at Covelo December 16, 1919. He arrived from
Missouri in 1875 with his family and ran a hotel for a time.

Samuel Duncan, a Hopland rancher, died at Ukiah May 16, 1915.   May 19, 1915
His brother, attorney Robert Duncan of Ukiah, survived.

J.L.Dunlap, an old settler of Covelo, died March 4, 1910.   Mar 23, 1910

Ores Dunlap, about 70, died on his Big River ranch   Dec 4, 1912
December 2, 1912. The funeral was in Willits December 5th.

Mrs.William (Victoria) <u>Dunn</u> died at Fort Bragg of heart
failure March 2, 1912. Born in Germany in 1836, she came to
the U.S.in 1862 and married William Dunn [died April 21, 1908]
in 1867. Seven children survived: Mrs.J.R.Reeves of
Inverness, Mrs.George Olson and Frank Dunn of Albion, Mrs.
George Stewart, Mrs.A.J.Lowell, Mrs.A.L.Anderson, and J.W.
Dunn of Westport. Rev.W.A.Chapman officiated at the funeral.

Mar 6, 1912

Mrs.K.<u>Dunsing</u>, 75, died north of Ukiah January 31, 1916.
Born in Germany February 27, 1841, she came to the Ukiah
valley where she lived 45 years. Her husband, five sons
and two daughters survived.

Feb 9, 1916

Frank <u>Dutra</u>, a woodsman in Mendocino and Caspar, was killed
in the Caspar woods June 6, 1913. Catholic rites were held
in Mendocino June 8th.

Jun 11, 1913

Mrs Mary A.<u>Dwelly</u> of Cleone died September 5, 1912.

Oct 2, 1912

The two week old child of Mr.& Mrs.<u>Dwinelle</u> of Mendocino
died at Ukiah April 24, 1910 of whooping cough.

Apr 27, 1910

Mrs.Frederick William <u>Earlich</u> was a suicide by drowning in
the Sacramento River. She was 45. [no date reported].

Jan 11, 1911

Mrs.Anna R.<u>Easton</u>, a former Mendocino resident, died in
San Francisco February 23, 1914. Formerly Anna Beaver of
Albion, the daughter of Stella Beaver Clow of Anderson
Valley, she was 49 years 10 months and 13 days old.

Mar 4, 1914

John <u>Eberhardt</u> of Chicago died suddenly at the Elk Horn
resort on Eel River June 5, 1915. Death was attributed to
heart disease. He was 44 years old. The body was shipped to
Oakland for cremation. [Elk Horn was about 50 miles from Fort Bragg.]

Jun 9, 1915

Reverend M.S.<u>Eby</u>, a Baptist minister, died in Healdsburg
"recently". His widow and six childen survived, one of whom
was Mrs.Mathews of Westport.

Dec 14, 1910

Mrs.C.E.<u>Eddy</u>, the wife of Dr.Eddy, died January 29, 1913 at
Fresno. Calvin Ruddock of Point Arena and Mrs.William
Cureton, her sister, survived.

Feb 5, 1913

Mrs.Holtie <u>Edwards</u>, the wife of Ward Edwards, died in Albion
August 9, 1917 at the age of 32. Born in New York, she was
the daughter of A.Samuelson. Her parents, husband and
children survived: Allen and John Samuelson, Miss Hannah,
Esther and Pearl Ward, Mrs.Sigurd Asquith and Mrs.Iley
Morton. The funeral was held at Fort Bragg August 12th.

Aug 15, 1917

James <u>Edwards</u>, born at Cuffey's Cove in 1886, died at
Willits February 2, 1911.

Feb 15, 1911

George <u>Eff</u>, a resident of the Ukiah Valley for 25 years,
died September 6, 1916.

Sep 13, 1916

Mrs.George <u>Eff</u>, a pioneer settler at Ukiah, died February 9,
1918. A native of Germany, she was buried February 11th.

Feb 13, 1918

Max <u>Eisner</u>, a sailor from the steamer *Klamath*, drowned in
the Fort Bragg harbor December 26, 1918 when a boat capsized.

Jan 1, 1919

Horace A.<u>Eldred</u>, 73, died at Ukiah November 3, 1912. He had
lived in Ukiah for 14 years.

Nov 6, 1912

William <u>Eldred</u>, manager of a livery stable, shot and killed
himself at Ukiah April 15, 1910. His widow and three
children survived.

Apr 20, 1910

Mrs.Ralph <u>Eldredge</u> died at Santa Rosa December 29, 1914. Her
brother-in-law was George Eldredge of Fort Bragg. The
funeral was held at Wendling December 31, 1914.

Dec 30, 1914

Tin Eli, 45, a Chinese who grew up in Mendocino, died in
Hong Kong "recently". He was the president of the Canton Bank
in San Francisco and was on a visit to his homeland.   Dec 3, 1919

Captain Charles Ellefson, aged 52, died in Berkeley   Feb 2, 1910
[no date reported].

The infant child of Mr.& Mrs.J.J.Elliott died at   May 4, 1910
Northwestern April 28, 1910.

Mrs.Rebecca J.Elliott, a former Ukiah resident, died in   Apr 9, 1919
Santa Rosa "this week".

George Ellis died at the County Farm near Ukiah February 10,   Feb 14, 1912
1912. A native of Scotia, he was over 70 years old.

Amanda Ellison, the wife of Edward Ellison of Mendocino,   Nov 5, 1919
died November 3, 1919 at the age of 23 years 4 months and
17 days. A native of Norway, she was a three year resident.
The funeral was held in Mendocino November 5th.

Albert H.Elmslie died at Fort Bragg September 30, 1917 from   Oct 3, 1917
heart trouble. Born in Massachusetts, he was 62 years
9 months and 5 days old. He came to California in 1886 and
settled at Caspar where he was a carpenter. His brother,
W.A.Elmslie, survived. The funeral was held at Caspar
October 3rd with Rev.W.A.Chapman officiating.

Mrs.M.B.Elmslie, aged 78 years 10 months and 11 days, died   Jan 19, 1910
at Caspar January 15, 1910. A native of Nova Scotia, Two
sons, W.A. and H.A.Elmslie of Caspar, survived.

William Albert Elmslie Jr., 23, died in France of a heart   Dec 26, 1917
complications from pneumonia. He was born and raised in Fort
Bragg and served with Company E, 20th.Forestry Engineers.

Mrs.Margaret Endicott, 81, died at Willits August 4, 1915.   Aug 11, 1915
She lived in the Little Lake Valley since 1861. Her son-in
-law, Charles Henry Wade, had died just 5 days earlier.

John England, a Stewart's Point rancher, was shot and killed   Aug 4, 1915
July 28, 1915 by M.J.Kennedy in a deer hunting accident.

Mrs.Dan English of Covelo died at Ukiah July 12, 1911.   Jul 19, 1911

Dennis English, a newcomer to Ukiah, was shot by Nicholas   Apr 25, 1917
Moldovean in Ukiah April 21, 1917 in a row over 30 cents   May 2, 1917
and died April 27th. Moldovean got life in prison.   Jul 4, 1917

Mrs.Wiley English died in Ukiah December 9, 1913. Born Hala   Dec 17, 1913
Neece January 22, 1836, the daughter of George Neece, she
came to California in September 1860 settling in the Ukiah
valley. She married Wiley English September 11, 1861. They
had eight children, one, Mrs.Della Fairbanks, died in 1906.
Mrs. Nanie Toney, George W., Robert M. of Imperial, Mrs.
Frankie Warren of Oakland, W.M., Haney English and Mrs.
Phronia Thomas of Ukiah.

Margaret Enright, the two month old daughter of Edmond   Feb 28, 1917
Enright of Inglenook, died February 24, 1917. Father
Brennan officiated at the funeral on February 25th.

The two year old daughter of John Erickson died May 2, 1913   May 7, 1913
south of Ukiah. She was buried in Ukiah May 3rd.

Mrs.Erickson, gave birth to a child on the South Fork of the   Jun 11, 1919
Noyo June 6, 1919 and died the next day from heart failure
triggered by the shock of the drowning of a five year old
boy, Viljo Sepantalo, left in her care.

Andrew Erickson, 35, hung himself near Northspur. His body   Jun 10, 1914
was found June 7, 1914.

Mrs.Andrew <u>Erickson</u>, 34, died in a San Francisco hospital August 4, 1918. A 20 year resident of Fort Bragg, she was the sister of Mrs.P.O.Hardell. A husband and child survived. The funeral was held August 8th led by Rev.J.J.Hillberg.

Aug 7, 1918

George <u>Erickson</u>, a Swedish Finn, was killed by a falling tree June 25, 1912 on the North fork of the Noyo River.

Jun 26, 1912

Mrs.Mina <u>Erickson</u> died at Albion February 14, 1910. She was 36 years old.

Feb 23, 1910

Otto <u>Erickson</u> died at Half Way House April 8, 1918 of TB. The funeral was held on April 10th.

Apr 17, 1918

Peter <u>Erickson</u>, formerly of Inglenook, died in San Francisco February 1, 1919 at the age of 89. He moved to the city in 1917 for his wife's health.

Feb 5, 1919
Feb 12, 1919

George <u>Escola</u> died at Mendocino June 11, 1914. Born in Finland, he was 76 years old. Five sons and two daughters survived.

Jun 17, 1914

The eleven month old son of M.<u>Evans</u> died March 21, 1916. His wife was the daughter of G.Ray Batt.

Mar 29, 1916

A.N.<u>Evans</u> died in Ukiah November 25, 1912. The funeral was held on the 27th. Born in Prince Edward Island, Canada, March 6, 1860, he came to Ukiah about 1847. A widow, two daughters and five sons survived.

Dec 4, 1912

W.A.<u>Evans</u>, 82, died at Ukiah August 11, 1911.

Aug 16, 1911
Aug 30, 1911

Edwin, the son of Emil <u>Evenson</u> drowned in a tub of water July 22, 1918 just one day short of his first birthday. The funeral was held July 24th.

Jul 24, 1918

Neniel K.<u>Everman</u>, a fisherman at Littleriver, died at Albion November 1, 1916. Born in Marin County, he was 68. A daughter, Mrs.G.M.Alexander of Albion, survived him.

Nov 8, 1916

Miss Susie Mae <u>Everson</u>, the daughter of Oscar Everson of Mendocino, died at Modesto "last week" from pneumonia. The funeral was held in San Francisco December 28, 1918.

Jan 1, 1919

Fred <u>Faas</u>, a native of Austria, died at Ukiah January 11, 1912.

Jan 17, 1912

Alfonza <u>Fagnani</u> was killed in a mill accident May 14, 1913. He was 51 years old and a resident for 26 years. Father White conducted the funeral May 18th.

May 21, 1913

Mrs.Elizabeth Jane <u>Fairbanks</u> died at Manchester April 22, 1917. Born in Iowa in 1841, she came to California in 1852. On January 25, 1855 she married Charles Schneider. After his death, she married again - to Barton Akuila Aull, and still later, to the late Clark Fairbanks (died July 17, 1902). From her first marriage there was one daughter, Mrs.Hillman. From the second, two daughters, Mrs.John Bilo of Washington and Mrs.George Gallagher of Fort Bragg. The third marriage produced three sons, Edward (deceased), Ernest and Herman Fairbanks. The funeral was April 24th.

May 2, 1917

Hiram H.<u>Fairbanks</u> died at Petaluma July 6, 1915. He was the father of A[ugustus] J.Fairbanks, Supervisor from Willits. Born in Indiana December 29, 1826, he relocated to Des Moines County, Iowa at age 19 and enlisted in the army to serve in the Mexican War. In 1849 he came to California and struck a rich vein. After returning to Indiana in 1851, he recrossed the plains in 1859 and settled at Petaluma where he ranched from 1860 to 1862. He then moved to San Francisco to engage in business. Later, he founded the Savings Bank of Petaluma and served as its president.

Jul 14, 1915

Alfred S.<u>Fairchild</u>, 86, died at Fort Bragg June 9, 1912.   Jun 12, 1912
Born in Pennsylvania in 1826, he enlisted in Company B,
7th California Infantry October 21, 1864. He lived in Sonoma
and Mendocino and was assistant postmaster at Inglenook. He
was buried in San Francisco.

Marianna <u>Fareira</u>, a former Mendocino resident, died in   Sep 17, 1913
Berkeley September 8, 1913. Her husband survived.

John A.<u>Faria</u>, a logging camp cook, died May 28, 1919 at   Jun 4, 1919
Mendocino. He was 70. His daughter, Maria Faria, a school-
teacher in Orange, New Jersey, survived.

Mrs.James <u>Farley</u>, 78, a former resident of Long Valley, died   May 15, 1912
at San Rafael May 9, 1912.

Silas <u>Farnsworth</u>, a 15 year resident of Willits and a   Jun 13, 1917
rancher in Sherwood Valley, died June 5, 1917.

Frank <u>Faro</u> died at Oakland "last week". He was born and   Jul 1, 1914
raised in Mendocino.

A.A.<u>Farrer</u> [also given as "Charles"] was a suicide north of   Oct 9, 1912
Mendocino October 3, 1912. The son of X.X.Farrer, his body   Oct 16, 1912
was found in the ocean with a fatal gunshot wound. His wife
had died two years before. Burial was in San Francisco.

John T.<u>Farrer</u>, 62, a merchant and former resident of the   Nov 27, 1918
Anderson Valley, died November 16, 1918 at Boonville.   Feb 5, 1919
His wife, Elizabeth, survived.

Mrs.<u>Fee</u>, 93, died at San Bernardino July 6, 1917.   Jul 11, 1917
Her son was George Fee of Westport.

The infant child of Jack <u>Fee</u> died at Westport July 20, 1913.   Jul 23, 1913

William A."Ahl" <u>Fee</u>, the oldest son of George Fee of   Apr 23, 1913
Westport, died April 19, 1913. Born there on a ranch, he was
32 years 7 months and 15 days old. The funeral was held
April 21st with Rev.W.A.Chapman officiating.

John <u>Figaro</u> died in New York June 2, 1919 enroute home from   Jun 4, 1919
service in France. He was the oldest son of Manuel Figaro
and brother of Antone Quaill and Herman Figaro.

The infant son of Peter <u>Filoon</u> died in Redwood Valley   Feb 21, 1912
February 11, 1912.

T.J.<u>Fine</u> died at Ukiah December 22, 1912. Born in Missouri   Dec 25, 1912
in 1897 [error, may be 1847], he crossed the plains with his
family as a lad of 15, settling in Sonoma County. He came to
Ukiah about 1877. A son, E.Fine of Crescent City, and two
daughters, Mrs.G.Sturtevant of San Francisco and Mrs.C.Stipp
of Eureka, survived.

Michael <u>Finn</u>, an old coaster, died "last week" at Greenwood   Jul 24, 1912
of bladder cancer. He was 79.

Thomas Columbus Benton <u>Finney</u> died at Ukiah July 14, 1912.   Jul 24, 1912
Born in Barry County, Missouri, May 15, 1843, his mother was
a niece of President Andrew Jackson.

Carl A.<u>Finstrom</u> died at Fort Bragg September 8, 1912 of   Sep 11, 1912
pneumonia. A native of Sweden, he had lived in California
for three years and worked at the Caspar Lumber Company.
Three sons survived. The funeral was held September 8, 1912
with Rev.J.C.Garth presiding.

Mrs.S.S.<u>Fisk</u>, the wife of the late Rev.Fisk of Caspar, died   Aug 22, 1917
at Tulare "last week". Her son was Frank Fisk of Albion.

Bud <u>Fitch</u>, 60, was killed in a runaway accident on his   Jul 5, 1916
ranch July 3, 1916. He had come to the coast from Nova Scotia
in June 1875. Here, he married Clara Hamilton. Survivors
included his father, two brothers, a sister and five children.

Ernest Demill <u>Fitch</u>, in military service, died at Walter   Jan 9, 1918
Reed hospital in Washington, D.C., January 5, 1918 of pneumonia.
[The son of Mrs.B.D.Fitch of Point Arena.]

George Albert <u>Fitch</u> was killed in action in France   Nov 13, 1918
October 4, 1918. About 26, he was the son of Mrs.B.D.Fitch
of Point Arena.

Mrs.Bessie McGarvey <u>Flaherty</u> died in San Rafael   Mar 5, 1913
February 25, 1913. Burial was at Ukiah.

John <u>Flanagan</u>, a pioneer of the coast and former County   Oct 9, 1912
Supervisor, died in Mendocino October 4, 1912. He was
survived by a son [Edward] and a daughter [Flossie].

Mrs.John <u>Flanagan</u> died at Mendocino May 31, 1910. Catholic   Jun 8, 1910
rites were performed there. Her husband and two children,
Edward John and Flossie survived as well as her sister,
Mrs.Ed Bouton of Vancouver.

Helen <u>Fleming</u>, the one year old daughter of F.N.Fleming of   Mar 29, 1911
Caspar, died at Caspar March 28, 1911. The funeral was   Apr 5, 1911
held on the 30th.

Arthur <u>Fletcher</u>, 28, a native of Minnesota, died   Nov 27, 1912
November 20, 1912 in Fort Bragg. A member of a touring actor
company, he had appeared on stage in the city. His funeral
was held November 23rd.

Emory <u>Flood</u> died at Mendocino September 3, 1910.   Sep 7, 1910
A Masonic funeral was held the next day.

Pete <u>Flrevca</u> (*sic*), an Italian about 26 years old, died at   Jan 22, 1913
Ukiah January 19, 1913.

Chay Yan <u>Fook</u>, *a.k.a.* Pat Kenny, died near Brush Creek where   Feb 2, 1916
he was a cook in a lumber camp. He had been on the coast for
40 years. The funeral was held at Mendocino with many of his
countrymen attending.

Mrs.W.H.<u>Foot</u>, *nee* Annie Albright of Fort Bragg, died in   Apr 2, 1913
Eureka March 21, 1913. A husband and two children survived.

The six week old daughter of Roy <u>Ford</u> of Ukiah died at   Jan 14, 1914
Sebastopol January 6, 1914.

Abraham <u>Ford</u>, 90, died on his ranch near Willits   Apr 30, 1919
April 24, 1919. He had been a 31 year resident.

Arnold <u>Ford</u>, a former Ukiah resident, died at Colorado   Mar 10, 1915
Springs, Colorado, March 2, 1915. He had come to California
in the early 1890*s*.

Mrs.A.W.<u>Ford</u>, 50, of Ukiah, died in a San Francisco hospital   Sep 22, 1915
September 15, 1915. She was a native of Sutter County.

Charles D.<u>Ford</u>, a former Mendocino resident, died in San   Jan 19, 1916
Francisco January 12, 1916. The son of Jerome and Martha
Ford, he left a wife, daughter (Mrs.Lewis Pierce), three
sisters and a brother, Jerome Chester Ford of San Diego.
Cremation was in San Francisco January 14th.

Mrs.J.C.<u>Ford</u>, the wife of a former superintendent of the   Jun 6, 1917
Mendocino Lumber Company, died in San Diego May 31, 1917.
She had moved there in 1901.

Mrs.Sarah Ford, the wife of W.M.Ford, died September 30, 1913. Born in Arkansas January 24, 1840, she came to California across the plains in 1853. In 1856 she married Ford, and they came to Ukiah in 1864. The husband and six children survived: James A.Ford, Mrs.Mary York, W.A.Ford, Mrs.Julia H.Ford, E.M.Ford and Mrs.Sarah Banker. The funeral was held October 1st in Ukiah.

Oct 8, 1913

William Ford, 89, died at Ukiah July 21, 1919. He was a pioneer settler of the area.

Jul 23, 1919

Frank Forich, a railroad laborer, was crushed by a falling boulder about six miles from Dos Rios on May 9, 1914.

May 13, 1914

A.Foster, a Ukiah merchant, died February 29, 1912 at 70.

Mar 6, 1912

A.W.Foster Jr., president of the Willits Water and Power Company and brother of W.A.S.Foster of Willits, died in San Francisco May 25, 1915 of a blood clot on the brain received from a fall in a squash game. He was the second son of A.W.Foster of San Rafael.

Jun 2, 1915

Arlington Foster died from injuries received in a fall from a bridge several weeks ago. The funeral was held at Ukiah March 3, 1912.

Mar 6, 1912

George Foster, 64, died at Northwestern January 13, 1914. He was a mill employee.

Jan 21, 1914

Mrs.Marion Burness Foster, wife of W.A.S.Foster, died at Northwestern July 20, 1913. Born in San Francisco in 1882, the daughter of John and Jennie Burness, she married Foster in 1906. The husband and three children survived: Jean, William & John. Burial was in San Rafael.

Jul 30, 1913

Mary V.Foster died at Muir's old mill January 8, 1911.

Jan 18, 1911

Edwin Foushee died in Fort Bragg August 2, 1913. Born in Bolivar, Polk County, Missouri, October 25, 1836, he went to Nevada and mined before coming to California in 1857 settling in Sonoma County. On November 27, 1867 he married Mary C.Hall and came to Mendocino in 1880. Later, in 1901, they moved to Fort Bragg, where he served as constable, assessor and worked for the lumber companies. The funeral was held August 5th with Rev.W.A.Chapman officiating.

Aug 6, 1913

Miss Laura T.Fower, formerly the principal of the Point Area grammar school, died in San Francisco "last week". She had come to California in 1862.

Oct 25, 1916

Mrs.Alice M.Foye died at Fort Bragg October 27, 1916. She was 53 years 6 months and 1 day old. Born in England, she came to California with her parents in 1869. In 1883 she married the late Henry M.Foye. Five children survived: Mrs.Gailen Hill of Portland, Oregon; Eugene Foye of Navarro, Florence A., Fred, and Arthur Foye of Fort Bragg. Her mother, Mrs.William Wells of Fort Bragg, five sisters: Mrs. George A.Cameron of Navarro, Mrs.Martin of Oakland, Mrs.R.Bohn of Fort Bragg, Misses Rose and Minnie of San Francisco, and a brother, J.Wells of Fort Bragg also survived. The funeral was held October 31st.

Nov 1, 1916
Nov 8, 1916

Henry Malcolm Foye died at Fort Bragg April 5, 1915. Born in Chelsea, Maine, May 28, 1851. He sailed to Mendocino arriving in August 1869. He was a foreman for the L.W.White Lumber Company for 9 years and 14 for Union Lumber Company. On January 7, 1883 he married Alice Weller and they had five children: Mrs.Gailen Hill, Eugene Foye of San Francisco, Florence, Fred and Arthur Foye of Fort Bragg. The funeral was held April 8th conducted by Rev.I.H.Wood.

Apr 7, 1915
Apr 14, 1915

William A.Foye, the brother of Henry Foye, died at the   Feb 24, 1915
Soldiers' Home in Sawtelle, Los Angeles County,
February 21, 1915. Born in Chelsea, Maine, he served in
the U.S.Navy during the Civil War. After the war he settled
on the coast amd was a resident for 40 years. He was 72.

Maurice Fraga drowned at Mendocino August 17, 1914.   Aug 19, 1914

The five month old son of John Fraki died of pneumonia   Feb 22, 1911
February 16, 1911. The funeral was held February 19th.

Mrs.J.C.Franks, 37, died at Fort Bragg February 18, 1914.   Feb 18, 1914
A three year resident in the area across Pudding Creek, she
left a husband and son. The funeral was held at the Presbyterian church in Fort Bragg February 20th.

Mrs.Fraser was killed in an automobile wreck on the   Oct 8, 1913
Navarro-Wendling road October 1, 1913.

James Fraser, formerly a coast woodsman, died in San   Jan 8, 1919
Francisco January 4, 1919 at the age of 74.

Mrs.Simon Fraser died at Mendocino February 2, 1914. Born in   Feb 4, 1914
Penn Brook, Ontario, she was an eleven year resident of
Mendocino. A husband and five children survived. The
funeral was held at the Presbyterian church February 5th.

Mrs.D.H.(Mildred) Frazier, the daughter of M.W.Edwards, died   Nov 6, 1918
in Berkeley November 1, 1918. Born and raised on the south
coast, she left a husband and daughter. Burial was in
Oakland on November 2nd.

Mrs.E.P.Freathy died at Caspar November 2, 1912. Born and   Nov 6, 1912
raised in Caspar, she was 46 years old. The funeral was
conducted November 4th by Rev.Hargraves.

A.W.Frederickson, formerly a resident of Irmulco, died in   Jul 3, 1918
San Francisco June 29, 1918. His funeral was held at
Mountain View June 30th.

Mrs.Charles Freeberg, a former Fort Bragg resident, died at   Dec 6, 1916
Talmage "last week". Her husband and two sons, Hugo and
Arthur Freeberg, survived.

Jacob Freeman, a shoemaker, was found dead in bed at Fort   Nov 27, 1912
Bragg November 25, 1912. The funeral was held November 27th.

Constantino Freitas was killed in the Albion woods   Nov 8, 1911
November 4, 1911 when a log rolled over him.

Jose Freitas, 50 and a native of the Azores, died at Mendo-   Aug 6, 1919
cino July 30, 1919. A wife and two sons survived.

Mrs.Elsie Frieberg of Greenwood died in Washington, DC,   Oct 23, 1918
October 21, 1918 of influenza. About 24 years old and a
native of Elk, she had been employed two months earlier as
a clerk in the War Industry Board.

Mrs.Annie Fritzsche died at Fort Bragg June 21, 1917. Born   Jun 27, 1917
in Germany in 1858, she came to New York with her family in
1860 and on to Oakland in 1875. In 1876 she married Frank
Fritzsche. They settled in Fort Bragg in 1895. Her husband
and five children survived: Mrs.Sam Shafsky, Arnold, Carl,
Frank and Fred Fritzsche. The funeral was held June 24th
in Fort Bragg.

John Frye dropped dead of heart failure in Westport   Apr 12, 1911
April 7, 1911. A resident of Westport for most of his life,
he was 31 years old. The funeral was held April 9th,
Rev.W.A.Chapman officiating.

Thomas Frye, 26, drove a truck into the side of a Northwestern Pacific Railroad train near McCann August 28, 1919
and died of his injuries. Born and raised at Westport, he
had served in France. His parents, sisters, Mrs.Charles
Anderson, Mrs.A.Hanson of Fort Bragg, Mrs.Archie Cameron of
Albion, Mrs.Ed Tracey of Portland, Oregon, and a brother,
Delwin Frye of Eureka, survived.   Sep 3, 1919

J.A.Fuller, the father of W.F.Fuller of Fort Bragg, died at
New Mines, Nova Scotia. He was about 85 and left seven
living children.   Feb 18, 1913

Major General Frederick Funston, 51, died at San Antonio,
Texas, February 19, 1917.   Feb 21, 1917

Eli Furgeson, a native of [lost] died at Ukiah March
[date lost account paper torn].   Apr 3, 1912

Mrs.Elizabeth Furlong, wife of the late Thomas P.Furlong,
died at Potter Valley December 7, 1917 at the age of
84 years and 7 months. A native of Ohio, she came to California in 1849 settling at Navarro. Two sons, Ed of Potter
Valley, and A.T.Furlong of Caspar, survived. The funeral was
held at Littleriver December 10th.   Dec 12, 1917

Joseph Gabac drowned in the Glen Blair millpond July 17,
1912. Catholic rites were held in Fort Bragg July 19th.   Jul 24, 1912

Charles Gage, an early lumber mill operator, died
in San Francisco "last week".   Sep 12, 1917

A six year old child of the Gahan's of Greenwood died in
San Francisco September 28, 1910 of appendicitis.   Oct 5, 1910

W.R.Gaine died of Point Arena died in San Francisco
September 5, 1912.   Sep 18, 1912

J.Gainsjager, a native of Austria aged 76, died at the
State Hospital in Ukiah January 16, 1911.   Jan 25, 1911

Mrs.Gallagher, nee Elsie Brown, the daughter of Dr.Artie
Brown a former Fort Bragg resident, died at Eldridge,
Sonoma County, November 11, 1918 of influenza. The funeral
was held in Alameda.   Dec 11, 1918

Peter Gallagher, formerly of Fort Bragg, disappeared from
Spokane, Washington in the Spring of 1919. His skeleton was
discovered December 23, 1919.   Dec 31, 1919

Mrs.Rodger Gallagher died in Eureka "last week". Her funeral
was held in Santa Rosa.   May 19, 1915

Louis Gallini, about 65, died at Albion July 2, 1918. He had
settled in Littleriver 41 years ago.   Jul 3, 1918

Mrs.James Galloway, 63, died November 30, 1917 of pneumonia.
A native of Germany, she lived on the coast 18 years.   Dec 12, 1917

Ed Gamberg, believed to have drowned in Ten Mile River   Feb 27, 1918
February 24, 1918, actually died in Pudding Creek where his Mar 6, 1918
body was found March 4th. The funeral was held at Fort Bragg
March 7th. His wife, two daughters, Fannie and Lena, and
three sons, Franz, August and Dave Gamberg, survived.

George Gamble, aged 55, died at the ranch north of Pudding   Sep 14, 1910
Creek September 8, 1910. A native of Canada, he was survived Oct 5, 1910
by eight children, four sons: George, Harold, Marvin and Guy
Gamble, and four daughters: Mrs.Maggie Kennedy, Mrs.Alice
Green, Mrs.E.Wellington and Mrs.E.Baker.The funeral was at
the Baptist church in Fort Bragg led by Rev.A.J.Sturtevant
and Rev.J.S.Ross. Samuel Shafsky was appointed guardian of
two minor children with W.H.Dixon acting as adminstrator.

The infant daughter of Henry Gamble died at Elk May 2, 1912.   May 22, 1912

John Gannon was found dead in his cabin at Ten Mile,   Sep 4, 1918
September 1918. He was about 50 and believed to have died
from natural causes.

Albert Garavanta was severly injured in a mill accident   Nov 20, 1912
November 17, 1912 and died the next day in the Fort Bragg   Nov 27, 1912
hospital. Catholic rites were held November 21st.

John Garth, the father of Rev.J.C.Garth a former pastor   Nov 26, 1913
at Fort Bragg, died at Petaluma November 17, 1913.

Joe M.Garvin, a former resident and merchant of Mendocino,   Mar 29, 1916
died in a San Francisco hospital [no date reported].

Edward Miligan Gaspar died at Point Arena June 16, 1915.   Jun 23, 1915
Born in Perry, Maine, November 20, 1853, he had come to
California in 1871. On October 25, 1878 he married Cora N.
Huntley and was the father of five children: Cecil M.Gaspar,
Orman C.Gaspar, Mrs.Millie Hackley, Mrs.Abbie Wilcox and
Edward Arthur Gaspar.

Joe Gaspari, 42, died in Mendocino November 1, 1915 of   Nov 3, 1915
pneumonia. In addition to his wife and six children, his
brother Rocco Gaspari of Point Arena survived. He was a
native of Italy.

Benjamin F.Gates, formerly of Fort Bragg, died in Oakland   Nov 27, 1918
"this week" at the age of 84. He was the father of Ruth A.
Wailes, Miss Amelia Gates and the late Rudolph Gates, all
raised in Fort Bragg.

Rudolph Gates of Tulare County, formerly of Fort Bragg, died   Aug 12, 1914
and was buried August 10, 1914 at Petaluma.

The 21 year old daughter of Charles Gear was buried   Jan 29, 1919
at Vallejo January 18, 1919. She died of influenza.

A.Germansen, a recent arrival from Portland, Oregon, was   Jun 3, 1914
found dead at the entrace to the Fort Bragg cemetery
May 30, 1914 - a suicide by poison.

Lewis M.Getchell, brother of G.L.Getchell of Fort Bragg,   Apr 6, 1910
died near Gualala March 18, 1910.

Louis Ghens, died at Fort Bragg January 14, 1919 from   Jan 15, 1919
influenza. His wife and four small children survived.

Neal Gianvall, the 18 year old son of Carl Gianvall, a Noyo   Oct 17, 1917
rancher, died October 16, 1917. The family had lived here
nine years.

Mrs.George Gibbs died at Fort Bragg July 29, 1913. Born and   Jul 30, 1913
raised in California, she was 37 years and 10 months old.
She lived in Fort Bragg for 20 years. Her husband, daughter
and son survived. The funeral was held from the Episcopal
church July 31st with Rev.John Barrett officiating.

Peter J.Gibney, an old resident of the Caspar area, died   Jan 12, 1910
January 4, 1910. The funeral was held at Mendocino
January 7th. His wife, two daughters and four sons survived.

Will Gibson died at Van Nuys June 1, 1914. Born in Ukiah   Jun 3, 1914
December 5, 1871, he had moved to Seattle about 1883.

T.J.Gillespie, an old resident of Eel River, died   Sep 17, 1913
September 8, 1913. His widow and several children survived.

W.E.Gillespie, a pioneer settler of the County, died at 82   Jul 26, 1911
in Hopland July 8, 1911.

Ike Gilley of Ukiah, 35, died September 9, 1913 following an   Sep 17, 1913
appendix operation. His wife and brother in Ukiah survived.

Mrs.L.Gilliam , a resident of Willits for more than 50   Mar 26, 1919
years, died there March 25, 1919. A sister of the Frost
brothers, pioneer settlers, she was past 80 years of age.

Mrs.Lily Gillmore and her sister, Miss Allie Akins, died at   Mar 11, 1914
Windsor, Sonoma County, March 3, 1914. Mrs.Gillmore was 26
and Miss Akins, 30. The latter died of heart failure. Their
joint funeral was held at Point Arena March 7, 1914.

H.E.Gilman, 21, was killed in an accident at the Greenwood   Mar 18, 1914
mill March 16, 1914. His folks lived in Seattle, Washington.

Mrs.Frederick Giorgone, nee Annie Figone, a daughter of A.   Jun 4, 1913
Figone of Ukiah valley, died at San Francisco May 30, 1913.

Dalle Giovani was found dying of exposure north of Clover-   Jan 12, 1916
dale January 10, 1916.

Mrs.Victor Giusti, 30, died October 16, 1919 in San Fran-   Oct 22, 1919
cisco from TB. Her husband and three small children survived.
Interment was in Fort Bragg October 21st.

F.G.Glander, 31, of San Francisco died at Needle Rock   Aug 9, 1911
August 5, 1911 of heat prostration and heart failure. The
body was shipped to San Francisco August 8, 1911. He left
a wife and three children.

Martin James Gleason died at his home on Juan Creek   Dec 22, 1915
December 16, 1915 of stomach cancer. Born in Ireland, he
was 61 years 1 month and 5 days old. A wife, four
daughters and a son survived. Catholic rites were held in
Fort Bragg by Father Blanderfield December 18th.

Louis Goetz was killed by a fellow inmate at the Ukiah State   Jan 27, 1915
Hospital in 1913.

Mrs.Grace Gofford died at Covelo December 27, 1915.   Jan 5, 1916

Mrs.David Goggins of Branscomb died October 9, 1919   Oct 29, 1919
in San Francisco of stomach cancer.

Con H.Goldberg, an attorney at Willits, died December 29,   Jan 3, 1917
1916. A native of Germany, he had lived in California from
childhood. The funeral was held in San Francisco.

A.L.Gonsalves died at Melburne July 22, 1915. Of the Azores,   Jul 28, 1915
he was 67. His wife and eight children survived: Mrs.L.
Pimentel, Mrs.May Skiffington, Mrs.Carrie Sanders, Louis,
Anna, Francis, Ethel and Lucy Gonsalves. Catholic rites were
held July 25th.

F.J.Goodall, a ranchhand from Covelo, fell from his horse   May 26, 1915
when fording the Eel River and drowned "last week"   .

Mrs.Emily M.Goodrich died January 12, 1915. A native of   Jan 20, 1915
Stratford, Kings County, she was 87 years 11 months and
4 days old. She came to Mendocino in 1900. Her son, George
Pease, survived. The funeral was January 16th at Mendocino,
with burial at Littleriver.

Ruel Sanford Goodwine died at Mendocino December 4, 1913.   Dec 10, 1913
Born in Maine in 1849, he lived on the coast for 40 years.
The Rev.J.H.Hargreaves of Caspar led the funeral in
Littleriver December 5th.

Mrs.Fred <u>Goranson</u> died at Fort Bragg December 9, 1919 when
giving birth by caesarian section. She was born on the
Garcia River December 2, 1891. Her husband, son, daughter,
infant son, brothers, Edward Bishop of Fort Bragg, and Fred
Bishop of Greenwood survived. The funeral was held at the
Episcopal church by Father Grant with burial at Fort Bragg.

Dec 10, 1919

Mrs.Walter <u>Goranson</u> died at Elk November 27, 1918 from
influenza. Her husband and three small children survived.

Nov 27, 1918

William John <u>Goudy</u>, a two year resident, died at Fort Bragg
January 9, 1919 from influenza. Burial there was January 11th.

Jan 15, 1919

William <u>Grace</u>, the father of Rev.Grace, died in Arkansas. He
was almost 81 years old. [no death date reported].

Mar 16, 1910

Joseph <u>Granskog</u> died at Mendocino February 6, 1919 from
pneumonia. A sister, Mrs.John Burbeck, [unnamed] brothers,
a wife and three children in Finland, survived.

Feb 12, 1919

Mrs.G.W.<u>Grant</u> died at age 70 in Hopland March 26, 1911.

Mar 29, 1911

Andrew <u>Granvall</u>, 57, died November 3, 1919 when struck by a
bicycle ridden by Will Bradley on the Noyo grade. He left a
wife and seven children. The funeral was held in Fort Bragg
November 6th with Rev.W.A.Chapman officiating.

Nov 5, 1919

Charles T.<u>Gray</u>, 67, a pioneer rancher and bakeryman of
Mendocino, died in Berkeley October 12, 1917. A native of
Maine, he came to California in 1861. The funeral was held
in Mendocino October 14th with Rev.Sutherland officiating.
In addition to his wife, two daughters, Mrs.Elizabeth
Ingalls and Mrs.Myrtle Gelston, and a brother, Prince W.
Gray, survived.

Oct 17, 1917

Mrs.Edith Dellett <u>Gray</u>, the wife of Lawrence A.Gray, died
October 29, 1918 at Wendling. The daughter of Henry J.
Dellett, she married Mr.Gray [October 18,] 1914. In 1916
they moved to Wendling. Her husband, a boy of three and a
girl of three months survived. The funeral was held at the
Episcopal church in Fort Bragg October 31st.

Oct 30, 1918

A son of Fred <u>Gray</u> died at Fort Bragg March 7, 1917. Burial
was in Santa Cruz.

Mar 14, 1917

The body of L.L.<u>Gray</u> was found in Jack Peters Gulch near
his home July 5, 1917. He had disappeared June 8th.

Jul 11, 1917

Lawrence Arden <u>Gray</u> of Wendling died in Fort Bragg
December 13, 1919 of spinal meningitis. Born near Santa Cruz
March 2, 1890, he came to Fort Bragg about 1903. A civil
engineer, he ran the Navarro Lumber Company's logging woods
at Wendling. His wife died October 29, 1918. His parents,
Frederick Gray of Wendling, two small children, two sisters,
Mrs.William Hartman of Mendocino, and Mrs.Howard Gray of
Ten Mile. The funeral was held at Fort Bragg December 16th.

Dec 17, 1919

Mrs.Mary Louise <u>Gray</u> died at Point Arena April 9, 1915. Born
in Holbrook, Massachusetts, December 5, 1851, she came to
California in 1869.

Apr 21, 1915

T.Bert <u>Greathouse</u>, 42, a rancher, was shot and killed by
Walter McClendon, a trapper, in a drunken row near Calpella
January 1, 1916. Greathouse was born at Elk and left a wife
and daughter in Humboldt County.

Jan 5, 1916
Jan 12, 1916

Mrs.Clara <u>Green</u> died at Mendocino December 1, 1914. Born in
Kentucky in April [date lost], she was [data lost] years old.
She lived in Missouri during the Civil War where her husband
was killed in front of her on the doorstep of their house.
Four children survived: Mrs.J.N.Rea of Mendocino, Mrs.E.A.
Wellman of Petaluma, George Edward Green of Petaluma and
Mrs.Francis [name lost] of the Phillipine Islands.

Dec 9, 1914

Isaac Green was found dead at Ukiah January 7, 1914 from
pneumonia. He was a veteran of the Spanish American war and
had served in the Phillipines.

Jan 14, 1914

Mrs.Rebecca J.Green, 65, died September 29, 1919 at Willits.
A native of Ireland, she came to San Francisco as a young
girl. She arrived in Willits in May 1918. Her son, P.R.
Green of Willits, survived.

Oct 8, 1919

Ralph Clifton Greenough, born September 11, 1879 at Littleriver, died at Fort Bragg April 4, 1915. He received his
teaching certificate at Ukiah in July 1896 and taught in
Albion and Mendocino, moving to Fort Bragg in 1906. His
health failed in 1912. The funeral was held at the Fort
Bragg Baptist church April 7th led by Rev.I.H.Wood.

Apr 7, 1915
Apr 14, 1914

Mrs.Gregory, a long time resident, died at Mendocino
February 16, 1918. Her husband, two daughters and two sons
survived. The funeral was held at Mendocino February 19th.

Feb 20, 1918

Mrs.Bessie Gregory died at Mendocino December 4, 1916. Born
in Mendocino January 23, 1862, she was the only daughter of
John Dougherty. Her husband, Albert Gregory, and son, John
Millard Gregory, survived. The funeral was December 10th.

Dec 13, 1916

Mrs.Bessie Howe Gregory, the wife of J.A.Gregory and
daughter of Mrs.Mary O.and the late S.B.Stevens, died in
Oakland May 3, 1919.

May 14, 1919

Thomas L.Gregory died at Caspar October 26, 1915. Born in
New Brunswick in 1849, he came to the U.S.in 1882 and was a
coast resident 30 years. His funeral was October 27th.

Oct 27, 1915

Mrs.Hannah Griffiths, 80, a native of South Carolina, died
at Ukiah November 22, 1915.

Dec 1, 1915

Mrs.S.R.Griffiths died in Upper Lake July 16[?], 1916. Born
in Placer County January 31, 1856, she came to Lake County
in 1861. She married John Griffiths in Big Valley. The
mother of five, she was widowed at 36. Sons, Ned of Big
Valley and Lorin of Ukiah and three daughters survived. The
funeral was conducted by C.W.Watson with burial at
Kelseyville July 18th [?].

Jul 26, 1916

Allie Grindle of Mendocino, the only child of Joshua Grindle,
was drowned in the sinking of the USS F-4, a submarine.

Mar 31, 1915

Alma Grist died in an Oakland hospital February 24, 1913.
The funeral was Fort Bragg led by Rev.J.C.Garth on the 28th.

Mar 5, 1913

George Grist died October 31, 1919 at Jackson, California,
of pneumonia. A pioneer of Round Valley, he was buried at
Covelo November 3rd.

Nov 5, 1919

Tom Grist, 75, died at Fort Bragg August 13, 1917. A native
of Ohio, he served in the 32nd Ohio Infantry during the
Civil War, coming to the coast over 30 years ago. The
funeral was at Fort Bragg August 14th by Rev.W.A.Chapman.

Aug 15, 1917

F.Grothe, 76 and a former County resident, died in
Briceland July 20, 1911 - burial in Laytonville.

Aug 16, 1911

M.Grubelick was killed at the Noyo chute when he was
knocked into the ocean and drowned August 9, 1912.

Aug 14, 1912

The son of Tom Gschwend died at Wendling February 10, 1917
of spinal meningitis. The funeral was at Philo February 13th.

Feb 21, 1917

Loigi Guatini, 24, died in Fort Bragg November 1, 1918 from
influenza. Italian, he was buried at Fort Bragg November 3rd.

Nov 6, 1918

Rock Gudenza, Sr. was killed at Elk when he fell from a
wagon May 12, 1912.

May 15, 1912
May 22, 1912

Joe Guenza was killed in a team runaway accident in   Mar 10, 1915
Point Arena March 6, 1915.

Joseph Guenza, a year old, died of burns November 11, 1915.   Nov 17, 1915
The funeral was held at Point Arena November 13th.

John Gunnar died at Littleriver January 19, 1916. He was   Jan 26, 1916
born in Albion. The funeral was held January 20th.

Mrs.Emma F.Gunning, the wife of Jack Gunning formerly of   May 21, 1913
Mendocino, died at Caspar May 16, 1913. Catholic rites
were held in Mendocino May 18th.

Mrs.Mary B.Guntley, 85, of Anderson Valley died near Philo   Jul 16, 1919
July 13, 1919.

Mrs.Lucy Gurley, 71, died at Mendocino July 30, 1914. A   Aug 5, 1914
native of Winchester, Virginia, she lived in Mendocino for
63 years. Two sons, James and Robert Gurley, survived.

The 15 month old daughter of Mr.& Mrs.Gustafson of Alpine   Dec 28, 1910
died December 27, 1910. The funeral was held the next day.

Arthur Gustafson died of stomach cancer at Fort Bragg   Sep 10, 1913
September 7, 1913. A native of Finland, he was in the U.S.
for 3½ years. A wife and child survived. His funeral was
held in Fort Bragg September 9, 1913.

Henry Gustafson died in Fort Bragg March 21, 1916 from   Mar 22, 1916
injuries received in the Glen Blair woods that day when
crushed by a log. The son of Peter Gustafson of near Glen
Blair, he was 26 years old.

Mary Gustafson, 24 years old, died from diphteria in Glen   Jan 4, 1911
Blair December 28, 1910. The funeral was held the same day.

Dakman Gustaphson, the eight year old daughter of the   Mar 1, 1911
Gustaphson's of Glen Blair, died February 26, 1911 of
diptheria. The funeral was held the 27th.

Mrs.Rosi Gusti, 52, died at Fort Bragg October 29, 1918.   Oct 30, 1918
A native of Italy, she left five daughters.

Charles G.Gustlander, a jeweler at Willits for 10 years,   Jul 12, 1916
died in San Francisco July 2, 1916 at the age of 58.

Donald Guthrie, the son of A.Guthrie of Mendocino County,   Apr 4, 1917
disappeared in November 1916. His body was discovered in
March 1917. Foul play was suspected.

Harold Guthrie drowned in the Eel River near Island Mountain Dec 6, 1916
November 26, 1916. He was the brother of Mrs.William T.Hearn.

George Haap was murdered at Upper Lake December 1, 1917; the Dec 5, 1917
body was discovered on December 2nd. Born in Phuladelphia,   Dec 12, 1917
Pennnsylvania, in 1862, he was a rancher. A brother, John
Haap of Oregon, and four sisters, Mrs.L.Mogle of Los Angeles,
Mrs.F.Werner of Westport, Mrs.C.V.Hannah and Mrs.F.C.Hunter
of Hayward, survived. Young Koko, an Indian, was held for
murder, but released for lack of evidence.

Mrs Maria Haap, 81, died at Westport January 31, 1917. She   Feb 7, 1917
was a 40 year resident of the area. Two sons and two
daughters survived. One daughter was Mrs.Fred Hunter of
Lake County.

August Haare, 55, of Greenwood died at Fort Bragg   Aug 29, 1917
August 29, 1917. He was a native of Germany.

Witt Hackley, 83, died at Ukiah January 1, 1912.   Jan 17, 1912

W.A.Hagans died at Ukiah July 15, 1911. Born in Illinois, he   Jul 19, 1911
came to Mendocino in 1863 and ran a hotel in Ukiah. Masonic
rites were performed at graveside.

Harry Haight, 57, a former resident of Fort Bragg, died at   Apr 3, 1912
Livermore, Alameda County, April 2, 1912.

John Calvin Hale, the son of John M.Hale of Willits, died   Sep 3, 1913
there August 23, 1913.

Mary P.Hale died at Chico December 1, 1911. The daughter   Dec 20, 1911
of J.D.Ball of Anderson Valley, she was born in Boonville
February 14, 1859.

Henry Hall, a native of Ireland aged 24, died at Elk   Apr 5, 1911
March 20, 1911.

Mrs.Ida B.Hall, a former resident of Round Valley, died at   Jun 7, 1911
Corona, Riverside County, June 4, 1911.

O.M.Hall died at Willits November 22, 1910. A farmer, he was   Nov 23, 1910
in Round Valley in 1855.

Mrs.P.L.Hall, 64, a resident of Little Lake Valley since   Jan 3, 1917
1864, died at Willits December 26, 1916.

Margaret J.Halliday, 61, died in San Francisco January 31,   Feb 12, 1913
1913. She was buried at Point Arena February 3rd.

Fred Halling died at Fort Bragg July 8, 1915 of pneumonia.   Jul 14, 1915
He was 78 years 7 months and [number days lost]. Born in Falun,
Sweden, November 16, 1836, he came to America in 1863 and to
Mendocino in 1869. He worked as a blacksmith and machinist
until retirement in 1902. His wife died [in San Francisco in
November] 1897. His daughter, Mrs.Harold Gray of Fort
Bragg survived. The funeral was held July 11th at Mendocino.

George Hallock, a cousin of P.W.Haggreen of Point Arena,   Dec 30, 1914
died at Compton "recently". A native of England, he was 73.

Charles Hamerstrong, a native of Sweden 52 years old, died   Jul 5, 1911
at Sherwood July 2, 1911 of heart failure.

Mrs.S.D.Hamilton, 60, died November 22, 1915 at Point Arena   Dec 1, 1915
where she had lived 29 years. Born in Santa Clara, she left
a husband and four children.

Mrs.R.E.Hamlin, formerly of Greenwood, died in San Francisco   Jun 12, 1912
June 1, 1912 of cancer. The daughter of Samuel Ayer, she was
25 years old.

Dr.Patrick W.Hammal was found dead in bed December 11, 1912   Dec 18, 1912
near Gualala.

Mrs.David Hammel died October 30, 1911 of injuries received   Nov 8, 1911
in a team runaway accident at Kelseyville.

Col.Charles M.Hammond, a Lake County rancher, died June 21,   Jun 23, 1915
1915 of heart failure. He was 54. His widow survived.

George Handley cut his throat November 22, 1916 at Caspar.   Nov 22, 1916
He had been a section foreman on the Caspar railroad and
came from Canada 30 years ago.

Mrs.Philo Handy, 72, died at Ukiah December 26, 1916. She   Jan 3, 1917
had lived in Ukiah and Covelo from 1864.

John W.Hansard died at Fort Bragg December 6, 1915 of   Dec 8, 1915
pneumonia. A native of California, he had been a resident
for 14 years. His wife and several children survived. The
funeral was held at the Baptist church December 7, 1915
led by Rev.I.H.Wood.

Mrs.E.L.Hansen, age 44, died at Navarro Ridge June 13, 1911. Jun 21, 1911

Margaret Vivian Hansen, born in Caspar June 27, 1896, died Dec 7, 1910
November 29, 1910.

Edward L.Hanson, 70, was found dead June 10, 1919 at Jun 18, 1919
Mendocino having died about May 26th. A native of Norway,
he ranched on Navarro Ridge. A brother and sister in Norway
survived his death.

Nels H.Hanson was killed at Wendling March 16, 1910 when a Mar 23, 1910
log fell on him.

Henry Harbig, a rancher at Comptche for 50 years, died at Aug 13, 1913
Fort Bragg August 12, 1913. The funeral was August 13th.

Mrs.Harbine, a former resident of Ten Mile and Fort Bragg, Jun 16, 1915
died at Santa Rosa "recently". She was about 65.

Frances Oscar Hardell, 34, died in Fort Bragg October 12, Oct 18, 1916
1916 of heart failure. A native of Sweden, he had been a
resident for 12 years working in his brother's (P.O.Hardell)
store. The funeral was held in Fort Bragg October 15th led
by Rev.John J.Hillberg. A wife and brother survived.

Helen C.Hardell, the 18 year old daughter of P.O.Hardell of Dec 19, 1917
Fort Bragg, died in San Francisco December 12, 1917 of
diabetes. The funeral was held in Fort Bragg December 16th.

Mrs.A.M.Hardie died at Ukiah November 3, 1912. Born in Cali- Nov 6, 1912
fornia, she was 57 years old and a resident of Ukiah since
1910. The funeral was held there November 4th.

John Hardika, 40, died at Wages Creek October 30, 1918 of Nov 6, 1918
influenza. A native of Finland, he was buried in Fort Bragg
November 2, 1918.

Mrs.R.A.Hardy, 75, died in Missouri February 25, 1917. She Mar 5, 1917
had operated a dairy with her husband on the Todd Ranch in
Noyo, but had moved away in 1900.

R.H.Hardy, a former old time coast resident, died in Mar 6, 1912
Chesterfield, Missouri, February 7, 1912.

Mrs.Charles Hargrave died near Russian Gulch February 10, Feb 12, 1913
1913. A husband and three sons: Walter of Covelo, Ed of
Vacaville, Charles Hargarve of Arizona, and five daughters:
Mrs.Florence Thompson of Northspur, Mrs.Anderson of Caspar,
Mrs.Agnews of Fort Bragg, Mrs.Waters of Irmulco and Mrs.
Olive Baker of Fresno, survived. The funeral was February 13th.

Rev.James Henry Hargreaves, 64, died at Caspar March 12, Mar 14, 1917
1917 as the result of injuries suffered in a team runaway Mar 21, 1917
accident November 14, 1916. Born in Lancashire, England, he
came to the United States and settled first at Fall River,
Massachusetts, where he married Mary A.Duckworth in 1874.
They went to Oregon where he was ordained as a Baptist
minister in 1889. Pastorates included Anderson in 1895, Red
Bluff, Dinuba and, finally, Caspar. His wife, daughter,
Miss Ethel Hargreaves of Caspar, and three sons, James H.
Hargreaves Jr.of Pasadena, G.W.of Readley and Carey
Hargreaves of Calpella, survived. The funeral was held in
Caspar March 15th followed by burial in Fort Bragg.

Mrs.Charlotte Harmon, 64, the wife of the late N.H.Harmon, Mar 28, 1917
died in Fort Bragg March 21, 1917 from pneumonia. Born in
Missouri, she came across the plains in an emigrant train
and was a resident from 1884 living at Inglenook and Fort
Bragg. Five children survived: W.S.Harmon, I.A.Harmon and
Mrs.C.Hanson, all of Fort Bragg, Mrs.Cox and Mrs W.W.Coats
of San Francisco. The funeral was held in Fort Bragg
March 24, 1917 under the direction of Rev. H.E.Lysinger.

Clyde Harrington, aged 19, was accidentally shot by his   Apr 12, 1911
brother, Ralph, while hunting near Hopland April 7, 1911.   Jun 7, 1911
He died of his wound June 6, 1911.

Charles C.Harris died at Ukiah December 21, 1913. He was   Dec 31, 1913
born in Illinois October 30, 1831. The funeral was
held December 23rd.

Supervisor J.W.Harris, about 45, died at Hopland   Dec 13, 1916
December 10, 1916. He also was cashier of the Bank of
Hopland. His wife and two children survived. The funeral
was held in Hopland December 12th.

Mrs.Laura Jane Harris, 44, died December 1, 1919 at Fort   Dec 3, 1919
Bragg. A three year resident, she ran the Alimo Rooming
House. Born and raised in Potter Valley, she was descended
from the Quesenberry family - one of the first to settle
there. Her daughter, Mrs.Alice Patterson, and son, Walter
Harris, survived. The funeral was in Ukiah December 2nd.

Sam Harris, who ran a general store at Middletown in Lake   May 13, 1914
County, was shot and killed by robbers. [no date reported].

Edward H.Hart died at Ross in Marin County September 26,   Oct 3, 1917
1917. Born in Cleveland, Ohio, in 1859, he came to
California in 1887.

J.S."Jack" Hart, a 47 year resident almost 73 years old,   Feb 26, 1919
died at Ukiah February 22, 1919. A native of New York, he
was a telegraph operator and Wells Fargo agent in Ukiah. His
widow, four sons and a daughter survived. The funeral was
February 25th.

Angus Marion Hartman died suddenly on the road July 25,   Jul 31, 1912
1912. He was born in California in 1858. A widow, son,
brother and sister survived. The funeral was held at the
Presbyterian church in Fort Bragg July 28th.

Frank Hartman died at Fort Bragg December 31, 1915 of   Jan 5, 1916
pneumonia. A native of Nevada County, California, he was
61 years 4 months and 24 days old. He had been a lumberman
most of his life. A wife, four sons and three daughters
survived: William, Frank, Harry, Opal, Mrs.Ada Wade,
Katheryn and Lennie Hartman. The funeral was held
January 2, 1916 in Fort Bragg.

Leroy Scott Hartman, son of Frank and Catherine Hartman,   Sep 13, 1911
died at Fort Bragg August 31, 1911. The fourth of seven
children, he was born in Fort Bragg and was 19 years
8 months and 20 days old. The surviving children were:
George, Will, Harry, Ada, Kitty and Minnie Hartman. The
funeral was held September 3rd at the Episcopal church with
services by Revs.Crook and Barrett.

Charles Harvey, an oiler on the steamer *Prentiss*, was killed   Jan 8, 1919
at sea January 2, 1919 when he slipped on some oil and fell
into the machinery. He died just before the ship reached
Albion harbor.

John Walter Harvey died in Mendocino February 24, 1910. Born   Mar 2, 1910
in Newport, Nova Scotia September 1, 1863, he came to California in 1886 and, at first, worked in the lumber mills
then managed a dairy in San Francisco. He married Emily Ada
Switzer of Mendocino September 21, 1892 in San Francisco.
In 1898 they prospected at Dawson, Yukon Territory, returning
to California in 1900. They resided at Oroville until 1907
when they moved to Arizona for a year. Survivors included a
wife and daughter.

W.A.Harvey, a resident of Hopland for 20 years, died   Apr 13, 1910
April 4, 1910. He was 69 years old.

Mrs.Guy Haskett, 57, died December 7, 1919 about two miles   Dec 10, 1919
north of Fort Bragg. A native Californian, she lived in
Willits until 1914 when she moved to Fort Bragg. Her husband
and six children survived: Mrs.Beth Martin of Santa Rosa,
Victor Haskett of Willits, Bessie Haskett of Fort Bragg,
Ellenor Haskett of Willits. Her mother,, Mrs.M.C.Angle Drew
of Ukiah and four brothers also survived: Carl Victor, D.A.
and Eugene Angle. The funeral was in Willits December 10th.

Mrs.Miranda Barnes Haskett died in Ukiah in January 1917   Jan 24, 1917
[exact date indeterminate]. Born in Illinois October 14,
1837, she was a California resident for 62 years, teaching
school from the 1860s over a fifty year span.

Mike Hastings, woodsman, died on the south coast   Nov 27, 1918
November 13, 1918 from influenza.

Mrs.B.S.Hatch, 78 years and three months old, died in   Feb 23, 1916
Leavenworth, Washington, February 12, 1916. She had come to
California in 1861 and lived at Sherwood and Ukiah.

E.M.Hatch, the son of the late H.T.Hatch of Fort Bragg, died   Aug 6, 1919
suddenly August 3, 1919 at Yellowstone National Park on a
vacation trip. He was 43. His wife, two children, two
brothers, J.F.Hatch of Healdsburg and S.B.Hatch of Ukiah,
survived.

W.R.Hatch, 58, died January 17, 1919 in Portland, Oregon,   Jan 29, 1919
following an operation. In the early days he was a mechanic
in the Fort Bragg mill and grew up in the Sherwood valley.
A wife, son and three brothers, J.F.Hatch of Healdsburg,
S.B.Hatch of Ukiah and E.M.Hatch of Portland, survived.

The 13 month old child of M.Hautala died at Albion   Mar 10, 1915
March 3, 1915.

The ten year old daughter of Mr.& Mrs.T.Hawkins died at Elk   Dec 21, 1910
Elk December 16, 1910.

Miss Georgia Hayden of Mendocino died November 30, 1918 at   Dec 4, 1918
Hopkin's ranch while on a visit.

Tom Hayden died at Round Valley June 10, 1913.   Jun 18, 1913

Matt Hayse, about 60, died at Albion June 24, 1919.   Jun 25, 1919
He had been employed by the Union Lumber Company.

Emett Kenneth Hayter, the one month old son of James Hayter   May 17, 1911
of Fort Bragg, died there May 16, 1911. The funeral was held
the same day.

Mrs.James Hayter, 26, died November 27, 1918 at Fort Bragg   Dec 4, 1918
influenza. She was the oldest daughter of Jack Gamberg and
was born and raised in Fort Bragg. Sisters included Mrs.
Fannie Young and Effie Gamberg, both of San Francisco.

Captain Henry Martin Hayward died of heart disease in San   May 29, 1912
Francisco May 25, 1912. He was at sea for 42 of his 64 years.
Five children survived one of whom was Mrs.Dr.Gregory.

Frank Heacock, 77 and a former Ukiah resident, died in   Jun 2, 1915
Modesto "last week". He had moved there in 1912.

Ernest Heckendorf, the son of L.Heckendorf, died at Grants   Jan 31, 1917
Pass, Oregon, of pneumonia [no date reported].

R.H.Hedden, an old resident of Pine Grove, died at Napa   May 15, 1912
"last week". He was over 80 years old.

Oliver Heeser, 36, Hans Johnson, 45, and Harry McKenzie, 55,   Dec 27, 1911
burned to death in a cabin on Cleone Point December 23, 1911.
They were said to have been very drunk when last seen in town.
[Name actually Kieser].

Jacob Heger, a pioneer tailor in Ukiah, died in Berkeley   Jan 22, 1919
January 15, 1919 at the age of 83. He had moved to Berkeley
in 1913. The funeral was held in Ukiah January 17th.

Askel Waldemar Heikkila, 17, the son of Mrs.Matt Markkula,   Oct 18, 1916
died October 16, 1916. The funeral was October 19th in Fort   Oct 25, 1916
Bragg led by Revs.John J.Hillberg and Burt.

Abe Heilala, 20, died suddenly July 15, 1919 of spinal   Jul 16, 1919
meningitis. He was the son of Jacob Heilala of Noyo.

Daniel Heldt, a coast resident for more than 30 years, died   Dec 22, 1915
at Inglenook December 18, 1915. Born in France, he was
73 years 2 months and 6 days old. He came to California
about 50 years ago. The funeral was held in Fort Bragg
December 20, 1915 led by Rev.I.H.Wood.

Mrs.A.H.Helela died at Ukiah in the State Hospital.   May 8, 1912
[date lost account torn original].

Lula Helela, 21, died in San Francisco October 3, 1917 from   Oct 3, 1917
TB. She was the daughter of John Helela of Noyo. The funeral   Oct 10, 1917
was held October 8th in Fort Bragg.

Leonard Helin, 57, died at Ukiah April 27, 1917 of TB. Born   May 9, 1917
in Finland, he ran the White House Hotel in Fort Bragg
thirty years ago, and later worked as a longshoreman in
San Francisco returning to work in the Greenwood woods. His
funeral was held in Fort Bragg April 29th. Two sisters,
Mrs.R.Mehtlan of Fort Bragg and Mrs.Hendrickson of Point
Arena, survived as did a brother back East, his wife and
two sons in San Francisco.

Fred Hellen, the son of the late Leonard Hellen [Helin], was   Oct 10, 1917
killed in an airplane crash in Ohio "this week".

Joseph Hellener died suddenly at his home in the Caspar   Feb 20, 1918
woods February 19, 1918 of heart failure. He was born in
Germany and left no relations. He had worked in the woods
for 25 years and was 67 years old and 5 days old at death.
The funeral was held at Fort Bragg February 21st with
burial in Littleriver.

Albert Henderson of Comptche accidentally shot himself when   Sep 23, 1914
cleaning a pistol, at Half Way House September 19, 1914.

Otto Hendrickson died at Keene's Summit March 22, 1918.   Mar 27, 1918
The funeral was held at Mendocino March 24th.

William Hendrickson was killed when he fell under moving   Dec 11, 1912
log cars on December 9, 1912. Born in Elk, he was 20 years
old. He was buried at Point Arena December 12th.

Gabrael Henrikson died of heart trouble March 30, 1913 at   Apr 2, 1913
the tie camp on the Noyo River. A native of Finland, he
was 57. The funeral was held in Fort Bragg April 3, 1913.

Della W.Henry, daughter of Mr.& Mrs.William Henry of Eureka,   Nov 9, 1910
died October 31, 1910 at the age 27 years and 23 days. She
was a former resident of Fort Bragg and had been engaged to
W.W.Brown of San Francisco. Her parents and two brothers,
Sankey and Percy Henry survived.

George Henry, 86, died in Ukiah November 9, 1919. A settler   Nov 12, 1919
since 1878, he left a widow and three daughters.

The two year four month old child of Mr.& Mrs.Hensley died   Oct 12, 1910
at Noyo October 5, 1910. The family formerly lived in the
Sacramento Valley. The funeral was in Fort Bragg October 6th.

Cloves Hensley, 5½, the son of C.L.Hensley, died   Dec 24, 1919
December 17, 1919 of scarlet fever.

Mrs.M.J.Hensley, an old resident of Mendocino County, died at Cloverdale June 20, 1910.

Jun 29, 1910

Mrs.Albert Hepworth died at Manchester June 23, 1911.

Jul 5, 1911

F.A.Herman died at Ukiah April 8, 1910.

Apr 13, 1910

August Hermansen, 20, was a suicide by shotgun in Fort Bragg June 17, 1919.

Jun 18, 1919

George Herring, 71, a veteran of the Civil War, died November 5, 1913 with burial at Cuffey's Cove.

Nov 12, 1913

Elmer Heryford died at Ukiah January 30, 1911.

Feb 1, 1911

C.E.Hewitt died at Hopland March 1, 1911.

Mar 22, 1911

Edward Ritter "Ned" Hickey, the son of H.B.Hickey, died in the Fort Bragg hospital November 24, 1918 of influenza. He was 26 years 1 month and 1 day old. Burial was in Oakland.

Nov 27, 1918

John Hickey died in the Noyo woods June 10, 1913.
He was an old time woodsman.

Jun 11, 1913

Mrs.Hickman, the mother of Mrs.Link Smith and late of Westport, died in Eureka April 14, 1918.

Apr 17, 1918

Captain Augustus "Gus" Daniel Higgins, 32, captain of the steamer *Fort Bragg*, died suddenly in Berkeley January 20, 1912. He was a cousin of Mrs.C.A.Scott of Fort Bragg.

Jan 24, 1912

John Higgins died at Ukiah October 20, 1916. He was 86 years 8 months and 12 days old. He settled in Mendocino County in 1856. A wife and five children survived.

Nov 8, 1916

Press Higgins, who lived at Noyo 25 years ago, died in the State Hospital at Talmage "last week".

Dec 17, 1913

W.J.Hildreth died suddenly on the street in Willits March 16, 1915. Born in Missouri August 17, 1834, he came to Mendocino in 1858 and was one of the first settlers on the Eel River where he raised stock. He married Miss Florence Bevans February 14, 1865, and they had 13 children.

Mar 24, 1915

Mrs.W.J.Hildreth, *nee* Florence Bevans, daughter of Joseph Bevans of Lewis County, Missouri, died suddenly on a train near New Orleans, Louisiana, November 27, 1915. Born in Missouri in 1850, she married W.J.Hildreth February 14, 1865, and they were the parents of 13 children, 10 of whom survived. They were: Mrs.Mary Ruddock, J.C., George, William, Lewis, Walter, Victor, Vincent, Mrs.Irene Bond and Miss Pauline Hildreth. The funeral was held in Ukiah.

Dec 1, 1915

Charles Hill, aged 33, died at Ukiah July 31, 1910.

Aug 3, 1910

Frank Hill, formerly a resident of Point Arena, died at Rocklin, Placer County, March 11, 1919.

Mar 26, 1919

Mrs.Iley Lawson Hill died in Lake County "last week" at the age of 104 years 8 months & 12 days.

Jan 22, 1913

Mrs.J.W.Hill died at Ukiah November 13, 1914.

Nov 18, 1914

Alex Hiltunen was killed in a woods accident April 7, 1910 at Alpine. Born at Noyo, he was about 23 years old. The funeral was held April 10th in Fort Bragg.

Apr 13, 1910

George Hinde, 46, died December 4, 1919 at Fort Bragg of TB. His sister, Mrs.Al Bangs, survived. Burial was in the Ocean View cemetery at Fort Bragg with Father Grant officiating.

Dec 10, 1919

Mrs.F.A.Hiniman died at Willits October 28, 1911.

Nov 1, 1911

Maurice <u>Hirsch</u>, an attorney from Ukiah, died suddenly in
San Francisco November 29, 1913. He was 43 years old and
left a wife and son.

Dec 3, 1913

Isaac <u>Hitchcock</u>, a pioneer settler at Gualala, died
August 27, 1912. A native of Missouri, he came to California in 1846 and lived at Point Arena for 50 years. His
grandfather was the first man to bring a team and wagon
over the mountains in 1843 or 1844. His widow and eight
children survived: Henry, Gaspar and Arthur Hitchcock;
Mrs.H.J.Randell, Mrs.S.E.Guilliee, Mrs.Howard Bishop,
Mrs.Lizzie Croswell and Mrs.James McFarland. The funeral
was held August 29th.

Sep 4, 1912

Thomas <u>Hitchcock</u> of Gualala, a stage driver, was killed in
an accident at Stewart's Point April 8, 1911. He was
32 years old and left a wife and two children. The funeral
was held at Gualala April 9, 1911.

Apr 12, 1911

Mrs.Mary F.<u>Hoak</u>, the wife of N.E.Hoak formerly of Comptche,
died at the State Hospital in Talmage April 7, 1913.

Apr 16, 1913
Apr 23, 1913

Newman E.<u>Hoak</u>, a former rancher at Comptche, died in Chico
August 27, 1915 at age 83. Three daughters survived: Mrs.
M.S.McIntyre of Chico, Mrs.R.Goodrich of Grass Valley, and
Miss Charlotte Hoak of Pasadena.

Sep 1, 1915

John <u>Hobbs</u>, about 69, died at the County Hospital in Ukiah
"last week". He had been a 25 year resident of the coast.

Feb 27, 1918

Mrs.John <u>Hobbs</u>, 68, died at Fort Bragg November 9, 1917. A
native of Ohio, she was a 20 year resident. Catholic rites
were led by Rev.Lawrence November 12th. Her husband survived.

Nov 14, 1917

Dr.David <u>Hodghead</u> died in San Francisco February 5, 1919.
His niece, Helen Hodghead of Mendocino, survived.

Feb 12, 1919

The three year old son of Mr.& Mrs.Charles <u>Hoe</u> died at
Willits May 13, 1910.

May 25, 1910

Charles <u>Hoe</u>, 40, a woodsman, died at Willits from injuries
suffered at Sherwood in a logging accident. A wife and
daughter survived.

Jan 12, 1916

Mrs.Lewis <u>Hofman</u>, the wife of a Ukiah merchant, died in
San Francisco December 2, 1919. Her husband and a
daughter survived.

Dec 3, 1919

William James <u>Hogadorn</u> was found dead at Caspar March 30,
1919 under mysterious circumstances. A two year resident, he
left a wife and two children in Seattle, Washington.

Apr 2, 1919

James <u>Hogan</u>, formerly a resident of Cleone, died in Los
Angeles March 14, 1910 of consumption. He was buried with
Catholic rites in Fort Bragg March 21, 1910. He was the
son of Peter Hogan and was 27 years old at his death.

Mar 23, 1910

Peter <u>Hogan</u>, 86 of Cleone, died November 22, 1914 at Fort
Bragg. Born in Ireland December 25, 1828, he came to the
U.S.in 1840. He lived in California for 50 years. Three
sons, John, Henry and Frank Hogan, and two daughters, Ollie
and Margaret, survived. The funeral was November 27th.

Nov 25, 1914

Andrew <u>Hoganen</u>, 45, strangled himself July 14, 1916 at
Albion. A native of Finland, his funeral was held in Fort
Bragg July 16th.

Jul 19, 1916

Mrs.Anne <u>Hoggreen</u>, a resident of Point Arena for 61 years,
died there June 22, 1919 at the age of 84. She had ten
children, three of them still living: Mrs.William Ketchum,
Porter Hoggreen of Point Arena and J.P.Hoggreen of Klamath
Falls, Oregon.

Jul 2, 1919

John D.Hollingsworth died at Ukiah May 9, 1912.   May 15, 1912

C.D.Holman was killed in a terroist bomb explosion in   Aug 2, 1916
San Francisco July 22, 1916.

Emil Holmberg died at Philo December 7, 1914. Born in   Dec 16, 1914
Finland, he settled in the Anderson Valley and established
orchards. He was well known on the coast as he peddled
fruit from his farm. He was 59 years 6 months and 10 days
old at his death. The funeral was held December 9th.

The 19 month old daughter of Herman Holquist died at Caspar   Feb 19, 1919
February 14, 1919. The funeral was held at Fort Bragg
February 16th led by Rev.Shaw.

Herman Holquist, the son of Mrs.Hulda Holquist of Caspar,   May 14, 1919
died May 12, 1919 in Caspar. He was 28 years 3 months and
28 days old. The funeral was held at Fort Bragg May 14th by
Rev.W.A.Chapman.

Charles Hopkins, 91, died at Potter Valley September 19,   Sep 25, 1918
1918. Seven children survived: Miss Ann McFarland of Madera
County, Mrs.Marin of San Francisco, Mrs.J.C.Hughes of
Potter Valley, Mrs.C.S.Wattenberg of Ukiah, C.W.Hopkins of
Coalinga, and C.L.Hopkins of Porter.

J.P.Hopkins 66, died at Lodi June 11, 1918. Formerly a   Jun 12, 1918
drayman at Fort Bragg, he left a widow.

Mrs.Margaret Hopkins, the wife of the late J.P.Hopkins, died   Jul 31, 1918
Lodi, San Joaquin County, July 28, 1918. A native of Prince
Edward Island, she came to the coast in 1875 settling first
at Greenwood, then at Noyo, and, finally, at Fort Bragg. She
was 60. The funeral was held August 1st at the Presbyterian
church in Fort Bragg.

R.J.Hopkins died at Ukiah October 5, 1914.   Oct 7, 1914

Walter Hopkins, 31, was killed in the woods at Greenwood   Nov 28, 1917
November 26, 1917 when hit by a log. The body was sent to
Woodland for burial.

Mrs.George Hopper died at Fort Bragg May 28, 1913. Just   Jun 4, 1913
25 years and 24 months [sic, probably meant days] old, she
old, she left a husband and two children. Her father, Steven
E.Pullen and three brothers also survived. Catholic rites
were held May 31st.

Harry Hopper, 49, employed by the Mendocino Lumber Company,   May 21, 1919
was found dead in his cabin May 18, 1919. He had been a
stableman and teamster.

Mrs.Mathilde Hoppner, 73, died February 15, 1917 in San   Feb 21, 1917
Francisco. Formerly of Fort Bragg, her two daughters were
left: Mrs.J.Burgett and Mrs. William Turner of Fort Bragg.

Arthur Horton, a resident of Ukiah to 1909, died in Oregon   Jan 24, 1912
"last week".

Mrs.Mary Host, formerly of Mendocino, died at age 83 in   Oct 26, 1910
Oakland October 23, 1910. She had been an invalid for
thirty years.

J.L.Houghtelling, an officer of the Union Lumber Company,   Aug 10, 1910
died in Illinois "last week".

Mrs.Alf Howard was buried at Westport May 15, 1910 under   May 25, 1910
Rev.W.A.Chapman's direction. Born in Missouri, she was
56 years old. Her husband, Alf, daughters, Mrs.Ed McFaul of
Union [Landing] and Mrs.Garland of San Francisco, and a
son, William Howard, survived. Her sister, Mrs.M.M.Cleveland
of Ukiah attended the service.

George <u>Howard</u> died at Westport April 22, 1918 from heart
failure. A native of Pennsylvania, he was 66 years 7 months
and 27 days old. He came to California about 1868 and settled
in Westport in 1880. He was an early day sawyer and worked in
the mills on the coast. A widow, son, Clifford Howard of
Westport, two daughters, Mrs.D.O.Lydick of Fort Bragg, Mrs.
Carrie Huntley of San Francisco, survived. The funeral was
held April 23rd in Fort Bragg led by Rev.W.A.Chapman.

Apr 24, 1918

John W.<u>Howard</u>, a printer, died of stomach cancer in Oakland
August 15, 1911.

Aug 23, 1911

Tom <u>Howard</u> died at Ukiah August 29, 1918. A widow and a son,
Mark Howard, survived.

Sep 4, 1918

W.Scott <u>Howard</u> died in Ukiah October 21, 1919. Born in
Missouri January 22, 1848, he came as a youth to Ukiah with
his family in 1858. His father was the late Mark Howard. He
married Mary Chase August 22, 1875. The widow, two daughters,
Mrs.Lulu Cox and Mrs.Ruth Howard, six brothers, Pete, Taylor,
William, Mack of Ukiah, James of Manchester, and Alf of
Westport, survived.

Oct 29, 1919

Newton P.<u>Howe</u>, former school teacher of Mendocino County,
died at Berkeley "last week" at 74. Sons, N.P.and Henry Howe
of Point Arena survived.

Jun 12, 1912

George <u>Howell</u> died January 31, 1915.

Feb 10, 1915

Mrs.Lucy W.<u>Hubbard</u>, an old Caspar resident, died
March 22, 1910. A native of Nova Scotia, she was 60 years
old. The funeral was held in Caspar March 24th led by
Rev.W.A.Chapman.

Mar 23, 1910

John <u>Huff</u>, a pioneer settler, died September 3, 1918 at
Mendocino. His widow, Mary Huff, survived. The funeral was
held September 5th.

Sep 4, 1918

Peter <u>Huff</u> died in Fort Bragg July 25, 1911 from an injury
received in Caspar when a pile of lumber fell on him. A
veteran of the Spanish-American War and a native of Pennsylvania, he was 45 years old. The funeral was July 28th
with the Rev.Crook of Ukiah officiating.

Jul 26, 1911
Aug 2, 1911

Mrs.Anna <u>Hufft</u> died at Ukiah November 14, 1916. Born in
El Dorado County January 31, 1858, she came to Mendocino
County about 1886.

Nov 22, 1916

J.B.<u>Hufft</u>, a resident of Ukiah for 15 years, dropped dead
December 27, 1919. A daughter and three sons survived. One
son was Clair Hufft, a civil engineer employed by the
Caspar Lumber Co.

Dec 31, 1919

Miss Harriet <u>Huggins</u>, the niece of Eri Huggins of Fort
Bragg, was killed by an automobile driven by Joseph F.
Carlston, the president of the Central National Bank, when
she stepped into a street in Oakland [no date reported]. A
native of Racine, Wisconsin, she was 45 and a schoolteacher.

Sep 24, 1919

C.A."Pony" <u>Hughes</u> died at Ukiah October 16, 1914. Born in
Missouri August 21, 1852 the son of James H.Hughes, he
crossed the plains with his family as an infant settling with
them Ukiah in 1866. His funeral was held at Ukiah
October 18th.

Oct 21, 1914

James <u>Hughes</u> died at Ukiah July 28, 1913 of TB.

Jul 30, 1913

Laurene E.<u>Hughes</u>, the daughter of F.D.Hughes of Point
Arena, died in Fort Bragg November 29, 1913. She was
17 years 4 months and 15 days at death. Burial was in
Point Arena December 2nd.

Dec 3, 1913

Mrs.Sarah Hulbert, 33, the daughter of Mrs.Badger of Fort
Bragg, died in San Francisco January 12, 1912. A son,
6 years old, survived. She was buried in Fort Bragg
January 21st. Rev.Garth officiated.

Jan 17, 1912

Mrs.William Humphrey died at Fort Bragg July 17, 1915
following an appendix operation. She was a visitor from San
Francisco and was taken ill at Boyle's camp on Big River.
The body was shipped to Oakland July 19th.

Jul 21, 1915

G.W.Hunt, a wellknown railroad man, died in Portland,
Oregon, "last week".

Mar 9, 1910

Charles Hunter died at Vallejo August 23, 1917 from TB. He
was born in Manchester April 28, 1861.His widow, two
daughters and two sons survived.

Sep 5, 1917

James Hunter, 94, died in San Francisco October 27, 1918. He
ran a store at Newport in the early days.

Nov 6, 1918

William Arthur Huntley, a 12 year resident of Cleone, died
May 21, 1919 at the age of 82. A native of Maine, he left a
widow and 7 children: Mrs.Emma Davis, Mrs.Deborah Knight
(a missionary in Central America), Mrs.Delia Torrence, Mrs.
Cora Schultz, Joseph, George and Eber Huntley.

May 28, 1919

Dennis Hurley, 87, died at Ukiah November 28, 1916. He
settled in Navarro flat in 1870. His wife died in 1890.
Three daughters survived: Mrs.J.Dolan, Mrs.J.Walsh of Fort
Bragg and Mrs.P.Connolly of Ukiah.

Nov 29, 1916

Mrs.Enoch Hurt died at Ukiah June 9, 1913.

Jun 18, 1913

Mrs.Mary J.Hurt died at Covelo December 23, 1915.
She was the mother of 16 children, 10 of whom lived.

Jan 5, 1916

William Hurt, 80, died in Round Valley August 31, 1910.

Oct 5, 1910

James Hutton, a pioneer settler of the County, died at Ukiah
February 20, 1912. A widow and eight children survived:
Mrs.James Doty, Mrs.Martha Kunzler, Mrs.Edna Helwich,
Mrs.M.Campbell, Nelson, Martin, P.and L.Hutton.

Feb 28, 1912

Mrs.Irene Hyland, the 27 year old daughter of the late Mrs.
Mollie Cox and a former Sherwood resident, was buried at
Willits August 12, 1919 of TB. Her husband and son survived.

Aug 13, 1919

John Hyman, Sr, a 37 year resident of Fort Bragg, died
August 7, 1918. He was 74 years and 3 months old. Born in
Finland May 1, 1844, he was a sailor before settling in Cali-
fornia as a rancher at Virgin Creek. He gave up the ranch in
1913. A widow, three sons, John Jr., Gustave of Alaska, and
Edward, also of Alaska, and a daughter, Mrs.Andrew Escola of
Navarro, survived. He was buried at Fort Bragg.

Aug 7, 1918

The body of May Gertrude Ilg of San Francisco was found at
Pebble Beach in Monterey County July 27, 1911.

Aug 2, 1911

H.H.Inman, a former Willits resident, was a suicide in San
Francisco "last week" by ingestion of illuminating gas.
A locomotive engineer on the Northwestern Pacific Railroad,
he had resigned account of poor health.

Mar 19, 1919

John Inman, 83, died at Manchester June 8, 1919. Born 1851
in Kentucky, he crossed the plains with his parents and
settled at Manchester in the early 1860s.

Jun 11, 1919

John Inman Jr.died in Eugene, Oregon, December 17, 1914 of
liver cancer. Born in Manchester October 20, 1870, he was a
resident until 1910 when he moved to Lorane, Oregon, where
he ranched. He married Maybelle Bishop October 26, 1911, and
a son was born in 1913.

Dec 30, 1914

Charles A.Irving, about 80, died September 16, 1914 at   Sep 16, 1914
Willits. He came to California in 1850 and was a principal
member of the Irving-Muir Lumber Company at Irmulco.

John Isaacson, a native of Finland about 58 years old, died   Oct 19, 1910
October 14, 1910. He had worked 18 years as a carpenter and
in milling at Glen Blair, Navarro, Fort Bragg and Elk. Rev.
John J.Hillberg conducted the service in Finnish with the
Red Men Fraternal Lodge holding graveside rites.

Oscar Itanen, 54, fell down the stairs at the Carob Hotel.   Jan 2, 1918
A cripple and a known drinker, his injuries were fatal. A
native of Finland, he left a brother, A.V.Itanen, a tailor.

Captain Nels Iversen, 82, died in San Francisco "last week".   Jun 26, 1912
A native of Denmark, he was an early sea captain on the coast
and Iversen's Landing was named for him. A widow and four
children survived: Mrs.Elsie Jensen, Mrs.Annie Johnson,
Iver Iversen, and Arthur Iversen.

A.D."Perry" Ives cut his throat March 16, 1912.   Mar 20, 1912

John Ivett, a jeweler, died at Fort Bragg of diabetes   Sep 9, 1914
September 6, 1914 at the age of 65. Born in England, he was
a resident of Mendocino. The funeral was held there
September 8th.

Evans Jackson was killed in a mining accident in Mexico   Nov 8, 1916
"this week". The brother of Joe Jackson, he left a wife and
five children.

Evans M.Jackson died at San Francisco December 18, 1911.   Jan 10, 1912
His widow and several children survived.

George Washington Jackson, an old resident of Ukiah,   Mar 6, 1912
died there February 26, 1912.

Mrs.J.G.Jackson, 99, the widow of J.G.Jackson founder of   Jul 23, 1919
the Caspar Lumber Company, died at San Francisco July 17,
1919. A daughter, Mrs.Abbe E.Wilkins, survived. She also
had a son, the late Charles G.Jackson.

Joseph Jackson, 34, was killed in an auto truck wreck five   Sep 2, 1914
miles north of Willits August 29, 1914. A native of California, he was buried in Oakland.

Lawrence Jackson, the six year old son of Joe Jackson, died   Jan 3, 1917
from scarlet fever December 31, 1916. Catholic rites were
held January 1, 1917 by Father Blanderfield.

Mrs.Sarah Jackson died in Comptche January 28, 1919. She   Feb 5, 1919
had been an invalid for some years. Her brother, Tatlow
Jackson of Comptche, survived. The funeral was held in
Mendocino February 2nd.

W.A.Jackson, a 51 year resident, died at Mendocino   Feb 9, 1916
February 3, 1916. His wife, Harriet Jackson, and two sons,
Walter and Clyde Jackson, survived as did three sisters and
two brothers. The funeral was held February 4, 1916 with
Revs.J.M.Fisher and [Duncan] Munroe officiating.

The three month old daughter of Jonas Jacobson died of the   Aug 31, 1910
whooping cough August 14, 1910 and was buried on the 16th.

Axel Jacobson, an employee in the Mendocino Lumber Company's   Aug 11, 1915
yard, died of heart failure August 8, 1915. A sister in
Denmark survived. His funeral was held August 11th.

Jonas Jacobson, 43, died November 3, 1918 from influenza.   Nov 6, 1918
A native of Finland, he operated a ranch on the Noyo. A
wife and five children survived. He was buried November 6th.

The two year old daughter of Jonas Jacobson died September 6, 1910 and was buried on September 8th.	Sep 7, 1910
Adulphus Jamison drowned in the Noyo River July 28, 1910 while on an outing with his family. Born November 16, 1858, he lived in Ukiah where the body was taken for burial. Bessie Baker, aged 16, drowned in the same incident. A wife and five children survived.	Aug 3, 1910
James A.Jamison died at Ukiah August 3, 1914. A 49er, he came to Mendocino County in 1858 and settled in the Anderson Valley. In 1866 he moved to Redwood Valley and on to Ukiah. He was elected county assessor in 1866 and served four years.	Aug 5, 1914
Mrs.James A.Jamison died at Ukiah November 2, 1914. Born in Illinois as Masse Shepherd June 14, 1831, she was married in California March 20, 1853 to Jamison [who died August 3, 1914]. They moved to Mendocino in 1858 and, in 1866, to Ukiah. There were five children: George and James J.Jamison, Mrs. Harry Linder, Mrs.William Cox and Mrs.Overmeyer. The funeral was held November 4th led by Rev.L.S.Jones.	Nov 11, 1914
Erick Jarf was shot and killed by Gus Dahl on the railroad between Moody and Andersonia September 30, 1913. Dahl, the brother of Charles Dahl of Fort Bragg, received 14 years in prison for the murder.	Oct 1, 1913 Oct 29, 1913 Dec 17, 1913
Mrs.Elizabeth Jarvis of Mendocino died February 8, 1919 at Claremont. Her daughter was Mrs.Florence Beggs of Claremont survived. A native of Maine, she was 61 years old and a Mendocino resident from 1882. Her husband was the late Frederick Jarvis who died [March 17, 1912]. The funeral was held in Mendocino February 13th.	Feb 12, 1919
Frederick A.Jarvis, 59, an old resident of Mendocino, died March 17, 1912. The funeral was March 19th. His wife, Elizabeth, had died February 8, 1919.	Mar 20, 1912 Feb 12, 1919
James Jeffries, 83, a 40 year resident of Mendocino County, died at Ukiah May 30, 1919. A native of Indiana, he lived in Cleone and other places. Rev.W.A.Chapman conducted his funeral with burial at Fort Bragg.	Jun 4, 1919
Nancy G.Jeffries, formerly a Caspar resident, died in Fort Bragg January 31, 1910 of pneumonia. She was 81. The funeral was led by Rev.W.A.Chapman in Fort Bragg February 2nd.	Feb 2, 1910
Mrs.Jenkins of Laytonville died January 15, 1911 in San Francisco where she had gone for medical treatment.	Jan 18, 1911
Judge George C.Jenkins, a California pioneer from 1853, died at Santa Clara April 14, 1910 at the age of 88. Born in Madison County, New York, he moved to Illinois in 1844 and was a friend of Abraham Lincoln. He married in 1853 and moved to California settling at Santa Clara. He was one of the early justice of the peaces elected.	Apr 20, 1910
Mrs.Jens Christian Jensen died at Pine Grove October 6, 1916. Rev.J.H.Hargeaves led her funeral October 9th.	Oct 11, 1916
Mrs.John Jensen died September 13, 1919 at 74 years 2 months and 29 days. She came to the coast in 1874 and lived "north of Pudding Creek" where the funeral was held September 16th led by Rev.W.A.Chapman. Her husband and three children survived.	Sep 17, 1919
Vanaer Jerdstrom, head brakeman on the Greenwood railroad was killed May 28, 1910. He left a wife and several children.	Jun 1, 1910
P.V.Johansen, a native of Sweden, escaped from the State Hospital at Talmage and was killed by a passenger train a few miles south of Ukiah on July 13, 1911. Being deaf, he apparently did not hear the locomotive's whistle.	Jul 19, 1911

A.W.W.John was found dead in his cabin near Sherwood
July 13, 1910 of apparent heart failure. A native of
Germany, he was 26 years old.   Jul 20, 1910

Mrs.Johns, the mother of Mrs.George Roach and a pioneer in
the Westport area, died October 20, 1916. The funeral was
held on the 22nd.   Oct 25, 1916

Charles Johns was found dead in his cabin in Reeves Canyon
near Ukiah April 9, 1910. A native of Germany, he was about
60 years old.   Apr 13, 1910

The infant child of August Johnson died at Melburne on
June 29, 1910.   Jul 13, 1910

The infant son of Emil Johnson died at Albion July 20, 1911. Aug 2, 1911

Johnson, a sailor on the steamer *Higgins*, drowned at Fort
Bragg January 7, 1915.   Jan 13, 1915

"Grandma" Johnson died June 3, 1911. The funeral was held
in Mendocino June 5th.   Jun 7, 1911

Mrs.Albert Johnson, 24, died at Fort Bragg January 7, 1918
of TB. A native of Ireland, she was a three year resident.
Four sisters survived: Mrs.Jack Scheper of Caspar, Mrs.Thomas
Croke, Miss Kittie & Susie Montague of New York. Catholic
rites were held at Fort Bragg January 9th.   Jan 9, 1918

Mrs.Alfred Johnson, *nee* Georgie Anna McClintock, died
September 25, 1910. A native of Pointe Fortune, [Quebec]
Canada, she was born February 8, 1852 and married
June 19, 1869. A former resident of Usal, she was
survived by her husband, sons Alfred, George, Everett
Ellsworth, Charles Clinock [sic] and daughters Ida Belle,
Katthryn May, Ethel Marguerite, Esther Irma and Mrs.Dave
Albert. Two brothers, W.and P.S.McClintock also survived.   Sep 28, 1910

Mrs.August J.(Agatha) Johnson, 78, a pioneer of Mendocino,   Nov 17, 1915
died November 14, 1915. She was the mother of Mrs.Lena   Nov 24, 1915
Bowman of Mendocino. The funeral was held November 17th.

C.V.Johnson, 40, was killed at Northwestern March 2, 1914
when crushed by logs. The funeral was held at Fort Bragg
March 5th.   Mar 4, 1914

Charles F.Johnson died in Fort Bragg February 28, 1919
following an appendix operation. Born and raised at Greenwood, he was 36 years 3 months and 10 days old. The funeral
was March 2nd. His wife, daughter, parents, the Fred
Johnsons, survived.   Mar 5, 1919

Edward Harold Johnson, son of Edward Johnson of Fort Bragg,
drowned while swimming in the ocean at Cliff House in San
Francisco September 7, 1914. He was 19 years old. The
funeral was held at Fort Bragg September 10th.   Sep 9, 1914

Emil Johnson died at Caspar August 29, 1913 of TB. His wife
and two children survived. His funeral was held at Caspar
August 31st.   Sep 3, 1913

Frederick Johnson, an old tie maker, died May 1, 1913. He   May 7, 1913
had lived near Melburne for 40 years. The funeral was held   May 14, 1913
May 4th at Mendocino with Rev.J.M.Fisher officiating.

G.C.Johnson, formerly of Ten Mile and father of Fort Bragg
City Clerk O.L.Johnson and two other sons, died May 20, 1911
in the soldiers' home in Yountville at age 67.   May 24, 1911

George Johnson was found dead in his cabin November 20,
1916. He was long time resident of Navarro ridge.   Nov 22, 1916

Deaths Reported	Issue Date

Mrs.H.C.Johnson, 54, was a suicide November 13, 1919 by drowning in Lake Merritt in Oakland. The body was found the next day. Two daughters, Mrs.H.C.Usinger and Miss Alice Johnson, survived. The funeral was in Oakland November 17th.

Nov 19, 1919

Hans Conrad Johnson, Superintendent of the Union Lumber Company's mill at Fort Bragg for 15 years, died at Arcata July 19, 1918. His funeral was held in Oakland July 25th. Born in Waupaca County, Wisconsin, March 20, 1864, he was the fourth child in a family of eight. Taking up black-smithing, he became a saw mill operator in Michigan before coming to California. A widow and two daughters, Mrs.Edith Usinger and Miss Alice Johnson, survived.

Jul 24, 1918

Mrs.Harry Johnson of Sunnyslope was killed in an automobile wreck at Christine December 8, 1919. The funeral and burial were at Mendocino. Her husband and daughter survived.

Dec 17, 1919

Jack Johnson, a woodsman, was killed April 19, 1915 at Greenwood. Very drunk, he went to sleep on the railroad track and was run over by a train. He was buried at Cuffey's Cove April 20th.

Apr 28, 1915

Mrs.Jane Johnson died in Fort Bragg August 2, 1912. Born in Iowa in 1839, she came to California in 1877 settling in Fort Bragg in 1887. Three sons survived: E.P. and A.S.Johnson of Fort Bragg and C.E.Johnson of Eureka. The funeral was held at Fort Bragg August 3rd led by Rev.W.A.Chapman.

Aug 7, 1912

Jim Johnson, 87, died near Point Arena October 1, 1914. He was born in Scotland.

Oct 7, 1914

John Johnson was found dead under the Jughandle bridge January 21, 1913. When last seen, he was very drunk and probably died of exposure.

Jan 22, 1913

Joseph Melville Johnson died of TB February 9, 1913 at Fort Bragg. Known as "Judd", he was born at Cuffey's Cove and was 35 years and 17 days old. He moved to Greenwood in 1906 and later worked as a saw filer at Union Lumber Company in Fort Bragg. The funeral was led by Rev.J.C.Garth February 11th.

Feb 12, 1913

Mrs.L.Johnson, 84, died in San Francisco "last week". A native of Nova Scotia, she settled in Mendocino in 1875. Three children survived: James Johnson, formerly of Fort Bragg, Mrs.C.T.Gray of Berkeley and Mrs.J.L.Clark of San Francisco.

Jun 11, 1919

Mary Johnson, 23, the daughter of John Johnson of "back of Noyo", died in San Francisco October 14, 1919 of peritonitis following an operation. Rev.Henry Shaw conducted the funeral at the Fort Bragg Presbyterian church October 16th.

Oct 22, 1919

Mrs.Mary Anna Johnson, the wife of Peter Johnson, died at Cleone April 7, 1918. A native of Finland, she was 73 and lived on the ranch for 43 years. The funeral was April 14th led by Rev.Franklin Bryan.

Apr 10, 1918

Otto Johnson was burned to death in his cabin March 21, 1915 in the Navarro woods. A brother, Jake Johnson of San Francisco, survived. He was buried March 23rd.

Mar 31, 1915

Pete Johnson died April 5, 1911 of injuries received in a railroad accident at Glen Blair the previous day. He was born in Cleone in 1872. A wife, three children, parents, two brothers and a sister survived.

Apr 5, 1911
Apr 12, 1911

Mrs.R.Johnson, 39, died at Willits January 14, 1914. She was a 20 year resident of Willits and Sherwood.

Jan 21, 1914

Tom Johnson, 80, a Civil War veteran, died at Westport May 10, 1914.

May 13, 1914

Thomas L.Johnson, the brother of C.R.Johnson, died in San   Oct 29, 1919
Francisco October 25, 1919 of double pneumonia. He had
served as superintendent of the Union Lumber Company for
8 or 9 years before being elected to the City Board of
Trustees in Fort Bragg in 1892. A native of Wisconsin, he
was 63 years old. His widow, brothers, C.R.Johnson, the
president of Union Lumber Company, Otis W.Johnson of Racine,
Wisconsin, and sisters, Mrs.H.S.Abbott, and Miss Janette
Johnson, survived. The funeral was held in San Francisco
October 27th.

William Johnson, a native of Sweden about 40 years old, died   Oct 30, 1918
in Fort Bragg October 27, 1918 of influenza. A one year
resident, he left a family in Sweden. Burial was
October 29th at Fort Bragg.

Isaac Jokela died at Comptche November 10, 1918. His wife   Nov 13, 1918
and several children survived. The funeral was held at
Fort Bragg November 12th.

Mrs.Jennie Jokela, 23, died August 13, 1915 "across Pudding   Aug 18, 1915
Creek" of TB. A daughter, Eli Sutta, survived. The funeral
was held August 15th at the Finn church.

Mrs.A.P.Jones, the wife of a Ukiah rancher, died in San   Aug 27, 1913
Francisco during an operation August 18, 1913.

B.G.Jones died near Willits April 27, 1910.   May 4, 1910

Billy Jones, an Indian, was shot and killed by Calico, also   May 19, 1915
an Indian, at Ukiah May 11, 1915.

Mrs.G.B.Jones of Willits died in San Francisco during an   Feb 23, 1910
operation [no date reported].

Mrs.Mathilda Jones of Willits died July 13, 1918 at Mendo-   Jul 17, 1918
cino at the home of her daughter, Mrs.John Salvador. The
deceased was the sister of the late Orrin Dunlap who settled
in Virginia City in 1849. She was 85. Burial was in Willits.

Mrs.W.G.Jones was a suicide at Fort Bragg June 15, 1914.   Jun 17, 1914
About 45 years old, she had come to Fort Bragg from Sonora,
California, about 1902.

Charles H.Joy, a veteran of the Civil War and long time   Dec 31, 1913
rancher on the south coast, died December 26, 1913 at Los
Gatos. Born in New Hampshire in 1842, he came to California
in 1869 and located at Navarro Ridge moving to Los Gatos in
1903. He was buried at Mendocino.

James Akester Joyce died at Noyo September 28, 1915. Born   Sep 29, 1915
in Unionville, Canada, in 1838, he came to California in
1800 [sic] with his family settling in Navarro. Two sons,
J.A.Joyce of Los Banos and A.J.Joyce, and two daughters,
Mrs.E.J.Rushing of Fort Bragg and Mrs.G.J.Handley of Noyo,
survived. The funeral was held October 1st.

Agnes Jylha was a suicide at Fort Bragg January 9, 1912.   Jan 10, 1912
Aged 26, she suffered from tuberculosis. Her funeral was
held January 11th.

Sophia Kaarto, 2 years 10 months and 3 days old, died at   Nov 29, 1911
Hardy woods November 21, 1911. The funeral was held at
Westport November 23rd.

Chris Kaisen died at Klintum, Germany, "last week" at age   Sep 27, 1911
79. He formerly lived in the Kaisen school district near
Ukiah with his brother in the early days of settlement.

Henry Kaiser, 63, died at Willits January 12, 1914. A wife   Jan 21, 1914
and daughter survived.

Patrick Kane, 60, dropped dead February 19, 1917 in the Ten   Feb 21, 1917
Mile woods. A native of Ireland, he had been a woods worker   Feb 28, 1917
for many years. The funeral was held February 20th in Fort
Bragg under the direction of Rev.W.A.Chapman.

Culo Karinen, an infant, died November 18, 1915 near   Nov 24, 1915
Comptche and was buried at Littleriver November 21st.

John Karo, 62, died at Fort Bragg August 2, 1912. A native   Aug 7, 1912
of Finland, he worked as a nurse. The funeral was held
August 4th with Rev.Otto Kaarto officiating.

J.G.Kaufman of Comptche was a suicide by gunshot   Jan 24, 1917
January 20, 1917. He was buried at Mendocino January 23rd.

The infant daughter of Thomas Kearns died at Littleriver   Sep 20, 1916
September 15, 1916.

Thomas Kearns Jr., 17, died at Littleriver January 10, 1918   Jan 16, 1918
of tuberculosis.

Mrs.T.Kearns died in Mendocino January 25, 1917 of pneumonia.   Jan 31, 1917
The funeral was at Littleriver January 26th. The deceased
was the daughter of the Lemmons of Mitchell Creek. A husband
and six children survived.

Mrs.Annie B.Kedon, 82, died December 22, 1914 at the State   Jan 13, 1915
Hospital and was buried on December 24th with Catholic rites.

Jing J.Kee, 67, an aged Chinese in ill health, poisoned   Oct 18, 1916
himself October 13, 1916. The funeral was held October 15th.

Miss Delia Kehoe, 34, died August 27, 1917 at Point Arena   Sep 5, 1917
where she was born and lived all her life.

Mrs.S.Keller, 76, died at Ukiah September 18, 1917. Eight   Sep 26, 1917
children survived: Mrs.J.B.Bucholz of Idaho, Mrs.C.J.Beckley,
Mrs.F.W. Parker, Mrs.C.W.Dahlstrom, G.A., H.A., E.A.Keller of
Ukiah and J.J.Keller of Willits.

Mrs.Elizabeth Kelly, almost 90, died September 25, 1914 in   Sep 30, 1914
Mendocino. A native of Prince Edward Island, she was the wife
of William Kelly and a 59 year resident of Mendocino. Two
daughters: Mrs.Daisy McCallum of Mendocino and Mrs.Elise
Dexter of San Francisco, survived as did one son, Otis Kelly
of San Francisco. The funeral was held September 27th.

Mrs.Mary Kelly, 69, burned to death October 14, 1912 at   Oct 16, 1912
Ukiah. She was buried the same day.

Richard Kelly died at Ukiah October 11, 1911. A native   Oct 25, 1911
of Ireland, he was 70 years old.

Soffa Kemppe, the wife of John Kemppe, died May 29, 1910.   Jun 1, 1910
A native of Finland, she was 31 years old.

Margaret Ann Kennedy, 81, died December 29, 1919 east of   Dec 31, 1919
Noyo. A native of Ireland, she lived in Illinois for
40 years before coming to California. Her daughter, Mrs.
Harris, and son, J.J.Kennedy, survived. Rev.H.Shaw led the
funeral service December 31st.

Thomas Kennedy, an old coast resident, died at Ukiah   Feb 14, 1912
February 9, 1912.

William Kennedy died "back of Noyo" August 14, 1919. A   Aug 20, 1919
native of Ireland, he was 78 years 4 months and 24 days
old. He came to California from Hanover, Illinois, with his
son, J.J.Kennedy, and daughter, Mrs.Ada Harris, in October
1919. His wife and children survived.

James <u>Kenny</u>, a veteran of the Mexican War, died in San Fran-   Feb 17, 1915
cisco February 11, 1915. He was 85 years old. Born in
Ireland, he came to Mendocino in 1853 and settled at Cuffey's
Cove. He had retired in 1890. Five children survived: Mrs.
Kate Gorman and Mrs.Mary Boyle of Mendocino; Mrs.Nellie
Carter and Mrs.Annie Kidwell of San Francisco and John Kenny
of Greenwood. The funeral was in San Francisco February 15th.

Dr.J.B.<u>Keough</u>, formerly a dentist at Point Arena, died   Feb 13, 1918
"this week".

Ellen <u>Kerr</u>, *nee* Meiklejohn, died January 17, 1916 in Fort   Jan 19, 1916
Bragg. Born in Fifeshire, Scotland, April 14, 1828, she   Jan 26, 1916
came to Canada at the age of 15. In 1846 she married   Feb 2, 1916
William Kerr and had eight children. She was a widow when
she came to California in 1887. Two sons, William and Robert,
were hotel operators at Whitesboro and Albion - Robert died
in 1910 [William's death date not mentioned]. The surviving
children were: Samuel of Republic, Washington, John of
Wilderville, Oregon, James of Ukiah, David of St.Maries,
Idaho, Mrs.J.W.Barton of Scotia and Mrs.J.A.Woodward of
Noyo. The funeral was held at Fort Bragg January 20, 1916
with burial at Littleriver. Rev.Sutherland officiated.

Robert <u>Kerr</u>, proprietor of a hotel at Albion, died in San   Mar 2, 1910
Francisco February 26, 1910. About 57 years old, he came to
the coast about 35 years ago.

Sam <u>Kerr</u>, a former coast resident, died in Republic, Wash-   Sep 24, 1919
ington, September 21, 1919. His sister, Mrs.J.A.Woodward of
Fort Bragg, survived.

Archie <u>Kesti</u>, died in Arizona "this week" He was born and   May 16, 1917
raised in Fort Bragg.

W."Billie" <u>Ketchum</u>, 60, died at Point Arena March 14, 1917   Mar 14, 1917
of asthma and a bad heart. Born on the Garcia River, he was
the brother of the late John Ketchum of Fort Bragg. A son,
Nels Ketchum, survived.

Mrs.<u>Kidd</u> died at Ukiah February 25, 1912.   Mar 6, 1912

J.L.<u>Kidwell</u> of San Francisco died in Germany July 1, 1912   Jul 10, 1912
where he had gone seeking medical treatment. His wife, the   Aug 7, 1912
former Annie Kenny of Cuffey's Cove, and four children
survived. He was buried in San Francisco.

Jim <u>Kimball</u>, a former Westport resident, died in Oakland   Jul 28, 1915
"recently".

John S.<u>Kimball</u>, over 70, died at Oakland June 4, 1918. A   Jun 5, 1918
lumberman from the early days on the coast, he operated
loading facilities first at Cuffey's Cove and, later, at
Westport. He built and operated a hotel at Westport and
owned several steam schooners, including the steamship
Sequoia at Fort Bragg, that worked the coastal ports.

Mrs.John S.<u>Kimball</u>, 73, died November 23, 1918 at Berkeley   Nov 27, 1918
from influenza. The wife of the late John S.Kimball, she
lived at Cuffey's Cove and other points along the coast. She
was the sister of the late C.E.White.

Mrs.Mary <u>Kincaid</u>, a prominent San Francisco educator, died   Jul 22, 1914
in that city July 18, 1914 at age 69. She owned the Redwood
Lodge at Noyo.

Dr.Edward Warren <u>King</u>, a pioneer doctor of the Ukiah valley,   Jan 14, 1914
died in San Francisco [no date reported]. The original head
of the State Hospital at Talmage from its construction to
1913, he was 82½ years old.

Ella May <u>King</u>, aged 44, died August 19, 1910 in San Francisco   Aug 31, 1910
She was buried in Westport. Her husband and three children
survived.

George R.<u>King</u>, a pioneer carpenter of Fort Bragg, died   Aug 13, 1919
August 9, 1919 at the age of 72 years 4 months and 29 days.
His wife and seven children survived. The funeral was held
at Fort Bragg August 12th led by Rev.W.A.Chapman.

Joseph <u>King</u> died at Mendocino August 9, 1915. A longtime   Aug 11, 1915
resident, he had worked in the lumber mills on the coast.
Catholic rites were held in Mendocino August 11th.

Willie <u>Kingsburg</u> died at Hardy February 22, 1910 of   Feb 23, 1910
apparent heart failure.
[probably should be KINGSBURY, see below].

Alme Roy <u>Kingsbury</u> died at January 16, 1911 at Tancred,   Jan 11, 1911
Yolo County. He had gone to Oakland for dental work and   Jan 18, 1911
caught a cold which developed into fatal pneumonia. He was   Jan 25, 1911
the son of Mr.& Mrs.C.W.Kingsbury of Hardy. Burial was in
Oakland's Mount View cemetery January 18th.

Oliver <u>Kingsbury</u>, a.k.a Texas Tom, died at the County Farm   Apr 12, 1911
near Ukiah April 8, 1911.

Willie <u>Kingsbury</u> died February 1910.   Jan 11, 1911

George D.P.<u>Kinlock</u> died September 1, 1913 at the age of   Sep 3, 1913
84 years 1 month and two days. Born at Monterey July 25,
1829, he was the first white child born in California. The
funeral was held at Ukiah September 2nd.

August <u>Kinnunen</u>, 60, died at Fort Bragg May 10, 1918. A   May 15, 1918
native of Finland, he was a 30 year resident living near
the Noyo tunnel. His wife and 12 children survived: Mrs.
Rose Saleman, Mrs.Annie Fernandez, Miss May, Olga, Niemi,
Ellen, Jennie, William, Edward, John, Van and Carl. The
funeral was in Fort Bragg May 15th led by Rev.O.Halla [?].

Alfred J.<u>Kinville</u>, a native of Canada 53 years old, was   May 18, 1910
killed in a logging accident May 9, 1910. A son in Fort
Bragg and his wife in Eureka survived. The body was
shipped to Wisconsin.

George <u>Kirkham</u> died at the State Hospital in Ukiah   Jan 25, 1911
January 10, 1911.

Peter <u>Kivi</u>, a native of Finland, was a suicide at the County   Jan 10, 1912
Farm near Ukiah "recently". He was 29 years old and had come
from Michigan recently. A wife and two children survived.

Charles <u>Klett</u> died at Ukiah May 20, 1911. Born in Germany,   May 24, 1911
he was 83 years old.

Fred G.<u>Knacke</u> of Mendocino was killed at Arcata   Feb 21, 1912
February 17, 1912.

Mrs.Herman <u>Knaesche</u>, *nee* Beekley, was murdered by her   Jun 25, 1919
husband July 9, 1919 in their home near Ukiah. They had been   Jul 16, 1919
married about two weeks. He claimed innocence, but the   Jul 23, 1919
sheriff produced enough evidence to cause Knaesche to   Aug 20, 1919
confess the shotgun murder on August 19, 1919. He received   Aug 27, 1919
a life sentence August 22nd.

Eli <u>Knight</u>, foreman of the Mendocino Lumber Company's lumber Aug 12, 1914
yard, died August 10, 1914. His wife, Nellie, a daughter,
Mrs.George Switzer, two sons, Linton and Charlie Knight, and
two brothers, Charles Knight of Mendocino and H.J.Knight of
San Francisco, survived.

George A.Knight, a San Francisco attorney who owned a ranch   Jul 5, 1916
at Longvale, died of pneumonia June 20, 1916.

Stephen W.Knowles, a former Mendocino County resident, died   Oct 4, 1911
at Cloverdale September 25, 1911.

Mrs.Peter Knudsen, a former Fort Bragg resident, died at   Sep 30, 1914
Lodi, San Joaquin County, September 28, 1914.

Martin Koenig, a native German, was shot in cold blood by   Jun 14, 1916
D.Gori, an Italian, in a wood camp near Sherwood June 4,   Sep 27, 1916
1916. The shooting was a result a drunken quarrel about the   Oct 4, 1916
European war. Gori got 15 years for second degree murder.

Otto Kogg, about 40 years old, died in the Eagle Hotel in   May 18, 1910
Fort Bragg May 16, 1910. A wife survived in Finland. His
funeral was held in Fort Bragg May 17th.

Mr.Komoda, a Japanese, cut his throat and died at Ukiah   Sep 5, 1917
September 3, 1917.

Marie Koopman, a nurse at the State Hospital, hanged herself Nov 8, 1916
October 30, 1916.

John Kopolo was killed by Stelio Karpantheno [also   Dec 2, 1914
Karfonthino], a Greek, near Willits November 28, 1914.   Jan 20, 1915
Karpantheno was freed by a jury at Ukiah in March 1915.   Mar 10, 1915

Matt Koskela drowned at Albion in an accident when loading   Jan 25, 1911
lumber on a steamer on January 18, 1911. His wife and five
children survived.

Mrs.Margaret Koski died March 27, 1911 in Fort Bragg. She   Mar 29, 1911
was born in Finland in 1837 and was a resident of Fort
Bragg from 1903. The funeral was held March 29th.

Elmer Kramer died at Willits October 3, 1911.   Oct 18, 1911

Blair Kucek, third son of Joe and Hattie Kucek, died at   Feb 15, 1911
Blair, Nevada, February 12, 1911. He was born in Fort Bragg
June 24, 1910.

Frank Kuharich of Caspar was shot June 5, 1919 by Chris   Jun 11, 1919
Hoyerdahl and died June 7th. Kuharich was attempting to
break into the Hoyerdahl home in a drunken rage and was shot
through the closed door.

Mrs.Mary Kuhn of Caspar, 72, died at Fort Bragg [no date   Dec 18, 1912
reported] of double pneumonia. A 40 year resident of Caspar,
three sons and five daughters survived. One son, Thomas Kuhn,
was of Fort Bragg. Catholic services were held by Father
Wright December 13th.

Mrs.Anna Kukko, 67, died at Noyo hill May 25, 1918. Born in   May 29, 1918
Finland, she had been a resident for 16 years. A husband and
four sons survived. The funeral was May 27, 1918 with
Rev.John J.Hillberg officiating.

Mrs.Louisa Lahm, 71, died in Willits February 18, 1913.   Feb 26, 1913

Vilma Lake, aged nine months, was badly burned in a house   Jan 12, 1910
fire on the "other side of Pudding Creek" January 8, 1910
and died on January 10th. Burial was on the 11th.

Anna Margaret Lamb, aged 14, died April 3, 1910. She was   Apr 13, 1910
the daughter of R.W.and G.L.Lamb.

Miss Annie Lamb died at Potter Valley March 28, 1910.   Apr 6, 1910
[Probably same as Anna Margaret Lamb above].

Russell W.Lamb died in Potter Valley "last week". Born in   Feb 15, 1911
Ohio, he came to California in the early days and engaged in
mining. He moved to Potter Valley in 1900. His widow, Gussie
Lamb, son, Hugh and three daughters, Mrs.W.A.(Geneva) Klinkie
of Elk, Rosalie and Olive, survived. Another daughter, Anna,
died in April 1910.

Washington Lambert, 80, died at Ukiah [June 2, 1916?]   Jun 7, 1916

L.H.Lamborn was killed in a terrorist bomb explosion in San   Aug 2, 1916
Francisco July 22, 1916.

W.P.Lampkin, 69, an old coast resident, died near Gualala   Nov 15, 1916
November 7, 1916. He was born in Virginia.

The body of Mr.Lamprey, formerly of Ukiah, was found near   Sep 13, 1911
Upper Lake [no date]. About 70 years, he was demented.

Charley Lancherio, *aka*.Captain Charlie, died at Point Arena   Jan 17, 1917
January 10, 1917. A Gualala Indian, he was reportedly over
100 years old.

Mrs.Mary Landrobe, who was raised at Westport, died recently   Oct 3, 1917
at Richmond. Two brothers, Sam Vann of Fort Bragg and
Orceneth Vann of Laytonville, and two sisters, Mrs.George
Johnson of Ukiah and Mrs.M.Pickerel of Gualala, survived.

Mrs.C.W.Lane, the mother of John C.Lane, died at Lakeport   Mar 2, 1910
February 18, 1910 and was buried at Manchester.

Mrs.George Lane died at Redwood Valley November 26, 1913.   Dec 3, 1913
Her husband survived.

William Ralph Lane, who was born and raised at Manchester,   Jan 22, 1919
died in Martinez, Contra Costa County, January 17, 1919. He
was assistant school principal there.

R.N.Langland, 48, was a suicide at Ukiah November 23, 1911   Nov 29, 1911
by drinking chloroform.

Carleton Langley, the 3 month old son of William Langley,   Dec 31, 1913
died December 25, 1913 and was buried the next day in Fort
Bragg. Rev.W.A.Chapman officiated.

Henry Langley died at Albion January 12, 1914. A woodsman,   Jan 21, 1914
he was 60 years old. The funeral was held in Mendocino.

Mrs.Lucy Langley, a native of Washington aged 45, died   Jul 13, 1910
July 11, 1910. Catholic services were conducted by Father
Michael. Two sons, William and Henry, and a daughter, Mrs.
Agnes Duffey, survived.

Mrs.Jeanette Langren died at Ukiah in October 1915 [date?].   Oct 27, 1915
She was 68 years 11 months and 2 [?] days old [data lost].

Solomon Lanto, aged 72, died September 13, 1910. A longtime   Sep 14, 1910
resident, he left a wife and two sons in Berkeley.

Mrs.Guy LaPorte, 27, the widow of the late Guy LaPorte, died   Mar 21, 1917
died at Fort Bragg March 15, 1917. She had just come from
Ukiah to her sister's home (Mrs.C.B.Melville). Her husband
died two months previously. She left a girl of 8 and a son,
6 years old. The funeral was held in Ukiah March 17th.

Albert Larsen, 10, shot in a hunting accident in Sanel   Oct 7, 1914
Valley September 29, 1914, died the next day.

Andrew Larsen, a farmer near the Albion River, died June 23,   Jun 25, 1913
1913 of injuries from a runaway accident on June 22nd. His
horse was frightened by a motorcycle near Comptche. A native
of Fort Bragg, he was 52 years old and left a wife and seven
children. The funeral was June 25th at Littleriver.

L.C.Larsen, 72 and a native of Norway, died at Comptche
May 23, 1912.

Jun 19, 1912

Oscar Larson, a resident for 25 years who moved to Sierra
Madre, Los Angeles County, in February 1916, died there
April 25th. A carpenter by trade and the operator the
Pacific Hotel in Fort Bragg, he was 43 years old. His wife
and two sons, Russel and Connie Larson, survived. His mother,
a brother and a sister, remained in Sweden. A brother, Emil
Larson, and a sister, Mrs.A.Swanson, were also mentioned.
The funeral was held in Fort Bragg April 30, 1916 led by
Rev.W.A.Chapman.

Apr 26, 1916
May 3, 1916

Mrs.Lenna LaSalle, 32, the wife of Edward LaSalle, died at
Fort Bragg November 2, 1918 from influenza. A native of
Finland, she had been a resident for 13 years. Her husband,
two children, her parents, the John Stroms, survived. She
was buried at Fort Bragg November 5, 1918.

Nov 6, 1918

The 19 day old infant daughter of Mr.& Mrs.Latvala died
May 1, 1910 "on the other side of Pudding Creek".

May 4, 1910

Adgelo Lavaggi, 25, died at Ukiah July 31, 1914. Catholic
rites were held on August 1st.

Aug 5, 1914

Mrs.G.Laviletta died at Talmage "last week". Her husband,
the gardener at the State Hospital, and nine children
survived.

Jan 14, 1914

Mabel Lawson, the 15 year old daughter of George Lawson of
Point Arena, died of TB "this week". This was the third
child of this Indian family to die in a short time.

Jun 27, 1917

Pvt.Roy Lawson from Point Arena died at Fort Dix, New
Jersey, and was to be buried December 5, 1918.

Dec 4, 1918

S.H.Lawson died at Santa Rosa September 24, 1913.
A County pioneer, he settled in Boonville in 1853.

Oct 1, 1913

Eric Lax, 36, dropped dead in the woods July 12, 1912.

Jul 17, 1912

Joe Layton, formerly of Westport, died "last week" of
influenza and was buried at Fort Bragg.

Nov 20, 1918

Dennis Lee was killed at summit tunnel on the railroad
May 22, 1912 in a steam shovel accident [details lost].
A brother, Patrick, came to Fort Bragg and took the body to
New York for burial.

May 29, 1912
Jun 5, 1912

Mrs.Sarah Lee died at Fort Bragg December 25, 1915. Born in
New York July 31, 1916, she was 99 years 4 months and 25 days
old. She came to California in 1885 and was a resident at
Fort Bragg for 11 years. Her daughter was Mrs.Elvira Raymond
of Fort Bragg. The funeral was held at the Baptist church
December 28th.

Dec 29, 1915

Gus LeFevre died at San Francisco January 5, 1913.
Four daughters survived.

Jan 8, 1913

Mrs.Sigrid LeFevre, wife of Gus LeFevre, died in Oakland of
heart failure, the body being found January 14, 1910. A
former resident of Fort Bragg, he was 48 years old. Four
daughters survived: Mrs.D.Haskins, Mrs.C.Lane, Mrs.A.Rowland,
and Miss Belle LeFevre of Bakersfield. The funeral was in
the Mountain View cemetery in Oakland January 17, 1910.

Jan 19, 1910
Jan 26, 1910

John W.Leffler drowned in the Garcia River January 14, 1910.
The body was found January 22nd. He was 41 years old and
left a wife and young son.

Jan 26, 1910
Feb 2, 1910

Mario Leggi, a native of Italy 30 years of age, died at the
State Hospital February 25, 1911.

Mar 8, 1911

Jack Leistner, a.k.a. "Happy Jack", was found dead with of a gunshot wound at his cabin on the south fork of Eel River August 6, 1918. About 65, he had worked at Usal in the early days. The coroner's jury called it an accidental death.

Aug 7, 1918
Aug 14, 1918

Mrs. Angeline Lemmon, wife of G.A. Lemmon, died near Noyo July 22, 1915. A 33 year resident of California and 12 of Noyo, she was 57 years and 10 months old. The funeral was conducted in Fort Bragg July 25th by Rev.W.A.Chapman. Her husband, three daughters and two sons survived.

Jul 28, 1915

Mrs. William Lemoine, 66, died February 17, 1915 on Albion ridge. A native of Canada, she lived on the coast for 40 years. Her husband and daughter survived. The funeral was held at Littleriver on February 19th.

Feb 24, 1915

Freddie Lemos, the youngest child of Antone Lemos, died July 5, 1918 of spinal meningitis. Catholic rites were performed at Mendocino July 7th.

Jul 10, 1918

Mrs. Doris Lempke died in Los Angeles July 24, 1914. She was a resident of Ukiah for 47 years. Born in Kellingheusen, Germany, in 1839, she arrived in New York in 1862, crossed the plains and settled in Ukiah Valley in 1867. Her husband, Peter Lempke, died in 1904 [August 19, 1903]. The funeral was held August 2nd in Ukiah.

Aug 26, 1903
Aug 5, 1914

Mrs. Lendrum died at San Francisco April 24, 1915. Her son, Dr.B.A.Lendrum of Fort Bragg, survived.

Apr 28, 1915

Henry Lentu, injured in a log car accident at Greenwood and died at Fort Bragg November 1, 1913. The funeral was held there November 2nd.

Nov 5, 1913

John Leonard was killed at Camp 3 May 6, 1910 by a rolling log. A native of Ireland, he was 28-30 years old. The body was sent to Nevada. [A later item reported his brother-in-law, John Fahey, took the body to San Francisco for burial.]

May 11, 1910
May 18, 1910

Mrs. Frank Leppo, daughter of Joseph Spottswood of Potter Valley, committed suicide in Santa Rosa October 28, 1911.

Nov 1, 1911

Mrs. LeValley, 58, died at Nordhoff, Ventura County [no date reported]. She was a pioneer of the Westport area. Her son, Don LeValley, survived.

Dec 26, 1917

The 3 month old son of J.M. Lewis died December 17, 1913 at Fort Bragg. Catholic rites were led by Rev.Edwards on the 19th.

Dec 24, 1913

Mrs. H. Lewis, formerly of Ukiah, died in Oakland "last week".

Dec 7, 1910

Richard Lewis, the second son of George Lewis, was kicked by a horse and died at Westport September 19, 1916. The funeral was held there on September 20th.

Sep 20, 1916
Sep 27, 1916

W.N. Lewis, 70, dropped dead at Glen Blair October 1, 1917. He had been a resident only three weeks.

Oct 3, 1917

Jeremiah Lierly, 81, died at Ukiah November 18, 1919. His widow and two children survived: Harry Lierly and Mrs. Catharine McGee of Potter Valley.

Nov 26, 1919

The 3 month old daughter of Alex Liimatainen died September 12, 1910.

Sep 14, 1910

John Samuel Lilley, 78, died August 14, 1919 in Littleriver. He was a ten year resident of Albion and had ranched near Albion before that. His wife and six children survived: William and James of Andersonia, Walter of Albion, John of Tuolumne County, Mrs.George Ottoson of Littleriver and Mrs.Ida Wolf.

Aug 20, 1919

Peter Linberg, an attorney from San Francisco, froze to   Mar 8, 1911
death 12 miles from Cummings. He was inspecting some
property in the north part of the county when caught in a
storm. The body was found February 22, 1911.

Nicholas Linc died in San Francisco where he had gone for   Jan 24, 1912
medical treatment, January 16, 1912. His funeral was held in
Westport on the 19th led by Rev.W.A.Chapman. He was 78 years
7 months and 16 days old.

Mr.Linderman's funeral was held at Fort Bragg March 8, 1910.   Mar 9, 1910

Gus Linderman, of the steamer National City, was believed to   May 30, 1917
have drowned in the Fort Bragg harbor May 19, 1917 as his
wife came from San Francisco looking for him when he failed
to return.

Mrs.John Lindquest, 70, died November 22, 1918 at Fort   Nov 27, 1918
Bragg. A native of Finland, she had been a 17 year resident.
The funeral was held at the Finnish church with Rev.John J.
Hillberg officiating on November 26th followed by burial in
the Fort Bragg cemetery.

Mrs.Mary Henley Lindsay, the daughter of L.C.Henley formerly   Dec 6, 1916
of Ukiah, died in Seattle, Washington, November 26, 1916.

Charles A.Linscott, born August 15, 1845 in South Windsor,   Apr 23, 1919
Maine, died at Point Area April 22, 1919. He came to California in 1863 locating at Noyo. On December 15, 1869 he
married Mrs.Ellen Bever. He worked as a sawyer in the
coastal mills and lived in Point Arena 30 years ago. His
wife and four of their six children survived: O.L.Linscott,
Mrs.Xarrissa McCallum, Mrs.B.Bishop and Mrs.Hazel Lawson.

Wilson B.Livermore, 62, died October 21, 1915 at Willits.   Nov 3, 1915
Born in Iowa, he was a 12 year resident.

W.A.Lobdell of Little Lake Road died September 26, 1910 at   Sep 28, 1910
Ukiah. He was the proprietor of the Half Way House resort.

Mrs.Charles Lockhart, an Indian, died October 23, 1918 in   Oct 30, 1918
Fort Bragg of influenza. She had lived 31 of her 40 years in
that city.

Gus Logan of Mendocino died in San Francisco "last week"   Aug 10, 1910
following surgery.

The four year old son of Peter Loggi was accidentally scalded   Feb 4, 1914
when he fell into a cauldron of hot milk on Albion Ridge
January 24, 1914 and died of the burns received.

Mrs.Mary Long, was shot in the leg by her halfbrother,   May 23, 1917
Charles Lee, in a drunken rage, near Willits May 1917. She   Jul 11, 1917
died of the wound July 5th. Lee also shot his own daughter,   Oct 10, 1917
but she recovered. Lee got 10 years in prison October 5th.

Fred Longland, the son of Mrs.George Longland, age 13, was   Aug 24, 1910
accidentally shot and killed by Roy Peacock in a hunting
accident [No date reported].

George Longland, a pioneer of Mendocino County, died at   Jan 20, 1915
Willits "last week". A native of England, he was 71. The
funeral was held in Willits January 17, 1915.

Pat Looney, a coast resident, died at Greenwood "last week".   Feb 16, 1910
A native of Boston, Massachusetts, he was 50 years old.

Mrs.Mary A.Lopps, 64, died at Mendocino April 1, 1912.   Apr 3, 1912

Bob Lord, a former Fort Bragg resident, died in San Fran-   Oct 10, 1914
cisco "last week".

Mrs.Josephine C.Lord dropped dead in the Union Lumber Co.   May 3, 1911
store in Fort Bragg April 27, 1911 of heart failure. A 13
year resident, she was 56. Catholic service was April 30th.

Rona G.Love, 64, died March 15, 1917 north of Fort Bragg   Mar 21, 1917
"across Pudding Creek". The funeral was held in Fort Bragg's
Episcopal church by Father Grant.

A son of the Lovejoys died on Eel River [no date reported].   Oct 19, 1910

Charles Lowell, Sr, a Covelo pioneer, died of heart   May 6, 1914
failure April 23, 1914.

Mr.Lucas, father of Mrs.Frank Douglas, died in Stockton   Apr 26, 1911
April 24, 1911.

A 3 month child of Mr.Lucas died at East Mendocino   Nov 22, 1911
November 18, 1911.

Addison Lucas died at East Mendocino March 5, 1912.   Mar 13, 1912

Elgar Samuel Lucas, the infant son of Mrs.L.F.Lucas, nee   Aug 6, 1919
Viola Buckbee, died in Lincoln, Los Angeles County. Mrs.
Lucas was the sister of Mrs.William J.Pedro of Fort Bragg.

The 5 month daughter of Mr.Luccia died at Albion   May 31, 1916
May 26, 1916 from pneumonia.

Rev.Charles Luce died at Fort Bragg March 28, 1917. He was   Apr 4, 1917
84 years 6 months and 16 days old. Born in Industry, Maine,
September 12, 1832, he came to California in 1855 via Panama
and mined in Grass Valley until 1861. He returned to Maine
and brought his parents to California in the Fall of 1865.
In April 1866 he married Mrs.Helen Cutts Viles of Maine.
Ordained in 1872, he moved to Ukiah in 1877.

Manuel Luce fell from a locomotive and was killed on the   Nov 23, 1910
Mendocino logging railroad November 10, 1910.

A.Lund, 22, died at Caspar October 14, 1912. His funeral   Oct 16, 1912
was October 16th led by Rev.W.A.Chapman.

Charles Lund, 56, a pioneer woodsman of the coast, died   Aug 7, 1918
August 4, 1918 of appendicitis. A native of Sweden, he had
worked in the Caspar woods for five years. The funeral was
in Fort Bragg August 7, 1918.

Peter Lundquist, a sailor from the steamer Klamath, drowned   Jan 1, 1919
in Fort Bragg harbor December 26, 1918 when a boat capsized.

Mrs.Lucy R.Lydick died above Cleone June 20, 1911. The   Jun 21, 1911
daughter of Jeridiah Dwelly, she was born in Crawford,   Sep 20, 1911
Maine, June 21, 1844. She married Isiah Lydick in 1870 and
came to California in 1876 settling at Cuffey's Cove before
moving to Cleone in 1883. Seven children were born of which
six survived: Ruel [s.] Lydick, Mrs.August Delmer of Fruitvale, Mrs.Harbour of Watsonville, Miss Lillie of Fort Bragg,
Mrs.Frost of Oregon and Mrs.Freitos of Scotia. A brother,
Jerediah Dwelly and a sister, Mrs.E.Smith, also survived.
Miss Lillie was the administrator of her mother's estate.

Mrs.Louise Lyle, 84, died at Ukiah August 10, 1911   Aug 16, 1911
[A Louise Lile reported as dying August 9th - same?]   Aug 30, 1911

Mrs.E.D.Lynch of Point Arena, died September 7, 1912.   Sep 18, 1912

Miss Vic Lynch, the daughter of D.M.Lynch, died after an   Apr 9, 1913
operation April 4, 1913.

Nick Lytala, aged 25, was killed in a team runaway about 4   Apr 27, 1910
miles south of Noyo April 23, 1910. The funeral was held in
Fort Bragg April 26th.

Thomas <u>Macedo</u>, a local boy, was killed in a submarine accident off the Connecticut coast in June 1918. Only 19 years old, he was a two year Navy veteran.

Jun 5, 1918

Mrs.O.M.<u>Mack</u>,33, died at Comptche May 13, 1911.

May 24, 1911

Dave C.<u>Mackay</u>, a Round Valley pioneer, died at Willits April 15, 1913. The funeral was at the Presbyterian church on April 16th.

Apr 23, 1913

George <u>Maddox</u> of Elk died December 4, 1918 from influenza. Born at Point Arena in 1881, he left a wife and two small children. Another child was born the day the father was buried. His parents and six sisters also survived: Mrs.Mike Iversen of Point Arena, Mrs.A.E.Grant of Cloverdale, Mrs. Frank Dilling of Miller, Mrs.W.Johnston of Bloomfield, Mrs. Walter Turnbull of Albion and Mrs.A.L.Dobner of Oakland.

Dec 11, 1918
Dec 18, 1918

Mrs.Robert <u>Maddox</u> died at Boonville August 21, 1916.

Aug 30, 1916

Margaret <u>Maderia</u>, 5, the daughter of Joseph Maderia of Mendocino, died November 17, 1918. The funeral was held there November 19th.

Nov 20, 1918

D.Caselli shot 4 people at the Maffini Hotel in Fort Bragg August 13, 1916 in a crazed attack fatally wounding two, John Bolson and A.<u>Maffini</u>, before turning the gun on himself. Maffini died the next day and was buried with Catholic rites at Fort Bragg August 17th. His wife and 2 children survived.

Aug 16, 1916
Sep 6, 1916

Mrs.E.<u>Maffini</u>, aged 23, died at Glen Blair January 24, 1911. Catholic rites were held in Fort Bragg January 25th.

Jan 25. 1911

Mrs.A.(Emilin) <u>Mahlman</u>, aged 76, died June 15, 1911 at Littleriver of pneumonia. She had been a resident for 40 years. The funeral was held June 18th. Five children survived: Mrs.Robert Pritchard, Mrs.James Porterfield, Mrs.James Barton, F.A.and W.T.Mahlman. Two brothers also survived: H.C. and P.L.Anderson.

Jun 21, 1911

Henry <u>Mahurin</u>, a former Caspar resident, was killed in a woods accident at Point Agnihis [sic], Washington, "this week". Born in Ukiah February 23, 1880, his mother, Mrs. Amandy Mahurin, two brothers, Charles and Amos Mahurin, and two sisters, Mrs.S.Gregory and Mrs.G.W.Appleton, survived. The funeral was held November 6, 1917.

Nov 7, 1917

John <u>Mahurin</u> died near Pine Grove "last week". Over 70 years old, he had been a resident of California for more than 50 years. His wife and six children survived.

Oct 19, 1910

Mrs.John <u>Main</u> died near Boonville May 7, 1914.

May 13, 1914

Mrs.<u>Makanen</u> died at age 52 June 23, 1912 about five miles "back of Noyo". A husband and three children survived. The funeral was held in Fort Bragg on June 25th.

Jun 26, 1912

Mrs.Anna <u>Makela</u>, 39, died in childbirth in Fort Bragg April 21, 1915. The twins were stillborn. A native of Finland, she had lived at Glen Blair. The funeral was held in Fort Bragg April 24th.

Apr 28, 1915

Mary <u>Maloney</u>, aged 70, died at the State Hospital in Ukiah February 28, 1911.

Mar 8, 1911

Clarence W.<u>Manchester</u> of Ten Mile died December 16, 1917 in France after contracting pneumonia following an attack of measles. Born at Ten Mile June 22, 1893, he was 22 years 5 months and 25 days old. The body was returned and buried at Fort Bragg October 24, 1920. [Dates no not add up.] He served with Company E of the 20th.Engineers. Burial was December 18, 1920. [Date suspect.]

Dec 26, 1917
Mar 13, 1918
Oct 27, 1920

Dorothy Manchester, 11 months and 22 days old, the daughter | Jan 29, 1919
of Luke Manchester, died in Fort Bragg January 22, 1919.
Rev.Sutherland led the funeral in Fort Bragg January 26th.

John Manchester died at Fort Bragg of kidney failure | Feb 9, 1916
February 2, 1916. He was 76 years 5 months and 8 days old.
A California resident for more than 60 years, he was born
in Wisconsin and crossed the great plains as a boy of 12.
The family settled in the Jackson Valley. He married Lena
Blair in 1865 (she died October 9, 1909). They were the
parents of seven children, six of whom survived: Mrs.Olive
Sparks of Kenny, Mrs.L.Branscomb of Inglenook, Mrs.Ed Gordon
of Fort Bragg, Iva Manchester of Sacramento, Lou Manchester
of Northspur and Irva Manchester of Vancouver. After his
wife's death he relocated to Ten Mile River.

Michele Manggeni, a native of Italy 20 years old, was | Oct 18, 1911
killed at Camp 10 October 12, 1911 when crushed by a log.
His funeral was held October 15th.

Mrs.Emily Mankins died at 81 in Ukiah September 28, 1910. | Oct 5, 1910

Zola R.Mankins, born July 1896, died July 25, 1917 | Aug 1, 1917
at Ukiah.

John Mannas died at Fort Bragg "last week" and was buried | Apr 9, 1913
April 6, 1913. Born in Finland, he was 42 years old.
Rev.R.C.Grace officiated at the funeral.

Thomas Manning, a former resident of Haywards, was killed | Sep 15, 1915
by a rolling log at Boyle's tie camp September 7, 1915.

Elizabeth Mannon, 13, the daughter of Charles Mannon died | Oct 30, 1918
October 24, 1918 from influenza.

Mrs.F.C.Marble died at Willits June 19, 1913. | Jun 25, 1913
The funeral was held June 21st.

James March, 68, died near Albion December 12, 1912. | Dec 18, 1912

C.H.Marders, a Wells Fargo agent, burned to death in his | Feb 18, 1914
express car in a tunnel accident February 12, 1914 at
Cumbres, Mexico. His father was Robert Marders of
Potter Valley.

Antone Marino drowned in Big River at Mendocino | Jun 16, 1915
June 13, 1915. He was a native of Italy.

Charles Marino, an Italian woodsman, was found dead on the | Nov 8, 1916
road between Albion and Greenwood November 6, 1916. It later | Nov 15, 1916
came out that he had been bludgeoned to death by Ermino
"Butch" Paganoni, about 24, on November 5, 1916.

Mrs.W.M.Marion of Irmulco died at Tacoma, Washington, where | Jul 28, 1915
she had gone for health reasons [no date reported].
Only 18 years old, she left a husband and daughter.

Isaac F.Markkula, a resident for 29 years, died | Sep 20, 1916
September 18, 1916. A native of Finland, he left a daughter,
Mrs.G.E.Bargqvist and two sons, Walter and Matt Markkula.

Adolph I.Marks, 30, died at Ukiah October 29, 1918 from | Nov 6, 1918
influenza. A native of Covelo, he was the manager of the
Cecile Hotel in Ukiah. His wife, child and mother survived.

Caroline Marks, a former resident of Ukiah and widow of the | Nov 30, 1910
late Seymour Marks, died at Ukiah November 20, 1910. A native
of Germany, she was buried in San Francisco with her husband.

Henry Marks, a pioneer merchant of Round Valley, died in | Jul 31, 1918
Oakland July 28, 1918. He was about 76. A widow, three sons
and a daughter survived.

Solomon Marks, a former Fort Bragg resident, died in San   Mar 23, 1910
Francisco "last week".

F.Maron was found dead in the road at Cox's Ranch near   Aug 17, 1910
Willits on August 12, 1910. A native of France, he was 61.

Harry Marsh, a 24 year resident of Fort Bragg, died March 13,   Mar 16, 1910
died March 13, 1910 of heart failure. He was 74 years
2 months and 13 days old. A native of Ohio, he resided at
Inglenook and DeHaven before moving to Fort Bragg. The
funeral was held March 15, 1910 led by Rev.Grace. His
widow survived.

John S.Marsh, a former Mendocino County resident, died in   Apr 30, 1919
Santa Rosa "last week" at the age of 90. Burial was in Ukiah.

Mrs.R.B.Marsh died at Fort Bragg April 8, 1914.   Apr 8, 1914

Asa Marshall, a resident of Pudding Creek and saw filer in   Nov 22, 1911
the mill, died November 20, 1911. A Civil War veteran, he
was over 70 years old. His wife, two daughters, Mrs.Semple
of Samoa and Mrs.Lawrence of Eureka, and sons, Jay in San
Francisco, Asa and Clifton in Los Angeles, survived.

C.L.Marshall fell into the Eel River at Andersonia and was   Mar 23, 1910
killed March 15, 1910.

Charles Marshall died May 24, 1915 and was buried   Jun 2, 1915
at Point Arena May 26th.

J.H.Marshall, 31, was shot and killed by George Spittler at   Dec 6, 1911
Longvale November 26, 1911 in a fight over the postmistress.   Jan 3, 1912
Spittler was acquited of murder December 27, 1911.

Mrs.Sarah Marshall, who lived on the coast before 1900, died   Apr 7, 1915
at Waltham, Massachusetts, "recently".

Mrs.Peter Martelle [Martella], nee Geni Previtali of Fort   Dec 10, 1913
Bragg, died in San Francisco [no date reported]. She was
19 years and 9 months old and married since May, 1913.

J.W.Martin of Willits, 37, died there of spinal meningitis.   May 1, 1918
His wife and two daughters survived. The funeral was held
April 29th.

Stephen Byron Martin, a veteran of the Civil War, died at   Sep 17, 1919
Willits September 15, 1919. He was born in Illinois
January 3, 1837.

Gabriel Martinetti, a hotel operator at Greenwood, died   Feb 10, 1915
there February 1, 1915. He was buried with Catholic rites
at Cuffey's Cove.

Mrs.Katherine Martinez received fatal injuries in a runaway   Jun 11, 1913
accident June 10, 1913. Her father was M.Martinez, an
Italian dairyman south of Ukiah.

Guido Martini was killed in a truck wreck at Virgin Creek   May 22, 1918
May 19, 1918. A native of Italy, he was 41 years and
26 days old.

Spirito Martino, 34, was run over by a locomotive when he   Jun 19, 1918
fell off in the Caspar woods June 14, 1918. A native of
Italy, he received Catholic rites June 17, 1918 with burial
at Fort Bragg.

Mrs.Lizzie Marvin, wife of Dr.Marvin, superintendent of the   Sep 18, 1912
State Hospital at Talmage, died in San Francisco "last week".
She was buried in Rohnerville, Humboldt County.

The infant daughter of Mr. Masolini died of severe burns from a gasoline stove accident at Cleone June 19, 1914. The funeral was held at Fort Bragg on June 21st.

Jun 24, 1914

George Masolini, 7, the son of Andrew Masolini of Cleone, died November 6, 1918. The funeral was held on November 9th.

Nov 13, 1918

H.H. Mason, a resident of Hardy Creek, was killed at Howard Creek July 11, 1912 when hit by a falling tree. His wife and three children survived.

Jul 17, 1912

Miss Bessie Mathews, the daughter of County Auditor J.J. Mathews, died at Ukiah March 13, 1919 at the age of 25. Her funeral was held March 15th.

Mar 19, 1919

Charles W. Mathews, the Mendocino County Auditor, died in San Francisco July 7, 1912. Born in New York December 14, 1859, he came to California about 1888 and to Mendocino County in 1890, first to Potter Valley and then to Ukiah. He married Jennie Briggs October 19, 1889. His widow and four children survived: Mabel Mathews of Seattle, Washington, and Charlie, Bessie and Paul of Ukiah.

Jul 10, 1912

Charles William Mathews was buried at Fort Bragg September 29, 1918 in rites at the Baptist church led by Rev. A.J. Sturtevant. Born in Ottawa, Canada, August 29, 1863 he came to California with his parents as a lad of eight. In 1889 he married Carrie Horton Blake of Massachusetts and moved to Fort Bragg about 1893 entering the banking field. His wife, son, William Mathews, two daughters, Inez and Phyllis, mother, Mrs. Obediah Mathews of Caspar, three brothers, James, Albert and Leonard, two sisters, Mrs. Albert Eagles of Caspar and Mrs. Benjamin Larkin of Berkeley, survived.

Oct 2, 1918
Oct 23, 1918
Nov 6, 1918

Mrs. Clyde Mathews nee Saide Betz a former Fort Bragg resident, died at Boise City, Idaho. The funeral was held at Fort Bragg April 12, 1910 led by Rev. A.J. Sturtevant.

Apr 6, 1910
Apr 13, 1910

James R. Mathews, 64, a druggist at Ukiah for 32 years, dropped dead in San Francisco December 25, 1919. He had sold his drug business in 1914 and was working for a San Francisco company. Born in Marysville, he left a sister there, Mrs. L.W. Burris. His widow and three children survived: Ernest J. Mathews, Mrs. E.A. LeFleur and Miss Grace Mathews.

Dec 31, 1919

Leta Mathews, a former Fort Bragg resident, died in Berkeley October 26, 1912 of a severe asthma condition. Born January 1888, she was 15 years old [sic!]. Her father died in Westport in 1911.

Oct 30, 1912

Obediah Mathews, 79, died at Caspar December 1, 1916. Born in England in 1837 [exact date lost], he came to Canada at age 24 and married Mary [surname lost], also of England. They came to Caspar in 1880 and engaged in ranching. They had eleven children: C.W. Mathews, J.W. Mathews of Fort Bragg, Mrs. Albert Eagles of Caspar, Mrs. Ben Larkin of Oakland [?], Leonard and Albert Mathews of Oakland. The widow also survived. The funeral was held at Caspar December 4th led by Rev. W.A. Chapman.

Dec 6, 1916

Rodney Mathews, age 3, the son of James Mathews, died January 19, 1917 of diptheria.

Jan 24, 1917

Walter Matson, 19, who accidentally shot himself August 20th, died September 5, 1919. The funeral September 7th was led by Rev. W.A. Chapman.

Sep 10, 1919

Sam Matthews, formerly of Mendocino County, died in Salinas, Monterey County, April 1, 1919.

Apr 9, 1919

Charles Mattila died January 15, 1919 "across Pudding Creek" from influenza. His wife and three children survived.

Jan 15, 1919

Deaths Reported	Issue Date
Isaac Mattila died June 22, 1912 at the age of 71. A nine year resident, his funeral was at Fort Bragg June 25th.	Jun 26, 1912
Victor Mattila died at Noyo May 4, 1919 at the age of 37 years 8 months and 6 days. He had operated the canning plant for two years. The funeral was held May 8, 1919 in Fort Bragg led by Rev.John J.Hillberg.	May 7, 1919
Andrew Mattson was killed at Westport August 12, 1910 when thrown from a wagon. He was 55 years old and left a wife and children.	Aug 17, 1910
Andrew Mauha died in Fort Bragg February 6, 1911 of pneumonia. The funeral was held there on the 10th.	Feb 8, 1911
Franklin P.May was killed February 18, 1915 on the Caspar railroad when he fell from the pilot of the locomotive and was run over by the train. A native of Iowa, he was a 30 year resident of the coast. He was 59 years 7 months and 7 days old at death. His wife and stepchildren survived.	Feb 24, 1915
Charles Mazzanti, a native of Italy, died at Ukiah May 2, 1912.	May 22, 1912
The five year old son of David McArthur died at Comptche August 2, 1911.	Aug 16, 1911
Albert McCabe [also reported as "Cave"] was shot and killed at Williams May 10, 1911. He formerly lived in Potter Valley. [A second item said he was a suicide.]	May 17, 1911
Mrs.McCallum, mother of John and Dan McCallum and a pioneer settler, died at Point Arena December 31, 1918. About 70 years old, her daughter was Mrs.Lyman of Vallejo.	Jan 1, 1919
Mrs.Eva McAbee McCanse, a graduate of the Ukiah highschool, died at Metropolis, Nevada "this week".	Dec 6, 1916
Marguerite McCanse, 14, the daughter of George McCanse of Greenwood, died there February 3, 1919 of influenza. Her funeral was held at Mendocino February 5th.	Feb 5, 1919
Mrs.Thomas McCarthy, formerly of Ukiah, died at LaMesa, San Diego County, on May 5, 1912.	May 22, 1912
William McCarthy Jr.died at Caspar June 15, 1912.	Jun 19, 1912
George McClain was killed in a handcar accident on the Greenwood railroad "last week". A pioneer in the area, he was 60 years old and a brother of Mrs.Henry of Fort Bragg.	Dec 17, 1913
Mrs.John W.McClellan, nee Lucy Michel, died at Bridgeville in Humboldt County January 26, 1919 from influenza. A native of Covelo, she was 40 years old.	Jan 29, 1919
George McClelland, about 65, died at Caspar March 28, 1917 of heart failure. A native of Michigan, he came to California in the early days, settling at Navarro and Caspar. After living for a time in Willits, he returned to Caspar in 1910. A wife and two sons, James and George McClelland of Oregon, survived. The funeral was April 1st led by Rev.W.A.Chapman.	Mar 28, 1917 Apr 4, 1917
Theresa F.McClelland died at McCloud, Siskiyou County, June 27, 1910 in childbirth. Her husband and two children survived. She was 33 years old. The funeral was held July 1, 1910 with the Rev.John Barrett officiating. Her mother and two brothers lived at Greenwood.	Jun 29, 1910 Jul 6, 1910
Mrs.Zila Elizabeth McClendon, 58, died March 17, 1913 at Ukiah of pneumonia. The funeral was held March 21st.	Mar 26, 1913

The eight year old son of N.T.McClure of Ukiah died in San
Francisco June 1, 1911 following an operation.

John McCornack, killed in a woods accident "last week",
was buried in Fort Bragg July 16, 1914.

Jul 22, 1914

Dr.William Andrew McCornack died in Oakland of heart
failure February 9, 1918. A pioneer doctor he had settled at
Littleriver about 45 years earlier and later moved to Mendocino and opened a hospital. In 1896 he moved to Fort Bragg
and founded a hospital there until finally moving to Oakland
in 1906. A native of Illinois, he was 70 years 4 months and
24 days old. The funeral was held in Oakland February 13th.
His wife, two daughters, Mrs.Edith Bigelow of Oakland, Mrs.
Emily Halliday of Portland, Oregon, and two sons, Alex of
Tuolumne and Roy McCornack of Shandon, California, survived.

Feb 13, 1918

John McDonald, 64, a pioneer rancher of Albion ridge, died
at the Alhambra Hotel in Mendocino of cancer. His wife, two
sons, John and Charles McDonald, and three daughters, Rose,
Lorne, and Forrest, survived. His funeral was held in
Mendocino October 26, 1916.

Oct 25, 1916
Nov 1, 1916

Mrs.John K.McDonald died near Caspar January 27, 1914 of
apparent heart failure.

Jan 28, 1914

Josephine Jean McDonald, the daughter of Edward McDonald,
died February 5, 1916 and was buried the next day.

Feb 9, 1916

James McDougall was shot and killed on his ranch in a
hunting accident by Frank Ferris July 11, 1913. A native of
Canada, he was about 53 years old. His aged mother, Mrs.Peter
McDougall of Santa Rosa, three sisters, Mrs.R.L.James of
Santa Rosa, Mrs.L.Campbell of Toledo, Oregon, Mrs.E.C.Kelson
of Santa Rosa, and two brothers, John McDougall of Washington
state, and W.S.McDougall of Santa Rosa, survived.

Jul 16, 1913

James McDowell, an old pioneer of Long Valley, died
December 8, 1910 at the age of 84.

Dec 14, 1910

Mrs.Pearl McEwen died of burns near Ukiah February 1, 1912.

Feb 7, 1912

Mrs.Sarah McFarland, a ten year resident of Ukiah, died
January 21, 1917. Her sister was Mrs.Randall.

Jan 24, 1917

Edson Jasper McFaul, 38, died February 21, 1916 at Fort
Bragg. Born in Littleriver, the family moved from Miller to
Hardy Creek in 1896. He lived most of his life at DeHaven.
A wife and two children survived. 3 brothers, Charles W.,
Arthur P., of Union Landing, and Wilson E.of Fort Bragg as
well as a twin sister, Stella (Mrs.Ed Dean of Fort Bragg),
survived. The funeral was held February 23rd led
by Rev.W.A.Chapman.

Feb 23, 1916

L.R.McFaul, 66, the brother of Charles McFaul of Union
Landing and an early day settler on the south coast, died
in San Francisco June 1, 1919. A native of Wisconsin, he
came to the coast in 1875 with his father and brother,
settling at Littleriver. He ranched for 20 years at
Bridgeport, Gualala and Stewart's Point.

Jun 4, 1919

Mrs.Mary Elizabeth McFaul, the wife of Charles A.McFaul,
died at Fort Bragg July 9, 1917. A native of Michigan, nee
Pond, she was 67 years 8 months and 11 days old. She came
to the coast about 1877, first to Bridgeport and then in
1899 to Union Landing. Her husband and three children
survived: Mrs.Ed Dean, William and Arthur McFaul. The
funeral was at Fort Bragg July 12th led by Rev.W.A.Chapman.

Jul 11, 1917

Mrs.Walter M.McGary, *nee* Susie Stoddard of Fort Bragg, died died suddenly at Lockford, San Joaquin County, February 28, 1917. The funeral was held in Fort Bragg March 4th led by Dr.Bryan. Born September 24, 1880 at Greenwood, she grew up in Fort Bragg, On April 15, 1903 she married Mr.McGary. Her husband and son, mother, Mrs.M.B. Stoddard, 4 sisters, Emily Rodgers of Fort Bragg, Ellen McKee of Stockton, Mabel Borges of San Francisco, Minnie Lilley of Andersonia, and a brother, E.T.Stoddard of Fort Bragg, survived.

Mar 7, 1917

Archie McGill died at Sanel [Hopland] May 20, 1911.

May 31, 1911

J.A.McGilvray, a former coast resident, died at Canyon City, Oregon, February 28, 1915 at age 69. A former timber cruiser, he had also served as a deputy sheriff.

Mar 3, 1915

Phocian McGimsey of Boonville was reported to be missing in action in France - August 1918.

Aug 21, 1918

Mrs.T.J.McGimsey, formerly of Ukiah, died in Sonoma "last week".

Dec 8, 1915

Mrs.McGough, a former resident of the Anderson Valley, died in San Francisco April 29, 1911.

May 10, 1911

Mrs.John McGough, formerly of Bridgeport, died in San Francisco "last week". She was about 50 years old and left a husband and three sons.

Aug 3, 1910

T.M.McGough, a former Ukiah resident, died of TB in San Francisco April 14, 1913.

Apr 23, 1913

Eugene McGowen, 23, died at Ukiah July 2, 1911.

Jul 19, 1911

Ruby McGuire, about 27, died at Ukiah December 24, 1911.

Dec 27, 1911

Alexander McIlree, a 20 year resident of the coast, died in Martinsburg, Iowa, August 29, 1913.

Oct 1, 1913

Henry J.McIntyre, 73, died at Oakland March 11, 1913. Born in New York, he was a prominent rancher at Cuffey's Cove. His widow, Mary E.McIntyre, survived.

Mar 19, 1913

Jim McKay, a pioneer woodsman, died November 2, 1918 at Ten Mile from influenza. He was over 60.

Nov 6, 1918

Frank H.McKee died at Shelter Cove April 18, 1910 of heart failure.

Apr 20, 1910

Dr.McKibbon, a dentist from Turlock, died suddenly at Point Arena August 23, 1916 from a ruptured appendix. His wife, nee Carrie Singley, survived.

Aug 30, 1916

William McKilva was shot and killed in a drunken row at Noyo May 6, 1915 when Antone Anderson fired an "unloaded" shotgun through a door which McKilva was attempting to break down. No relatives were found, and he was buried May 26th. Anderson was convicted of manslaughter June 9th and sentenced to four years in the San Quentin penitentiary.

May 12, 1915
May 26, 1915
Jun 2, 1915
Jun 16, 1915
Jun 23, 1915

Mrs.Robert McKindley died at Ukiah March 30, 1918. [Balance of text lost]. She was the aunt of the Dean brothers, Ed and Alfred.

Apr 3, 1918

Duncan McKinley, former congressman of the coast district (1904), died of apoplexy in San Francisco December 30, 1914. After his stint in Washington, he was appointed to the post of surveyor for the port of San Francisco in 1910.

Jan 6, 1915

Charity Eliza McKinna, 81, died April 3, 1919 near Willits. She had been a resident for 31 years.

Apr 9, 1919

Belle McKinney, nee Belle Hall of Fort Bragg, died in San   Sep 3, 1913
Francisco August 27, 1913. The funeral was September 3rd.

Robert McKinzie, a woodsman, was buried at Fort Bragg   Nov 6, 1912
November 1, 1912.

Daniel McLean of Upper Lake died in a team runaway accident   Oct 16, 1912
October 14, 1912.

Oliver McLeod drowned in San Francisco Bay the "first of   Oct 30, 1918
last week". Born in Mendocino he was an employee on a ferry-
boat when he fell into the bay. His wife and sister, Mrs.
W.B.Gorman, survived.

James McMahon, the third cook at Mendocino State Hospital,   Jan 13, 1915
died January 4, 1915.

Patrick McManus, Sr. of Caspar died August 7, 1914. The   Aug 12, 1914
funeral was held in Mendocino August 10th. A daughter and
son survived.

George McMaster of Caspar died January 20, 1919 in Fort   Jan 22, 1919
Bragg. The funeral was to be held January 25th.

V.C.McMurry, about 55, dropped dead March 19, 1918 at Ten   Mar 20, 1918
Mile from heart failure. He had been employed there for
three months. A wife and family in Sacramento survived.
The body was shipped to Napa.

Mrs.Alice McNamara, the widow of Patrick McNamara who was   Dec 24, 1919
killed many years ago in a fall at the Mendocino mill, died
in San Francisco "last week" at the age of 75.

Mary McNamarra , 35 years of age, died in San Francisco   Jul 27, 1910
"last week". Burial was at Westport July 18, 1910.

Allie McNeil of Point Arena died at Healdsburg   Jul 20, 1910
July 13, 1910.

J.McNeil, a former resident of Point Arena, died at Newport,   Dec 25, 1918
Oregon, December 5, 1918 while in government employment.
Born at Point Arena March 8, 1887, the son of Ollie McNeil,
he left a wife, three small children, mother, sister and
three brothers.

Mrs.Justin McNeil died December 8, 1918 at Freemont [sic],   Jan 15, 1919
Oregon. Her husband died December 5th. Three small children
were orphaned.

J.H.McPeak, 83, a pioneer Ukiah resident, died in Santa Rosa   Mar 26, 1913
[date not reported]. His daughter, Mrs.McKinley, survived.

Mrs.J.H.McPeak, 75, died January 12, 1913. She came to Ukiah   Jan 22, 1913
in 1875 and was the mother of eight children, six of whom
survived. Her husband and three sisters: Mrs.King of Willits,
Mrs.Mahon of Los Angeles and Mrs.LeSieuer of Oregon survived.
The funeral was held on January 13th.

J.L.McPherson, about 55, was a suicide at Ukiah   Jun 16, 1915
June 14, 1915.

Martin McPherson died at Ukiah February 14, 1912.   Feb 28, 1912
A native of Scotland, he was 69 years old.

Mrs.Mary J.McRay died at Kibesillah June 23, 1911 and was   Jun 28, 1911
buried at Newport June 25, 1911. Born in Missouri April 1,
1858, she came to California with her parents, Mr.& Mrs.
Anderson, who settled at Cuffey's Cove in 1859. They moved
to Kibesillah about 1869. She married and had 12 children,
seven of which survived her.

Albert Mead died June 29, 1913 at Coyote Valley near Ukiah.   Jul 2, 1913

Mrs.I.Meador died at Ukiah October 23, 1910.   Oct 26, 1910

Mrs.J.D.Mecum, *nee* Sarah Ann Pope, died at East Mendocino   Jan 7, 1914
December 27, 1913. Born in New York in 1848, she was 65
years old. She married a Mr.Henderson and had a son who died
in 1912 of TB. She married again in 1880 and was J.D.Mecum's
second wife. Mecum died in 1903. A stepson, Stephen Mecum
survived. The funeral was held January 4, 1914.

George Meditz cut his throat at Willits September 2, 1913.   Sep 10, 1913

Elizabeth Meech died October 25, 1910. Born 67 years ago in   Oct 26, 1910
Connecticut, she lived on the coast for 24 years. A son,
Ervin Meech, and a daughter, Mrs.Scott, survived.

Eugene Meehan, a former Fort Bragg resident, died at   Jan 31, 1912
Burlingame January 27, 1912. Burial was in San Mateo.

Richard Mehtlan, 57, died November 19, 1917 at Boyle's Camp   Nov 21, 1917
on Big River from heart failure. A 35 year resident, he came
to Fort Bragg in 1895. His wife and nine children survived:
Aner, Otto, Charles, Ben, Lempie, Nan, Mary, Mamie and Millie
Mehtlan. The funeral was at Fort Bragg November 21, 1917.

Ben Melton, 52, died in San Francisco May 5, 1914. Mother,   May 6, 1914
Mrs.Thompson, a daughter, two brothers: Robert and William
Melton, and two sisters survived. The funeral was May 10th.

Joseph Melvis, father of Mrs.F.Rowland, died near Ukiah   Feb 19, 1913
February 12, 1913 at age 62.

D.Merga, 46, died January 8, 1914 of heart failure. He was   Jan 14, 1914
a 13 year coast resident. Catholic rites were held by
Father Lawrence January 11th.

Charles Merrill, who lived near Mendocino, was a suicide.   Feb 14, 1912
His body was recovered February 13, 1912. A native of   Feb 21, 1912
Maine, he came to California in 1874 and worked as a
woodsman. He was 62.

Rev.Richard Messenger died at Alameda and was buried on   Jun 28, 1916
June 25, 1916. Born in Berkshire, England, in 1842, he came
to Canada and, in 1888, to California where he held pastorates
in Navarro, Fort Bragg, Healdsburg, Roseville and Greenville.

Oliver Meyers, a former Hopland resident, died in   May 20, 1914
San Francisco May 18, 1914.

G.C.Meyser was killed when a boulder fell on the caboose of   May 14, 1913
a Northwestern Pacific Railroad train near Dos Rios
May 10, 1913.

John Michaelson, 50, section boss on the Albion railroad,   Aug 4, 1915
was killed in an automobile accident near Melburne August 1,
1915. Riding as a passenger, he unaccountably grabbed the
steering wheel causing the car to turn over.

John Michaelson was struck and killed by a falling limb in   Aug 13, 1919
the woods at Ten Mile August 12, 1919.

Francisco Michetti died at Albion March 17, 1913.   Mar 26, 1913

Mary A.Millar, a Fort Bragg resident until 1911, died in San   Mar 19, 1913
Francisco March 11, 1913. A recent resident of Ross in Marin
County, she was born in Dundee, Scotland, December 27, 1869,
and came to the U.S.in 1872 with her parents. Three brothers:
Dave, George and James Millar of Fort Bragg, and two sisters,
Mrs.H.B.Simpson and Mrs.Lillian McCullough of San Francisco,
survived. Cremation occured March 15th.

Albert Miller, injured by a log at Boyle's camp on Big River   Oct 16, 1912
October 9, 1912, died the next day. He was a native German.

Mrs.Carrie Miller, the wife of George Miller of Point Arena, died on board the steamer *Sea Foam* in heavy weather off Point Arena March 4, 1916. She was 67 years old and suffered a heart attack.   Mar 8, 1916

Elisha Miller died at Fort Bragg June 19, 1916. He was 72 years and 10 months old. Born in Illinois, he was a California resident for 50 years and ran the harness shop in the Pioneer Livery stable. The funeral was held June 21st led by Rev.W.A.Chapman.   Jun 21, 1916

Elisha B.Miller of Ukiah died from wounds received in battle in France [no date reported].   Nov 13, 1918

Mrs.J.M.Miller died at Westport January 29, 1912. Her husband, daughter and three sons survived. A native of Denmark, she was 51 years old. Rev.W.A.Chapman led the funeral January 30th.   Feb 14, 1912

Jack Miller was killed when the stage he was driving ran away and overturned at the railhead in Willits. The body was shipped to San Francisco. [No date reported].   Jun 22, 1910

John Miller, 67, was found dead at McNutt's camp near Willits February 5, 1912. The cause of death was pneumonia.   Feb 7, 1912

R.Miller, formerly of Ukiah, was killed at Coalinga, Fresno County, June 21, 1912 in an oil field accident.   Jul 10, 1912

Mrs.Rose A.Miller died near Point Arena June 15, 1919. The mother of Charles Ledford, she was a California resident for 29 years.   Jun 25, 1919

Newell Milliken, a native of Mendocino, died suddenly at Claremont, Los Angeles County, August 17, 1919. His daughter, Ruth Milliken, was a teacher in the local highschool.   Aug 20, 1919

Benjamin Mills, a Civil War veteran formerly of Point Arena, died in the Soldier's Home at Yountville October 14, 1912.   Oct 23, 1912

S.D.Mills, aged 76, died at Yorkville of heart failure [no date reported].   Jun 21, 1911

Mrs.John Minton, 92, died at Willits January 6, 1914. She was a California resident for 26 years.   Jan 14, 1914

Ebenezar Mitchell died at DeHaven May 9, 1918 of cancer. His funeral was May 10th with Rev.Schnall presiding. A widow and children survived.   May 15, 1918

T.R.Mockler, a Ukiah attorney for three years, died there November 27, 1918. He was 56. A wife and two sons survived.   Dec 4, 1918

George Monroe received a fatal fracture to his skull when horse was frightened by an automobile, bolted and became entangled in its lines, falling on him, near Mitchell Creek October 15, 1916. Born in Washington July 27, 1872, he came to California with his parents in the same year. His wife, two daughters: Mrs.Henry Madsen and Mrs.Alice Reed, a brother, John Monroe, survived. The funeral was held at the Presbyterian church in Fort Bragg October 21st.   Oct 18, 1916
                                    Oct 25, 1916

Peter Monson, an old time resident of Fort Bragg, died January 18, 1912 at the age of 67. His wife and several children survived. The funeral was held at the Baptist church January 20th.   Jan 24, 1912

Vinenzo Montini, an Italian aged 19, died in Fort Bragg February 10, 1911. The funeral was held on February 12th.   Feb 15, 1911

L.A.Moody of Moody, died at Santa Rosa March 30, 1912.   Apr 3, 1912

The 2 year old son of Clarence <u>Moore</u> of Sausalito died of   Jul 12, 1911
scalds on a camping trip near Branscomb July 8, 1911.

Nathan A.<u>Moore</u> died at Point Arena July 21, 1913.   Jul 30, 1913

Mrs.Reuben <u>Moore</u> died at Ukiah January 29, 1914. She had   Feb 4, 1914
been a resident since 1856.

Thomas <u>Moorehead</u>, 87, died at Santa Rosa [no date reported].   Jan 10, 1917
A son, A.E.Moorehead of Ukiah, survived.

Lewis <u>Moran</u> was crushed to death at Caspar by a log at the   Aug 14, 1912
log dump August 10, 1912. Born and raised at Caspar, the
funeral was held there August 12th.

Charles <u>Morand</u>, born in Caspar in 1873, died there March 30,   Apr 2, 1913
1913 of TB. His wife and one child survived. Catholic rites
were held in Mendocino April 2nd.

Mrs.Elizabeth <u>Morand</u>, 70, died November 5, 1914 "back of   Nov 11, 1914
Noyo". The funeral was held at Mendocino November 7th.

Hugh <u>Morehead</u>, formerly of Ukiah Valley, died "last week".   Aug 27, 1913

Jose J.<u>Mores</u>, Portuguese about 25 years old, was killed when   Oct 18, 1911
riding on a locomotive. A log car behind the engine derailed
causing a log to slide forward and crush him. He had been in
the county about five months.

Mrs.Mary J.<u>Moriarty</u>, wife of Daniel Moriarty, a former Fort   May 8, 1912
Bragg resident, died at Oakland April 30, 1912.

John C.<u>Morley</u>, 57, died at Santa Rosa March 27, 1919. A   Apr 2, 1919
six year resident of Fort Bragg, his son, Albert Morley of
that city, survived.

John Wesley "Curley" <u>Morris</u>, 41, was killed at Glen Blair   Nov 20, 1918
November 15, 1918 when run over by a locomotive. He had been
a long time coast resident.

The infant child of Mr.& Mrs.Frank <u>Morrison</u> of Inglenook   Jun 15, 1910
died June 8, 1910 at the age of 1 month and 19 days.

E.L.<u>Morrison</u> died at Ukiah February 16, 1910.   Feb 23, 1910
He was born in Walker Valley in 1880.

Ed <u>Morrison</u>, the brother of Mrs.Anna Morrison Reid and well   Sep 7, 1910
known on the coast, died in Oroville, Butte County, "last
week" at the age of 53.

Mrs.Mattie <u>Morrison</u>, a pioneer of Ukiah and the former wife   Sep 17, 1913
of Dr.Pressy who practiced there 40 years earlier, died at
San Francisco September 3, 1913 at age 68, burial in Ukiah.

J.B.<u>Morse</u>, an old resident of Ukiah, died January 11, 1912.   Jan 17, 1912

Mrs.<u>Morton</u>, mother of Mrs.Swales and sister of Mrs.Huggins   May 8, 1912
of Fort Bragg, died in San Francisco May 5, 1912. She was
the wife of Professor Frank W.Morton, the educator.

Dick <u>Moseberger</u> of Crockett, the son-in-law of W.T.Saxon,   Aug 6, 1919
fell from a cliff near Laurel Dell, Lake County, on August 3,
1919 and sustained fatal injuries. He left a wife and two
small children.

Tom <u>Mosher</u>, 57, dropped dead of heart failure in a new   Aug 9, 1911
Wages Creek saloon August 3, 1911. A pioneer settler of the
coast, he was a timber cruiser based in Albion. The funeral
was held in Fort Bragg August 6, 1911 led by Rev.J.C.Garth.

Mrs.Catherine A.<u>Moss</u>, 81, died January 6, 1919 in Fort   Jan 8, 1919
Bragg. She had lived on a ranch north of Cleone many years.   Jan 15, 1919

Mrs.Anna Moungovan, a 30 year resident of Point Arena,   Aug 20, 1919
died August 15, 1919. She was 58 years old.

Andrew Munroe died at the State Hospital in Ukiah   Feb 8, 1911
January 25, 1911.

P.Murphy was striken with sunstroke in the woods and died   Jun 4, 1913
on the train to Fort Bragg May 31, 1913. He had arrived from
San Francisco on May 29th and begun work on May 30th.

Patrick S.Murphy, 61, died at Ukiah April 24, 1919. About   Apr 30, 1919
1892 he ran a cigar factory at Fort Bragg and then went
ranching in the Potter Valley until 1913 when he moved to
Willits.

R.P.Murphy died in the Greenwood woods of heart failure   Dec 8, 1915
December 2, 1915.

Mrs.T.F.Murphy died at Fort Bragg March 19, 1911. She was   Mar 22, 1911
79 years 11 months and 17 days old. Catholic rites were
held March 21st by Father Brennan. She was born in Wales
and came to the U.S.with her parents in 1861 settling
first in Scranton and later in Danville, both in Pennsylvania. In 1863 they moved to Buffalo, New York and
returned to Danville where they stayed from 1865 to 1875
coming to California in July with her husband. They first
lived at Elk Creek, then Newport, Bear Harbor, Westport
and moved to Fort Bragg about 1908. Two daughters: Mrs.
Charles Murray of Willits and Mrs.Frank Wegner of Fort
Bragg, and three sons: Jerry, Tim and John Murphy, survived.

Carl Murray died at Mendocino January 19, 1917. Born and   Jan 24, 1917
raised in Mendocino, he had worked in San Francisco for some
time and returned to the coast for health reasons, working
at the Mendocino *Beacon* newspaper. A sister, Mrs.Susie Taft
of Oakland, and brother, John Murray of Mendocino, survived.
Catholic services were held in Mendocino January 21, 1917.

Charles Murray, a former Glen Blair resident, died at   Feb 26, 1913
Santa Rosa February 20, 1913.

Dayton Murray, a native of Mendocino 29 years old, died at   Apr 12, 1911
San Leandro April 4, 1911 of pneumonia. He was a brother of
J.P.Murray of Mendocino.

Mrs.Isaac Murray died at Willits July 5, 1913.   Jul 16, 1913
She was 31 years and 11 months old.

Timothy Murray, 77, died in Sonora May 6, 1915. He had lived May 12, 1915
in Mendocino, Fort Bragg and Littleriver for many years.

The infant son of D.Myers died at Willits July 28, 1913.   Aug 6, 1913

Edwin P.Myers, the brother of Mrs.Ben Byrnes of Fort Bragg,   Mar 12, 1919
died at Colorado Springs, Colorado, March 3, 1919. The son
of Mrs.F.C.Handy of Ukiah, he was born at Littleriver
June 21, 1885.

Mrs.Elmer Myers, 18 years and 4 months of age, died at   Sep 3, 1913
Willits August 27, 1913.

John B.Myring died December 21, 1910.   Jan 5, 1910

Laura Ivy Myring, the 2 year old daughter of J.L.Myring,   Oct 15, 1913
died at Albion ridge "last week".

Erich Nabb died December 25, 1910 in Fort Bragg and was   Dec 28, 1910
buried on the 27th.

E.Nanni was killed in the Albion woods March 8, 1919 when a   Mar 12, 1919
log rolled over him.

Isabelle Neal, 15, the daughter of Mrs.Beamer, died in Fort Bragg January 15, 1919 from influenza. — Jan 15, 1919

Sam Neal, an old Potter Valley resident, died May 28, 1911. — May 31, 1911

Richard Neckritz, a rancher 61 years old, died near Albion January 9, 1914. — Jan 21, 1914

The seven year old daughter of Mr.& Mrs.Neighbor died at Hearst October 29, 1910. — Nov 9, 1910

Mr.Nelson died in the lumber yard at Albion May 17, 1914. — May 20, 1914

The three year old son of Nelson fell into scalding hot wash water and subsequently died - on Elk Creek "this week". — Jan 26, 1916

Alfred Nelson died at Mendocino July 14, 1911. A sawyer by trade and a pioneer settler, he was born in Oldtown, Maine, June 17, 1842. He served as deputy sheriff and constable. He married Catherine O'Meara April 14, 1867 and was the father of six children, two of whom survived: Mrs.George Lammers and Mrs.Joseph Nichols. — Jul 19, 1911

Amelia Nelson died in San Francisco hospital June 25, 1918. A son, C.L.Berry, three daughters, Mrs.J.P.Harvey, Mrs.T.H. Dunn and Mrs.F.O.Knacke, survived. Her funeral was at Mendocino June 27th. — Jul 3, 1918

Christopher Nelson died at Greenwood December 13, 1915. A native of Norway, he was 55 years old. His wife and two sons survived. — Dec 22, 1915

Erick Nelson, a Noyo fisherman, was shot and killed by Phil Roselle February 2, 1912. The funeral was February 5th. — Feb 7, 1912 / Feb 14, 1912 / Feb 21, 1912

John Nelson, aged 68, died at Ukiah July 11, 1911. — Jul 19, 1911

Justin Nelson, 27, died at Mendocino July 10, 1917. He was born and raised at Mendocino. The funeral was July 13th. — Jul 18, 1917

Peter Emil Nelson, coast woodsman, drowned in a ditch February 20, 1919. He was under the influence of strong drink and fell into the ditch when on the way home. A native of Sweden, he was 49 years old and a resident for 13 years. — Feb 26, 1919

R.F.Nelson, 31 year resident of Little Lake Road, burned to death in his cabin sometime "last week". Unmarried, he was a native of Denmark about 55 years old. The remains were buried at Mendocino after the inquest. — Nov 23, 1910

Frank Nenicco, Italian, was found dead in the Longvale tunnel 9 miles north of Willits August 4, 1912. — Aug 7, 1912

Samuel Nesbitt, the night watchman at Willits, died October 22, 1918 from influenza. — Oct 30, 1918

Arthur Ness, formerly of Point Arena, was reported killed in France. He arrived home safely in May 1919. — Apr 30, 1919 / Jun 4, 1919

John Ness died of stomach cancer March 8, 1913. He came to California 35 years earlier and settled north of Fort Bragg in 1910. He was 55 years 4 months and 11 days old. A wife and three sons survived. The funeral was held at the Presbyterian church by Rev.R.C.Grace March 11th. — Mar 12, 1913

Mrs.Nestell of Fort Bragg, 56, was a suicide January 2, 1912. The funeral was held January 4th. — Jan 3, 1912

J.S.Neto died "last week" at Mendocino at the age of 68. A son, Dr.J.R.Neto of Oakland and two stepsons, J.L.Armas of San Francisco and R.R.Armas of Mendocino survived. — Jul 24, 1912

Deaths Reported	Issue Date

H.L.Nevin died at Wendling of diptheria "last week".   Nov 23, 1910

Elizabeth Newman, 85, died at the State Hospital at   Sep 10, 1913
Talmage August 25, 1913. Catholic rites were held in Ukiah
August 29th by Father Brennen.

Mrs.John Newman, the daughter of Robert Dartt of Bridgeport,   Nov 14, 1917
died in Berkeley "recently". She was 32.

Matt Newman was killed in a woods accident near Caspar. Born   Nov 17, 1915
on Noyo Hill, he was 25 years old.

The daughter of Otto Newman died "last week". The family   Nov 12, 1913
lived between Wendling and Comptche.

H.Newton fell off the rocks at Caspar while fishing and   Nov 7, 1917
drowned November 4, 1917. He was a carpenter by trade and
about 50 years old.

William N.Newton, 37 and a machinist at Caspar, died from   Jan 15, 1919
influenza January 12, 1919. He left a widow and two small
children. Masonic rites were held in Mendocino January 14th.

James Albert Nichols, formerly of Mendocino, died at Oakland   Nov 13, 1918
November 10, 1918 from influenza. A native of Maine, he was
70 years 9 months and 15 days old. A veteran of the Civil
War, he worked in the woods at Mendocino becoming superintendent of the Mendocino Lumber Company. Later he operated a
store and moved to Mendocino in 1916. He married Katie
Carlson, the daughter of J.E.Carlson. On October 15, 1879
he served on the posse that pursued an outlaw gang and was
wounded when posse members William Wright and Thomas Dollard
were killed. His wife, two children, Edith and Herbert
Nichols, survived. A brother, Joseph Nichols of Mendocino
also survived. His funeral was held at Oakland November 12th.

Joseph Frances Nichols, 22, of Mendocino was killed in   Oct 30, 1918
action in France September 29, 1918. He was the first
Mendocino County boy killed in battle.

Mrs.J.W."Grandma" Nicholson died March 28, 1917 in Fort   Mar 28, 1917
Bragg. Born April 10, 1832 in Indiana, she married at age 22
to the late J.W.Nicholson and lived in Illinois for 15 years.
They then came to California and settled first in Santa Rosa
and, later, in Inglenook and Fort Bragg. Survivors included
a son, William Nicholson of Fort Bragg, and a daughter, Mrs.
Ben Jarvis of San Francisco.

The young son of Conrad Nicks died March 7, 1912 at Point   Mar 13, 1912
Arena of pneumonia.

Joseph Nicols, about 47, died November 4, 1919 at Mendocino.   Nov 5, 1919
He ran an icecream parlor and motion picture show. His wife
and eight children survived: Ardelle, Jessie, Naomi, George,
Alfred, Grace, Laura and a baby. Rev.Ingram conducted the
funeral at Mendocino's Presbyterian church November 6th.

Issac Niemi, 65, was crushed by a log in the Ten Mile woods   Dec 26, 1917
December 21, 1917. A native of Finland, his son, Manuel
Niemi, of Fort Bragg survived. The funeral was held in Fort
Bragg December 23rd with Rev.John J.Hillberg officiating.

Oscar Niemi, 55, died in Fort Bragg June 8, 1919. A native   Jun 11, 1919
Sweden, he was a 27 year resident. The funeral was held
June 9th under Rev.J.J.Hillberg's direction.

William Nissen, a 41 year resident of Point Arena, died   Aug 26, 1914
there August 20, 1914. Born in Copenhagen, Denmark, in 1838,
he left a wife, daughter and six sons.

Mrs.L.L.Noble died at Ukiah November 23, 1911. She was born   Dec 6, 1911
New York in 1838.

Mrs.M.M.Nobles, almost 86, died November 4, 1914. She came   Nov 11, 1914
to California in 1853. A husband and eight children survived.
The funeral was held November 6th.

Marion M.Nobles, 78, a resident of Point Arena, died of   Feb 21, 1917
pneumonia while on a visit to Palo Alto February 17, 1917.

Yell Nobles was killed in a team runaway accident near   Mar 23, 1910
Ukiah March 19, 1910.

Mrs.Millard Nolan of Caspar, nee Bertha Brinzing of Pine   Dec 24, 1913
Grove, suddenly died December 21, 1913 of pneumonia. She   Dec 31, 1913
was 25 years 3 months and 21 days old. [She married Millard Nolan
October 12, 1912.] The funeral was held in Caspar December 22nd
led by Rev.Hargreaves and Rev.Fisher with burial in Fort Bragg.

Mrs.Nancy Jane Nonis, 80, died February 12, 1919 at Ukiah   Feb 19, 1919
where she had been a 30 year resident.

The two year old son of Mrs.John Norbeck died February 4,   Feb 6, 1918
1918. The funeral was held at Fort Bragg February 5th.

The infant son of J.E.Norberry of Mendocino died and was   Oct 1, 1913
buried September 29, 1913.

Charles Norberry, about 42, died at Coquille, Oregon,   Nov 27, 1918
"several days ago". His wife and two children in Fort Bragg
survived. His brothers were Charles and John Norberry. He
was buried at Littleriver.

Mrs.Emily Noyer, the daughter of Manuel Perreria of Mendo-   Nov 6, 1918
cino died at Antioch November 1, 1918 from influenza. Her
husband and two children survived.

Joseph G.Noyo, a native of the Azores aged 24, died in Fort   Jun 23, 1915
Bragg June 17, 1915 from injuries received in an accident
in the Caspar woods when he was jammed between a railroad
car and a log landing. Catholic rites were held June 20th.

Evelyn Ruth Nurnberger died February 20, 1913 of typhoid.   Feb 25, 1914
She was 4 years old and lived east of Fort Bragg with her
family who had been there about a year. The funeral was held
at the Presbyterian church February 22nd led by Rev.R.C.Grace.

Herman Nygard, 59, died July 13, 1911 of stomach cancer.   Jul 19, 1911
Born in Finland, he was a resident of the state for 22 years.
The funeral was July 16th led by Rev.R.C.Grace. A daughter,
Mrs.Ness, survived.

John Alexander Nylund, a carpenter for 17 years at Fort   Aug 27, 1919
Bragg, died August 22, 1919. A native of Finland, he was
54 years 9 months and 26 days old. The funeral was held in
Fort Bragg August 24th led by Rev.Itanen.

Maurice F.O'Brien died October 23, 1919 in Fort Bragg of   Oct 29, 1919
acute jaundice. A native of Elizabeth, New Jersey, and a   Nov 5, 1919
woods worker, he was buried with Catholic rites at Fort B
ragg October 31st.

Timothy O'Connor, a pioneer and former resident of Fort   Feb 11, 1914
Bragg, died in San Francisco February 11, 1914. He had
worked in the mills on the coast until 1899 when he retired
and moved to San Francisco.

Thomas O'Grady, 70, died at the State Hospital in Talmage   Nov 10, 1915
"last week".

John S.O'Neil died September 14, 1914 at Ukiah. Born in   Sep 23, 1914
Australia June 21, 1842, he came to California as a baby in
1844 and, later, came to Mendocino County in 1856 settling
at Round Valley. He moved to Ukiah in 1902. A daughter,
Mrs.J.H.Laughlin of Ukiah, survived.

Charles <u>Ohlson</u>, 50, died at Fort Bragg October 14, 1918.   Oct 16, 1918
A native of Sweden, he had been a 30 year resident. He was
buried October 15th at Fort Bragg.

Emil <u>Ohlson</u> died June 30, 1912 while hunting on Ten Mile   Jul 3, 1912
River. A native of Sweden, he was 42 years and four months
old and a resident of Fort Bragg for 20 years. A wife and
three children survived. The funeral was held in Fort Bragg
July 3rd with Rev.R.C.Grace officiating.

Frank <u>Olds</u>, an old settler at Fort Bragg, died at Ukiah   Apr 24, 1918
"last week".

Mrs.Frank <u>Olds</u> died at Fort Bragg September 29, 1912. The   Oct 2, 1912
funeral was held at the Baptist church in Fort Bragg
October 1st with burial in Mendocino.

Walter <u>Olney</u> died at Gibbs' tie camp at Sherwood   Mar 19, 1913
March 14, 1913.

Mrs.Margaret <u>Olsen</u> died at Point Arena October 5, 1914. A   Oct 10, 1914
native of England, she was about 80 years old. The funeral
was held October 7th.

Mrs.A.<u>Olson</u> died at Point Arena January 31, 1918. Seven   Feb 6, 1918
children survived.

Ben <u>Olson</u> of Inglenook, 58, died December 24, 1916 in Fort   Dec 27, 1916
Bragg of peritonitis. A native of Sweden, he was a 29 year   Jan 3, 1917
resident. The funeral was held December 26th at the
Inglenook school with Rev.W.A.Chapman officiating.

John <u>Olson</u>, a brick mason of Fort Bragg, died in the County   Jul 2, 1913
Hospital at Talmage June 29, 1913.

Mrs.I.<u>Onyon</u>, *nee* Hattie Powell, died in Burlingame "last   Jun 19, 1918
week". She grew up in Fort Bragg. Five children survived.

W.H.<u>Oppenlander</u> Jr., the son of W.H.Oppenlander of   Apr 9, 1913
Comptche, died April 6, 1913.

Ed <u>Ordway</u>, 45, died at Petaluma January 3, 1919 of Bright's   Jan 8, 1919
disease. He ran the Union Lumber Company's ranch for 12 years
and later went into a meat and stock raising business with
his brother, Ira Ordway of Willits. His wife and 3 children
survived. The funeral was in Petaluma January 6th.

Miss Jesse <u>Orr</u>, 18, the daughter Thomas Orr, died in Fort   Sep 9, 1914
Bragg September 5, 1914 of typhoid. The funeral was
September 7th with Dr.Graham presiding.

S.M.<u>Orr</u> died near Calpella June 4, 1910.   Jun 8, 1910

Mrs.Will <u>Orr</u>, the wife of a rancher, died of influenza at   Oct 23, 1918
Redwood Valley October 18, 1918.

Mrs.Mathilda <u>Osborn</u>, 56, died at the State Hospital   Oct 25, 1916
October 19, 1916. She had been an employee there for 22 years.

Miss Clara <u>Osborne</u> died at Ukiah January 9, 1911.   Jan 18, 1911

Violet <u>Osborne</u>, the infant daughter of Joaquin Osborne, died   Nov 6, 1918
at Mendocino November 4, 1918 from influenza. Catholic rites
were held in Mendocino November 5th.

Mrs.Carl <u>Osimaa</u>, 74, died at Noyo December 7, 1913. Born in   Dec 10, 1913
Kentucky, she lived in California 50 years. She was the
former Mrs.Saye of Fort Bragg. The funeral was held in Fort
Bragg December 9th with Rev.W.A.Chapman presiding.

Ole <u>Oss</u>, a laborer on the Northwestern Pacific Railroad   May 19, 1915
extension, was killed by a landslide "last week".

Mrs.Lenora <u>Overmeyer</u>, a long time Ukiah resident, died   Sep 19, 1917
there September 10, 1917.

C.E.<u>Owens</u> died at Ukiah February 17, 1911. He was born in   Mar 1, 1911
Virginia September 28, 1837.

Walter V.<u>Owens</u> of Caspar died January 12, 1918 in Fort   Jan 16, 1918
Bragg. Born at Salmon Creek, he was raised on the coast and   Jan 23, 1918
worked with his father in the shingle mill at Caspar for
20 years. He was 34 years 9 months and 6 days old. His
parents, brothers, Ray, Ed and Cecil Owens, sister, Mrs.
H.L.Long of the British East Indies, survived. His funeral
was held in Fort Bragg January 13th.

C.O.<u>Packard</u>, a pioneer druggist of Mendocino, died there   Jun 13, 1917
June 8, 1917. A native of Maine, he was 69 years old and
had lived in Mendocino 48 years. He purchased the drugstore
in 1878. A wife and six children survived: Mrs.J.Salvador,
George Calvert and Hazel Packard of Mendocino, Harold C.,
Mrs.G.N.Rouse and Mrs.W.L.Clyme of Portland, Oregon. Two
brothers, Justin E.Packard of Augusta, Maine, and George
E.Packard of Seattle, Washington, also lived. His funeral
was held in Mendocino June 10th.

Charles Wilfred <u>Packard</u> died at Mendocino November 11, 1911   Nov 15, 1911
of tuberculosis contracted when working in Oregon. He was
20 years old. Five sisters and two brothers survived. The
funeral was held November 13th.

Hannah May <u>Packard</u>, the daughter of C.O.Packard of Mendo-   Jun 23, 1915
cino, died June 18, 1915 at the age of 26.

Mrs.George <u>Paddleford</u>, formerly of Mendocino, died in   Nov 3, 1915
Los Angeles [no date reported].

Mrs.M.J.<u>Paddleford</u> died September 3, 1917 in a San Franciso   Sep 12, 1917
hospital. A resident of Mendocino for 20 years, she was the
sister of John Walsh of that place. Her husband, daughter,
Nettie, and two sons, Almon and George Paddleford, survived.
The funeral was held in San Francisco September 5th.

Mr.<u>Palfarro</u>, an Italian, was killed in the Caspar woods by   Jun 11, 1919
a rolling log June 9, 1919.

P.<u>Paporn</u>, an Italian brakeman on the Northwestern Pacific   Nov 23, 1910
Railroad, was killed at Echo Station November 14, 1910 by
a southbound train.

Fernando <u>Pardini</u> drowned in Noyo Harbor when fishing on   Jan 3, 1917
December 31, 1916. The body was not recovered. [Age lost].

Freeman <u>Parker</u> and Joe Saunders were killed in an automobile   Sep 30, 1914
accident near Ukiah September 29, 1914.

Mrs.Ira (Josephine) <u>Parrish</u> died near Noyo June 6, 1914.   Jun 10, 1914
About 26 years old, she was born and raised at Noyo.

W.E.<u>Parsons</u>, 86, a Hopland rancher for 52 years, was struck   Mar 11, 1914
killed by an automobile in Santa Rosa "last week".

John <u>Paul</u>, formerly of Garcia, died in San Francisco   Dec 18, 1918
November 21, 1918. He had been a blacksmith on the south
coast for a number of years.

Dave <u>Paxton</u> died at Ukiah in November 1916 [exact date   Dec 6, 1916
indeterminate]. He was a 30 year resident.

William <u>Payne</u>, the father of the late Mrs.W.A.Chapman, died   Jan 21, 1914
in Boston, England, January 2, 1914.

H.A.<u>Peabody</u>, former editor of the Ukiah *Dispatch*, died at   Jun 9, 1915
Santa Ana April 24, 1915.

The thirteen year old son of J.Peacock died at Willits   Jan 18, 1911
January 6, 1911.

George Pease died at Fort Bragg of a paralytic stroke   Apr 24, 1918
April 19, 1918. He was 72 years and 9 months old. His wife
died on April 11th. A native of New York, he came to California about 1878 settling at Littleriver and Mendocino. His
wife had died April 11, 1918. His funeral was held as a
double ceremony with burial at Littleriver.

Mrs.George Pease died at Mendocino April 11, 1918.   Apr 17, 1918
She came to California in 1872, the daughter of   Apr 24, 1918
Alfred Gowell, settling at Littleriver. Her father,
husband, George Pease, and two brothers, Alfred
Gowell of Ukiah and Park Gowell of Klamath Falls,
Oregon, survived. The funeral was held April 16th
at Mendocino with burial at Littleriver. The next
week on April 21st her husband's funeral was held
with interment as a double ceremony.

Philander W.Peck died at Greenwood, New York, July 13, 1914.   Aug 12, 1914
His son, Joe Peck of Fort Bragg, survived.

Charles Pedrotti, 55, died at Richmond May 24, 1918 of heart   Jun 5, 1918
failure. He once ran a hotel at Fort Bragg. Three children
survived. The funeral was held at Fort Bragg May 28, 1918.

Mrs.C.Pedrotti, about 40, died at Richmond February 1, 1916.   Feb 9, 1916
Her husband, two sons and a daughter survived.

Mrs.H.J.Peirsol died at Oakland September 1, 1916.   Sep 6, 1916

Joe Peletti, an Italian woodsman, cut his throat   Feb 20, 1918
February 15, 1918 near Greenwood after receiving a letter
containing the news that his brother had been killed in
battle in Europe. His funeral was at Greenwood February 17th.

John Peltoma, 46, died at Fort Bragg April 13, 1913. He was   Apr 16, 1913
an 18 year resident of Fort Bragg. A wife and daughter in
Finland survived. The funeral was held April 16th.

Pete Pennche, brakeman on a log train at Wendling was killed   Apr 29, 1914
when run over by the train April 23, 1914. A native of
Italy, his funeral was conducted by Father Lawrence.

Mrs.Minerva Pennell, a resident of Redwood Valley   Nov 19, 1913
aged 65, died November 14, 1913.

Alfred Pennington died at Oakland July 18, 1919. He was   Jul 23, 1919
60 years 10 months and 9 days old. A native of Illinois,
he came to California over 40 years ago and worked as a
printer in San Francisco. He purchased a half interest in
the *Ukiah Republican Press*, and later, started the *Little
Lake Herald*. He married Ora Smart, who survived with her
twelve year old son.

William Higham Pennington, an old resident of Westport, died   Jan 10, 1912
January 9, 1912. Born in Preston, England, August 3, 1825,   Jan 17, 1912
he moved to the U.S.in 1857 and served in the Federal army
for 3½ years during the Civil War. After the war, he
lived with his family in Philadelphia where his wife and
five children died of cholera within one week. One child
survived. He came to California about 1872 and to Westport
ten years later. He married a second time: to Ellen Aiken
November 1, 1883, and they had a son, Albert E., born
December 5, 1884. Funeral services were held January 11th
led by Rev.W.A.Chapman.

Annie Pentila, 19, died of tuberculosis January 24, 1912   Feb 7, 1912
and was buried on the 25th. Her parents, brothers and
sisters survived.

Oscar Pentilla, aged 21, died of TB August 14, 1910.   Aug 17, 1910

Ben Penwell, formerly of Fort Bragg, died in Trinity   Dec 4, 1918
County September 13, 1918.

Mr.Percy died at Ukiah August 11, 1914 of heart failure.   Aug 12, 1914
His son, Ed Percy of Fort Bragg, survived.

Imogene Perkins, 56, died at El Monte December 10, 1917.   Dec 12, 1917
Born at Littleriver, she was the widow of the late Hillman
Perkins and sister of the Pullen brothers of Littleriver and
Mrs.L.W.Babcock. The funeral was at Littleriver December 13th.

Casimir Peronette was shot and killed by Louis Robilliard   Jun 1, 1910
May 25, 1910.

Mrs.Joe Perreira, aged 35 years and 4 months, died May 29,   May 31, 1911
1911. A resident of Fort Bragg, her husband and child
survived. The funeral was held on May 30th.

Ernest Perry, a former Fort Bragg resident, died July 14,   Jul 31, 1912
1912 in San Luis Obispo. A mother and two sisters survived.
He had worked in the Mendocino mill for some time.

Frank Perry died at San Francisco March 15, 1919 from   Mar 19, 1919
Bright's disease. A car repair foreman for the Northwestern
Pacific Railroad at Willits, he was a 16 year resident. A
wife and 3 children survived.

Mrs.Mary C.Perry, formerly of Mendocino in the early days,   May 21, 1919
died in Santa Barbara "last week" at 88. Three children,
Mrs.Effie Perry of Richmond, E.B.Perry of Oakland and Mrs.
Fredericks, survived.

Walter Perry was killed in a mill accident north of Covelo   Jul 27, 1910
July 21, 1910.

William Perry, one time County Recorder, died at Ukiah   Jan 3, 1912
December 25, 1912.

Adam Pershbaker, 79, an old Point Arena resident, died at   Feb 28, 1917
Prosper, Oregon, "recently".

Louis Petersen died at Fort Bragg November 2, 1910. Born in   Nov 9, 1910
Copenhagen, Denmark, August 5, 1856, he came to America in
1886. He settled at Cuffey's Cove, later moving to Greenwood
where he lived for 15 years. In 1904 he moved to Fort Bragg
to engage in business. In 1888 he married Mary Forsberg and
was the father of a daughter, Amy. The funeral was held
November 4, 1910 led by Rev John Barrett. Masonic rites were
held at graveside. His wife and daughter, Amy, survived.

The infant son of R.Peterson died Juky 11, 1910.   Jul 13, 1910

Al Peterson drowned in the Noyo River; his body was found   Feb 1, 1911
January 28, 1911. An old timer on the coast, he worked in
livery stables most of his life. The funeral was held in
Fort Bragg on January 29th.

Andrew Peterson, 58, suffered a broken back caused by his   Apr 18, 1917
cow falling on him, dying at Comptche on April 17, 1917.   Apr 25, 1917
The funeral was held April 21st led by Rev.Henry Shaw. His
wife, son and daughter survived.

Andrew P.Peterson was found dead on the sand on his ranch   May 24, 1916
near Ten Mile May 22, 1916. A resident for 33 years, he had
gone to take the cows out in the morning and died from heart
failure. He was 69 years 4 months and 7 days old. His wife
and daughter survived. The funeral was May 25 led by
Rev.W.A.Chapman.

Mrs.Andrew <u>Peterson</u>, 60, 26 year resident of Comptche, died   Feb 6, 1918
"this week". Her husband was killed [April 17, 1917] when
the cow he was milking fell on him breaking his back. A son,
John Peterson and daughter, Mrs.Ada Jaakola, survived.

Carl <u>Peterson</u>, brother of the late L.Peterson of Fort Bragg,   Jan 1, 1913
died in Grand Rapids, Michigan, November 7, 1912.

Gus <u>Peterson</u>, 31, was crushed by logs and died at Westport   Jun 4, 1913
June 2, 1913. The funeral was held in Fort Bragg June 5th.

Gust <u>Peterson</u>, the father of the late Mrs.Mary Dilling, died   Mar 15, 1916
in Portland, Oregon, March 12, 1916. A native of Kansas, he
arrived in Fort Bragg about 25 years ago and moved to
Portland in 1906. He was nearly 85 years old. The body was
shipped to Fort Bragg for burial.

John <u>Peterson</u> died at Albion of pneumonia. [No date reported   Jan 12, 1916
but probably was January 10, 1916.] A resident for more than
30 years, he was survived by one daughter, Mrs.John Nelson.

Mrs.John <u>Peterson</u> died at Mendocino September 16, 1911. The   Sep 20, 1911
funeral was held on the 18th.

Oscar <u>Peterson</u>, 25, born and raised in Fort Bragg,   Jan 5, 1916
died in San Francisco January 2, 1916.

Preston <u>Peterson</u>, 14, the son of W.Peterson, died at Fort   Oct 23, 1912
Bragg October 16, 1912 from injuries received in an accident
on the railroad in the Caspar woods October 14th. His
funeral was held October 19th.

Captain Thomas H.<u>Peterson</u>, a former Coast resident, died at   Jul 14, 1915
Seattle, Washington, July 2, 1915. He was a shipbuilder at
Littleriver for some years. His daughter, Mrs.H.H.Brown of
Mendocino, survived.

Tom <u>Peterson</u> died at Fort Bragg July 29, 1916. Born in   Aug 2, 1916
Finland, he was 65.

William H.<u>Peterson</u>, a 50 year coast resident with twelve at   Oct 15, 1913
Mendocino, died October 3, 1913 at the age of 73 years
8 months and 1 day.

Mrs.William H.<u>Peterson</u> died at Mendocino December 12, 1915.   Dec 15, 1915
Her husband died October 3, 1913. The funeral was held
December 15th in Mendocino.

Mrs.A.H.<u>Petrie</u>, 63, died at Long Valley January 2, 1914. A   Jan 14, 1914
daughter, Annie LeValley of Westport, survived.

C.<u>Pezzola</u> was fatally injured at Gualala November 28, 1914   Dec 2, 1914
in a fight with Antone Mostachetti, dying the next day.

Scott <u>Philbert</u> was struck and killed by an automobile near   Apr 7, 1915
Manchester March 31, 1915. About 66 years old, he was a
native of Indiana.

Mrs.Dudley Orville <u>Philbrick</u> of Comptche died near Ukiah   Oct 18, 1911
October 9, 1911.   Dec 28, 1938

G.<u>Picca</u> was crushed by logs in a woods accident at Elk   Aug 10, 1910
August 3, 1910. He was buried in the Catholic cemetery at
Cuffey's Cove. He had no relatives in this country.

Emma <u>Pickkola</u>, the 3 year old daughter of Gus Pickkola, died   Jan 11, 1911
January 6, 1911. The funeral was in Fort Bragg January 7th.

John F.<u>Pickle</u>,82, a Potter Valley resident, died   Jul 26, 1916
July 16, 1916. Eleven children survived.

Mrs.R.W.Pickle died in Potter Valley February 4, 1915. Her funeral was held February 6th. — Feb 10, 1915

The four year old daughter of Wiley Pickle was fatally burned when her clothes caught fire, in Potter Valley December 13, 1911. — Dec 20, 1911

Joe Pierra, was accidentally killed by a .22 caliber bullet at Camp 1 on Ten Mile May 6, 1917. Only 19 years old, he was the son of Manuel Pierra. — May 9, 1917

Mr.Pietilla, a native of Finland, died at the County Hospital near Ukiah "last week." — Feb 7, 1917

Thomas Frank Pike, the 8 year old son of Tom Pike, died at Point Arena December 29, 1913. — Jan 7, 1914

Robert Pilati, an Italian 28 years old, was killed in the Albion woods March 25, 1914 when a log rolled on him. — Apr 1, 1914

Tony Piris was struck and killed by falling rock while operating a steam shovel on the Northwestern Pacific Railroad at Woodman Creek [no date reported]. — Apr 21, 1915

J.B.Pitman, 82, died at Willits June 22, 1912. — Jul 3, 1912

Mrs.Platt, the daughter of Mrs.R.E.Reese, died in San Jose in 1919. — Sep 24, 1919

Mrs.George Plowman of Caspar, 36, died January 5, 1914. Her husband and 14 year old son survived. The funeral was held at Fort Bragg January 8th led by Rev.J.H.Hargreaves. — Jan 7, 1914

Louisa Plumb died in Ukiah July 28, 1910. — Aug 3, 1910

Albert Plummer, 45, choked himself to death in the Fort Bragg jail January 1, 1918. A heavy drinker, he had lived on the coast for ten years. — Jan 2, 1918

C.B.Plummer, 54, of Fort Bragg died at Covelo where he had gone to set up a movie house, August 4, 1915. The funeral was in Fort Bragg August 6th. — Aug 4, 1915 / Aug 11, 1915

W.P.Plummer, president of the First National Bank in Fort Bragg, died in San Francisco February 5, 1912. He was 62 years and 11 months old. His wife and son, Harold, survived. He had also served as superintendent for Union Lumber Company. Burial was in San Francisco February 7th. — Feb 7, 1912

Mrs.N.G.Poggie, 72, died near Gualala April 14, 1916. Born in Jacksonville, Illinois, she came to California in 1871. Burial was in Gualala April 16th. — Apr 26, 1916

Mrs.Pollard, the landlady of the hotel since 1901, died at Greenwood September 17, 1916. A 25 year resident, she left a sister in San Francisco, Mrs.Frank Drew. — Sep 20, 1916

Henry Gustafson accidentally shot and killed Italo Polonelle, a young boy, with a .22 rifle at Glen Blair November 17, 1910. Italo was a native of San Francisco and was 12 years old. The funeral was held in Fort Bragg November 20th. — Nov 23, 1910

Will Pond was killed in a hunting accident on Signal Ridge by Conway Brayton December 25, 1910. The victim, 49, was single. — Dec 28, 1910

Peter Pontane, an Albion rancher, died December 7, 1915. A native of Finland, he had been a resident for four years. He left a wife and several children. The funeral was held at Littleriver December 8, 1915. — Dec 8, 1915

J.R.Porter, a 30 year resident of Annapolis, died March 5, 1914 while sowing grain. — Mar 4, 1914

Thomas H.Porter, 52, died at Willits November 18, 1912 of   Nov 27, 1912
cancer. The funeral was held November 20th.

George Harold Porterfield, 19, the son of James Porterfield   Sep 4, 1918
of Mendocino, died at Manila, Phillipine Islands, August 7,   Nov 6, 1918
1918 of pneumonia while on active duty with the Infantry.   Nov 20, 1918
His was the first war related death for a Mendocino county
resident. He was born at Bridgeport March 14, 1889. His body
was returned for burial November 13th at Littleriver.
Rev.H.P.Ingram officiated.

Erick Pott, a railroad brakeman of Finnish birth, died at   May 11, 1910
Salsig April 28, 1910.

Eber W.Potter, Sr. was a suicide by gunshot in Oakland   Apr 23, 1919
April 20, 1919. He had located in Santa Rosa about 1899 and
established a plumbing and hardware business.

Mrs.George Potter died in Covelo March 19, 1914.   Apr 1, 1914
Her husband and two children survived.

Alexander Powell, 50, died October 23, 1918 in San Francisco.   Oct 30, 1918
His parents once operated the White House hotel at Fort Bragg.

Mrs.C.Prate, a pioneer settler in Anderson Valley,   May 8, 1912
died at Philo April 24, 1912.

Maurice R.Prather, 42, died at Philo August 31, 1914.   Sep 9, 1914

Mrs.Charles Preston, sister of P.Brubeck, died in Oakland   Jan 17, 1917
January 9, 1917. The funeral was in Concord January 11th.

H.L.Preston died in Tennessee September 4, 1919. Born in   Sep 10, 1919
1843, he served in the Confederate army. After the war, he
served as sheriff, probate judge, assemblyman and state
senator. He was the president of the Woodbury Bank. His sons,
John, Hugh, and Howard Preston, secretary of the Fort Bragg
Commercial Bank, survived.

Mrs.Harrison Price, a former Ukiah resident, died at   Feb 9, 1910
Oakland "last week".

Herbert Price, formerly of Ukiah, was killed by a train at   Jul 20, 1910
Port Costa July 13, 1910.

Bertrim Pritchard, 13, son of Robert Pritchard of Little-   Apr 3, 1918
river, died April 1, 1918 of spinal meningitis. The funeral
was held there April 3rd.

Thomas Probst, a newcomer to Glen Blair, was killed in a mill   Apr 6, 1910
accident April 2, 1910. The funeral was April 5th led by
Rev.W.A.Chapman.

Herman Puck, 76, died at the Soldiers' Home in Los Angeles   Feb 27, 1918
"recently". A native of Germany, he first came to the coast
in 1867 as a U.S.soldier, later returning and living here
for 25 years until going to the Home about four months ago.

Mrs.Elizabeth Pullen, 95, died at El Monte, Los Angeles   Apr 11, 1917
County, April 8, 1917. A pioneer settler of Littleriver,
she was the mother of Mrs.L.W.Babcock and Mrs.Imogene
Perkins, formerly of Ukiah.

Howard Purcell, a former resident of Fort Bragg and Scotia,   Oct 19, 1910
was accidentally electrocuted October 12, 1910. Burial was
in Covelo. His parents were residents of Mendocino County.

Luigi Pusca died at Elk of injuries received when run over   Sep 22, 1915
by a log car on the railroad. [No date reported]..

Mrs.Anna W.Pyhalnoto died at Fort Bragg April 9, 1910. A   Apr 13, 1910
husband and child survived. The funeral was April 11th.

Frank Quaill died at Mendocino January 29, 1919 of TB and   Feb 5, 1919
influenza. Catholic rites were held there February 1st.

Emil Quass, 70, died near Willits "last week". He was a   May 31, 1916
native of Germany.

Christopher Queen, a pioneer of the south coast, died at   Oct 2, 1918
Berkeley September 25, 1918. A native of France, he was 76.
His wife, Mrs.Lucinda D.Queen, daughter, Mrs.Guy R.Stewart,
and a sister [in-law?], Mrs.D.Queen, survived.

Mrs.T.Quinliven of Willits died May 19, 1912. She had lived   Jun 5, 1912
many years at Calpella.

Charles Quinn, about 30, died March 6, 1918 in San Francisco   Mar 13, 1918
of pneumonia. He was buried in there March 11th.

Leung Yong Quoi, a.k.a.Jim the Chinaman, was found dead in   Mar 19, 1919
his cabin on DeHaven beach March 14, 1919. He probably died
March 12th. About 80 years old, he had lived on the beach
for 17 years. Burial was in Fort Bragg March 16th.

A daughter was born to the wife of Frank Radnick of Comptche   May 7, 1913
April 25, 1913. The child died soon after birth.

M.Radokomie, a native of Greece, died September 30, 1911 in   Oct 4, 1911
Willits from a blow to the head on the railroad extension
north of the city.

Mrs.Elizabeth Raffety died February 16, 1912 at the age of   Feb 21, 1912
82 years 3 months and 14 days. A native of Pennsylvania, she
settled at Inglenook in 1881*. Daughters, Mrs.W.W.Ware and Mrs.
Whistler of Largo and son, Mr.Raffety of Boonville survived.
The funeral was February 19th at Rockport, Rev.W.A. Chapman.
    *from Mendocino County Remembered, Vol II, 1976, page 267:
    [Married William Raffety in 1848, moved from Ohio to Illinois where seven
    children died and her husband got TB. She brought him to California in
    1881, but he died in 1882. She then took up a timber claim on the Ten
    Mile River about twelve miles from Inglenook.]

Keene Raffety, 24, son of A.L.Raffety, died at Ukiah   Nov 28, 1917
November 24, 1917. He was born at Inglenook. A service was
held at the Ukiah Baptist church November 27th led by
Dr.Franklin Bryan.

Fred E.Rafter, the son of the late Jerome Rafter, died at   Dec 15, 1915
Greenwood December 2, 1915. Born at Cuffey's Cove, he was
about 35 years old. His wife, two brothers, Charles and Romie
Rafter of Fort Bragg, and a sister, Felecitas Rafter of Greenwood, survived. The funeral was December 14th at Cuffey's Cove.

Jerome H.Rafter died at Greenwood November 16, 1913. Born   Nov 19, 1913
in Maine, he lived at Cuffey's Cove and Greenwood for
40 years. The funeral was held November 18th at Cuffey's
Cove. His wife, three sons: J.H., Charles of Fort Bragg and
Fred Rafter, and a daughter: Felecitas Rafter, survived.

William Ramus, a representative of the Burroughs Adding   Oct 8, 1919
Machine Company, fell onto rocks by the ocean in Fort Bragg
when a suspension bridge collapsed. He struck his head and
drowned - October 7, 1919. He was about 20 years old.

H.J.Randall died at Ukiah May 1, 1914. Born in Yountville   May 6, 1914
January 13, 1859, he came to Mendocino County in the 1870s.
The funeral was held May 3rd.

Maria Rani, 24, of Albion, died at Fort Bragg May 13, 1917.   May 16, 1917
A husband and son survived. She was buried May 15th.

Mrs.August Rantala, 42, died February 24, 1917 and was   Feb 28, 1917
buried on the 26th in Fort Bragg. Father Grant officiated.
A native of Finland, she left a husband, three sons,
August, Everett, Axel, and a daughter, Blanche Rantala.

Mrs.August <u>Raudio</u>, 37, died December 16, 1912 on Little Lake
Road. The funeral was December 19th.

Dec 25, 1912

Charles <u>Raudio</u> died at Fort Bragg October 28, 1918 of
influenza. A daughter had been born to his wife on
October 26th. His son, Charles Raudio Jr., was a fireman on
the California Western Railroad.

Oct 30, 1918

Charlotte Lucele <u>Raudio</u> of Noyo was severly burned
November 23, 1911 dying therefrom December 3, 1911. She was
4 years 1 month and 25 days old. The funeral was conducted
by Rev.R.C.Grace December 4th.

Dec 6, 1911

Thomas E.<u>Rawles</u>, 64, a Boonville pioneer, died in San
Francisco "last week".

Jan 14, 1914

J.N.<u>Rea</u> dropped dead in Ukiah "yesterday" [thought to be
June 2, 1916]. He was formerly a resident of Mendocino.

Jun 7, 1916

Lewis Woodlie <u>Redwine</u> died at Fort Bragg December 7, 1913.

Dec 10, 1913

Sanford <u>Redwine</u>, 58, was a suicide by gunshot at the County
Hospital August 5, 1917. He had been a patient in the State
Hospital for some time. Born in El Dorado County, he was
buried in Covelo. His wife, son and daughter survived.

Aug 8, 1917

I.C.<u>Reed</u>, 93, died at Ukiah April 26, 1919. His daughter,
Mrs.Hatch of Ukiah, survived.

Apr 30, 1919

Mrs.R.E.<u>Reese</u>, the wife of Dr.Reese who formerly practiced
in Fort Bragg, died in San Jose in July 1919 of acute asthma.

Sep 24, 1919

Mrs.C.A.<u>Reeves</u>, widow of the late Warren Reeves, died in
Oakland January 5, 1911.

Jan 11, 1911

Samuel <u>Reilinger</u> was found dead in the lake in Golden Gate
Park, San Francisco, under mysterious circumstances "last
week". He was 56 years old. The funeral was held in Oakland
October 1, 1912.

Oct 2, 1912

Mrs.Katheryn <u>Reilly</u> died in Fort Bragg May 14, 1916. She was
70 years 8 months and 16 days old. She had come to San Francisco in 1866 and to Fort Bragg in 1910. Her husband, three
sons and a daughter, Mrs.William Harmon, survived.

May 17, 1916

Mrs.Therese <u>Reinke</u> died September 13, 1911 at Noyo. Born in
Germany, she was 31 years old and a resident of the Caspar
woods for two years. A husband and two children survived.
The funeral was held September 17th by Rev.J.C.Garth.

Sep 20, 1911

Mrs.Ruth <u>Reinking</u>, 83, of Manchester died September 11, 1919.

Oct 1, 1919

E.<u>Renckly</u>, 53 and a native of France, was fatally crushed by
a log at Ten Mile June 8, 1917

Jun 13, 1917

Katrina <u>Reskada</u>, 24, died at Ukiah August 29, 1911.

Sep 6, 1911

M.<u>Revis</u> pulled a razor and was shot and killed by
M.Valenzuela in self defense at Outlet camp north of Willits
July 11, 1910.

Jul 20, 1910

Mrs.Dora <u>Reynolds</u>, 40, died December 21, 1915 in Sacramento.
Born and raised in Point Arena, she left a husband, three
sons and a daughter.

Jan 5, 1916

J.A.<u>Reynolds</u> died at Ukiah November 21, 1916. A two year
resident, he left a wife and two children.

Nov 29, 1916

Robert <u>Reynolds</u>, 70, died at Mendocino January 11, 1913.
[Another account gave his age as 68.] He was a resident of
Ukiah for 40 years. A wife, two sons and a daughter lived.
The funeral was held at Ukiah January 14th.

Jan 15, 1913
Jan 22, 1913

Stephen Rice, a former Mendocino resident, died at age 61 in   Aug 27, 1913
in San Francisco. [No date reported].

William Isaac "Billie" Rice, the father of Mrs.Bourns, died   May 7, 1913
at Willits May 1, 1913, age 67, and was buried there May 4th.   May 14, 1913

Pete Ricetti, died at Boyle's Camp on Big River   Feb 23, 1910
February 21, 1910. He was a native of Italy.

Chester Rich, 30, was shot and killed by an Indian east of   Sep 23, 1914
Fort Bragg in a quarrel over a card game. [No date reported].

The infant daughter of E.Ridley died at Hardy of whooping   Aug 19, 1914
cough "last week".

Mrs.Jessie Fee Ridley, aged 20 and a resident of Westport,   Apr 19, 1911
was buried April 14, 1911 with services at the Presbyterian
church led by Rev.W.A.Chapman.

Edward Riffe, 37, the donkey boss at Ten Mile, died   Oct 30, 1918
October 29, 1918 of influenza. His wife and two children
survived. The funeral was held October 30th in Fort Bragg.

Ben Rigden, a saw filer and old time resident of the coast,   Feb 21, 1912
died at Hardy February 18, 1912. The funeral was held in
Westport on the 19th. [A second account said the name was Ben "Rigdon"
gave his death as February 19th.]

Ben Rigdon see: Ben Rigden.   Feb 21, 1912

Mrs.Minnie Riggs died at Willits April 3, 1913.   Apr 9, 1913

Electa Riley of Point Arena died July 27, 1910.   Aug 3, 1910

George Rinke was killed at Mendocino February 3, 1912 when   Feb 7, 1912
helping to raise a flag pole at the new school at East
Mendocino. His funeral was held on February 7th.

William Risco, aged 40, died in San Francisco from injuries   Jun 14, 1911
received in a railroad accident at Greenwood. [no date given].

Charles Rivett, a former Fort Bragg resident, died in a San   May 24, 1916
Francisco hospital "last week". Born in Point Arena, he was
31 years old. His mother, Mrs.A.Rivett, two brothers,
Benjamin and Henry Rivett, and a sister, Mrs.Minnie Hollis
survived. He had worked in a furniture store in Eureka.

Alfredo Rivetti was killed on the Greenwood railroad   Jan 26, 1916
extension January 20, 1916 when a steam shovel turned over
in soft ground crushing him and Giacomo Digoncelli.

Hattie Rivington died at Ukiah July 21, 1914.   Jul 22, 1914

Patrick Roach, 91, died at Westport July 6, 1915. Born in   Jul 7, 1915
Ireland, he had been a resident of Westport for 50 years.   Jul 14, 1915
The funeral was held July 8th led by Rev.W.A.Chapman.

Mrs.Roberts died at Elk June 21, 1911.   Jun 28, 1911

Mrs.Elmer E.Robinson died in San Francisco in childbirth at   Jul 23, 1919
the age of 20 years and 9 months. She was the daughter of
Frank H.Gould. Her husband, infant daughter and mother lived.

Mrs.Emma Robinson died at Covelo December 22, 1915.   Jan 5, 1916

Miss Edith Rodda, 25, an artist from San Francisco, drowned   Aug 23, 1916
in the Noyo August 20, 1916. She was a visitor of Alice
Swanson, the daughter of Captain Erick Swanson, and was on
an outing in the woods. A graduate of the University of
California in 1914, she was the daughter of Mrs.Anna F.Rodda
of San Francisco and a sister of attorney A.G.Rodda.

Mrs.Margaret <u>Rodger</u> died east of Fort Bragg May 7, 1915.   May 12, 1915
Born in Fifeshire, Scotland in 1862, she married Henry Rodger
there and had nine children, three dying in infancy and the
eldest, David, died in San Francisco in 1905. In 1891 she
came to San Francisco and moved to Fort Bragg in 1905. Her
husband, two daughters, Miss Agnes and Mrs.R.Donaldson of
Fort Bragg, and three sons, two in Washington state, William
of Bryans and James of Bremerton, and Andrew of Los Angeles,
survived. The funeral was held in Fort Bragg May 9th.

The daughter of T.<u>Rodriguez</u> died December 5, 1915 north of   Dec 8, 1915
Pudding Creek. The funeral was in Fort Bragg on December 6th.

George H.<u>Roelke</u> died at Kelsey, El Dorado County, [no date   Apr 19, 1916
reported]. A veteran of the Mexican War, he was 87 years old.
Mr.Roelke was a personal friend of James Marshall who
discovered gold at Sutter's Mill in 1848. His daughter, Mrs.
P.W.Smith of Fort Bragg, survived.

Mary A.<u>Roesman</u>, a former resident of Point Arena, died in   Apr 12, 1911
Oakland March 28, 1911.

Thomas <u>Roesman</u>, formerly a businessman in Point Arena, died   Sep 13, 1916
in Oakland September 2, 1916. A native of Ireland, he left
three sons and five daughters.

Mrs.A.T.<u>Rogers</u>, a former Mendocino resident, died at Eureka   Aug 30, 1911
August 23, 1911. She was the sister of Mrs.Frank Allen of
Fort Bragg. A husband and six children survived.

Carter W.<u>Rohrbough</u>, accidentally shot himself while riding a   Jan 19, 1916
mule near Covelo - the date of death is uncertain. Formerly   Jan 26, 1916
an attorney he worked for his brother, John S.Rohrbough,
known as the cattle king of Round Valley. Given to being
alone, he was known to use his shotgun as a whip and, as it
had a broken safety, it probably discharged as he struck the
mule with the butt of the gun.

Mrs.Al <u>Roland</u>, the daughter of W.T.Coffer and a former   Mar 29, 1916
Fort Bragg resident when her husband worked for the Cali-
fornia Western Railroad, died in Riverside March 8, 1916.

Miss Vina E.<u>Rolf</u>, a native of Willits, died at Cloverdale   Aug 12, 1914
August 8, 1914.

C.H.<u>Roper</u>, a former coast resident, died at Healdsburg "this   Jun 20, 1917
week" following an operation.

Edgar A.<u>Roper</u>, 46, a native of New Zealand, died at Willits   Dec 1, 1915
November 28, 1915.

Andrew <u>Ropla</u> died while gardening March 21, 1911. Born in   Mar 22, 1911
Finland, he was 57 years old. He was a U.S.resident for   Mar 29, 1911
30 years and left a wife in Finland. The funeral was held
in Fort Bragg March 23rd.

Gus <u>Rose</u>, 46, died at the County Hospital October 25, 1916.   Nov 1, 1916
A native of the Azores, he was a former Fort Bragg resident.

Mrs.M.<u>Rose</u>, a resident of the Anderson Valley, died at Ukiah   Apr 19, 1916
April 13, 1916. Born in Napa in 1854, she was 59 years old.
The funeral was held at Boonville April 15th.

Ray <u>Rosewarn</u> of Andersonia went missing March 7, 1915 after   Mar 17, 1915
a dancehall quarrel. His body was found in the Eel River   Mar 24, 1915
near Andersonia March 18th. As no marks of violence were
found, he was judged to have drowned in a drunken accident.

Eugene <u>Ross</u>, nephew of W.W.Ware, was killed in France   Dec 12, 1917
[no date or details reported].

I.W.Ross, a former Point Arena resident, died in Alameda   Mar 8, 1911
"last week."

William Ross, a former woodsman on the south coast, died in   Jan 12, 1916
San Francisco "last week" at the age of 71. His wife, two
sons and a daughter survived.

P.Rossini, injured in a saw mill accident at Fort Bragg when   Feb 21, 1912
he fell on his head February 15, 1912, died of his injuries
on the 19th.

The infant child of Mr.Rossolti died at Elk May 5, 1916 and   May 10, 1916
was buried with Catholic rites the next day.

Eugene Rouse was shot and killed in a hunting accident by   Oct 1, 1913
Gustave Hagne near Round Valley September 25, 1913. A wife
and child survived.

Eugene Roussan, a fireman, was fatally injured when jumping   Apr 29, 1914
from a runaway locomotive April 22, 1914. He was buried at
Healdsburg April 25th.

Dr.Ciussius M.Rowe died in Fort Bragg of gangrene append-   Sep 3, 1913
icitis August 31, 1913. Born in Millville, Shasta County,
July 25, 1886, he was a dentist. The funeral was held in
Willits September 2nd.

Addison Rucker died near Willits May 25, 1914 at the age of   Jun 3, 1914
87 years 8 months and 29 days. Born in Missouri, he crossed
the plains in 1849.

Clara Rucker, 72 years 4 months and 2 days, died four miles   May 7, 1913
east of Willits May 3, 1913.

Miles Rucker, a resident of Potter Valley, died at age 35   Mar 1, 1911
February 19, 1911.

Mrs.Paul Rudd died at Comptche November 18, 1918. Her   Nov 20, 1918
husband and four small children survived.

L.M.Ruddick, a 50 year resident of Ukiah, died there   Jun 29, 1910
"last week".

Lewis S.Ruddick died at Ukiah August 27, 1919 following an   Sep 3, 1919
an appendix operation. Born and raised in Ukiah, he was 28.
His mother and 10 brothers and sisters survived.

J.C.Ruddock, a prominent Democratic politician, died in   Jan 14, 1914
Ukiah January 10, 1914 at the age of 64. He had served as
school superintendent of Mendocino County, chief clerk in
the U.S.Surveyor General's office in San Francisco and
cashier of the Mercantile Bank. His widow and three children
survived.

Mrs.Maude Hayter Ruddock died at the Vallejo hospital   Dec 4, 1918
November 27, 1918 from influenza. She was the sister of
R.Hayter.

Andrew David "Jack" Ruderick died October 14, 1919 from a   Oct 15, 1919
bad cold. He had been in business with Tom Hale in Fort
Bragg and lived with the Hales for 25 years. A native of
Missouri, he was 62 years 10 months and 12 days old. The
body was cremated in Oakland.

Mrs.W.C.Ruscoe died south of Ukiah February 13, 1910. She   Feb 16, 1910
was born in San Francisco in 1866.

Kenneth Russ, 10, drowned in a beach pond at Greenwood   Jun 21, 1916
June 18, 1916. The funeral was held there on the 20th.

William Russ, a 20 year veteran woodsman about 56 years old,   Jul 23, 1919
died in Fort Bragg July 22, 1919 from pneumonia.

John Ruttikainen, 37, died November 29, 1918 at Fort Bragg
of influenza. A native of Finland, he was a 15 year resident.
He was buried in Fort Bragg December 1st.

Dec 4, 1918

Mrs.Matt Ruuska died "east of Noyo" October 18, 1919 of TB.
She was 25 years and 10 months old. Her husband and two small
children survived. The funeral was held October 22nd with
burial at Fort Bragg.

Oct 22, 1919

George Ryan, of the Northwestern Pacific Railroad, was found
dead on the cookhouse steps at Albion January 31, 1914. A
brother in the Anderson Valley, William Ryan, survived.

Feb 4, 1914

William Ryan, a veteran of the Civil War and a pioneer
settler in the Anderson Valley, died in the Soldiers' Home
in Yountville April 30, 1919.

May 7, 1919

Adrian Ryerson of Crescent City died January 11, 1916. He was
the son of Mrs.Trefry of Marysville.

Jan 19, 1916

The son of Mr.Saaaijarvi [sic] drowned in Pudding Creek
north of Fort Bragg July 1, 1914.

Jul 1, 1914

John Saari died recently at Fort Bragg. His wife, Eva,
survived. [No date reported].

Oct 10, 1917

Mrs.John Sacks died in San Francisco January 15, 1917 and
was buried in Potter Valley.

Jan 31, 1917

Mrs.A.A.Sakett died at Ukiah December 27, 1911.

Jan 3, 1912

Frank Salameda, 21, was killed by a falling tree on Juan
Creek June 22, 1912. The funeral was at Westport June 23rd.

Jun 26, 1912

Mrs.John Sallinen died December 5, 1918 at Mitchell Creek.
The funeral was held December 8th in Fort Bragg. Her
husband, eight sons and a daughter survived.

Dec 11, 1918

Peter Sallinen, 26, died below Noyo December 18, 1918 of
influenza. The funeral was at Fort Bragg December 20th.

Dec 18, 1918

Walter Salmela was fatally injured by a falling tree at
Juan Creek June 14, 1912. The son of Matt Salmela, his
funeral was at Westport June 24th.

Jun 19, 1912
Jun 26, 1912

William Salmi fell off a log in the Fort Bragg millpond and
drowned December 12, 1917. A native of Finland, he was 25.

Dec 19, 1917

Oliver Salsbury, 21, died at Ukiah August 15, 1913.
The funeral was held August 16th.

Aug 20, 1913

Mrs.Rachael Francana Sampson, aged 64 years 11 months and
2 days, died of T.B. at Berkeley August 16, 1911. A former
Littleriver resident, she was survived by a daughter, Dr.May
Sampson, and two sisters, Mrs.M.D.Gray of Fort Bragg and Mrs.
Wilder Pullen of Littleriver. The funeral was August 20, 1911.

Aug 23, 1911

Mrs.John Samuelson, nee Lucile Handley, died of kidney
failure at Noyo October 16, 1915. Born in Caspar in 1896,
she married John Samuelson [May 31], 1914. The funeral was
held at the Baptist church in Fort Bragg led by Rev.I.H.Wood.
Burial was in Fort Bragg.

Oct 20, 1915

John Samuelson, an old time resident on the coast, died near
Comptche February 25, 1910.

Mar 9, 1910

Dr.Franklin H.Sanborn died in Fort Bragg January 11, 1916 of
heart failure and pneumonia. Born in Indianapolis, Iowa,
probably Indianola, Warren County, Iowa] in 1869, he was
46 years and 3 months old. His wife survived as did two
brothers in Bakerfield. The funeral was held January 13th
in Fort Bragg led by Rev.W.A.Chapman.

Jan 12, 1916

John <u>Sanders</u> of Covelo and a former Ukiah resident received   May 28, 1913
fatal injuries when thrown from a stage "last week".

Alexander <u>Sanderson</u> died at Fort Bragg April 16, 1913. Born   Apr 23, 1913
in New York, he was 69 years 6 months and 9 days old. He
came to California in 1869 and married Johanna Penwell
January 31, 1877 on Ten Mile River. The family moved to Fort
Bragg in 1888. The widow and eight children survived: Mrs.
Evelyn Browne, Mrs.George Holt of Fruitvale, Mrs.Lenora
McManus of Eureka, Mrs.Fred Hanson, Mrs.T.Cooney, Mrs.T.
Welch, Miss Wilma and David Sanderson of Fort Bragg. The
funeral was in Fort Bragg April 18, 1913 led by Rev.J.C.Garth.

Mrs.Alexander <u>Sanderson</u> died February 17, 1915 at Fort Bragg. Feb 24, 1915
February 17, 1915. Born in Ohio as Johanna the daughter of
Aron Penwell, she came to California with her parents and
lived at Ten Mile. [On January 31, 1877 she married Sanderson, who
 died April 16, 1913.] In 1895, they moved to Fort Bragg. She
was 59 years 1 month and 10 days old. The funeral was held
February 20th led by Rev.W.A.Chapman. Three sisters survived:
Mrs.Moore of Idaho, Mrs.McFarland at Eureka, and Mrs.Strawn
of Lake County. There were seven children: Mrs.E.Browne,
Mrs.Annie Holt, Mrs.Leona McManus, Mrs.Hattie Hanson, Mrs.
Lorraine Welch, Mrs.Lena Cooney and Miss Wilma Sanderson.

David Alexander <u>Sanderson</u> died December 20, 1913 in Fort   Dec 24, 1913
Bragg following an appendix operation. Born in Fort Bragg
May 2, 1891, he was the only son in a family of eight. The
funeral and burial were December 23rd led by Rev.W.A.Chapman.
Survivors included: Mrs.E.Browne, Mrs.Annie Holt, Mrs.Lena
McManus, Mrs.Lorraine Welch, Mrs.Lena Cooney and Miss Wilma
Sanderson.

Tom <u>Sanderson</u>, an old time resident of the coast, was found   Feb 16, 1910
dead February 13, 1910. The cause of death was pneumonia.
He was about 60 years old.

Antone <u>Sankovich</u>, a Croat, died at Fort Bragg May 10, 1915   May 19, 1915
from pneumonia. A California resident for 11 years and a
woods worker in the Fort Bragg area for the past four, he
was 42 years old. The funeral was May 13th in Fort Bragg.

Michael <u>Sankovich</u>, a former Fort Bragg resident, died in San   Nov 15, 1911
Francisco November 9, 1911 of tuberculosis. Catholic rites
were held at Fort Bragg November 12, 1911.

N.<u>Sanzoni</u> was a suicide by drowning January 4, 1910. A   Jan 5, 1910
of Italy, he was about 50 years old and had lived at
Wendling for three years.

R.F.<u>Sargentini</u> was buried with Catholic rites at Fort Bragg   Sep 17, 1919
September 16, 1919. He was 8 years 2 months and 17 days of
age and died of acute enteritis.

J.C.<u>Sarowski</u>, 73, an old resident of the coast, died at   Mar 6, 1912
Mendocino February 27, 1912. A native of Germany, he owned
and operated a brewery north of Mendocino.

Mrs.J.C.<u>Sarowski</u> died near Mendocino January 13, 1910 of   Jan 19, 1910
heart failure. A husband survived.

Dr.<u>Satchell</u> of the State Hospital at Talmage died of   Nov 13, 1918
influenza [no date reported].

J.H.<u>Saunders</u> died at Ukiah July 5, 1911. He was the son of   Jul 12, 1911
G.D.Saunders, a resident of Fort Bragg.

Freeman Parker and Joe <u>Saunders</u> were killed in an automobile   Sep 30, 1914
accident near Ukiah September 29, 1914.

Mrs.L.<u>Saunders</u> died at Ukiah June 9, 1915 from uremic   Jun 16, 1915
poisoning. She was about to give birth when she died.

Rev.M.K.Sawyers, 80, died at Willits November 8, 1915. A   Nov 10, 1915
native of Missouri, he came to Willits in 1866.

Lawrence Saxon, the son of W.T.Saxon of Willits, died in an   Apr 23, 1919
Oakland hospital April 19, 1919 from pneumonia following an
influenza attack. Born at Arbuckle, Colusa County, July 23,
1889, he came to the Ukiah Valley as a baby. A graduate of
the University of California, he was employed as a statist-
ician. His wife and three small children survived.

Mrs.W.T.Saxon of Willits died January 17, 1916 in San Fran-   Jan 19, 1916
cisco. Mr.Saxon was president of the Commercial Bank and
vice-president of the Irvine and Muir Lumber Company. Her
funeral was held January 18th in Willits.

B.Sbrana, a native of Italy and a ten year resident of Fort   Jan 19, 1916
Bragg, died January 14, 1916 at the age of 73. Catholic rites
in Fort Bragg were led by Father Blanderfield January 16th.

Mrs.Ed Scarry, an employee at the State Hospital, died   Oct 25, 1916
October 17, 1916.

Amelio Scesco, 51, was found dead in the southern part of   Sep 27, 1911
the county. Known as a "wild man", he had recently been
released from the San Quentin penitentiary.

Charles Christian Schaeffer, a 40 year coast resident, died   Oct 4, 1916
on Navarro flat September 30, 1916. A native of Pennsylvania,
he came to California in 1871 and worked as a sawyer. He was
64 years 11 months and 5 days old. His wife, three daughters:
Mrs.Duncan of Colusa; Mrs.E.P.Thurston of Ukiah; and Mrs.H.
Nystrom of Albion, and a son: Charles Schaeffer of Fort Bragg,
survived. The funeral was October 2nd led by Rev.W.A.Chapman
with burial in Littleriver.

Dewey Schaeffer, the 12 year old son of Charles Schaeffer of   May 17, 1911
Navarro, died of pneumonia at Mendocino May 11, 1911.

Gus Schamp, 55, died in the railroad camp near Willits   Mar 20, 1912
March 13, 1912.

Mrs.Emma Schapp, 81, died August 1, 1914. Born in Germany,   Aug 5, 1914
she was a Ukiah resident for 30 years. The funeral was held
August 3rd.

Antonio Scherini was electrocuted at Caspar February 9, 1916   Feb 16, 1916
when a loading cable touched a powerline. A native of Italy,
he was 36 years old. He left a wife and three children in
Italy. Catholic rites were held in Fort Bragg February 13th.

Mrs.A.W.Schiller, of about six miles east of Elk, died   Feb 21, 1917
February 17, 1917. Her husband and daughter, Mrs.Dollie
Swanson, survived.

Charles Percival Schlacter died October 13, 1913 in Point   Oct 22, 1913
Arena. Born there, he was 24 years 11 months and 7 days old.
His wife and son survived.

Francis Schnitker, 25, a former Ukiah resident, died in   Nov 29, 1916
Arizona November 23, 1916. Burial was in Ukiah.

George Schnitker, proprietor of a shoe shop in Ukiah, died   Sep 3, 1913
there August 30, 1913. Born in Germany, he had been a
resident for 18 months.

The old blacksmith, Henry S.Schnoor, died at Mendocino   Jul 24, 1912
July 17, 1912. Born in Germany and a veteran of the U.S.
Civil War, he was 81 years old.

Mrs.Mary Scholl died in Fort Bragg May 22, 1914 at the home   May 27, 1914
of her daughter, Mrs.Enders. A former resident of Ukiah for
20 years, she was born in Ohio and was 69 years 6 months and

Mrs.Mary Scholl *(continued)*
23 days old. Survivors included her husband, two daughters,
Mrs.R.R.Enders of Fort Bragg, Mrs.W.Caldwell of Bakersfield,
and a son, Fred Scholl, of Ukiah. The funeral was held in
Ukiah May 24th led by Rev.Elbert Holland.

Henry Schreiber committed suicide August 13, 1910 at Point   Aug 17, 1910
Arena by shooting himself in the head and heart.

Mrs.Johanna Schultz, aged 81, died June 25, 1910 at Mendo-   Jun 29, 1910
cino. She was a resident for 42 years.

Mrs.Johanna Schultz died at Mendocino March 18, 1917. Three   Mar 21, 1917
daughters, Mrs.James Gordon of Oakland, Mrs.Alma Nolte of
Tacoma, Washington, Miss Edna Schultz of Mendocino, and 3
sons, Paul, Otto and Henry Schultz of Mendocino, survived.

Mrs.Scott died in Missouri January 1, 1917 at the age of   Jan 17, 1917
85 years and nine months. Her son, George H.Scott of Fort
Bragg, survived. Mr.Scott died at the age of 87 in 1914.

Otto Schultz, a former resident of Willits, held up a saloon   Aug 19, 1914
in San Francisco and shot himself when about to be arrested.
A native of Germany, he was about 50 years old and said to
be drunk most of the time.

August Schwantner, about 60, a rancher on Navarro ridge,   Jan 16, 1918
died January 11, 1918 and was buried in Oakland.

Chester A.Scott died August 2, 1915 in Fort Bragg. Born in   Aug 4, 1915
Cleone March 1885, he left a wife and two children, one of
whom was George A.Scott of Fort Bragg. Two brothers: Saxon
Scott of San Francisco and Ben Scott of Fort Bragg also
survived as well as a sister, Mrs.Ned Bull of Northspur.
The funeral was held August 4th.

Mrs.Joe Scott, *nee* Mae Meech, died in March 28, 1911 in   Mar 29, 1911
San Francisco after an operation.

John Scott, 68, a Willits blacksmith, died there   Jul 3, 1918
June 25, 1918 when he fell down a mountain.

Martin L.Scott, the son of Frank O.Scott, died at Calpella   Apr 21, 1915
April 12, 1915 at the age of 20.

Sarah Scott, the widow of the late Hiram Scott, died at the   Sep 17, 1919
County Hospital [no date reported]. A pioneer settler of
Covelo, she was 90 years old.

Steve Scotten, a printer, was killed May 29, 1911 at Fortuna   Jun 7, 1911
when he slipped while boarding a moving NWP train.

Mrs.Mabel Seaton, the wife of J.F.Seaton of Fort Bragg, was   Nov 22, 1911
badly burned when her clothes caught fire November 3, 1911,
dying on November 19th. She was 32 years old and left a
husband and two children. Burial was in Murphys, Calaveras
County.

John James Seery, 50, was found dead in his cabin at Alpine   Jun 14, 1916
June 12, 1916. A native of County Fermannah [*sic*], Ireland,   Jun 21, 1916
he was a nine year resident. Unmarried, he was survived by
two brothers and a sister in Ireland.

Mrs.Jacob Sene, 70 a native of Sweden, died July 3, 1912   Jul 10, 1912
"back of Noyo". The funeral was held July 6th in Fort Bragg
with the service conducted by Rev.Otto Kaarto.

Viljo Sepantalo drowned in the South Fork of the Noyo   Jun 11, 1919
June 6, 1919. He was 5 years, 4 months and 12 days old.
Under the care of Mrs.Erickson, the shock of his death
caused her heart to fail the next day.

Mrs.Ella Seppa, 24, died at Fort Bragg April 8, 1915 of TB.   Apr 14, 1915
She lived on the south fork of the Noyo and had been in the
U.S. for 5 years. The funeral was led by Rev.John J.Hilberg
April 10th.

Matt Serlija, 28, died November 27, 1918 in Fort Bragg   Dec 4, 1918
of influenza and buried there December 1st.

Fred A.Severance, brother of Mrs.Bertha Boyd of Navarro,   Apr 24, 1918
died at Santa Cruz April 18, 1918 of pneumonia while on
furlough from the battleship *Oregon*.

Frederick Seymour, an old pioneer, died at Mendocino   Mar 18, 1914
March 13, 1914 of pneumonia.

Mrs.Fred Seymour died at Noyo May 4, 1910. A county native,   May 11, 1910
she was survived by four sons and three daughters.

John Seymour, a pioneer resident of Mendocino, died at the   Apr 10, 1918
Odd Fellows' Home in Saratoga "the first of last week".

Mrs.C.Donald Shane, *nee* Ethel Haskett the daughter of Guy   Jan 22, 1919
Haskett, died of influenza in Tacoma, Washington [no date
reported]. Born near Willits August 12, 1890, she grew up
there, taught school including two years at the University
of California, and was appointed secretary to the director
of the Lick Observatory near San Jose. There she met her
husband and married him December 23, 1917. They went to
Tacoma where she was stricken. Her husband and a two week
old son survived.

Joseph Shaw, 40, died at Willits July 1, 1912.   Jul 3, 1912

Palmer H.Shaw of Antioch was scalded to death while cleaning   Feb 28, 1917
a hot boiler in the paper mill [no date reported].

Clarence Shelton, the oldest son of T.Shelton, died in   May 16, 1917
Prescott, Arizona, May 13, 1917 of TB. Born and raised in   May 23, 1917
Fort Bragg, he was about 21 years old. The funeral was held
in Fort Bragg May 19th.

Michael Sheridan, a former Mendocino resident, died at age   Apr 23, 1913
62 April 4, 1913. He was the brother of Father Sheridan,
the former parish priest.

James Schoolcraft Sherman, the Vice President of the U.S.,   Nov 6, 1912
died at Utica, New York, October 30, 1912 of Bright's
disease. Known as "Sunny Jim", he was born in Utica
October 24, 1855.

The three year old son of Joe Sherwood died at Manchester   Apr 16, 1913
April 14, 1913.

Mrs.Andrew Sherwood, formerly of Comptche, Sherwood Valley   Apr 30, 1919
and other local places, died April 26, 1919 in Santa Rosa.
Her son, Henry, died of pneumonia while in military service
and her son, Homer, died on the battleship *U.S.S.Brooklyn*.
[Note: erroneously given as U.S.S.Oregon.]

Mrs.Foster Sherwood died at Stege February 2, 1918 from   Feb 6, 1918
scarlet fever and pneumonia. She was the former Ida Bever of
Mendocino. Her brothers, Sam and Charles Bever, husband and
two children survived.

Homer Sherwood, formerly a ranch hand at Glen Blair for ten   Dec 18, 1918
years, was killed by an explosion in a coal bunker while
serving as a fireman on the warship *U.S.S.Brooklyn*
believed to have been in Russian waters at the time of the
accident. Born and raised in Comptche, he was the grandson
of the late Alfred Sherwood, namesake of the Sherwood Valley.

Robert Foster Sherwood died at Manchester August 24, 1915.   Sep 1, 1915
Born in Kings County, New Brunswick, January 22, 1845, he
came to California by way of Panama in 1875. Settling at
Manchester in March 1896, he worked as a carpenter. In 1873
he married Medora Bishop and was the father of seven children
- five of whom lived: Charles Henry Sherwood of Manchester,
Mrs.James McCosker of Oakland, Mrs.C.W.Reinking of Point
Arena, Foster Elijah Sherwood of Stege, California,and
Joseph Addison Sherwood of Manchester. The funeral was
held August 27th. [Widow died February 19, 1937].

A young boy named Shields, died in Round Valley of   Jun 25, 1919
influenza [no date reported].

Nelson Shields, a rancher in Mendocino County, died at   Jan 15, 1919
Ukiah January 8, 1919 from influenza.

Robert Larue Shimmin, 62, died at Willits of TB   Mar 5, 1913
March 1, 1913.

Mrs.Harriet A.Shinn, the wife of S.D.Shinn of Fort Bragg,   Nov 5, 1913
died in San Francisco November 3, 1913 at the age of
75 years 3 months and 3 days. Born in Somerset, Perry County,
Pennsylvania, she was a 20 year resident of the coast. Her
husband, a daughter, Addie McSwegen, and two sons, George
and Frank Shinn, survived.

Mrs.Elizabeth Shoemaker died near Ukiah December 22, 1912.   Dec 25, 1912
She was born in Tulare March 21, 1855. The funeral was
December 23rd.

John G.Shores, 78, was found dead from exposure at Point   Dec 23, 1914
Arena December 13, 1914. A native of Illinois, he was buried
December 15th.

D.E.Shull, the principal of the Greenwood school, was shot   Feb 9, 1910
and killed in 1891 by Frank Roads, pardoned after 14 years.

Alfred Sibbis, 45, drowned in Salmon Creek August 24, 1914   Sep 2, 1914
when drunk. A native of Finland, he had been a coast
resident for 20 years. The funeral was held at Fort Bragg
August 26th.

David Sibley, 66, died at Albion May 22, 1913. He worked in   May 28, 1913
the lumber camps on the coast for more than 30 years.

A.W.Sifton, former owner of the Fort Bragg Dispatch, died in   Oct 19, 1910
Fitchburg, Massachusetts, recently.

Hilja Siipola, 35, died at Wages Creek October 30, 1918 from   Nov 6, 1918
influenza. The wife of John Siipola, she was a native of
Finland and a six year resident. Her husband and two children
survived. The funeral was held in Fort Bragg November 6th.

Mrs.Anna K.Silberhorn, 90, died at Calpella April 30, 1913. A   May 7, 1913
pioneer of Redwood Valley, she was buried in Ukiah May 2nd.

The three year old daughter of L.Silva died in Fort Bragg   Aug 17, 1910
August 10, 1910.

Mrs.Maria Silva, the wife of Joe King Silva, died at Fort   Oct 24, 1917
Bragg October 20, 1917 following the birth of a son on
October 18th. A resident of Mendocino for 16 years, she was
36 years old. Her husband and four children survived.
Catholic rites were held in Mendocino October 22nd.

Sebastian Silva died at Mendocino "last week". Catholic   Sep 18, 1918
rites were held there September 15, 1918.

William Silva, 12, the son of Antone Silva, died in   Nov 6, 1918
Wendling November 1, 1918 of influenza. He was buried
November 5th in Fort Bragg.

Tonie Silvera, 29, died at Fort Bragg July 16, 1912.   Jul 17, 1912

C.A.Silveria died at Fort Bragg November 8, 1918 from spinal   Nov 13, 1918
meningitis and double pneumonia. He had been in the under-
taking and furniture business. A wife and four children
survived. The funeral was held November 10th.

Theodore Silveria, a former Mendocino resident, died in   May 27, 1914
Oakland May 13, 1914.

Henry Silverstine, a drygoods salesman on the coast, died   May 28, 1919
in San Francisco "this week".

James L.Silverthorn of Calpella died June 20, 1914 at age   Jun 24, 1914
69. His wife died the next day. Both were born in Kentucky.

Mrs.James L.Silverthorn of Calpella died June 21, 1914 at   Jun 24, 1914
age 63. Her husband died the previous day. Both were born
in Kentucky.

Mrs.Barbara Silvia, 85, died at Mendocino January 6, 1915. A   Jan 13, 1915
native of the Azores, she left a son, John Silvia and a
daughter, Mrs.Mary Ramus. Catholic rites were held in Mendocino January 7th.

J.G.Silvia died at Fort Bragg July 18, 1912. Catholic rites   Jul 24, 1912
were held July 20th.

Mrs.G.Simmerley of Spy Rock died October 1918 [no date   Oct 23, 1918
reported]. Born and raised in Westport as Ruth Devilbiss,
she left a husband, three children, parents, and a sister,
Madge Devilbiss of San Francisco. Burial was in Willits.

L.G.Simmons died at Ukiah March 11, 1910 at the age of 77.   Mar 16, 1910

Pat Simms died at Fort Bragg May 21, 1912 from injuries in   May 22, 1912
a mill accident May 17th. Catholic rites were May 28th.   May 29, 1912

Julius Simon of Hearst accidentally shot and killed himself   Sep 15, 1915
September 10, 1915. Born in Germany, he was 61. A widow and
two children survived.

John Simonds, a rancher at Usal, died in San Francisco   Sep 27, 1916
"recently".

Battista Simonini, an Italian, was burned to death in a   Oct 2, 1918
fire at Guidiville October 1, 1918.

Zacharias Simonson of Little Lake Valley, died at Healdsburg   Jun 11, 1919
June 8, 1919. Born in Norway March 24, 1833, he came to
California in 1854 and was engaged in ranching from 1865.

Henry Simpson, 30, was killed at Decker's Camp on Little   Nov 27, 1918
Lake Road November 21, 1918 when a log rolled on him. His
wife, child [William Henry], mother, two brothers, Thomas
and William Simpson, and a sister, survived.

Mike Singleton, a Willits resident, died December 18, 1910.   Dec 21, 1910

Mrs.Sarah Singley died in Ukiah August 11, 1916. Born in   Aug 16, 1916
1840, she crossed the plains with her family in 1851. Two
sons survived her death.

Eskil E.Sjolund, born in Mendocino July 1886, died in   Mar 22, 1911
Sunnyvale, Santa Clara County, March 18, 1911.

N.P.Sjolund, aged 95, died near Mendocino October 25, 1910.   Nov 9, 1910

Mrs.Skiffington died at Melburne October 10, 1910. Born in   Oct 19, 1910
Michigan, she was 54 years old. Her husband, five sons and
a daughter survived. Burial was in the Catholic cemetery at
Mendocino.

John <u>Skiffington</u> died at Melburne September 21, 1911. Born in Canada, he was 56 years old.	Sep 27, 1911
John <u>Skiffington</u>, the postmaster at Melburne, died on October 13, 1912 from injuries received in an automobile accident near Mendocino on October 2nd that also claimed the life of Mrs.Dearborn.	Oct 16, 1912
Ernest <u>Sloan</u>, 9, the son of George Sloan, died of TB March 10, 1917 "back of Noyo".	Mar 14, 1917
The four year old son of George <u>Sloan</u>, died March 13, 1917 of TB "back of Noyo".	Mar 14, 1917
Andrew <u>Slotte</u>, a resident of Greenwood, died September 28, 1916 at Ukiah. Three daughters survived: Mrs.Edith Bridgeford and Mrs.E.Rinaldson, both of Elk, and Mrs.E.West of Albion.	Oct 4, 1916
Joseph <u>Smedley</u>, 64, died in San Francisco October 8, 1914. A native of Wales, he left a widow and two daughters: Mrs. Minnie Morris of Point Arena and Bertha Taylor of Healdsburg.	Oct 10, 1914
Albert <u>Smidt</u> died at Albion November 15, 1911 when he fell from a handcar on the railroad. Born in Germany, he was 68 years old. Burial was in Mendocino.	Nov 22, 1911
The 3 month old son of J.C.<u>Smith</u> died August 2, 1913 at Fort Bragg. Burial was in that city August 4th.	Aug 6, 1913
Rev.Mr.<u>Smith</u>, formerly the Methodist pastor at Point Arena and Manchester, died at age 60 June 16, 1919. His health was seriously weakened by an attack of influenza last winter.	Jun 18, 1919
Mrs.<u>Smith</u>, 76, died in Avon, Idaho [no date reported]. Born in Louisiana, she came to Placer County in 1852. Two sons survived: B.F.Smith of Avon, and Professor P.W.Smith of Fort Bragg.	Dec 20, 1916
Albert <u>Smith</u> died at Mendocino May 26, 1915. Born in Mendocino in 1895, he had worked in tie camps in the area - the heavy work was believed to have caused his kidneys to fail. His mother, Mrs.Julia Finlayson, and sister, Mrs.Charles Tyrell of Mendocino, survived.	Jun 2, 1915
Alex <u>Smith</u>, 69, died at Fort Bragg May 15, 1916 from injuries received at the Shake City bark camp that day when caught between two logs. A native of Finland, he had been a resident for 40 years. His wife had died several months earlier. A son living in Eureka survived.	May 17, 1916
Ana J.<u>Smith</u>, 82, died at Long Valley December 13, 1915. Born in Chile, she was a resident for 56 years. Seven of her children survived.	Dec 29, 1915
C.W.<u>Smith</u>, a resident of Willits, died August 15, 1918. Born Born in New York December 1840, he served in the entire U.S. Civil War until discharged in 1865.	Aug 28, 1918
Charles <u>Smith</u>, a native of Louisiana aged 58, died at Ukiah September 5, 1911.	Sep 20, 1911
Charles H.<u>Smith</u>, 56, died at Westport June 24, 1919 from an accidental gunshot wound received the preceding day. A coast resident all his life, he was buried at Kibesillah June 27th.	Jun 25, 1919 Jul 2, 1919
Mrs.Charles P.<u>Smith</u> died in Ukiah November 1, 1912. Born in Mendocino October 1, 1855 *nee* Sarah C.Crockett, the daughter of David C.Crockett, JP, she was married January 1, 1877 to Charles P.Smith at Ukiah. They had two children: Charles F. Smith and Mrs. Maurice (Mabel) Hirsch. Her sister was Mrs.Belle Hanes.	Nov 6, 1912

Mrs.Elizabeth Brooks <u>Smith</u>, the wife of Marshal F.J.Smith of
Fort Bragg, died December 22, 1913. Born in Cincinnati, Ohio,
she was 48 years 11 months and 23 days old and came to Fort
Bragg about 1903. Three daughters survived: Ruth, Daisy Hill
and Helen Smith. A sister, Mrs.Kate Monroe of Mendocino, and
a brother, Fred Keller of Cincinnati, survived. The funeral
was held December 27th led by Rev.T.T.Denhardt.

Dec 24, 1913

Emil <u>Smith</u>, 27, was killed in an automobile wreck at Chad-
bourn Gulch August 20, 1917. He was the brother of Otto Smith
of Greenwood.

Aug 22, 1917

Mrs.Emma <u>Smith</u> died at Fort Bragg May 3, 1915. Born in
Finland, she lived in Fort Bragg for 30 years. Her husband,
two daughters: Mrs.Joe Larson of Modesto and Mrs.Pickkola of
Fort Bragg, and a son: John Smith, survived. The funeral was
held at the Finn church May 6th by Rev.Westerbury.

May 5, 1915

F.C.<u>Smith</u>, about 48, a woodsman on the coast, died in San
Francisco March 17, 1918.

Mar 20, 1918

Mrs.F.J.<u>Smith</u> died at Fort Bragg December 23, 1913 and was
buried there December 26th.

Dec 31, 1913

Frederick Hale <u>Smith</u> died at Inglenook August 12, 1911. Born
1853 in Wisconsin, he was a farmer and 9 year state resident.
Rev.J.S.Ross led the funeral service on August 13th.

Aug 16, 1911

Mrs.George <u>Smith</u> died at Butte, Montana, February 26, 1914.
Born in Machias, Maine, she was 84 years old. Her son,
Marshal F.J.Smith of Fort Bragg, survived.

Mar 4, 1914

Henry <u>Smith</u>, a woodsman and ten year resident on the coast,
died suddenly January 12, 1919 from too much alcohol.

Jan 15, 1919

J.P.<u>Smith</u>, 90, died at Ukiah September 6, 1917. In 1857 he
was the second white man to settle in Ukiah. Three sons
survived: C.P., Henry and H.B.Smith. The funeral was held
September 8th.

Sep 12, 1917

Mrs.J.W.<u>Smith</u> was found frozen to death at the Garberville
gate on the Harris Road November 28, 1914. She had been
involved in a robbery with her husband at Willits for which
crime he was sent to San Quentin prison. Released on parole,
they had headed back to Humboldt County on foot. He deserted
her on the road.

Dec 9, 1914

Mrs.M.B.<u>Smith</u>, wife of the late sheriff, died August 16,
1912 and was buried at Ukiah August 18th.

Aug 28, 1912

Mart T.<u>Smith</u>, a veteran of the Mexican war, died on Ten Mile
January 24, 1913. Born in Goffstown, New Hampshire, July 31,
1829, he was the son of Benjamin and Mary (Hartin) Smith. He
moved with his family to Alton, Illinois, and later attended
Shurtleff college there. On June 12, 1846 he enlisted in the
2nd.Illinois Volunteer Infantry and served until August 1847.
In 1849 he came to California across the plains later settling
in Point Arena (1856). He engaged in a shipping business at
Fish Rock until 1861, selling out to go into farming for five
years in Yolo County. In 1874 he moved to Ten Mile and established a ranch. On September 22, 1859 he married Carrie O'Neal,
died June 10, 1865 leaving two children: Jennie and Carrie.
[Carrie was killed in an accident at Greenwood December 27, 1877.]
On June 24, 1880, Mart married again, to Minnie E.Johnson,
with whom he had three children: Frank M., Fred H.and Perry
M.Smith (deceased). Mart's funeral was January 27, 1913.

Jan 29, 1913

Nancy A.<u>Smith</u>, the wife of W.W.Smith of Mendocino, died
there at age 63 on January 25, 1913.

Jan 29, 1913

Peter <u>Smith</u> a woodsman, died at Albion September 28, 1910.
A native of Holland, he was 46. Burial was in Mendocino.

Oct 5, 1910

Robert <u>Smith</u> drowned in the woods at Camp A near Comptche   Jul 1, 1914
June 29, 1914. Two brothers in Oregon and one in Arcata
survived.

Mrs.Theora <u>Smith</u> died at Placerville March 28, 1912 at the   Apr 3, 1912
home of her daughter, Mrs.Albert Shafsky. She was the sister
of Mrs.John Dennen of Fort Bragg. Burial was at Littleriver
April 2, 1912.

Wallace <u>Smith</u> accidentally shot and killed himself while   Dec 10, 1913
hunting near Willits December 7, 1913. The funeral was held
December 9th.

Warner C.<u>Smith</u> was shot and killed by John V.Wilt, a former   Feb 16, 1916
resident of Mendocino, February 14, 1916 at Willows, Glenn   Apr 26, 1916
County. Wilt had robbed a store where Smith and T.Jensen   Nov 22, 1916
were working and took them as hostages down the railroad,   Dec 6, 1916
shooting them both - Jensen only being wounded. On June 30,   Feb 21, 1917
1916 Wilt was convicted of murder and was sentenced to hang.
The date set was February 9, 1917, but the execution
actually occured a week later on the 16th.
[In another item name given as "Joseph V.Wilt" or "Wilts".]

Mrs.Emilia (Peterson) <u>Snell</u>, daughter of Eric Peterson of   Feb 4, 1914
Fort Bragg, died in Honolulu, Hawaii, January 18, 1914.
Born March 21, 1883, she was 30 years 9 months and 28 days
old. She had married Albert Snell August 6, 1908 in San
Francisco. Her husband, parents, four brothers and three
sisters survived.

Mrs.Ed <u>Snickers</u> of Bridgeport died at the Point Arena Hot   Oct 5, 1910
Springs October 1, 1910.

Mrs.D.<u>Snider</u> died at Navarro February 2, 1915. The funeral   Feb 10, 1915
was held at Philo February 5th.

The body of Charles <u>Snow</u>, about 70, was found on the "other   May 31, 1916
side of the Noyo" in the woods. He had last been seen in
Fort Bragg March 11, 1916.

Hazel Oletha <u>Snow</u>, the wife of W.Clyde Snow, died at Fort   Jan 8, 1919
Bragg January 1, 1919 from influenza. Born in Nebraska
February 28, 1899, she came to California in 1913 with her
parents, T.L.Snook. She married Mr.Snow on March 23, 1916.
Her husband, two year old child, parents, three sisters and
four brothers residing in Westwood, Lassen County, except
Lloyd M.Snook of Fort Bragg, survived.

Amos <u>Snuffion</u>, aged 81, died near Ukiah March 24, 1911. He   Apr 5, 1911
was a native of Ohio.

Emil <u>Snugg</u>, 22, was killed May 1, 1916 in a automobile   May 3, 1916
accident on the Navarro grade. A native of Greenwood, he   May 10, 1916
had lived in Fort Bragg for 11 years. The funeral was held
at Fort Bragg May 4th with Rev.W.A.Chapman officiating.
A brother survived.

Erich <u>Snugg</u> died at Fort Bragg April 19, 1915 of TB. Born   Apr 21, 1915
in Finland, he came to California in 1888 operating a hotel
in Fort Bragg for 9 years. Two sons survived. The funeral
was held April 21st with Rev.W.A.Chapman officiating.

Esther <u>Snugg</u>, the daughter of Erick Snugg of Fort Bragg,   Mar 12, 1913
died at the age of 16 years 11 months and 6 days
March 10, 1913. The funeral was March 12th.

Mrs.Lena <u>Snugg</u>, the wife of Erick Snugg, died January 30,   Feb 1, 1911
1911 of TB. She was 40 years old. Her husband, two sons and
a daughter survived. Her funeral was held February 1st.

Joseph <u>Sodini</u> was killed in a runaway accident at Glen Blair   Jun 14, 1916
June 9, 1916. A native of Italy, he was 22 years old. The
funeral was held in Fort Bragg June 11th.

Khristian Sorola, 42, die at Fort Bragg "last week". Born   Mar 4, 1914
in Finland, he left a wife and six children. The funeral
was held in Fort Bragg February 25, 1913.

Mrs.Fannie Southard, a former Mendocino resident, was run   Feb 12, 1919
over and killed by a train "last week" at Selma, Fresno
County. She was the sister of Nellie Sherwood of Sherwood.

Mrs.J.F.Speer died at Ukiah May 25, 1911.   May 31, 1911

H.A.Spencer, of Potter Valley, died at North Port,   Nov 29, 1916
Washington. [No date reported].

Bob Spini, 23, was killed by a log at Greenwood "last week".   Aug 27, 1913
He was a native of Italy.

J.W.Spotswood, a pioneer rancher in Potter Valley, died   Mar 6, 1912
March 1, 1912.

Mrs.Clair Sprague, nee Sophie Koskela of Albion, died at   Dec 15, 1915
Reno, Nevada, "last week" after an appendix operation. Her
husband and daughter survived.

Mrs.Ellis Springer, nee Lydia Rice the daughter of Louis   Dec 6, 1916
Rice, died at Willits "this week". She first married Amos Cox
about 1904 and had one child. Moving to Willits in 1908 she
later [December 16, 1914] married Ellis Springer.

Mrs.C.Stager, formerly of Point Arena, died at Bakersfield   Nov 20, 1918
November 9, 1918 from influenza.

Mrs.Sarah Charity (Clay) Standley, widow of the late   Dec 17, 1913
J.M.Standley, died at Willits December 15, 1913. Born in
Keithsburg, Missouri, August 26, 1851, she crossed the
prairies and mountains with her family in 1857 and located
in Manchester in 1859. In September 1868 she married J.M.
Standley and moved to Willits. They had four children: Mrs.
Minnie Jamison, Mrs.Nellie Gibson, Mrs.James Hildreth of
Ukiah and Lt.Hale Standley, USN, at Mare Island. Four sisters
survived: Mrs.Isaac Crispin, Mrs.Joseph Bishop, Mrs.William
Lynch and Mrs.Henry Bowen. Four brothers: W.H., Harris,
Charles, and Dr.Louis Clay also survived. The funeral was
held at the Methodist church in Ukiah December 17th.

Mrs.William Standley, 28, died November 6, 1918 at Glen   Nov 13, 1918
Blair of influenza. The daughter of H.H.Button of Santa
Rosa, she had been a nurse in the Fort Bragg hospital. The
funeral was held in Santa Rosa November 8th.

Dick Stanley was thrown from a bucking horse and killed   Oct 19, 1910
October 18, 1910 at Point Arena. His troupe of rough riders
had performed at Fort Bragg on October 9th and 10th.

O.L.Stanley, formerly of the Mendocino coast, died in   May 24, 1911
Lakeport May 20, 1911 of tuberculosis. A former newsman,
he left a wife and several children.

Felix Stark, 50, a woodsman, died at Ukiah "last week".   Jul 16, 1919

John T.Stark, 67, died at Ukiah October 15, 1911.   Oct 25, 1911

Charles Starkey, a little son of Mrs.Starkey, died at   Jun 8, 1910
Ukiah June 6, 1910.

David Stauer died at San Francisco November 11, 1918 of   Nov 13, 1918
pneumonia. He worked at the Union Iron Works in the city.   Nov 20, 1918
His sister, Miss Rose Stauer of San Francisco, survived.

Mrs.Nellie Stauer died December 31, 1916 in San Francisco.   Jan 3, 1917
Born in Nova Scotia as Nellie Buchanan, she married the
late Jacob H.Stauer in 1883. (Mr.Stauer was killed in a
railroad accident enroute to Chicago in June 1893.) Five

Mrs.Nellie Stauer (continued)
children survived: H.J.and Dave Stauer of Mendocino, Mrs.
Kate Peterson of San Francisco, Mrs.Anna Atkinson of Rands-
burg, and Miss Rose Stauer of San Francisco. Two brothers,
C.J. and Hugh Buchanan of Elk, and two sisters, Mrs.Anna
Huot of San Francisco, and Miss Flora Buchanan of Fruitvale.
The funeral was held January 4, 1917.

Mrs.Sarah C.Stayton, 65, died in San Francisco [no date   Mar 13, 1918
reported]. A native of Illinois, she came to California as
a young girl and settled at Fort Bragg spending her last
ten years at Westport. Of her 14 children, 9 survived:
Mrs.J.R.Briones, John, Charles, Robert and Archie Stayton,
Mrs.H.Helms, Mrs.Dan Grant, Mrs.Charles Shelton, and Mrs.
Will Standley. The funeral was held at Westport March 10,
1918 with Rev.W.A.Chapman officiating.

Mrs.C.Stebi died at Annapolis May 4, 1917. Born in Scotland,   May 16, 1917
she was 62 years and 8 months old and came to California
about 1884.

Perry Stedham, a ranchhand, was a suicide December 23, 1911.   Dec 27, 1911

L.L.Sternberg died at San Francisco "last week". His   Dec 17, 1919
brother, Charles Sternberg, and Mrs.Rebecca Leiser, survived.

H.Steudeman, 42, died at Redwood City December 2, 1918 of   Dec 4, 1918
stomach cancer. Born in Santa Cruz, he had ranched on Big
River for 14 years. His funeral was held with Masonic rites
in Redwood City December 3rd. A wife and two daughters,
Eileen and Grace Steudeman, survived.

Frank Stevens, a former resident of Fort Bragg, died at   Nov 23, 1910
the County Farm in Ukiah "last week' at the age of 86.

Isaac Stevens, an old resident and pioneer of Caspar, died   Jul 17, 1912
July 11, 1912. He was 63. The funeral was held at Caspar
July 14th.

J.O.Stevenson, 83, died at Ukiah June 8, 1917. A pioneer of   Jun 13, 1917
Fort Bragg, he was born in Tennessee and crossed the plains
to California in 1852. Three daughters and five sons
survived: Mrs.Katheryn Hartman of Willits, Mrs.Lacy of Los
Angeles, Mrs.Joe Jackson of Fort Bragg, George Stevenson of
Portland, Oregon, William Stevenson of Red Bluff, LeRoy
Stevenson of Richmond, Joe Stevenson of Cleone, and James
Stevenson of Fort Bragg. The funeral was June 11th.

Isaac Stewart died at Holtville, Imperial valley. He had   Feb 11, 1914
been a harness maker at Mendocino until 1902.

Mrs.T.J.Stewart died at Greenwood February 27, 1918. An   Feb 27, 1918
early settler at Bridgeport, she came to Greenwood 42 years
ago. She also lived in Calistoga for 15 years. Her husband
of Fort Bragg and two daughters, Mrs.Bert Thompson of Elk
and Mrs Dan Evans of Nevada, survived.

W.P.Stewart, a piano tuner of San Francisco who regularly   Dec 17, 1913
visited the coastal towns, died in Reno, Nevada,
December 11, 1913.

William A.Stewart was a suicide by hanging in Wendling   Dec 10, 1919
sometime in November 1919. The body was discovered
December 3rd. He had worked in the Albion woods about three
months. Burial was at Fort Bragg.

Mrs.A.T.Stickney died near Ukiah September 9, 1915. Born in   Sep 15, 1915
Maine, she was 89 and had lived at Littleriver for over 40
years. There were four living children: Mrs.N.E.Perkins of
Littleriver, F.W.Stickney of Caspar, Dr.F.W.Stickney of San
Francisco, and Mrs.C.D.Flowers of Ukiah. The funeral was
held September 12th.

Mrs.J.Stillwell died at Little Valley July 8, 1915 of TB.   Jul 14, 1915
She was the wife of C.W.Stillwell. Rev.W.A.Chapman conducted
the funeral followed by burial at Inglenook.

John Stilwell, 27, died at Noyo December 10, 1917   Dec 12, 1917
and was buried at Fort Bragg the next day.

Mrs.Minnie Hall Stoddard died in San Francisco June 2, 1918   Jun 5, 1918
following an operation. Born at Green Springs, California,
June 18, 1852, the daughter of Captain J.Hall, an early
settler of Mendocino County, she lived at Albion. At the
age of 13 she lost one arm because of a severe burn. Despite
her handicap, she taught at Albion and Navarro Ridge schools.
On June 4, 1871 she married Mark B.Stoddard. Five daughters
and one son survived: E.T.Stoddard, Mrs.L.C.Rogers of Fort
Bragg, Mrs.F.Sharratt of Miranda,(Humboldt County), Mrs.W.G.
Lilley of Andersonia and Mrs.J.S.McKee of Stockton. Two
sisters, Mrs.Scott Saunders and Mrs.R.McCutcheon, both of
Fort Bragg, and two brothers, L.Hall of Garberville and
Eugene Hall of San Francisco, also survived. Dr.Franklyn
Bryan led the funeral June 4th at the Baptist church
followed by burial at the Fort Bragg cemetery.

Mrs.Victoria Stodulsk of Elk, accidentally died of asphyxia   Jul 5, 1916
from illuminating gas while visiting her sister in San Francisco July 1, 1916. A native of Russia, 25, she was the
wife of Michael Stodulsk.

Joe Stokes, 62, died in Fort Bragg of stomach cancer   Jul 19, 1916
July 13, 1916. Born in Fitsville, Pennsylvania, he drove a
stage at the age of 19 in Arizona and came to California in
1880 where he continued to drive stages for the past twenty
years. His daughter, Verna Stokes of Fort Bragg, survived.

Isaac Stolpe, 24, a woodsman, died January 28, 1919 in Fort   Jan 29, 1919
Bragg. Born in Finland, he had been a five year resident.

Charles B.Stone, a veteran of the Civil War, died in Los   Oct 9, 1912
Angeles September 29, 1912.

Mrs.A.C.Storer, an old resident of Point Arena, died   Dec 6, 1911
December 1, 1911.

James L.Storner died at Garcia December 19, 1909.   Jan 5, 1910

A.Stornetta, a south coast rancher, died November 24, 1918   Nov 27, 1918
from influenza. He was about 35 years old.

Leslie Stornetta died at the Belmont Sanitarium in San Mateo   May 14, 1919
May 2, 1919 of TB. Born at Manchester September 20, 1894, he
was 25 years 4 months and 19 days old. His mother, Pauline
Stornetta, two sisters, Mrs.Charles Galletti and Mrs.M.Mael,
three brothers, A.O.,J.O. and Fred Stornetta survived.

Raymond Stornetta was killed in a team runaway accident in   Sep 18, 1912
Point Arena September 15, 1912. He was the father of Mrs.J.
Male of Albion.

Leland Stout died at Ukiah June 10, 1913.   Jun 18, 1913

C.V.Street, an old resident of Potter Valley, died   Feb 19, 1913
February 17, 1913 at the age of 70.

Mrs.E.B.Street, the wife of Will Street, died May 2, 1919 in   May 7, 1919
Santa Rosa. A native of California, she was 30 and left a
child 20 months old.

Ray J.Strond, the husband of Hilda Strond, nee Torstrom, was   Mar 28, 1917
killed in a mining accident in El Dorado County and was
buried in Fort Bragg March 28, 1917.

Mrs.Edna <u>Stuart</u> died at Point Arena February 25, 1910.   Mar 2, 1910

Selmia A.<u>Sunfari</u>, aged 18 years and 11 months, died on the   Feb 16, 1910
"other side of Pudding Creek" February 10, 1910 of TB. The
funeral was held February 13th.

Matt <u>Suranto</u> died in Fort Bragg December 22, 1911 of TB. A   Dec 27, 1911
native of Finland, he was 36 years old. The funeral was
held on December 26th.

William J.<u>Surryhne</u>, a former Fort Bragg resident, died in   Dec 17, 1913
San Francisco December 13, 1913 at the age of 51 years
6 months and 16 days. He was a JP in Fort Bragg in 1890 and
engaged in the painting and paper hanging business until
moving to San Francisco about 1901. His wife, two daughters
and a son survived.

John <u>Sutherland</u>, an old settler, died at Wages Creek   Jul 27, 1910
"last week".

L.H.<u>Sutherland</u> died in the Fort Bragg hospital November 28,   Dec 10, 1913
1913 after an operation in which his hand was removed.

Robert L.<u>Sutherland</u>, 54, a coast woodsman, was severly   Feb 19, 1919
injured in the Ten Mile woods when struck by a limb
February 15, 1919. Taken to Fort Bragg, he died the same
day. The funeral was held there February 18th.

David <u>Sutton</u>, a patient at the State Hospital at Talmage,   Jul 26, 1916
hanged himself July 22, 1916.

Peter <u>Sutton</u>, 72, died on Navarro ridge April 23, 1913. A   Apr 30, 1913
son-in-law, John Ray, survived. He was buried at Cuffey's
Cove April 25, 1913.

Matt <u>Sverko</u> was murdered by Joe Stokes [date not reported]   Oct 28, 1914
and was buried at Fort Bragg October 25, 1914. A native of
Austria, 27, he was an eight year resident of Fort Bragg.

Thomas <u>Swanson</u>, a resident of Greenwood, died in Fort Bragg   Sep 1, 1915
August 27, 1915 of pneumonia at age 38. A wife and several
children survived. The funeral was held at Cuffey's Cove
August 28th.

Peter <u>Swartz</u>, 66, an old coast resident, died at the County   Mar 3, 1915
Hospital February 26, 1915.

Benjamin <u>Sweet</u> died in Fort Bragg August 20, 1914 from   Aug 26, 1914
injuries received in a woods accident at Northspur. Born and
raised in Santa Cruz, he was 34 years old. The funeral was
held August 25th.

Clara Moore <u>Switzer</u>, the wife of Albert Switzer formerly of   Sep 9, 1914
Westport, died at Oakland August 24, 1914 [probably should be
August 17th]. She came to California from Wisconsin in the
early 1870s. The funeral was held August 21st.

George <u>Switzer</u> suffered a stroke April 26, 1911 and died   May 3, 1911
on the 28th. Born in Kingston, Canada, June 18, 1839, he
came to California in 1863 via Panama where he lived six
years before returning to California. In 1870 he married
Elizabeth Hopkins and moved to Caspar. In 1871 they moved to
Westport and farmed with his brothers Albert and Peter and
A.W.Boyd. Later he moved to Mendocino and operated a livery
business with Boyd. They expanded to Fort Bragg where he
retired in 1907. His wife, five daughters and four sons
survived. The funeral was held April 30th with Revs.R.C.
Grace and J.S.Ross officiating.

Peter <u>Switzer</u>, formerly of Westport, died   Dec 28, 1910
December 11, 1910 at Atwood, Ontario, Canada.

William "Curley" Syres of Covelo died in Round Valley   Nov 19, 1913
November 15, 1913. He used creosote to plug a bad tooth
and was consequently fatally poisoned.

The four week old infant of Jesse Tallman died at Fort   Sep 1, 1915
Bragg August 26, 1915. The funeral was held August 28th.

Andrew Talus was killed when struck by a log at Howard   Oct 17, 1917
Creek October 16, 1917. Born in Finland, he was 35.

Ernest Tamagini, aged five months, died of pneumonia at   Nov 16, 1910
Ten Mile and was buried at Cleone November 11, 1910.

George Tanner's remains were found at Usal about   Feb 18, 1914
February 15, 1913. He had been missing for some time.

Mrs.Annie T.Tanney died at Covelo May 5, 1911.   May 24, 1911

Martin Tappines, aged three months, died November 11, 1910   Nov 16, 1910
and was buried on November 13th.

Giaccomo Tarro, a native of Italy and a new arrival to   Nov 29, 1911
the coast, died at Fort Bragg November 25, 1911. He was over
26 years of age. Catholic rites were conducted November 26th.
Mrs.Mary Taylor, wife of Coroner John Taylor, died   May 31, 1911
at Ukiah May 26, 1911.

The 22 month old daughter of Mr.& Mrs.G.F.Teale died at   Dec 14, 1910
Willits December 5, 1910.

Guiseppe Tenchio, 30, died at Fort Bragg November 8, 1918.   Nov 13, 1918
He left a family in Italy. He was buried at Fort Bragg
November 11th.

W.W.Thatcher, 83 of Hopland, died January 1, 1916 of   Jan 5, 1916
gangrene poisoning. A native of Ohio, he came to California
in the 1850s and was a resident of Mendocino County from
1868. A widow and five children survived: Mrs.J.W.Kemp and
Mrs.Dr.William R.Hill of Los Angeles, Mrs.M.F.Prosser of
Honolulu, Hawaii, and A.Thatcher, an attorney in Eureka
[one child not named]. The funeral was held January 4, 1916.

Mrs.Ariana L.Thomas died at Ukiah November 11, 1918. A   Nov 20, 1918
native of Georgia, she came to Mendocino with her husband,
Rev.J.P.Thomas, in 1871 settling on a ranch in Redwood
Valley. Seven children survived: C.R.Thomas, Mrs.Fannie
McCowen, W.P., H.P., J.R., and J.G.Thomas.

Mrs.Phronia English Thomas, the wife of attorney J.R.Thomas   Apr 3, 1918
of Ukiah, died there March 29, 1918. She was the daughter of
Wiley English.

The Mendocino County Assessor, W.A.Thomas, died in San   Jul 31, 1912
Francisco July 29, 1912. Born December 10, 1846 in Macon,   Aug 7, 1912
Georgia, he served in the Confederate army and came to
Mendocino in 1878. He was assessor for 16 years.

J.S.Thomason, a Ukiah nurseryman, dropped dead   Mar 19, 1913
March 17, 1913.

Mrs.Thompson, 70, died at Eureka August 4, 1919. Her son,   Aug 13, 1919
Moses Williams of Willits, survived.

August Thompson, 36, was a suicide by cutting his wrist.   Sep 25, 1918
Born in Norway, he was a local fisherman. A wife and two
children survived. He was buried September 22, 1918.

Mrs.Fred Thompson, the sister of Ernest Vann of Westport,   Jun 12, 1918
died at Ferndale June 5, 1918. She was born at Covelo
November 27, 1877.

George Thompson of Littleriver killed himself June 15, 1910. He was a painter and paperhanger and had been drinking at the time of his death.	Jun 22, 1910
John Thompson died at Mendocino May 29, 1915. He came to California in the 1860s and worked in the woods. His wife and two children, Mrs.Mable Crawford of San Jose and A.D. Thompson of Elk, survived.	Jun 2, 1915
John Thompson, of Tunnel Hill, died January 6, 1916. He was 72 years 5 months and 21 days old. Born in Finland, he lived at Noyo for 33 years. A widow and two sons survived. The funeral was held January 8th at the Finn Hall with Rev.John J.Hillberg officiating.	Jan 12, 1916
Mrs.John Thompson, 60, died east of Fort Bragg February 12, 1916. A native of Finland, she lived in Fort Bragg 19 years. Her husband, daughter and son survived as did a sister, Mrs.M.Mattson of Fort Bragg. The funeral was February 13th conducted by Rev.John J.Hillberg.	Feb 16, 1916
John S.Thompson of Ukiah was found dead on Orr's Creek January 30, 1912. A widow and two children survived.	Feb 7, 1912
Joseph Thompson, a former Inglenook resident, died at Santa Rosa "last week".	Sep 29, 1915
Peter Thompson, 36, was hit by a falling tree in the Glen Blair woods November 8, 1916 and died the same day in Fort Bragg from the injuries received. A native of Norway, he was a Californian for 15 years working at Wendling for 6. Two brothers, Chris and Bernt of the coast, and parents in Norway survived. The funeral was in Fort Bragg November 12th.	Nov 15, 1916
Robert D.Thompson died at Ukiah April 10, 1915. Born in Ottawa, Canada, in 1832, he came to California in 1868. He was 82 years and 6 months old.	Apr 21, 1915
S.R.Thompson was killed in an accident at the Fairbanks mill near Willits May 30, 1911.	Jun 7, 1911
An infant child of A.R.Thornton of Caspar was killed when thrown from an automobile in a wreck caused by a tire coming off the rim as the family traveled between Noyo and Caspar July 22, 1917.	Jul 25, 1917
The seven week old daughter of Ross Thornton died July 29, 1913 about two miles north of Fort Bragg. The funeral was held July 30th.	Jul 30, 1913
Mrs.Martha A.Thrush, the widow of William Thrush, died at Fort Bragg April 22, 1914 at the age of 79 years 2 months and 7 days. Born in Cleveland, Ohio, February 16, 1835, she was a coast resident for 30 years at Inglenook and Fort Bragg. The funeral was held at the Baptist church in Fort Bragg April 25th. Mrs.Nettie Kukendall of Amador County and DeForrest Thrush of San Francisco survived.	Apr 29, 1914
William Thrush died at the Soldiers' Home in Yountville August 6, 1911. Born in Wayne County, Ohio, November 16, 1832, he served in Company E, 119th.Iowa Infantry during the Civil War. He came to California in 1875. His wife survived. Burial occured August 8th.	Aug 9, 1911 Aug 16, 1911
Miss Winnie Thrush, 21, died at Napa June 16, 1918. The daughter of Mrs.Lena Penwell, she was born and raised at Inglenook and later lived in Fort Bragg. Her funeral was held at Fort Bragg June 19th led by Dr.Franklyn Bryan.	Jun 19, 1918 Jun 26, 1918
Edwin Thurlow died at the State Hospital May 1914. A coast pioneer and a Civil War veteran, he lived in the sand dunes near Ten Mile River.	Feb 10, 1915

Len Thurston, a former Mendocino resident, died at Bakersfield February 1, 1913.	Feb 5, 1913
Mrs.C.D.Tindall, a former Fort Bragg resident, died at Highline, Imperial County, August 8, 1916. A former teacher, his funeral was held in El Centro.	Aug 16, 1916
Charles W.Tindall, former Supervisor for Mendocino County and businessman at Lakeport, died there from heart failure triggered by an automobile accident a few weeks earlier. He served in the State Assembly in 1893 and ran stores in Petaluma, Upper Lake, Point Arena and Fort Bragg. In the last three years he ran a mail stage in Lake County. His widow and three children survived.	Dec 4, 1918
Elsie Tock, the 11 year old daughter of P.H.Tock, fell from a bluff into the ocean and drowned October 7, 1919. The body was discovered October 15th.	Oct 15, 1919 Oct 22, 1919
Mrs.Katherine Tock, a pioneer settler at Fish Rock, died in San Francisco "last week".	Jun 25, 1919
Antoneo Tores, a native of Portugal, died in Fort Bragg July 4, 1915. He had been in California for 12 years and was 36 years old.	Jul 7, 1915
Clarence Tracy, 25, was shot in the back and slain when riding horseback near Cummings May 28, 1915. The killer was unknown. Recently, Tracy had been successful in a land suit and may have been killed for revenge. Millard Means was accused of the deed but was acquitted by the jury. Tracy was the son of Ed Tracy.	Jun 2, 1915 Aug 4, 1915 Jan 30, 1929
Joseph Triguerio, 54, the father of J.Triguerio, the local operator of the movie projector, died at Mendocino November 24, 1919. The funeral was held at the Catholic church there by Father Gregory November 27th.	Nov 26, 1919
James Tritchler, a woodsman, died at Decker's camp from pneumonia January 18, 1919 following an influenza attack. A native of California, he was 40 years old and left a wife and two sons. The funeral was January 23rd in Boonville.	Jan 22, 1919
John Trodsen, 59, died at San Jose September 5, 1916. Born in Sweden, he worked on the coast for 33 years. He was buried at Mendocino September 8th.	Sep 13, 1916
Martin Luther Turner died June 30, 1910. A native of Eddington, Maine, he came to the coast in 1861. He was 70 years old. Rev.A.J.Sturtevant conducted the funeral. A brother, William C.Turner, survived in New Hampshire.	Jul 6, 1910
Mrs.E.C.Tuttle, a formerly of Willits and Redwood Valley, died at Napa February 18, 1910.	Feb 23, 1910
L.B.Tuttle, 71 and the brother-in-law of Frank Bowman of Fort Bragg, died at Covelo February 26, 1919. He came to the U.S. in 1860, and spent his working life as a rancher in the Ukiah valley.	Mar 5, 1919
Alfred Tyler, who died the first of the week, was buried in Fort Bragg January 24, 1912. Rev.Garth officiated.	Jan 24, 1912
Miss Pearl Tyson, 19, died November 14, 1918 at Fort Bragg. She was the daughter of Sam Tyson of Inglenook. Burial was at Fort Bragg November 15th.	Nov 20, 1918
Twin daughters were born to the wife of Robert Tyson at Mendocino May 25, 1913. One baby died June 18, 1913.	Jun 4, 1913 Jun 25, 1913

William F.Tyson, 73, died at Yountville August 31, 1914. A
Civil War veteran who volunteered at 19, he was a 35 year
resident of Mendocino County. Six sons survived: Charles
Tyson of Lake County, Pulaski, Sam, Archie and Bert of
Inglenook and Fred Tyson of Noyo. The funeral was held at
Fort Bragg September 3rd.

Sep 2, 1914

M.Uncina, a native of Austria, drowned in Outlet Creek near
Long Valley July 16, 1911. He worked on the railroad
extension north from Willits.

Jul 19, 1911

Miss Ada Underhill, 22, started a cooking fire with gasoline
instead of coal oil by mistake and was fatally burned in the
resulting explosion, at Willits. Burial was January 19, 1918.

Jan 23, 1918

Mrs.Millie Underhill, 76, died November 7, 1915 at Sherwood.
Born in Missouri, she came to California in 1849. Three sons
and three daughters survived. The funeral was in Santa Rosa.

Nov 17, 1915

Arthur W.Upp was killed at Willits when unloading timbers
June 24, 1910.

Jun 29, 1910

The three month old daughter of Manuel Valadao died
August 23, 1917 and was buried the next day at Mendocino
with Catholic rites.

Aug 29, 1917

The son of Gaspar Valena died at Mendocino July 25, 1914.

Jul 29, 1914

Gaudenzio Valenti, native of Italy, died March 8, 1916 at
Elk where he operated a hotel. His widow and daughter,
Mrs.V.Bacci, two sons, Pio and Edward Valenti, survived.
He was 68 years old.

Mar 15, 1916
Mar 22, 1916

Pio Valenti, about 35, a rancher near Greenwood, died
November 24, 1918. His family survived.

Nov 27, 1918

Don A.Valentine was severely hurt at Boyle's Camp July 17,
1918 when coupling loaded log cars which then ran away. He
jumped off just as the cars crossed a trestle bridge. He
died in Fort Bragg on July 18th, the funeral being held on
the 21st. The body was cremated in Oakland.

Jul 24, 1918

Mrs.Frances Van Allen, 64, died January 16, 1916 at Fort
Bragg. A native of New York, she was a California resident
for 33 years, settling in Ukiah in the early 1880s. She
moved to Los Angeles for a short time and then came to Fort
Bragg. Her husband, two daughters, two sons and a sister,
Mrs.McDonald of Los Angeles, survived. The children were:
Mrs.Katherine Greenough of Fort Bragg, Mrs.J.J.Carpenter of
Fort Bragg, Dr.Van Allen of Ukiah, M.C.Van Allen of Los
Angeles. The funeral was held in Fort Bragg led by Rev.
W.A.Chapman.

Jan 19, 1916

Fred Van Allen, proprietor of the *Tulare Register* and a
former Ukiah resident, died at Tulare February 22, 1912.

Feb 28, 1912

Mrs.Harriet A.Van Allen, a missionary, died at Madura,
India, of cholera June 5, 1911. Her husband, Frank was a
cousin of Mrs.J.J.Carpenter of Fort Bragg.

Jul 12, 1911

William Van Allen died at Los Angeles [no date reported].
A pioneer of the Ukiah area where he settled in the 1880s.
Two daughters survived: Mrs.R.C.Greenough and Mrs.J.J.
Carpenter, both of Fort Bragg.

Apr 5, 1916

Mrs.Mary L.Van Damme died at Fort Bragg May 2, 1913. She had
come to California 45 years earlier and lived at Littleriver
until moving to Fort Bragg about 1897. She was 68 years
10 months and 22 days old. Survivors included: Miss Josie Van
Damme of Fort Bragg, C.F.,T.B.,V.D.Van Damme of San Francisco
and another [unnamed] son. Catholic rites were held May 7th.

May 7, 1913

Fred Van Dike of Ukiah, the youngest son of the County   Oct 30, 1918
Assessor, died of pneumonia and influenza in Washington
where he was attending a special school [no date reported].
His widow, *nee* Verda Edwards, and an infant son survived.
The funeral was held in Willits.

Mrs.Alice Van Dyne, 52, died at Ukiah May 3, 1914. The   May 6, 1914
funeral was May 5th. Her husband, son and daughter survived.

William Van Fleet, a resident of Potter Valley, died in   Mar 8, 1911
Petaluma February 24, 1911. Born in 1831, he came to California in the early days.

Mrs.Leslie Vann, *nee* Geneva Johnson, died at Ukiah   Feb 19, 1913
[no date reported].

T.S.Vann, a pioneer settler of Mendocino County, died in   Mar 31, 1915
Jackson Valley March 18, 1915 at the age of 80. Born in
Missouri, he crossed the plains in 1856 and came to Mendocino about 1875 settling in Potter Valley in 1877 ranching
for 10 years.

John Van Nader, a former Fort Bragg resident, died at Ukiah   Jul 26, 1916
July 15, 1916.

Claude Van Voast died at Ukiah October 19, 1910.   Oct 26, 1910

James Vassar died at Hopland February 17, 1912 of diptheria.   Feb 21, 1912

Ethel Vegman, a woman of the Fort Bragg tenderloin district,   Apr 5, 1911
was shot by John Brown, *aka* John Fager, March 30, 1911.   May 24, 1911

Mrs.D.Venturi died of ptomaine poisoning at Hardy   Dec 24, 1913
December 22, 1913.

Charles F.Vincent died at Willits July 17, 1917.   Jul 25, 1917
He was born there October 1882.

Perry Vivian of Laytonville was accidentally shot in a   Nov 21, 1917
hunting accident November 10, 1917 by Ed Downing and died
of the wound November 14th.

Miss Elizabeth Waara, the daughter of the late [Oscar] John   May 2, 1917
Waara, was stricken with a brain tumor at the the age of 21   Jun 6, 1917
in May 1917. She died May 5, 1919 [Mrs.Oscar Waara cited as the Jun 27, 1917
parent in 1919] after a long illness. Born and raised on Noyo   May 7, 1919
Hill near Fort Bragg, she was 23 years 11 months and 12 days
old at death. The funeral was held May 8th at Fort Bragg
with Rev.John J.Hillberg officiating.

Oscar Waara, 55, of Noyo hill was fatally injured in a team   Nov 11, 1914
runaway accident on Little Lake Road November 7, 1914, dying
the next day. A 30 years resident, he left a wife, three sons
and three daughters survived. The funeral was November 11th.

Charles Henry Wade, 58, died at Willits July 31, 1915. Born   Aug 11, 1915
in the Anderson Valley, he was a teamster by trade. His
mother-in-law, Margaret Endicott, died August 4, 1915.

Lem Wade, formerly of Fort Bragg, dropped dead in Oakland   Mar 6, 1918
February 27, 1918 of heart failure. He had been a camp cook
in the north coast woods.

S.R.Wade, a former coast resident, died at Campbell   Oct 8, 1913
October 5, 1913.

N.Wagenseller, a resident of Ukiah and a county pioneer,   May 4, 1910
died at Redding April 25, 1910 at the age of 83.

Mrs.O.F.Waggoner died in a San Francisco hospital   Feb 23, 1916
February 18, 1916 following an appendix operation. Born in
Point Arena, she was 33 years 11 months and 26 days old and
had just moved to Willits from Fort Bragg.

Carl Wagner, aged 10, was shot by Ed Nieberger, aged 12.   Jan 11, 1911
[no date reported].

Elmer Walcott died at Ukiah December 25, 1909.   Jan 5, 1910

H.R.Waldo, a former Fort Bragg resident, died May 12, 1910.   May 25, 1910
Born in Royalton, Vermont, he was a Civil War veteran.
Survivors included his wife, three sons, Walter, Ben and
Bert, and two daughters, Mrs.Emil Larsen of Fort Bragg and
Mrs.L.Dotta of Santa Cruz.

Emerson Waldron died at Fort Bragg February 16, 1916. Born   Feb 16, 1916
in New Brunswick, he was more than 59 years old. He came to
California in 1876, settling at Greenwood.

William R.Walker, 96, died October 30, 1919. A native of   Nov 5, 1919
Missouri, he crossed the plains in 1849 to mine for gold.
In 1867 he came to Mendocino County, settling in the Ukiah
Valley where he farmed until moving to Westport. Later he
went to Oregon where he died. Six sons, two of whom, Will
and David lived in Willits and Aaron, in southern Humboldt
County, survived as well as one daughter.

W.T.Wallace, one time justice of the peace at Greenwood,   Jul 20, 1910
died at Schiller's Ranch near Greenwood July 12, 1910. A
native of Canada, he was interred at Greenwood.

Mrs.William Wallach, about 72, died September 28, 1919 at   Oct 1, 1919
Boonville. He was a pioneer settler in the Anderson Valley.
Rev.William Shaw of Fort Bragg officiated at the funeral.

John Walsh died at Mendocino February 27, 1919 of Bright's   Mar 5, 1919
disease. Two brothers, Frank of Los Angeles, and George
Walsh of San Francisco, and a niece, Mrs. Nettie Paddleford,
survived. The funeral was held March 2nd at Mendocino.

Patrick Walsh, about 87, died at Point Arena August 24,   Sep 3, 1913
1913. He was a native of Ireland.

Harvey J.Walters was killed in a boiler room accident at the   May 14, 1913
Union Lumber Company mill in Fort Bragg May 10, 1913. He was
41. A wife and two daughters survived. The funeral was held
in the Baptist church May 13th led by Rev.J.C.Garth.

Roland Walters, [also given as "Rowland"] died at Hardy   Jun 12, 1912
June 10, 1912. The funeral was held there June 14th; Rev.   Jun 19, 1912
Rev.W.A.Chapman officiated. A sister, Theresa Walters
survived.

Ben Walton of Westport, died there May 13, 1915. Born in   May 19, 1915
Illinois August 7, 1834, he was 80 years 9 months and 6 days
old. He had settled in Westport in 1880 and was a hotel
operator in the early days. His wife died in 1883. His
funeral was held at Westport May 16, 1915.

Mrs.Mary E.Waltrip, an early settler at Willits, died in   Sep 12, 1917
Oakland "last week". She crossed the plains in 1857. Six
children were born and two survived: M.V.Baker and Mrs.T.L.
Young of Willits formerly of Westport.

Mrs.S.Ward, a former resident of Ukiah, died at Oakland   Jun 5, 1912
June 3, 1912.

George Block [later report "George Ward"] was shot and   Dec 10, 1913
killed by Mrs.Fabian Reyes [later report "Flora Reyes]   Dec 17, 1913
northwest of Covelo December 2, 1913.

Mrs.Nora Ward, the wife of George Ward of Kibesillah, died   Mar 5, 1913
in a San Francisco hospital March 1, 1913. The funeral was
held at Graton, Sonoma County, March 4th.

William C.Ward was shot and killed while riding in the
caboose of a logging train August 19, 1911. He was accidentally shot by Jesse Davis, aged 14, who was hunting. Burial
was in Healdsburg where a wife and son survived.

Aug 30, 1911

Erick Warner, an old resident of Mendocino, died there
"last week' at age 62.

May 15, 1912

B.H.Warren, an early coast lumberman, died at Point Arena
July 23, 1919 at the age of 84. He came to California via
Cape Horn in the early 1850s. He established a sawmill at
Fish Rock in 1858. In 1860 he went to Gualala. Three sons,
Fred H., S.L.Warren of Tonopah, Nevada, and C.L.Warren in
the East, survived.

Jul 30, 1919

Cecil Washburn, a former Willits resident, drowned in a
millpond at Tuolumne May 21, 1919. Born and raised in
Mendocino County, he was 19.

Jun 4, 1919

M.T.Washburn, 67, died near Ukiah March 17, 1912 of heart
failure. A native of Indiana, he had recently come from
Sonoma County.

Mar 20, 1912

John Watson, an old resident of Inglenook, died in the
County Hospital at Ukiah "this week".

Mar 6, 1918

Mary Watson, the 3½ month daughter of Henry Ward, died at
Fort Bragg August 25, 1913. The funeral was held on
August 27th.

Aug 27, 1913

Mrs.Rachel Watson, a three year resident of Point Arena,
died there January 3, 1916.

Jan 12, 1916

Elmer Waugh, about 29, died January 5, 1919 from influenza.
His widow, nee Miss Kunzler of Point Arena, and two
children survived.

Jan 8, 1919

J.A.Waymire, a former judge, died at Alameda April 16, 1910
of ptomaine poisoning.

Apr 27, 1910

Mrs.Martha A.Webb of Willits died April 7, 1914 at Fort
Bragg. She was enroute from Willits when she was taken ill
at Half Way House and later dying in Fort Bragg. She was 81.
The funeral was held April 10th.

Apr 8, 1914

S.W.Webb was killed at Seattle [no date reported]. He had
been in the lighthouse service.

Apr 30, 1913

William Webster of Mendocino died July 24, 1915 at Fort
Bragg. Born in Morrow, Prince Edward Island, in 1846, he
came to the coast in 1896 working ten years at Glen Blair
and then moving to Mendocino. The funeral was held July 26th
in the Mendocino Presbyterian church.

Jul 28, 1915

William Weeks of the Anderson Valley died at Santa Rosa
October 16, 1910 of heart failure.

Oct 19, 1910

Francis M.Weger, a 49 year resident of Ukiah, died
April 25, 1918. He served in the State Assembly 1902-04 and
was a prominent Democrat. He ran the County Hospital for
some time. A widow and two children, Oscar Weger and Mrs.
Maude Brown, survived.

May 1, 1918

Mrs.Christy Weiss, the wife of Frederick Weiss of Caspar,
died March 4, 1912. A native of Nova Scotia, she was 68 and
had lived at Caspar for 20 years. The funeral was held
there March 6, 1912.

Mar 6, 1912

Albert Welch, a brakeman, was killed in a railroad accident
north of Willits when the work train he was riding on hit
three mules and was derailed, November 28, 1913.

Dec 10, 1913

Dayton E.Weldon died at Ukiah March 30, 1913. He was born in New York in 1832.

Apr 2, 1913

Mrs.Harry Weldon died at Ukiah April 3, 1913.

Apr 9, 1913

Mrs.T.J.Weldon of Ukiah, suddenly died in San Francisco May 6, 1916 when enroute to San Diego with her husband to visit the exposition. She had taught school in Ukiah for thirty years.

May 10, 1916

Mrs.C.H.Weller, the wife of Charles H.Weller, died at San Rafael June 27, 1910. Her husband, sister, Mattie Weller, and brother, J.E.Guy, survived.

Jun 29, 1910

Mrs.Horace A.Weller died at her daughter's home at Morgan Hill in Santa Clara County March 26, 1914. Born Helen Elvira Cooper in Warrensville, Ohio, April 12, 1846, she moved to Hillsdale, Michigan, in 1864 and attended college there. In 1869 she married Horace A.Weller of Athens, Pennsylvania, and moved with him to Kibesillah in 1873 and later, in 1886, to Fort Bragg. The funeral was held March 29th in Fort Bragg with Revs.J.S.Ross, W.A.Chapman and A.J.Sturtevant participating. She was the mother of 7 children - 5 girls and 2 boys: Flossie (died at age 4), Mrs.A.D.(Minnie) Flagler of Orange County, California, Maude French of Sonora, Horace Weller, Delia Scott of San Francisco, Charles R.Weller of Fort Bragg, and Mrs.T.A.(Marguerite) Cheal of Morgan Hill. Two sisters also survived: Mrs.Edward F.Adams of San Francisco and Mrs. Calvin Stewart of Petrolia.

Apr 1, 1914

Lucile Weller, about 24, died suddenly while visiting friends at Sea Bright near Santa Cruz September 17, 1918. The cause of death was heart failure. Her funeral was held in Fort Bragg September 20th with Fathers Crook of Ukiah and Grant of Fort Bragg officiating.

Sep 18, 1918
Sep 25, 1918

E.D.Wellman, 67, died in Ukiah August 2, 1919. A former resident of a ranch at Orr's Hot Springs, he later moved to Ukiah to run a hardware business. His wife, five sons and a daughter survived.

Aug 6, 1919

Edward N.Wells, a former Ukiah resident, died at Vallejo January 28, 1912 at the age of 63. A widow and three sons survived.

Feb 7, 1912

Eli Henry Wells, postmaster at Willits for 13 years, died there September 3, 1914.

Sep 9, 1914

Fred Wells was a suicide November 11, 1913 in Jackson Valley. A dentist, he was forced to give up his practice when stricken with TB. He married B.F.Branscomb's youngest daughter [name not reported].

Nov 19, 1913

Miss Naomi Wells, 19, was reported to have died in Denver, Colorado, January 19, 1919 from TB and influenza. She had been in charge of the Western Union offices in Fort Bragg and Ukiah before going to Colorado. The report proved to be incorrect.

Jan 29, 1919
Feb 5, 1919

Mrs.Viola Wells, 61, died at San Francisco July 1, 1916. She was a 15 year resident of Willits.

Jul 12, 1916

William Bennett Wells died at Ukiah July 6, 1915. Formerly of Mendocino, his funeral was July 9th, Rev.Sutherland.

Jul 7, 1915
Jul 14, 1915

George Wenke of Westport died January 11, 1912 from stomach trouble. He was buried on the 12th.

Jan 17, 1912

Botto Alberto and Gust Wesala were killed in a blackpowder explosion while widening a cut on the California Western Railroad near Camp 3 April 25, 1915. The funerals were held April 29th.

Apr 28, 1915

Mrs.Erich <u>West</u> died at Albion December 8, 1918 from   Dec 11, 1918
influenza and pneumonia. Born and raised in Greenwood, she
was 23 years 7 months and 10 days old. Her husband and three
small children survived. The funeral was held at Greenwood
December 11th with Rev.Henry Shaw presiding. Burial was at
Cuffey's Cove.

Sylvester P.<u>West</u> died at Covelo May 10, 1914. Born in   May 20, 1914
Dubuque, Iowa, May 8, 1852, he came to California in 1876
settling first at Cahto and then moving to Covelo in 1898.
The funeral was held at Ukiah May 13th.

Hilda <u>Westberg</u>, aged 15, died of a ruptured appendix in   May 17, 1911
Fort Bragg May 12, 1911. Her funeral was held on the 14th.

Annie <u>Westerberg</u>, 17, was found dead in a well four miles   Jul 22, 1914
east of Noyo. Her funeral was held at Fort Bragg July 22, 1914.

Mrs.Mary E.<u>Westfelt</u>, 70, died at home in the Caspar woods.   Dec 3, 1919
The funeral was held November 30, 1919 at the Fort Bragg
Baptist church with Rev.W.A.Chapman officiating.

Mr.<u>Wethern</u> was killed in an automobile accident on   May 15, 1918
Rattlesnake grade near Cummings [May 1918] - his wife
and child survived.

Charles <u>Wheeler</u>, formerly a Ukiah attorney, dropped dead   Mar 20, 1912
in San Francisco "last week".

Mrs.E.W.<u>Wheeler</u>, a 40 year resident of Mendocino County,   Mar 10, 1915
died at Willits March 8, 1915. She was 79.

William J.<u>Wheelock</u>, 67 years and 19 days old, died in Fort Jul 16, 1919
Bragg July 11, 1919. A native of Nova Scotia, he was a
resident of California for 46 years, 20 of them in Fort
Bragg where he worked as a tallyman on the wharf. The
funeral was in Fort Bragg July 15th led by Rev.W.A.Chapman.

Elisha Lathrop <u>Whipple</u> died in Philo October 21, 1915. A   Oct 27, 1915
pioneer in the Anderson Valley, he was 85 years old.

A.L.<u>White</u> was killed when struck by a backline at Muir's   Sep 7, 1910
mill September 5, 1910. A native of Maine, he was 70.

Mrs.Clarence U.<u>White</u> died at Ukiah December 7, 1914.   Dec 9, 1914
Nee Mary L.Cleland, the daughter of J.M.Cleland, she was
born in Iowa in 1861 and came to California as a child in
1865. She married White in 1888 and moved to Fort Bragg
about 1900. There were four children: two sons, Valmer C.
and Erwin White, two daughters, Hilda and Ula. Two brothers
also survived: T.M. and B.L.Cleland. The funeral was held
at Ukiah December 9, 1914.

Mrs.H.H.<u>White</u> died at Ukiah January 30, 1912.   Feb 7, 1912

Henry M.<u>White</u>, the brother of Judge J.Q.White of Ukiah,   Nov 18, 1914
died near Windsor November 11, 1914. He crossed the plains
to California in 1853.

Jack Augustus <u>White</u>, 76, father of Mrs.T.Hale of Fort Bragg, Mar 13, 1912
died March 9, 1912. A resident of Fort Bragg for only three
months, he was born in Vermont and came to California in
1849, residing in Tuolumne County for 41 years. He was
buried in San Francisco.

Jim <u>White</u>, Chinese, died at Willits July 10, 1919. He came Jul 16, 1919
to California about 50 years earlier and worked as a cook.
He was supposed to be about 104 years old. The funeral was
held in Fort Bragg July 12, 1919.

Lillian <u>White</u> died [no date reported].   Apr 29, 1914

Mrs.Maud <u>White</u>, 68, the wife of Manley White, died at Santa   Mar 7, 1917
Rosa March 2, 1917. An early resident of Littleriver and
Caspar, she moved to Santa Rosa around 1907. The funeral
was held at Littleriver March 5th. A daughter, Mrs.Fred
Close of Santa Rosa, survived.

Mrs.Priscilla <u>White</u>, 78, died near Point Arena April 23,   May 3, 1916
1916. A more than 40 year resident of Ukiah, she was the
mother of the late editor of *The Ukiah Republican Press*,
W.C.White.

William Orvile <u>White</u>, editor of the *Ukiah Republican Press*, Aug 18, 1915
died at Ukiah August 13, 1915 following an appendix
operation. Born and raised in Mendocino County, he was
38 years old. He had started in the printing business at
age 14 and purchased the *Press* in 1902. His wife and two
children survived, Veta S.White and William Orvile White Jr.
A sister, Mrs.P.Moungovan of Gualala, also survived.
Services were at Ukiah August 15th.

J.<u>Whited</u> was killed in a mill accident at Wendling June 2,   Jun 8, 1910
1910. He was a native of Iowa.

Carroll <u>Whitney</u>, 15, was accidentally shot and killed by a   May 15, 1912
.22 caliber rifle by Chester Roffee, 13, at Willits
May 5, 1912. [The item's date of April 9, 1912 may be an error
for May 9th]. The funeral was held two days later.

George <u>Whittche</u> of Roseville died [no date reported]. His   Nov 6, 1918
grandparents were the Frank Arnolds of Inglenook.

Mrs.Joe <u>Whitted</u> died in Willits May 27, 1911 of   May 31, 1911
Bright's disease.

Dietrich <u>Wichmann</u> died in the woods "last week".   Jul 16, 1913
He was buried in Fort Bragg July 9, 1913.

Mrs.Melinda <u>Wilbur</u>, a former Mendocino resident, died in   Nov 1, 1911
Portland, Oregon, October 22, 1911 at the age of 65.

Nathan <u>Wilcox</u>, father of Mrs.Penland of Ukiah, died there   Jan 22, 1913
January 18, 1913 at age 85.

Mr.<u>Williams</u>, 14, drowned in the Gualala River near   Jun 4, 1919
Sea View at Del Mar June 1, 1919.

E.C.<u>Williams</u>, 93, died at Oakland March 1, 1913. He had   Mar 5, 1913
been a superintendent of the Mendocino Lumber Company in
the early days.

E.J.<u>Williams</u>, assistant caretaker of a Leonard Lake estate,   Nov 13, 1918
was found dead in his cabin November 9, 1918.

Ed <u>Williams</u>, about 20, was killed January 24, 1913 on his   Jan 29, 1913
his job as nightwatchman on the railroad when a stump
rolled down a bank and crushed him. Burial was at Willits.

George <u>Williams</u> of Willits died at Ukiah March 27, 1911   Mar 29, 1911
of tuberculosis.

George <u>Williams</u>, 21, the son of Mrs.Matt Erickson, died in   Jan 22, 1919
Fort Bragg January 17, 1919 from influenza. He was buried in
Fort Bragg January 19th.

John "Jack" <u>Williams</u> of Mendocino died from severe burns   Sep 20, 1911
received when fueling a stove, September 13, 1911. A coast
pioneer, he was 86. Three sons and a daughter survived.

John Andrew "Jack" <u>Williams</u> died at Fort Bragg July 15,   Jul 17, 1918
1918. His sister, Mrs.Lillie O'Donnell of San Francisco, and
two brothers, Jim and George Williams of Mendocino, survived.
The funeral was held at Mendocino July 17th.

John H.Williams of Willits died March 25, 1919 of typhoid fever. His wife and two children survived but were also stricken with the disease.

Mrs.M.Williams, the widow of the late E.C.Williams, died in Oakland April 16, 1916. E.C.Williams was one of the founders of Mendocino.

Apr 26, 1916

Moses B.Williams died at Willits July 5, 1919. Born in Springfield, Ohio, July 12, 1830, he came to California in 1849 returning East to serve in the Union Army during the Civil War 1861-1865. He came west again as an Indian Scout. Married 52 years, his wife and four children survived.

Jul 9, 1919

Samuel J.Williams, 19, was a suicide by gunshot October 4, 1915. The funeral was held in Fort Bragg October 9th with Rev.I.H.Wood presiding.

Oct 6, 1915

August Williamson, was a suicide by gunshot at Glen Blair February 14, 1915. He had been a coast resident for 22 years.

Feb 17, 1915

Elige Williford died November 28, 1919 at Point Arena where he had come with his parents in 1857. Born in Merced County, he was 64 years 10 months and 21 days old. On November 24, 1904 he married Terisa Rochelle. The widow and son, Warl Williford, survived as did four sisters: Mrs.Louise Bowles, Mrs.S.Reynolds of Point Arena, Mrs.Greek of Riverside, and Mrs.Schroof of Kansas. Three brothers, Thomas of San Francisco, Dave and Henry of Point Arena, were also left.

Dec 3, 1919

Rev.F.M.Willis, an early day Methodist pastor at Point Arena, died at Pacific Grove December 3, 1918 at the age of 87. He left the south coast in 1894. The funeral was held December 6th. Nine children survived: Mrs.W.F.Fuller, Mrs. J.O.Ross, Mrs.T.L.Hopper, Mrs.J.I.Wilson, Mrs.J.K.Allen, William, George, Went and Leon Willis.

Dec 4, 1918

Hiram Willits, the brother of George Willits and a former Willits resident, died in Oakland April 25, 1915 at 52.

May 5, 1915

R."Rube" H.Willits died at Point Arena August 25, 1912.

Aug 28, 1912

Matt Willpola died at Fort Bragg March 19, 1917. A sister, Mrs.Ness, survived.

Mar 21, 1917

Mrs.M.Wilming died at Willits August 3, 1918. She was born in Denmark December 3, 1857.

Aug 14, 1918

Mrs.Briita Maria Wilson, 54, died October 27, 1911 of cancer of the stomach. She lived in Pudding Creek area. Her funeral was October 29, 1911 at Fort Bragg led by Rev.Westerberg.

Nov 1, 1911

C.D.Wilson was killed in a mill accident at Willits September 9, 1916. The funeral was held next day.

Sep 13, 1916

C.E.Wilson, a lead attorney for the Union Lumber Company, died in San Francisco October 7, 1916.

Oct 11, 1916

Mrs.Charles Wilson died at Ukiah June 13, 1911.

Jun 21, 1911

Devoie Wilson, 48, native born in Mendocino County, died at Point Arena July 29, 1917. His widow and five children survived.

Aug 1, 1917

Ernest Wilson, 33, died at Willits February 11, 1917.

Feb 21, 1917

George Wilson died of heart failure at Camp 10 on the Noyo River October 12, 1911. A native of England, his funeral was held October 15th.

Oct 18, 1911

Mrs.John Wilson, of Pudding Creek, died December 21, 1919. The funeral was held in Fort Bragg December 25th.

Dec 24, 1919

Oscar <u>Wilson</u> died at Whitesboro "last week" of alcoholism.   Jul 10, 1912
He was a woods worker.

William <u>Wilson</u>, about 30, died at Westport February 21,   Feb 25, 1914
1913. The funeral was held February 23rd with burial in
Laytonville.

William <u>Wilson</u>, 29, was shot at a gypsy camp in Caspar when   Apr 21, 1915
tried to molest the wife of Peter Mitchell. Although only
struck in the legs by shotgun pellets, he died later the
same day, April 16, 1915, in Fort Bragg. The funeral was
held at Fish Rock April 19th.

William M.<u>Wilson</u> died at Potter Valley September 26, 1914.   Apr 7, 1937

Zenas <u>Wilson</u> died at Nordyke, Nevada, of typhoid fever   Oct 8, 1913
October 5, 1913. He was a nephew of Mrs.S.Ross of Mendocino
and Mrs.W.Fuller of Fort Bragg.

Frederick Joseph <u>Windlinx</u>, a 40 year resident of Fort Bragg, Jul 9, 1919
died there July 7, 1919. Born in Belgium in 1850, he went
to Canada when he was about 20 years old and then to Mexico
before arriving in California about 1879. He worked in the
lumber trade until 1903 when he opened a hardware and
plumbing business. The funeral was held at Fort Bragg
July 10th.

Emery <u>Wing</u>, a Point Arena resident 30 years ago, died at   Aug 13, 1919
Eureka August 6, 1919 at the age of 88. His wife and four
sons survived.

Walter William <u>Winkley</u>, a salesman representative for   Oct 23, 1918
Dodge-Sweney Company and well known on the coast, died in
San Francisco October 19, 1918 of Spanish influenza.

James <u>Winters</u>, about 38 years old, was killed in the Fort   Jan 12, 1910
Bragg woods January 10, 1910. The funeral was held in Fort
Bragg on January 15th.

Charles <u>Wintzer</u>, a resident of Fort Bragg from 1903, died   Jan 29, 1913
January 28, 1913. Born in Hanover, Germany, September 24,
1826, the son of Arnold L.and Charlotte (Wehrkamp) Wintzer,
he came to New York in September 1848 and lived in Nashville,
Tennessee, until 1856 when he came west to the Jacksonville,
Oregon, gold rush. Later he located in the Anderson Valley
and at Navarro where he operated a store and shingle mill.
He also served for 30 years as postmaster. He married Mary
Ann Tarwater, who was born in Maryland and reared in Cali-
fornia. She died at the age of 39 in 1885. Two children
survived: Arnold L.Wintzer and Mrs.Charles E.Wright, both of
Fort Bragg. His funeral was held at Fort Bragg January 29th.

Mrs.Frankie <u>Wintzer</u>, nee Frankie Dodson, the daughter of   Aug 13, 1919
L.Dodson of Point Arena, died in Los Angeles July 30, 1919.
Her mother, sister, Mrs.Alice Petty of Los Angeles, and a
brother, Fred Dodson of Point Arena, survived.

The 14 month old daughter of C.<u>Wirtanen</u> of Navarro was   Dec 16, 1914
buried at Fort Bragg December 7, 1914.

Mrs.Alice L.<u>Witherell</u> died at Ukiah July 11, 1911.   Jul 19, 1911

Mrs.Mary Welch <u>Wittrock</u>, mother of Thomas Welch of Fort Bragg, Nov 27, 1912
died there November 27, 1912. She was born in Germany   Dec 4, 1912
December 17, 1848. A member of the Baptist church, her funeral
was conducted in the Presbyterian church in Fort Bragg. Five
children survived: Mrs.Edward Sherman of San Francisco, Mrs.
Charles Kramer of Tacoma, Fred Welch of Caspar, Thomas Welch
and Mrs.Paul Racine, both of Fort Bragg.

Dr.G.A.<u>Woelffel</u> died in San Francisco August 21, 1917. He   Aug 29, 1917
had practiced dentistry at Willits for 17 years.

Richard Woelffel, formerly of Mendocino County, died in San   Dec 18, 1912
Francisco December 5, 1912. He was the father of Emma and May
Woelffel who once taught in the Fort Bragg Grammar School.

Tow Chung Wong, a log camp cook, died at Fort Bragg   Nov 12, 1913
November 5, 1913 at the age of 63.

Mrs.Wood, 78, died in Vermont "last week". She was the   Oct 9, 1918
mother of W.N.Wood of Fort Bragg.

Daniel T.Woodman was fatally burned in his cabin when a   Sep 11, 1918
forest fire swept through the Dobbyn Creek area. His
daughter was Mrs.T.F.Rowe of Albion. The funeral was held
in Eureka.

Robert Woods committed suicide by standing on the track in   Jun 18, 1913
front of an approaching locomotive at Ukiah June 9, 1913.

J.D.Worden, 80, died at Westport September 20, 1915 and was   Sep 22, 1915
buried September 22nd with Rev.W.A.Chapman officiating.   Sep 29, 1915

James Workman, a U.S.marine. was killed by Fred Meyers, a   Jun 26, 1912
former Fort Bragg resident, in a barroom fight in Vallejo
June 8, 1912.

Mrs.T.Workover died at Two Rock April 25, 1915.   May 5, 1915
She came to California in 1857.

Berry Wright, 80, died at Ukiah [no date reported]. Born in   Mar 10, 1915
Franklin County, Virginia November 2, 1835, he came to California in 1853 and to Ukiah in 1857.

Mary Wright, aged 51, died suddenly of heart failure in   Jan 25, 1911
Willits "last week".

Wilbur Wright of Dayton, Ohio, died of typhoid fever   Jun 12, 1912
May 30, 1912.

William Wright of Ukiah died in France of pneumonia. [1918].   Sep 11, 1918

Simon Wurtenburg, 89, died at Ukiah April 19, 1916. Born in   Apr 26, 1916
Germany, he had resided in the U.S.for 57 years.

Agnes M.Wylie, born in Littleriver, died of TB in Fort Bragg   Dec 21, 1910
at the age of 22. She had tried living in San Bernardino for
her health, but seeing that her health was failing, came
home to die. Father, Thomas Wylie, a brother in San Luis
Obispo and a sister in Detroit, Michigan, survived. Rev.Grace
conducted the funeral services December 19, 1910.

William Harrison Wyrick, a former resident of Greenwood and   Nov 18, 1914
Mendocino, died in San Francisco November 8, 1914. Born in
Eureka, he was 55. His widow survived.

Jack Yale, a traveling salesman for the Levi Strauss Company   Feb 14, 1912
and well known on the coast, died in San Francisco
February 3, 1912.

L.H.Yates, 80, died at Laytonville August 27, 1914.   Sep 9, 1914

Andrew Jackson Yeary, a veteran of the Civil War and a 16   Jul 17, 1918
year resident of Fort Bragg, died July 11, 1918. A native of
Virginia, he had moved to Missouri where he married in 1866.
A widow, son, George Yeary of Humboldt County, and a daughter,
Mrs.William Bartley of Navarro, survived. His funeral was
held in Fort Bragg July 13th led by Rev.W.A.Chapman.

Meredith York, 68, died at Ukiah January 5, 1913.   Jan 8, 1913

Richard York, a pioneer settler of the County, dropped dead   Jan 17, 1912
at Yorkville January 10, 1912.

Mrs.Yost, the mother of R.M.Yost of Fort Bragg, died   Mar 12, 1919
March 11, 1919. The funeral was March 12th led by Rev.
W.M.Sutherland. Burial was in Ypsilanti, Michigan.

Al Young died at Eureka of apoplexy "this week. He operated   Jun 11, 1919
a hotel and restaurant business.

Mrs.M.B.Young died near Ukiah of measles "last week".   Apr 27, 1910

Mrs.Susan Young, died at Willits February 17, 1910 at the   Feb 23, 1910
age of 90 years and nine months.

F.W.Youree, 78, a longtime Covelo resident, died at Ukiah   Sep 26, 1917
"this week".

The infant son of John Zarucchi died at Fish Rock from a   Aug 16, 1911
scorpion bite July 17, 1911.

Mrs.Mary Zeferina, 75, died at Fort Bragg December 10, 1911.   Dec 13, 1911
Burial was in Mendocino December 12th. Her husband survived.

Mrs.Adelide Zeferino died at Fort Bragg May 29, 1918. A   Jun 5, 1918
native of Portugal, she was 44 years old. The funeral was
held at Fort Bragg May 31st.

Mrs.Ella Flora Zeigler, the daughter of Mrs.W.A.Menafee,   Sep 10, 1913
died at Willits September 3, 1913.

John Zetterlund, a.k.a John Strom, died at the County Farm   Mar 3, 1915
near Ukiah February 22, 1915. A native of Sweden, he had
lived in the U.S. for 30 years. The funeral was held
February 25th.

Joseph Zill died at Albion July 24, 1912.   Aug 7, 1912

Mrs.Florence Zincan, 44, died at Gualala May 27, 1913. A   Jun 4, 1913
native of West Virginia, she had lived on the coast for
35 years. Three sons survived.

Alphabetized by groom's name; bride's name in Index

Marriages Reported	Issue Date
Andrew <u>Abramson</u> obtained a license to wed Esther <u>Lillkola</u> [also "Lillekela"].	Sep 30, 1914 Nov 4, 1914
E[lmer] R.<u>Ackley</u> married Alice McManus in Catholic service at Mendocino June 2, 1917. They were both residents of Caspar.	Jun 6, 1917
M.Earle <u>Adams</u> married [bride's name not given] in Los Altos June 25, 1913. Adams was editor of the *Ukiah Times*.	Jul 2, 1913
W.<u>Adams</u> obtained a license to wed Miss E.A.Allison, both of Mendocino.	Aug 21, 1912
J.P.<u>Agee</u> married Mrs.May Alice Dixon in San Franc- isco February 20, 1917. The groom was a contractor in Berkeley and a brother of Mrs.M.S.Scott of Point Arena. Nettie Agee left her husband in May 1917.	Feb 28, 1917 May 9, 1917
Guy B.<u>Aikins</u>,32, of Hopland married Eugenia Josephine Swan, 18, of Northwestern at that place March 17, 1912.	Mar 20, 1912 Mar 27, 1912
F.G.<u>Ainslie</u>, 26, the son of the late Joe Ainslie of Point Arena, obtained a license to wed Clara L.Paiva, 22.	Apr 11, 1917
J.M.<u>Alagoinha</u> married Carrie Gomes at Fort Bragg February 9, 1918. Judge Frank A.Whipple presided.	Feb 13, 1918
Frank H.<u>Albert</u> of Eureka married Ella Stewart at Petrolia, Humboldt County, March 2, 1910. The bride was the daughter of Mr.& Mrs.Calvin Stewart of Petrolia. Rev.N.L.Freeman conducted the ceremony.	Mar 16, 1910 Mar 23, 1910
Charles <u>Alberts</u>, 45, of Seattle, Washington, got a license to wed Nellie Anderson, 35, of Ukiah.	Jan 17, 1917
Edward J.<u>Albrecht</u>, 23, married Zoe A.Neal, 22, in Berkeley June 1, 1916.	Jun 7, 1916
Frank <u>Albrecht</u> married Sophia Raudio at Fort Bragg February 23. 1913.	Feb 26, 1913
Sabin A.<u>Aldrich</u> of Ukiah married Madge Laird of Lakeview, Oregon, in San Francisco "last week".	Aug 6, 1919
Charles <u>Alexander</u> married Lena Osborn at Ukiah "last week".	Jan 19, 1910
E.F.<u>Alexander</u> Sr.married Mrs.Helen Garvin at Santa Rosa December 26, 1917.	Jan 2, 1918
Gerard <u>Alexander</u> of Albion married Viola Weger, formerly of Fort Bragg, in San Francisco November 22, 1912.	Nov 27, 1912
Antone A.<u>Allen</u> of Albion obtained a license to wed Maryan F.Callierena of Mendocino.	Jan 1, 1913
Antone A.<u>Allen</u> of Albion married Jennie Simona of Albion in San Francisco October 29, 1913.	Nov 5, 1913
Professor Clifford G.<u>Allen</u> of Stanford married Alice Chalfant of Ukiah December 30, 1912.	Jan 8, 1913
James Kirke <u>Allen</u> married Blanch Perkins at the Willits Baptist church October 25, 1914. Rev.W.C.Whitaker presided. The bride was the sister of J.S.Ross of Mendocino and W.F.Fuller of Fort Bragg.	Oct 28, 1914

Albert Anderson of Albion married Flossie Flanagan of Mendocino at Ukiah March 24, 1911. The bride was the daughter of John Flanagan of Mendocino. Mar 29, 1911

Alex Anderson wed Ruth Froman in Oakland December 26, 1915. Dec 29, 1915

Anton Anderson married Manda Dahl, both of Noyo, in Fort Bragg October 25, 1911. Judge F.A.Whipple presided. Nov 1, 1911

Charles Anderson obtained a license March 30, 1914 to wed May Marshall. Apr 8, 1914

Ernest Anderson, the youngest son of N.A.Anderson of Albion, married Hattie Handelin in San Francisco [no date reported]. May 14, 1919

F.C.Anderson, 26, of Samoa obtained a license to wed Bessie Lovejoy, 23, of Branscomb. Sep 13, 1916

George P.Anderson married Della McKay in San Francisco October 6, 1914. Both were residents of Ukiah; she was the daughter of Andrew McKay, formerly of Fort Bragg. Rev.P.R.Dickey officiated. Oct 7, 1914

Harry H.Anderson got a license to wed Goldie Thrailkill. Jul 16, 1913

Andrew Andreis, 35, obtained a license to wed Togana Maria, 28, both were from Fort Bragg. Jan 24, 1917

William Gus Andrews, 26, obtained a license to wed Matilde Margiute De Slaef, 20, both of Hopland. Jul 12, 1911

Florine Anker wed Bessie Larrison in Ukiah June 27, 1913. Jul 23, 1913

Edgar Arens married Mary F.Case of Willits at Ukiah July 6, 1914. Jul 8, 1914 / Jul 15, 1914

George Aristen got a license to wed Catherine L.McManus. Nov 27, 1912

Elmer Aronen, 33, obtained a license to wed Tilda Menkkinen, 23, both of Eureka. Dec 24, 1919

Christopher Atkinson of Berkeley obtained a license to wed Alma M.Atkinson of Ukiah. Aug 10, 1910

Witherle N.Atwood of Oakland married Inez M.Valentine, the daughter of Mrs.L.H.Valentine of East Mendocino, at that place October 17, 1914. Rev.J.Melville Fisher officiated. Oct 21, 1914 / Nov 4, 1914

Fred Aulin married Adeli L.Rukka of Fort Bragg in that city June 24, 1911. Rev.Stadins presided. Jul 5, 1911

Harry W.Auser married Cecille Witherell of Anderson Valley "recently". Dec 2, 1914 / Dec 9, 1914

Joe R.Avelar married Amelia Perry at Mendocino May 8, 1910. May 25, 1910

W.J.Azbill got a license to wed Nina Caldwell of Covelo. Aug 4, 1915

Fred Jackson Babbitt married Sadie Marguerite Watson of Fort Bragg at the Catholic church in that city December 25, 1912. Jan 1, 1913

David Elijah Babcock married Lenore Rawles at Ukiah August 11, 1913. Both were residents of Boonville. Aug 13, 1913

Harry S.Babcock married Mrs.Laura M.Lilley in Noyo June 19, 1915. Rev.J.H.Hargreaves officiated. Jun 23, 1915

Dr.Raymond A.Babcock, the son of L.W.Babcock of Ukiah (County Superintendent of Schools), married Boonie Moore, daughter of J.E.Moore, pastor of the M.E.church in Ukiah, July 28, 1913. Jul 30, 1913

T.F.Babcock got a license to wed Orpha V.Weimer.   May 19, 1915

Thomas S.Bacon married Viola May Lockhart at Mendocino   Jan 22, 1913
"last week".   Feb 12, 1913

Alfred L.Bainbridge of Fort Bragg married Jessie Devilbiss Oct 24, 1917
in Ukiah October 13, 1917. The groom worked in a Wendling
store and the bride was a schoolteacher at Cottoneva.

Harold [Octave] Bainbridge married Anna Gilbrenson of   Mar 12, 1919
Tacoma, Washington, in that place March 5, 1919.   Apr 2, 1919

E.M.Baker married Henrietta Tallman of Albion   Dec 23, 1914
in Oakland "last week".

George Paul Baker, 30, married Edith Eberhardt, 25, in   Dec 24, 1919
Willits December 14, 1919.

Ray C.Baker of Willits married Marie Redwine of Covelo   Oct 24, 1917
at Ukiah October 20, 1917.

Sidney Baker of Gualala married Miss Clyde Ball of   Apr 3, 1918
Point Arena in Ukiah March 28, 1918.

William Baldwin married Aileen O'Brien, a former Fort Bragg Aug 14, 1918
resident and daughter of Mrs.A.L.Boon, in San Francisco
August 9, 1918.

Ernest Ball of Ukiah obtained a license to wed   Jul 9, 1919
Marguerite Davidson of San Francisco.

Fred E.Ball of Northspur married Helen Boyd of   Nov 1, 1916
Albion in Ukiah October 28, 1916.

Ned Ball married Adeline Scott, daughter of   Apr 22, 1914
G.H.Scott of Fort Bragg, April 18, 1914.

William Ball obtained a license to wed Leonora Gardella.   Sep 14, 1910

Earnest Banks, 19, married Zelma Eaton, 16, in Ukiah   Nov 19, 1913
November 14, 1913. Residents of Redwood Valley, they   Aug 29, 1917
separated March 1916 and filed for divorce.

Elbert A.Banks of Fort Bragg married Elsie Alice   Jul 9, 1913
McCandless of Ukiah at Ukiah July 3, 1913.
Rev.J.C.Garth officiated.

Lester Jones Banks of Hopland married Mrs.Dortha Enola   Jan 13, 1915
Rouse January 4, 1915.

Bert B.Banta of Tracy married Amelia Armstrong in Berkeley Jan 1, 1919
December 16, 1918. The bride was the daughter of F.A.Arm-
strong of Fort Bragg and a sister of Marguerita Armstrong.

Eugene Barley of Mendocino married Minnie Wainwright of   Jun 14, 1911
Albion ridge June 11, 1911.

A.P.Barnes married Miss Mabel(?) Mallory of Littleriver in Dec 27, 1916
Santa Rosa "last week".

Earl Desmond Barnett married Ella Brown Clark at Redlands, Jan 10, 1917
San Bernardino County, January 3, 1917.

Abraham Barnwell remarried I.Barnwell at Willits   Jul 8, 1914
June 18, 1914.

Bey J.Barnwell, 28, of Willits, obtained a license to marry Nov 8, 1916
Lena Lulu Hurt, 20, of Covelo.

Joe Baroni obtained a license to wed Eudora Lora.   Sep 22, 1915
Both were from Greenwood.

Oliver Barron, 40, obtained a license to wed Hazel
Barron, 25, both of Ferndale and not related.   Mar 5, 1912

Pietro Barrossi obtained a license to wed Giossa Severian.   Jun 7, 1911

Giuseppe Barsotti, 32, of San Francisco, obtained   Jan 26, 1916
a license to wed Rose Lucchincetti, 21, of Gualala.

Roberto Bartolemeo obtained a license to wed Anastasia   Nov 5, 1913
Martini, both of Fort Bragg.

Joe Barzone obtained a license to wed Pia Vannuchi   Dec 6, 1916
of Pine Mountain.

Louie Bassi got a license to wed Inez Battani of Manchester. Jan 3, 1912

James R.Bates of Fort Bragg married Ludy May Rice   Apr 9, 1913
of Irmulco in Ukiah "last week".   Apr 16, 1913

Elmer M.Batt wed Elsie I.Brown of Dry Creek July 17, 1913.   Jul 30, 1913

Mazza G.Battista got a license to wed Emma Cornaggia.   Jun 30, 1915
                                                             Jul 21, 1915
John Bauer wed Ida Waldner at Willits September 22, 1911.   Oct 4, 1911

Robin Bauer, a Round Valley farmer, married Alva Rupe, the   Dec 24, 1919
oldest daughter of John Rupe and a schoolteacher, in Willits
December 22, 1919. Rev.A.J.Sturtevant officiated.

Wilhelm Baumgartner, head keeper of the Point Cabrillo   Jul 19, 1911
lighthouse, married Lena Seaman of Mendocino at Ukiah
July 10, 1911.

Dr.Francis Baxter of San Francisco married Pauline   Oct 25, 1916
Hildreth of Ukiah in San Francisco October 23, 1916.

Frank W.Beach married Mabel Howard of Portland, Oregon, at   Jun 11, 1919
that place "last week". He formerly worked for the
Mendocino Beacon newspaper.

Charles C.Bean obtained a license to wed   Nov 23, 1910
Bertha A.Hensley, both of Fort Bragg.

Lester Clarence Bean obtained a license to wed   Sep 30, 1914
Josephine L.Palmer.

Oakley Beaver of Ukiah obtained a license to wed   Oct 15, 1913
Ida Adams of Fort Bragg.

M.S.Beck married Ester Olsen in Santa Rosa "last week".   Jun 27, 1917

Milton E.Beecher married Adah Lane of Manchester   Sep 20, 1911
in Oakland "recently".

Harry Bell married Vera Smith, the daughter of   Sep 15, 1915
J.R.Smith of Mendocino, in Napa September 5, 1915.

L.Bellumomino obtained a license to wed   May 27, 1914
Miss G.Bellumoni at Willits May 14, 1914.

Alfred Benedetti obtained a license to wed   Feb 18, 1914
Angelina Puccinelli.

Dante Beneditti obtained a license to wed   May 27, 1914
Emelia Ginignati at Willits.

Grant Bennett obtained a license to wed Emma   Sep 4, 1918
Harris of Covelo.

W.H.Bennett of Caspar obtained a license to wed   Aug 21, 1912
May Brown of Albion.

Erick Berg married Mary A.Sjostrom in Fort Bragg   Jan 22, 1913
January 25, 1913. Judge J.K.Peirsol presided.   Jan 29, 1913
[Given as "Eric Burg" in the last item.]

William Bergerson married Mary Brown June 1, 1913.   Jun 4, 1913
Rev.W.C.Whitaker officiated.

Archie Berkovits, a tailor, married Fern Anderson of Point   Mar 11, 1914
Arena at Ukiah March 5, 1914. Judge J.Q.White presided.

Ottavio Bernardeni married Geni Galli, the daughter of Dan   Nov 29, 1916
Galli, in Fort Bragg November 25, 1916. Judge F.A.Whipple
officiated.

Lodorico Bernardini, 26, married Mary Tamborini, 17, at Fort May 8,1918
Bragg May 4, 1918 by Judge F.A.Whipple.

Archie T.Berryhill married Hazel M.Sawyers in Santa Rosa   Aug 27, 1919
August 25, 1919.

Grover C.Berryhill got a license to wed Hazel Ackerman.   Sep 20, 1911

John Bertolini obtained a license to wed Mary Gabrino.   Oct 8, 1919

J.S.Bertrand of Albion married Myrtle Robinson at   Jun 18, 1913
Mendocino June 14, 1913.

Frank E.Bertsch married Alice McClure, daughter of   Jul 30, 1913
Nelson McClure, at Ukiah July 27, 1913.

Lester Jacob Bertsch married Edith Johnson, daughter of the   Dec 10, 1913
County Treasurer G.A.Johnson, at Ukiah December 9, 1913.

Lester Bertsch, on active service with the U.S.Army, married Oct 9, 1918
Mrs.Mary DeBuhr at Santa Cruz [no date reported]. The bride
was a telephone operator at Fort Bragg.

J.F.Betts married Grace Jakway of Caspar at Point Arena   Mar 11, 1914
March 6, 1914. Rev.D.McManus officiated.   Mar 18, 1914

Charles Albert Bever married Myrtle Winifred Sweetser of   Aug 14, 1918
Mendocino in Fort Bragg Presbyterian church August 14, 1918. Aug 21, 1918
Rev.W.M.Sutherland officiated. The bride was a nurse in the
local hospital.

J.R.Biaggi married Eva Bree of Healdsburg "last week".   May 2, 1917

James Biaggi Jr.of Manchester got a license   Jun 6, 1917
to wed Florence Ciapusci of Gualala.

Samuel Bibby, 45, of Fort Bragg, obtained a license   Oct 29, 1919
to wed Nellie Christine Boulton, 29, of Antioch.

Garret A.Bigelow married Edith Forrest McCornack in   Feb 12, 1913
Berkeley April 30, 1913. She was the oldest daughter of   May 7, 1913
Dr.and Mrs.W.A.McCornack, former residents of Fort Bragg.

John Bigiooli married Annie Bositos. [No date reported].   Jul 13, 1910

J.W.Bills obtained a license to wed Magarette Canada.   Aug 5, 1914

Grover C.Binkley married Mary Krause on August 29,   Sep 6, 1911
1911 at Ukiah where they were residents.

Alfred Bishop married Anita Brigden at Point Arena in   Jun 12, 1918
June 1918.

Chester E.Bishop married Cordelia E.Crispin, the daughter of Feb 28, 1917
Charles Crispin of Manchester, in San Francisco [no date].

Earl Bishop obtained a license to wed Mildred Williams.   Jan 3, 1912

Edwin Carl Bishop of Fort Bragg married Leta M.Bell, the daughter of Mrs.K."Betty" Bell of Fort Bragg, in Oakland March 9, 1919. — Mar 5, 1919 / Mar 19, 1919

Ernest E.Bishop of Manchester married Ruth E.Merrill of Soquel at Manchester September 11, 1917. — Sep 19, 1917

Fred Bishop married Blanche Linscott of Point Arena at Ukiah August 17, 1910. — Aug 31, 1910

Leslie Bishop married Grace Reinking in Fort Bragg April 30, 1916 which also happened to be the bride's birthday. — May 3, 1916

Noble M.Bishop of Madera married Eva Bowden, the daughter of B.J.Bowden of Albion, June 3, 1919. — Jun 11, 1919

Charles Bjarkas got a license to wed Betty Johnson. — Dec 23, 1914

Anton P.Black obtained a license to wed Sophie Samuelson. — Feb 10, 1915

Freeman Bleakely married Beatrice Hansen in the Fort Bragg Presbyterian church October 23, 1912. Rev.R.C.Grace officiated. [Probably "Blakely"] — Oct 30, 1912

Oscar C.Bley, a pharmicist in San Francisco, married Mabel Kuhn in Fort Bragg April 30, 1916. Father Blanderfield performed the Catholic service. — May 3, 1916

Roy Blosser, the son of John Blosser of Willits, married Sadie Milliken, the daughter of the late Dr.J.W. and Lizzie Milliken of Berkeley, in that city June 23, 1914. Rev.B.B. Connor of Fruitvale officiated. — Jul 1, 1914

Albert Blume, former Fort Bragg resident, was married in San Francisco September 1910. [Name of bridge not reported.] — Mar 1, 1911

Frank L.Bohn was to marry Aileen Corwin at Oakland October 1, 1914 — Sep 30, 1914

Arthur D.Borden of Palo Alto married Geneva Swain of Point Arena at that place May 9, 1914. — Jun 3, 1914

A.Borneman married Embie Mann, the daughter of John Mann of Fort Bragg, at Santa Rosa October 22, 1917. — Oct 17, 1917

Henry Boseton got a license to wed Mamie Pony. — Sep 29, 1915

F.Bota obtained a license to wed Miss E.Melo. — Nov 18, 1914

W.P.Botkin obtained a license to wed Edna K.Morgan of San Francisco. — Jul 26, 1916

Elwin J.Boundy of San Jose married Gertrude Claire Fuller, the daughter of W.F.Fuller of Fort Bragg, in San Francisco March 17, 1913. [engagement notice said "Edwin J.Boundey"] — Jan 8, 1913 / Mar 19, 1913

T.L.Bourns, a prominent druggist of San Francisco born in and the brother of Thomas Bourns, married Florence Oliver in San Francisco March 16, 1910. — Mar 23, 1910

William Carlton Bouton of Portland, Oregon, married Elizabeth Richards of Havre, Montana, September 19, 1914. The groom was the son of Ed Bouton, formerly of Noyo. — Sep 30, 1914

Irving Bowden married Nellie Vaughn, formerly of Mendocino, in Ukiah October 18, 1919. — Oct 22, 1919

Arthur R.Bowen, 37, of Navarro, obtained a license to wed Nellie Frances Hartley, 23, of Boonville. — Dec 19, 1917

Bert Bowman of Santa Rosa married Mabel Piper, the daughter of John Piper of Schooner Gulch, at that place "recently". — Sep 3, 1919

Henry Bowman married Hilda Flowers in Zanesville, Ohio,   Nov 19, 1919
November 9, 1919. The groom was born and raised in
Mendocino County.

J.L.Bowman of Mendocino obtained a license to marry   Aug 21, 1912
Anna Dougherty.

Constable J.D.Boyd of Salt Point Township married   Jan 7, 1914
Adeline May Nobles near Annapolis December 25, 1913.

O.Boyd obtained a license to wed Irene Cromwell,   Mar 6, 1918
both were of Westport.

H.B.Braden married Nellie Nelson, the daughter of Gus Nelson,   Mar 3, 1915
at Fort Bragg March 2, 1915. Judge F.A.Whipple officiated.

Quin Bradley got a license to wed Belle Price, both of Philo.   Jan 9, 1918

Roy Hudson Bradley, 28, of Fort Collins, Colorado,   Jan 24, 1912
got a license to wed Nellie Ward, 21, of Philo.

W.P.Bradley obtained a license March 25, 1914 to   Apr 8, 1914
wed Alice Mecham of Ukiah.

Roy A.Brady married Gertrude Murray of Caspar at Piedmont   Jul 22, 1914
July 18, 1914. Rev.Thomas A.Boyen presided.

Leo Brandon, the son of Dave Brandon, obtained a license to   Jun 6, 1917
wed Sadie Forsythe of Howard Creek, in San Francisco
June 4, 1917.

LeRoy Verne Brant of Fort Bragg married Beatrice Clayton   Feb 4, 1914
of San Jose at Fort Bragg February 3, 1914. The groom was
a music teacher. Rev.R.C.Grace presided.

Jesse M.Brayton, 28, of Northwestern obtained a   Dec 27, 1911
license to wed Blanch M.Lewis, 18, of Willits.

Charles J.Breen married Vesta Irene Johnson in Fort Bragg   Jun 4, 1919
May 29, 1919. Rev.W.M.Sutherland officiated.

W.E.Brewer of Ukiah married Reva D.Sweet of San Francisco   May 12, 1915
in that city "last week".

J.Albert Brien married Marie Iversen at Mendocino April 3,   Apr 7, 1915
1915 in Catholic rites conducted by Father Raymond. Both
were school teachers.

Chester Briggs wed Barbara Frazer at Albion May 14, 1916.   May 17, 1916

L.C.Briggs married Gladys Gantz at Ukiah July 28, 1915. Both   Aug 4, 1915
were from Redwood Valley.

Walter N.Briggs obtained a license to wed Ida Williams   Dec 18, 1912
of Ukiah.

James Madison Brines obtained a license to wed   Nov 24, 1915
Mary M.Sweetser of Ukiah.

Walter P.Brinkman obtained a license to wed Emma L.Dane,   Nov 15, 1911
both of Fort Bragg.

Martin L.Brinzing obtained a license to wed Grace Eagle   Aug 5, 1914
of Caspar.

Indiana Darville Brochier married Nicey Alma Beal   Apr 22, 1914
of Caspar at that place April 25, 1914.   May 13, 1914

Darville Brochier of Albion married Mrs.Juliette   Sep 24, 1919
Raudio of Fort Bragg at Ukiah "last week".

Harry Broo of Albion obtained a license to wed Mary Ronn   Sep 6, 1911
of Fort Bragg.

C.Brooks, 23, obtained a license to wed Mabel Carner, 21.   Nov 17, 1915
Both were from Potter Valley.

Claude Brooks married Louise Steimle June 1, 1919 in Oakland.   May 7, 1919
[The bride's name on the license was reported as "Stimley".]   Jun 4, 1919

M.E.Brooks of San Francisco obtained a license to wed   Oct 25, 1911
Sarah March of Willits.

Henry Brovelli obtained a license to wed Rosa Malinari.   Sep 2, 1914
                                                                 Sep 9, 1914
E.P.Brower got a license to wed Phyllis L.Ingram.   Dec 2, 1914

Rev.A.Brown, the former pastor of the Caspar Baptist church,   Mar 26, 1913
married Susie Gibson of Ukiah in San Francisco "last week".

Austin Brown married Nellie Bowen at Lakeport July 14, 1916.   Aug 2, 1916

Allie Brown, the son of Albert Brown of Mendocino, was to   Nov 19, 1919
marry Bessie Sprinkle in San Francisco November 21, 1919.

Charles Brown, the son of George Brown of Fort Bragg, wed   Jul 26, 1916
Elizabeth Handley, the daughter of George Handley of Noyo,   Aug 2, 1916
in Fort Bragg July 16, 1916. Rev.W.M.Sutherland officiated.

Eugene A.Brown married Janet Louise Shudy at St.Helena,   Nov 12, 1919
Napa County, November 3, 1919.

George Brown got a license to wed Agnes Rodger.   Aug 11, 1915

H.A.Brown, a civil engineer with the California Western   Dec 3, 1913
Railroad, married Mrs.Leona Wallace in Willits
November 29, 1913.

Herbert Brown married Ethel A.Bailey at Willits   Oct 20, 1915
October 9, 1915.

Howard G.Brown of Mendocino married Elizabeth M.Ballard of   Aug 30, 1911
Oakland in that city August 21, 1911.

John M.Brown of Comptche obtained a license to wed   Sep 27, 1916
Nellie F.Raab of Branscomb.

Joseph A.Brown of Mendocino married Amy Torrence, the   Feb 6, 1918
daughter of Dayton Torrence of Cleone, February 3, 1918 at
Fort Bragg. Judge J.K.Peirsol officiated.

Leslie A.Brown married Ora Spellman of Anchorage, Alaska,   Sep 27, 1916
in that city August 29, 1916. The groom was the son of
Henry H.Brown of Mendocino.

Walter Brown of Mendocino wed Mrs.Mabel Winkler of Sonoma   Sep 6, 1916
County at San Francisco August 21, 1916. Mr.Brown was the
brother of Mrs.Frank West and Miss Olive Brown of Mendocino.

Wilson J.Brown of Willits married Helen Olmstead of   Jul 25, 1917
Petaluma July 18, 1917.

R.O.Brunk got a license to wed Zelphia R.Rawles.   Nov 25, 1914

Henry C.S.Brush obtained a license to wed   Aug 3, 1910
Gertie Barkdoll of Covelo.

R.J.T.Brush got a license to wed Edna I.Smith.   Nov 18, 1914

E.G.Bryant of San Francisco obtained a license to wed Irma   Feb 12, 1919
Roper of Santa Cruz, a graduate of Point Arena highschool.

Virgilio <u>Bucchioni</u> married Elsie Susan Burr at Fort Bragg   Jul 21, 1915
July 17, 1915. Judge F.A.Whipple presided.

Cole <u>Buchanan</u> Jr.married Mrs.Ellen Kingren in San   Dec 1, 1915
Francisco November 27, 1915. Judge Roach presided.
Both were residents of Greenwood.

Frank <u>Buchanan</u>, 27, obtained a license to wed   Sep 11, 1918
Emma Biaggi, 22, both of Greenwood.

John <u>Buckbee</u> married Olive Douglass, the daughter   Oct 8, 1913
of F.A.Douglass, at Fort Bragg October 3, 1913.   Mar 4, 1914
Judge F.A.Whipple officiated.

George R.<u>Bunch</u> got a license to wed Ethel Beatrice Clow.   Mar 10, 1915

August <u>Burbeck</u> married Dena Ingman, both of Fort Bragg, at   Apr 9, 1919
that place April 5, 1919. Rev.Ohman officiated.

Horace E.<u>Burger</u> married Helen M.Newberry of Boonville   Dec 29, 1915
[married December 23, 1915; Separated August 1, 1929].   Dec 6, 1939

E.J.<u>Burke</u> got a license to wed Hattie Nobles of Point Arena.   Sep 13, 1911

Walter E.<u>Burke</u> of Cazadero married Evelyn R.Shuster of   Jan 3, 1912
Willits January 14, 1912.   Jan 17, 1912

Bruce Leroy <u>Burlingame</u> married Hazel Genevieve Doty at   Dec 26, 1917
San Jose December 10, 1917.

William <u>Burnstein</u> married Ida Saunders, daughter of W.S.   Feb 7, 1912
Saunders of Fort Bragg, in San Jose February 1, 1912.

Judge Leslie <u>Burr</u> married Blanche Mast, the daughter of   Jun 4, 1919
George Mast of Willits, in Hawaii April 4, 1919. The bride
taught school there.

Edward <u>Bush</u> of Portland, Oregon, married Maria Brown, a   Aug 30, 1916
former Mendocino resident and daughter of Walter Brown,
formerly of Albion. [No date reported].

Harry Gerald <u>Butler</u> married Vivian Taylor, daughter   Jun 11, 1913
of Harris Taylor, at Santa Rosa June 4, 1913.

John F.<u>Butler</u> wed Ethel Eastlick at Ukiah October 31, 1915.   Nov 3, 1915

Earl Frazier <u>Butts</u> got a license to wed Emily H.Stevens.   Sep 6, 1916

Walter D.<u>Butts</u>, of Healdsburg, was engaged to wed   Nov 5, 1913
Rena C.Laughlin, daughter of Mrs.William Laughlin.

Chester P.<u>Byrne</u> married Eva D.Talbot in Point Arena   Jul 5, 1911
July 3, 1911.

John P.<u>Byrnes</u>, 33, of San Francisco married Mayme Jefferson,   Dec 21, 1910
aged 32 of Fort Bragg, in San Francisco December 16, 1910.
Rev.A.C.Bane officiated.

Dr.C.B.<u>Caldwell</u>, a former Fort Bragg resident, married   Dec 11, 1912
Myrtle Therese Burnes of Sacramento there November 28, 1912.

Richard <u>Caldwell</u> obtained a license to wed   Oct 5, 1910
Samantha L.James of Westport.

Archie <u>Cameron</u> of Northspur obtained a license   May 21, 1913
to wed Myrtle Parsons of Berkeley.

Roderick <u>Cameron</u> married Mamie C.Snider, the daughter of   Jul 8, 1914
Abe Snider of Westport, at Fort Bragg July 2, 1914.   Jul 15, 1914
Rev.W.A.Chapman officiated.

William <u>Cameron</u> obtained a license to wed [name lost].   May 22, 1912

Alex Cammers married Irene Ramsdell in San Francisco
December 29, 1910.   Jan 4, 1911

Robert Cannaar married Grace T.Sloan in Fort Bragg
February 18, 1917.   Feb 21, 1917

Guilo Cantieri obtained a license to wed
Enrichetti Rizzoli.   Sep 9, 1914

Frank Carboni married Eliza Merini April 2, 1916 at Mendo-   Apr 5, 1916
cino in a Catholic ceremony. The groom was employed at
Boyle's tie camp; the bride had just arrived from Italy.

Thomas D.Cardwell, 30, obtained a license to wed
Mary E.Bills, 30, of Alder Point.   Jan 24, 1917

John D.Carey, formerly of Fort Bragg and now a resident of   Jul 27, 1910
Monrovia, married Mary Maloney recently.

Romie "Jerry" Carey married Helen Hanson in San Francisco   Nov 29, 1916
about November 25, 1916.

W.F."Bill" Carey, the son of Maurice Carey, formerly of Fort Jul 9, 1919
Bragg, got a license to wed Rita H.McCarren. Both were from
San Francisco.

Robert J.Carlisle of San Francisco obtained a license to wed Dec 12, 1917
Leona Curtis, formerly of Mendocino, in Solano County.

Charles Carlson of Eureka married Mrs.William Carlson   Mar 18, 1914
at Eureka "last week".

Charles R.Carlson married Leonora J.Wolfe of Albion at that   Dec 24, 1913
place December 25, 1913.   Dec 31, 1913
[License application gave bride's name as "Leonoria"]   Jan 21, 1914

Emil Carlson obtained a license to wed Katie Olsen of   Dec 20, 1911
Fort Bragg.

Thomas Carlson married Edith Semple, both of   Jan 29, 1913
Caspar, January 28, 1913. Rev.McKee officiated.

William Carlson obtained a license to wed   May 24, 1911
Selma Joutsen of Fort Bragg.

E.P.Carman got a license to wed Ada B.Gamman of Sebastopol.   Nov 1, 1911

William D.Carothers married Alice Myrtle Scott   Nov 1, 1911
at Ukiah October 30, 1911.

B.L.Carpenter got a license to wed Lela Hiatt.   May 31, 1911

Herbert W.Carr obtained a license to wed   Sep 6, 1911
Rena DeCarli, both of Mendocino.

George A.Carter obtained a license to wed Maud   Aug 3, 1910
Mae Van Arsdale of Laughlen.

W.H.Carter got a license to wed Lena Oakes, both of Willits. Oct 18, 1911

W.T.Carter of Santa Rosa obtained a license to wed   Nov 9, 1910
Laura Gill of Hopland.

Neal J.Carver of Washington obtained a license to   Sep 17, 1919
wed Hazel L.Begley of Covelo.

Hallie Case married Shirley Whited at Willits June 18, 1916. Jun 21, 1916

Leon A.Cassaouri obtained a license to wed Marie Baradat.   Aug 28, 1912

S.J.Cassel got a license to wed Agnes Hamilton of Caspar.   Aug 10, 1910

Felix Casthaux [Cozahoux?] obtained a license to   Sep 9, 1914
wed Georgia W.Zitska of San Francisco.

Joe Catherina married Margaret Robinson, the oldest   Jul 8, 1914
daughter of Mrs.Julia Robinson, at Mendocino July 2, 1914. Jul 15, 1914
[Name on license J.Cataninch,]

A.Cerretini got a license to wed Angelina Figone.   Jul 7, 1915

E.D.Cerruti married Alvira Lepori, the daughter of John   May 21, 1919
Lepori of Point Arena, in San Francisco May 3, 1919.

James Chaffin, 43, obtained a license to wed Abbie Seidner, Mar 27, 1912
16, of Irma, Humboldt County.

E.W.Chalmers married Bertha H.Baker in Santa Rosa   Sep 15, 1915
September 8, 1915. Rev.Baker, the bride's father, officiated.

A.B.Chamberlain obtained a license to wed Gertrude Harman May 21, 1913
of Petaluma.

John Hadley Chambers obtained a license to wed   May 24, 1911
Elizabeth Milliken of Mendocino.

Clarence Chapin, the proprietor of the Grand Hotel in Fort Oct 25, 1916
Bragg, married Miss Genevieve Wilson of Nevada, in San   Nov 15, 1916
Francisco November 15, 1916.

Rev.W.A.Chapman married Miss Harriet E.Langstaff   Jul 12, 1916
of Boston, England, in Fort Bragg on July 4, 1916.
Rev.Hargreaves of Caspar officiated.

William Floyd Chapman of San Francisco married   Dec 29, 1915
Blanche Dodge of Point Arena in Berkeley
December 23, 1915. Rev.Arthur Hicks officiated.

Norman R.Charman married Elsie Baechtel at Willits   Jul 5, 1916
July 2, 1916.

Dr.Thomas A.Cheal married Helen Weller in Fort Bragg   Dec 27, 1911
December 27, 1911 at the Baptist church.
Rev.J.C.Garth officiated.

Charley Chester married Birdie Geitner   Jan 24, 1912
January 21, 1912. Rev.Grace officiated.

William Chisholm married Gussie Cyphers in Eureka   Oct 4, 1916
October 1, 1916.

Harry H.Christian, 27, obtained a license to wed   Feb 6, 1918
Alma Rose Hood, 20 - both of Gualala. [A second item reported Feb 13, 1918
Harry Christian of Elk marrying Zena Hood of Gualala "last week".]

H.G.C.Christianson obtained a license to wed Irene L.Elder. Jul 29, 1914

Myren A.Christy married Etta M.Pickle at Ukiah May 5, 1911. May 17, 1911

E.A.Clark obtained a license to wed Mary Wilsey of Westport. Sep 11, 1918

Edward Clark married Marie Newman of Ukiah at that city on Feb 10, 1915
February 3, 1915.

Ernest Clark, a former Ukiah resident, married in Idaho   Feb 9, 1910
"last week" [bride's name not reported].

Ethan Clark married Nellie Rogers at Ukiah March 17, 1912. Mar 20, 1912

William Clark married Mrs.Minnie Young, the daughter of   Oct 21, 1914
Mrs.E.F.Rich of Sherwood October 18, 1914. Rev.W.C.Whitaker Oct 28, 1914
officiated at the ceremony.

Frank Clatts was licensed to wed Leta M.Williams of Willits. Mar 11, 1914

Albert Clay, 33, married Grace Bullock, 30,   Oct 25, 1916
October 15, 1916. Both were Willits residents.

Dr.H.O.Clelland, the only son of T.L.Clelland, married   Apr 25, 1917
Marguerite Thomas, the daughter of attorney W.P.Thomas and
president of the Commercial Bank in Ukiah, at that place on
April 22, 1917.

Grover Cleveland married Ethel Lambert at Ukiah   Mar 20, 1912
March 16, 1912. Judge White officiated.

James Cleveland, 43, obtained a license to wed Ida Bell   Jan 3, 1917
Wages, 30 - both of Ukiah.

Frank M.Cloyd obtained a license to wed Emily C.Gibson.   Sep 30, 1914

Oscar Cohard of Covelo obtained a license to wed   Nov 9, 1910
Marie Buss of Mill Valley.

Roy Colburn married Alice Barnes of Caspar at Ukiah   Jun 29, 1910
May 25, 1910.

Cyrus Joseph Cole married Hazel J.Gillespie, both of   Feb 4, 1914
Willits, at that place January 26, 1914. Elder John H.   Feb 11, 1914
Clark officiated.

Ludwig Coleman of Navarro obtained a license to wed Vera   Dec 13, 1916
Irene Palladay of Boonville.

Amzi K.Compton, 60, obtained a license to wed Clara   Jul 7, 1915
Anderson, 19. Both were from Ukiah.   Jul 14, 1915

T.Condon obtained a license to wed Pearl Grafe.   Jun 30, 1915

James E.Conway married Mrs.Imogene Hardeman Givens, a local   Jul 23, 1919
schoolteacher, at Santa Barbara June 30, 1919.

Clifford G.Cook, the son of the late Horatio Nelson Cook,   Mar 3, 1915
married Violet M.Cook, the daughter of Norton L.Cook, in San
Francisco March 1, 1915.

R.S.Coon, 22, married Ruby Lillian Bail, 19, of Guerneville,   Feb 28, 1912
in Ukiah February 29, 1912. [License application said T.S.Coon Mar 6, 1912
and Lillian Bail].

Jim Cooney, formerly of Greenwood, married Miss B.Kirk of San   Dec 23, 1914
Francisco in that city December 17, 1914.

John Cooney, formerly of Mendocino, was engaged to wed   Oct 31, 1917
Claire Ansel of Alameda.

Robert T.Cop obtained a license to wed Kittie Miller of   Sep 14, 1910
Hopland.

Alba B.Copsey, 30, of Ukiah, obtained a license   Nov 8, 1916
to wed Edith May Court, 24, of Willits.

Frank Corbett wed Nellie Donlon at Ukiah February 1, 1912.   Feb 7, 1912

Fred Corbett married Lillian Talbot September 18, 1911 at   Nov 1, 1911
Modesto. Miss Talbot was a former Inglenook resident.

Robert Corbett married Verna Whitman of Willits   May 21, 1913
at Ukiah May 18, 1913. Rev.Charles Luce presided.

Wilbur Cotrel got a license to wed Ruby Wright.   Jun 16, 1915

James Cowan of Elk was wed to Alberta Orr in Santa Rosa   Jan 3, 1912
"last week".

E.A.Cox got a license to wed Pearl May Strider of Ukiah.   Jun 14, 1911

G.W.Cox obtained a license to wed Olive Kees of
Blocksburg, Humboldt County.

May 31, 1911

Samuel Cox married Grace Rhinehart in San Francisco "last
week". Both were employees at the State Hospital in Talmage.

Dec 29, 1915

Felix Cozahoux [Casthaux] obtained a license to marry
Georgia W.Zitska of San Francisco.

Sep 9, 1914

Fred Crabtree got a license to wed Merle A.Wilsey of Covelo.

Jul 1, 1914
Jul 15, 1914

Leroy Craig of Point Arena married Della Grace Bishop of
Inglenook at that place December 31, 1919.
[Engagement announcement gave groom's name as "Walter"].

Dec 17, 1919
Jan 7, 1920

J.D.Craighan celebrated a 50th wedding anniversary,
December 31, 1915. Their daughter was Mrs.Charles R.Weller
of Fort Bragg.

Jan 5, 1916

George Crawford of San Jose married Maybelle Thompson of
Mendocino at San Jose June 24, 1914.

Jul 1, 1914

O.R.Crester married Mabel Fortune of Ukiah, in San Diego.
[No date reported.]

Jan 30, 1918

Omar Crester of Fort Bragg married Clare Talbot of Albion
January 28, 1916. Rev.Sutherland presided. Clara Crester
died October 12, 1917.

Feb 2, 1916
Oct 24, 1917

Charles Joseph Cretser, 21, obtained a license
to wed Beatrice K.Gitner, 16, of Fort Bragg.

Jan 31, 1912

George Crnac married Mary Colbert in Fort Bragg
January 11, 1919. Judge Frank A.Whipple officiated.
[The license gave the groom's name as "Cernia"].

Jan 15, 1919

John T.Crockett, 54, obtained a license to wed
Edith Castle Hudson, 22, both of Ukiah.

Dec 6, 1911

J.Crossweight [also "Crossthwaite"]. married Birdie
[also "Bertie"]. Jackson at Albion July 11, 1915.

Jul 21, 1915

William H.Cummings, 26, obtained a license to wed
Mary L.James, 22 - both of San Francisco.

Aug 1, 1917

Carlton A.Curtis married Dorothy Kincaid in Berkeley on
June 3, 1916. Mr.Curtis was Superintendent of the California
Western Railroad at Fort Bragg and the son of A.A.Curtis of
San Rafael. His bride was the daughter of George Frank
Kincaid of Berkeley. Bishop William Ford Nichols presided.

Apr 5, 1916
May 31, 1916
Jun 7, 1916

Eugene Cussins, 23, of Covelo obtained a license
to wed Mable Staffler, 15, of San Francisco.

Sep 18, 1912

Ernest J.Cuthbertson, a teacher at the Manchester school,
married Mary A.Bishop at Manchester "last week".

Feb 3, 1915
Feb 24, 1915

The R.H.Cuthbertsons celebrated their 50th wedding
anniversary in Fort Bragg April 15, 1917.

May 2, 1917

Aner Dahl married Gladys Dean at Los Gatos
"several weeks ago".

Dec 11, 1918

Victor Dahl obtained a license to wed Anna K.Rush,
both of Fort Bragg.

Oct 1, 1919

John A.Dahlberg obtained a license to wed Hilma I.Anderson.

Jul 1, 1914
Jul 15, 1914

C.W.Dahlstrom married Martha Keller at Ukiah July 11, 1915.

Jul 21, 1915

Charles Dallerup of San Rafael married Lena Hansen of Caspar
in Ukiah August 13, 1913. Judge White officiated.

Aug 20, 1913

Chester <u>Dalmas</u> obtained a license to wed Phoebe May Smith of Willits.   Mar 22, 1911

Frank W.<u>Dane</u> of Fort Bragg married Alice Smith of Santa Cruz at Fort Bragg June 4, 1913. Judge F.A.Whipple officiated.   Jun 11, 1913

George M.<u>Dane</u> obtained a license to wed Sarah M.Conger, both of Fort Bragg.   May 30, 1917

Arthur Wesley <u>Daniels</u>, 24, married Sene Seman, 27, December 17, 1919 in Ukiah. Judge J.Q.White officiated. Both parties were from Mendocino.   Dec 24, 1919

Cassius W.B.<u>Darling</u> married Gladys Rae Renick at Willits June 24, 1914.   Jul 1, 1914
                                                      Jul 8, 1914

Byron Austin <u>Davis</u> obtained a license to wed Eva Mary Morrison of Covelo.   Dec 13, 1916

D.R.<u>Davis</u> married Berenice Brown, the daughter of Henry Brown of Mendocino, at that place February 13, 1915.   Feb 17, 1915

G.<u>Davis</u> married Kate White in Fort Bragg May 18, 1911.   May 31, 1911

Leroy Allison <u>Davis</u> of Oakland, 21, obtained a license to wed Blanch N.Nieghbors [Neighbors?], 20, of Hearst.   Mar 13, 1912

Paul <u>Davis</u>, 22, obtained a license to wed Ida Haylor, 20.   Feb 28, 1912
[Another report gives the bride's name as "Haydon"].   Mar 6, 1912

Roy Ellis <u>Davis</u>, 22, of Harris, obtained a license to wed Elizabeth Lynn Johnson, 17, of Covelo.   Dec 1, 1915

W.B.<u>Davis</u>, 25, obtained a license to wed Lillian M.Garfield, 27. Both were from Harris.   Dec 1, 1915

Will <u>Davis</u> of Albion married Ida Norris of Lakeport at that place August 18, 1914.   Aug 19, 1914

Charles Christopher <u>Day</u> obtained a license to wed Eva B.Fry of Comptche.   Aug 2, 1916

Alva <u>Deacon</u> married Vivian Wilson in a double ceremony at Ukiah December 25, 1919 with Bert Thompson and Leta Wilson.   Dec 24, 1919

Fred <u>Dean</u> married Grace Wallace in Oakland August 13, 1916.   Sep 6, 1916

Joe <u>Dean</u> married Mae Jahnigen in Fort Bragg June 25, 1913.   Jun 25, 1913

F.E.<u>DeCarli</u>, 27, obtained a license to wed Henrietta M.Martinazzi, 21 - both of Ukiah.   Dec 1, 1915

S.P.<u>DeCarli</u> of Manchester obtained a license to wed Ella Elva Logue of Point Arena.   Sep 7, 1910

Vincienzo <u>Deghi</u> got a license to wed Aladina Giusti of Elk.   Dec 29, 1915

Pietro <u>Della Maggiora</u> married Angelina Bertini in Fort Bragg November 15, 1912 in a Catholic ceremony by Father Brennen.   Nov 20, 1912

Mathew <u>Delli Fatti</u> married Winnie Estes at Ukiah October 27, 1919. Both were from Boonville.   Oct 29, 1919

E.<u>Del Poggretto</u> obtained a license to wed Madalene Mazzetta of Greenwood.   Aug 5, 1914

Agostino <u>Del Re</u> obtained a license to wed Maria Del Re.   Feb 23, 1910

Martin <u>Del Re</u> obtained a license to wed Maria Losa.   Feb 23, 1910

Warren <u>DeMerritt</u> married Ethel McKinley at Talmage June 9, 1910.   Jun 15, 1910

J.Dempsey obtained a license to wed Pauline Monson.   Dec 4, 1912

Arthur L.Dennen married Elsie V.Brown in San Francisco   Dec 4, 1918
November 20, 1918. Both were from Fort Bragg.

Byron James Dennison married Alice Ballad in San Francisco   Jun 11, 1919
June 9, 1919.

Juilio Derosa got a license to wed Lena Sichi.   Nov 3, 1915

Gail DeShiell got a license to wed Edith Dempsey.   Sep 15, 1915

Clarence R.Devereux of Cleone married Bernice Randall of   Jun 26, 1912
Concord, Contra Costa County, at that place June 20, 1912.
Catholic services were conducted by Father Campbell. The
bride was the eldest daughter of E.J.Randall of Concord.
Her sister was Grace D.Randall.

Edwin A.Devereux married Lila Joy in Fresno [no date reported].   Jul 12, 1911
Rev.Duncan Wallace officiated. The groom's parents lived in
Cleone.

A.E.Dexter, a marine stationed at Vallejo, married Mrs.Edna Sep 17, 1919
Bunch, the daughter of Lee Cunningham of Ukiah, on
September 7, 1919.

Edward DeYoung married Mary K.Estes at Boonville   Nov 19, 1913
November 23, 1913. Both were from that place.   Nov 26, 1913

Owen L.Dickinson, 28, of San Francisco obtained a license to May 10, 1916
wed Vera Mason, 24, of Dixon. The bride-to-be was a former
Inglenook resident.

J.H.Dickey Jr.married Annie M.Sagehorn at Ukiah   Oct 7, 1914
October 3, 1914. Both were residents of Willits.

W.B.Dickey wed Myrtle Elaine Anker in Ukiah July 3, 1910.   Jul 6, 1910
                                                            Jul 13, 1910
Otto Dietsche obtained a license to wed Julia Main.   Jan 8, 1913

John Dietz of Albion, a woodsman, married Mrs.Helen Scott of Mar 9, 1910
Comptche at Ukiah March 8, 1910.

Sgt.Joseph Alfred Dixon, the son of W.G.Dixon of Fort Bragg, Jul 18, 1917
married Louise Boudreau, the daughter of F.J.Boudreau who   Jun 12, 1918
once ran the Grand Hotel in Fort Bragg, in Tacoma,
Washington, "last week".

P.H.Dixon married Mary Colkhoun of Montreal, Canada, in   Oct 19, 1910
San Francisco [no date reported].

Arthur Dodge of Mendocino married Alma L.Hopkins   Jul 13, 1910
at Santa Rosa July 2, 1910.

Charles P.Dodge married Alice Amelia Richmond in   Sep 29, 1915
Fort Bragg September 27, 1915.   Oct 13, 1915

H.A.Doidge married Florence Foye at Ukiah July 16, 1917. The Aug 1, 1917
groom was the head of the gent's clothing department at the
Union Lumber Company store in Fort Bragg; the bride, the
daughter of the late Henry Foye, was a local school teacher.

Massino Domenigoni married [bride's name unreported was Teresa   Sep 3, 1913
Lafranchi], a niece of John Lafranchi, "last week" in Fort   Mar 4, 1914
Bragg. Judge F.A.Whipple officiated.

M.A.Donahue of Fulton obtained a license to wed   Aug 21, 1912
Clara E.Faught of Hopland.

Alexander Donaldson got a license to wed May J.Wilkey.   Oct 27, 1915

D.H.Donnan, 33, of Covelo, obtained a license to
wed Josephine Smith, 20, of Santa Rosa.

Mar 20, 1918

Sylvester H.Donohoe, 45, obtained a license to
wed Ida J.Morrison, 43, of San Francisco.

Feb 14, 1912

Thomas Arthur Dornan of Albion married Florence Ramona
Woodward near Noyo October 16, 1910. Rev.J.S.Ross officiated.

Oct 19, 1910

Frances Dougherty of Point Arena obtained a
license to wed Ruby Philbert of Lytton Springs.

Sep 7, 1910

Peter C.Dougherty wed Alice Trueman at Caspar
December 10, 1914.

Dec 23, 1914

S.Downie obtained a license to wed Lucy Agnes Palmer of
Sebastopol, Sonoma County.

Sep 7, 1910

Chester R.Downing married Rosella Quinliven at Ukiah
September 30, 1916.

Oct 4, 1916

Lauren J.Downing, 20, of Laytonville, obtained a
license to wed Ethel Betts, 19, of Covelo.

Jul 7, 1915
Jul 14, 1915

Walter Hampton Downing, 28, married Ethel May Watkins, 27,
at Ukiah July 30, 1915. Both were from Chicago, Illinois.

Jul 28, 1915
Aug 4, 1915

J.Doyle of Portola married Miss M.Adams, the daughter of
Mr.Nye formerly of Point Arena, on September 16, 1916.

Sep 27, 1916

Thomas E.Doyle married Mrs.Eva Freeman of Mendocino
at that place February 1, 1919 by Judge Wallace.

Jan 29, 1919
Feb 5, 1919

Harry Drenkle married Hanna Crozer at Alamo, Contra Costa
County, July 12, 1913.

Jul 23, 1913

Theodore Driver married Emma E.McNamara February 14, 1914.

Feb 18, 1914
Mar 4, 1914

John Duarte obtained a license to wed Belle Fitch.

Mar 11, 1914

Edward F.Duchaine obtained a license to wed Leila May
Iversen.

May 7, 1913

Albert Duffey married Mrs.Ed McFaul, the daughter
of Alf Howard, in Fort Bragg January 16, 1918.

Jan 16, 1918

Ray Duncan obtained a license to wed Agnes Ackerman, both
of Covello.

Sep 6, 1911

Leslie Raymond Dunlap, 20, obtained a license to
wed Ruby Myrtle Cummins, 20, both of Covelo.

Jul 12, 1911

Frances A.Dunnebeck obtained a license to wed
Viola P.Bowen of Lakeport.

Sep 30, 1914

H.D.Dunsmore, 21, obtained a license to wed
Freta L.McClellan, 19, both of Ukiah.

Feb 14, 1912

Edgar Kirkand Dun Van obtained a license to wed
Hazel Venre Hamlin of Laytonville.

Jun 28, 1911

George Dunwall married Esther Sands at Fort Bragg
June 27, 1914. Judge F.A.Whipple officiated.

Jul 1, 1914
Jul 8, 1914

Attorney C.D.Dutton, formerly of Ukiah and now in Oakland,
was to marry Laura Weir of Vacaville "soon".

Jan 19, 1910

Edgar Dutton, the son of D.C.Dutton, married
Eva Thomas at Oakland December 16, 1915.

Dec 22, 1915

D.H.DuVander of Santa Rosa married Mary Cordano   Jan 18, 1911
of Windsor at Ukiah January 11, 1911.

Raymond Dyer married Ruby Standley of Westport at Fort Bragg   Jan 24, 1912
January 13, 1912. Rev.W.C.Chapman officiated.

William S.Dyer married Blanche Anderson, the daughter of   Dec 25, 1918
N.P.Anderson a Fort Bragg resident until 1917, in Oakland
December 3, 1918. The groom was a conductor on the Key
System of street railways.

Henry M.Eagan married Edith M.Leger, both of Wendling,   May 8, 1912
at Ukiah April 29, 1912.

Earl Edison married Florence Larsen in San Francisco   Jan 17, 1917
August 17, 1916. Rev.John Brewer presided. The wedding was
kept secret until January 1917.

J.W.Edwards obtained a license to wed Henrietta Bilnde   Oct 5, 1910
of Willits.

W.E.Edwards of Willits obtained a license to wed   Mar 8, 1911
Kate Craft of Kennet, Shasta County.

William Eggers got a license to wed Ida Elamix.   Jan 15, 1913

Mark Egland married Mrs.Myrtle Scott [date uncertain].   Jul 3, 1918

Victor Eickhoff obtained a license to wed   Nov 23, 1910
Margaret Lamotte of San Francisco.

Eugene Earl Eldredge, 35, married Elwilda Francis Tracy, 27, Aug 30, 1916
in Lake County August 21, 1916. Both were from Christine and
were married by Superior Judge M.S.Sayre.

Robert Leroy Eldredge, the only son of George Eldredge   Jan 19, 1916
of Fort Bragg, married Adeline G.Lerman of San Jose
January 14, 1916.

Edward Ellison of Mendocino married Amanda "Mandy"   Dec 12, 1917
Larsen of Fort Bragg at Mendocino December 15,   Dec 19, 1917
1917. Rev.John J.Hillberg officiated.

Lars A.Ellison of Mendocino married Miss A.Markkula of Fort   Jul 4, 1917
Bragg July 1, 1917 at Mendocino by Rev.J.J.Hillberg.

Harry Ells of Stege, California, married Mabel Perry,   Jan 8, 1913
formerly of Mendocino, in Santa Barbara December 21, 1912.

M.A.Ely obtained a license to wed Hazel H.Eastlick.   Aug 11, 1915

Bert Enders married Eva Triplett, the daughter of Henry   Dec 18, 1918
Triplett, at Fort Bragg December 14, 1918. Dr.Franklin Bryan
officiated at the ceremony.

Joe Ennes obtained a license to wed Mary Pereira.   Jan 8, 1913

C.Enright married Margaret Josephine Leonard in San Fran-   Jul 8, 1914
cisco June 28, 1914. Father Ryan officiated. Both were
residents of Willits.

Frederick C.Ensey of Harris obtained a license   Sep 2, 1914
to wed Alice Elaine Young of Coaledo, Oregon.   Sep 9, 1914

W.A.Erbe married Mrs.Holcomb in San Francisco "last week".   Jul 22, 1914

A.P.Erickson of Inglenook celebrated their 50th.wedding   Mar 13, 1912
anniversary February 27, 1912. They were residents of the
county since 1886.

John Erickson married Sifla West in Fort Bragg by Judge   Sep 27, 1911
Frank A.Whipple September 22, 1911. Declaration filed 1917.   Feb 21, 1917
[Bride's name "Sophia" on license application of September 21, 1911.]

Lloyd Erwin, 23, of Talmage, obtained a license
to wed Bertha B.Bush, 20, of Covelo.   Nov 1, 1916

E.H.Escher, electrical engineer with Pacific Telephone and   May 6, 1914
Telegraph, married Hazel Taylor, the daughter of George
Taylor and a 1910 graduate of the Fort Bragg highschool, at
the Baptist church in Ukiah May 2, 1914. Rev.Fox presided.

John S.Escola married Nannie M.Flood at Littleriver   Jun 24, 1914
June 18, 1914.

Joe Etchart married Clara Casanega at Ukiah   Apr 16, 1913
April 7, 1913. Judge Crockett presided.

Will Evans, formerly of Ukiah, married Miss Williams, the   Nov 12, 1913
daughter of J.E.Williams, in Santa Rosa November 3, 1913.

Edward A.Eversole married Bess Gwartney of Oakland   Jan 6, 1915
at Ukiah December 31, 1914.

Keith C.Eversole, an attorney in Ukiah, obtained   Jan 19, 1916
a license to wed Ina Tutt of Oakland.

J.D.Fair married Leila Price [sometime between   Jul 4, 1917
July 4 and 10, 1917].

Herman Fairbanks married Loretta Studebaker of   Jul 12, 1916
Manchester at that place July 10, 1916.   Jul 19, 1916

Hiram T.Fairbanks obtained a license to wed   Aug 18, 1915
Mrs.Gertrude Keller of Willits.

J.Fairbanks married Miss Baechtel, both of   Jul 12, 1911
Willits, in San Francisco June 30, 1911.

Pearl R.Fairbairn obtained a license to wed   Nov 5, 1913
May E.Winey, both of Talmage.

P.R.Fairbarn wed Edna Jean Miline at Talmage May 18, 1912.   May 22, 1912

Vernon Nathan Fales obtained a license to wed   Aug 9, 1916
Annie Laura Leah, both of Dos Rios.

C.W.Falli got a license to wed Mary Crabtree of Round Valley.   Mar 8, 1911

R.E.Farrelly got a license to wed Anna E.Jones.   Jul 7, 1915

Ernest E.Farrer of Boonville married Ella Agnes Eten of   Feb 27, 1918
Philo at Santa Rosa February 23, 1918.

Attorney William Dudley Farthing of St.Louis, Missouri,   Jul 8, 1914
married Hattie Garrigus, the sister of Mrs.J.Melville Fisher,
in St.Louis June 18, 1914.

Arthur Fawler obtained a license to wed Edith Harriman   May 31, 1911
of San Francisco.

Herman C.Fayal married Amelia Costa of New Bedford,   Dec 30, 1914
Massachusetts, at the Mendocino Catholic church   Jan 13, 1915
December 24, 1914. Father Raymond led the ceremony.

John Costa Fayal, 27, obtained a license to wed   Oct 18, 1916
Amelia Costa, 17, of Mendocino.
[A second account gives the bride's name as "Maria M.Costa"].   Oct 25, 1916

J.H.Fee married Gertrude LeValley in Fort Bragg   Dec 4, 1912
November 28, 1912. Rev.W.A.Chapman officiated.

Leland Frank Feiden married Wilmae Mae Sanderson July 6,   Mar 12, 1919
1918 at the First Presbyterian church in Seattle;
Rev.M.A.Mathew officiated. The wedding was kept secret
until March 1919.

Harry Feliz obtained a license to wed Mary Stevens.   Jan 27, 1915

E.E.Ferguson, a wealthy rancher, married Mrs.Marie   Mar 19, 1919
Case, formerly of Willits, at Healdsburg "last
week". The bride was the daughter of Zack Simonson.

Frank Fernandez obtained a license to wed Maria   Feb 26, 1919
Augusta of Fort Bragg.

Joseph L.Fernandez married Pearl Crews of Santa Cruz in   Mar 17, 1915
Catholic rites at Fort Bragg March 13, 1915 conducted by
Father Wright.

Manuel Fernandez wed Annie Kinnanen November 5, 1916.   Nov 15, 1916

Frank L.Fertato of Caspar was engaged to wed   Oct 9, 1918
Georgia Wolfe of Albion.

Joseph Fevelli married Leta Moretti, the daughter   Jul 2, 1919
of A.Moretti, at Mendocino June 29, 1919.

A.Field of Oakland obtained a license to wed   Sep 6, 1916
Florence Golden of Fort Bragg.

John Figone, 23, obtained a license to wed   Nov 1, 1916
Rosa Mazzini, 21 - both of Willits.

Laurence [Lawrence] Filosi married Delphina DelTorchio on   Oct 19, 1910
October 22, 1910 in a Catholic service conducted by   Oct 26, 1910
Father Brennan. Both were residents of Inglenook.

Domenico Fiorina married Maria Maffini in Fort Bragg   Jan 27, 1915
January 30, 1915.   Feb 3, 1915
[License application: "Domingo Fiorina and Josephini Maffini".]

Charles E.Firebaugh obtained a license to wed   Aug 6, 1919
Elva Hollingsworth of Covelo.

Charles D.Fisher obtained a license to wed   Oct 7, 1914
Jennie B.White of Oakland.

F.L.Fisk married Austa Haarby in San Francisco   Sep 16, 1914
September 8, 1914. Both were from Albion.

Pietro Fistolera obtained a license to wed Caterina Delke.   Dec 30, 1914

Harry Douglass Fitch, 24, married Mary Violet White, 23,   Sep 30, 1914
September 29, 1914. Both were residents of Albion, Judge
M.S.Sayre officiated.

E.L.Fitzhugh obtained a license to wed Henrietta M.Cortze.   Aug 5, 1914
[Probably Cortez.]

George Fleming obtained a license to wed Carrie G.Paulson.   Jun 15, 1910

William Flemming married Thora Olsen at Hilton, Sonoma   Jan 8, 1919
County, January 1, 1919. The bride had been a nurse at
Sebastopol.

A.E.Flint obtained a license to wed Elizabeth Susan Crofts   Aug 28, 1912
of Penhryn, Eldorado County.

Hanby A.Ford, a rancher in the Ukiah valley, married Ula   Oct 17, 1917
White, a former Fort Bragg resident, in Ukiah "this week".

J.A.Ford married Mrs.Hattie Hayes in Santa Rosa   Dec 31, 1913
December 17, 1913.

Kirby L.Ford, 19, obtained a license to wed   Nov 1, 1916
Pamelia McLintock, 19. Both were from Calpella.

Russell Ford wed Leta Alberton at San Rafael January 8, 1916. Jan 19, 1916

Wesley M.Ford married Hazel Gertrude Lucas at
Ukiah February 11, 1911.

Feb 8, 1911
Feb 15, 1911

William Arnold Ford obtained a license to wed
Margaret Van Dyke of Ukiah.

Jul 9, 1919

Emil Forsman married Annie Ness of Fort Bragg in that place
December 28, 1912. Judge J.K.Peirsol officiated.

Dec 25, 1912
Jan 1, 1913

John Forsman married Miss A.Aspholm on September 24, 1910 at
the residence of Gus West in Fort Bragg by F.A.Whipple, JP.

Sep 28, 1910

F.L.Fortado obtained a license to wed Rose Castillo
of Greenwood.

Mar 8, 1911

Walter H.Foster obtained a license to wed
Ida M.Dale of Covelo.

Nov 24, 1915

George Fowler, 46, of Hopland obtained a license
to wed Elizabeth Burns, 45, of Oakland.

Sep 18, 1912

L.Fox married Lillian Burke of Ukiah in San Francisco
"recently".

Feb 23, 1910

William A.Fratis married Mrs.Joaquina S.Valadao of Mendocino
January 2, 1914. He was the son of Mike Fratis, a rancher at
Pine Grove, and she was the widow of Antone Valadao.

Dec 17, 1913
Jan 7, 1914
Feb 4, 1914

Melville Millar Frazer of Mendocino wed Mildred H.Johnson of
Point Arena October 1, 1916. Rev.Duncan Munro officiated.

Oct 11, 1916

Claude Frazier married Lillian Ellis at Fort Bragg
December 14, 1918. Judge Frank A.Whipple presided.

Dec 18, 1918

Hugh Frazier got a license to wed Hattie Martin of Hardy.

Jul 16, 1913

Walter G.Frederickson of Berkeley married Grace Chubb of
Willits [no date reported].

Aug 27, 1913

John Fredson married Alma Carlson at Sequoia Hall
in Fort Bragg May 14, 1910. F.A.Whipple presided.

May 4, 1910
May 18, 1910

Oliver F.Freeland married Mrs.Catherine Arfstean in Fort
Bragg December 23, 1915. Judge F.A.Whipple officiated.
Both were from Greenwood.

Dec 29, 1915

Earl Freeman was licensed to wed Dora Hassard of Fort Bragg.

Dec 27, 1916

Isaac Freeman married Laura Crouch at Ukiah May 5, 1919.
He was a veteran of the 343rd artillery.

May 14, 1919

Lester Freeman obtained a license to wed Flossie
Glatfeldera of Santa Rosa.

Jan 15, 1913

Lewis Freeman married Eva [surname unknown] at Navarro
May 20, 1893. The couple sought a divorce in October 1917.

Oct 31, 1917

Louis Freitas obtained a license to wed Rena Williams
of Fort Bragg.

Aug 30, 1911

Edwin J.Freshour obtained a license to wed Marie Boys.

Sep 29, 1915

Elbert Frost of Willits married Dorothy "Dolly" G.Smith at
at Willits November 11, 1911.

Nov 8, 1911
Nov 15, 1911

Orville M.Frost married Isabel O.Hoyt, a Willits highschool
teacher, in Berkeley "this week".

Oct 4, 1916
Nov 8, 1916

W.F.Fuller of Marysville married Mrs.Nellie Carlisle, a
former resident of Fort Bragg and daughter of Mr.Triplett.
[No date reported].

Mar 15, 1916

W.P.<u>Fuller</u> married Ora Hargis, daughter of Rev.Hargis of
Ukiah on September 30, 1916.   Oct 4, 1916

T.A.<u>Galer</u> obtained a license to wed Minerva Washington.   May 20, 1914

Ed <u>Gallagher</u> wed Adelia Williford January 1, 1917.   Jan 3, 1917

J.J.<u>Gallagher</u> married Blanche Bunker of Cloverdale   Jun 14, 1911
at Midlake, Lake County, June 11, 1911.

Roger <u>Gallagher</u> married Myrtle Cooper in Fort Bragg   Oct 25, 1911
October 22, 1911. Rev.J.S.Ross officiated.

August E.<u>Gamberg</u> married Ethel Monroe at Fort Bragg   Jan 5, 1916
December 24, 1915. Rev.Hillberg officiated.

Franz Jacob <u>Gamberg</u> married Kathryn K.Karl in Fort Bragg   Sep 9, 1914
September 5, 1914.   Sep 23, 1914

George <u>Gamble</u> married Hazel Schultize in Catholic services Apr 7, 1915
at Mendocino April 4, 1915 conducted by Father Raymond.

Arthur <u>Garason</u> got a license to wed Alice Driver of Hardy.   Dec 28, 1910

Amerigo <u>Gargini</u> obtained a license to wed Laura Gargina   Nov 8, 1911
of Riverside.

Stanley <u>Garoutte</u> married Gertrude Baffico at Ukiah   Aug 13, 1919
August 7, 1919.

C.M.<u>Garrett</u> got a license to wed Pearl L.Deal of Oakland.   Oct 7, 1914

John O.<u>Garvine</u> obtained a license to wed Helen Dott Boyd   Sep 7, 1910
of Mendocino.

Cecil M.<u>Gaspar</u> married Miss A.D.Birderman August 27, 1913. Sep 3, 1913
Rev.B.H.Baker of the Presbyterian church officiated.

Edward A.<u>Gaspar</u> obtained a license to wed Cordelia   Nov 13, 1918
Gillmore of Ukiah.

R.<u>Gaspari</u> married N.Mazzetta at Point Arena January 2, 1910. Jan 19, 1910

J.A.<u>Geary</u> married Daisy H.Underhill at Ukiah June 7, 1911.   Jun 14, 1911

Redames <u>Giannini</u> obtained a license to wed Agnes L.Rielli. Jul 1, 1914
["Riello" in another item.]

Peter <u>Gibney</u> married Alice Lilley at Mendocino   Jun 25, 1913
June 21, 1913.

Charles B.<u>Gibson</u> of Caspar obtained a license   Jun 5, 1918
to wed Amelia Bowman of Fort Bragg.

E.A.<u>Gibson</u> married Pansy G.English in Ukiah June 29, 1910. Jul 6, 1910

F.A.<u>Gibson</u> married Grace Mae Griffiths of Potter Valley at Oct 26, 1910
Ukiah October 23, 1910.

G.L.<u>Gibson</u> of Ukiah married Emma Travers of Sebastopol at   Sep 20, 1911
Santa Rosa September 10, 1911.

Herman W.<u>Gibson</u> of Gilroy obtained a license to marry   Aug 8, 1917
Cora E.Berry of Point Arena.

William N.<u>Gibson</u> married Elsie E.Barnes at Wendling   Jul 1, 1914
June 28, 1914.   Jul 8, 1914

Claude <u>Gignoux</u> married Daisy Hill January 10, 1917 in San   Jan 10, 1917
Francisco in a Catholic ceremony. The bride was formerly of
Fort Bragg and taught in the Ukiah Grammar School.

Orin <u>Gillmore</u> of Point Arena married Leona Bishop, the   Jan 12, 1916
daughter of Howard Bishop, at Bridgeport January 8, 1916.

Charlie <u>Gin</u>, Chinese, married Miss Shun Foy of San Francisco   May 31, 1916
in Fort Bragg May 24, 1916. Judge J.K.Peirsol officiated.

F.I.<u>Giorons</u> obtained a license to wed Annie Figone.   Oct 12, 1910

Max <u>Gold</u> married Leonora Moore in San Francisco in   Oct 25, 1916
April 1916 but was kept secret until October.

Allen <u>Golden</u> married Margaret Carey at Fort Bragg   Jun 23, 1915
June 17, 1915 in a Catholic service by Father Lawrence.

Johnny <u>Golden</u> obtained a license to wed Miss Munson,   May 18, 1910
formerly of Fort Bragg. [No date reported].

Thomas <u>Golden</u> married Madeline Vogel at the Fort Bragg Pres-   Nov 3, 1915
byterian church October 30, 1915. Rev.Sutherland officiated.

Antonio Joe <u>Gomes</u>, 21, got a license to wed Maria [May]   Sep 20, 1916
Hortense Andre, 18 - both of Mendocino.
[Maria was born June 11, 1900 at Sao Miguel, Azores, and came to
Mendocino in 1904. "Tony" and Maria were married September 16, 1916.]

John Antonio <u>Gomes</u> married Angelina Maderia-Saudades of Fort   Sep 8, 1915
Bragg in Catholic services at Mendocino September 18, 1915.   Sep 22, 1915

Louie <u>Gonsalves</u> married Miss M.E.Sutton of San Jose   Jan 12, 1910
January 9, 1910.

Roy <u>Good</u>, the Willits grammar school principal, obtained   Aug 30, 1916
a license to wed Marietta R.Hardin of Willits.

Edward <u>Gordon</u> obtained a license to wed   Aug 6, 1919
May K.Wilson of Manchester.

George H.<u>Gordon</u> married Bertha M.Standley in Ukiah   Nov 1, 1916
October 25, 1916. Both were residents of Westport.

Henry <u>Gordon</u> wed Mrs.Etta Hatch at Ukiah January 4, 1910.   Jan 5, 1910

William B.<u>Gorman</u> of San Francisco married Irene McLeod,   Aug 28, 1912
formerly of Mendocino, in San Francisco. [No date reported].

Hiram Elmer <u>Gowan</u> married Grace Higgins, the daughter of   Oct 13, 1915
John Higgins of Ukiah, at Ukiah October 6, 1915.   Oct 20, 1915

P.D.<u>Gowell</u> married Mrs.Dolly Hodghead August 14, 1918.   Aug 21, 1918
Rev.H.P.Ingram officiated.

W.R.<u>Grady</u>, a Noyo rancher, married Mary E.Oden in Fort Bragg   Apr 12, 1916
April 8, 1916. Rev.W.A.Chapman officiated. The couple were   Apr 26, 1916
new arrivals from Los Angeles. A second item reported the
marriage as occuring in Fort Bragg April 22, 1916.

Malcolm D.<u>Grant</u>, 22, obtained a license to wed   Dec 24, 1919
Sophie Hellen, 20, both were from Fort Bragg.

Arthur <u>Gray</u>, the son of M.D.Gray of Fort Bragg, married   Apr 23, 1913
Margaret Cameron, the daughter of A.Cameron a rancher at
Comptche, at Willits April 15, 1913.

Harold <u>Gray</u> married Emily Halling of Mendocino.[No date reported].   Jun 15, 1910

Lawrence A.<u>Gray</u>, the son of A.J.Gray of Northspur, married   Oct 21, 1914
Edith F.Dellett, daughter of Henry Dellett of Fort Bragg, at   Oct 28, 1914
that place October 18, 1914. Rev.Dawson of Sacramento presided.

W.A.<u>Gray</u> wed Bertha Patton at Round Valley February 26, 1913.   Mar 5, 1913

Henry A.<u>Green</u> obtained a license to wed Ethel DeMerrit of   Aug 2, 1916
Ukiah.

Perry W.Green obtained a license to wed Eva Sutherland
of Willits.   Aug 28, 1912

Paul B.Greenough, 39, of San Francisco obtained
a license to wed Irma Farho, 35, of Albion.   Sep 3, 1919

A.L.Gregor married Mary Mahurin of Caspar at Mendocino
September 10, 1911.   Sep 20, 1911

Hugh Griffin married Mary Gibson in Fort Bragg
January 6, 1910. Rev.Grace presided.   Jan 12, 1910

L.Grothe of Humboldt County married Kate Gibson of Ukiah in
Santa Rosa June 20, 1916.   Jun 7, 1916

William Grotz of Mendocino wed Nellie B.Holt of Stockton,
San Joaquin County, April 30, 1912.   May 22, 1912

Guiseppe Guenza got a license to wed Geovanina Mayestris
of Elk.   Aug 2, 1911

Paolo Guerra obtained a license to wed Cesira Paulinella
of Albion.   Dec 13, 1916

William Guest married Ivah Brett, the daughter of James
Brett of Albion, in San Francisco December 18, 1915.   Dec 22, 1915

Vitola Guesti obtained a license to wed Maria Angelino
of Fort Bragg.   May 31, 1911

Emilio Guidi obtained a license to wed Luiza Fosca
of Ukiah.   Aug 5, 1914

Gabrielo Guisti got a license to marry Gena Pagancelli.   Sep 30, 1914

Aino Rutti Gummerus married Elmi Sipila at Fort Bragg   Jan 1, 1919
January 9, 1919. Judge F.A.Whipple officiated.   Jan 15, 1919

Dr.Gunn of Willits married Miss E.Pilot of Fond du Lac,
Wisconsin, in San Francisco November 6, 1914.   Nov 11, 1914

Herbert A.Guptell of Albion married Alma Mitchell of Willits   Jul 7, 1915
in Fort Bragg July 3, 1915. Rev.W.A.Chapman presided.   Jul 14, 1915
                                                               Jul 21, 1915
Arthur Gustafson of Mendocino obtained a license   Feb 28, 1912
to wed Sibyl Martin of Fort Bragg.

Emil Gustafson obtained a license to wed Hilda Simeasson,
both of Manchester.   Sep 8, 1915

Fred Hahn of Wichita, Kansas, obtained a license
to wed Isabelle Robinson, 22, of Westport.   Nov 22, 1916

Clyde Haight, son of Harry Haight formerly of Fort Bragg,   May 24, 1911
married in Redding, Shasta County, May 15, 1911.
[Bride's name unreported.]

Sidney B.Hale obtained a license at Elk to wed Minnie West,   May 6, 1914
April 24, 1914.

Horace Lyman Hall, president of the Hall Lithograph Company   Sep 10, 1913
of Topeka, Kansas, married Martha A."Mattie" Weller, the   Dec 3, 1913
daughter of M.J.Weller of Fort Bragg, in San Francisco
November 26, 1913.

James L.Hall obtained a license to wed Agnes Dunham
of Laytonville.   Aug 14, 1918

Parker Hall married Mrs.Dorcas Whited June 14, 1917 at
Willits. They were pioneer settlers of the Willits area.   Jun 20, 1917

Ben F.Halliday, the son of J.C.Halliday of Point Arena,   Feb 28, 1917
married Hilda O.Nelson of Fresno February 14, 1917.

Charles <u>Halliday</u>, of Ukiah, married Mrs.Sydney
Gaillard in San Francisco July 29, 1912.

Jul 31, 1912

James Albert <u>Halliday</u> of Portland, Oregon, married Emily B.
McCornack, daughter of Dr.W.A.McCornack, formerly of Fort
Bragg and later of East Oakland, in Oakland April 17, 1916.
The groom was the son of J.C.Halliday of Fort Bragg.

Jan 5, 1916
Apr 19, 1916

C.J.<u>Hamer</u> married Relia Hill at Inglenook October 15, 1912.
Rev.J.S.Ross officiated.

Oct 16, 1912

Lloyd Lawrence <u>Hamilton</u> of Point Arena married Golda Schaaf
of Manchester at Point Arena August 18, 1918.
August 18, 1918.

Aug 21, 1918
Sep 4, 1918

Lovel [Lowell?] <u>Hamilton</u> married Helen Hunter in Petaluma
"this week".

Jul 19, 1916

Clayton J.<u>Haney</u>, 21 of Escondido, San Diego County, married
Ruth A.Donohoe, daughter of the ex-sheriff, at Ukiah
February 19, 1912.

Feb 21, 1912

Charles H.<u>Hansen</u> of Benecia obtained a license
to wed Zola Marie Hotell of Cloverdale.

Aug 18, 1915
Sep 1, 1915

Hans L.<u>Hansen</u>, 26, married Mrs.Signa McCarthy, 25,
in Mendocino "this week". Both were from Albion.

Nov 22, 1916
Nov 29, 1916

Louis <u>Hansen</u>, 31, of Cedarville, Modoc County, obtained a
a license to wed Mabel Jane Brower, 23, of Potter Valley.

Jan 3, 1917

Louis A.<u>Hanses</u>, 48, of Northwestern, obtained a
license to wed Mrs.Ethel McLean, 38, of Los Angeles.

Nov 8, 1916

Albert F.<u>Hanson</u>, 22, obtained a license to wed
Gwenlian McCallum, 19, both of Mendocino.

Mar 21, 1917

Arthur C.<u>Hanson</u> married Miss V.Frye in San Francisco
August 10, 1915. Mr.Hanson was a conductor on the California
Western Railroad.

Aug 25, 1915

Dewey <u>Hanson</u>, a jitney operator of Westport, eloped with
Verda Cromwell, 16, a telephone operator also of Westport.
An intensive search resulted in their arrest in Stockton
on March 18, 1919. Hanson was reported to have also married
Myra Hagney of Westport in Stockton. A daughter was born in
June 1919.

Jan 29, 1919
Mar 12, 1919
Mar 19, 1919
Jun 18, 1919

P.O.<u>Hardell</u> married Jennie M.Walgren in Fort Bragg
July 16, 1914. Judge F.A.Whipple officiated.

Jul 22, 1914

Albert M.<u>Hardie</u> married Bertha Louise Romer
at Willits June 12, 1915.

Jun 16, 1915

Louis J.<u>Hardie</u> of Ukiah married Iris Neighbors of Willits
June 29, 1916. The groom was a manager of Pacific Telephone
and Telegraph office.

Jun 28, 1916
Jul 5, 1916

S.A.<u>Hargreaves</u> of Minneapolis married Ella McMurry
of Ukiah at Omaha, Nebraska, November 7, 1911.

Nov 29, 1911

Frances S.<u>Harmon</u> of Littleriver obtained a license
to wed Bessie M.Quinliven of Willits.

Dec 30, 1914
Jan 6, 1915

Roy <u>Harmon</u> married Jean Philbrick, the daughter of
D.O.Philbrick of Comptche, at Petaluma January 31, 1916.

Feb 9, 1916

W.A.<u>Harpe</u> of Hopland married Gladys Fortune of
Ukiah at that place February 28, 1911.

Mar 1, 1911

Frank <u>Harrington</u>, 35, obtained a license to wed
Lillian Blockson, 16, both of Hopland.

Jul 12, 1911

Ray B.Harrington, 21, married Mary E.Ingram, 18, — Sep 6, 1911
on August 31, 1911 at Ukiah, home of both.

Clarence E.Harris married Lillie E.Worley September 2, 1911 — Sep 13, 1911
at Ukiah. [License was "G.E.Harris" and "Lilli Wareley".]

George Harris married Effie Gamberg of Fort Bragg — Mar 12, 1919
in Stockton April 3, 1919. — May 14, 1919

Merriman C.Harris of Los Angeles married Gladys Knight, — Dec 29, 1915
the daughter of C.L.Knight of Mendocino, at the Mendocino — Jul 26, 1916
Presbyterian church July 16, 1916.

George M.Hartman, the son of Frank Hartman of Fort Bragg, — Nov 4, 1914
married Agnes M.Rosskoff at Eureka October 24, 1914.

Henry Hartman married Amenda Adams June 10, 1912 in Fort — Jun 12, 1912
Bragg. Judge F.A.Whipple officiated. Since the bride was not
yet 18 and the parents had not consented to the marriage,
steps were taken to have the marriage annulled.

Earl Harvey got a license to wed Lois Simons of Hullville, — Dec 25, 1912
Lake County.

Leo Hasel, a boot and shoe maker, married Mrs.Mary Feider, — Dec 31, 1913
formerly of Fort Bragg, at Lakeview, Oregon, December 17,
1913. Rev.G.A.Crawford of the Presbyterian church presided.

H.M.Haskett married Isabelle M.Windsor at Santa Rosa — Dec 23, 1914
December 17, 1914.

Victor Haskett married Elizabeth Boyd at Willits — Oct 10, 1917
October 4, 1917.

James Hatton married Nellie Good of Willits at Ukiah — Dec 3, 1913
November 29, 1913.

Ernest Franklin Hawn of Ukiah obtained a license to marry — Jan 1, 1913
Jennie W.McGlashan.

Benjamin Haydon obtained a license to wed Ruth Hamilton — Apr 11, 1917
of Covelo.

Thomas B.Hayes, 21, of San Francisco, obtained a — Apr 30, 1919
license to wed Madge E.Craig, 19, of Point Arena.

W.Hayes married Carrie Tullener, the daughter of Mr.& Mrs. — May 4, 1910
Tullener of Point Arena, in Oakland April 23, 1910.

James E.Hayter married Olga M.Gamberg at Fort Bragg on — Jun 1, 1910
May 28, 1910. F.A.Whipple, JP, presided.

Ralph Hayter married Minnie Banker at Ukiah July 12, 1910. — Jul 13, 1910

Roy B.Hayter of Albion married Della Finkle of — Aug 16, 1911
Mendocino at that place August 19, 1911.

Walter S.Hayter of Albion wed Charlotte May Cummings of Cas- — Nov 5, 1913
par at Mendocino November 29, 1913. Judge Wallace presided.

S.M.Heathcock, 21, of Fort Bragg, obtained a license to wed — Oct 25, 1916
Verna May Connor, 15, of Caspar.

Ernest Heckendory married Eva Richey at Ukiah May 5, 1911. — May 17, 1911

Joseph Heidvick married Juanita Southard, the — Apr 9, 1919
daughter of Bert Southard, at Oakland "last week".

John Jacob Helela got a license to wed Mary Galliani. — Jul 15, 1914

Homer Helm obtained a license to wed Christine Bohn of — Jul 26, 1916
Fort Bragg.

Frank <u>Helmick</u> married Edna Hutton at Ukiah May 9, 1910.

May 11, 1910

Henry William <u>Henderson</u> married Hazel M.Stevenson, the only
daughter of George Stevenson, at Westport August 3, 1919.
Rev.F.S.Shinall officiated.
[The wedding account gives the groom's name as "Hendrickson".]

Aug 6, 1919

J.F.<u>Henderson</u> got a license to wed Idah M.Haynie.

Jul 28, 1915

Maurice <u>Henever</u> married Carla Nordwall at Fort Bragg
March 26, 1913.
[License application "Mauric Havener" and "Charla Norwall"]

Apr 2, 1913
Apr 9, 1913

Edward <u>Henley</u>, an attorney from Ukiah, married Bessie Reed
of Mayfield in San Francisco October 31, 1915.

Nov 3, 1915

Lloyd <u>Henley</u>, a former Ukiah resident, married Kathleen Dunn
of Campbell, Santa Clara County, "last week".

Jul 23, 1913

Victor <u>Henley</u> married Madge Brown at Ukiah July 13, 1910.

Jul 20, 1910

W.G.<u>Henricks</u> got a license to wed Gladys C.Burris.

Jul 29, 1914

Francis J.<u>Henry</u> married Mrs.Dora Winans in San Francisco
November 23, 1915. Both were of Willits.

Dec 1, 1915

John William <u>Henry</u> obtained a license to wed Audelaide A.
Nutter, both of Covelo.

Sep 6, 1911

August <u>Herrling</u> got a license to wed Hulda Snickers.

Apr 21, 1915

E.C.<u>Hiatt</u> married Miss S.I.Rose. [No date reported].

Jul 13, 1910

Milton <u>Hicks</u> of Sebastopol obtained a license to
wed Mildred Leila Meredith of Healdsburg.

Jul 3, 1918

William Paul <u>Hicks</u> obtained a license to marry
Elizabeth Miller - both of Hopland.

Jun 27, 1917

Charles E.<u>Higgins</u>, 28, of Santa Rosa obtained a
license to wed Daisy McKinley, 17, of Ukiah.

Feb 14, 1912

John Victor <u>Hildreth</u> obtained a license to wed
Goldie M.Peters.

Jun 17, 1914

Louis <u>Hildreth</u> married Jessie Standley of Ukiah
December 28, 1910.

Jan 4, 1911

Chester <u>Hill</u> married Annie Raudio, 16, the daughter of
Charles Raudio of Fort Bragg, in Ukiah July 7, 1917. In
October 1917 she asked the Draft Board to release her husband
from service at Fort Lewis, Washington, account he was
improperly examined by the medical board.

Jul 11, 1917
Oct 24, 1917

Gaylord R.<u>Hill</u> of San Francisco married Abbie L.Foye, the
daughter of Henry Foye of Fort Bragg, in San Francisco "last
week". Mr.Hill was a salesman for a drug company.

Aug 27, 1913

James A.<u>Hill</u> obtained a license to marry Hannah Howard
of Point Arena.

Jan 27, 1915

Henry <u>Hinkson</u> obtained a license to wed Anna S.Patton.

Jun 8, 1910

Harry <u>Hoddiuott</u> obtained a license to wed Maggie Galvin of
Point Arena.

Apr 26, 1911

Edwin <u>Hogan</u> married Mrs.Ella Prather, both of Anderson
Valley, at Ukiah May 12, 1917.

May 16, 1917

N.D.<u>Holland</u> married Emma Molise in San Francisco "recently".
The bride was a schoolteacher at Greenwood.

Aug 6, 1919

Harry <u>Holliday</u> wed Edna Ball of Ukiah December 14, 1911.

Dec 20, 1911

John E.Hollingsworth obtained a license to wed Ida Cyrus.   Sep 23, 1914

Jeremiah Vandermeer Hollinseed, 49, of Woodside, San Mateo   May 22, 1912
County, obtained a license to wed Annie Maria [surname lost],
36, of Taunton, Mass.

Herman Holquist obtained a license to wed Birdie   Jul 25, 1917
Shelton - both were from Caspar.

Edward F.Holtz obtained a license to wed Anita L.Fowler   Jul 9, 1919
of San Francisco.

C.E.Hopper obtained a license to wed Nancy M.Hopper.   Apr 6, 1910

C.Z.Hopper obtained a license to wed Miss H.C.Gibbons   Jul 26, 1916
Sylvandale.

Herbert Hopper married Alberta Helen Argelsinger of Willits   Feb 5, 1913
January 28, 1913. Rev.A.S.Jackson officiated.

J.C.Hopper of Wendling married Elva Tallinan of Albion   May 31, 1911
[another item says "Tallman"] at Middle Ridge near Albion   Jun 7, 1911
June 4, 1911.

J.F.Hopper obtained a license to wed Lillie G.Stinson.   Nov 18, 1914

W.L.Hopper obtained a license to wed Grace Augusta Koffee,   Jun 28, 1911
both of Willits.

E.W.Horton obtained a license to wed Georgia W.Nichols of   Sep 11, 1918
Arcata, Humboldt County.

Emil Host got a license to wed Mary Newgard of Fort Bragg.   Apr 29, 1914

Albert O.Hotell [also Elbert Hotel] of Boonville married   Dec 23, 1914
Alda Nunn of Philo at Wendling December 16, 1914.   Jan 6, 1915

Alfred Carter Howard got a license to wed Sophie Handley.   Nov 2, 1910

Carl Howard, 24, of Fort Bragg, married Mabel Dunsing, 16,   Jun 7, 1916
of Ukiah. [No date reported, but probably May 31, 1916.]

Elmer Howard of Ukiah married Mrs.M.Gates of   Apr 29, 1914
Oakland at Ukiah April 23, 1914.

James L.Howard married Victoria E.Perkins in Fort Bragg   Sep 13, 1911
September 5, 1911. Rev.J.C.Garth officiated.

Leroy Arthur Howard obtained a license to wed   Dec 4, 1912
Lillie Ethel Tracy of Cummings.   Dec 18, 1912

William Howard of DeHaven married Dorothy C.Corley at Fort   Dec 8, 1915
Bragg December 4, 1915. Rev.W.A.Chapman officiated. Mr.Howard
was a rancher and Miss Corley, the local school teacher.

Dr.W.O.Howell, a former Hopland resident, married   Sep 27, 1911
Miss A.Saling in Honolulu July 26, 1911.

J.H.Hub obtained a license to wed Winifred L.Long.   Dec 2, 1914

Elbert O.Hubbard of Potter obtained a license   Aug 28, 1912
to wed Fannie May Stover of Redding.

John Huber of Camp Fremont obtained a license to   Feb 27, 1918
wed Agnes Merry of Fort Bragg.

George W.Huffer of Raymond, Washington, married Ida   Oct 16, 1918
Charron, the daughter of Mrs.J.E.Charron, "recently".

Flint W.Hufford married Vivian Blackwell of Alabama   Mar 12, 1919
March 10, 1919 in Fort Bragg. Rev.W.A.Chapman officiated.

Clair Hufft wed Lucille Edwards at Ukiah November 7, 1914.   Sep 2, 1914
                                                                    Nov 25, 1914

Andrew Hughes wed Edna Seward at Ukiah January 17, 1911.   Jan 25, 1911

Harry Hughes of Ukiah married Ida Raudio, the   Dec 24, 1919
daughter of Charles Raudio of Fort Bragg, in Ukiah
December 19, 1919.

Nilas Hughes married Edna McNab, the daughter of   Apr 16, 1913
A.V.McNab of Largo, on April 12, 1913. Rev.J.E.Moore
officiated.

Walter S.Hughes married Margaret Kelly, both of   Jan 31, 1912
Potter Valley, at Ukiah January 5, 1912.

W.S.Hull obtained a license to marry Lurena Margaret   Dec 29, 1915
Medcalf of Garberville.

E.J.Hunt Jr.of Alameda married Helen Silveria of Sherwood   Dec 20, 1911
in San Francisco December 19, 1911.

Harry Hunter obtained a license to wed Viola C.E.C.Williams   Aug 18, 1915
of Willits.

J.B.Hunter got a license to wed Florence Mason.   Dec 6, 1916

Judge J.C.Hurley of Ukiah married Lillian Alexander   Jun 14, 1916
of Mendocino at Ukiah in May 1916 [day not reported].

John J.Hurley married Lillian Hansen, the daughter   May 2, 1917
of Theodore Hansen of Mendocino, April 25, 1917.

Arthur N.Hurst obtained a license to wed Irene H.Tolle.   Jul 1, 1914

George Thomas Hurst, 23, got a license to wed   Jul 31, 1918
Leona Josephine Girand, 25, both of San Francisco.

Byron L.Hurt married Wilda May Ornbaun at Round Valley   Jun 3, 1914
May 31, 1914.

Enoch Hurt obtained a license to wed Lena May Williams   Dec 18, 1912
of Calpella.

Frank Hyman of Fort Bragg was engaged to wed Cleone Ward   Dec 25, 1912
of Kibesillah December 25, 1912 at Santa Rosa.

Fred Hyman married Mae Height at Cleone April 12, 1913.   Apr 16, 1913
Rev.J.S.Ross officiated.

Chester A.Hymen, 26, of Willits, obtained a license   Jun 7, 1916
to wed Marthena Moore, 24, of Fort Bragg.

John Ingman married Mrs.Porter at Willits "recently".   Nov 4, 1914
Rev.Duncan Munro officiated.

Thomas Irwin married Josephine Wolfe at Albion   Oct 1, 1913
September 27, 1913.

Marion C.Isaacson obtained a license to wed   Jan 6, 1915
Violet A.Gray of Willits.   Jan 13, 1915

Samuel A.Iversen, 30, of Fort Bragg, obtained a license   Jul 14, 1915
in 1915 to wed Bertha J.McRay, 18, of Westport. They were   Nov 15, 1916
married in Westport November 6 [or November 13], 1916.
[The marriage notice said Arthur Iversen; bride's name lost.]

Stephen E.Jackaway, 21, of Elk obtained a license   Jul 23, 1919
to wed Violet Leheney, 18, of Alameda.

Joseph Jacks obtained a license to wed Martha Lou.   Jul 22, 1914

Gus Jackson of Albion married Miss T.E.Anderson
of San Francisco in that place "last week".   Dec 17, 1913

Josiah Jackson obtained a license to wed Martha Levi
of Covelo.   Jul 8, 1914

Thomas P.Jackson married Edna A.Antrim in Berkeley
November 21, 1913.   Nov 26, 1913

Walter Jackson of Mendocino married Edna Buck of
Mendocino at Ukiah July 23, 1919.   Jul 23, 1919

Oscar E.Jacobs, 25, obtained a license to wed
Hattie J.Muir, 21, both of Willits.   Aug 1, 1917

C.E.Jacobson obtained a license to wed Bessie C.Boog
of Los Angeles.   Jun 28, 1911

Harvey Jacobson obtained a license to wed Selma Bjork.   Aug 28, 1912

Clay Webster Jamison obtained a license to wed
Ada Cyrus of Covelo.   Nov 24, 1915

Gust Jarf married Selma Norrgard in Fort Bragg
June 10, 1916. Judge J.K.Peirsol officiated.   Jun 14. 1916

Paul Ivan Jenks got a license to wed Pearl Briones.   Aug 9, 1916

Jewel Jensen of Caspar married Mary Rist in Oakland
"last week".   Jul 9, 1919

Abraham Johnson, 44, the son of Peter Johnson of Cleone,
married Alina Gronross, 31, in San Francisco "this week". Jan 8, 1919

Albert J.Johnson, 33, married Josephine A.Montague, 23, at Nov 8, 1916
Fort Bragg November 15, 1916 in a Catholic service led by Nov 15, 1916
Father Blanderfield. The bride was the sister of Mrs.John
Scheper of Caspar.

August Johnson married Mrs.Fraski at Fort Bragg
November 8, 1917. Judge Frank A.Whipple presided.   Nov 14, 1917
The groom was a local rancher and cannery operator.

August A.Johnson married Annetta Peterson at   Jul 3, 1889
Caspar "last week". Rev.J.S.Ross officiated.   Sep 18, 1912

Bert D.Johnson of Ukiah obtained a license to
wed Laura Keller of Healdsburg.   Aug 3, 1910

Carl A.Johnson obtained a license to wed   May 27, 1914
Anna L.Olson May 20, 1914.   Jun 10, 1914

Charles J.Johnson married Anna S.Monna at Fort Bragg   Sep 23, 1914
September 16, 1914. Judge Peirsol officiated.   Sep 30, 1914
[Bride's name also given as "Mauna"].

E.J.Johnson married Mrs.May H.Pierce at Comptche
June 16, 1914. Mr.Johnson was a local rancher.   Jun 17, 1914

Harold Johnson married Violet Rasmussen, the daughter of
Pete Rasmussen, in a Catholic service at Fort Bragg   Jun 18, 1919
June 16, 1919 with Father Lawrence officiating.

Joseph M.Johnson, 33, obtained a license to wed
Evelyn F.Simonds, 32, both of Fort Bragg. Miss   Jan 3, 1912
Simonds was a teacher in the local schools.

Louis Johnson, depot agent for the Northwestern Pacific
Railroad at Ukiah, married Mrs.Addie H.Rogers   Dec 25, 1912
of Ukiah "last week". Judge White officiated.

O.Johnson married Myrtle Watenberg at Fort Bragg   Apr 19, 1911
April 16, 1911. Rev.R.C.Grace officated.

Oliver H.Johnson married Myrtle M.Helm at Fort Bragg   Dec 1, 1915
November 30, 1915 by Judge F.A.Whipple. Both bride and
groom were from Caspar.

Oscar Johnson obtained a license to wed Hazel   Oct 10, 1914
Hollenbeck of Comptche.   Oct 28, 1914

Otis R.Johnson, assistant superintendent of the Union Lumber   Jun 5, 1912
Company's Fort Bragg mill, married Marian Marvin on June 5,   Jun 12, 1912
1912. Otis was the son of Charles R.Johnson of Fort Bragg
and the bride was the daughter of Harvey A.Marvin of
San Francisco.

Robert N.Johnson of Cloverdale obtained a license   Apr 17, 1918
to wed Nettie A.Cavanagh of Fort Bragg.

T.J.Johnson obtained a license to wed Phoebe Davis of   Nov 15, 1911
Willits.

Joseph E.Jokie of San Francisco, 23, obtained a   Aug 7, 1918
license to wed Hannah Hatjie, 28, of Fort Bragg.

A.Jones married Mrs.Verna Burnes Tucker June 9, 1919 at   Jun 11, 1919
Willits. The bride was the daughter of Mrs.J.Burnes.

J.M.Jones obtained a license to wed Hattie Purcell.   Nov 17, 1915
Both were from Covelo.

J.T.Jones, foreman of the Domestic Steam Laundry of Fort Jan 6, 1915
Bragg, married Clutilda E.Dupras of Willows "last week".

Thomas O.Jones obtained a license to wed   Dec 29, 1915
Evagene Hall of Fort Bragg.

William Gaston Jones married Sigrid Fogerholm in   Apr 28, 1915
Fort Bragg April 25, 1915. Rev.W.A.Chapman presided.

Ben Joseph of Salinas married Goldie Sapp at Ukiah   Jan 21, 1914
January 11, 1914.

Arba V.Joslin married Grace Marie Adams at Ukiah   Jun 30, 1915
[date indeterminate]. Rev.W.T.Adams presided.

Horace Edward Joy of Mendocino married Nellie M.Clifton   Jun 25, 1913
of Piedmont at Los Gatos June 1, 1913.

Professor James A.Joyce married Mrs.Evelyn Leith   Mar 22, 1911
at Los Banos "last week".

Robert Juhola of Comptche married Jennie Ikola of   Oct 10, 1917
Mendocino October 4, 1917. Rev.J.J.Hillberg officiated.

Oliver P.Justice of Santa Ana obtained a license   Jul 8, 1914
to wed Lulu B.Fisher of Angels Camp, Calaveras County.

Charley Kamemoto got a license to wed Shix Nagamura.   May 20, 1914

George Kammus got a license to wed Lydia Typpie.   Sep 7, 1910

William Kane obtained a license to wed Bell Cropley.   Dec 3, 1913
William Kane got a license to wed Belle Copley.   Dec 2, 1914

Attorney Charles Kasch of Ukiah married Ruth Shinn   Dec 23, 1914
at Niles, Madera County, January 6, 1915.   Jan 13, 1915

Eugene Otto Kaufman married Hazel E.Woodward near   Oct 19, 1910
Noyo October 16, 1910. Rev.J.S.Ross officiated.
Mr.Kaufman was a resident of Fort Bragg.

John Kaun got a license to wed Aili Mammi of Fort Bragg.   Apr 12, 1911

J.J.Keller married Una Smart at Willits May 28, 1910.   Jun 1, 1910

William Lyndall Kellogg married Mrs.Tillie (Carmichael) Body   Dec 2, 1914
at the Mendocino Presbyterian church November 25, 1914.   Dec 9, 1914
Rev.J.M.Fisher presided.

[Waino] Frederick Kemppe married Ada Strom of Lake County in   Sep 22, 1915
San Francisco September 15, 1915.

John Kemppe obtained a license to wed Hilda Lavola   Dec 14, 1910
of Fort Bragg.   Dec 21, 1910

L.E.Kendall married Mrs.Mabel Inman at Manchester   Jan 15, 1919
January 11, 1919. Rev.John Swift officiated.

Ernest Kern obtained a license to wed Elizabeth A.Bates   Dec 20, 1911
of Redwood Valley.

Dave Kerr, formerly of Albion, obtained a license   May 29, 1918
to wed Helen Johnson of St.Marys, Idaho.

James M.Kerr, 58, of Ukiah, obtained a license to   Mar 5, 1917
wed Elizabeth C.Woodman, 57, of San Francisco.

Elbert Ketchum, the son of Mrs.George Gallagher of Fort   Feb 19, 1913
Bragg, married Ethel Kennedy at San Jose February 9, 1913.

George Riley King, 72, obtained a license to wed   Aug 20, 1919
Ellen Barton, 60, both of Fort Bragg.

J.J.King, 33, obtained a license to wed Florence Alice   Jan 10, 1917
Laurence, 20, both of Mendocino.

Percy A.King married Rose Gaspar in Fort Bragg   Nov 28, 1917
December 15, 1917. Judge F.A.Whipple officiated.   Dec 19, 1917

J.W.Kingren obtained a license to wed Verga Gillmore.   Nov 2, 1910

J.R.Kingwell of Cloverdale obtained a license to wed Hazel   Jun 28, 1911
H.Hiatt of Hermitage.

C.C.Kirk got a license to wed Leila Alice Medcalf.   Jun 30, 1915

Roy W.Kirkbride obtained a license to wed Lola Etta Stone.   Oct 12, 1910

Vernon Kjeldsen, the son of C.R.Kjeldsen, married   Mar 12, 1919
Rose Gibbons in Santa Rosa March 7, 1919.

Herman Knaesche married Frieda Beekley at Ukiah "this week".   Jun 25, 1919
She was murdered July 9, 1919 by her husband.   Jul 16, 1919

Mr.Knudsen married Ester Bowen at Westport   Feb 21, 1917
February 17, 1917. Judge Roache presided.

Peter Knudsen of Lodi married Jessie Gilles in San Francisco   Oct 13, 1915
October 6, 1915. He was formerly a merchant in Fort Bragg.

Paul B.Koary, 28, obtained a license to wed   Nov 17, 1915
Bridget Lacientas, 29. Both were from Ukiah.

Frank Kocher obtained a license to wed Mabel Woolley   May 12, 1915
of Redwood Valley.

Alfred Koistinen of South Dakota married Helen Torstrom,   Apr 17, 1918
the daughter of Carl Torstrom, in Berkeley "this week".

Jonas Koivisto married Annie Mammela at Fort Bragg   Jul 31, 1912
July 27, 1912. Rev.John J.Hillberg officiated.

Oscar William Koponen married Ida A.Walley in a double   Aug 8, 1917
ceremony at South Fork August 7, 1917 with John W.Mantell
and Anna L.Kerm.

Jack Kopsa got a license to wed Hinni Methala.   Oct 30, 1912

Abram Koski, a Fort Bragg merchant, married Katherin   Sep 5, 1917
Korhonen in Fort Bragg September 1, 1917. Rev.John J.
Hillberg officiated.

John Koski obtained a license to wed Aline   Mar 8, 1911
Erickson of Fort Bragg.

Oscar Koski obtained a license to wed   Mar 1, 1911
Anna Murkala of Fort Bragg.

J.R.Koskinen married Ella Simila at Albion July 23, 1911.   Aug 2, 1911

Mike Kotila married Jennie Hardell at Fort Bragg   Sep 11, 1918
September 8, 1918. Rev.J.J.Hillberg officiated.

F.F.Krainek of Vallejo married Bertha Lammers of Ukiah   Feb 23, 1910
February 22, 1910.

Oley Harold Kroh got a license to wed Mrs.Mary Hazel Rader.   Aug 9, 1916

Frank Kuharich, 28, married Agnes L.Giunnini, 30, in Fort   Dec 11, 1918
Bragg December 7, 1918. Judge F.A.Whipple officiated.

Arch Kunzler married Elma Donohoe, a teacher at the Garcia   Sep 12, 1917
school, at Point Arena August 29, 1917.

Clarence LaBoyteaux, foreman of the Glen Blair yard, married   Jun 26, 1912
Belle Carson, daughter of Milton Carson of Fort Bragg, at
Fort Bragg June 25, 1912.

Giovanni Lacorti obtained a license to wed   Oct 11, 1916
Mary Gomes, both of Glen Blair.

John Lafranchi of Fort Bragg married Mary D.Antone   Dec 18, 1918
of Santa Clara December 14, 1918. Judge Charles
Thompson presided.

L.Lafranchine of Plumas County married Jennie Biaggi at   Dec 7, 1910
Ten Mile November 30, 1910.

Frank G.Lagergren married Julia Larson, both of Elk, in   Jan 11, 1911
Greenwood on January 14, 1911. He was section boss on the   Jan 18, 1911
railroad, and she worked in the hotel. [His name also "Legreen"?].

E.Lamb wed Lillie B.King of Ukiah at Willits July 4, 1912.   Jul 10, 1912
[Another item says "John Lamb"].

James E.Lambert obtained a license March 31, 1914   Apr 8, 1914
to wed Elizabeth Burnham.

L.W.Lambert, an attorney from Cloverdale, married   Mar 4, 1914
Inez Shore at Palo Alto February 25, 1914.

Lewis R.Lambert, 35, of Fort Bragg married Hilda Thompson,   Dec 17, 1919
34, of Salinas, Monterey County.

Bert Lane of Calpella obtained a license to wed   Aug 28, 1912
Urith McClellan of Ukiah.

G.W.Lane obtained a license to wed Ida Lax.   Feb 28, 1912

George W.Lane of Ukiah obtained a license to wed   Jul 9, 1919
Irma J.Neuhaus of Ferndale, Humboldt County.

Laurence J.Lane married Hilda B.Wilming of Willits at   Jul 12, 1916
that place July 2, 1916.

R.G.Lane, 25, of Sherwood, obtained a license to wed Olina Marie Hellesoe, 23, of Willits.	Dec 1, 1915
Will Langley was married to Nellie Dempsey by Father Sebastian on September 11, 1910. Both were of Fort Bragg.	Sep 14, 1910
William Patrick Langley married Alexie D.Chisholm of Fort Bragg at Willits May 21, 1913. Judge Whitney officiated.	May 21, 1913
George A.Lantz married Nora Hill in Willits December 22, 1915. Both were from Dos Rios.	Dec 29, 1915
Ellerth Larson married Alma Wickstrom of Fort Bragg in Oakland June 16, 1917.	Jun 20, 1917
Louis Larson married Annie Wheeler of Willits "last week".	Jan 1, 1919
Pete Larson of Northwestern wed Kate Hartman of Fort Bragg at that place May 19, 1918. Judge F.A.Whipple presided.	May 22, 1918 / May 29, 1918
Russel Larson, the oldest son of Oscar Larson, married Stella Culder at Fort Bragg January 6, 1914. Rev.R.C. Grace officiated.	Jan 7, 1914
Alonzio Lawranson married Ruth Moffit at Willits December 4, 1918. Rev.A.J.Sturtevant presided.	Dec 11, 1918
Edward B.Lawrence married Carrie Bowman of Fort Bragg July 28, 1918. Judge F.A.Whipple presided.	Jul 31, 1918
Warren Lawrence got a license to wed Lizzy Stransberry.	Jan 6, 1915
Matt Lax obtained a license to wed Saund Maia Mantili.	Apr 6, 1910
Arch Layton of Ukiah married Hazel Klein of Berkeley at Pacific Grove, Monterey County, July 7, 1915.	Jul 14, 1915
Frank Lazarus of Mendocino wed Laura Pimental "last week".	May 7, 1919
Ernest V.Leek, 23, of Hopland married Lee McMullen, 18, of San Francisco at Ukiah September 4, 1912.	Sep 11, 1912
L.E.Lefleur of San Francisco married Genevieve Mathews, the daughter of J.R.Mathews of Ukiah, on January 29, 1913.	Feb 5, 1913
Earl E.LeFrampus obtained a license to wed Naomi Van Dyne. Both were from Ukiah.	Sep 23, 1914 / Sep 30, 1914
George C.Lemmon, 21, married Ella O.Ferm [Fern], 22, both of Fort Bragg, at Mitchell February 10, 1912. Judge F.A.Whipple officiated. The bride' sister was Mrs.Frank Sallinen.	Feb 14, 1912 / Apr 29, 1914
Loyal A.Lemmon married Mary J.Sallinen, the daughter of John Sallinen, at Mitchell Creek February 22, 1913. F.A.Whipple presided. [Lemmon was a locomotive engineer on the Caspar railroad.]	Feb 26, 1913
Matt Lemponen got a license to wed Lusa Mastamaki.	Oct 27, 1915
Loring William Lenard, 19, of Santa Rosa, obtained a license to wed Bessie L.Davis, 18, of Hanford.	Dec 24, 1919
Robert W.Leroux, 27, married Myrtle Howard, 16, in San Francisco May 4, 1916. Both were of Fort Bragg.	May 10, 1916
Fred LeValley, a stage driver, married Myrtle Woodward, the daughter of Al Woodward of Fort Bragg, at Sand Dunes Ranch north of Cleone October 26, 1913. Rev.J.S.Ross officiated.	Oct 29, 1913
George Lewis, proprietor of the Westport cannery, married Alice Devilbiss, a teacher, at Ukiah December 21, 1913. Father Brennen officiated.	Dec 24, 1913

Miguel S.Lewis obtained a license to wed Mayme Mendosa, the   Dec 16, 1914
daughter of F[rank].J.Mendosa of Mendocino.

Vern T.Lewis of Willits married Miss Alma A.Frederickson of   Dec 21, 1910
Irmulco at her parents' home there December 18, 1910. Rev.
W.A.Chapman presided.

Agostino Lezzoni obtained a license to wed Teresa Ricetti of   Aug 3, 1910
Mendocino.

Dr.J.Liftchild of Ukiah married Mrs.Ida Lance   Jan 19, 1910
in San Francisco January 16, 1910.

James Lilley of Littleriver married Amy Dodds of Mendocino   May 8, 1918
at Fort Bragg May 1, 1918 by Rev.Sutherland. The couple made
their home in Andersonia.

Chester G.Limebarger obtained a license to wed   Oct 15, 1913
Elsie Caroline Ruff of Willits.

John Lind obtained a license to marry Hannah Gummerus   Apr 5, 1911
of Fort Bragg.

John Lind obtained a license to wed Emma Swedberg   Sep 13, 1911
of Northwestern.

Emil Lindkvist married Wendla Sofia Erickson in Fort Bragg   Oct 18, 1916
October 14, 1916. Rev.John J.Hillberg officiated.

James Linn of Ukiah married Estella Edith Rose of   Feb 15, 1911
Boonville at Ukiah February 16, 1911.   Mar 1, 1911

John Linn, 35, of Orr's Hot Springs obtained a   Jan 17, 1917
license to wed Grace Haley, 35, of Ukiah.

D.E.Llewellyn, 24, of Blocksburg, obtained a   Jan 17, 1917
license to wed Iva M.Nobles, 23, of Talmage.

Phil Lobree married Annie Miller, both of Point Arena, in   Oct 20, 1915
San Francisco "last week".

Charles Locatall obtained a license to wed Mary Luchesi.   Oct 27, 1915

Nick Locicero obtained a license to wed Elsie Josephine   Feb 12, 1913
Cristina of San Jose.

William Loescher of Fort Bragg married Rhoda Irene Berryhill   Apr 3, 1912
at the Sand Dunes Ranch north of Cleone April 1, 1912.
Rev.J.S.Ross officiated.

B.Lombardo got a license to wed Rose Guidi of Ukiah.   May 31, 1911

Harvey LeRoy Long married Hildegard Owens March 5, 1916 at   Mar 8, 1916
Caspar. The couple went to Borneo where he managed a Shell
Oil facility. She was a graduate of San Francisco Normal.

Frederick N.Loring, the editor of the *Willits News*, obtained   Oct 15, 1913
a license in San Francisco October 11, 1913 to wed
Estelle Shimmin.

C.A.Lorrenson got a license to wed Hattie L.Grotevant.   May 27, 1914

George Lorri got a license to wed Olevi Tari of Largo.   Feb 12, 1913

Robert T.Lovejoy married Inice R.Ells of Covelo in Santa   Dec 17, 1919
Rosa December 5, 1919. Judge C.N.Collins presided.

Charles H.Lovell got a license to wed Jennie Brush.   Mar 17, 1915
[Married at Covelo September 19, 1915; separated September 19, 1934.]

W.L.Lowe married Sadie O.Evans at Ukiah December 12, 1915.   Dec 15, 1915

Harold <u>Lowenthal</u> married Jennie Forsythe Dougherty of Fort Bragg in San Francisco February 11, 1919.	Feb 12, 1919
Charles <u>Lowery</u> obtained a license to wed Nettie McKee of Briceland in Humboldt County.	Mar 1, 1911
Charles Edward <u>Lownes</u>, 21, obtained a license to wed Myrtle Agnes Short, 18, both of Ukiah.	Mar 13, 1912
Mony <u>Lucas</u> got a license to wed Nola Cannon of Blocksburg.	Jul 8, 1914
Guido <u>Lucchesi</u> obtained a license to wed Maria Moffini.	Jan 12, 1910
Marcelli <u>Lucchesi</u>, 22, obtained a license to wed Mary Ruschetti, 18, both of Fort Bragg.	Dec 27, 1911
Antone <u>Luce</u> married Rose Jerome at Mendocino in a Catholic ceremony January 1, 1916.	Jan 5, 1916
Charles C.<u>Luiz</u> of Mendocino married Ella Gordon of Littleriver August 29, 1911. Both were from Mendocino. The service was held in the Presbyterian church by J.Melville Fisher.	Sep 6, 1911
Peter <u>Lulich</u> obtained a license to wed Ana Bozicevic of Fort Bragg.	Feb 25, 1914
A.<u>Luoma</u> married Ella Stevens of Fort Bragg, in Tonopah, Nevada, March 15, 1919.	Apr 2, 1919
Charles <u>Luoma</u> of Virginia, Minnesota, married Jennie Luoma in that place "recently". The parties had the same surname but were not related.	Aug 6, 1919
Jacob <u>Luomo</u> married Ida Hyman, "across Pudding Creek" June 28, 1913. Judge F.A.Whipple officiated.	Jul 2, 1913
John <u>Luoto</u> got a license to wed Ida Jaakola of Comptche.	Sep 10, 1919
Ruel S.<u>Lydick</u>, 40, of Cleone married Adelina Giorno, 36, of Ukiah, there on January 21, 1912.	Jan 24, 1912
Emmett D.<u>Lynch</u> married Luella M.Rasmussen, the daughter of Pete Rasmussen of Fort Bragg, in a Catholic service at Fort Bragg August 24, 1919 conducted by Father Lawrence.	Aug 27, 1919
Orin C.<u>Lynch</u> married Marka M.Packard of Wages Creek at Westport November 8, 1914. Father Brennen officiated.	Nov 11, 1914 Nov 25, 1914
Grover <u>Lyons</u> of Talmage obtained a license to wed Bessie Burkhardt of Potter Valley.	Nov 27, 1912
W.B.O.<u>Macgregor</u> obtained a license to wed Eva McGinty of San Francisco.	Jul 16, 1913
John <u>Machedo</u> obtained a license to wed Annie Salvador.	May 26, 1915
Walter <u>Mackay</u>, 24, obtained a license to wed Faith Thom, 21, of Oregon.	Nov 17, 1915
The Duncan <u>MacKerrichers</u> celebrated their 50th wedding anniversery October 14, 1914. They were married in Dalesville, Canada, October 14, 1864. Soon thereafter, they came to California via Panama settling at Cleone. There were six children: Russell, Mrs.R.Tibbotts of Oakland, Mrs.Austin Lord of Noyo, Mrs.J.S.Cotton of Fort Bragg, Edward of Fort Bragg and Mrs.Geary of Red Bluff. [Another son, William, died of typhoid fever in Santa Rosa January 8, 1894.]	Oct 21, 1914
J.D.<u>Maddrill</u> wed Mrs.A.Tisdale at Ukiah January 15, 1911.	Jan 18, 1911
Charles A.<u>Madeiros</u> obtained a license to wed Viola Hartley.	Oct 12, 1910
Merle <u>Madeiros</u> of Butte City married Lilly B.Tallman.	Dec 23, 1914

Philip Joseph <u>Madero</u> of Mendocino married Edna Eleanor   Aug 21, 1918
Berkovits of Fort Bragg in Ukiah August 17, 1918.
[The license showed the groom's name as "Maderia"].

Robert <u>Madison</u> married Genevieve M.White, both of   May 19, 1915
Fort Bragg, in Oakland May 3, 1915.

Frank <u>Maffina</u> obtained a license to wed Barunzion   Oct 18, 1911
Carolina; both were from Fort Bragg.

George L.<u>Magneson</u> married Luzanne H.Schutz at Berkeley   Jun 19, 1918
June 15, 1918. They later resided in Redwood Valley.

John <u>Magulas</u> of Oakland obtained a license to   Mar 19, 1913
wed Louise Garaventa of Ukiah.

J.<u>Mahaffey</u>, 30, of Laurel Dell, obtained a license   Jul 28, 1915
to wed Hilda Cann, 25, of Lakeport.

Oscar <u>Mahler</u> of San Francisco married Hellen Wright, the   Oct 23, 1918
daughter of W.H.Wright, in Fort Bragg October 17, 1918. She
was born and raised there.

Paul William <u>Mahler</u> married Elsie J.Wright, the daughter   Sep 23, 1914
of W.H.Wright of Fort Bragg, in Catholic rites
September 20, 1914 conducted by Father Edwards.

Amos <u>Mahurin</u> obtained a license to wed Ella M.Tibbitts.   Oct 21, 1914

Amos <u>Mahurin</u> of Caspar married Stella Simpson of Healdsburg Aug 2, 1916
at Caspar July 29, 1916. Rev.J.H.Hargreaves officiated.   Aug 9, 1916

Rupert T.<u>Mahurin</u> married Mabel Purdy, daughter of   Oct 27, 1915
Carl Purdy of Ukiah, October 18, 1915.

Jack <u>Majors</u> married Lillian F.Lydick of Fort Bragg   Oct 14, 1914
October 10, 1914. Rev.W.A.Chapman officiated.

Niko <u>Makinen</u> got a license to wed Lisi Anterson.   Sep 17, 1913

John G.<u>Male</u> obtained a license to wed Mary Stornetta   Sep 14, 1910
of Point Arena.

James G.<u>Maltman</u> married Beryl Ross, formerly of Fort Bragg, May 3, 1916
in Oakland April 21, 1916. The bride was the daughter of the
late Robert Ross and Mrs.J.L.Brown of Alameda.

John L.<u>Manchester</u> obtained a license to wed   Feb 25, 1914
Annie Ellen Dale of Fort Bragg.

Luke <u>Manchester</u> of Ten Mile married Lena M.Gummerus, the   Jun 9, 1915
daughter of J.H.Gummerus of Fort Bragg in Mendocino
June 3, 1915.

John <u>Manners</u> married Annie Anderson at the Eagle Hotel in   Feb 28, 1912
Fort Bragg February 24, 1912. F.A.Whipple officiated.
[A second account gives groom's name as "Mannus"].

Paul M.<u>Manss</u>, the son of F.H.Manss, Superintendent of the   Jul 28, 1915
Albion Lumber Company, married Edith F.Ebey, daughter of
R.L.Ebey, Superintendent of the South San Francisco water
works, in San Francisco on July 22, 1915.

John W.<u>Manteli</u> married Anna L.Kerm in a double ceremony at   Aug 8, 1917
South Fork August 7, 1917 with Oscar W.Koponen and
Ida A.Walley.

J.E.<u>March</u> obtained a license to wed Helen W.Busch.   Jun 16, 1915

Harry <u>Marion</u> obtained a license to wed Norma   May 6, 1914
Huelbert at Ukiah April 22, 1914.

Adolph Marks married Jessie Gray of Ukiah in
San Francisco August 9, 1915.   Aug 18, 1915

Peter Martella married Clementina Preirtali at Fort Bragg   Sep 23, 1914
September 17, 1914.   Sep 30, 1914
[Groom's name also given as "Pietro Martelle"].

Peter Martella married Geni Previtali in Fort Bragg "last   May 14, 1913
week". Judge F.A.Whipple officiated.

Mr.Martin married Miss Lizzie Jordan, formerly   May 25, 1910
a resident of Fort Bragg, in Oakland "last week".

Alfred W.Martin obtained a license to wed   Aug 2, 1916
Ethel A.Millen, both of Oakland.

Charles Martin married Ethel Blake, a former resident of   Feb 22, 1911
Potter Valley, in Portland, Oregon, February 7, 1911.

Clifford A.Martin, a telegraph operator for the Southern   Aug 28, 1912
Pacific Railroad at Oakland, married Minnie M.Peterson in
Fort Bragg August 21, 1912. Father Brennen officiated.

C.G.Martindale obtained a license to wed Elizabeth   Jul 21, 1915
Schmidt of Two Rivers [Dos Rios].

John Martinen obtained a license to wed Mary Soldani of   Jan 3, 1912
Point Arena.

Ray E.Martinez obtained a license to wed   Jul 21, 1915
Maria R.Uresti; both were from Fort Bragg.   Jul 28, 1915

Domenico Martini obtained a license to wed Pucetti Puriona.   Jun 8, 1910

Guy Mason married Lulu Davis of Willits in   Nov 15, 1911
San Francisco "last week".

Frank Masotti wed Olive Halick at Hopland August 24, 1911.   Sep 6, 1911

C.L.Masters obtained a license to wed Gertrude H.McPherson   Sep 27, 1916
of Healdsburg, Sonoma County.

Ed Mathews was engaged to wed Miss A.Servaty in January   Dec 11, 1918
1919. She was a schoolteacher in the Point Arena highschool.

F.S.Mathews married Josephine Gibson of Ukiah at San Diego   Mar 22, 1911
February 12, 1911. He was a contractor and builder in
Southern California and she was a daughter of Ellen Gibson.

William Charles Mathews married Florence May Mason   Aug 18, 1915
August 15, 1915. Rev.I.H.Wood officiated. The bride was a
native of New York and had made a business career in Los
Angeles as the secretary of the Indian Tea and Coffee Company.

Charles Mathison of Wendling married Irma Brown of   Aug 8, 1917
Boonville in Santa Rosa July 28, 1917.

George Mattocks married Grace McCormick, the daughter of   Oct 22, 1919
William McCormick, for many years the woods superintendent
for Albion Lumber Company, at San Jose October 18, 1919.

Harry McAinick married Lillian McKenzie in San Francisco   Jun 22, 1910
"last week", both were from Talmage.

Frank McAnich, 34, obtained a license to wed   May 22, 1912
Verna Wilcox, 24, both of Willits.

John A.McCallum married Byrd G.Baker, the youngest   Oct 20, 1915
daughter of Rev.B.H.Baker, at the Presbyterian
church in Point Arena October 12, 1915.

Robert McCammon married Mrs.Margaret Nichols, the sister of   Feb 28, 1917
W.A.Kirkland, at Bloomfield February 23, 1917.

Lloyd Farrer McCarthy obtained a license to wed   Dec 27, 1916
Mabel O'Farrell of Spy Rock.

Frank T.McClendon wed Bessie Wycoff at Ukiah May 28, 1913.   Jun 4, 1913

George W.McClendon of Ukiah married Carrie Linser   Dec 28, 1910
of Sherwood at Ukiah December 22, 1910.

Elmer H.McClure got a license to wed Edith Betts.   Dec 9, 1914

W.McClure, formerly of Ukiah, married Miss J.Goodwin in   Mar 2, 1910
Plumas County March 1, 1910.

Ralph Vernon McCombs obtained a license to wed   May 4, 1910
Mabel A.Begley of Covelo.

Alexander McCornack married Dora M.Sturn at Ukiah   Jul 5, 1911
October 30, 1915 on a four year old license. Judge Young   Nov 10, 1915
presided. The 'bride' thought they had been married when
they got the license and had filed it in a trunk.
Threatened with arrest as a 'white slaver', McCornack went
through the ceremony. They had had three children.

Hale McCowen Jr., the District Attorney, married   Dec 22, 1915
Hazel Minnie Blosser, the daughter of Mrs.Ora
Blosser of Willits, at Willits December 27, 1915.

A.E.McCown obtained a license to wed Edith R.Thompson   Aug 5, 1914
of Hopland.

Charles W.McCoy obtained a license to wed   Sep 30, 1914
Inez L.Copple of Hopland.

B.McCreary married Myrtle Grant in Fort Bragg   Nov 29, 1911
November 25, 1911. Judge F.A.Whipple presided.

Alexander McDonald, 31, of Hardy married Elizabeth Edna   Dec 27, 1911
Tullis, 24, of Fort Bragg December 25, 1911.
Rev.W.A.Chapman officiated.

Alexander J.McDonald married Mollie Randolph, the oldest   Mar 12, 1913
daughter of J.W.Randolph of Fort Bragg, in Oakland
March 9, 1913.

Angus A.McDonald of Northspur married Ida Jacobson   Sep 6, 1916
at Mitchell Creek September 3, 1916.   Sep 13, 1916

Edward McDonald of Comptche obtained a license to   Jan 3, 1912
wed Rosalind Feldman of Melburne.

John Daniel McDonald, 24, of Philo, got a license   Feb 14, 1912
to wed Georgia Hathaway, 24, of Point Arena.

Malcolm McDonald of Sonoma County obtained a   Dec 15, 1915
license to wed Flora Margaret Murchison of Oakland.

John Andrew McDonnel married Hilma Sophia Jacobson   Mar 11, 1914
at Mitchell Creek April 25, 1914.   Apr 29, 1914
[Name of groom as reported as "McDonald"].   May 14, 1914

Arthur P.McFaul, the son of C.McFaul of Union   Aug 25, 1915
Landing, married Artie E.Riggs at Fort Bragg
August 22, 1915. Rev.Sutherland presided.

C.H.McGahan got a license to wed Alice Kiniker.   Jun 30, 1915

W.T.McGarvey obtained a license April 1, 1914 to   Apr 8, 1914
wed Freda Van Dusen.

Edward Jasper McGhaney, a fireman on the California Western Jul 19, 1916
Railroad, married May Johnson, the daughter of Robert
Johnson of Fort Bragg, in Willits July 13, 1916.

Charles L.McGimsey of Boonville married Nora Keithly of   Jul 26, 1911
Kelseyville at Boonville July 19, 1911.

Andrew L.McKean, of Concord, California, married Mable   Oct 29, 1913
Juanita Saxon of Willits at that place October 25, 1913.

Thomas McKenzie married Eunice Ellen Craig near   Jul 30, 1913
Iversen July 20, 1913.

Edwin Lawrence McKinley married Edna Milliken in San Jose   Jan 8, 1913
December 31, 1912. Rev.James Falconer of the Santa Clara
Presbyterian church officiated.

C.E.McKinney, 33, of New York, married Florence   Aug 4, 1915
Bertha Eilken, 23, of San Francisco, August 2, 1915.

Edward McKnight obtained a license to wed Maude Ray.   Sep 30, 1914
Both were from Ukiah.   Oct 7, 1914

Daniel McLean married Leta Muir at Ukiah   Aug 20, 1913
August 18, 1913. Both were residents of Boonville.

George McMullen married Victoria [surname unknown] in Ukiah   Oct 23, 1895
August 30, 1887. They had a son named Russell, aged 14 in   Sep 28, 1910
in 1910. [Born to the wife of George McMillan October 16, 1895.
Divorce action by Mrs McMullen September 1910].

Robert McMurchy of Fort Bragg married Lillian Fuller of   Mar 28, 1917
Everett, Washington, March 22, 1917 in Portland, Oregon.

David T.McMurphy, 37, of Mendocino, married   Jan 31, 1912
Ruby M.Allenby, 18, at Willits January 24, 1912.
She was the daughter of James Allenby of Willits.

Mr.McNamer of Willits married Miss Foster of Eureka in   Feb 28, 1912
Fort Bragg "last week". Judge F.A.Whipple officiated.

Oscar McNary of Oakland married Lenore Willoughby   Feb 21, 1912
of Ukiah February 11, 1912.

E.R.McOmber obtained a license to wed Maude R.Brooks.   Nov 18, 1914

C.McPherson of San Francisco married May Werener   Jul 23, 1913
of Westport at San Francisco "last week".

Clark Mead married Florence McNamara at Westport   Jul 16, 1919
July 24, 1919 by Judge Roach.   Jul 30, 1919

Millard E.Means of Eureka obtained a license to   Sep 17, 1913
wed Nellie Corey of Cummings.

Foster S.Meders obtained a license to wed   Apr 12, 1911
Francis B.Olives of Mendocino.

Edward Meek obtained a license to wed Elva Peterson,   Jul 9, 1919
the daughter of John Peterson of Mendocino.

Al Meister was engaged to wed Amy Beale, both of Caspar.   Mar 26, 1919
Al Muster Jr.[sic] married Amy Beal [sic], the daughter of   Jul 9, 1919
J.H.Beal of Caspar, at that place "last week".

Peter Mencucci obtained a license to wed Zeffera   Jul 26, 1916
Giaconda Bacci.

Howard M.Merritt, Fairbanks Telephone Company manager,   May 31, 1911
wed Miss M.Lovetto Mero of Mendocino in Fairbanks, Alaska,
[no date reported].

Henry Merrow obtained a license to wed Della Pinches of   Oct 15, 1913
Laytonville.

Arthur N.Miller, 45 obtained a license to wed Myrtle Terry,   Feb 28, 1912
33, of Ashland, Oregon.   Mar 6, 1912

Curtis A.Miller, a Ukiah realtor, married Mrs.Isabella Feb 4, 1914
Fuller of San Jose "last week".

G.Whitmore Miller, 24, of Mare Island obtained a license to Jan 29, 1919
wed Lois I.Cureton, 20, of Boonville.

George Miller married Hilda Stump in San Francisco Jul 16, 1913
December 25, 1912.

George Miller of Point Arena obtained a license Jul 25, 1917
to wed Sigue Siverts of San Francisco.

Herman Miller of Westport married Wilma Johnson of Fort Dec 29, 1915
Bragg January 2, 1916. Rev.John J.Hillberg officiated. Jan 5, 1916

Alden J.Milliken of Nogales, Arizona, married Mabelle Lyons Dec 13, 1911
of Mendocino at that place December 9, 1911.
Rev.J.S.Ross officiated.

First Lieutenant Charles Morton Milliken married Pansy Sep 20, 1916
Frances Painter at Johnson City, Tennessee, [no date reported].
He was the nephew of H.F.Milliken of Fort Bragg.

Gerald Mish of San Francisco was engaged to Apr 6, 1910
wed Sara Hoffman of Ukiah.

Claude H.Mitchell obtained a license to wed Aug 6, 1919
Marion F.Elliott, both of Ukiah.

Shelby Mitchell obtained a license to wed Almira Cassade. Jun 17, 1914

Ansfgelo [sic] Moffino, 30, obtained a license to wed May 22, 1912
Emma Isabelle, 26, both of Fort Bragg.

Jack Moisala married Annie Madsen at Tunnel Hill Sep 27, 1911
October 15, 1911. Rev.Hillberg officiated. Oct 18, 1911

Frank Molise got a license to wed Amy Guidinger. Jan 15, 1919

Richard Molsberger of Northwestern married Hazel G.Saxon of Dec 16, 1914
Willits at Ukiah December 9, 1914. Rev.Dahl officiated.

Clarence E.Montgomery married Florence M.McDonald Apr 2, 1913
in Fort Bragg March 28, 1913. F.A.Whipple presided.

Camillo Montini obtained a license to wed Theresa Garoni. Sep 22, 1915

Alexander Moore obtained a license to wed Mabel Salomon. Jan 15, 1913

Bernard Dudley Moore obtained a license to wed Jan 1, 1913
Sidna Squires of Ukiah.

John Moore obtained a license to wed Lulu Morrison Sep 11, 1918
of Stockton.

Sodorico Moranda obtained a license to wed Ellen Herren of Apr 21, 1915
Lakeport.

Hale C.Morgan obtained a license to wed Clara Theresa Reilly. Jan 6, 1915

John Moriel obtained a license to wed Louisa Salomon. Jan 15, 1913

Antone Moroni obtained a license to wed Irene Vannucchi. Oct 15, 1913

J.M.Morris obtained a license to wed Fanny V.Bauer. Nov 18, 1914

Richard Morris married Mrs.D.D.Burrough of Tennessee. Oct 31, 1917
[Date thought to be October 30, 1917.]

William Morrison of Oakland married Mrs.C.C.Scott Sep 24, 1919
of Fort Bragg in San Francisco September 21, 1919.

H.L.Morrow, formerly of Fort Bragg, married Edith Blume in Redwood City, San Mateo County, January 6, 1916.   Jan 26, 1916

Howard Morrow, a former Fort Bragg resident, married Beulah M.Drew of San Francisco April 25, 1917.   May 2, 1917

Lee Morsberger obtained a license to wed Elizabeth M.Silva.   Aug 25, 1915

Stewart Morton married Ilie Samuelson at the Episcopal church in Fort Bragg February 5, 1917. Rev.L.H.Grant officiated. [License said "Stuart Morton" and "Ileen Samuelson".]   Jan 31, 1917 Feb 7, 1917

Roy Mott obtained a license to wed Alice Delaney.   May 19, 1915

Sgt.Thomas O.Moungovan of Point Arena, married Mabel Evans of Hampshire, England, over there September 12, 1918.   Oct 16, 1918

Milton J.Moyles obtained a license to wed Dora Vivian Whitten of Point Arena.   Dec 13, 1916

Ray Muir obtained a license to wed Edith B.Lewis of Willits.   Dec 18, 1912

Henry Mummel got a license to wed Sopie Cannon of Ukiah.   Nov 24, 1915

William Munk married Gail Barnwell of Willits at Santa Rosa "last week".   Jul 8, 1914

J.R.Munroe married Theresa Wagner at St.Helena, Napa County, April 23, 1914.   May 6, 1914

J.C.Murray of Hopland obtained a license to wed Josephine Drake of Windsor.   Aug 2, 1916 Aug 9, 1916

Elmer A.Myers of San Mateo obtained a license to wed Esther Williams of Willits.   Nov 27, 1912

Frederick Naiducci, 24, obtained a license to wed Corinna Taleri, 18, both of Greenwood.   Jan 31, 1912

Frank C.Nash married Minnie Bishop, the second eldest daughter of Joseph Bishop of Point Arena, in San Francisco July 19, 1913.   Jul 23, 1913

J.E.Neff of Willits married Elsie Adams in San Francisco June 7, 1910.   Jun 29, 1910

Lauretz Carl C.Neilsen, 60, of Vallejo obtained a license to wed Martha A.Bean, 60, of Branscomb.   Oct 22, 1919

Peter W.Neilson obtained a license to wed Alice M.Jensen.   Sep 10, 1919

William Nellest married Fannie Underhill in Oakland May 30, 1914.   Jun 3, 1914

H.F.Nelson married Ruby Orletta Gowell in Ukiah January 20, 1917.   Jan 31, 1917

John Nelson married Mrs.Lilly O'Donnell in Fort Bragg June 28, 1919.   Jul 2, 1919

Leroy Nelson married Mary Madalene Chapman, sister of John Geary of Ukiah, at Ukiah December 30, 1914.   Jan 6, 1915

Nels Nelson married Alina Erickson February 20, 1915 at Fort Bragg. Rev.J.J.Hillberg officiated at the Finnish Methodist church.   Feb 24, 1915

Norman Nelson married Mable Barnes of Caspar in San Francisco "last week".   Sep 3, 1913

Sam Nesbit obtained a license to wed Lolita J.Caraway.   Dec 9, 1914

Edwin <u>Ness</u> married Ida Wilppalo in Fort Bragg   Mar 25, 1914
March 21, 1914.

John A.<u>Ness</u>, 34, obtained a license to wed May   Jul 14, 1915
Goodenow, 21; both of San Francisco.

William Niel <u>Newton</u> of London (England) married Mable   Jul 6, 1910
Carlson of Caspar at Caspar June 22, 1910. Rev.Boyington
presided at the ceremony.

Harry V.<u>Nichols</u>, 45, of Elk, married Louise Larson,   Jun 4, 1919
26, of Fort Bragg (and late of San Francisco) in   Jun 11, 1919
Fort Bragg June 8, 1919.

Joseph H.<u>Nicols</u> married Mamie Nelson, both of   Jan 21, 1914
Mendocino, at Oakland January 8, 1914.

Alfred <u>Nicolai</u> obtained a license to wed Eva Valenti.   Feb 23, 1910

Elmer <u>Nielsen</u> married Gladys Gray, the daughter of   Jan 24, 1917
M.D.Gray Sr., at Fort Bragg January 20, 1917.
Rev.J.H.Bryan officiated.

Earl E.<u>Nimela</u>, in Army service at Camp Kearney, got a   Mar 12, 1919
license to wed Lena E.Smith, both of Albion.

Roy <u>Nissen</u>, a former resident of Point Arena, married   Dec 4, 1918
Frances Pole "recently". The bride formerly taught school in
Point Arena.

M.<u>Nolan</u> of Caspar married Bertha S.Brinzing of Pine Grove   Oct 16, 1912
in San Francisco October 8, 1912. Rev.G.A.Bernthal presided.

M.A.<u>Nolan</u> married Olga Wahlstrom in May 1918 [exact date   May 22, 1918
indeterminate] Both were from Caspar.

Ralph <u>Noreil</u> got a license to wed Eva J.Lovell of Willits.   Sep 4, 1918

Clarence A.<u>Norris</u> of Camp Fremont married Eva Fairbanks,   Oct 30, 1918
formerly of Mendocino, in San Jose October 4, 1918. The
bride was the sister of Mrs.Carl Nystrom of Mendocino.

Charles R.<u>Norton</u> obtained a license to wed Mrs.Zella Mason   May 21, 1913
of San Francisco.

James E.<u>Norton</u> married Miss T.Hargis, a former Ukiah   Feb 28, 1912
resident, in Honolulu [Hawaii] "recently".

Joseph J.<u>Noyer</u> married Emily Agnes Perreria at Mendocino   Jul 21, 1915
September 2, 1915. Father Raymond officiated.   Sep 8, 1915
                                                        Sep 22, 1915
L.V.<u>Nye</u> obtained a license to wed Grace Simmerly of Redwine.   Feb 22, 1911

William <u>Nye</u> married Tyyna Oquest in San Francisco   Oct 25, 1916
October 24, 1916.

Olof R.<u>Nylander</u> married Rhoda L.Williams at the   Feb 21, 1917
Fort Bragg Baptist church February 17, 1917.

Dr.Edward S.<u>O'Brien</u> married Mrs.Francis L.Hartley   Mar 18, 1914
in Berkeley March 11, 1914. Dr.O'Brien was a
former Mendocino resident and had moved to Merced.

Henry J.<u>O'Brien</u> married Susie Berry of Boonville in San Jose   Dec 27, 1911
December 18, 1911.

T.<u>O'Brien</u> of San Francisco married Clara Walsh of Point   Sep 17, 1919
Arena at Santa Rosa September 5, 1919.

John <u>O'Donnell</u> married Atalkia McArthur at Ukiah   May 30, 1917
"last week".

John W.Odell got a license to wed Manny M.Tuck.	Dec 9, 1914
Henry Oja, 34, obtained a license to wed Ida Solola, 36, both of Fort Bragg.	Aug 28, 1918
Ole P.Oleson obtained a license to wed Rosa Cavallini.	Jul 25, 1917
Hilmer Olsen of Mendocino married Edna Freeman of the Anderson Valley at Ukiah June 19, 1915.	Jun 23, 1915 Jun 30, 1915
Oscar Olsen married Katie Anker of Ukiah in San Francisco "last week".	Jan 10, 1912
Carl A.Olson, 22, of Elk obtained a license to wed Estelli M.Gordon, 21, of Santa Rosa.	Apr 9, 1919
Frank Olson married Lena Fagerholm in Fort Bragg December 25, 1910. Rev.Grace officiated.	Dec 28, 1910
William Oppenlander of Comptche married Lulu Smith of Littleriver in Ukiah August 17, 1910.	Aug 24, 1910
Byron Ordway married Myrtle Winfield at Fort Bragg November 16, 1913. Judge F.A.Whipple presided.	Nov 19, 1913
Cavalini Oreste obtained a license to wed Rosi Bogni.	Jan 11, 1911
James C.Ornbaun married Mrs.Lulu H.Williams in Fort Bragg October 16, 1914. Judge F.A.Whipple presided.	Oct 28, 1914
Ferdinand William Orr obtained a license to wed Cora M.Mead.	Oct 27, 1915
Mattie Osborn married Maryan Catherena at Mendocino November 9, 1913. Father O'Gorman officiated.	Nov 12, 1913
Miss Phoebe Osborn, the daughter of Charles Osborn formerly of Comptche, married Dr.George Chamberlain at Anchorage, Alaska, August 17, 1919.	Dec 10, 1919
Charles Osgood married Irene Wright two weeks ago in Fort Bragg in a secret ceremony.	Sep 19, 1917
J.G.Ossman, 60 of Philo, married Mrs.Susan Markham, 59, in Santa Rosa September 29, 1915.	Oct 6, 1915
J.M.Owen married Lena Brunner in Oakland "last week". Both were residents of Ukiah.	Mar 2, 1910
Francis C.Owenby, 34, of Ukiah, obtained a license to wed Harriette M.Turner, 32, of San Francisco.	Mar 20, 1918
Will H.Owens wed Effie Wisecarver at Ukiah August 2, 1914.	Aug 5, 1914
H.C.Packard of Mendocino married Janetta M.Longmire in in Dallas [The Dalles], Oregon, "last week".	Apr 5, 1911
John F.Packard, 30, obtained a license to wed Emma Faucett, 23 - both were from Upper Lake.	Nov 8, 1916
Ernest Page obtained a license to wed Addie Hicks.	Apr 22, 1914
Henry Clayton Palmer married Edith Swanson, the daughter of August Swanson, June 25, 1919 at Fort Bragg. Father Grant of the Episcopal church officiated.	Jun 25, 1919
John Palmer obtained a license to wed Lizzie Pudas.	Feb 10, 1915
George Pardi obtained a license to wed Arggene Del Basso. A second item reported the divorce of Joseph Pardi who married Aiginni [last name lost] at Fort Bragg January 14, 1919 and separated in February, 1919.	Jan 15, 1919 Jul 9, 1919

John Pardini got a license to wed Rosa Sanini of Greenwood.   Sep 27, 1916

Mr.Parks of Crescent City married Theresa Carey   Dec 7, 1910
of Fort Bragg in San Francisco "last week".

Edwin Parr married Pearl Beach, the daughter of Frank W.   Jan 8, 1913
Beach formerly of Mendocino, in San Francisco
December 31, 1912.

Ira Parrish of Caspar married Florence Bowman at   Apr 30, 1919
Westport April 22, 1919. Rev.Shinall officiated.

Mark L.Parrish married Myrtle C.Clow at Noyo   Sep 23, 1914
September 16, 1914. Rev.W.A.Chapman officiated.   Sep 30, 1914

Robert Parrish married Josephine Sallinen at Noyo   May 11, 1910
May 7, 1910. F.A.Whipple, JP, presided.

E.M.Partin obtained a license to wed Cecille M.Granger   Dec 16, 1914
of Willits.

Emile Banness Partout obtained a license to wed Frances   Apr 18, 1917
Martin Brown.

W.H.Partridge, of Oakland, married Emma Gilliam, the   Jan 12, 1916
daughter of W.A.Gilliam of Oakland, a former Fort Bragg   Aug 23, 1916
resident, at Berkeley August 21, 1916. The bride's sister
was Mrs.C.A.Scott of Fort Bragg.

Joseph L.Pate married Mrs.Phoebe Snuffin at Ukiah   Dec 28, 1910
December 24, 1910.

Charles L.Patten wed Martha Barton in Scotia "this week".   Dec 8, 1915

Robert E.Patterson obtained a license to wed   Sep 9, 1914
Maud E.Miller of Los Angeles.

De Los Patton of Ukiah married Esma Dutton in   Jan 5, 1910
San Francisco December 25, 1909.

Earl Patton married Helen May Wheeler at Willits   Jul 29, 1914
July 25, 1914. Judge Whitney officiated.

Fred D.Patton married Ada L.B.Hughes of Point Arena   Jul 5, 1911
June 21, 1911.

A.Pavino obtained a license to wed Maria Brovelli.   Jul 19, 1911

Dr.Harper Peddicord of Fort Bragg married Gertrude Gish   Mar 22, 1916
of Portland, Oregon, [no date reported].

Mr.Pedretti married Miss A.Soldani in San Francisco on   Dec 7, 1910
November 19, 1910. Both were from Point Arena.

William J.Pedro married Mrs.Georgia Williams "last week".   Jul 2, 1919
Both were from the Mitchell Creek area. She had a son,
Leo Williams.

L.R.Pedrotti married Frances Packard Whipple, the daughter Nov 27, 1912
of Judge Frank A.Whipple, in Fort Bragg November 20, 1912.
Judge Whipple officiated at the ceremony.

P.Pelascini obtained a license to wed Giovana Stoppa of Elk. Apr 8, 1914

Angelo Pelliei obtained a license to wed Johanna Brusa.   Jan 21, 1914

J.Pelligrini married Miss E.Sala May 16, 1914.   May 27, 1914

Bennett Edward Pemberton married Ollie Barrett in the Bay   Dec 31, 1919
area December 24, 1919. The bride was the head nurse at
the Fort Bragg hospital.

Jose Pereira obtained a license to wed Velaida   Oct 18, 1911
DaSilva; both being from Fort Bragg.

Arthur Stanley Perkins, 31, obtained a license to marry   Jul 31, 1918
Lela Finkle, 20, both of Caspar.

Charles R.Perkins married Kathleen Randolph of Oakland in   Jul 21, 1915
that place July 14, 1915. He was a game warden from
Mendocino County.

David Perkins obtained a license to wed Rachael B.Martin.   Jan 15, 1913

Attorney Lester Perry wed Eleanor Brown in Walnut Creek,   Sep 26, 1917
Contra Costa County, September 12, 1917. The groom was
formerly the clerk of the Fort Bragg city council and the
bride taught in the local schools.

Walter Perry, a Navarro rancher, married Edna Straw,   Dec 19, 1917
an Albion schoolteacker, "this week".

Walter Edward Perry married Sara Genevia Hoxie at Covelo   Jul 19, 1911
July 16, 1911.   Jul 26, 1911

Willis Perry of Ukiah married Esther Inez Triplett, the   Apr 30, 1919
daughter of Henry Triplett of Fort Bragg, in that place   May 7, 1919
April 27, 1919. The groom was an automobile repair mechanic.

Robert S.Peters married Alice Badger in San Francisco   Apr 21, 1915
April 10, 1915. The bride was born in Westport, the
daughter of W.H.Badger a former Fort Bragg resident later
of San Leandro, Alameda County.

George Peterson obtained a license to wed Julia Alber.   Feb 8, 1911

Gus Peterson wed Alice Pearl White at Albion July 10, 1915. Jul 21, 1915

John Peterson obtained a license to wed Bessie Fisher.   Dec 30, 1914

Julius Peterson married Mrs.Emil Ohlson in Oakland   Jul 4, 1917
July 1, 1917.

Louis W.Peterson obtained a license to wed Gladys   Dec 3, 1919
Whitney, both of Gualala.

Oscar Peterson, a former Mendocino resident, married   Jun 17, 1914
Wilma Burge at Coronado June 11, 1914.

John Petroni got a license to wed Narcisa Sichi.   Jan 27, 1915

Arthur C.Phelps got a license to wed Georgia Brown.   Aug 18, 1915
[Married August 2, 1915 according to divorce proceedins].   May 3, 1933

Clarence Lee Phillips obtained a license to wed   May 4, 1910
Crystal Delia Watson of Upper Lake.

William M.Phillips of Fort Bragg married Alice Watson at   Oct 15, 1913
Westport November 23, 1913. JP Standley presided. Phillips Nov 26, 1913
had obtained the license with the bride's name kept secret.

Peetro Picaatte (sic) obtained a license to wed   Jan 21, 1914
Adele Azzalini of Fort Bragg.

P.Picalotte obtained a license to wed Vaglini Rosa.   Jan 11, 1911

Henry Pickle obtained a license to wed Florence Carter   Apr 22, 1914
of Potter Valley.

Galileo Pierotti obtained a license to wed Cisisa Giusti. May 26, 1915

John J.Pimental wed Laura R.Boreca, the daughter of Manuel Dec 16, 1914
Boreca of Fort Bragg, at that place December 12, 1914.
Father Sebastian conducted the service.

Marriages Reported	Issue Date

Claude W.<u>Pinches</u>, 19, married Georgia E.Holmes, 21, of
Laytonville in Ukiah September 9, 1912.   Sep 11, 1912

George <u>Pinches</u> obtained a license to wed Mabel Pinches.   Oct 30, 1912

Oswell <u>Pinches</u> of Laytonville married Norah Dyer
of Willits December 16, 1914.   Dec 23, 1914

William A.<u>Piner</u>, 43, obtained a license to wed
Pearl Bulen, 35; both of Oakland.   Jul 14, 1915

Arthur A.<u>Pitt</u>, 38, of Ukiah married Mrs.Clarissa G.Flinn,
41, a former Fort Bragg resident, September 29, 1914. Judge   Sep 30, 1914
Ornbaun officiated.

Louis <u>Piva</u> obtained a license to wed Ramona Hansard.   Oct 8, 1919

C.B.<u>Plummer</u> married Mrs.Gallagher, both of Fort Bragg, in   Sep 18, 1912
San Francisco [no date reported].

Harold <u>Plummer</u>, son the the late W.P.Plummer, married Doris   Sep 2, 1914
Wilshire in San Francisco September 8, 1914.   Sep 9, 1914

David <u>Poe</u>, an Indian, obtained a license to wed Blanche   Jul 23, 1919
Feliz, a Spaniard. Both were from the Indian Reservation
at Covelo.

Philip Oscar <u>Poe</u>, 27, married Ida Conner, 43, of
Lakeport at Ukiah July 5, 1911.   Jul 12, 1911

Robert <u>Poe</u> married Sarah Kinsey in Healdsburg "this week".   Nov 19, 1919

Oscar M.<u>Polin</u> married Bessie Marie Busch in Potter Valley   Jul 6, 1910
July 4, 1910.   Jul 13, 1910

A.<u>Polly</u>, a Fort Bragg tailorshop owner, married   Jan 12, 1916
Olga Wertnen in Willits January 2, 1916.

Denie <u>Pomon</u> wed Edna Livingston at Willits June 19, 1919.   Jun 25, 1919

H.F.<u>Pool</u> obtained a license to wed Orpha Pearl Clendennin   Jan 6, 1915
of Lakeport, Lake County.   Jan 13, 1915

William L."Lon" <u>Pool</u> married Mrs.Mary Florence Morris   Aug 13, 1913
"week before last".

Clarence E.<u>Poole</u> of Petaluma obtained a license to wed   Sep 2, 1914
Hattie E.Rowe of Willits.   Sep 9, 1914

Burton Claud <u>Porter</u> obtained a license to wed   Dec 13, 1916
Dollie M.Tracy of Laytonville.

J.R.<u>Porter</u> obtained a license to wed Della Perotti of Kenny.   Dec 27, 1916

Nicholas <u>Posti</u> married Sofia Maria Laurila at Fort Bragg   Dec 9, 1914
December 5, 1914. Judge F.A.Whipple officiated.

E.W.<u>Powell</u> obtained a license to wed Elsie M.Bell,   Feb 15, 1911
both were residents of the north County.

Harvey D.<u>Prather</u> got a license to wed Helen McGimsey.   Sep 8, 1915

Lloyd W.<u>Prather</u> obtained a license to wed Allie Witherell.   Jul 19, 1916

Guido <u>Pratolo</u> obtained a license to wed Annita Guisti.   Jan 15, 1913

Cecil G.<u>Prentious</u> of Fort Bragg obtained a license   May 22, 1918
to wed Minnie E.Curtis of Ukiah.

C.M.<u>Presley</u> of Ukiah married Margaret T.McMahon of   Aug 30, 1911
Visalia, Tulare County, at Ukiah August 22, 1911.

John Prest, 28, obtained a license to wed Esther Miller, 19,   Oct 11, 1916
both of Stewart's Point.

H.L.Preston married Florence Ruddock of Ukiah in   Aug 1, 1917
Berkeley July 25, 1917.

H.P.Preston of Ukiah wed Effie Case, daughter of Dr.Case,   Dec 21, 1910
November 7, 1910. The wedding was kept secret.

Frank Pullen married Emma Russe at Ukiah June 28, 1919.   Jul 9, 1919

Elmer C.Purdy got a license to wed Effie Goddard of Ukiah.   Dec 25, 1912

Antone J.Quaill married Fina Figaro in Mendocino   Nov 17, 1915
November 15, 1915.

Joseph J.Quaill married Eleanor Perreria at Mendocino in   Jul 17, 1918
a Catholic service July 14, 1918.

E.W.Quinliven married Bessie Mason of Willits in   Nov 23, 1910
Richmond, Contra Costa County, November 12, 1910.

M.J.Rademaker obtained a license to wed Miss C.A.Cross.   Nov 25, 1914

Charles Rafter of Greenwood married Blanche Berryhill of   Jan 11, 1911
Fort Bragg in Ukiah January 3, 1911. The groom was employed
by the lumber company at Weed, Siskiyou County.

Jack Raininen, 29, of Albion, wed Sadie Pyorre, 16, of Noyo,   Jun 7, 1916
Fort Bragg on June 1, 1916. Judge F.A.Whipple officiated.

Frank Raines of Talmage obtained a license to wed Blanche   Jan 3, 1912
Wellman of Ukiah.

Charles P.Ralstron of Spy Rock obtained a license   Dec 27, 1916
to wed Mary A.Pratt of Stockton.

Martin A.Ramiez married Elba Patterson August 14, 1914 at   Aug 19, 1914
Ukiah. Both were residents of Hopland. Judge J.Q.White
conducted the ceremony.

Wade Ransdell obtained a license to wed Eva Smith of   Feb 10, 1915
Santa Rosa.

August Ranta, 39, obtained a license to wed Sauna Maria   Mar 27, 1912
Sippola, 28, both of Fort Bragg.

Allan Rasmussen of Roseville married Margaret Escola at   Apr 9, 1919
Auburn, Placer County, March 15, 1919. The bride was the
sister of Annie Escola of Sacramento.

Charles Raudio wed Julette Reynaud in a Catholic ceremony at   Nov 24, 1915
Fort Bragg November 20, 1915. Father Blanderfield presided.
The groom was employed by the California Western Railroad.

George Rause of Portland, Oregon, was engaged to wed Mrs.   Aug 9, 1916
Kirkwood, the daughter of C.O.Packard of Mendocino.

Vernon Rawles of Boonville obtained a license to marry   Oct 24, 1917
Martha Wood of Wendling, local school teacher.

Avon C.Ray got a license to wed Edna Van Zandt of Philo.   Apr 9, 1913

Charles Quincy Ray obtained a license to wed Mildred F.   Sep 17, 1919
Biddings, both of Arcata, Humboldt County.

Sam M.Ray obtained a license to wed Theresa Kramer of Ukiah.   Jul 9, 1919

Joe Raymond married May Berryhill, the daughter of George   Oct 21, 1914
Berryhill of Fort Bragg, in Oakland October 19, 1914.

Manuel Raymonda obtained a license to wed Sigrid Avilla.   Mar 10, 1915

Guy Redwine, the County Surveyor, married Emma Luhrman   Sep 11, 1912
at San Jose "last week".

George C.Reed, 28, obtained a license to wed Ruth Crawford,   Jan 10, 1917
17. Both were from Lakeport.

Lilfred Warren Reed obtained a license to wed Daisy Hazel   Jul 9, 1919
Brightenstine.

Charles D.Reese obtained a license to wed Marie C.M.Henry.   Jun 17, 1914

Lewis B.Reese, 24, of Ukiah, obtained a license to wed   Oct 4, 1916
Elsie Hounton, 21, of Hopland.

Mumm Reid wed Ida Ann Arthur in San Francisco "last week".   Mar 19, 1913

Serafini Reidi obtained a license to wed Giulia Grambelli   Mar 8, 1911
of Mendocino.

George Patrick Reidmiller married Winifred Bardin of   Sep 20, 1916
Salinas, Monterey County, in that place September 12, 1916.
She was the daughter of Sesse Bardin and the sister of
Judge J.A.Bardin. Rev.W.A.McClean officiated.

J.W.Reilly of Healdsburg obtained a license to wed   Sep 4, 1912
Winnie Atkinson.

Gustave A.Reinke married Viola Baird at the Alhambra Hotel   Dec 4, 1912
in Albion November 25, 1912. Rev.M.Black officiated.

Victor Remmer married Eillen Stahl in Oakland "last week".   Dec 15, 1915

Robert E.Remstedt obtained a license to wed Emily Gillmore.   Oct 5, 1910

Sam Remstedt married Ora Gillmore, both of Point Arena, at   Aug 30, 1911
Ukiah August 23, 1911.

Harold G.Renner, 38, obtained a license to wed   Jul 14, 1915
Miss F.May McClary, 37; both of Los Angeles.   Jul 28, 1915

Carl Rennick obtained a license to wed Josephine   Nov 15, 1911
McDonald of Comptche.

Oscar Restolia obtained a license to wed Selma Katrina Koski   May 31, 1911
of Fort Bragg.

George Rheinhart married Ida Florence Heyward, a native   Sep 2, 1914
of Point Arena, in San Francisco August 15, 1914.

Charles Lewis Rice, 24, married Ethel Amelia Willson, 18,   Mar 6, 1912
both of Willits, at Irmulco March 3, 1912.   Mar 13, 1912
[License reported name of bride as "Wilson"].

J.Rich obtained a license to wed Cora M.Studdert.   Jun 24, 1914

George Richards married Irene Seymour at Fort   Dec 30, 1914
Bragg December 24, 1914. Judge F.A.Whipple presided.

Walter Richmond married Mrs.Florence Stanley at Point Arena   Jul 19, 1911
July 5, 1911.

Dr.T.B.Ricks, manager of the Henshaw ranch in Eden Valley,   Jan 20, 1915
married Grace Beattie of Willits in San Rafael
January 16, 1915.

Arnold Ridgway obtained a license to wed Margaret G.Stutsman.   Dec 10, 1913

Edward Ridley married Nina E.Walters, both of Hardy, at Fort   Jun 12, 1912
Bragg on June 5, 1912. Rev.W.A.Chapman officiated.

Lester Riffe got a license to wed Helen Terry of Covelo.   Jan 3, 1912

Bert Rimmer, formerly of Fort Bragg, married Elsie   Oct 31, 1917
Christensen of Elk in San Francisco October 23, 1917.

Andrew Rinaldo obtained a license to wed Julia Soldina   Jul 5, 1911
of Point Arena.

Raymond Ritschel wed Edna M.Scott at Willits March 24, 1914. Apr 1, 1914

Harold Roberts of Newport married Marian Dunn of Westport   Sep 30, 1914
at Ukiah September 26, 1914.   Oct 7, 1914

J.Roberts of Elk obtained a license to wed Lilly F.Johnson May 31, 1911
of Albion.

Max Roberts married Hilda Raudio, the daughter of Charles   Aug 23, 1916
Raudio of Fort Bragg, in Los Angeles August 18, 1916. The
groom was employed by the Southern Pacific Railroad.

Clarence A.Robinson got a license to wed Clara B.Stevens.   Nov 13, 1918

Elmer E.Robinson, formerly of Fort Bragg, married Doris E. Sep 26, 1917
Gould, the daughter of attorney Frank Gould, in San Francisco September 26, 1917.

J.W.Robinson, 63, of Sparks, Nevada, got a license   Nov 27, 1918
to wed Mrs.Delia Bishop, 42, of Point Arena.

Mario J.Rocca obtained a license to wed Louisa   Jul 9, 1919
Yturriaga of San Francisco.

Charles Rodgers was engaged to wed Engelena Ward, the   Sep 12, 1917
daughter of W.B.Ward of Fort Bragg, in San Francisco.

M.Roebke married Norma McClintock, formerly of   Feb 23, 1916
Fort Bragg, in San Francisco February 7, 1916.

Arthur Romer, the son of L.J.Romer of Ukiah valley, married Jan 19, 1916
Leila Rose of Wendling on January 6, 1916.

Edward T.Roney got a license to wed Thelma A.Montgomery.   Jun 23, 1915

W.J.Rosewarne obtained a license to wed Laura Green.   Sep 9, 1914

Constanti Rositti obtained a license to wed Rosa Guigui.   Jan 15, 1913

David Ross of Melburne married Leta Howard of Wendling   Dec 11, 1918
in Ukiah "last week".

R.A.Ross, a rancher at Rocklin and son of the late Abram and Mar 1, 1916
Mary Ross, married Mildred R.Smith, daughter of P.W.Smith of
Fort Bragg, at Sacramento [no date reported].

R.R.Ross wed Mrs.Jessie Orr in Willits November 22, 1910.   Nov 23, 1910

Robert Ross married Grace Devereux at Cleone June 20, 1918. Jun 26, 1918

C.Rossetti married Carmelino Martinelli in Santa Rosa   Oct 10, 1917
"last week". Both were from Albion.

Delbert S.Rossiter married Florence Hepworth at   Dec 6, 1916
Manchester November 23, 1916.

Richard W.Rowan married Natalie Elizabeth Rasmussen at Fort Aug 20, 1919
Bragg September 16, 1919 with Dr.Bryan officiating. She was Sep 17, 1919
the chief operator of the Fort Bragg telegraph office.

Joel E.Royman married Mrs.Luella Carmichael, formerly of   May 7, 1913
Fort Bragg, April 19, 1913 in Astoria, Oregon, where Mr.
Royman was cashier of the Scandanavian American Bank.

Walter S.Royster married Mabel Harriet Sweney in   Nov 13, 1912
San Francisco April 6, 1913, by Rev.C.L.Meil.   Apr 16, 1913

William Rucker obtained a license to wed
Lottie Sagehorn of Willits.

Jan 3, 1912

G.E.Ruckstill of San Francisco obtained a license
to wed Eugenia Klipstein of Bakersfield.

Sep 7, 1910

Joseph Rudd married Viola Elizabeth Chapman in
Ukiah January 24, 1914. Rev.S.L.Jones officiated.

Feb 4, 1914
Mar 11, 1914

Paul Rudd, 26, obtained a license to wed Emma Smith, 30,
of Comptche.

Mar 13, 1912

Herbert Ruddick obtained a license to wed Rose Etta
Salladay of Covelo.

Dec 25, 1912

C.J.Ruddock married Maude Hayter, daughter of
R.M.Hayter, at Ukiah July 9, 1914.

Jul 15, 1914

Fred Rudolph obtained a license to wed Susan Dodge.

Nov 2, 1910

John Ruonavaara, formerly of Albion, wed Ethyle Perry in
Fort Bragg May 6, 1916. The bride was the daughter of Rube
Perry of Cleone. The service was led by Judge J.K.Peirsol.

May 10, 1916

Charles F.Rupe of Fort Bragg married Myrtle Reynolds of
Alameda in Oakland December 24, 1910. Rupe was in charge of
the Irmulco Lumber Company yard at Noyo.

Dec 28, 1910
Jan 4, 1911

Ernest Rupe married Bessie Hall at Willits April 25, 1917.

May 2, 1917

William Russ married Ella Rena Irish, both of Elk, of Ukiah
"this week".

Apr 18, 1917

J.E.Russell married Marie Nelson of Pasadena in
Fort Bragg September 18, 1914.

Sep 23, 1914
Oct 10, 1914

Matt Ruuska married Ninnie Sipila, the daughter of John
Sipila of Noyo Hill, by Rev.J.J.Hillberg May 5, 1917.

May 9, 1917

Edgar B.Ryan got a license to wed Emma L.Koch.

Jul 30, 1913

C.E.Rynearson married Ester [sic] Wilson October 16, 1910.
Rev.R.Grace officiated.

Oct 19, 1910

Edward Salanave of San Francisco married Ethel Allen in Fort
Bragg July 23, 1915, Rev.Sutherland presiding. The bride was
the daughter of Sam Allen of Fort Bragg and a graduate of
the University of California.

Jul 28, 1915

Christopher L.Sallinen obtained a license to wed
Sophia L.Makin of Noyo.

Dec 20, 1911

S.T.Sallinen got a license to wed Rosa E.Kinnunen.

Sep 15, 1915

Ellis Salmen applied for a license to wed Carina Telen of
Northspur at Ukiah May 23, 1916, but was refused as the girl
was under 16 years old and had no parents or guardian. The
couple were married by Judge J.K.Peirsol in Fort Bragg
June 10, 1916.

May 31, 1916
Jun 14, 1916

Thomas W.Salo was married to Elvina Hautala in Fort Bragg
August 8, 1917.

Aug 8, 1917

J.L.Salomon of Sherwood obtained a license to wed
Miss T.Effie Taylor of Glenn County.

Sep 27, 1916

Charles Salvador of Mendocino obtained a license
to wed Lena Seymour of Noyo.

Aug 2, 1911

John Salvador married Sine Packard [no date reported
but probably in December 1912. Her name also given as "Seine"].

Jan 8, 1913

Donald Sampson married Eliza Berchtold in Ukiah   Sep 29, 1915
September 16, 1915.

Gus Myer Sampson of Berkeley married Nellie Cameron at   Jul 8, 1914
Willits June 30, 1914. Miss Cameron taught at Albion.

Alan Samuelson obtained a license to wed Carrie Southard. Mar 3, 1915

John Samuelson of Albion married Lucile Handley, the   Jun 3, 1914
daughter of George Handley of Noyo, May 31, 1914. Rev.
Hargreaves officiated.

Dr.Frank H.Sanborn married Lillian E.Eagle in Fort Bragg Sep 3, 1913
August 30, 1913. Judge F.A.Whipple officiated.   Mar 4, 1914

Walter Sand from South Dakota married Evelyn Sand in Fort Mar 19, 1919
Bragg March 15, 1919, with Rev W.M.Sutherland officiating.

Earl Sanel wed Mrs.Jessie Story at Napa. [No date reported]. Jun 7, 1916

Matt Sankovich married Mary Klobas in Fort Bragg   Sep 27, 1916
September 30, 1916. Judge J.K.Peirsol officiated.   Oct 4, 1916

J.C.Sarowski obtained a license to wed Amanda C.Warnell, Apr 27, 1910
both of Mendocino.

Joseph M.Satndads [sic] got a license to wed Mary G.Andes. Sep 20, 1911

John M.Saudade married Mrs.Marie E.Clemente in Mendocino Dec 25, 1912
January 5, 1913. Catholic rites were led by Father Raymond. Jan 8, 1913

Herman Saukkar of Eureka obtained a license to wed   Jul 9, 1919
Sofa Hendrickson of Caspar.

W.O.Saukko wed Teresa Breen in Fort Bragg October 22, 1919. Oct 22, 1919

Eugene W.Saunders of Fort Bragg obtained a license   Dec 16, 1914
to wed May Pearl Blosser of Willits.

Lawrence R.Saunders married Beulah Jones at the Episcopal Jun 17, 1914
church in Ukiah June 14, 1914. Rev.Crook officiated.   Jul 1, 1914

Tom R.Saunders wed Pearl Begley in Covelo October 17, 1914. Oct 28, 1914

Carl Savo wed Sany Lehtimaki in Fort Bragg July 15, 1916. Jul 19, 1916
Judge F.A.Whipple officiated.   Jul 26, 1916

H.C.Sawyers, 23, obtained a license to wed Luella   Jul 25, 1917
May Mitchell, 23, both of Navarro.   Aug 1, 1917

Louis D.Sawyers married Hazel McClintock at Ukiah   Jan 5, 1910
December 29, 1909.

Laurence Saxon married Hazel White in Willits   Aug 20, 1913
August 15, 1913. Rev.Funk officiated.

Albert Schandri got a license to wed Johanna Magistries. Aug 18, 1915

Dr.F.M.Scheele married Emma Edwards, the daughter of Bob Dec 8, 1915
Edmonds of Fort Bragg, in Waukesha, Wisconsin,
December 1, 1915.

J.B.Schibi married Kittie Emerick in San Francisco   Mar 3, 1915
February 27, 1915.

Herman Schmidt obtained a license to wed Romilda Mariani. Oct 27, 1915
[Also "Romilda da Mariani".]

Julius Schmidt obtained a license to wed   Jan 29, 1913
Lillian Lafranchi of Hopland.

Joseph Schranth obtained a license to wed Laura Westergart Dec 25, 1912
of Talmage.

Fred Schonbeck obtained a license to wed Canideva Morrison   Jun 14, 1911
of Covelo.

Leon Schuhl of Los Angeles obtained a license to marry   May 28, 1913
Delia Cook of San Francisco.

Charles J.Schwartz, 47, of Willits, married Sophie Walli,   Nov 15, 1916
36, of Eureka in Ukiah November 6, 1916.

William Scoble, 23, of San Francisco obtained a   Dec 6, 1911
license to wed Laura Wirth, 15, of Willits.

James W.Scoggen married Mrs.Eugene Haydon, the widow of the   Apr 9. 1919
late Frank Haydon of Round Valley, in Ukiah April 1, 1919.

E.S.Scott of Fort Bragg married Frances McGowan of   Aug 26, 1914
Yerington, Nevada, at that place August 23, 1914.
The bride was the sister of W.N.Wood of Fort Bragg.

George R.Scott obtained a license to wed Nevada Brooks   Dec 24, 1913
of Potter Valley.

George Wiley Scott obtained a license to wed Minnie Card.   Feb 12, 1913

H.B.Scott celebrated their 50th wedding anniversary at   Jun 26, 1918
Manchester. They were married there by Rev.Haskett on
May 18, 1868. Mrs.Scott, was the daughter of S.S.Hoyt who
came to the coast in 1859. Mr.Scott, a native of Illinois,
crossed the plains in 1864 settling first at Fish Rock and
later farming in the Manchester area. He served two terms
as Supervisor and also as a justice of the peace. Six
children, four sons and two daughters were born.

Lloyd B.Scott of Upper Lake obtained a license to   Dec 25, 1912
wed Gertrude A.Pool of Lakeport.

Otto Harrison Scott married Hannah Gummerus in Willits by   Jul 22, 1914
Judge Whitney [no date].Both were from Fort Bragg.

Dr.Saxon Scott married Cora Jordan December 23, 1911 in San   Dec 27, 1911
Francisco. Rev.A.J.Sawyer of the Baptist church officiated.
Dr Scott, a dentist, was a former resident of Fort Bragg.

Will Scott, 30, of the Presidio in San Francisco,   Mar 20, 1918
obtained a license to wed Helma Lake, 27, the
daughter of Matt Lake a merchant of Fort Bragg.

Paul Seammon married Ida May Heckendorf in Ukiah   Dec 31, 1913
December 16, 1913.

Volney R.Seawell married Ethel Leota Elledge at Ukiah   Feb 8, 1911
February 1, 1911.

Guiseppe Senini obtained a license to wed Maddalena Senini.   Jan 15, 1913

S.A.Senteny obtained a license to wed Edna Woodworth of   Oct 30, 1912
Geyserville, Sonoma County.

R.Seymore of Noyo obtained a license to wed   Jul 5, 1911
Gertrude Buehl of Caspar.

Harry Shafsky married Hazel M.Mero at Ukiah   Jul 30, 1913
September 24, 1913. Father Brennen officiated.   Sep 24, 1913

Fred Sharp obtained a license to wed Juanita Neighbor.   Oct 8, 1919

Fred Franklin Sharp married Charlotte Annie Lawson at   Feb 12, 1913
Willits February 5, 1913. Rev.W.C.Whitaker officiated.

Frank G.Sharratt, a rancher at Bear Buttes, Humboldt County,   Aug 1, 1917
married Mabel Stoddard Borges in San Francisco July 28, 1917.

George <u>Sharrock</u> obtained a license to wed Ferol V.Gibson, both of Ukiah.

Dec 3, 1913

W.J.<u>Shattuck</u> of Ukiah married Miss E.Reed of Petaluma at Santa Rosa March 12, 1911.

Mar 15, 1911

William <u>Shaw</u> of Mendocino obtained a license to marry Lizzie Hendrickson of Comptche.

Sep 4, 1918

William T.<u>Shaw</u>, a petty officer U.S.Navy, married Agnes Ayers of Willits "a year ago".

Jul 29, 1914

Robert Edward <u>Shean</u> married Daisy Margaret Cahill in San Francisco December 22, 1912. Rev.S.J.Sawyer of the Baptist church performed the ceremony.

Dec 25, 1912

Thomas <u>Shelton</u> obtained a license to marry Belle V.Starr of Fort Bragg.

Jun 28, 1911

Homer <u>Sherwood</u> of Westport married May Young of Willits February 17, 1914. Rev.W.A.Chapman officiated. The groom was the town druggist and the bride, the daughter of Thomas Young, formerly of Westport.

Feb 11, 1914

L.A.<u>Shibley</u>, the son of J.H.Shibley of Fort Bragg, married Miss Towlamen in San Francisco September 19, 1915.

Sep 22, 1915

William E.<u>Shields</u> obtained a license to wed Anna Whipple.

Aug 18, 1915

Earnest <u>Shoemake</u> married Mary Woods at Ukiah June 1, 1913. Rev.Clark officiated.

Jun 4, 1913

Paul <u>Sholtz</u> married Olive Dorwaad in Napa December 31, 1918.

Jan 8, 1919

Sam <u>Shore</u> of Two Rivers obtained a license to wed Meda Cleveland of Chico. [Two Rivers became Dos Rios.]

Mar 19, 1913

Russell <u>Sierck</u>, a brakeman on the Northwestern Pacific Railroad, married Margaret Perry, the daughter of J.D.Perry of Willits, at that place September 7, 1919.

Sep 10, 1919

Fred <u>Sill</u> married Goldie E.Cohen in San Francisco September 28, 1913.

Oct 1, 1913

William James <u>Sill</u> obtained a license to wed Sarah Cole, both of Northwestern.

Jun 28, 1911

Leander <u>Siltanen</u> married Emma Anttila at Fort Bragg February 11, 1915. Rev.John J.Hillberg officiated.

Feb 17, 1915

Antone <u>Silva</u> married Mayme Costa at the Mendocino Catholic church December 24, 1914.

Dec 30, 1914

John M.<u>Silveria</u> married Anna F.Silvia in Mendocino June 25, 1911.

Jun 7, 1911
Jul 5, 1911

Joseph M.<u>Silveria</u> married Cecilia J.Silvia, both of Mendocino, in Oakland May 14, 1913. Three Silveria brothers married three Silvia sisters: John married Annie and Manuel married Belle.

May 21, 1913

Manuel <u>Silveria</u> married Belle Silvia December 29, 1912. The bride was the daughter of Casimiro Silvia of Mendocino. Catholic services were conducted by Father Raymond.

Dec 4, 1912
Jan 8, 1913

Milo <u>Silverthrone</u> married Alba Metzler in Santa Rosa November 26, 1913. Both were from Willits.

Dec 3, 1913

Charles A.<u>Simkins</u> obtained a license to wed Leonora L.Owens of Ukiah.

Sep 17, 1919

Gary S.Simmerly of Redwine wed Ruth Edna Devilbiss of Hardy   Nov 29, 1911
at Rockport November 23, 1911. Father Brennan officiated.   Dec 6, 1911

J.Simonin, 33, obtained a license to wed Miss C.Johnson, 16.   Nov 17, 1915
Both were from the Round Valley Indian reservation.

Arthur Simpson obtained a license to wed Ethel Fraine   Jan 17, 1912
of Boonville.

Henry Simpson of Fort Bragg married Mary Dashiell of   Dec 28, 1910
Westport in Fort Bragg December 25, 1910. Rev.W.A.Chapman
presided at the ceremony.

Thomas B.Simpson, 28, of Crockett, married Wanda B.Lawson,   Feb 20, 1918
27, of San Leandro "this week". She was the daughter of
former Supervisor Lawson of the Hopland district and had
taught school at Albion.

Capt.Ernest A.Sinclair, the son of J.A.Sinclair of Glen   Apr 9, 1919
Blair, married Helen Harris, the daughter of the late C.P.   May 7, 1919
Harris of Moncton, New Brunswick, on April 30, 1919.

Angelo Sirizzotti obtained a license to wed Mary Sarina.   Mar 4, 1914

F.M.Slack of Point Arena married Lurine Freeman   Sep 17, 1919
at Eureka, Humboldt County, August 30, 1919.

William Slack of Point Arena married Agnes Bryant   Jun 27, 1917
in San Francisco "this week".

Julian Sleeper obtained a license to wed Gladys Green.   Dec 4, 1912

Preston Slye married Zella Zelsworth of Placerville   Feb 27, 1918
at Arcata, Humboldt County, February 24, 1918.

Carolino Smith obtained a license to wed Ellin Williams.   Oct 30, 1912

Charles L.Smith got a license to wed Belle Hayden.   Apr 18, 1917

Clair Smith married Mabel Stitt at Ukiah June 19, 1912.   Jun 19, 1912
The bride was the daughter of James Stitt.

Frank Smith married Inez Stayton in Fort Bragg   Dec 6, 1916
December 2, 1916. Judge Frank A.Whipple officiated.

George A.Smith married Josephine E.Van Winkle at Willits   Dec 31, 1913
December 23, 1913. Rev.Chrysler presided.   Feb 11, 1914

George M.Smith obtained a license to wed Marguerite Vaughn Apr 9, 1913
of Potter Valley.

Gordon A.Smith obtained a license to wed Elsie [data lost]. Jun 12, 1912

Henry Smith got a license to wed Mary Steele of Covelo.   Jan 17, 1912

J.J.Smith of Fort Bragg obtained a license to wed   May 22, 1918
Alice Morand of Caspar.

John S.Smith obtained a license to wed Lelia T.Clawson.   Jan 12, 1910

L.S.Smith obtained a license to wed Clara Rose.   Jun 17, 1914

R.E.Smith married Mollie Wright at Ukiah September 7, 1910. Sep 7, 1910

David M.Snodgrass on April 25, 1918 obtained a   May 1, 1918
license to wed Ethel Mendel of Caspar.

Bert Snyder, a U.S.Navy veteran, married Erika Hartland in Dec 11, 1912
Fort Bragg December 9, 1912. Rev.Grace officiated.   Dec 18, 1912
[Bride's name also given as "Ericka Northland"].

Percey A.Sobey married Mary A.Neary of Cleone in   Jun 5, 1912
Fort Bragg June 2, 1912. F.A.Whipple officiated.

Marriages Reported	Issue Date

Toivo <u>Sold</u> married Hilda Ojolo in Fort Bragg
August 29, 1912. F.A.Whipple presided. — Sep 4, 1912

James <u>Somersel</u> of Ukiah obtained a license to wed
Nora White of Laytonville. — Apr 22, 1914

S.M.<u>Sorensen</u> obtained a license to wed Laura Hysong, both
of Point Arena. — Aug 16, 1911

Peter <u>Sousi</u> obtained a license to wed Mary Baird. — Oct 27, 1915

C.E.<u>Southard</u> obtained a license to wed Mary Jacinta,
both of Willits. — Oct 18, 1911

John <u>Souza</u> married Amelia Silveria January 2, 1916 at
Fort Bragg in a Catholic service conducted by
Rev.Blanderfield. — Jan 5, 1916

Homer C.<u>Spoonemore</u> obtained a license to wed Anna M.Swanson
of Eureka, Humboldt County. — Sep 4, 1918

Gus <u>Spotswood</u>, a rancher of Potter Valley, married
Olga Richter in San Jose June 22, 1919. — Jun 25, 1919

E.C.<u>Springer</u> wed Lydia Rice at Willits December 16, 1914. — Dec 23, 1914

Ellis <u>Springer</u> married Ethel Patterson of Fort Worth, Texas,
at Santa Rosa July 2, 1919. — Jul 9, 1919

George E.<u>Squires</u> obtained a license to wed Edna S.Jamison
of Covelo. — Aug 10, 1910

Roscoe <u>Squires</u> married Jeneveve Patton at Willits.
[No date reported]. — Apr 29, 1914

Lord Hendrix <u>Stampe</u> of Denmark married Myrtle Harvery
of Mendocino County at Oakland September 5, 1919.
Rev.Alexander Allen officiated. The couple met in Hawaii. — Sep 10, 1919

Amos <u>Standley</u> obtained a license to wed Helene Nichols
of Westport. — Nov 8, 1911

William Raymond <u>Standley</u> married Ella Button in Fort Bragg
December 10, 1917. Rev.W.A.Chapman presided. The bride was
a nurse. — Dec 19, 1917

Archie C.<u>Stayton</u>, formerly of Fort Bragg and lately
of San Rafael, obtained a license to wed Mayme E.
Thorpe of San Francisco. — Jun 7, 1916

John D.<u>Stayton</u> married Inez J.McRae June 12, 1910.
Rev.W.A.Chapman officiated. — Jun 15, 1910

Donald <u>Steel</u> of Palo Alto married Alice Cuthbertson of
Manchester in Palo Alto September 6, 1913. — Sep 10, 1913

Bert <u>Steele</u> obtained a license to wed Mary Meyers. — Oct 5, 1910

Clifford A.<u>Steele</u> married Lois Allingham at Ukiah
January 10, 1919. The bride had been a schoolteacher
in the Anderson Valley. — Jan 15, 1919

Fred William <u>Steele</u> of Gualala obtained a license
to wed Rose B.Dawson of Irmulco — Jul 8, 1914 / Jul 15, 1914

Winifred <u>Steele</u> married Gladys Mallory, a former
Mendocino resident, in Holton, Kansas,
"a short time ago". — Jul 18, 1917

Henry <u>Steimle</u> of Fort Bragg married Emma Rang of Gualala
at that place March 14, 1912. — Mar 20, 1912

Alex Stenberg, formerly of Fort Bragg, married   Feb 23, 1916
Ruth Winlund of Oakland in San Francisco   Nov 1, 1916
November 4, 1916. Rev.B.L.Carlton officiated.   Nov 15, 1916

Joe Stevenson married Blossom Cretser in Santa Rosa   Jul 22, 1914
April 6, 1914. Both were from Fort Bragg.

Calvin C.Stewart of Needle Rock married Frances Eastman   May 11, 1910
formerly of Ferndale, Humboldt County, in San Anselmo, Marin
County, April 14, 1910. The bride was the daughter of
E.G.Eastman and the groom, the son of Calvin Stewart of
Petrolia, Humboldt County.

Allen George Stipp, 21, obtained a license to   Jan 24, 1912
wed Nellie Burke, 18, both of Ukiah.

Arthur Stipp married Clara Fine at Ukiah January 2, 1910.   Jan 5, 1910

G.L.Stock obtained a license to wed Miss G.E.Andrews. Jul 15, 1914

John Stolpe got a license to wed Regina Bjork of Greenwood.   Oct 25, 1911

A.G.Stone of Mendocino married Annie L.Brown in Oakland   Nov 15, 1911
November 7, 1911.

L.G.Stone married Alice R.Ross in Willits November 22, 1910.   Nov 23, 1910

R.M.Stone obtained a license to wed Miss A.M.Nowlin,   Aug 9, 1916
both of Branscomb.

William Stone married Amenda Dahl in Fort Bragg   Jul 23, 1913
July 20, 1913. Judge F.A.Whipple officiated.

A.Stornetta married Mary Acquistapace in Point Arena   Jul 30, 1913
July 19, 1913.

J.O.Stornetta got a license to wed Louise Salla.   Jul 7, 1915

John Stornetta of Point Arena married Louise Ciapuscia,   Jun 12, 1918
the daughter of A.Ciapuscia, the operator of the Gualala
hotel, at Ukiah June 8, 1918.

Fred A.Stoschke, 23, of Hopland, obtained a license to wed   Jul 14, 1915
Dorothy E.Gray, 18, of the Anderson Valley.

Tom I.Strand married Isabelle Elvira Wahlberg, the daughter   Apr 30, 1919
of Mrs.E.J.Wahlberg of Fort Bragg, in San Francisco "last
week". Strand was a contractor and builder in the Bay area.

Raymond J.Stroud, 24, of Idaho Falls, Idaho, got a license   Dec 20, 1916
to wed Hilia Thorstrom, 19, the daughter of J.Thorstrom of
Fort Bragg tunnel.

Andrew Sturtevant, the son of Rev.A.J.Sturtevant, obtained   Nov 11, 1914
a license to wed Rhoda Mitchell in Oakland November 6, 1914.

J.Succeti obtained a license to wed Angeline Del Prete.   Nov 15, 1911

Arthur Summerville of Usal obtained a license to   Jul 26, 1911
wed Mary Murphy of Monroe.

Charles L.Sumner of San Francisco obtained a license to wed   Jul 25, 1917
Irwa F.Vercoutere of Berkeley.

Joseph Sverko got a license to wed Jelena Zmak, Fort Bragg.   Oct 18, 1911

F.P.Swan married Georgia Shaver in Spokane, Washington,   Mar 28, 1917
"recently".

Alfred Swanson, the son of August Swanson of Fort Bragg,   Nov 12, 1919
married Annie Lind, the daughter of Mrs.Lind in San Francisco November 10, 1919.

Carl Emil <u>Swanson</u>, 29, of Mendocino married Catherine   May 31, 1916
Lammers, 23, the daughter of George Lammers of Mendocino,   Jan 3, 1917
at that place January 1, 1917. Rev.H.P.Ingram officiated.

Gustaf <u>Swanson</u> married Jennie Olsen, both of Mendocino at   Jan 1, 1913
Caspar December 31, 1912. Rev.J.H.Hargraves officiated.

Lawrence <u>Sweeney</u> obtained a license to wed Grace Barney   Jun 2, 1915
of Covelo.   Jun 23, 1915

Archie Lee <u>Sweetser</u> married Inez Ethel Elmslie   Jan 18, 1911
February 5, 1911 at the Fort Bragg Presbyterian church, Rev.   Feb 8, 1911
R.C.Grace officated. Both parties were residents of Caspar.

Emory H.<u>Sweetser</u> married Johanna C.Gallop in Oakland   Oct 4, 1916
"last week".

George H.<u>Switzer</u>, a Fort Bragg teamster, married Mrs.Ethel   Feb 12, 1913
Beckman, the daughter of Eli Knight of Mendocino at Ukiah
February 3, 1913.

John R.<u>Switzer</u> of Fort Bragg obtained a license to wed   Jul 5, 1911
Mae E.Dixon, also of Fort Bragg, in Oakland June 3, 1911.

John C.<u>Sypriano</u> obtained a license to wed Mamie C.Cortez.   Oct 10, 1914

C.A.<u>Tarwater</u> obtained a license to wed Alma Dalton.   Sep 9, 1914

Anderson <u>Taylor</u>, attorney, married Carmel Ostrom   Aug 27, 1913
at Ukiah August 19, 1913. Father Clark officiated.

Austin <u>Taylor</u> married Mamie Brooks in Santa Rosa   May 9, 1917
May 2, 1917.

Ernest M.<u>Taylor</u> married Ruby Frederickson, the daughter of   Nov 18, 1914
A.W.Frederickson of Irmulco, at Ukiah November 10, 1914.   Dec 2, 1914

Mervin Earl <u>Taylor</u> obtained a license to wed   Oct 15, 1913
Elna Hatch of Ukiah.

W.R.<u>Taylor</u> married Nellie Senteney of Mendocino in Napa   Apr 25, 1917
April 16, 1917.

Wharton [Shields] <u>Taylor</u> married Ellen Lind July 7, 1918 in   Jul 10, 1918
Fort Bragg. Rev.Franklyn Bryan officiated. The groom was a
bugler in the 319th Engineers; the bride, a schoolteacher.

H.A.<u>Taylos</u>, 60, of Lakeport, married Lena M.Jones,   Nov 8, 1916
40, of Fort Bragg at Ukiah November 1, 1916.

L.C.<u>Terry</u> of Mina obtained a license Ethel E.Cummings   Nov 13, 1918
of Bell Springs.

Max <u>Thelen</u>, state road commissioner, married Ora Muir,   May 7, 1913
the daughter of H.B.Muir of Willits, at Berkeley May 1,   Apr 28, 1920
1913. Mr.Thelan was head of the California Railroad
Commission and was appointed Director General of the
U.S.RRs in 1920.

Eugene Clifford <u>Therrien</u> obtained a license to   Jun 3, 1914
wed Henrietta Connor of Covelo.

Frank <u>Thomas</u> of Ukiah married Mattie Snider   Nov 1, 1911
October 25, 1911.

Isom <u>Thompson</u> of Scotia married Ellen Dougherty at   Jun 7, 1911
Point Arena "last week".

Henry <u>Thurman</u> married Hazel Wikstrom, the daughter   Jan 5, 1916
of Mrs.E.Wikstrom, in Fort Bragg January 1, 1916.
Rev.W.A.Chapman presided.

John Edward <u>Thurman</u> obtained a license to wed
Haidee L.Brayton, both of Point Arena.   Nov 23, 1910

E.P.<u>Thurston</u>, a printer, married Hattie Schaeffer of Navarro   Feb 16, 1910
[no date reported]. [He was later to be the co-publisher of the
Fort Bragg Advocate and the Ukiah Press Democrat].

Herbert <u>Tichenor</u> of Vallejo obtained a license to   Sep 17, 1913
wed Lulu Pearl Girschel of Stockton.

James Wilson <u>Todd</u> married Eunice Elizbeth Barnes, both of   Sep 11, 1912
Caspar, at Ukiah September 4, 1912. Rev.Moore officiated.

Elijah G.<u>Tolle</u>, 21, obtained a license to wed   Aug 20, 1919
Elizabeth M.Jacobson, 18, both of Fort Bragg.

Alvin S.<u>Tollman</u> married Effie St.Louis of Arcata,   May 22, 1912
Humboldt County, at Albion ridge May 15, 1912.

Guy Ray <u>Torrence</u> of Cleone married Cleo F.Tolle "across   Nov 25, 1914
Pudding Creek" November 21, 1914. Rev.W.A.Chapman presided.   Dec 9, 1914

John <u>Torsman</u> got a license to wed Amanda Aspholm.   Mar 4, 1914

Carl Oscar <u>Torstrom</u>, the son of Carl Torstrom,   Aug 2, 1916
married Elna Harkonen in Berkeley July 30, 1916.

A.<u>Toscocci</u> got a license to wed Minnie Bassi of Fort Bragg.   Oct 19, 1910

John Francis <u>Towle</u> married Lilian Harper McClure   Feb 23, 1916
February 10, 1916.

G.<u>Towson</u> obtained a license to wed Matilda Schamber.   Jan 8, 1913

Charles Maxwell <u>Tucker</u> married Rose Mary Grothe   Jul 12, 1916
of Cummings in Ukiah July 14, 1916.   Jul 19, 1916

Earl <u>Tucker</u> obtained a license to wed Della M.Hunt   Aug 5, 1914
of Redwine.

Charles <u>Tyrell</u>, driver of Barnard's auto stage, married   Mar 19, 1913
Emily Smith of Mendocino in Fort Bragg March 22, 1913.   Mar 26, 1913
Judge J.K.Peirsol officiated.

Arch <u>Tyson</u> married Rosie Dashiell December 9, 1916 in Fort   Dec 13, 1916
Bragg, Judge F.A.Whipple officiating. Both were of Westport.

E.H.<u>Tyson</u>, principal of the Mendocino grammar school, wed   Jul 27, 1910
Miss A.Roberts "last week" in San Francisco. The bride
formerly resided at Ten Mile River.

Irving G.<u>Utschig</u> married Gladys A.Handley, the daughter of   Aug 8, 1917
George Handley, in Fort Bragg August 5, 1917. Father Grant
officiated at the ceremony.

J.S.<u>Valadao</u> married Miss M.Schroter, formerly of Eureka,   Jan 2, 1918
Humboldt County, at Mendocino December 31, 1917.

William <u>Valadoa</u> married Mrs.Sybil Gustafson at Mendocino   Aug 30, 1916
in a Catholic ceremony August 23, 1916.

Harry <u>Van Bebber</u> of Eureka obtained a license to marry   May 22, 1918
Hattie Bunch of Willits.

Lt.H.D.<u>Vandiver</u> of Fort Baker married Edith Naomi Nichols   Sep 11, 1918
of Mendocino at that place September 11, 1918.

Claude <u>Van Dyke</u> of Ukiah married Bertha L.Steele   Jul 25, 1917
of Willits at that place July 21, 1917.

Volney <u>Van Dyke</u>, the son of County Assessor Van Dyke,   Jun 27, 1917
married Ethel Ford, the daughter of Supervisor E.M.Ford,
secretly in May 1917.

Frederick Van Loo, 46, obtained a license to wed   Mar 12, 1919
Ida Finley, 39, both of Irmulco.

George L.Vann obtained a license to wed Rena May Shields   Jan 27, 1915
of Ukiah.

Leslie G.Vann of Longvale obtained a license   Jan 31, 1917
to wed Emma G.Brown of Covelo.

Arthur M.Van Winkle of Vallejo married Lois J.Martin at Fort   Nov 13, 1918
Bragg November 12, 1918. The bride was a sister of Mrs.
F.H.Hyman of Fort Bragg.

James A.Vassar married Edna Lorine Ward at Willits   Jul 9, 1913
July 6, 1913.

Peter Venturelli obtained a license to wed Louisa Persico   Sep 13, 1911
of Willits.

Octavio Venturi obtained a license to wed Argentina Tombini   Jun 14, 1911
of Willits.

Mr.Vermason of Hanford married Adeline Deering at Ukiah   Mar 19, 1913
March 15, 1913.

Arthur Vick obtained a license to wed Annie Simonin of   Aug 14, 1918
Covelo. Both were Indians.

John Joseph Vieira married Maria S.Neto September 13, 1913.   Sep 17, 1913

Frederick Ludwick Viemann obtained a license to wed   Jun 3, 1914
Mrs.Elizabeth Gartina Helm.

Frank J.Vieria married Anna Josephine Rose, both of   Dec 3, 1913
Melburne, at Mendocino November 29, 1913.
Judge Wallace presided.

Pietro Caetano Vieirra married Conceiccio Madira Ramus in   Jul 19, 1916
a Catholic ceremony at Mendocino August 6, 1916.   Aug 9, 1916

Frank Volfi got a license to wed Aurelia Sala of Albion.   Dec 17, 1913

Eugene Voreis obtained a license to wed Bernice Woodward   Dec 3, 1913
of Laurel Dell.

Charles R.Waara of Fort Bragg married Jennie Niemela of   Nov 10, 1910
Navarro November 4, 1910. Judge J.K.Piersol officiated.

Edward H.Wade married Ada Marie Hartman at Fort Bragg   Jan 1, 1913
December 25, 1912. Rev.J.C.Garth of the Baptist church
officiated at the ceremony.

O.F.Waggoner of Fort Bragg married Hattie Winsboro of Cement,   Aug 27, 1913
Sonoma County, in Santa Rosa August 21, 1913.

Grant Wagner wed Gertrude Rich at Willits July 2, 1911.   Jul 12, 1911

Imer W.Wainie of Fort Bragg obtained a license to marry   Nov 16, 1910
Aili Hyman of Pudding Creek north of Fort Bragg.

Thomas A Wait obtained a license to wed Alma T.Waidi   Nov 29, 1911
of Willits.

George W.Waite obtained a license to wed Jennie A.Farnell.   Sep 22, 1915

Charles Walbridge, a former resident of Mendocino, married   Apr 25, 1917
Frances Whittaker of Long Beach, Los Angeles County, at that
place "this week".

Ben Waldo of Fort Bragg obtained a license to marry Maretta O.   Sep 7, 1910
Shibley of Greenwood.

Walter W.Waldo of Greenwood married Gertrude James of Union
Landing in Fort Bragg December 18, 1912. Judge J.K.Peirsol
officiated at the ceremony.   Dec 11, 1912

Aaron Walker got a license to wed Gladys M.Wade.   Nov 3, 1915

C.M.Walker, 54, obtained a license to wed Alta Luck, 33.   Jan 24, 1917
Both were from Elk.

Cecil E.Walker of Willits obtained a license to wed   Sep 7, 1910
wed Miss I.S.Riggs.

Elmer L.Walker was to marry Ella Fairbanks of Manchester.   Mar 24, 1915

Raymond H.Walker married Emma McWaters of Willits   Jan 1, 1919
at Ukiah December 28, 1918.

Roy Walker wed Mary Hill of Willits at Ukiah "last week".   Oct 29, 1913

W.A.Walker obtained a license to wed Christine   Jan 11, 1911
Burnham, both of Ukiah.

William Walker married Ethel Wilson at Point Arena   Sep 12, 1913
"this week". Both were from Manchester.

Alex Wall of Ukiah married Lydia Backlund of Fort Bragg in   Sep 27, 1916
that city September 26, 1916, Rev.J.J.Hillberg officiating.

Jacob Wallace of Covelo obtained a license to wed   Nov 16, 1910
Lizzie Trammell of Potter Valley.

Thomas S.Wallace, the son of W.T.Wallace, married Lash A.   Sep 2, 1914
Demeris of Eureka at Mendocino August 30, 1914. Rev.J.   Sep 9, 1914
Melville Fisher officiated.

William Wallace married Ethel Hicks, the oldest daughter of   Mar 11, 1914
William Bartley of Fort Bragg, at that place May 31, 1914.   Jun 3, 1914
Rev.W.A.Chapman officiated.

Charles Wallach married Edna Sweet of Bell Valley   Jun 24, 1914
at Ukiah June 22nd [possibly June 15th]. Both were
residents of the Anderson Valley.

Ray W.Waller married Zinobia ["Zenolia" in another item] May   Sep 27, 1911
Creston, both of Fort Bragg September 18, 1911. Rev.R.C.
Grace officiated.

Louis Walsh married May Titus at Ukiah "last week".   Jun 6, 1917
It was rumored they were not of age.

G.E.Ward, the son of C.M.Ward, married Geraldine Stanley,   Jan 26, 1916
the daughter of W.Stanley, at Ukiah January 23, 1916.

G.K.Ward got a license to wed Charlotte Wayland.   Nov 18, 1914

Clyde Ware, the son of W.W.Ware the Fort Bragg postmaster,   Oct 1, 1919
married in San Francisco "this week". Clyde was employed by
the Sterling Furniture Company in San Francisco.
[Bride's name not reported].

Elmer J.Ware obtained a license to wed Mary Houx of   Jul 26, 1916
Fellows, Kern County.

Leiland P.Ware, 27, obtained a license to wed Myrtle P.   Nov 15, 1916
Burrows, 34. Both were from Ukiah.

James Warten married Mrs.Mary Dickenson, a former Newport   Dec 6, 1916
resident, in San Francisco "this week".

Claude Waymire, 25, of Westport obtained a license to marry   Sep 27, 1911
Katy May Binner, 21, of Willits.

Rudolph Waymire obtained a license to wed Minnie Averill.   Dec 4, 1912

Isaac E.Weaver got a license to wed Emma J.Carver.

Apr 18, 1917

G.C.Webster obtained a license to wed Enex F.Smith
of Covelo.

Oct 5, 1910

George F.Weeks got a license to wed Ellen B.Dailey.

Aug 18, 1915

Thomas Welch married Lorraine Sanderson in Fort Bragg
March 25, 1911.

Mar 29, 1911
Apr 5, 1911

John Weisse married Esther Golden January 6, 1916 in Fort
Bragg. Rev.Sutherland officiated.

Jan 5, 1916
Jan 12, 1916

C.H.Weller, the son of M.J.Weller of Fort Bragg, married
Charlotte Polk, both of San Francisco, on November 28, 1912
in San Francisco.

Dec 4, 1911

Horace A.Weller married Mrs.Florence Corbaley of Los Angeles
November 17, 1915.

Nov 24, 1915

James Weller married Dorothy Waugh in San Francisco
in September 1919 [exact date not reported].
Rev.Barrett, formerly of Fort Bragg, officiated.

Oct 1, 1919

David C.Wellman of Ukiah married Vendel Sjolund of
Mendocino December 22, 1913.

Dec 31, 1913

Walter Wells obtained a license to wed Bernice Keenan.

Jul 29, 1914

L.A.Wemple of Laytonville married Alma N.Clifton of Covelo
August 31, 1910.

Oct 5, 1910

Ned West married Ruth Donohoe at Lakeport September 26, 1915.

Oct 6, 1915

J.V.Westerlund obtained a license to wed Tyne Makinen.

May 13, 1914

Joseph F.Westphalen got a license to wed Della Shimmin.

Oct 27, 1915

Henry W.Whipple married Lulu Madsen, daughter of J.G.Madsen
of Fort Bragg, in that place August 4, 1916. Judge Frank A.
Whipple, father of the groom, officiated.

Aug 9, 1916

Woodie Whipple, 33, obtained a license to wed
Josephine Smith, 28 - both of Covelo.

Nov 8, 1916

Clarence Whitcomb married Alice Hicks at Santa Rosa
September 9, 1919.

Sep 17, 1919

George Whitcomb married Laura E.Shelton in Fort Bragg
[no date reported]. Judge F.A.Whipple officiated.

Jun 30, 1915
Jul 14, 1915

Percy Whitcomb married Mabel Spotswood at the Ukiah Baptist
church May 4, 1919. Rev.A.J.Sturtevant presided. The groom
was employed by the Northwestern Pacific Railroad. The bride
was born and raised in Potter Valley.

May 7, 1919

Carleton White, the son of C.L.White, secretary of the Union
Lumber Company, of San Rafael obtained a license to wed
Helen Hathaway of Oakland.

Apr 11, 1917

George Edward White, aged 33, of Zenia, Humboldt County, got
a license to wed Ethel Gladys Brightenstine, 18, of Covelo.

Jul 12, 1911

Judge J.Q.White was engaged to wed Harriet Ortley
of Santa Clara County February 19, 1913.

Feb 19, 1913

Robert D.White married Carrie Olsen in Fort Bragg
March 18, 1911. Judge F.A.Whipple presided.

Mar 22, 1911

R.E.Whited, 29, married Grace Elaine Johnson, 20,
of Willits in Lakeport September 27, 1916.
Rev.Mallory Flanagin officiated.

Oct 4, 1916

Captain E.L.Whitney of Mobile, Alabama, married
Olga O'Connor at Fort Bragg September 28, 1918.   Oct 2, 1918

Frank Whitney married Mable Sellers in Willits "last week".   Jul 6, 1910

L.F.Wilcox married Miss L.A.Gaspar at Manchester   Dec 21, 1910
December 17, 1910.

Charles Wiles obtained a license to wed Edna Raymond. Both   Nov 27, 1912
were from Willits.

J.B.William of Potter Valley obtained a license   Dec 21, 1910
to wed Olive A.Eten of Philo.

George M.Williams obtained a license to wed Effie Ray.   Jul 9, 1919

Grover Williams obtained a license to wed Ruth Chapman.   Mar 22, 1911

J.Williams married Laura Kaiser at Ukiah April 9, 1911.   Apr 12, 1911

Merrill Williams married Beth Wakeley of Laytonville in   Feb 28, 1917
Ukiah February 22, 1917. The groom was the postmaster and
son of L.J.Williams, a prominent local rancher.

William W.Williams married Violet I.Lilley at Caspar   Jun 9, 1915
June 5, 1915. The Rev.J.H.Hargreaves conducted the ceremony
in the Baptist parsonage.

William Williamson obtained a license to wed Edna Moran.   Oct 5, 1910

Charles O.Williford of Point Arena married Vivian Hackley of   Sep 6, 1916
San Francisco and Brush Creek September 10, 1916.   Sep 13, 1916

Alexander Willimaa obtained a license to wed Selima Santala.   Jan 12, 1910

Will Willis married Deena Hanson, the daughter of Jesse   Sep 18, 1912
Hanson, "last February". Willis' sister was Mrs.W.Fuller
of Fort Bragg.

Arthur A.Willoughby married Elsie Peterson of Mendocino in   Feb 9, 1916
Sacramento January 24, 1916. A second item reported the   Jun 7, 1916
marriage in San Francisco in June 1916. He was editor of
the Chronicle.

Melville W.Wilsey of Ukiah married Myrtle M.Mallory, the   Dec 30, 1914
daughter of C.B.Mallory of Littleriver, at that place
December 25, 1914. Rev.J.M.Fisher officiated.

Henry Wilson obtained a license to wed Louise E.Dowling,   Jan 9, 1918
both of New York.

James Wilson married May Aberley near Willits   Jul 10, 1912
July 3, 1912. Judge Whitney officiated.

John Wilson married Rose Howard March 31, 1913. Judge   Apr 9, 1913
E.M.Whitney presided. [License gave groom's name as "Arthur Wilson"]

William Wilson married Ada [surname not reported] at Modesto   Apr 24, 1918
October 15, 1917. They sought a divorce in April 1918.

F.W.Windlinx married Ruby L.Berry of Anchor Bay at that place   Jul 31, 1912
July 31, 1912.

Fred Windlinx married Etta Smith at the Fort Bragg Baptist   Nov 25, 1914
church November 22, 1914.

William Winta married Jenny Niema at the Pioneer Hotel in   May 11, 1910
Fort Bragg May 7, 1910. F.A.Whipple, JP, presided.

Kaarl Wirtanen obtained a license to wed Hilya Ritonieni   Apr 9, 1913
of Fort Bragg.

Adolph Wittrock wed Mrs.Welch in Caspar January 30, 1919.   Feb 2, 1910

H.H.Wonacott obtained a license to wed Lulu Robertson,   Feb 22, 1911
both were residents of Willits.

K.N.Wonacott wed Bessie Montgomery at Willits "last week".   Jan 21, 1914

J.A.Wood got a license to wed Grace E.Babcock.   Nov 9, 1910

J.Bertram Wood of Indianapolis, Indiana, was engaged to   Jul 25, 1917
marry Hazel Adams Hartman, a former Fort Bragg resident,
in San Francisco.

Harry C.Woodham married Edna Clara Banks at Ukiah   Jan 6, 1915
January 3, 1915. Rev.P.T.Lynn officiated.   Jan 13, 1915

Roy Woodhead of Branscomb married Frances Mary Stewart   Jan 24, 1917
of San Francisco in Ukiah January 21, 1917.

H.Woodman married Mabel Johnson in Ukiah October 29, 1917.   Oct 31, 1917
Both were from Caspar.

Horace Rupert Woodward of San Francisco obtained   Aug 18, 1915
a license to wed Myrtle Eleanor Lewin of San Jose.   Aug 25, 1915

Alex Wouri married Marian Soffia at Fort Bragg   Sep 4, 1912
August 31, 1912. F.A.Whipple presided.

Augustus Wright married Lora Nellie James at Willits   Sep 14, 1910
September 11, 1910.

Isak Yaakla, 22, obtained a license to wed   Dec 27, 1911
Ida Mary Peterson, 19, both of Comptche.

Lee Yates got a license to wed Lulu Pardee Sargent   Jul 12, 1916

George Yeary of Fort Bragg married Laurel Connick at Eureka,   Dec 7, 1910
December 2, 1910. Rev.Walter B.Reed presided.

Meredith York, 67, obtained a license to wed   Sep 27, 1911
Elizabeth Ann Herman, 75, of Ukiah.

F.M.Young married Elvira S.Sandkula at Elk July 11, 1915.   Jul 21, 1915

Harry Young married Fannie Gamberg, the daughter of J.   Dec 31, 1913
Gamberg, at Fort Bragg December 25, 1913.   Feb 11, 1914
Rev.R.C.Grace officiated.

Garfield N.Zabits of Mendocino married Leonora E.Clark   Jan 3, 1912
Fort Bragg December 31, 1911. Rev.W.A.Chapman officiated.

James F.Zachary obtained a license to wed Lola M.Wilgus   Sep 17, 1913
of Ukiah.

W.Zachman of Ukiah obtained a license to wed   Dec 13, 1916
Inez Tomlinson of Philo.

John Zaina obtained a license to wed Felicita Gare   Jun 2, 1915
of Fort Bragg.

Frank Zeek obtained a license to wed Bertha Riffe.   Jan 6, 1915

Henry Phillip Zill obtained a license to wed Alma Standley   Jul 10, 1918
of Westport.

Walter Zimmerman married Iva Tolle of Fort Bragg   Apr 23, 1919
in San Francisco "last week".

George E.Zinkard married Christina Iversen at   Sep 3, 1913
Fort Bragg "last week". Rev.R.C.Grace officiated.

W.F.Zwicken married Monica Young at Ukiah "last week".   Apr 16, 1913

MENDOCINO COUNTY MEN IN WORLD WAR I

1917-1918

The United States entered the Great European War, or World War I as it was later known, on April 6, 1917. Prior to that date the *Fort Bragg Advocate* carried relatively little information about the war and its battles. A few local men went off to Canada to enlist in the army, but the great numbers of European nationals that worked in the Mendocino County woods, were little affected until America entered the war. Recognizing that volunteers for military service could not provide the numbers of men needed, the Government instituted a draft based on a lottery of registered able bodied men. All eligible men were registered and assigned a number in July 1917. The July 18th newspaper carried the local men's names and numbers. Beginning on July 20, 1917 in Washington, DC, and running for 16½ hours, far into the wee hours of the 21st, 10,499 capsules containing individual numbers on bits of paper were drawn by blindfolded college students to determine the sequence for men to be called to service. The first, #258 and the last #3217, were not held by any Mendocino County men.

The newspaper reported lists of men certified as fit, *i.e.*, passed a physical, called to active duty, registered for the subsequent 1918 draft, failed to return their questionaire (for one reason or another not often reported), listed some as "slackers", and those reporting for duty. Mercifully, casualties were light and largely due to illness or accident both stateside and overseas. Letters from men in the training camps, and later, France, appeared now and again in the paper. Note: The Mendocino County Draft Board went out of business on December 7, 1918.

For convenience to researchers, these lists were merged and presented as a part of the 1910-1919 volume. Comparison with obituary and marriage records, more correct spelling of some individual names was sometimes achieved.

In later years many of these men were active in veterans' organizations in the County, were accorded honors and remembrances in their lives and, after death, were interred in special sections of the cemeteries. Sadly, many of the men who served in France received wounds or suffered illness especially from poison gas attacks that often resulted in shortened lives.

The following material by no means represents any individual's complete service record. These are only names and events as reported in the *Fort Bragg Advocate* during 1917-1918.

MENDOCINO COUNTY MEN IN WORLD WAR I

Name	Postoffice	Event	Issue Date
[Ernest?] Alfred Ackerman		Registered #2355	Jul 18, 1917
Oscar Ackerman		Registered #2350	Jul 18, 1917
Elmer R. Ackley	Caspar	Listed as a slacker Reported for exam.	Mar 27, 1918 Apr 3, 1918
Frank Acquistapace		Registered #2104	Jul 18, 1917
Vincenzio Acquistapace	Gualala	Certified as fit Called to active duty	Aug 22, 1917 Oct 3, 1917
I. Agipatos	Willits	Delinquent questionaire	Oct 23, 1918
Guiseppe Aggi	Comptche	Called to active duty	Apr 17, 1918
Pietro Aggi	Fort Bragg	Registered #2356 Listed as a slacker Called to active duty	Jul 18, 1917 Mar 27, 1918 Apr 17, 1918
Cia Agostino	Fort Bragg	Registered #2359 Called to active duty	Jul 18, 1917 Jun 12, 1918
Charles Aho		Registered #2106	Jul 18, 1917
Matti A. Ahvenlampi	Fort Bragg	Called to active duty	Apr 17, 1918
John Martin Alaganinha [Alagaminha]	Fort Bragg	Registered #1723 Listed as a slacker Called for active duty	Jul 18, 1917 Mar 27, 1918 Apr 17, 1918
Erik F. Alanko		Registered #2358	Jul 18, 1917
Giuseppe Alberto	Fort Bragg	Registered #2351 Listed as a slacker	Jul 18, 1917 Mar 27, 1918
Charles Albine		Registered #1724	Jul 18, 1917
Charles Albini	Fort Bragg	Called to active duty	Jul 10, 1918
Frank Adalpi Albrecht		Registered #2240	Jul 18, 1917
Chester A. Aldrich		Certified as fit	Nov 6, 1918
Winthrop Aldrich	Ukiah	Certified as fit Called to active duty	Aug 22, 1917 Oct 3, 1917
E. F. Alexander Jr.	[Westport]	Registered #28	Jul 18, 1917
Samuel Alexander	Mendocino	Called to active duty	Jun 12, 1918
William James Allard	Ukiah	Registered June 5th	Jun 19, 1918
Arthur Allen	Ukiah	Called to active duty Called to active duty	Apr 17, 1918 Jun 12, 1918
Firmin Allue	Willits	Certified as fit	Aug 22, 1917
John Alta		Registered #2357	Jul 18, 1917
Sinesio Perez Alustisa	Fort Bragg	Registered June 5th	Jun 19, 1918
Peter Alvarez	Westport	Called to active duty Called to active duty	Apr 17, 1918 Jul 24, 1918
Glenn Alverley	Fort Bragg	Registered June 5th	Jun 19, 1918

Name	Postoffice	Event	Issue Date
Peter Alves	Westport	Listed as a slacker	Mar 27, 1918
Eugene Ambrose		Called to active duty	Oct 3, 1917
Joas Chrisostomo Amorim		Registered #1668	Jul 18, 1917
Arthur Anderson	Covelo	Called to active duty Called to active duty	Apr 17, 1918 Jun 12, 1918
Arthur M.E.Anderson	Fort Bragg	Registered #1725 Listed as a slacker Called to active duty	Jul 18, 1917 Mar 27, 1918 Jun 12, 1918
James C.Anderson	Albion	Called to active duty	Jul 10, 1918
Lowe Anderson	Potter Valley	Registered June 5th	Jun 19, 1918
Ragnar E.E.Anderson	Caspar	Called to active duty Failed to report	Oct 3, 1917 Oct 10, 1917
Russell P.Anderson		Registered #2352	Jul 18, 1917
Walter Anthony Andrews	Calpella	Registered June 5th	Jun 19, 1918
Andrew Andrich		Registered #2108	Jul 18, 1917
Tony Andris	Albion	Certified as fit	Aug 22, 1917
Cialini Antonio	Mendocino	Listed as a slacker Called to active duty	Mar 27, 1918 May 22, 1918
Matt Aquist	Fort Bragg	Delinquent questionaire	Nov 27, 1918
Giovanni Arcuri		Registered #2353	Jul 18, 1917
James Armstrong		Registered #2105	Jul 18, 1917
W.St.Paul Armstrong	Ornbaun	Registered June 5th Called to active duty	Jun 19, 1918 Jul 24, 1918
Kirk Arthur	Ukiah	Certified as fit	Aug 22, 1917
Manuel Silvera Arvila		Registered #2038	Jul 18, 1917
Edward Aulin		Registered #27	Jul 18, 1917
Carl Jon Auttila		Registered #2360	Jul 18, 1917
Matti A.Avenlanmpi	Fort Bragg	Listed as a slacker	Mar 27, 1918
John Ayle	Westport	Listed as a slacker Called to active duty	Mar 27, 1918 Apr 17, 1918
Fred Nelson Aylward		Registered #1726	Jul 18, 1917
George Azuzaroff	Westport	Delinquent questionaire	Oct 23, 1918
Fred Babbitt	[Fort Bragg]	Registered #2342	Jul 18, 1917
David Bacci	Fort Bragg	Registered #2334 Called to active duty	Jul 18, 1917 Jul 10, 1918
Francisco Bacci		Registered #2347	Jul 18, 1917
Oscar Bacci	Albion	Called to active duty	Jun 12, 1918
A.Backland	Fort Bragg	Certified as fit	Aug 22, 1917

Name	Postoffice	Event	Issue Date
W.K. Bailey	Ukiah	Certified as fit	Aug 22, 1917
Alfred L. Bainbridge	Navarro	Called to active duty	May 22, 1918
Harold Octave Bainbridge	Fort Bragg	Registered #31 Certified as fit Called to active duty	Jul 18, 1917 Aug 22, 1917 Apr 10, 1918
F.B. Bake	Mina	Certified as fit	Aug 22, 1917
Jack Baker	Westport	Listed as a slacker Called to active duty	Mar 27, 1918 Jul 10, 1918
George Baldini	Albion	Registered June 5th	Jun 19, 1918
John Baldoni	Fort Bragg	Registered #2113 Listed as a slacker	Jul 18, 1917 Mar 27, 1918
Clifford Ball		Registered #1722	Jul 18, 1917
Fred E. Ball	[Northspur]	Registered #2116	Jul 18, 1917
Manuel J. Ballado	Caspar	Called to active duty	Dec 5, 1917
F.F. Banker	Ukiah	Certified as fit	Aug 22, 1917
William Jennings Banker	Ukiah	Registered June 5th	Jun 19, 1918
M. Barberio		Called to active duty	Oct 3, 1917
Antonio Bariloni	Albion	Certified as fit Called to active duty	Aug 22, 1917 Oct 3, 1917
R. Barnett	Albion	Called to active duty	Aug 14, 1918
Audillo Barelli		Registered #2337	Jul 18, 1917
Davino Barsonti		Registered #1709	Jul 18, 1917
Joe Bartlett	Calpella	Certified as fit	Aug 22, 1917
Joe Bartlett	Ukiah	Called to active duty	Jun 12, 1918
W. Bartlett	Talmage	Called to active duty	Jun 12, 1918
Idone Bartolomei	Ukiah	Registered June 5th	Jun 19, 1918
R.L. Bartow	Willits	Registered June 5th Called to active duty	Jun 19, 1918 Jul 24, 1918
Daverio Basanti	Fort Bragg	Certified as fit	Aug 22, 1917
H.C. Batty	Comptche	Certified as fit	Aug 22, 1917
Roy Lee Beamer		Registered #985	Jul 18, 1917
Don Carlos Bean	Fort Bragg	Registered #2432 Certified as fit Called to active duty	Jul 18, 1917 Aug 22, 1917 Oct 3, 1917
Adolph Beckland		Registered #2109	Jul 18, 1917
Harry Begley	Elk	Called to active duty Failed to report	Oct 3, 1917 Oct 10, 1917
John Bell		Registered #1721	Jul 18, 1917
Laerto Benedith		Registered #1717	Jul 18, 1917

Name	Postoffice	Event	Issue Date
Gino **Benedetti**	Northwestern	Certified as fit Called to active duty	Aug 22, 1917 Oct 3, 1917
E.G.**Bennett**	Covelo	Called to active duty	Apr 17, 1918
William C.**Bennina**	Fort Bragg	Delinquent questionaire	Nov 27, 1918
Beauford Jay **Benning**		Registered #1718	Jul 18, 1917
Michaele **Bergamini**	Fort Bragg	Certified as fit Draft No.14	Nov 6, 1918 Nov 13, 1918
Archie **Berkovits**		Registered #2339	Jul 18, 1917
Arwa R.**Berkovits**		Registered #2343	Jul 18, 1917
Frank H.**Berkovits**	Fort Bragg	Registered #1716 Called for active duty	Jul 18, 1917 Dec 5, 1917
Franz Herman **Berkovitz**		Registered #2333	Jul 18, 1917
Lodovico **Bernardini**		Registered #2340	Jul 18, 1917
Ovidio **Berrattini**		Registered #1710	Jul 18, 1917
John **Bertilini**	Mendocino	Certified as fit	Aug 22, 1917
Pietro **Bertolli**	Sherwood	Called to active duty	Apr 17, 1918
Lester Jacob **Bertsch**	Fort Bragg	Registered #32 Called to active duty	Jul 18, 1917 Apr 24, 1918
Joas Maniz **Betencurto** [Bettancurto]	Fort Bragg	Registered #2177 Certified as fit	Jul 18, 1917 Aug 22, 1917
William **Bettencourt**	Mendocino	Called to active duty	Jul 3, 1918
Giuseppe **Bettiga**		Registered #2251	Jul 18, 1917
Harry **Betts**		Killed in action	Jan 15, 1919
Ottavio **Beunaidini**		Registered #2335	Jul 18, 1917
John **Biaggi**	Manchester	Certified as fit	Aug 22, 1917
Guiseppe, **Biagini** [Name reversed in paper]		Registered #2346	Jul 18, 1917
Ambragio **Bianchi**	Mendocino	Registered #1711 Called to active duty	Jul 18, 1917 Jun 12, 1918
Orlando G.**Bianchini**	Albion	Listed as a slacker Called to active duty	Mar 27, 1918 Jul 10, 1918
Austin Elijah **Bishop**	Manchester	Registered June 5th	Jun 19, 1918
B.**Bishop**	Point Arena	Called to active duty	Jun 12, 1918
Edwin Carl **Bishop**	[Fort Bragg]	Registered #1720	Jul 18, 1917
August Werner **Bjarkholm**		Registered #1712	Jul 18, 1917
Bozo **Bjelobrk**		Registered #2115	Jul 18, 1917
Carl **Bjorkas**		Registered #2117	Jul 18, 1917
William James **Black**	Fort Bragg	Registered #33 Called to active duty	Jul 18, 1917 Apr 24, 1918
Freeman Jasper **Blackly**		Registered #2175	Jul 18, 1917

Name	Postoffice	Event	Issue Date
Marvin E. Blaylock		Registered #2338	Jul 18, 1917
Edward Charles Bloom	Elk	Delinquent questionaire	Nov 27, 1918
Winnis Boggs	Manchester	Listed as a slacker	Mar 27, 1918
Richard Edward Bohn	Fort Bragg	Registered #970 Certified as fit	Jul 18, 1917 Aug 22, 1917
Harold Thomas Bolden	Fort Bragg	Registered June 5th	Jun 19, 1918
Allesio Boldi	Philo	Certified as fit	Aug 22, 1917
Hong Bon	Navarro	Listed as a slacker	Mar 27, 1918
Guiseppe Bonanetti		Registered #2345	Jul 18, 1917
Giacomo Bonetto	Albion	Listed as a slacker Called to active duty	Mar 27, 1918 Jun 12, 1918
Alvin R. Bonnifield	Potter Valley	Certified as fit Called to active duty	Aug 22, 1917 Oct 3, 1917
Adamo Boschi	Mendocino	Listed as a slacker Called to active duty	Mar 27, 1918 May 22, 1918
Antonio Goncalves Botar		Registered #2119	Jul 18, 1917
Perry F. Bowman	Kenny	Certified as fit	Aug 22, 1917
Adolphus O. Boyd	Westport	Called to active duty	Jul 10, 1918
John Boyes	Elk	Certified as fit	Aug 22, 1917
Clifton Lloyd Boyle	Mendocino	Certified as fit Enlisted	Aug 22, 1917 Aug 22, 1917
John Boziech		Registered #1713	Jul 18, 1917
Mate Brajkovish		Registered #1356	Jul 18, 1917
Aquililo Branchini		Registered #2110	Jul 18, 1917
Carlo Branchini	Philo	Certified as fit Called to active duty	Aug 22, 1917 Oct 3, 1917
Joe Branchini		Registered #2114	Jul 18, 1917
Leo Brandon		Registered #971	Jul 18, 1917
Andrew A. Brandstrom	Elk	Called to active duty	May 22, 1918
LeRoy Verne Brant		Registered #2176	Jul 18, 1917
William Brazill	Caspar	Certified as fit	Aug 22, 1917
H.W. Bredehoft	Covelo	Certified as fit Called to active duty	Aug 22, 1917 Oct 3, 1917
F.A. Breen		Registered #2341	Jul 18, 1917
Johann F.G. Brener		Registered #2166	Jul 18, 1917
George Briggs	Covelo	Certified as fit	Aug 22, 1917
George Ervine Brooks	Sherwood	Registered June 5th	Jun 19, 1918
Wilbur Broughton		Registered #2336	Jul 18, 1917

Name	Postoffice	Event	Issue Date
Charles James Brown		Registered #2036	Jul 18, 1917
Charlie Arthur Brown		Registered #2348	Jul 18, 1917
Eugene McKinley Brown	Covelo	Registered June 5th	Jun 19, 1918
Francis Martin Brown	Covelo	Registered June 5th	Jun 19, 1918
J.H. Brown	Willits	Called to active duty	Jun 12, 1918
Justin Kent Brown	Yorkville	Registered June 5th	Jun 19, 1918
L.W. Brown	Covelo	Certified as fit	Aug 22, 1917
W.J. Brown	Willits	Called to active duty	Aug 14, 1918
Philip W. Brubeck	Fort Bragg	Draft No.159	Nov 13, 1918
Albert Brusa	Mendocino	Called to active duty	Jun 12, 1918
Martin A. Brush	Covelo	Called to active duty	May 8, 1918
Virgileo Bucchiani		Registered #2118	Jul 18, 1917
Pete Buchini		Registered #2344	Jul 18, 1917
		Called to active duty	Oct 3, 1917
	Merced Falls	Failed to report	Oct 10, 1917
Andrew Buck		Registered #2112	Jul 18, 1917
John Sampson Buckbee		Registered #2037	Jul 18, 1917
Robert Harold Buckman	Hopland	Registered June 5th	Jun 19, 1918
Roy A. Bullard	Hopland	Certified as fit	Aug 22, 1917
		Called to active duty	Sep 5, 1917
George R. Bunch	Elk	Called to active duty	Jul 10, 1918
J.L. Bunker	Navarro	Certified as fit	Aug 22, 1917
Fred H. Bunton	Caspar	Delinquent questionaire	Oct 23, 1917
Wade B. Burger		Called to active duty	Oct 3, 1917
William George Burger		Registered #969	Jul 18, 1917
James G. Burke	Mendocino	Listed as a slacker	Mar 27, 1918
		Error-in France since September 6, 1917.	Apr 10, 1918
John Axel Burke		Registered #34	Jul 18, 1917
George Burkhart	Potter Valley	Certified as fit	Aug 22, 1917
		Called to active duty	Jun 12, 1918
John T. Burman		Registered #30	Jul 18, 1917
Thomas Burnie		Registered #29	Jul 18, 1917
C.V. Burr	Caspar	Certified as fit	Aug 22, 1917
Walter L. Burr	Fort Bragg	Registered June 5th	Jun 19, 1918
		[died Nov 25, 1921]	Nov 30, 1921
		American Legion list	May 27, 1927
Herbert Burris		Called to active duty	Oct 3, 1917
Joan S. Butin	Elk	Delinquent questionaire	Oct 23, 1918

MENDOCINO COUNTY MEN IN WORLD WAR I

Name	Postoffice	Event	Issue Date
Frank W. Butts	Willits	Certified as fit	Aug 22, 1917
		Called to active duty	Oct 3, 1917
James Cabassi	Gualala	Called to active duty	Jun 12, 1918
Stefano Cabassi	Caspar	Registered June 5th	Jun 19, 1918
Robert E. Caldwell		Registered #2331	Jul 18, 1917
Andrew Johnnie Calli		Registered #51	Jul 18, 1917
G. Callina	Mendocino	Certified as fit	Aug 22, 1917
James Camata		American Legion list	May 27, 1927
William Archibald Cameron		Registered #2171	Jul 18, 1917
Charles Campbell	Elk	Called to active duty	Oct 3, 1917
		Failed to report	Oct 10, 1917
Dewey Campbell	Caspar	Delinquent questionaire	Nov 27, 1918
Fernando Campbell	Laytonville	Called to active duty	Jun 12, 1918
Frank McLean Campbell		Registered #1707	Jul 18, 1917
Martin Campbell	Fort Bragg	Registered #1708	Jul 18, 1917
		Called to active duty	Jul 10, 1918
Matti Alfred Ahven Campi		Registered #2178	Jul 18, 1917
Nicola Cancline	Albion	Certified as fit	Nov 6, 1918
		Draft No. 101	Nov 13, 1918
Anthony Canclini	Comptche	Certified as fit	Aug 22, 1917
L. Cappeleti	Point Arena	Called to active duty	Apr 17, 1918
Raffaello Cardinotti	Fort Bragg	Registered June 5th	Jun 19, 1918
Jerome C. Carey		Registered #41	Jul 18, 1917
Hugo Carli	Albion	Certified as fit	Aug 22, 1917
		Called to active duty	Oct 3, 1917
Alex Carlson		Registered #1729	Jul 18, 1917
Earl Charles Carlson		Registered #27	Jul 18, 1917
Fred Leander Carlson		Registered #965	Jul 18, 1917
Iver Carlson	Fort Bragg	Registered #2332	Jul 18, 1917
		Listed as a slacker	Mar 27, 1918
Thomas Henry Carlson		Registered #2329	Jul 18, 1917
Eugene F. Carter	Calpella	Registered June 5th	Jun 19, 1918
Harry H. Carter	Potter Valley	Certified as fit	Aug 22, 1917
		Called to active duty	Oct 3, 1917
Walter Henry Castor		Registered #966	Jul 18, 1917
Ngo Guillo P. Catanari	Sherwood	Certified as fit	Aug 22, 1917
Grant Cater		Registered #40	Jul 18, 1917
Achille Catlani [Cateloni]	Fort Bragg	Registered #1727	Jul 18, 1917
		Certified as fit	Aug 22, 1917

Name	Postoffice	Event	Issue Date
Attilio <u>Cattini</u>	Glen Blair	Called to active duty	Jul 10, 1918
Michael <u>Caughlin</u>		Registered #1706	Jul 18, 1917
Frank <u>Cavaco</u>	Fort Bragg	Delinquent questionaire	Oct 23, 1918
Charles Clinton <u>Cavanagh</u> [Fort Bragg]		Registered #1705	Jul 18, 1917
C.<u>Chahon</u>	Willits	Certified as fit Called to active duty	Aug 22, 1917 Sep 5, 1917
Arthur W.<u>Challman</u>		Registered #1703	Jul 18, 1917
John L.<u>Chalmers</u> [James L.	Fort Bragg	Registered #35 Called to active duty	Jul 18, 1917 Jul 10, 1918
Frank H.<u>Chandler</u>		Registered #2330	Jul 18, 1917
Herbert R.<u>Chapman</u>	Fort Bragg	Delinquent questionaire Papers returned, lost	Nov 27, 1918 Dec 4, 1918
William S.<u>Chase</u>	Covelo	Certified as fit	Aug 22, 1917
Roberto <u>Chicchi</u>	Navarro Santa Rosa	Certified as fit Called to active duty	Aug 22, 1917 Oct 3, 1917
Quong <u>Chin</u>		Registered #2173	Jul 18, 1917
Lum <u>Chong</u>	Fort Bragg	Registered June 5th	Jun 19, 1918
Harry G.<u>Christian</u>	Gualala	Called to active duty	Jun 12, 1918
Henry A.<u>Christianson</u>	Point Arena	Listed as a slacker	Mar 27, 1918
Henry A.<u>Christy</u>	Ukiah	Called to active duty	Jun 12, 1918
Wong <u>Chung</u>		Registered #2174	Jul 18, 1917
Battista <u>Ciolina</u>		Registered #1715	Jul 18, 1917
Norris Alkire <u>Clark</u>	Littleriver	Registered June 5th	Jun 19, 1918
Russell Allen <u>Clark</u>		Registered #967	Jul 18, 1917
Frank Leslie <u>Clay</u>		Registered #1704	Jul 18, 1917
Standley <u>Clay</u>	Willits	Delinquent questionaire	Nov 27, 1918
Ernest J.<u>Cockrill</u>	Hopland	Called to active duty	May 8, 1918
Emilio <u>Codiroli</u>		Registered #1701	Jul 18, 1917
Francisco Rodrisgues <u>Coelho</u>	Fort Bragg	Registered #1702 Called to active duty Reported for duty	Jul 18, 1917 Oct 3, 1917 Oct 10, 1917
Hiram Gladstone <u>Coffee</u>	Ukiah	Delinquent questionaire	Oct 23, 1918
Adolph Berton <u>Colberg</u>		Registered #2172	Jul 18, 1917
LeRoy Harrison <u>Colburn</u>		Registered #38	Jul 18, 1917
Loyde Nelson <u>Cole</u> [Lloyd M.]	Fort Bragg	Registered #39 Listed as a slacker Called to active duty	Jul 18, 1917 Mar 27, 1918 Jul 10, 1918
August <u>Colija</u>	Dos Rios	Called to active duty	Jun 12, 1918
C.<u>Colli</u>	Manchester	Called to active duty	Jun 12, 1918
Pietro <u>Comaita</u>		Registered #2327	Jul 18, 1917

Name	Postoffice	Event	Issue Date
Jim Comuita [Comanita]	Fort Bragg	Registered #1728 Called to active duty	Jul 18, 1917 Dec 5, 1917
Leslie A. Conner	Covelo	Called to active duty	Apr 17, 1918
Antonio Constanti	Irmulco	Called to active duty Failed to report	Oct 3, 1917 Oct 10, 1917
Harold Daniel Cook		Registered #2235	Jul 18, 1917
Peter Copes	Caspar	Called to active duty	Apr 17, 1918
Raymond Copsey	Calpella	Certified as fit Called to active duty	Aug 22, 1917 Sep 5, 1917
Giovanni Corrzza		Called to active duty	Oct 3, 1917
Natale Costa		Registered #2326	Jul 18, 1917
Michael Coughlin	Fort Bragg	Listed as a slacker Called to active duty	Mar 27, 1918 Jul 10, 1918
F. LaMar Courtenay	Ukiah	Called to active duty	Jun 12, 1918
Russel Harrison Cox		Registered #2236	Jul 18, 1917
Wesley Cox	Ukiah	Registered June 5th	Jun 19, 1918
Chester Clyde Craddock		Registered #968	Jul 18, 1917
C. Craig	Glen Blair	Called to active duty	May 8, 1918
Walter A. Craig	Point Arena	Called to active duty	Jun 12, 1918
Andrew Crass	Eastport	Certified as fit	Aug 22, 1917
Tony Crnac		Registered #2107	Jul 18, 1917
James B. Cross	Albion	Listed as a slacker	Nov 27, 1918
Oliver S. Cross		Called to active duty	Oct 3, 1917
Felice Crosto [Crosta]	Fort Bragg	Registered #2328 Listed as a slacker	Jul 18, 1917 Mar 27, 1918
Guiseppe Cuidotti	Point Arena	Certified as fit	Aug 22, 1917
John Curti	Manchester	Called to active duty	Jun 12, 1918
John Curtis	Fort Bragg	Registered #36 Called to active duty	Jul 18, 1917 Apr 17, 1918
Antonio da Costa		Registered #1697	Jul 18, 1917
Andrew Dahl		Registered #1730	Jul 18, 1917
Carl Jacob Dahl	Fort Bragg	Registered #1699 Listed as a slacker	Jul 18, 1917 Mar 27, 1918
J. C. Dahl	Manchester	Called to active duty	Jun 12, 1918
Negie Dalson	Covelo	Called to active duty	Jun 12, 1918
Joe Darisih		Registered #1365	Jul 18, 1917
Harry E. Daubeneck	Caspar	Certified as fit Draft No. 10	Nov 6, 1918 Nov 13, 1918
John Douglas Davis		[died Jan 16, 1926] American Legion list	Jan 20, 1926 May 27, 1927

Name	Postoffice	Event	Issue Date
Roy Clyde Davis		Registered #2323	Jul 18, 1917
Silas M. Davis	Ukiah	Delinquent questionaire	Nov 27, 1918
T.M. Davis	Dos Rios	Certified as fit	Aug 22, 1917
William Davis		Died in service American Legion list	Jan 9, 1918 May 27, 1927
George Dawe		Registered #2321 Called to active duty	Jul 18, 1917 Oct 3, 1917
Ruel W. Day	Philo	Certified as fit Killed in action	Aug 22, 1917 Dec 4, 1918
J. DeCarli	Ukiah	Called to active duty	Jun 12, 1918
Byron DeEstell		Called to active duty	Oct 3, 1917
Pietro Deghi [Peter]		Registered #2170 Called to active duty	Jul 18, 1917 Oct 3, 1917
Martin L. Delaney	Caspar	Called to active duty	Apr 17, 1918
Michele Del Chiaro		Registered #1698	Jul 18, 1917
Albert Del Fiorentini	Fort Bragg	Registered #2316 Certified as fit	Jul 18, 1917 Aug 22, 1917
Pete Della Bosca		Registered #1714	Jul 18, 1917
Jacinto Bento De Lousa		Registered #2149	Jul 18, 1917
James Dempsey		Registered #2035	Jul 18, 1917
Ellsworth A. Denning		Registered #1700	Jul 18, 1917
Byron James Dennison		Registered #2033 [2023?]	Jul 18, 1917
Merl DeShiell	Albion	Called to active duty	Jun 12, 1918
A.M. De Silveria	Mendocino	Called to active duty	May 22, 1918
Peter Desjardin	Westport	Certified as fit Called to active duty	Aug 22, 1917 Oct 3, 1917
Frank Detamasi	Sherwood	Delinquent questionaire	Oct 23, 1918
Henry Aden Dickey	Potter Valley	Registered June 5th	Jun 19, 1918
Adolph Dinucci	Irmulco	Certified as fit Called to active duty	Aug 22, 1917 Oct 3, 1917
Joseph Alfred Dixon	Fort Bragg	Registered #43 Certified as fit Called to active duty	Jul 18, 1917 Aug 22, 1917 Sep 5, 1917
W.D. Dolan	Fort Bragg	Registered #2325 Called to active duty	Jul 18, 1917 Apr 17, 1918
William A. Donovan	Ukiah	Called to active duty Called AWOL in error	May 22, 1918 Jul 31, 1918
John H. Dorffi	Noyo	Certified as fit	Aug 22, 1917
Thomas Arthur Dornan	Albion	Registered #2324	Jul 18, 1917
Claude E. Doty		Called to active duty	Oct 3, 1917
A. Downing		Called to active duty	Oct 3, 1917

Name	Postoffice	Event	Issue Date
James Moss <u>Doyle</u>	Fort Bragg	Registered #42 Listed as a slacker	Jul 18, 1917 Mar 27, 1918
Neil A. <u>Doyle</u>	Fort Bragg	Registered #2322 Certified as fit	Jul 18, 1917 Aug 22, 1917
Oscar J. <u>Doyle</u>	Fort Bragg	Registered #2319 Certified as fit	Jul 18, 1917 Aug 22, 1917
William T. <u>Driver</u>	Gualala	Called to active duty	Jun 12, 1918
Laton V. <u>Duffy</u>		[died Sep 3, 1920] American Legion list	Sep 8, 1920 May 27, 1927
John <u>Dukellis</u> [Donkellis]	Ukiah	Certified as fit Called to active duty	Aug 22, 1917 Sep 6, 1917
F.H. <u>Duncan</u>	Covelo	Certified as fit	Aug 22, 1917
Fred <u>Duncan</u>	Ukiah	Delinquent questionaire	Nov 27, 1918
Ray I. <u>Dunham</u>	Cummings	Registered June 5th Called to active duty	Jun 19, 1918 Jul 24, 1918
Emil Henry <u>Dutzi</u>		Registered #2320	Jul 18, 1917
Vernon K. <u>Dyer</u>	Inglenook	Called to active duty	Jun 12, 1918
Woodrow John <u>Dymons</u>		Registered #2132	Jul 18, 1917
W.J. <u>Eagle</u>	Caspar	Registered June 5th Called to active duty	Jun 19, 1918 Jul 24, 1918
Esidro <u>Ebarreta</u>		Registered #1694	Jul 18, 1917
D.H. <u>Eberhart</u>	Fort Bragg	Registered #1695 Listed as a slacker Called to active duty	Jul 18, 1917 Mar 27, 1918 Jun 12, 1918
Roman L. <u>Eberhardt</u>	Willits	Certified as fit Called to active duty	Aug 22, 1917 Sep 5, 1917
Joseph <u>Ehiopello</u>	Spy Rock	Failed to report	Oct 10, 1917
Grover Cleveland <u>Elbert</u>		Registered #2318	Jul 18, 1917
Robert Leroy <u>Eldredge</u>		Registered #45	Jul 18, 1917
Harry <u>Elliott</u>	Ukiah	Certified as fit	Aug 22, 1917
Rafe <u>Elliott</u>	Talmage	Called to active duty	Jun 12, 1918
Charles Emil <u>Ellison</u>	Mendocino	Registered June 5th	Jun 19, 1918
John August <u>Ellison</u>		Registered #44	Jul 18, 1917
Lars A. <u>Ellison</u>	Mendocino	Called to active duty	Jun 12, 1918
William Albert <u>Elmslie</u>	Fort Bragg	[died Dec.26, 1917] died from accident American Legion list	Dec 4, 1918 May 27, 1927
Otto H. <u>Elvers</u>	Caspar	Certified as fit	Aug 22, 1917
D.L. <u>Emerson</u>	Calpella	Certified as fit Called to active duty	Aug 22, 1917 Oct 3, 1917
Frank <u>Engler</u>	Ukiah	Certified as fit Called to active duty	Aug 22, 1917 Oct 3, 1917

Name	Postoffice	Event	Issue Date
Oscar W.Erickson	Elk	Called to active duty	May 22, 1918
William Emerson Erickson	Ukiah	Registered June 5th	Jun 19, 1918
Charles A.Escola	Mendocino	Certified as fit Draft No.44	Nov 6, 1918 Nov 13, 1918
George H.Estes		Called to active duty	Oct 3, 1917
Talbot N.Evans	Ukiah	Certified as fit Draft No.28	Nov 6, 1918 Nov 13, 1918
Andrew Faqqi	Elk	Registered June 5th	Jun 19, 1918
Americo Fagnani	Ukiah	Delinquent questionaire	Oct 23, 1918
Richard Franklin Fain	Fort Bragg	Registered #986 Listed as a slacker Called to active duty	Jul 18, 1917 Mar 27, 1918 Apr 24, 1918
Charles H.Fairbanks	Manchester	Certified as fit Called to active duty	Aug 22, 1917 Oct 3, 1917
Harry McGregor Fallas	Ukiah	Certified as fit	Aug 22, 1917
John Fambrini	Willits	Registered June 5th	Jun 19, 1918
Pete Farina		Registered #1733	Jul 18, 1917
Frank J.Farrell	Glen Blair	Listed as a slacker Called to active duty	Mar 27, 1918 Jul 10, 1918
Leland Frank Feiden	Fort Bragg	Registered #46 Certified as fit Called to active duty	Jul 18, 1917 Aug 22, 1917 Sep 5, 1917
Necho Feliz	Hopland	Called to active duty	Jul 24, 1918
C.A.Fenton	Boonville	Certified as fit Called to active duty	Aug 22, 1917 Oct 3, 1917
Bacci Ferdinando		Registered #2241	Jul 18, 1917
Bacci Ferdinando		Registered #2242	Jul 18, 1917
Jerima Fernandeo		Registered #57	Jul 18, 1917
Frank Fernandez		Registered #49	Jul 18, 1917
Joseph L.Fernandez	Fort Bragg	Registered #56 Listed as a slacker Called to active duty	Jul 18, 1917 Mar 27, 1918 Apr 17, 1918
Manuel Fernandez		Registered #2313	Jul 18, 1917
William Henry Fernandez		Registered #48	Jul 18, 1917
Vittorio Ferrano	Covelo	Certified as fit	Aug 22, 1917
John Harvey Ferrill	Albion	Registered June 5th Called to active duty	Jun 19, 1918 Jul 24, 1918
Nelson H.Ferry	Caspar	Listed as a slacker Called to active duty	Mar 27, 1918 May 22, 1918
Chinn Ginns Fhons		Registered #1691	Jul 18, 1917

MENDOCINO COUNTY MEN IN WORLD WAR I

Name	Postoffice	Event	Issue Date
John Figaro	Mendocino	Certified as fit Active duty-Sep.1917	Aug 22, 1917
		Died June 2, 1919	Jun 4, 1919
		American Legion list	May 27, 1927
Mauriel Figueiredo		Registered #2168	Jul 18, 1917
Manuel Filippo		Registered #1690	Jul 18, 1917
Battista Filosi		Registered #2312	Jul 18, 1917
Louis Filosi	Fort Bragg	Registered #1732	Jul 18, 1917
		Certified as fit	Aug 22, 1917
		Called to active duty	Sep 5, 1917
Albino Fiori	Mendocino	Called to active duty	Oct 3, 1917
		Failed to report	Oct 10, 1917
Albert B.Firentino	Fort Bragg	Certified as fit	Aug 22, 1917
Lester A.Fisher	Ukiah	Certified as fit	Nov 6, 1918
		Draft No.16	Nov 13, 1918
Ernest Demill Fitch	Manchester	Died Washington,DC-pneumonia Jan 5, 1918	Jan 9, 1918
		American Legion list	May 27, 1927
George Albert Fitch	Manchester	Certified as fit	Aug 22, 1917
		Killed in action	Nov 13, 1918
		Oct 4, 1918	Dec 4, 1918
		American Legion list	May 27, 1927
Martin Foley		Called to active duty	Oct 3, 1917
Carl Fontana		Registered #1731	Jul 18, 1917
Junz Wah Foon		Registered #2169	Jul 18, 1917
Lou P.Foster	Willits	Certified as fit	Aug 22, 1917
		Called to active duty	Sep 5, 1917
Arthur L.Foye	Fort Bragg	Registered June 5th	Jun 19, 1918
Frederic Malcolm Foye		Registered #1693	Jul 18, 1917
John Framacchi		Registered #1626	Jul 18, 1917
Salvatore Franceschi	Northwestern	Called to active duty	Apr 17, 1918
DeAndrea Francisco		Registered #2354	Jul 18, 1917
Fred Franklin	Fruitland	Called to active duty	Apr 17, 1918
Frank Silveria Fratis		Registered #1692	Jul 18, 1917
Ernest Frazer	Fort Bragg	Certified as fit	Aug 22, 1917
Carl Saverine Fredson		Registered #2314	Jul 18, 1917
John Fredson		Registered #1734	Jul 18, 1917
Hugo Valdemer Freeberg		Registered #47	Jul 18, 1917
Arthur Freeburg	Fort Bragg	Registered June 5th	Jun 19, 1918
Oliver F.Freeland	Westport	Delinquent questionaire	Oct 23, 1918
Isaac Freeman		Served in 343rd Artilery	May 14, 1919

Name	Postoffice	Event	Issue Date
Joe Fretas		Registered #2317	Jul 18, 1917
Lester Frink	Cloverdale	Certified as fit Called to active duty	Aug 22, 1917 Oct 3, 1917
Arnold Otto Fritzsche		Registered #55	Jul 18, 1917
E.Fuller	Ukiah	Certified as fit	Aug 22, 1917
G.Fuorini		Called to active duty	Oct 3, 1917
A.F.Furtado		Registered #2315	Jul 18, 1917
J.L.Furtado	Elk	Certified as fit Called to active duty	Aug 22, 1917 Oct 3, 1917
Pasquale Gaeomella		Registered #1687	Jul 18, 1917
James Edward Gallagher		Registered #2311	Jul 18, 1917
Roger Gallagher		Registered #1689	Jul 18, 1917
Albert P.Galliani	Fort Bragg	Delinquent questionaire Ill with flu-will comply	Nov 27, 1918 Dec 4, 1918
John Galliani	Fort Bragg	Registered June 5th	Jun 19, 1918
Charles D.Galloway		Called to active duty	Oct 3, 1917
Franz Jacob Gamberg		Registered #1738	Jul 18, 1917
H.W.Gamble		Called to active duty	Oct 3, 1917
Harold William Ganelo		Registered #2304	Jul 18, 1917
Charles M.Gardner	Cloverdale	Called to active duty	Jun 12, 1918
Amerigo Gargini		Registered #1685	Jul 18, 1917
John Henry Garner	Glen Blair	Listed as a slacker Called to active duty	Mar 27, 1918 Jul 10, 1919
Luther Garrett	Northwestern	Certified as fit	Aug 22, 1917
Ballista Garsini	Albion	Called to active duty	Jul 3, 1918
Andrew Garzini	Ukiah	Called to active duty Called to active duty	Apr 17, 1918 May 8, 1918
John Garzini	Calpella	Certified as fit	Aug 22, 1917
Edward A.Gaspar	Ukiah	Certified as fit	Aug 22, 1917
Roy H.German	Ukiah	Called to active duty	May 22, 1918
Pasquale Giacomella	Fort Bragg	Called to active duty	Jul 10, 1918
Guiseppe Giacopazzi		Registered #2297 Called to active duty	Jul 18, 1917 Oct 3, 1917
Pietro Gianicchia	Fort Bragg	Called to active duty	Dec 5, 1917
G.Gianini	Albion	Certified as fit	Aug 22, 1917
Ottairo Giannecchini		Registered #2305	Jul 18, 1917
Settino Gianneidini		Registered #2309	Jul 18, 1917
Lorenzo Giannini		Registered #2308	Jul 18, 1917

Name	Postoffice	Event	Issue Date
Luigi Giannini [Louis]	Elk	Called to active duty	Jun 12, 1918
F.E.Gibson	Hopland	Certified as fit	Aug 22, 1917
Otto Emil Gielow	Ukiah	Registered June 5th	Jun 19, 1918
Biagini Giuseppe		Registered #2346	Jul 18, 1917
Giovanni Giglio	Spy Rock	Called to active duty	May 22, 1918
Che Lung Gime		Registered #2150	Jul 18, 1917
Yim Mun Ging	Northwestern	Delinquent questionaire	Oct 23, 1918
Quintino Gini	Mendocino	Called to active duty Reported for duty	Oct 3, 1917 Oct 10, 1917
Frankie Giraud	Hopland	Certified as fit	Aug 22, 1917
Pietro Gisnicchini		Registered #1760	Jul 18, 1917
G.Giusti	Albion	Certified as fit	Aug 22, 1917
Lorenzo Giusti	Navarro	Certified as fit	Aug 22, 1917
Raffello Giusti	Navarro	Certified as fit	Aug 22, 1917
Borneo Givoconni		Registered #1688	Jul 18, 1917
Guy N.Glenn		Called to active duty	Oct 3, 1917
F.J.Gonsalves	Navarro	Certified as fit Called to active duty	Aug 22, 1917 Oct 3, 1917
Archie Feliz Gordon	Mendocino	Registered June 5th Called to active duty	Jun 19, 1918 Jul 24, 1918
Philip R.Gorman		[died Jul 22, 1922] American Legion list	Aug 2, 1922 May 27, 1927
Aquilino Gotti		Registered #1737	Jul 18, 1917
Martin Gotti		Registered #1736	Jul 18, 1917
Morandni Grazandio		Registered #1686	Jul 18, 1917
Henry A.Graziana	Fort Bragg	Certified as fit Draft No.115	Nov 6, 1918 Nov 13, 1918
Antone Grbac	Fort Bragg	Registered #58 Certified as fit Called to active duty	Jul 18, 1917 Aug 22, 1917 Oct 3, 1917
Lester Gregory	Fort Bragg	Delinquent questionaire	Nov 27, 1918
August Groher	Laytonville	Certified as fit Draft No.118	Nov 6, 1918 Nov 13, 1918
Fred Grondorf	Ukiah	Called to active duty Failed to report	Oct 3, 1917 Oct 10, 1917
Gaitano Grosini	Sherwood	Delinquent questionaire	Oct 23, 1918
Wein M.Grothe	Cummings	Certified as fit Called to active duty	Aug 22, 1917 Oct 3, 1917
John Gryurch		Registered #2310	Jul 18, 1917

Name	Postoffice	Event	Issue Date
Ellis G. Gschwend	Navarro	Called to active duty	Jun 12, 1918
Lutt Guatini [Luis Guattini] [Luis Guattini]	Fort Bragg	Registered #1735 Certified as fit Called to active duty	Jul 18, 1917 Aug 22, 1917 Oct 3, 1917
Benjamin Guererro		Registered #50	Jul 18, 1917
Alberto Guisti	Fort Bragg	Registered #2306 Listed as a slacker	Jul 18, 1917 Mar 27, 1918
Ettare Guisti	Albion	Registered June 5th	Jun 19, 1918
Aino Rutti Gummerus		Registered #2167	Jul 18, 1917
Erik Gustafson [Eric] [Erick]	Fort Bragg	Registered #1739 Listed as a slacker Called to active duty	Jul 18, 1917 Mar 27, 1918 Jul 3, 1918
Martin Haarby		Registered #964	Jul 18, 1917
A. Theo Haggblom	Albion	Called to active duty Reported for duty	Oct 3, 1917 Oct 10, 1917
Robert F. Hague	Covelo	Called to active duty	Jun 12, 1918
Elmer Linwood Haile	Fort Bragg]	Registered #2298	Jul 18, 1917
Albert Hale	Ukiah	Certified as fit	Aug 22, 1917
Sidney B. Hale		Registered #2302	Jul 18, 1917
Lloyd Lawrence Hamilton	Point Arena	Certified as fit	Aug 22, 1917
Lowell R. Hamilton	Point Arena	Delinquent questionaire	Nov 27, 1918
Emil Hamm	Littleriver	Called to active duty	May 8, 1918
Lawrence V. Hammett		Registered #2299	Jul 18, 1917
Charles Hamula	Albion	Listed as a slacker Called to active duty	Mar 27, 1918 Jul 24, 1918
Bert Hansen	Ukiah	Certified as fit	Aug 22, 1917
Arthur Chester Hanson		Registered #963	Jul 18, 1917
Oscar Edwin Hanson	Caspar	Certified as fit	Aug 22, 1917
Charles D.M. Hardwick	Willits	Registered June 5th Called to active duty	Jun 19, 1918 Jul 24, 1918
Rea. P. Harper	Willits	Delinquent questionaire	Oct 23, 1918
Ralph J. Harrington	Hopland	Registered June 5th	Jun 19, 1918
Emerson Ralph Harris	Covelo	Delinquent questionaire	Nov 27, 1918
Charles Harrison		Registered #1741	Jul 18, 1917
Eugene Benjamin Hartman		Registered #962	Jul 18, 1917
F. Hartman	Glen Blair	Called to active duty	Dec 5, 1917
Harry Emerson Hartman		Registered #54	Jul 18, 1917
Maurice Hartwing	Point Arena	Called to active duty	Jul 3, 1918
Jack Haskell	Point Arena	Certified as fit	Aug 22, 1917

Name	Postoffice	Event	Issue Date
Harold V. Haskett	Willits	Called to active duty	Oct 3, 1917
Martin W. Hasselmeir	San Francisco	Registered June 5th Called to active duty	Jun 19, 1918 Jul 24, 1918
G.F. Hawkins	Elk	Certified as fit	Aug 22, 1917
F. Harold Haydon	Covelo	Registered June 5th	Jun 19, 1918
Stacy Miller Heathcock		Registered #2160	Jul 18, 1917
Henry August Heitmeyer		Registered #2031	Jul 18, 1917
Daniel Heldt	Fort Bragg	Registered June 5th Called to active duty	Jun 19, 1918 Jul 24, 1918
John Jacob Helela		Registered # 125	Jul 18, 1917
Albert E. Helgeson	Westport	Called to active duty	Apr 17, 1918
A.N. Hellesoe	Willits	Registered June 5th	Jun 19, 1918
Matti Edward Hellman		Registered #2032	Jul 18, 1917
Thomas O. Helm	Caspar	Certified as fit Called to active duty	Aug 22, 1917 Oct 3, 1917
Andrew Hendrickson		[died Nov 3, 1922] American Legion list	Nov 15, 1922 May 27, 1927
Fred Hendrickson	Point Arena	Registered June 5th Called to active duty	Jun 19, 1918 Jul 24, 1918
Clyde W. Henry	Fort Bragg	Registered June 5th	Jun 19, 1918
B. Henthorn	Covelo	Called to active duty	Jun 12, 1918
Manuel Herrera	Ridgewood	Called to active duty	May 22, 1918
Claude R. Heryford	Albion	Delinquent questionaire	Nov 27, 1918
William Paul Hicks	Hopland	Called to active duty	May 8, 1918
Johannes Hietacuori	Navarro	Listed as a slacker	Mar 27, 1918
Vaini J. Hietavouri	Comptche	Called to active duty	Apr 24, 1918
Herman Clinton Hight	Fort Bragg	Registered #53 Called to active duty	Jul 18, 1917 Jul 10, 1918
George Reginald Hildreth	Ukiah	Registered June 5th	Jun 19, 1918
C.S. Hill	Ukiah	Certified as fit	Aug 22, 1917
Charles Hill		Registered #1740	Jul 18, 1917
Chester Arthur Hill	Fort Bragg	Registered #2303 Certified as fit	Jul 18, 1917 Aug 22, 1917
Thomas B. Hill	Caspar	Listed as a slacker Called to active duty	Mar 27, 1918 Jul 3, 1918
Helmer Taulinus Hinanan		Registered #2301	Jul 18, 1917
You Hing		Registered #2165	Jul 18, 1917
Frederick Hirt	Seattle, WA	Called for active duty	Apr 24, 1918
Wong Tin Ho		Registered #2163	Jul 18, 1917

Name	Postoffice	Event	Issue Date
James Hogan	Fort Bragg	Delinquent questionaire	Oct 23, 1918
G.A. Hollenbeck	Comptche	Called to active duty	Jun 12, 1918
Herbert Holquist	Caspar	Called to active duty	Jul 3, 1918
Peter E. Holzreiter Jr.		Registered #2300	Jul 18, 1917
David Honkonen	Fort Bragg	Registered June 5th	Jun 19, 1918
Julius Honkonen		Registered #2164	Jul 18, 1917
Prosper E. Hontou	Hopland	Called to active duty	May 22, 1918
Percy H. Hopper	Hopland	Certified as fit	Aug 22, 1917
Everett C. Hoskins		Registered #52	Jul 18, 1917
Johannes Hostinen	Mendocino	Called to active duty	Jun 12, 1918
Melvin Hotell	Cloverdale	Certified as fit	Aug 22, 1917
Elmer Houx	Hearst	Certified as fit Called to active duty	Aug 22, 1917 Oct 3, 1917
Andy L. Huff	Ukiah	Delinquent questionaire	Oct 23, 1918
Loren V. Hufft	Ukiah	Called to active duty	Jun 12, 1918
Russell Hughes	Ukiah	Called to active duty Failed to report Called to active duty	Oct 3, 1917 Oct 10, 1917 Apr 17, 1918
Roy Hull	Caspar	Called to active duty Failed to report Listed as a slacker Called to active duty	Oct 3, 1917 Oct 10, 1917 Mar 27, 1918 Apr 17, 1918
Lucio Hunter	Irmulco	Certified as fit	Aug 22, 1917
Enoch Hurt	Ukiah	Certified as fit	Aug 22, 1917
G. Hurt	Ukiah	Called to active duty	Aug 14, 1918
J. Hurt	Ukiah	Called to active duty	Aug 14, 1918
Frank Jacob Hyman		Registered # 126	Jul 18, 1917
Herman Edward Hyman		Registered #2161	Jul 18, 1917
Oscar Emanuel Hyman		Registered #2162	Jul 18, 1917
Frans Ilmar Hyvari		Registered #2159	Jul 18, 1917
Ralph K. Inman	San Francisco	Called to active duty	May 8, 1918
Charles Ivers		Registered #1742	Jul 18, 1917
Frank Iversen	Point Arena	Certified as fit Called to active duty	Aug 22, 1917 Oct 3, 1917
John Lambert Iversen	Point Arena	Registered June 5th Called to active duty	Jun 19, 1918 Jul 24, 1918
William Jackson		Registered #2029	Jul 18, 1917
Simon Andrew Jacobson [Simon E.]	Fort Bragg Fort Bragg	Registered #61 Called to active duty	Jul 18, 1917 Jul 10, 1918
Rodney A. Jamison	Talmage	Certified as fit	Aug 22, 1917

Name	Postoffice	Event	Issue Date
Jack Herman Jansen		Registered #987	Jul 18, 1917
Kalle Jarseisalo [Raale J.Jarscisalo] [Kalle S.Jarseix]	Fort Bragg	Registered #2294 Listed as a slacker Called to active duty	Jul 18, 1917 Mar 27, 1918 Jul 10, 1918
Algernon Johnson	Caspar	Certified as fit	Aug 22, 1917
Arthur Johnson	Gualala	Called to active duty	Jul 3, 1918
Charles E.Johnson	Fort Bragg	Delinquent questionaire	Oct 23, 1918
Clarence Johnson		[died Jun 13, 1920] American Legion list	Jun 16, 1920 May 27, 1927
Earl W.Johnson	Fort Bragg	Registered June 5th	Jun 19, 1918
Ernest Johnson		Registered #1743	Jul 18, 1917
Frank A.Johnson		Registered #2296	Jul 18, 1917
Frank Gardner Johnson		Registered #2157	Jul 18, 1917
Fred Johnson	Westport	Certified as fit	Aug 22, 1917
Harold Johnson	Fort Bragg	Certified as fit Draft No.127	Nov 6, 1918 Nov 13, 1918
Henry Edward Johnson	Comptche	Called to active duty Killed in action [Sep 30, 1918] American Legion list	May 8, 1918 Dec 4, 1918 Jan 4, 1922 May 27, 1927
Wallace R.Johnson		[died Jun 13, 1920] American Legion list	Jun 16, 1920 May 27, 1927
John Jola	Spy Rock	Called to active duty Failed to report Called to active duty	Oct 3, 1917 Oct 10, 1917 Apr 17, 1918
Clarence Deveur Jones		Registered #2232	Jul 18, 1917
Clarence F.Jones	Westport	Certified as fit Called to active duty	Aug 22, 1917 Jul 3, 1918
J.A.Jones	Ukiah	Certified as fit	Aug 22, 1917
Phillip Jose	Talmage	Listed as a slacker	Nov 27, 1918
Arthur Carl Josephson	[Fort Bragg]	Registered #988	Jul 18, 1917
Junz Jim Jrain		Registered #2158	Jul 18, 1917
Jung Jim Jram	Fort Bragg	Listed as a slacker	Mar 27, 1918
Carl Sivan Junker		Registered #2295	Jul 18, 1917
Carnaggia Junocente		Registered #1628	Jul 18, 1917
Erkki Justue Kaamis		Registered #2293	Jul 18, 1917
Sam Kaive	Fort Bragg	Registered #2290 Called to active duty	Jul 18, 1917 Jul 3, 1918
John Henry Kandelberg		Registered #2292	Jul 18, 1917
John August Karjamaki		Registered #2153	Jul 18, 1917
John E.Kastis	Talmage	Called to active duty	May 22, 1918

Name	Postoffice	Event	Issue Date
Tom You Kee		Registered #1684	Jul 18, 1917
Archie Isaac Kemppe		Registered #2291	Jul 18, 1917
Waino Frederick Kemppe		Registered #2154	Jul 18, 1917
Dwight N.Kent	Littleriver	Certified as fit	Aug 22, 1917
Carl A.Kesti	Fort Bragg	Draft No.164	Nov 13, 1918
Adolph King		Registered #2155	Jul 18, 1917
Percy A.King	Fort Bragg	Called to active duty	Jul 10, 1918
William Andrew Kinnunen	Fort Bragg	Registered #2025 Certified as fit Called to active duty	Jul 18, 1917 Aug 22, 1917 Oct 3, 1917
Harold Kirk	Calpella	Certified as fit	Aug 22, 1917
Tom Klobas		Registered #1744	Jul 18, 1917
Herman Knaesche	Talmage	Called to active duty	Jun 12, 1918
J.K.Knight	Ukiah	Called to active duty	Jun 12, 1918
L.Ewing Knight	Mendocino	Registered June 5th Called to active duty	Jun 19, 1918 Jul 24, 1918
Constantino Kohatsis Koliatsis	Spy Rock	Reported for duty Called to active duty	Oct 10, 1917 Oct 3, 1917
Oscar William Koponen		Registered #2156	Jul 18, 1917
Andreas Kuharich		Registered #1745	Jul 18, 1917
Frank Ervine Kuher		Registered #1683	Jul 18, 1917
Emil J.Kunzler	Elk Camp	Certified as fit	Aug 22, 1917
Ralph W.Kunzler	Elk	Registered June 5th	Jun 19, 1918
Oscar Laaksonen [Oskar Laaksonon]	Fort Bragg	Registered #2437 Listed as a slacker Called to active duty	Jul 18, 1917 Mar 27, 1918 Jul 10, 1918
Mike Ladika		Registered #1624	Jul 18, 1917
Frank Lade	Fort Bragg	Registered #1676 Certified as fit	Jul 18, 1917 Aug 22, 1917
Saino Ladovici	Mendocino	Called to active duty Reported for duty	Oct 3, 1917 Oct 10, 1917
Amedio Laducci	Sherwood	Called to active duty	Apr 17, 1918
Paul Lamperti	Ukiah	Registered June 5th	Jun 19, 1918
Frank Lampi [F.Lampati] [Lampa]	Fort Bragg	Registered #2148 Called to active duty Listed as a slacker Called to active duty	Jul 18, 1917 Oct 3, 1917 Mar 27, 1918 Apr 17, 1918
Giuseppi Landi		Registered #1748	Jul 18, 1917
Cornelius Lane		Registered #1679	Jul 18, 1917
Elmon Lane	Covelo	Certified as fit Called to active duty	Aug 22, 1917 Oct 3, 1917

Name	Postoffice	Event	Issue Date
Ernest Lyford Lane		Registered #60	Jul 18, 1917
P.M. Lane	Willits	Called to active duty	Jun 12, 1918
Walfrid E. Lane	Noyo	Certified as fit	Aug 22, 1917
Henry Joseph Langley		Registered #1750	Jul 18, 1917
William Patrick Langley		Registered #1747	Jul 18, 1917
Walter Larsen		Registered #2289	Jul 18, 1917
Nels Larson	Fort Bragg	Registered #2288 Called to active duty	Jul 18, 1917 Jun 12, 1918
Alonzo F. Laurason	Northwestern	Certified as fit	Aug 22, 1917
J. Lavaletta	Talmage	Certified as fit	Aug 22, 1917
Victor Laviletta	Talmage	Certified as fit Called to active duty	Aug 22, 1917 Oct 3, 1917
Alvah W. Lawranson	Irmulco	Certified as fit	Aug 22, 1917
Roscoe V. Lawson	Albion	Delinquent questionaire	Nov 27, 1918
Roy E. Lawson	Point Arena	Died of wounds [buried Dec 5, 1918] American Legion list	Dec 4, 1918 May 27, 1927
L.J. Layton	Ukiah	Called to active duty	Aug 14, 1918
Charles L. Leavitt	Fort Bragg	Registered #2243 Called to active duty	Jul 18, 1917 Apr 24, 1918
William R. Ledford	Yorkville	Certified as fit Called in active duty Died from accident	Aug 22, 1917 Sep 5, 1917 Dec 4, 1918
Bert Leggett	Covelo	Certified as fit	Aug 22, 1917
Jesse Edward Leggett	Spy Rock	Registered June 5th	Jun 19, 1918
M.H. Leggett	Spy Rock	Certified as fit Called to active duty	Aug 22, 1917 Oct 3, 1917
Alfredo Leippi		Registered #2278	Jul 18, 1917
Jose Moniy Lema	Fort Bragg	Registered #2152 Certified as fit	Jul 18, 1917 Aug 22, 1917
Aladino Lencioni		Registered #2286	Jul 18, 1917
Enrico Leoni	Mendocino	Certified as fit Called to active duty Failed to report Listed as a slacker Called to active duty	Aug 22, 1917 Oct 3, 1917 Oct 10, 1917 Mar 27, 1918 Apr 17, 1918
David Leskinen	San Francisco	Registered #2287 Called to active duty	Jul 18, 1917 May 22, 1918
Frederick LeValley		Registered #59	Jul 18, 1917
Walter A. Lewis	Willits	Certified as fit Called to active duty	Aug 22, 1917 Sep 5, 1917
John Duncan Lewthwaite		Registered # 123	Jul 18, 1917

Name	Postoffice	Event	Issue Date
Alfred W.Liljeberg	Elk	Registered June 5th Called to active duty	Jun 19, 1918 Jul 24, 1918
Manuel Lima		Registered #1681	Jul 18, 1917
Lee C.Ling		Registered #2151	Jul 18, 1917
Thomas Linn	Orrs	Certified as fit Called to active duty	Aug 22, 1917 Oct 3, 1917
Matti Ossian Linnala	Fort Bragg	Registered #1338 Listed as a slacker Called to active duty	Jul 18, 1917 Mar 27, 1918 Jun 12, 1918
John R.Long		[died Mar 5, 1924] American Legion list	Mar 12, 1924 May 27, 1927
Antone T.L.Lopps	Mendocino	Died of disease American Legion list	Dec 4, 1918 May 27, 1927
Marola Lorenza		Registered #1677	Jul 18, 1917
Herbert L.Loveall	Calpella	Draft No.176	Nov 13, 1918
Marcello Lucchisi		Registered #1680	Jul 18, 1917
Limusi Lumei		Registered #1776	Jul 18, 1917
Charles Lund		Registered #1749	Jul 18, 1917
Eric Ralph Luomi	Mendocino	Called to active duty	Jul 10, 1918
Gust Luoto	Leadville,CO	Called to active duty Failed to report	Oct 3, 1917 Oct 10, 1917
Lee Hin Lun	Fort Bragg	Registered June 5th	Jun 19, 1918
Giacoma Luzzi	Point Arena	Delinquent questionaire	Oct 23, 1918
Thomas Myles Lynch		Registered #62	Jul 18, 1917
Arthur A.Lyons	Covelo	Called to active duty	Jul 24, 1918
Thomas Macedo		Killed in action	Jun 5, 1918
Claude Mack	Caspar	Registered June 5th	Jun 19, 1918
Fred Mack	Albion	Delinquent questionaire	Oct 23, 1918
John Madeira	Mendocino	Enlisted.Served 8th.Inf. Sverko, *Portuguese Families*, p 337]	
Michael Madison	Fort Bragg	Registered June 5th	Jun 19, 1918
Carl William Madsen		Registered #1461	Jul 18, 1917
John Waino Madsen		Registered #2020	Jul 18, 1917
A.Magala	Sherwood	Called to active duty	Jun 12, 1918
Paul William Mahler		Registered #2019	Jul 18, 1917
Allen D.Main	Boonville	Certified as fit Draft No.105	Nov 6, 1918 Nov 13, 1918
Cecil M.Main	Boonville	Delinquent questionaire	Nov 27, 1918
William H.Main	Mountain House	Called to active duty	Jun 12, 1918
Samuel Maksente	Ornbaun	Registered June 5th	Jun 19, 1918

Name	Postoffice	Event	Issue Date
Clarence W.Manchester	Fort Bragg	Registered #1031	Jul 18, 1917
		Certified as fit	Aug 22, 1917
		Reported dead of disease	Dec 4, 1918
		Died Dec 16, 1917	Oct 27, 1920
		American Legion list	May 27, 1927
James Thomas Manchester		Registered #1033	Jul 18, 1917
John L.Manchester		Registered #2427	Jul 18, 1917
Pompilio Manicusi		Registered #2284	Jul 18, 1917
John Manili		Registered #2280	Jul 18, 1917
Arthur Arvid Mann		Registered #2018	Jul 18, 1917
John William Manteli		Registered #66	Jul 18, 1917
Dan Mantila		Registered #64	Jul 18, 1917
Giacomo Marando		Registered #1664	Jul 18, 1917
Marchesi Marco		Registered #1751	Jul 18, 1917
Siri Marco		Registered #2021	Jul 18, 1917
John Marisa	Fort Bragg	Registered #1666	Jul 18, 1917
		Listed as a slacker	Mar 27, 1918
Emanueli Markkula		Registered #2283	Jul 18, 1917
Sebastio Marques		Registered #1669	Jul 18, 1917
C.B.Martin	Willits	Certified as fit	Aug 22, 1917
Frank Everett Martin		Registered #65	Jul 18, 1917
Jesse Elmer Martin		Registered #1752	Jul 18, 1917
Karl A.Martin		Registered #2281	Jul 18, 1917
Ottavio Martinelli	Philo	Certified as fit	Aug 22, 1917
		Called to active duty	Oct 3, 1917
Pete Massavelli	Willits	Certified as fit	Aug 22, 1917
Bello Massimo	Mendocino	Certified as fit	Aug 22, 1917
Stephen Massoletti	Ukiah	Certified as fit	Aug 22, 1917
John Matana		Registered #1670	Jul 18, 1917
Edward R.Mather	Elk	Registered June 5th	Jun 19, 1918
		Called to active duty	Jul 24, 1918
William Charles Mathews		Registered #2144	Jul 18, 1917
Robert Mathison	Mendocino	Certified as fit	Aug 22, 1917
Giovanni Mattinzzo	Caspar	Called to active duty	Apr 17, 1918
William A.May	Willits	Registered June 5th	Jun 19, 1918
Waino Mayala		Registered #2285	Jul 18, 1917
George A.Maze	Ukiah	Certified as fit	Aug 22, 1917
		Called in active duty	Oct 3, 1917
[Dave]		Failed to report	Oct 10, 1917
Pietro Mazzetta	Manchester	Registered June 5th	Jun 19, 1918

MENDOCINO COUNTY MEN IN WORLD WAR I

Name	Postoffice	Event	Issue Date
Battisa <u>Mazzina</u>	Sherwood	Called to active duty	Jul 24, 1918
Vittorio <u>Mazzina</u>	Sherwood	Certified as fit	Aug 22, 1917
B.<u>Mazzini</u>	Point Arena	Called to active duty	Aug 14, 1918
William C.<u>McCabe</u>	Willits	Died in Arizona [December 7, 1920]	Dec 15, 1920
Asa R.<u>McDowell</u>	Yorkville	Certified as fit	Aug 22, 1917
Floyd L.<u>McElroy</u>	Mendocino	Delinquent questionaire	Oct 23, 1918
Edward Jasper <u>McGhaney</u>		Registered #1663	Jul 18, 1917
James <u>McGill</u>	Ukiah	Certified as fit	Aug 22, 1917
Alva P.<u>McGimsey</u>	Boonville	Certified as fit Called to active duty	Aug 22, 1917 Oct 3, 1917
Jack A.<u>McGimsey</u>	Boonville	Certified as fit	Aug 22, 1917
Phocian <u>McGimsey</u>	Boonville	Missing in action	Aug 21, 1918
Joe <u>McGuinness</u>		Registered #1662	Jul 18, 1917
Cecil Charles <u>McGuire</u>		Registered #63	Jul 18, 1917
Earl E. <u>McLaughlin</u>	Caspar	Delinquent questionaire	Oct 23, 1918
D.F.<u>McMannis</u>	Caspar	Certified as fit	Aug 22, 1917
Archie <u>McWhinney</u>	Ukiah	Certified as fit	Aug 22, 1917
John <u>Medeiros</u>		Registered #1675	Jul 18, 1917
Argie <u>Medicas</u>		Registered #1671	Jul 18, 1917
Lucius O.<u>Medicas</u>	Fort Bragg	Registered #1673 Certified as fit	Jul 18, 1917 Aug 22, 1917
Sidney Clarence <u>Medicas</u>	Fort Bragg	Delinquent questionaire	Nov 27, 1918
John J.<u>Meehan</u>	Talmage	Called to active duty	May 22, 1918
Warren L.<u>Meese</u>	Ukiah	Delinquent questionaire	Oct 23, 1918
Aner Jack <u>Mehtlan</u>	Fort Bragg	Registered #2146 Called to active duty	Jul 18, 1917 May 8, 1918
Otto <u>Mehtlan</u>	Fort Bragg	Registered #2145 Certified as fit Called to active duty	Jul 18, 1917 Aug 22, 1917 Oct 3, 1917
Emil Edward <u>Meminen</u>		Registered #2142	Jul 18, 1917
Antone J.<u>Mendosa</u>	Mendocino	U.S.Army Batt.C CAC	
Frank Joseph <u>Mendosa</u>	Mendocino	Called to active duty U.S.Army Co.L 21st Infantry	May 22, 1918
John Sylvester <u>Mendosa</u>	Mendocino	Certified as fit Called to active duty	Aug 22, 1917 Oct 3, 1917
Joseph Albert <u>Mendosa</u>	Mendocino	Enlisted Marines 1917 Served with 36th company	
Jose J.<u>Mendosa</u>	Manchester	Called to active duty	Jun 12, 1918

MENDOCINO COUNTY MEN IN WORLD WAR I

Name	Postoffice	Event	Issue Date
William Arthur Mendosa	Mendocino	Registered June 5th Served with 48th Mach.gun	Jun 19, 1918
Joseph Micheletti	Ukiah	Certified as fit Called to active duty	Aug 22, 1917 Oct 3, 1917
Frank J.Middleton		Registered #1674	Jul 18, 1917
J.E.Millard	Mendocino	Called to active duty	Jun 12, 1918
John F.Miller	Albion	Called to active duty	Jul 3, 1918
Joseph Miller	Fort Bragg	Delinquent questionaire	Oct 23, 1918
Howard Moffit	Willits	Registered June 5th	Jun 19, 1918
Newton Charles Mohn	Ukiah	Certified as fit	Aug 22, 1917
Leonard Mokka		Registered #2282	Jul 18, 1917
Manuel Monis		Registered #1667	Jul 18, 1917
Carl W.Monsen	Fort Bragg	Registered June 5th	Jun 19, 1918
Clarence C.Montgomery		Registered #2078	Jul 18, 1917
Elbert P.Montgomery	Caspar	Certified as fit	Aug 22, 1917
J.E.Montgomery	Potter Valley	Called to active duty	Oct 3, 1917
J.P.Montgomery	Potter Valley	Certified as fit	Aug 22, 1917
W.D.Montgomery	Potter Valley	Called to active duty	Jun 12, 1918
Walter H.Moore	Pittsburg	Called to active duty	May 22, 1918
Los A.Morby	Ukiah	Certified as fit Called to active duty	Aug 22, 1917 Oct 3, 1917
Christian Morley	Fort Bragg	Registered #2147 Certified as fit	Jul 18, 1917 Aug 22, 1917
Milton Morrison	Ukiah	Delinquent questionaire	Oct 23, 1918
James L.Moyles	Gualala Point Arena	Called to active duty Called to active duty	Jun 12, 1918 Jul 3, 1918
Guy E.Muir	Willits	Called to active duty	Jul 24, 1918
Walter Mullis		Called to active duty	Oct 3, 1917
Fred Murk	Fort Bragg	Registered #1672 Listed as a slacker	Jul 18, 1917 Mar 27, 1918
Antonio Mussetti	Willits	Called to active duty	May 22, 1918
Isaac Nabb	[Fort Bragg]	Registered #1360	Jul 18, 1917
Joe Nadal		Registered #2274	Jul 18, 1917
Adolph Emil Neckritz	Albion	Registered June 5th Called to active duty	Jun 19, 1918 Jul 24, 1918
Kenneth Neighbors	Willits	Registered June 5th	Jun 19, 1918
Arthur Nelson	Elk	Called to active duty	Jun 12, 1918
Arthur C.Nelson	Caspar	Called to active duty	Jun 12, 1918
Charles Theodore Nelson		Registered #2016	Jul 18, 1917

Name	Postoffice	Event	Issue Date
Enoch M. Nelson	Fort Bragg	Registered June 5th	Jun 19, 1918
Jacob Arvid Nelson		Registered #2017	Jul 18, 1917
Rea Alvin Nelson		Registered #958	Jul 18, 1917
Robert Nelson	Fort Bragg	Registered #2276 Listed as a slacker Called to active duty	Jul 18, 1917 Mar 27, 1918 Jun 12, 1918
Carl Walfred Ness		Registered #1755	Jul 18, 1917
Oscar Irwin Ness	Point Arena	Registered June 5th Called to active duty	Jun 19, 1918 Jul 24, 1918
J. Nevin	Ukiah	Certified as fit	Aug 22, 1917
George B. Newberg	Fort Bragg	Listed as a slacker	Mar 27, 1918
George Burnhart Newbury		Registered #2015	Jul 18, 1917
Jacob Andrew Newman	Noyo	Certified as fit	Aug 22, 1917
Joseph Frances Nichols	Mendocino	Killed in action [Sep 29, 1918] American Legion list	Oct 30, 1918 Dec 4, 1918 May 27, 1927
Alfred Nicholson	Littleriver	Called to active duty	Jun 12, 1918
Pinoli Nicomeda	Mendocino	Called to active duty	Jun 12, 1918
Elmer Lawrence Nielsen		Registered #67	Jul 18, 1917
Oscar Niemi		Registered #2275	Jul 18, 1917
Jack Niemla	Fort Bragg	Registered June 5th	Jun 19, 1918
Emil E. Nieminen	Fort Bragg	Called to active duty	Jun 12, 1918
Juhan Eelis Nikula		Registered #2143	Jul 18, 1917
Earl E. Nimela		In service Camp Kearney	Mar 12, 1919
Emil Edward Nimele	Albion	Registered June 5th	Jun 19, 1918
Herman Nohf	Fort Bragg	Delinquent questionaire	Oct 23, 1918
Manuel G. Nola	Fort Bragg	Registered June 5th	Jun 19, 1918
John Norback		Registered #2273	Jul 18, 1917
Comrado Nunon	Elk	Delinquent questionaire	Oct 23, 1918
Fred Nybeck		American Legion list	May 27, 1927
Albin Nyberg		Registered #1754	Jul 18, 1917
Francis Willard Nye		Registered #989	Jul 18, 1917
Herbert O'Connor		Registered #1387	Jul 18, 1917
D. O'Sullivan	Willits	Called to active duty	Jun 12, 1918
Alva E. Ogle	Ornbaun	Certified as fit Called to active duty	Aug 22, 1917 Oct 3, 1917
F. Cecil Ogle	Ornbaun	Registered June 5th	Jun 19, 1918
Carl Archie Winter Olsen [Olson]	Elk	Registered June 5th Called to active duty	Jun 19, 1918 Jul 24, 1918

Name	Postoffice	Event	Issue Date
Frank Almer Olsen		Registered #2272	Jul 18, 1917
Ole Peter Louis Olsen	Fort Bragg	Registered #2012 Certified as fit	Jul 18, 1917 Aug 22, 1917
Swanti H.Olson		Killed in action (mother got $10,000 ins.) American Legion list	Aug 25, 1920 May 27, 1927
Dong On	Sherwood	Called to active duty Failed to report	Oct 3, 1917 Oct 10, 1917
C.F.Oppenlander	Comptche	Draft No. 184	Nov 13, 1918
C.L.Ord	Gualala	Certified as fit	Aug 22, 1917
Tob Ordway		Registered #2271	Jul 18, 1917
A.D.Organ	Hopland	Called to active duty Called to active duty	Apr 17, 1918 Jun 12, 1918
Jesse L.Ornbaun	Marysville	Called to active duty	Jul 24, 1918
Raymond C.Ornbaun	Boonville	Registered June 5th Called to active duty	Jun 19, 1918 Jul 24, 1918
Winfield Shipley Ornbaun		Registered #1468	Jul 18, 1917
Arthur Orre		Registered #1756	Jul 18, 1917
John Ottoson	Comptche	Certified as fit Called to active duty	Aug 22, 1917 Sep 5, 1917
John Paloposki	Fort Bragg	Registered June 5th	Jun 19, 1918
M.Pamentilla		Called to active duty	Oct 3, 1917
Value Paoli	Mendocino	Delinquent questionaire	Nov 27, 1918
Elia Paolini	Navarro	Registered June 5th	Jun 19, 1918
Dide Papera	Hopland	Certified as fit	Aug 22, 1917
Charles Parage	Talmage	Certified as fit Called to active duty	Aug 22, 1917 Oct 3, 1917
Pete Parasdi		Registered #1759	Jul 18, 1917
Joseph Parasei		Registered #71	Jul 18, 1917
Frank Pardini	Fort Bragg	Registered #1661 Called to active duty	Jul 18, 1917 Jul 3, 1918
Grovanini Pardini		Registered #2266	Jul 18, 1917
Nat Pardini	Fort Bragg	Registered #1657 Called to active duty	Jul 18, 1917 Dec 5, 1917
Pietro Pardini	Albion	Registered June 5th	Jun 19, 1918
Harry Parker		Registered #2269	Jul 18, 1917
Lynn H.Parker	Laytonville	Certified as fit Called to active duty	Aug 22, 1917 Oct 3, 1917
Steve Parun		Registered #2270	Jul 18, 1917
Jaas Jacintho Patricio		Registered #1656	Jul 18, 1917
Fred D.Patton	Point Arena	Delinquent questionaire	Oct 23, 1918

Name	Postoffice	Event	Issue Date
Julius R.Paulson	Cummings	Delinquent questionaire	Oct 23, 1918
Lemuel Raymond Pedratti		Registered #2138	Jul 18, 1917
Louis Pedretti	Elk	Delinquent questionaire	Nov 27, 1918
William J.Pedro	Noyo	Certified as fit	Aug 22, 1917
Alcide Pelletti	Navarro	Registered June 5th	Jun 19, 1918
Joseph E.Pello		Called to active duty	Oct 3, 1917
Bennett Edward Pemberton	Fort Bragg	Registered #1660 Certified as fit Called to active duty	Jul 18, 1917 Aug 22, 1917 Oct 3, 1917
Thomas Pencetta		Registered #73	Jul 18, 1917
Dick George Penlan	Ukiah	Registered June 5th	Jun 19, 1918
L.H.Pepper	Hopland	Certified as fit Called to active duty	Aug 22, 1917 Oct 3, 1917
Guido Pera		Registered #2267	Jul 18, 1917
Michele Pera		Registered #1655	Jul 18, 1917
Avelino Pereira		Registered #70	Jul 18, 1917
John Pereira	Mendocino	Called to active duty	Jun 12, 1918
Thomas Perereia	Mendocino	Registered June 5th Called to active duty	Jun 19, 1918 Jul 24, 1918
Antonio Peres	Fort Bragg	Registered #1652 Called to active duty Failed to report	Jul 18, 1917 Oct 3, 1917 Oct 10, 1917
D.H.Petersen	Cloverdale	Certified as fit	Aug 22, 1917
Richard Lee Phelan	Noyo	Delinquent questionaire	Nov 27, 1918
Herbert Philbert	Fort Bragg	Called to active duty	Jul 3, 1918
Archie Ray Phillips	Willits	Registered June 5th	Jun 19, 1918
James E.Pickerell	Gualala	Certified as fit	Aug 22, 1917
Gilbert Tamage Picou	Ukiah	Registered June 5th	Jun 19, 1918
W.H.Pierce	Willits	Certified as fit	Aug 22, 1917
Matt Piipola	Fort Bragg	Called to active duty	Jul 10, 1918
Silvester G.Pimental		Registered #69	Jul 18, 1917
Anton Pinnoli		Registered #1654	Jul 18, 1917
Jose Francisco Pires		Registered #1757	Jul 18, 1917
Diego Pisnoli		Registered #1758	Jul 18, 1917
John Pitkanen		Registered #2264	Jul 18, 1917
Joe Piva		Registered #2268	Jul 18, 1917
Louie Piva		Registered #2265	Jul 18, 1917
Harry Americo Pocai	Mendocino	Listed as a slacker	Mar 27, 1918

MENDOCINO COUNTY MEN IN WORLD WAR I

Name	Postoffice	Event	Issue Date
William A. Pollock	Westport	Listed as a slacker	Mar 27, 1918
Elias Pomon	Willits	Called to active duty	Apr 17, 1918
Poll Pomon	Willits	Called to active duty	Oct 3, 1917
	San Francisco	Failed to report	Oct 10, 1917
P. Pomonon	Willits	Certified as fit	Aug 22, 1917
Pedro Ponce	Fort Bragg	Registered #1653	Jul 18, 1917
		Listed as a slacker	Mar 27, 1918
		Called to active duty	Jun 12, 1918
Fred J. Popoff	Willits	Delinquent questionaire	Oct 23, 1918
Michael Porro	Willits	Certified as fit	Aug 22, 1917
George Harold Porterfield		[died Aug 7, 1918]	Sep 4, 1918
		American Legion list	May 27, 1927
Pit Prevostini		Registered #2141	Jul 18, 1917
Fred R. Prichard	Littleriver	Called to active duty	Jul 10, 1918
Arthur A. Pritchard	Littleriver	Called to active duty	Apr 17, 1918
James W. Pritchard		American Legion list	May 27, 1927
Clarence L. Prothero	Laytonville	Registered June 5th	Jun 19, 1918
James Calvin Pruitt		Registered #2139	Jul 18, 1917
John Anderson Pruitt		Registered #68	Jul 18, 1917
William Franklin Pruitt		Registered #72	Jul 18, 1917
John Dee Pugh	Ukiah	Registered June 5th	Jun 19, 1918
William Harrison Pullen		Registered #1659	Jul 18, 1917
Matt Pulola		Registered #2140	Jul 18, 1917
John H. Purdy	Laytonville	Certified as fit	Aug 22, 1917
Joseph Quadrio	Willits	Called to active duty	May 22, 1918
Frank Quaill	Mendocino	Failed physical Aug 1917	
Martini Quaini [Martin?]	Elk	Called to active duty	May 22, 1918
Charles Joseph Quinn [Jerome?]		Registered #1651	Jul 18, 1917
Don Quong		Registered #1650	Jul 18, 1917
Ah Quoon	Fort Bragg	Registered June 5th	Jun 19, 1918
Nikola Radosevic	Fort Bragg	Registered June 5th	Jun 19, 1918
Joseph Vincent Ramus	Fort Bragg	Registered #76	Jul 18, 1917
		Called to active duty	Dec 5, 1917
Victor Frederick Ramus		Registered #77	Jul 18, 1917
Albert Edward Rang	Fort Bragg	Registered #1646	Jul 18, 1917
		Called to active duty	Jul 10, 1918
Isak Rantanen		Registered #2438	Jul 18, 1917

MENDOCINO COUNTY MEN IN WORLD WAR I

Name	Postoffice	Event	Issue Date
Frank Raspi		Registered #1764	Jul 18, 1917
Charles Raudio	[Fort Bragg]	Registered #1765	Jul 18, 1917
Austin N. Rawles	Boonville	Registered June 5th	Jun 19, 1918
Earnest Everett Rawles	Boonville	Registered June 5th	Jun 19, 1918
McDonald Rawles	Boonville	Called to active duty	Jun 12, 1918
Vernon R. Rawles	Boonville	Certified as fit	Aug 22, 1917
Gus Ray		Registered #1762	Jul 18, 1917
John Ray		Registered #1766 Called to active duty	Jul 18, 1917 Oct 3, 1917
Sam M. Ray	Ukiah	Certified as fit	Aug 22, 1917
Sam Redmond	Westport	Listed as a slacker Called to active duty	Mar 27, 1918 May 22, 1918
George Patrick Reidmiller		Registered #75	Jul 18, 1917
Carl Rennick		Registered #1647	Jul 18, 1917
Raymond Reyes	Westport	Listed as a slacker Called to active duty	Mar 27, 1918 Jul 3, 1918
George Richards		Registered #2005	Jul 18, 1917
C.A. Richey	Ukiah	Called for active duty	Apr 17, 1918
G. Ricney	Ukiah	Certified as fit	Aug 22, 1917
B.H. Rigby		Called to active duty	Oct 3, 1917
Guiseppe Rinaldo	Point Arena	Called to active duty	Apr 24, 1918
Pinocchi Rinardo [Ricardo] [Ricardo]	Fort Bragg	Registered #1658 Certified as fit Called to active duty	Jul 18, 1917 Aug 22, 1917 Oct 3, 1917
Sakari A. Rinne	Branscomb	Called to active duty	May 22, 1918
P. Rira	Gualala	Registered June 5th	Jun 19, 1918
Emil Riskee		Registered #1474	Jul 18, 1917
Lauri Risky		Registered #1761	Jul 18, 1917
Theodore J. Ritcher [Richter]	Talmage	Called to active duty Failed to report Called to active duty	Oct 3, 1917 Oct 10, 1917 Apr 17, 1918
Mathust Robak		Registered #1648	Jul 18, 1917
E.H. Robbins	Dos Rios	Certified as fit	Aug 22, 1917
C. Robejohannes	Comptche	Called to active duty	May 8, 1918
Amilcare Roberts [Amil Carl]	Albion	Listed as a slacker Called to active duty	Mar 27, 1918 Jul 10, 1918
Clarence E. Robinson		Called to active duty	Oct 3, 1917
Frank Rochetti	Fort Bragg	Registered June 5th	Jun 19, 1918
Antonia Rodriguer		Registered #1645	Jul 18, 1917

Name	Postoffice	Event	Issue Date
Manoel Rodrigues		Registered #1763	Jul 18, 1917
Manuel John Rodrigues		Registered #74	Jul 18, 1917
Enrique Rodriquez	Westport	Listed as a slacker Called to active duty Called to active duty	Mar 27, 1918 Apr 17, 1918 Jul 24, 1918
Charles Myron Rogers		Registered #957	Jul 18, 1917
Evan F. Rohrbough	Covelo	Certified as fit Called to active duty	Aug 22, 1917 Sep 5, 1917
Giacinto Romeri	Fort Bragg	Registered #1343 Certified as fit Called to active duty	Jul 18, 1917 Aug 22, 1917 Oct 3, 1917
Emil Rosa		Registered #2137	Jul 18, 1917
Eugene Ross		killed in action	Dec 12, 1917
Lorin B. Ross	Ukiah	Certified as fit	Aug 22, 1917
Julius Rotluff	Potter Valley	Certified as fit	Aug 22, 1917
John B. Rucchetti		Registered #1649	Jul 18, 1917
Ernest V. Ruddick	Ukiah	Certified as fit	Aug 22, 1917
Vernon Ruddock	Ukiah	Certified as fit	Aug 22, 1917
Adam Rudrisk	Fort Bragg	Delinquent questionaire	Oct 23, 1918
Willard E. Runk	Upper Lake	Registered June 5th	Jun 19, 1918
Matt Rupola	Fort Bragg	Listed as a slacker	Mar 27, 1918
G. Rusca	Willits	Called to active duty	Jun 12, 1918
P.B. Ruschetti	Fort Bragg	Registered #2263 Certified as fit Called to active duty	Jul 18, 1917 Aug 22, 1917 Sep 5, 1917
A. Guiseppe Rusconi [Pusconi]	Glen Blair Glen Blair	Listed as a slacker Called to active duty	Mar 27, 1918 Jul 10, 1918
L. Russell	Ukiah	Called to active duty	Jun 12, 1918
W. St. John	Boonville	Certified as fit	Aug 22, 1917
Ellis Saiva		Registered #2277	Jul 18, 1917
Thomas William Sala		Registered #2426	Jul 18, 1917
Guilio Salir		Registered #1631	Jul 18, 1917
Charles A. Sallinen	Noyo	Called to active duty	Jun 12, 1918
Robert Arthur Sallinen	Noyo	Certified as fit Buried Fort Bragg American Legion list	Aug 22, 1917 Aug 10, 1921 May 27, 1927
Ellis Salmen	Fort Bragg	Registered #1768 Listed as a slacker Called to active duty	Jul 18, 1917 Mar 27, 1918 Jul 10, 1918
William Salmi		Registered #2134	Jul 18, 1917
P.G. Same	Hopland	Certified as fit	Aug 22, 1917

Name	Postoffice	Event	Issue Date
J.G. Samuelson	Comptche	Certified as fit	Aug 22, 1917
John Samuelson	Fort Bragg	Registered #2254	Jul 18, 1917
		Called to active duty	Jun 12, 1918
Frank W. Sandelin	Ukiah	Registered June 5th	Jun 19, 1918
Walter Leander Sandkulla		Registered #85	Jul 18, 1917
Joe Sandroni [Gio]	Fort Bragg	Registered #959	Jul 18, 1917
		Listed as a slacker	Mar 27, 1918
		Called to active duty	Jun 12, 1918
Matt Sankovich		Registered #1638	Jul 18, 1917
Andrey Sarja		Registered #2133	Jul 18, 1917
Albert L. Saunders	Fort Bragg	Registered June 5th	Jun 19, 1918
Jack Sauso		Registered #2279	Jul 18, 1917
Antonio Sauza		Registered #1634	Jul 18, 1917
Joe Sauza		Registered #1635	Jul 18, 1917
Carl Savo		Registered #2256	Jul 18, 1917
Bruno Sbrana		Registered #1719	Jul 18, 1917
Settimo Sbregia		Registered #1770	Jul 18, 1917
Settino Sbroggia	Fort Bragg	Listed as a slacker	Mar 27, 1918
		Called to active duty	Jun 12, 1918
R. Scampini		Called to active duty	Oct 3, 1917
Charles F. Schaeffer		Registered #1642	Jul 18, 1917
Kuno Schamber	Ukiah	Certified as fit	Aug 22, 1917
E. Schmidt	Philo	Certified as fit	Aug 22, 1917
Herman Schmidt	Philo	Certified as fit	Aug 22, 1917
Ray J. Schulz	Ukiah	Certified as fit	Nov 6, 1918
		Draft No.40	Nov 13, 1918
Benjamin Scott	Fort Bragg	Registered June 5th	Jun 19, 1918
Otto Harrison Scott		Registered #2129	Jul 18, 1917
Ralph M. Scott	Calpella	Registered June 5th	Jun 19, 1918
George C. Scrader		Registered #1644	Jul 18, 1917
H.F. Semple	Willits	Certified as fit	Aug 22, 1917
Augusti Seppala [Agusti]	Fort Bragg	Registered #1368	Jul 18, 1917
		Listed as a slacker	Mar 27, 1918
Emelio Seri	Inglenook	Certified as fit	Aug 22, 1917
		Called to active duty	Oct 3, 1917
James Sertori	Sherwood	Delinquent questionaire	Oct 23, 1918
Mauriel Seva		Registered #2135	Jul 18, 1917
H.T. Seward	Calpella	Certified as fit	Aug 22, 1917
Albert Charles Seymour	Albion	Registered #78	Jul 18, 1917
		Called to active duty	Jul 10, 1918

Name	Postoffice	Event	Issue Date
Ronald Seymour	Fort Bragg	Registered #79 Called to active duty	Jul 18, 1917 Jun 12, 1918
Fred F. Sharp	Willits	Called to active duty	Jun 12, 1918
Dong She [Sher]	Point Arena	Certified as fit Listed as a slacker	Aug 22, 1917 Mar 27, 1918
John J. Sherman	Cummings	Delinquent questionaire	Oct 23, 1918
Harry Sherwood	Comptche	Certified as fit Called to active duty	Aug 22, 1917 Oct 3, 1917
Lawrence T. Sherwood	Sherwood	Certified as fit	Aug 22, 1917
Harry LeValley Shields	Comptche	Certified as fit Called to active duty	Aug 22, 1917 Oct 3, 1917
M. Shiminowsky	Willits	Called to active duty	Jun 12, 1918
B. Shimonwsky	Willits	Certified as fit	Aug 22, 1917
Claude A. Shipley	Covelo	Certified as fit	Aug 22, 1917
J.B. Shire	Willits	Delinquent questionaire	Oct 23, 1918
Serefino Shringhelli	Comptche	Called to active duty	Jul 10, 1918
C.H. Shular		Called to active duty	Oct 3, 1917
Piacentini Sialdini		Registered #2307	Jul 18, 1917
Piacentini Sialviani	Fort Bragg	Listed as a slacker	Mar 27, 1918
Leander Siltanen	Fort Bragg	Registered #2127 Listed as a slacker	Jul 18, 1917 Mar 27, 1918
Joe R. Silva	Caspar	Called to active duty	Apr 24, 1918
Tony L. Silva		Called to active duty	Oct 3, 1917
Seth Simmonds [Simmons]	Fort Bragg	Registered #1639 Certified as fit	Jul 18, 1917 Aug 22, 1917
Ernest Simmons	Fort Bragg	Registered #1637 Called to active duty	Jul 18, 1917 Jun 12, 1918
Johnnie Simmons		American Legion list	May 27, 1927
Alfred Simoni		Registered #1632	Jul 18, 1917
Henry Simpson	[Fort Bragg]	Registered #1034	Jul 18, 1917
Capt. Ernest A. Sinclair	Glen Blair	marriage in New Brunswick	Apr 9, 1919
Walter J. Sipe	Ukiah	Called to active duty	May 22, 1918
Matt E. Sipila	Noyo	Called to active duty	Jun 12, 1918
Agusta Sippala	Fort Bragg	Called to active duty	Jun 12, 1918
James Skeleton	Elk	Called to active duty	Jul 10, 1918
Emanuel Skroza		Registered #1682	Jul 18, 1917
Bud M. Sloan	Sherwood	Delinquent questionaire	Oct 23, 1918
Harold C. Sloper	Ukiah	Delinquent questionaire	Nov 27, 1918
Irvine Erving Slye		Registered #83	Jul 18, 1917

Name	Postoffice	Event	Issue Date
Andrew J.Smith	Ukiah	Called to active duty	Jun 12, 1918
Charles M.Smith	Covelo	Delinquent questionaire	Nov 27, 1918
George Smith	Willits	Delinquent questionaire	Oct 23, 1918
John Smith	Caspar	Called to active duty	Jul 10, 1918
John F.Smith	Comptche	Called to active duty	Jul 10, 1918
John Henry Smith	Fort Bragg	Registered #81 Listed as a slacker Called to active duty	Jul 18, 1917 Mar 27, 1918 Jul 3, 1918
John Jacob Smith		Registered #82	Jul 18, 1917
Luther Smith	Covelo	Called to active duty	Jun 12, 1918
P.H.Smith	Bonner,MT	Called to active duty	May 22, 1918
Albert Snickers	Elk	Called to active duty	Jul 10, 1918
David M.Snodgrass	Caspar	Certified as fit Called to active duty	Aug 22, 1917 Oct 3, 1917
Lloyd Melvin Snook		Registered #2260	Jul 18, 1917
John Victor Soderland	Caspar	Delinquent questionaire	Oct 23, 1918
Matt Sosich		Registered #1633	Jul 18, 1917
Michael Sosie		Registered #2136	Jul 18, 1917
John Sousa	Elk	Delinquent questionaire	Nov 27, 1918
Manuel Carreia C.Souza	Fort Bragg	Registered #2128 Certified as fit	Jul 18, 1917 Aug 22, 1917
Nello Spadoni		Registered #1640 Called to active duty	Jul 18, 1917 Oct 3, 1917
Emmett Spencer	Covelo	Called to active duty Called to active duty	Apr 24, 1918 Jun 12, 1918
Emmet G.Srack		Registered #1641	Jul 18, 1917
William Raymond Standley		Registered #960	Jul 18, 1917
Charles R.Stayton	Point Arena	Delinquent questionaire	Nov 27, 1918
Bob Steffanetti		Registered #80	Jul 18, 1917
William Stemile		Registered #1643	Jul 18, 1917
Henry Steumbee		Registered #2130	Jul 18, 1917
E.C.Stevens	Westport	Called to active duty	Dec 5, 1917
Herman A.Stevens	Caspar	Called to active duty Called to active duty	Jun 12, 1918 Jul 10, 1918
Steve Stevens	Caspar	Certified as fit Called to active duty	Aug 22, 1917 Oct 3, 1917
Archie Stevenson	Ukiah	Called to active duty	Jun 12, 1918
Charles Thomas Stevenson		Registered #1772	Jul 18, 1917
H.Charles Stillwell	Willits Caspar	Registered June 5th Called to active duty	Jun 19, 1918 Jul 24, 1918

Name	Postoffice	Event	Issue Date
Samuel M. Stillwell		Registered #1771	Jul 18, 1917
Perley A. Stilwell	Ukiah	Delinquent questionaire	Nov 27, 1918
Robert Stilwell	Covelo	Called to active duty	Jun 12, 1918
Harold Harrison Stiter [probably Switzer]		Registered #961	Jul 18, 1917
Alex Stolpe		Registered #1769	Jul 18, 1917
Carl Stolpe		Registered #1767	Jul 18, 1917
William O. Stowe		Called to active duty	Oct 3, 1917
Charles Strait	Ukiah	Certified as fit	Aug 22, 1917
Edgar Ernest Strait	Potter Valley	Called to active duty Failed to report	Oct 3, 1917 Oct 10, 1917
Homer Strong	Fort Bragg	Registered #2262 Listed as a slacker	Jul 18, 1917 Mar 27, 1918
Hugo W. Strong	Elk	Certified as fit Called to active duty	Aug 22, 1917 Oct 3, 1917
William P. Struss [Struzz]	Hopland	Certified as fit Called to active duty	Aug 22, 1917 Oct 3, 1917
J.G. Struz	Hopland	Called to active duty	Apr 17, 1918
Alvin L. Studebaker	Fort Bragg	Registered June 5th	Jun 19, 1918
Irvin E. Studebaker	Philo	Certified as fit	Aug 22, 1917
Benjamin Stump	Comptche	Registered June 5th Called to active duty	Jun 19, 1918 Jul 24, 1918
Emil Stump	Comptche	Called to active duty	Jun 12, 1918
Alberto Suffregini	Irmulco	Called to active duty	Jun 12, 1918
Thomas Sullivan	Albion	Certified as fit	Aug 22, 1917
Arthur R. Sutherland	Albion	Registered June 5th	Jun 19, 1918
T.W. Sutherland		Called to active duty	Oct 3, 1917
Gerhard Svendsen	Ukiah	Called to active duty	Jun 12, 1918
John Sverko		Registered #2258	Jul 18, 1917
John Sverko		Registered #2261	Jul 18, 1917
Joseph Sverko		Registered #2257	Jul 18, 1917
Alfred Donald Swanson	Fort Bragg	Registered #84 Listed as a slacker Error by Draft Board	Jul 18, 1917 Mar 27, 1918 Apr 3, 1918
Walter Swanson	Fort Bragg	Registered #1636 Listed as a slacker Error by Draft Board Called for active duty	Jul 18, 1917 Mar 27, 1918 Apr 3, 1918 Apr 17, 1918
H.O. Sweeney	Potter Valley	Called to active duty	Apr 17, 1918
Archie Lee Sweetser		Registered #2131	Jul 18, 1917

Name	Postoffice	Event	Issue Date
Emery C. Sweetser	Mendocino	Certified as fit [died Sep 13, 1925] American Legion list	Aug 22, 1917 Sep 16, 1925 May 27, 1927
Harold Harrison Switzer	Fort Bragg	Certified as fit	Aug 22, 1917
Frank Symns	Willits	Certified as fit	Aug 22, 1917
Frank C. Taboas	Ukiah	Draft No.169	Nov 13, 1918
Jesse James Tallman		Registered #955	Jul 18, 1917
Kiriatos Taramontanas	Lodi	Called to active duty Failed to report	Oct 3, 1917 Oct 10, 1917
C.P. Taylor	Willits	Certified as fit	Aug 22, 1917
Nat Milton Taylor	San Francisco	Registered June 5th	Jun 19, 1918
Wharton Shields Taylor		Registered #2229 319th Engineers	Jul 18, 1917 Jul 10, 1918
Guido Tazzari		Registered #1678	Jul 18, 1917
Frank R. Tenny	Willits	Delinquent questionaire	Oct 23, 1918
John S. Terin	Los Angeles	Registered June 5th	Jun 19, 1918
A. Thompson	Covelo	Called to active duty	Jun 12, 1918
Thomas Ernest Thompson	Fort Bragg	Registered #87 Listed as a slacker	Jul 18, 1917 Mar 27, 1918
John Clayton Larkin Thorn		Registered #1629	Jul 18, 1917
Albert Ross Thornton		Registered #1630	Jul 18, 1917
Philip George Timerman		Registered #956	Jul 18, 1917
P. Tomagno	Mendocino	Called to active duty	Dec 5, 1917
John Tomelo	Albion	Listed as a slacker Called to active duty	Mar 27, 1918 Jul 24, 1918
Domenico Tonelli [Domenoico]	Albion	Listed as a slacker Called to active duty	Mar 27, 1918 Apr 17, 1918
Giovanni Tonelli	Santa Rosa	Called to active duty	Apr 24, 1918
Zuong Tong		Registered #1627	Jul 18, 1917
Urban Tooley	Albion	Delinquent questionaire	Nov 27, 1918
Guy Raymond Torrence		Registered #2230	Jul 18, 1917
Giuseppe Tosana		Registered #2252	Jul 18, 1917
L. Tracey		Called to active duty	Oct 3, 1917
G.T. Tracy	Covelo	Called to active duty	Jun 12, 1918
Clemento Trinzoni	Mendocino	Registered June 5th	Jun 19, 1918
Louis Tumontassi	Sherwood	Delinquent questionaire	Oct 23, 1918
Mate Tumpich		Registered #1773	Jul 18, 1917
Waino Richard Tura [W.C. Tura]	Fort Bragg	Registered #86 Called in active duty Reported for duty	Jul 18, 1917 Oct 3, 1917 Oct 10, 1917

MENDOCINO COUNTY MEN IN WORLD WAR I

Name	Postoffice	Event	Issue Date
Irving G. Utschig	Fort Bragg	Registered June 5th	Jun 19, 1918
Antonio Valadoa	Caspar	Called to active duty	Apr 17, 1918
Albert Valentine	Ukiah	Certified as fit	Aug 22, 1917
Raymond Van Bebber	Willits	Certified as fit Draft No.33	Nov 6, 1918 Nov 13, 1918
T.J. Van Bebber	Potter Valley	Called to active duty	Jun 12, 1918
W.H. Van Bebber	Willits	Certified as fit	Aug 22, 1917
Fred Van Dyke	Ukiah	Registered June 5th	Jun 19, 1918
Chester C. Van Egidy [Von Egily]	Fort Bragg	Registered #1696 Called to active duty	Jul 18, 1917 Jun 12, 1918
Dianizio Vannetti		Registered #2249	Jul 18, 1917
E.D. Vassar	Hopland	Certified as fit	Aug 22, 1917
William D. Vaughn	Mendocino	Certified as fit **Active duty-Sep.1917**	Aug 22, 1917
Frederick Ludwick Viemann		Registered #954	Jul 18, 1917
Manuel Vierra	Fort Bragg	Registered #2250 Called to active duty	Jul 18, 1917 Apr 24, 1918
Antonio Visini	Sherwood	Called to active duty	Apr 17, 1918
Ezio Vittolini	Albion	Listed as a slacker	Mar 27, 1918
Vincent Viviani	Elk	Called to active duty	Jun 12, 1918
Philip Vogel		Registered #1625	Jul 18, 1917
Harold Erick Von Krusze (Von Kruze)	Ukiah	Registered June 5th Called to active duty	Jun 19, 1918 Jul 24, 1918
Herman Vosbrink		Registered #2008	Jul 18, 1917
Charles Robert Waara		Registered #1358	Jul 18, 1917
Eddie Oscar Waara	Fort Bragg	Registered #2247 Certified as fit	Jul 18, 1917 Aug 22, 1917
W. Wagner	Covelo	Certified as fit	Aug 22, 1917
Jeow You Wah		Registered #2126	Jul 18, 1917
Karl Hjalmar Waino		Registered #990	Jul 18, 1917
Thorn Waldsen	Elk	Delinquent questionaire	Oct 23, 1918
Raymond H. Walker	Willits	Called to active duty	Jun 12, 1918
William Earle Wallace		Registered #2122	Jul 18, 1917
Roy Wessley Wallger		Registered #952	Jul 18, 1917
Eino Wallonius		Registered #1774	Jul 18, 1917
Walter Walsky		Registered #2124	Jul 18, 1917
Raymond Walters	Fort Bragg	Registered June 5th	Jun 19, 1918
Ernest Ward	Covelo	Certified as fit	Aug 22, 1917

Name	Postoffice	Event	Issue Date
Raleigh J.Ward	Covelo	Certified as fit Draft No.92	Nov 6, 1918 Nov 13, 1918
Raymond E.Ware	Fort Bragg	Registered June 5th	Jun 19, 1918
John Warre	Albion	Called to active duty Failed to report	Oct 3, 1917 Oct 10, 1917
Samuel Warren	Ukiah	Called to active duty Failed to report	Oct 3, 1917 Oct 10, 1917
Gust Weed	Fort Bragg	Registered #1775 Listed as a slacker Called to active duty	Jul 18, 1917 Mar 27, 1918 Jul 3, 1918
Leyland P.Weir		Called to active duty	Oct 3, 1917
Walter Howard Weisse		Registered #88	Jul 18, 1917
Elisha B.Weller	Ukiah	Died of disease	Dec 4, 1918
T.O.Weller	Ukiah	Certified as fit	Aug 22, 1917
Sam J.Wellman	Ukiah	Certified as fit	Aug 22, 1917
Roy Elsworth Wells		Registered #2123	Jul 18, 1917
Walter R.West	Dos Rios	Called to active duty	Apr 17, 1918
C.A.Westerberg	Noyo	Called to active duty	Jun 12, 1918
Fred J.Westfall	Laytonville	Called to active duty	Jun 12, 1918
James A.Wheeler	Northspur	Certified as fit Called to active duty	Aug 22, 1917 Oct 3, 1917
Alfred White	Laytonville	Delinquent questionaire	Nov 27, 1918
Edward B.White	Ukiah	Certified as fit	Aug 22, 1917
Ermin Ulmer White		Registered #953	Jul 18, 1917
Lewis B.White	Ukiah	Killed in action	Dec 4, 1918
Robert White	Laytonville	Certified as fit Called to active duty	Aug 22, 1917 Jun 12, 1918
W.F.Whitney	Willits	Certified as fit Draft No.59	Nov 6, 1918 Nov 13, 1918
William C.Whittaker Jr.	Willits	Certified as fit	Aug 22, 1917
Hannes Wikeli		Registered #2248	Jul 18, 1917
Howard F.Wilkinson	Willits	Registered June 5th	Jun 19, 1918
Alfred Williams	Ukiah	Listed as a slacker	Nov 27, 1918
J.R.Williams	Potter Valley	Certified as fit Called to active duty	Aug 22, 1917 Oct 3, 1918
John Isaac Williams		Registered #2246	Jul 18, 1917
Earl L.Willis		Called to active duty	Oct 3, 1917
J.M.Wilsey	Covelo	Certified as fit	Aug 22, 1917
Perle Wilsey	Comptche	Called to active duty	Jun 12, 1918
Frank Edwin Wilson		Registered #2121	Jul 18, 1917

Name	Postoffice	Event	Issue Date
John William Wilson		Registered #991	Jul 18, 1917
Richard W. Wilson	Willits	Delinquent questionaire	Oct 23, 1918
Francis W. Windlinx		Registered #89	Jul 18, 1917
Ralph Witherell	Boonville	Certified as fit Draft No. 94	Nov 6, 1918 Nov 13, 1918
Thomas C. Witherell	Boonville	Certified as fit	Aug 22, 1917
A.R. Wonacott		Called to active duty	Oct 3, 1917
William Wright	Ukiah	Died of wounds	Dec 4, 1918
Arvid Wuoltoenaho		Registered #2125	Jul 18, 1917
Ah Yew	Elk	Registered June 5th	Jun 19, 1918
T. Yokum	Willits	Certified as fit	Aug 22, 1917
Charles H. York	Caspar	Certified as fit Draft No. 68	Nov 6, 1918 Nov 13, 1918
Mark D. York	Calpella	Called to active duty	Jun 12, 1918
Lee Young	Albion	Delinquent questionaire	Oct 23, 1918
William McKinley Young	Hopland	Registered June 5th	Jun 19, 1918
Wo Jung Yuen		Registered #2120	Jul 18, 1917
Paola Zaina	Sherwood	Certified as fit Called to active duty	Aug 22, 1917 Oct 3, 1917
Augustino Zani	Fort Bragg	Registered #1622 Called to active duty Reported for duty	Jul 18, 1917 Oct 3, 1917 Oct 10, 1917
Francisco Zatti	Comptche	Delinquent questionaire	Oct 23, 1918
Felix Zermoski		Registered #1621	Jul 18, 1917
Henry Phillip Zill		Registered #2244	Jul 18, 1917
Joseph Zinach		Registered #1623	Jul 18, 1917

ROLL OF THE DEAD

From the *FORT BRAGG ADVOCATE AND NEWS* of May 27, 1927.

AMERICAN LEGION POST

Walter <u>Burr</u>

James <u>Camata</u>

Douglas <u>Davis</u>

William <u>Davis</u>

Laton V.<u>Duffy</u>

William Albert <u>Elmslie</u>

John <u>Figaro</u>

Ernest Demill <u>Fitch</u>

George Albert <u>Fitch</u>

Philip R.<u>Gorman</u>

Andrew <u>Hendrickson</u>

Clarence <u>Johnson</u>

Henry Edward <u>Johnson</u>

Wallace R.<u>Johnson</u>

Roy E.<u>Lawson</u>

John R.<u>Long</u>

Antone <u>Lopps</u>

Clarence W.<u>Manchester</u>

Joseph Frances <u>Nichols</u>

Fred <u>Nybeck</u>

Swanti <u>Olson</u>

George Harold <u>Porterfield</u>

James W.<u>Pritchard</u>

Robert Arthur <u>Sallinen</u>

Johnnie <u>Simmons</u>

Emery <u>Sweetser</u>

A

BEAL, Albert 61 Amy 217 Charles 61
    Edward 61 Harold 61 J H 61 Mrs J H
    61 Leslie 61 Nicey Ann 185
BEALE, Amy 217
BEAMER Mrs 136 Roy Lee 245
BEAN, Carl 61 Charles C 182
    Don Carlos 245 George 61 Lester
    Clarence 182 Louisa Maye 61
    Luther 3 Martha A 219
BEANE, Walter 3 H H 61 Mrs Ida 61
BEASLEY, Ira 3
BEATTIE, Carl 3 E H 61 Edward 61
    Grace 226 Karl S 61 Thomas F 61
    Mrs Thomas F 61
BEAVER, Anna 87 Oakley 182
BECHTOL, F L 3
BECK, Chris 61 Christopher Jr 61
    Ed 3 Emma 62 Mrs Henry 61 M S 182
BECKLAND, Adolph 245
BECKLEY, C J (Mrs) 115
BECKMAN, Mrs Ethel 235
BEEBE, Napoleon 62 T 3 William 3
BEECHER, Milton E 182
BEEF, C 3
BEEKLEY, Frieda 117 209
BEGGS, Mrs Florence 111 Thomas H 62
BEGLEY, Harry 245 Hazel L 188 Mabel A
    216 Pearl 229
BELKNAP, E S 62   Roy Stanley 62
BELL, Betty 184 Elsie M 224 Harry 3
    182 John 245 Mrs K 184 Leta M 184
BELLAH, Mrs Nancy Ann 62
BELLUMOMINO, L 182
BELLUMONI, G 182
BELTRANNI, Pete 62
BENDETTI, A 3 P 3
BENEDETTI 3 Alfred 182 Dante 182
    Gino 246
BENEDITH, Laerto 245
BENNETT, E G 246 Grant 182 Joe 62
    W H 182 William 62
BENNINA, William C 246
BENNING, Beauford Jay 246
BENOIT, J L 3
BENTON, C B 4
BENZ 4 W F 4
BERCHTOLD, Eliza 229
BERG, Erick 183
BERGAMINI, Michaele 246
BERGER, Mrs Hattie 62
BERGERSON, Louis 62 William 62 183
BERKE, Edward 62 Mrs Hattie Noble 62
BERKOVITS, Archie R 183 246 Arwa R
    246 Edna 214 Frank H 246 Franz
    Herman 246 Herman 62
BERKYACA, John 62
BERNARDENI, Ottavio 183
BERNARDINI, Lodorico 183 Lodovico 246
BERNSTEIN, Mrs Ida 62
BERRATTINI, Ovidio 246
BERRINGER, P 4 Perley 4 Simon 63
BERRY 63 C L 136 Cora E 199
    Grandma 63 J C 4 J E 63 Ruby L 240
    Susie 220
BERRYHILL, Archie T 63 183
    Blanche 225 Elmer M 63 Frank D 63
BERRYHILL (Continued)
    George 4 63 George H 63 Gladys H 63
    Grover C 183 Hazel E 63 Joseph T 63
    Margerite 63 May 225 Melvin 63
    Myrtle A 63 Pearl O 63 Rhoda Irene
    212 Ruth M 63
BERSTEN, B 63
BERTILINI, John 246
BERTINI, Angelina 192 Otto 4
    Ulissme 63
BERTOLA, Mrs Angelina 63
BERTOLLI, Pietro 246

BERTOLINI, John 183
BERTRAND, J S 183
BERTSCH, Lester Jacob 183 246
BETENCURTO, Joas Maniz 246
BETTANCURTO, Joas Maniz 246
BETTENCOURT, William 246
BETTIGA, Giuseppe 246
BETTS, Edith 216 Edward 63 Ethel 194
    Harry 63 246 J F 183 May 63 Minnie
    63 Ross 63
BETZ, Fred 63 I 63 Saide 127
BEUNAIDINI, Ottavio 246
BEVANS, Florence 105 Joseph 105
BEVER, Ben 63 Benjamin 63 64 Charles
    Albert 63 155 183 Ellen 122 Ida 155
    Mrs Mary 63 Napoleon B 63 Robert 63
    Samuel 63 64 155 Thomas 63 64
BIAGGI, Emma 70 187 J R 183 James 70
    James Jr 4 183 Jennie 210 John 246
BIAGINI, Giuseppe 246
BIANCHI, Ambragio 246
BIANCHINI, Orlando G 246
BIBBY, Samuel 183
BICKFORD, David 64 George 64
BIDDINGS, Mildred F 225
BIEBER, Mrs Pauline 64
BIGELOW, Mrs Edith 129 Garret A 183
    G A 4
BIGGAR, Arthur W 64 George Milton 64
    William J 64 William James 64
BIGGERS, A W 64 Charles 64 Mrs W J 64
BIGGS, Charles 64
BIGIOOLI, John 183
BIGLOW, Arthur B 64
BILLINGS, Edward 64 Mrs Polly 64
BILLODEAU, Louis 64
BILLS, J W 4 183 Mary E 188
BILNDE, Henrietta 195
BILO, Mrs John 89
BINKLEY, Fred 64 Grover C 183
BINNER, Katy May 238
BIRDERMAN, A D 199
BISHOP, A 4 Alfred 183 Anna Maria 18
    Austin 4 B 246 Mrs B 122 C 4
    Charles 64 Chester E 4 183
    Mrs Delia 227 Della Grace 191 E 4
    Earl 183 Ed 4 Edward 97 Edwin Carl
    184 246 Ernest E 184 Fred 4 97 184
    Harry 64 Herbert 4 Mrs Howard 106
    John 64 Joseph 219 Mrs Joseph 161
    Leona 200 Leslie 184 Mary A 191
    Maybelle 109 Medora 156 Minnie 219
    Noble M 184 Perry 4
BISKOP, Mary 18
BITHER 4 Mrs Clara Isbelle 64 L H 64
BITTENBENDER, Dwain 4
BJARKAS, Charles 184
BJARKHOLM, August Werner 246
BJELOBRK, Bozo 246
BJORK, Regina 234 Selma 207
BJORKAS, Carl 4 246
BLACK, Anton P 184 William James 246
BLACKLEDGE 5
BLACKLY, Freeman Jasper 246
BLACKMAN, Daniel 65
BLACKWELL, Vivian 205
BLAIR, Austin 65 Jennie M 65 Lena 125
    Rufus C 65 Samuel 65 Mrs Samuel 65
    William J 65 William S 65
BLAKE, Carrie Horton 127 Ethel 215
    Mrs Martha 65
BLAKELY, Clarence 65 Freeman 5 65 184
BLAKESLEY, Charles 65
BLALOCK, Z V 65
BLANK, Edith T 65
BLAYLOCK, Marvin E 247
BLEAKELY, Freeman 184
BLEY, Oscar C 184

BLOCK, George 65 170 Henry 65
BLOCKSON, Lillian 202
BLOOM, Edward Charles 247
BLOSSER, Fred 65 Hazel 65 Hazel
    Minnie 216 Mrs J T 65 John 184
    John Adam 65 May Pearl 229
    Nicholas J 65 Mrs Ora 216 Roy 5 65
    184 Tobias 65
BLUME, Albert 184 Edith 219
BLUNCK, John 65
BODINE, Mrs Emma 65
BODY, Mrs Tillie Carmichael 209
BOGGS, Winnis 247
BOGNI, Rosi 221
BOHN, Mrs Aileen 66 Christine 203
    Frank L 203 Mrs R 92 Mrs Richard 73
    Richard Edward 247
BOLDEN, Harold Thomas 247 T R 5
BOLDI, Allesio 247
BOLES, Mrs E E 66
BOLSON, John 66 75 124
BON, Hong 247
BONAMICI, Mrs M 66
BONANETTI, Giuseppe 247
BOND, Mrs Irene 105
BONEE, Elmer G 66 Wiilliam 66
BONESTEEL, Q A 66
BONETTO, Giacomo 247
BONI, Ben 5
BONINI, O 5
BONNIFIELD, Alvin R 247
BONOMINO, Mario 66
BONZANI, Eugenio 66
BOOG, Bessie C 207
BOON, Mrs A L 181
BOOS, Victor 66
BORDEN, Arthur D 184
BORECA, Laura R 223 Manuel 223
BORELK, Gugilo 66
BORGES, Mrs Mabel 130
    Mabel Stoddard 230
BORGNA, Ernest 66 Joe 66 Joseph 66
BORNEMAN, A 184 Mrs A 66
BORTOLOMEI, Anastasia 5 66 Mrs N 66
    Roberto 5 66
BOSCACCI, Emico 66
BOSCHI, Adamo 247
BOSETON, Henry 184
BOSITOS, Annie 183
BOTA, F 184
BOTAR, Antonio Goncalves 247
BOTKIN, W P 181
BOULEN, Mrs Newni 68
BOULTON, Nellie Christine 183
BOUNDEY, Edwin J 184 Elwin J 184
BOUDREAUX, F J 193 Louise 193
BOURNE, Chester 5
BOURNS Mrs 148 T L 184 Thomas 184
BOUTON, Ed 184 Mrs Ed 91 William
    Carlton 184
BOWDEN, B J 184 Eva 184 Irving 184
BOWEN, Arthur R 184 Ester 209
    Mrs Henry 161 Lillie S 66 Minnie 66
    Nellie 186 Viola P 194 W 66
    William M 66
BOWER, Edwin 5
BOWERS, John P 67
BOWLES, Atley 5 Mrs G R 67
    Mrs Louise 175
BOWMAN, Amelia 199 B 5 Bert 184
    Carrie 211 E B 67 F M 67
    Florence 222 Frank 167 Henry 185
    J L 185 James 5 Mrs Lena 112
    Perry F 247

BOYD, Adolphus O 247 Alexander
    William 67 164 Mrs Bertha 155
    Elizabeth 203 George 67 Mrs George
    67 Helen 181 Helen Dott 199 J D 185
    O 185
BOYES, John 247
BOYLE, Clifford Lloyd 247
    Mrs Mary 116
BOYS, Marie 198
BOZANI, Antone 6
BOZIADH, Antoine 67
BOZIAH, Antoine 67
BOZICEVIC, Ana 213
BOZIECH, John 247
BRACE, W A 67
BRADEN, H B 185 Harry 67 Mrs Harry 67
    J H 67
BRADLEY, Mrs Bertram 67 Fred 5 Paul 5
    Quin 185 Roy Hudson 185 W P 185
    Will 97
BRADY, Filix 67 Leonard C 67 Levi 67
    Michael 67 Roy A 67 185 Stanly T 67
    Walter G 67
BRAJKOVISH, Mate 247
BRANCHINI, Aquililo 247 Carlo 247
    Joe 247
BRANDON, Dave 185 Mrs Dave 85 Leo 185
    247
BRANDSTROM, Andrew A 247
BRANDT, A E 67 C B 67 G W 67
    Mrs G W 67 Henry 67 R P 67 WM 67
BRANDON, Leo 5 L 5
BRANSCOMB, Arthur 5 67 Benjamin 68
    Mrs Jane 68 Mrs L 125
BRANT, LeRoy Verne 185 247
BRAUDWELL, William 68
BRAYTON, Mrs B C 67 Haidee L 236
    Jesse M 185
BRAZILL, William 247
BREDEHOFT, H W 247
BREE, Eva 183
BREEN, Charles J 185 F A 247
    Patrick 68 Teresa 229
BRENDEN, Herbert 68
BRENER, Johann F G 247
BRENNER, Charles 68 Tom 68
BRETT, Ivah 201 James 201 Maggie 77
BREWER, Mrs C 68 C C 68 S 68 W E 185
    Mrs W E 68
BRIDGEFORD, Mrs Edith 158
BRIEN, Albert 5 68 Charles 78
    Elizabeth 78 J Albert 185
    John 68 78
BRIGDEN, Anita 183
BRIGGS, Chester 5 185 Elizabeth
    Potter 68 George 247 Jennie 127
    Kit 247 L C 185 Peter C 68
    Walter N 185
BRIGHTENSTINE, Daisy Hazel 226
    Ethel Gladys 239
BRINES, James Madison 185
BRINK, C 6
BRINKMAN, Walter P 185
BRINKS, Harry 82
BRINZING, Bertha 138 Bertha S 220
    Mrs Margaret J 68 Martin L 185
BRIONES, Mrs J R 162 Pearl 207
BRITTON, Ella 27 Joseph J 68
BROBACK, Mrs C W 81 Charles 68
    Charles Jr 68 Mrs Charles 68
    Clarence 6 68 G W 68 Walter 68
BROCHIER, Alden 69 Darville 185
    Indiana Darville 185 Mrs Nicey 61
BROCK, Henry 6 69 Mrs William 69
BRODERICK, A 69
BRONKINI, Henry 69
BRONNENBERG, Ernest 69 Mrs Lettie
    Wilson 69

BROO, Harry 186
BROOKS 69 A C 6 C 186 Claude 186
 Clyde 6 George Ervine 247 John S 69
 M E 186 Mamie 235 Maude R 217
 Nevada 230
BROUGHTON, Wilbur 247
BROVELLI, Henry 186 Maria 222
 Vergilio 69
BROWER, Con 69 E P 185 Hirschel 69
 Mabel Jane 202
BROWN, Rev A 186 A M 6 Albert 186
 Allie 186 Annie L 234 Arthur 69
 Dr Artie 94 Austin H 69 186
 Berneice E 82 192 Blevins M 69
 Charles 6 69 186 Charles James
 Brown 248 Charlie Arthur Brown 248
 Dan 69 Eleanor 223 Mrs Ella
 Bartlett 69 Mrs Ellen 69 70 Elsie
 94 Elsie I 182 Elsie V 193 Emma G
 237 Eugene A 186 Eugene McKinley
 248 Francis Martin 222 248 Frank 69
 George 186 Georgia 223 H A 186
 Henry 82 192 Henry H 186 Herbert 6
 186 Howard 6 Howard G 186 Hubert F
 69 Irma 215 J H 248 Mrs J L 214
 Mrs J Q 70 J McAllen 6 James 6 69
 70 John 70 169 John M 186 Joseph A
 186 Joseph E 69 Justin Kent 248
 L W 248 Leslie A 186 Lew 70 Madge
 204 Maria 187 Marie 7 Mrs Maude 171
 Mary 183 May 182 Mayme 70 Olive 186
 R L 6 Richard 70 Susan Agnes 70 W J
 248 W W 104 Walter 186 187 William
 64 William M 70 Wilson J 186
BROWNE, Mrs Evelyn 152
BROWNELL, A E 70
BRUBECK, Philip W 248
BRUCKRIDGE 6 Bert 6
BRUEHL, Henry 70
BRUMAN, Erick 70 Henry 70 Victor 70
BRUNGES, Mrs Helena Schneider 70
 John 70
BRUNK, R O 186
BRUNNER, Lena 221
BRUSA, Albert 248 Johanna 222
BRUSH, Den 6 Henry 6 Henry C S 186
 I 6 Jennie 212 Martin A 248
 Mrs Nelson 70
BRYANT, Agnes 232 E G 186
BUCCHEONI, Victor 6
BUCCHIANI, Virgileo 248
BUCCHIONI, Virgilio 187
BUCHANAN, C J 162 Cole Jr 187 Colin J
 70 Donald 70 Edward 70 Flora 162
 Frances 70 Frank 187 Mrs Frank 70
 Hugh 162 Mrs Hugh 85 Mrs Mary
 McMaster 70 Nellie 161 Willie 70
BUCHINI, Pete 248
BUCHOLTZ, Alex 70 F Oscar 71
BUCHOLZ, Mrs J B 115
BUCK, Andrew 248 Edna 207
BUCKBEE, John 187 John Sampson 248
 Viola 123
BUCKLEY, D J 71
BUCKMAN, J R 71 John 71 Robert
 Harold 248
BUCKNELL, H 6 Nellie 71
BUDD, E R 74
BUEHL, Gertrude 230
BULEN, Pearl 224
BULL, F C 6 Mrs Ned 154
BULLARD, Roy A 248 Mrs Tom 71
BULLIS, J W 6
BULLOCK, Grace 190
BUNCH, Mrs Edna 193 George R 187 248
 Hattie 236
BUNKER, Blanche 199 J L 248
BUNTON, Fred H 248

BURBECK, August 187
BURBEK, Andrew 71
BURG, Erick 183
BURGE, Wilma 223
BURGER Mrs 71 H E 187 William
 George 248
BURGESS, C F 71
Burgess, John 71
BURGETT, Mrs J 107
BURK, Neil 71
BURKE, E J 187 Jack 71 James G 248
 John Axel 248 Lillian 198 Nellie
 198 W A 6 W C 7 Walter E 187
 William 7 Mrs William 84
BURKHART, George 248
BURKHARDT, Mrs Alvina 71 Bessie 213
 M V 71
BURLINGAME, Bruce Leroy 187
BURLINGAME, Homer S 71
BURMAN, John T 248
BURMEISTER, F C 71
BURNES, Mrs J 208 Myrtle Therese 187
BURNESS, Jennie 92 John 92 Marion 16
BURNETT, Ed 71 J O 7
BURNHAM, Christine 238 Elizabeth 210
 Joseph 71
BURNIE 71 Thomas 248
BURNMAN, Joseph 71
BURNS 7 Carrie B 72 Chris 7 72
 Elizabeth 198
BURNSTEIN, William 187
BURR, Elsie Susan 187 J L 7 Mrs J L 7
 L 7 Leslie 187 Walter L 248 282
BURRIS, Gladys C 204 Herbert 248
 Mrs L W 127
BURROUGH, Mrs D D 218
BURROUGHS, Mrs Mary A 72
BURROWS, Myrtle P 238
BURT, Anna 72 J A 72
BURTON, Andrew 72 John 7
BUSCH, Bessie Marie 224 Ed 7 Helen W
 214 J G 72
BUSH, Bertha B 196 David 7 Edward 187
BUSS, Marie 190
BUTIN, Joan S 248
BUTLER, Harry Gerald 187 Jane 63
 John F 187
BUTTON, Ella 233 H H 161
BUTTS, Earl Frazier 187 Frank W 249
 W M 7 Walter D 187
BUZDON, Mrs Mary 72
BYERS, Harry 7
BYRNE, Chester 7 Chester P 187
 Mrs Fred 72 G 7 James 72 Moore 72
BYRNER, Walter 72
BYRNES, Mrs Ben 135 Jack 7 John 72
 John P 187 Ralph 7
BYRON, Mrs Alice 72 Mrs Alice M 77
 C A 72 J H 72

C

CABASSI, James 249 Stefano 249
CABLE 7
CAHILL, Daisy Margaret 231
CAIN, David F 72
CALDWELL, Dr C B 187 Nina 180
 Richard 7 187 Robert E 249
 Mrs W 154
CALL, Derunda 72 Melville 72
CALLAHAN, Patrick 72
CALLI, Andrew Johnnie 249 J 7
CALLIERENA, Maryan F 179
CALLINA, G 249
CAMATA, James 249 282

CAMERON, A 7 200 Alex 73 Archie 8 73
187 Mrs Archie 94 Archie Jr 7
Duncan 73 Edwin F 73 Edwin H 73
George 73 Mrs George A 82 Guy O 73
John 73 Margaret 200 Mrs Margaret
73 Nellie 42 229 Rod 8 Roderick 73
Roderick 73 187 William 187 William
Archibald 249
CAMMERS, Alex 188
CAMPBELL 8 C W 73 Charles 249
Dewey 249 F McLain 8 Fernando 249
Flora 73 Frank McLean 249 Fred 8
Joseph G 73 Mrs L 129 Mrs M 109
Martin 249 S B 8 Sam 73
CAMPI, Matti Alfred Ahven 249
CANADA, Magarette 183 W C 73
CANCLINE, Nicola 249
CANCLINI, Anthony 249
CANN, Hilda 214
CANNARR, Robert 188
CANNON, Nola 213 Sopie 219
CANTIERI, Guilo 188
CAPELL, Charles 73 Estell 73
CAPPELETI, L 249
CARAWAY, James 73 Lolita J 219
CARBONI, Frank 188
CARD, Minnie 230
CARDINOTTI, Raffaello 249
CARDWELL, Thomas D 188
CAREY, Jerome C 249 John 73
John D 188 Margaret 200 Mary D 73
Maurice R 8 188 Romie 188 S F 8
Theresa 222 W F 188
CARLESON, John 73
CARLI, Hugo 249
CARLISLE, Robert J 18 Mrs Nellie 198
CARLSON, Agnes 73 Alex 73 74 249 Alma
198 Charles 188 Charles R 188 Earl
Charles 249 Edward 73 Emil 188
Mrs Emil 73 Fred 74 Fred Leander
249 Glenn 73 J E 137 John Edward 74
John Erick 74 Iver 249 Karie 137
Lucien 73 Mrs Lucy 73 Mable 220 R 8
Ray 73 Thomas 188 Thomas Henry 249
Victor 74 William 8 74 188
Mrs William 188
CARLSTON, Joseph F 108
CARMAN, E P 188
CARMICHAEL, Bert 8 Ethel 74 Mrs James
73 Mrs Luella 227 Thomas 8
CARNER, B 8 Elmer 8 James 74
Mabel 186
CAROLINA, Barunzion 214
CAROTHERS, T L 74 William D 188
CARPENTER 74 A O 74 Aurelius 74
B L 188 Mrs B L 74 Mrs Helen M 74
Mrs J J 168 W A 8
CARR, Herbert 8 Herbert W 188
CARRANZA, Lupie 74
CARRICK, William 74
CARRETO, Leonardo 74
CARROLL, Charles A 77
CARSON, Belle 210 Milton 210
CARTER, Alberta Ozetta (Mrs) 75
Buck 8 Eugene F 249 Florence 223
George A 188 Harry H 249 Mrs Nellie
116 R H 8 W H 188 W T 188
William 8
CARVER, Emma J 239 Neal J 188
CARY, Mrs Tolman E 75
CASANEGA, Clara 196
CASE Dr 225 E G 75 Effie 225 Hallie
188 James 75 Mrs Marie 197
Mary F 180
CASELLI, D 66 75 124
CASEY, C L 75 Matt 9
CASK, Frank 75
CASSADE, Almira 218 L 75

CASSAOURI, Leon A 188
CASSEL, S J 188
CASSIDY, Peter 75
CASTHOUX, Felix 189
CASTILLO, Rose 198
CASTNER, Mrs Ellis 85
CASTOR, Walter Henry 249
CATANARI, Ngo Guillo P 249
CATANINCH, J 189
CATELONI, Achille 249
CATER, Grant 249
CATHERENA, Maryan 221
CATHERINA, Joe 189
CATLANI, Achille 249
CATTINI, Attilio 250
CAUGHEY, Charlie 75 Dot 75 Mrs Ellen
75 F L 75 Lavinia 75 Robert 75
William 75
CAUGHLIN, Michael 250
CAVACO, Frank 250
CAVALLINI, Rosa 221
CAVANAGH, Charles Clinton 250 Ed 9
Edward 75 Elizabeth 75 Mrs Ellen 75
Nettie A 208 Mrs Sarah 75
Thomas E 75
CAVE, Albert 75
CEDARQUIST, J A 9
CELERI, Silva 76
CERNIA, George 191
CERRETINI, A 189
CERRUTI, E D 189
CHAFFIN, James 189
CHAHON, C 250
CHALFANT, Alice 179
CHALLMAN, Arthur W 250
CHALMERS, E W 9 189 James L 250
John L 250
CHAMBERLAIN, A B 189 Dr George 221
CHAMBERS, Gladys 76 Hadley 76
John A 76 Mrs John A 76 John Hadley
189 Hadley 9 Laing 76
CHANDLER, Francis 9 Frank H 250 H D 9
W R 9 Mrs William R 76
CHAPIN, Clarence 189 H C 9
CHAPLIN Mrs 56
CHAPMAN, Herbert R 250 Mrs J T 76
Mrs Mary 76 Mary Madalene 219
Oliver L 76 Ruth 240 Viola
Elizabeth 228 Rev W A 76 189
Mrs W A 76 140 William Floyd 189
CHAPRALIS, George 76
CHARLTON, Mrs Thomas 76
CHARMAN, Norman R 189
CHARRON, Ida 205 Mrs J E 205
CHASE, Mary 108 Samuel 9
William S 250
CHEAL, Dr Thomas A 9 189
Mrs Thomas A 172
CHESTER, Charley 189 Theodore 9 76
CHICCHI, Roberto 250
CHILDERS, Nathan B 76
CHILLSON, D W 76 Mrs O A 76
CHIN, Lee 76 Quong 250
CHISHOLM, Alexie D 211 William 189
CHONG, Lum 250
CHRISTENSEN, Charles 76 Elsie 227
CHRISTIAN, Harry G 250 Harry H 189
CHRISTIANI, Mike 9
CHRISTIANSON, H G C 189 Henry A 250
CHRISTINA, Elsie Josephine 212
CHRISTY, Henry A 250 Myren A 9 189
CHUBB, Grace 198
CHUNG, Wong 250
CHURCH, V 9
CHUTE, Mrs Lydia A 76
CIAMBELLI, Pietro 76
CIAPUSCI, Florence 183

CIAPUSCIA, A 234 Louise 234
CIANCIO, Charles 9
CINCHES, John 76
CIOLINA, Battista 250
CITTONI 9
CLARK 76 A H 9 Charles B 77 E A 189
    Edward 189 Elizabeth Reed 77 Ella
    Brown 181 Ernest 189 Ethan 189
    Frank 9 J J 77 Mrs J L 113 L S 9
    Leonora E 241 Norris Alkire 250 Mrs
    Oleva 71 Russell Allens 250 Scott 9
    W H 10 W M 10 William 77 189
CLATTS, Frank 189
CLAWSON, Lelia T 232
CLAY, Albert 190 Charles 161 Frank
    Leslie 250 Harris 161 Henry 77
    Dr Louis 161 Sarah Charity 161
    Standley 250 W H 161
CLAYTON, Beatrice 185 George 77
CLELAND, B L 173 J M 173 Mary L 173
    T M 173
CLELLAND, Mrs H J 77 Dr H O 190
    T L 190
CLEMENT, Mrs C J 77 George 77
CLEMENTE, Mrs Marie E 229
CLENDENNIN, Orpha Pearl 224
CLEVELAND, Mrs Ann Howard 77 Grover
    190 James 190 Mrs M M 107 Meda 231
    Oliver 77
CLIFTON, Alma N 239 Edward 77
    Nellie M 208
CLINTON, Michael 77
CLOSE, Mrs Fred 174
CLOW, Ethel Beatrice 187 Myrtle C 222
    Stella Beaver 87 W A 10
CLOYD, Frank M 190
CLYMA, Lester 10
CLYME, Mr W L 140
COATES Mrs 77
COBB, John 77
COCKRILL, Ernest J 250
CODIROLI, Emilio 250
COELHO, Francisco Rodrisgues 250
COFFEE, Hiram Gladstone 250
COFFER, J W 77
COHARD, Oscar 190
COHEN, Goldie E 231
COKE, Hugh M 77
COLBERG, Adolph Berton 250
    Burger Nathaniel 77
COLBERT, Mary 191
COLBURN, Horations 77 LeRoy Harrison
    250 J F 77 Joe 77 R L 77 Roy 190
    S B 77 W A 10 77 Mrs W A 77
COLBY, P 10 Percy 10
COLE, Cyrus Joseph 10 190 Lloyd M 250
    Loyde Nelson 250 Sarah 231 W T 78
COLEMAN, Ludwig 190
COLI Mrs 78
COLIJA, August 250
COLKHOUN, Mary 84 193
COLLBROUGH, Mrs M 78
COLLI, C 250 J 10
COLLIER, Howard 78
COLLINS, Mrs T 54
COMAITA, Pietro 250
COMANITA, Jim 251
COMPTON, Amzi K 190 E S 10
COMUITA, Jim 251
CONDON, T 190
CONGER, Sarah M 192
CONKEY, Dave 78 W 10
CONNAUGHTON, Michael 78
CONNER, Ida 224 Leslie A 251
CONNICK, Laurel 241
CONNOLLY, Mrs P 109
CONNOR, Henrietta 235 Verna May 203
    W R 10

CONOLY, Tom 78
CONRAD (Grandma) 78 George 60
CONSTANTI, Antonio 251
CONWAY, Edward 251 James E 78
    Mrs Jane 78 John 78 John Sr 78
    Joseph 78 Lizzie 78 P J 10
COOK, C E 10 Clifford G 190 Clarence
    78 Delia 230 Mrs Edith 78 Harold
    Daniel 251 Horatio Nelson 190
    Leroy D 78 Norton L 190 Tom 78
    Vera 10 Violet M 190
COOKE, Weldon B 78
COOLEY, E A 78
COOMBS, Callie M 79 Caroline 79 Lois
    Vadalia 79 Marcissa P 79 Richard 79
    Richard R 79 Silas 79 W B 10
    Mrs Will
COON, R S 190 T S 190
COONEY 10 79 Mrs Andrew 85 Elizabeth
    79 Jim 190 John 10 190 Mrs Lena 152
    Mrs T 152
COOPER Mrs 10 Mrs Anna 72 Mrs
    Flora 72 Helen Elvira 172 Joe 79
    Myrtle 199 Mrs Newton Sidney 79
COP, Robert T 190
COPELAND, Nat 10 Nathaniel 79 Tom 79
COPES, Peter 251
COPLAND, A 10
COPLEY, Belle 208
COPPLE, Inez L 216
COPSEY, Alba B 190 Raymond 251
CORBALEY, Mrs Florence 239
CORBET, B Jr 10
CORBETT, Ed 11 Frank 190 Fred 190
    Robert 190
CORDA, Charles 11
CORDANO, Mary 195
COREY, Nellie 217
CORLEY, Dorothy C 205
CORNALE, Giovanni 79
CORNAGGIA, Emma 182
CORNELL, S C 55
CORRELL, Eugene P 79
CORRIGAN, Mrs Emma Harris 79 J S 79
CORRZZA, Giovanni 251
CORTEZ, Antonio 79 George 79
    Henrietta M 197 Mamie C 235
CORTZE, Henrietta M 197
CORVILLE, R 11
CORWIN 66 Aileen 184
COSKA, M 11
COSTA, Amelia 196 Manuel 80
    Maria M 196 Mayme 231 Natale 251
COTREL, Wilbur 190
COTTON, Mrs J S 213
COUGHLIN, Michael 251
COURT, Edith May 190 J G 11
COURTENAY, F LaMar 251
COVINGTON, Sidney 80
COWAN, James 190
COWLES, W S 11
COWLING, Mrs M E 80
COX Mrs 101 Amos 161 Amy 80 E A 190
    Elbert 11 G W 191 Hugh 80 J F 11
    Joseph 80 Mrs Lulu 108 Mrs Mollie
    109 Russel Harrison 251 Samuel 191
    W A 11 W M 80 Wesley 251
    Mrs William 111
COZAHOUX, Felix 189 191
CRABTREE, Fred 191 Mary 196
CRADDOCK, Chester Clyde 251
CRAFT, Kate 195 Robert William 80
CRAIG, C 251 Eunice Ellen 217 J 80
    Leroy 191 Madge E 203 Walter A 191
    251
CRAIGHAN, Mrs Augusta Lorentz 80
    J D 80 191 J F 80 L A 80 N L 80

DENNING, Ellsworth A 252
DENNISON, Byron James 193
DEROSA, Juilio 193
DeSHIELL, Gail 193 Merl 252
DE SILVERIA, A M 252
DESJARDIN, Peter 252
DE SLAEF, Matilde Margiute 180
DETAMASI, Frank 252
DEVEREUX, Clarence 83 Clarence R 193
    Edward 83 Edwin A 193 Grace 83 227
    John 83 William 83
DEVILBISS, Alice 211 Andrew J 83
    Edgar 83 Ethel 83 H A 83 Harrie 83
    Irene 83 Jessie 181 John 83
    Mrs Julia Lowell 83 Madge 157
    Ruth 157 Ruth Edna 232
DEXTER, A E 193 Mrs Elise 115
DEYOE, Mrs Frank 83
DeYOUNG, Edward 193
DIAS, Joseph 12 83 Mrs Maria 83
DIBBLE, William 83
DICKENSON, Mrs Mary 238
DICKINSON, Alonzo 83 Alonzo S 83
    Owen L 193
DICKEY, Henry Aden 252 J H Jr 193
    W H 193
DIETSCHE 13 Otto 193
DIETZ, John 193
DIGGLES, Grace 83
DIGHTMAN, Mrs C I 84
DIGONCELLI, Giacomo 84 148
DILL, John M 84
DILLING, Albert 13 84 Cecile 84 Ed 84
    Frank 13 84 Mrs Frank 124
    Mrs George 84 Harry 84 Mrs I B 84
    James 84 Jim 84 Mabel 84 Mrs Mary
    84 143 Oscar 84 Verona 84
DINI 13
DINUCCI, Adolph 252
DIXON, John 84 Joseph Alfred 193 252
    Mae E 235 Maude 79 Mrs May Alice
    179 P H 84 193 Pete 13 Mrs Pete 84
    W G 193 W H 94
DOBNER, Mrs A L 124
DODDS, Amy 212
DODGE 84 Arthur 84 193 Blanche 189
    Bud 84 Charles 84 Charles P 84 193
    Charlie 84 Dave 84 David L 84
DODGE (Continued)
    F A 84 Fred 13 84 G O 84 H 13
    Mrs Harry 84 P W 84 Rebecca Plato
    84 Susan 228 W J H 84
DODSON, Frankie 176 Fred 176 L 176
DOIG, James 13 Mrs James 84
DOIDGE, H A 193
DOLAN, Mrs J 109 W D 252
DOLLAR, Mrs Margaret 85
DOLLARD, Thomas 13 85 137
DOMENIGONI 13 Massino 193
DOMINOGONI 13
DONAHUE, M A 193
DONALDSON, Alexander 193 Harry 85
    Mrs R 149 Robert 13 85
DONALVITCH, Jim 85
DONEGAN, Dan 85
DONKELLIS, John 253
DONLON, Nellie 190
DONNADIEU, Milton 85
DONNAN, D H 194
DONOHOE, Mrs Ellen 85 Elma 210
    Emmett 85 Fred 85 J H 85
    Katheryn 85 Martin 13 85 Michael 85
    Mrs Michael 85 P R 13 Ruth 239
    Ruth A 202 Sylvester H 194 Ves 85
DONOVAN, William A 252
DOOLEY, Arthur W 85 Marvin 13
DORNAN, Andrew 85 Thomas 13 Thomas
    Arthur 194

DORWAAD, Olive 231
DOTTA, Mrs L 170
DOTY, Claude E 252 Hazel Genevieve
    187 Mrs James 187
DOUGHERTY, Anna 185 Ellen 235 F 13
    Frances 194 Mrs G 85 Jennie
    Forsythe 213 John 85 98 Mrs Kate 85
    Peter C 194 William 85
    Mrs William 85
DOUGLAS, Mrs R H 68
DOUGLASS, F A 187 Olive 187
DOWD, Jesse Dixon 85
DOWLEN, Mrs Emily 86
DOWLING, Mrs J R 86 Louise E 86
DOWNEY, Jack 86
DOWNIE, S 194
DOWNING, A 252 Chester R 194 Ed 169
    Mrs Ethel 63 Lauren J 194 Walter
    Hampton 194
DOYLE, Dan 86 J 194 James Moss 253
    John 86 Neil A 253 Oscar J 253
    Thomas E 194 Tom 86 Valve 86
    Walter 86 William 86
DRAKE 13 Josephine 219
DRENKLE, Harry 194
DREW, Beulah M 219 Mrs Frank 144
    Mrs M C Angle 103
DRIVER, Alice 199 Theodore 194
    William T 253
DRYDEN, Fay 13
DUARTE, F 86 John 194
DUCHAINE, Edward F 194
DUCKWORTH, Mary A 101
DUFFEY, A D 86 Mrs Agnes 119 Albert
    86 194 Almyra 86 Mrs Annie S 86
    Fred 86
DUFFY, Laton V 253 282
DUKELLIS, John 253
DUNATI, Joe 86
DUNCAN Mrs 153 Anne J 86 F H 253
    Mrs Fannie Holliday 86 Frank 86
    Fred 253 George W 86 J J 86
    Ralph 13 Ray 194 Robert 86 Samuel
    86 Samuel M 86
DUNHAM, Agnes 201 Ray I 253
DUNLAP, J L 86 Leslie Raymond 194
    Ores 86 Orrin 114 Roy 13
    Theodore 13
DUNN, Frank 87 J W 87 Kathleen 204
    Marian 227 Mrs T H 136 Mrs Victoria
    87 William 87 Mrs William 87
DUNNEBECK, Frances A 194
DUNSING, Mrs K 87 Mabel 205
DUNSMORE, H D 194
DUNVAN 194
DUNWAL 13
DUNWALL, George 194
DUPRAS, Clutilda E 208
DUSICK, Albert H 14
DUTRA, Frank 87
DUTZI, Emil Henry 253
DUTTON, C D 194 D C 194 Edgar 194
    Esma 222
DU VANDER, D H 195
DWELLY, Jerediah Jr 123 Jerediah Sr
    123 Lucy R 123 Mrs Mary A 87
DWINELLE 87 Jesse 14
DYER, Ed 14 Norah 224 Raymond 14 195
    Vernon K 253 William S 195
DYMONS, Woodrow John 253

E

EAGAN, Mrs H 62 Henry M 195
EAGLE, Bert 14 Elsie 69 Grace 185
    Jane 66 Joe 66 Lillian E 229
    W J 253

FERRIS, Frank 129
FERRY, Nelson H 254
FERTATO, Frank L 197
FEVELLI, Joseph 197
FHONS, Chinn Ginns 254
FIELD, A 197 Marion 73
FIGARO, Fina 225 Herman 90 John 90
   225 282 Manuel 90
FIGONE, 15 A 96 Angelina 189 Annie 96
   200 John 197
FIGUERIDO, Mauriel 255
FILIPPO, Manuel 255
FILOON, Peter 90
FILOSI, Battista 255 Lawrence 15 197
   Louis 255
FINE, Clara 234 E 90 T J 90
FINKLE, Della 203 Lela 223
FINLAYSON, Mrs Julia 158
FINLEY, Ida 237
FINN, Michael 90
FINNEY, Thomas Columbus Benton 90
FINSTROM, Carl A 90
FIORI, Albino 255
FIORINA, Domenico 197 Domingo 197
FIREBAUGH, Charles E 197
FIRENTINO, Albert B 255
FISHER, Bessie 223 Charles D 197
   J M 15 Mrs J Melville 196
   Lester A 255 Lulu B 208 William 15
FISK, F L 197 Rev S S 90 Mrs S S 90
FISTOLERA, Peter 15 Pietro 197
FITCH, B D 91 Mrs B D 91 Belle 194
   Bud 91 Ernest Demill 91 255 282
   George Albert 91 255 282 Harry
   Douglass 197
FITZHUGH, E L 197
FLAGLER, Mrs A D 172
FLAHERTY, Mrs Bessie McGarvey 91
FLANAGAN, Edward John 91 Flossie 91
   180 John 180 Mrs John 91
FLEMING, F N 91 George 197 Helen 91
FLEMMING, William 197
FLETCHER, Arthur 91
FLINN, Mrs Clarissa G 224
FLINT, A E 197
FLOOD, Emory 91 Nannie 14 196
FLOWERS, Mrs C D 162 Hilda 185
FLREVCA, Pete 91
FOGERHOLM, Sigrid 208
FOKES, Mrs A 76
FOLEY, Martin 255
FONTANA, Carl 255
FOOK, Chay Yan 91
FOON, Junz Wah 255
FOOT, Mrs W H 91
FORD, Mrs A W 91 Abraham 91 Arnold 91
   Charles D 91 E M 92 236 Ethel 236
   Henry 15 J A 15 197 J C 91 James 16
   James A 92 Jerome 91 Jerome Chester
   91 Mrs Julia H 92 Kirby L 197
   Martha 91 Roy 16 91 Rissell 197
   Mrs Sarah 92 W A 92 W M 92
   Wesley M 198 William 16 92
   William Arnold 198
FORICH, Frank 92
FORSBERG, Mary 142
FORSMAN, Emil 198 John 198
FORSTER 16
FORSYTHE, Sadie 185
FORTADO, F L 198
FORTUNE, Gladys 202 Mabel 191
FOSCA, Luiza 201
FOSTER Miss 217 A 92 A W 92 A W Jr 92
   Arlington 92 George 92 Jean 92
   John 92 L H 16 Lou P 255 Mrs Marion
   Burness 92 Mary V 92 W A S 16 92
   Walter H 198 William 92
FOUSHEE, Edwin 92

FOWER, Laura T 92
FOWLER, Anita L 205 George 198
FOX, L 198 W 16
FOY, Shun 200
FOYE, Abbie L 204 Mrs Alice M 92
   Arthur 92 Arthur L 255 Eugene 92
   Florence A 92 193 Fred 92 Frederic
   Malcolm 255 Henry 204 Henry Malcolm
   92 93 193 William A 93
FRAGA, Maurice 93
FRAINE, Ethel 232
FRAKI, John 93
FRAMACCHI, John 255
FRANCESCHI, Salvatore 255
FRANCISCO, DeAndrea 255
FRANKLIN, Fred 255
FRANKS, Mrs J C 93
FRASER Mrs 93 James 93 Mrs Simon 93
FRASIER, Mrs D H 93 Mrs Mildred 93
   W L 16
FRASKI Mrs 207
FRATIS, Frank Silveria 255 Michael
   198 William A 198
FRAZER, Barbara 185 Ernest 255
   Melvin Miller 198
FRAZIER, Claude 198 Hugh 198
FREATHY, Mrs E P 93 Ed 16
FREDERICKS Mrs
FREDERICKSON, A W 93 235 Alma A 212
   Ruby 235 Walter G 198
FREDSON 16 Carl Saverine 255 Charles
   16 J 16 John 198 255
FREEBERG, Arthur 93 Mrs Charles 93
   Hugo Valdemer 93 255
FREEBURG, Arthur 255
FREELAND, Oliver F 198 255
FREEMAN, Earl 198 Edna 221 Mrs Eva
   194 G E 16 Isaac 198 255 Jacob 93
Freeman (Continued)
   Lester 198 Lewis 198 Lurine 232
FREITAS, Constantino 93 Joaquin 16
   Jose 93 Louis 198
FREITOS Mrs 123
FRENCH, Mrs Maude 172
FRESHOUR, Edwin J 198
FRETAS, Joe 256
FRIEBERG, Mrs Elsie 93
FRINK, Lester 256
FRITZSCHE, Mrs Annie 93 Arnold Otto
   93 255 Carl 16 93 Frank 93 Fred 93
FROMAN, Ruth 180
FROST Mrs 123 Elbert 198
   Orville M 198
FRY, Eva B 192
FRYE, Delwin 93 John 93 Thomas 94
   V 202
FULLER, Della 47 E 256 Gertrude
   Claire 184 Mrs Isabella 218 J A 94
   Lillian 217 Mrs W 176 W F 179 184
   198 W P 199
FULTON, T C 16
FUNKE, Louis 16
FUNSTON, Frederick 94
FUORINI, G 256
FURGESON, Eli 94
FURLONG, A T 94 Ed 94 Mrs Elizabeth
   94 Mrs Jack 85 Thomas P 94
FURTADO, A F 256 J L 256

G

GABAC, Joseph 94
GABRINO, Mary 183
GAEOMELLA, Pasquale 256
GAGE, Charles 94
GAHAN 94
GAILLARD, Mrs Sydney 202
GAINE, W R 94

GORDON, Archie Feliz 257 Ed 200
    Mrs Ed 125 Ella 213 Estelli M 221
    George 18 George H 200 Henry 200
    Mrs J 84 Mrs James 154
GORI, D 118
GORMAN, Mrs Kate 116 Philip R 257 282
    Mrs W B 131 William B 200
    William D 18
GOTARI, Louis 18
GOTTI, Aquilino 257 Martin 257
GOUDY, William John 97
GOULD, Doris E 227 E 18 Frank H 148
GOWAN, Hiram Elmer 18 200
GOWELL, Alfred 141 P D 200 Park 141
    Mrs Parker 65 Ruby Orletta 219
GOWEN 19
GRACE, William 97
GRADY, W R 200
GRAFE, Pearl 190
GRAMBELLI, Giulia 226
GRANGER, Cecille M 222
GRANSKOG, Joseph 97
GRANT, Mrs A E 124 Mrs Dan 162 E A 19
    Ed 19 Malcolm D 200 Myrtle 216
    Theodore 19
GRANVALL, Andrew 97
GRASS 19
GRAY, A J 200 Arden H 19 Arthur 200
    Arthur J 19 Mrs C T 113 Charles T
    97 Dana 19 Donald Cameron 19
    Dorothy E 234 Mrs Edith Dellett 97
    Fred 97 Frederick 97 Gladys 220
    Harold 19 200 Mrs Harold 100 Mrs
    Howard 97 Jessie 215 L 19 L L 97
    Lawrence A 200 Lawrence Arden 97
    M D 200 Mrs M D 151 M D Sr 220
    Mary Louise 97 Prince W 97
    Violet A 206 W A 200
GRAZANDIO, Morandni 257
GRAZIANA, Henry A 257
GRBAC, Antone 257
GREATHOUSE, T Bert 97
GREEK Mrs 175
GREEN, Mrs Alice 94 Mrs Clara 97 E A
    19 George Edward 97 Gladys 232
    Henry A 200 Isaac 98 Laura 227 P R
    98 Perry W 201 Mrs Rebecca J 98
GREENOUGH Mrs 68 F H 19 Mrs Katherine
    168 Paul B 201 Ralph Clinton 98
GREGOR, A L 201
GREGORY Mrs 98 103 Albert 98
    Mrs Albert 85 Mrs Bessie 98
    Mrs Bessie Howe 98 J A 98 John
    Millard 98 Lester 257 Mrs S 124
    Thomas L 98
GRIFFIN, Hugh 201
GRIFFITHS, F A 19 Grace Mae 199
    Mrs Hannah 98 John 98 Lorin 98
    Ned 98 Mrs S R 98
GRINDLE, Allie 98 Joshua 98
GRIST, Alma 98 Mrs Della George 66
    Tom 98
GROHER, August 257
GRONDORF, Fred 257
GRONROSS, Alina 207
GROSINI, Gaitano 257
GROSSE, A Mrs 19
GROSZ, A Mrs 19
GROTEVANT, Hattie L 212
GROTHE, F 98 Franz 19 L 201 Rose Mary
    236 Wein M 257
GROTZ, William 201
GROVER, L E 76 Leon L 19 M M 76
GRUBELICK, M 98
GRYURCH, John 257
GSCHWEND, Ellis G 258 Tom 98
GUATINI, Loigi 98 Luis 258 Lutt 258
GUDENZA, Rock Sr 98

GUENZA, Guiseppe 201 Joe 19 99
    Joseph 99
GUERERRO, Benjamin 258
GUERRA, Paolo 201
GUEST, William 201
GUESTI, Vitola 201
GUIDI, Emilio 201 Rose 212
GUIDINGER, Amy 218
GUIGUI, Rosa 227
GUILLIEE, Mrs S E 106
GUISTI, Alberto 258 Annita 224
    Ettare 258 Gabrielo 201
GUMMERUS, Aino Rutti 201 258
    Hannah 212 230 J H 214 Lena M 214
GUNN Dr 201
GUNNAR, John 99
GUNNING, Mrs Emma P 99 Jack 99
GUNTLEY, Mars Mary B 99
GUPTELL, Herbert A 201
GURLEY, James 99 Mrs Lucy 99
    Robert 99
GUSTAFSON 99 Arthur 99 201 Emil 201
    Eric 258 Erick 258 Erik 258
    Henry 99 144 Mary 99 Mrs Sybil 236
GUSTAPHSON, Dakman 99
GUSTI, Mrs Rosi 99
GUSTLANDER, Charles G 99
GUTHRIE, A 99 Donald 99 Harold 99
GUY, J E 172
GWARTNEY, Bess 196

H

HAAP, George 99 John 99 Mrs Maria 99
HAARBY, Austa 197 Martin 258
HAARE, August 99
HACKABOUT, J 19
HACKLEY, Edwin 19 Mrs Millie 95
    Vivian 240 Witt 99
HAGANS, W A 100
HAGGBLOM, A Theo 258
HAGGREEN, P W 100
HAGNE, Gustave 150
HAGNEY, Myra 202
HAGUE, Robert F 258
HAHN, Fred 201
HAIGH, Frances A 68
HAIGHT, Clyde 201 Harry 100 201
HAILE, Elmer Linwood 258
HALE 19 Albert 258 J M 19 John Calvin
    100 John M 100 Mary P 100 Sidney B
    201 258 Mrs T 173 Tom 150
HALEY, Grace 212
HALICK, Olive 215
HALL Mrs 82 Belle 131 Bessie 228
    Eugene 163 Evagene 208 Harry 100
    Horace Lyman 201 Ida B 100 J 163
    James L 201 L 163 Mary C 92 O M 100
    Mrs P L 100 Parker 201
HALLIDAY, Ben F 201 Charles 202
    Mrs Emily 129 Henry J 19 J C 20 202
    J H 20 James Albert 202 Margaret J
    100
HALLING, Emily 200 Fred 100
HALLOCK, George 100
HAMBLIN, O A 20
HAMER, C J 202
HAMERSTRONG, Charles 100
HAMILTON, Agnes 188 Clara 91 L 20
    Lloyd Lawrence 292 258 Lovel 292
    Lowell R 202 258 Ruth 203 Mrs S D
    100
HAMLIN, Hazel Venre 194 Mrs R E 100
HAMM, Emil 258
HAMMAL, Dr Patrick W 100
HAMMEL, Mrs David 100
HAMMER 20

HENDRICKSON Mrs 104 Andrew 258 282
   Fred 259 Lizzie 231 Otto 104
   Sofa 229
HENEVER, Maurice 204
HENGEVELD, K N 21
HENLEY, Edward 204 Lloyd 204
   Victor 204
HENNINGSEN, Albert 21 Mrs Albert 68
HENNSEN 22
HENRICKS, W G 204
HENRIKSON, Gabrael 104
HENRY Mrs 128 Clyde W 259 Della W 104
   Francis J 204 George 104 Harriet 59
   John William 204 Marie C M 226
   Percy 104 Sankey 104 William 104
   Mrs William 104
HENSLEY 104 Bertha A 182 C L 22 104
   Cloves 104 L C 122 M J 105
HENTHORN, B 259
HENTON, Bert 22
HEPWORTH, Mrs A 80 Mrs Albert 105
   Florence 227
HERMAN, Elizabeth Ann 241 F A 105
HERMANSON, August 105
HERREN, Ellen 218
HERRERA, Manuel 259
HERRING, George 105
HERRLING, August 204
HERSEY, Mrs R 58
HERYFORD, Claude R 259
HERYFORD, Elmer 105 Frank 22
HESEL Mrs 84
HESS, Verda 73
HEWITT, C E 105
HEYWARD, Ida Florence 226
HIATT, E C 204 Hazel H 209 Lela 188
HICKEY, Edward Ritter 105 H B 105
HICKMAN Mrs 105 I 22
HICKS, Addie 221 Alice 239 Ethel 50
   238 Mrs John S 54 Milton 204
   William Paul 204 259
HIETSCUORI, Johannes 259
HIETAVOURI, Vaini J 259
HIGGINS, Augustus Daniel 105
   Charles E 204 E 22 Grace 200 John
   105 Press 105 Walter 22
HIGHT, Herman Clinton 259
HILDRETH, George 105 George Reginald
   259 J C 105 Mrs James 161 John
   Victor 204 Lewis 105 Louis 204
   Pauline 105 182 Victor 22 105
   Vincent 105 W J 105 Walter 22
   William 105
HILL, A W 22 C S 259 Charles 105 259
   Chester Arthur 22 204 259 Daisy 17
   199 Frank 105 Gailen 92 Gaylord R
   204 Mrs Iley Lawson 105 J W 105
   James A 204 Mary 238 Nora 211 Relia
   202 Thomas B 259 Mrs William R 165
HILLARD, F 22
HILTUNEN, Alex 105
HINAMEN, Helmer Taulinus 259
HINDE, George 105
HING, You 259
HINIMAN, Mrs F A 105
HINKSON, Henry 204
HIRSCH, Mrs Mabel 158 Maurice 106
   Mrs Maurice 158
HIRT, Frederick 259
HITCHCOCK, Arthur 106 Gaspar 106
   Henry 106 Isaac 106 Thomas 106
HO, Tom 22 Wong Tin 259
HOAK, Charlotte 106 Mrs Mary F
   N E 106 Newman E 106
HOBBS, John 106 Mrs John 106
HODDIUOTT, Harry 204
HODGHEAD, Dr David 106 Mrs Dolly 60
   200 Helen 106

HOE, Charles 106 Tom 22
HOFF, H J 22
HOFMAN, Mrs Lewis 106
HOFFMAN, Sara 218
HOGADORN, William James 106
HOGAN, Edwin 204 Frank 106 Henry 106
   James 106 260 John 106 Margaret 106
   Ollie 106 Peter 106
HOGANEN, Andrew 106
HOGGREEN, Mrs Anne 106 J P 106
   Porter 106
HOGLUND, Emil 22
HOLBERG, Andrew 22
HOLCOMB Mrs 195
HOLLAND, N D 204
HOLLENBECK, G A 260 Hazel 208
HOLLIDAY, Harold 22 Harry 204
HOLLINGSWORTH, Elva 197 John D 107
   John E 205 Oscar 22
HOLLINSEED, Jeremiah Vandermeer 205
HOLLIS, Mrs Minnie 148
HOLM, Aila 7 Dora 7
HOLMAN, C D 107
HOLMBERG, Emil 107
HOLMES, Georgia E 224 Harry 22
HOLQUIST, Charles 22 H 22 Herbert 260
   Herman 107 205 Mrs Hulda 107
HOLT, Mrs Annie 152 Mrs George 152
   Nellie B 201
HOLTZ, Edward F 205
HOLZHAUSER, L J 23
HOLZREITER, Peter E Jr 260
HONKONEN, David 260 Julius 260
HONTOU, Prosper E 260
HOOD, Alma Rose 189 Zena 189
HOPKINS, Alma L 193 C L 107 C W 107
   Charles 107 Elizabeth 164 F E 23
   J P 107 Mrs Margaret 107 R J 107
   Walter 107
HOPPER, Bert 23 C 23 C E 205 C Z 205
   Ed 23 Mrs George 107 Harry 107
   Henry 23 Herbert 205 J C 205 J F
   205 L C 23 Nancy M 205 Percy H 260
   Mrs T L 175 W L 205 Winifred 23
HOPNER, Mrs Mathilde 107
HORNBUCKLE, Thomas 78
HORTON 23 Arthur 107 E W 205
HOSKINS, Everett C 260
HOST, Emil 205 Mrs Mary 107
HOSTINEN, Johannes 260
HOTEL, Elbert 205
HOTELL, Albert O 205 Melvin 260
   Zola Marie 202
HOTZ, Lloyd 23
HOUGHTELLING, J L 107
HOUTON, Elsie 226
HOUX, Elmer 260 Mary 238
HOWARD, Alf 107 108 194 Mrs Alf 107
   Alfred Carter 205 Carl 23 205
   Clifford 108 Elmer 205 George 108
   Mrs George 108 Hannah 204 James 108
   James L 205 John W 108 Leroy Arthur
   205 Leta 227 Mabel 23 182 Mack 108
   Mark 108 Myrtle 211 Pete 108 Rose
   240 Ruth 108 Taylor 108 Tom 108
   W Scott 108 William 23 107 108 205
HOWE, C F 23 Henry 108 N P 108
   Newton P 108
HOWELL, A S 23 George 108 Dr W O 205
HOXIE, M C 23 Sarah Genevia 223
HOYERDAHL, Chris 118
HOYT, Isabel O 198 S S 230
HUB, J H 205
HUBBARD, Elbert O 205 Frank 23
   Mrs Lucy W 108
HUBER, John 205
HUDSON, Edith Castle 191
HUELBERT, Norma 214

HUFF, Andy L 260 John 108 Mary 108
    Peter 108
HUFFER, George W 205
HUFFORD, Flint W 205
HUFFT, Mrs Anna 108 Clair 108 206
    Clarence 23 J B 108 Loren V 260
HUGGINS Mrs 134 Eri 108 Harriet 108
HUGHES, Ada L B 222 Andrew 206 C A
    108 F D 108 Harry 206 Mrs J C 107
    James 108 James H 108 Laurene E 108
    Nilas 23 206 Quin 23 Russell 260
    Walter S 206
HULBERT, Mrs Sarah 109
HULL 23 Amos 23 B 24 Roy 260 W S 206
HUMPHREY, William Arthur 109
HUNT, Della M 236 E J Jr 206 G W 109
    Mrs J B 59 Milton 24
HUNTER, Charles 24 109 Mrs Eva 54
    Mrs Fred C 99 Harry 206 Harold 24
    Helen 202 J B 206 James 109
    Lucio 260
HUNTLEY, Mars Carrie 108 Cora N 95
    Eber 109 George 109 Joseph 109
    William Arthur 109
HUNTTING, L G 24
HUOT, Mrs Anna 162
HURLEY, Dennis 109 J C 24 206
    John J 206
HURLING, Oscar 24
HURT, Enoch 260 Mrs Enoch 109 G 260
    J 260 Lena Lulu 181 Mrs Mary J 109
    William 109
HURST, Arthur N 206 George Thomas 206
HURT, Byron L 206 Enoch 206
HUTSON Bert 24
HUTTON, Edna 204 James 109
    Mrs James 109 L 109 Martin 109
    Nels 24 Nelson 109 P 109
HYLAND, Mrs Irene 109
HYMAN, Aili 237 Edward 109 Mrs F H
    237 Frank 24 206 Frank Jacob 260
    Fred 206 Gustave 109 Herman Edward
    260 Ida 213 John Sr 109 Mrs John Sr
    109 John Jr 109 Oscar Emanuel 260
HYMEN, Chester A 206
HYSONG, Laura 233
HYVARI, Frans Ilmar 260

I

IELMONI, Joe 24
IKOLA, Jennie 208
ILG, May Gertrude 109
INGALLS, Mrs Elizabeth 97
INGMAN, Dena 187 John 206
INGRAM, Mary E 203 Phyllis L 186
INMAN, H H 109 John 24 109 John Jr
    109 Mrs Mabel 209 Ralph K 160
IRISH, Ella Rena 228
IRVING, Charles A 110
IRWIN, Thomas 206
ISAACSON, John 110 Marion C 206
ISABELLE, Emma 218
ITANEN, Oscar 110
IVERS, Charles 260
IVERSEN, Arthur 110 206 Christina 241
    Daisy 24 Frank 260 Mrs Garfield 241
    Henry 24 Iver 110 John Lambert 260
    Leila May 194 Marie 185 Mrs Mike
    124 Nels 110 Samuel A 206
IVES, A D 110
IVETT, John 110

J

JAACKALA, Isaac 24
JAAKOLA, Mrs Ada 143 Ida 213

JACINTA, Mary 233
JACKAWAY, Stephen E 206
JACKS, Joseph 206
JACKSON, Pres. Andrew 90 Bertie 191
    Birdie 191 Charles G 110 Clyde 110
    Evans 110 Evans M 110 George
    Washington 110 Gus 207 Harriet 110
    J A 24 J G 110 Mrs J G 110 Joe 24
    110 Mrs Joe 162 Joseph 110 Josiah
    207 Lawrence 110 Sarah 110 Tatlow
    110 Thomas 24 Thomas P 207 W A 110
    Walter 110 William 260
JACOBS, Oscar E 207
JACOBSON, Axel 110 C E 207 Elizabeth
    M 236 Harvey 207 Hilma Sophia 216
    Ida 216 Jonas 110 111 Simon Andrew
    260 Simon E 260
JAHNIGEN, G R 24 Mae 192 J R 24
JAKWAY, Grace 183
JALDINI, A 24
JAMES, Gertrude 238 Mary L 191 Lora
    Nellie 241 Mrs R L 129 Samantha L
    187
JAMESON, Frank 24 Tom 24
JAMISON, Adulphus 59 111 Clay Webster
    207 Edna S 233 Earl 24 George 111
    James J 111 Mrs Minnie 161
    Rodney A 260
JANSEN, Jack Herman 261
JARF, August 25 Erick 111 Gust 207
JARSCISALO, Ralle J 261
JARSEISALO, Kalle 261
JARSEIX, Kalle S 261
JARVIS, Mrs Ben 137 Elizabeth 111
    Frederick A 111
JEFFERSON, Mayme 187
JEFFRIES, James 111 Nancy G 111
JENKS, Paul Ivan
JENKINS Mrs 111 George C 111
JENSEN, Alice M 219 Carrie 42 Dan 25
    Mrs Elsie 110 Mrs Jens Christian
    111 Jewel 207 John 111 T 160
JERDSTROM, Vanaer 111
JEREMIAS, C 25
JEROME, Rose 213
JOHANSEN, P V 111
JOHN, A W W 112
JOHNS Mrs 112 Charles 112
JOHNSON 112 A R 25 A S 113 Abraham
    207 Mrs Agatha 112 Mrs Albert 112
    Albert J 207 Alfred 112 Mrs Alfred
    112 Algernon 261 Alice 40 113
    Mrs Annie 110 August 112 207
    August A 207 Mrs August J 112
    Bert D 207 Betty 184 C 232 C D 25
    C E 113 C F 25 Mrs C F 73 C R 28
    114 Mrs C R 81 C V 112 Carl A 207
    Charles 25 Charles Clinock 112
    Charles E 261 Charles F 112
    Charles J 207 Charles R 208
    Clarence 261 282 E J 207 E P 113
    Earl W 261 Edward 112 Edith 183
    Edward Harold 112 Elizabeth Lynn
    192 Emery 25 Emil 25 112 Emily 28
    Esther Irma 112 Ethel Marguerite
    112 Everett Ellsworth 112 Frank 25
    Frank A 261 Frank Gardner 261 Fred
    25 112 261 Frederick 112 G A 183
    G C 112 Geneva 169 George 112
    Mrs George 119 Grace Elaine 239
    "Grandma" 112 Mrs H C 113 H E 25
    H G 251 Hans 103 Hans Conrad 113
    Harold 207 261 Mrs Harry 113 Helen
    209 Henry Edward 261 282 Ida Belle
    112 Jack 113 Jake 113 James 113
    Mrs Jane 113 Janette 114 Jim 113
    John 113 Joseph M 207 Joseph

JOHNSON *(Continued)*
 Melville 113 Kathryn May 112 L 25
 113 L M 25 Lilly F 227 Louis 207
 Mabel 45 241 Mary 113 Mrs Mary Anna
 113 May 216 Mildred H 198 Minnie E
 159 O 208 O E 25 O L 112 O R 25
 Oliver H 208 Oscar 208 Otis R 208
 Otis W 114 Otto 113 Pete 113 Peter
 113 207 Mrs R 113 Robert 216
 Robert N 208 T D 25 T J 208
 Thomas L 114 Mrs Thomas L 114 Tom
 113 Vesta Irene 185 Wallace R 261
 282 William 114 Wilma 218
JOHNSTON, A E 25 Mrs Al 57 Mrs W 124
 William 25
JOKELA, Isaac 114 Mrs Jennie 114
JOKIE, Joseph E 208
JOLA, John 261
JONES, A 208 Mrs A P 114 Anna E 196
 B G 114 Beulah 229 Billy 114
 Clarence Deveur 261 Clarence F 261
 E T 26 Mrs G B 114 J A 261 J M 208
 J T 208 Lena M 235 Mrs Mathilda 114
 Mrs Minnie 73 Phillip Jose 261 R 26
 Thomas R 208 Mrs W G 114 William
 Gaston 208
JORDAN, Cora 230 Lizzie 215
JOSEPH, Ben 26 208
JOSEPHSON, Arthur Carl 261
JOSLIN, Arba V 208
JOUTSEN, Selma 188
JOY, Charles H 114 Horace Edward 208
 Lila 193
JOYCE, A J 114 J A 114 James A 208
 James Akester 114
JRAIN, Junz Jim 261
JRAM, Jung Jim 261
JUHOLA, Robert 208
JUNKER, Carl Sivan 261
JUNOCENTE, Carnaggia 261
JUSSEL, M 26
JUSTICE, Oliver P 208
JYLHA, Agnes 114

K

KAAMIS, Erkki Justue 261
KAARTO 26 John 26 Sophia 114
KAISEN, Chris 114
KAISER, Henry 114 Laura 240
KAJAMAKI 26
KAMEMOTO, Charley 208
KAMMUS, George 208
KANAANEN, August 26
KANE, Patrick 115 William 208
KARINEN, Culo 115
KARJAMAKI, John August 261
KARL, Kathryn K 199
KARO, John 115
KARVONEN, Herman 26
KASCH, Charles 208
KASTIS, John E 261
KAUFMAN, Eugene Otto 208 J G 115 N 26
KAUN, John 209
KEARNS, Thomas 26 115 Mrs Thomas 115
 Thomas Jr 115
KEDON, Mrs Annie B 115
KEE, Jing J 115 Tom You 262
KEENAN, Bernice 239
KEES, Olive 191
KEHOE, Delia 115 Ed 26
KEITHLY, Nora 217
KELLER, E A 115 Fred 159 G A 115
 Mrs Gertrude 196 H A 115 J J 115
 John Jr 26 Laura 207 Martha 191
 Mrs S 115 William Lyndall 209

KELLY, Eleanor 52 Mrs Elizabeth 115
 Frank 52 J W 26 Margaret 206
 Mrs Mary 115 Otis 115 Richard 115
 William 115
KELSON, Mrs E C 129
KEMP, Mrs J W 165
KEMPPE, Archie Isac 262 Fred 26 John
 115 209 Soffa 115 Waino Frederick
 209 262
KENDALL, Alfred 26 L E 209
KENNEDY, Ethel 209 J J 115 M J 88
 Mrs Maggie 94 Margaret Ann 115
 Thomas 115 William 115 115
KENNY, James 116 John 116 Pat 91
KENT, Dwight N 262
KEOUGH, Dr J B 116
KERM, Anna L 210 214
KERN, Ernest 209
KERR, Dave 209 David 116 Ellen 116
 James 116 James M 209 John 116
 Robert 116 Samuel 116 William 116
KESTI, Archie 116 Carl A 262
KETCHUM, Elbert 209 John 116 Nels 116
 W 116 Mrs William 106
KIDD Mrs 116
KIDWELL, Mrs Annie 116 J L 116
KIESER, Oliver 103 [Heeser]
KIMBALL, Jim 116 John S 116
KINCAID, Dorothy 191 George Frank 191
 Mrs Mary 116
KING Mrs 131 Adolph 262 Dr Edward
 Warren 116 Ella May 117 George R
 117 George Riley 209 J J 209
 Joseph 117 Lee 26 Lillie B 210
 Percy A 209 262
KINGREN, Mrs Ellen 187 J W 209
KINGSBURG, Willie 117
KINGSBURY, Alme Roy 117 C W 117
 Oliver 117 Willie 117
KINGWELL, J R 209
KINIKER, Alice 216
KINLOCK, George D P 117
KINMAN, Jennie E 69
KINNANEN, Annie 197
KINNUNEN, August 117 Mrs August 117
 Carl 117 Edward 117 Ellen 117
 Jennie 117 John 117 May 117 Niemi
 117 Olga 117 Rosa E 228 Van 117
 William 117 William Andrew 117
KINSEY, Sarah 224
KINVILLE, Alfred J 117
KINYON, Oliver 26
KIRK, B 190 C C 209 Harold 262
KIRKBRIDE, Roy W 209
KIRKLAND, W A 215 William 26
KIRKHAM, George 117
KIRKWOOD Mrs 225
KIVI, Peter 117
KJELDSEN, C R 26 209 Vernon 209
KLEIN, Hazel 211
KLETT, Charles 117
KLINKIE, Mrs Geneva 119 Mrs W A 119
KLIPSTEIN, Eugenia 228
KLOBAS, Mary 229 Tom 262
KNACKE, Mrs F O 136 Fred G 117
 Frank 26
KNAESCHE, Herman 117 209 262
 Mrs Herman 117
KNAPP, Winnie 71
KNIGHT, C L 203 Charles 117 Charlie
 117 Mrs Deborah 109 Eli 117 235
 George A 118 Gladys 203 H J 117
 J K 262 L Ewing 262 Linton 117
 Nellie 117
KNOWLES, Stephen W 118
KNOX, Mrs Ellen 79

M

MACEDO, Thomas 124 264
MacGREGOR, W B O 213
MACHEDO, John 213
MACK, Claude 264 Fred 264 Mrs O M 124
MacKAY, Dave C 124 Walter 213
MacKERRICHER, Duncan 213 Edith 47
    Edward 213 Russell 29 213
    William 213
MacPHERSON, Charles 29
MADDOX, G E 29 George 29 124
    Mrs Robert 124
MADDRILL, J D 213
MADEIRA, John 264 Joseph 29 124
    Margaret 124
MADEIRA-SAUDADES, Angelina 200
MADEIROS, Charles A 213 Merle 213
MADERIA, Philip Joseph 214
MADERO, Philip Joseph 214
MADISON, Lillian Bernhardine 29
    Michael 264 Robert 29 214
MADSEN, Annie 218 Carl William 264
    J G 239 John Waino 264 Henry 29
    Mrs Henry 133 Lulu 239
MAEL, Mrs M 163
MAFFINA, Frank 214
MAFFINI, A 66 75 124 Angelo 29 Mrs E
    124 Frank 29 Josephini 197
    Maria 197
MAGALA, A 264
MAGISTRIES, Johanna 229
MAGNESON, George L 214
MAGULAS, John 214
MAHAFFEY, J 214
MAHLER 29 Helen Wright 29 Oscar 29
    214 Paul William 214 264
MAHLMAN, Mrs A 124 Mrs Emilin 124
    F A 124 W T 124
MAHON Mrs 131
MAHURIN, Amandy 124 Amos 29 124 214
    Charles 124 Henry 124 John 124
    Mary 201 Rupert 30 214
MAIN, Allen D 264 Cecil M 264 Mrs
    John 124 Julia 193 William H 264
MAJORS, Jack 30 214
MAKANEN Mrs 124
MAKELA, Anna Mrs
MAKIN, Sophia L 228
MAKINEN, Niko 214 Tyne 239
MAKSENTE, Samuel 264
MALE, Jack G 30 214
MALINARI, Rosa 186
MALLORY, C B 240 Cecil 30 Gladys 233
    Mabel 181 Myrtle M 240
MALONEY, Mary 124 188 T J 30
MALTMAN, James G 214
MAMMELA, Annie 209
MAMMI, Aili 209
MANCHESTER, Clarence W 124 265 282
    Dorothy 125 Irva 125 Iva 125 James
    Thomas 265 John 125 John L 214 265
    Lewis 30 Lou 125 Luke 30 125 214
MANGGENI, Michele 125
MANICUSI, Pompilio 265
MANILI, John 265
MANKINS, Mrs Emily 125 Zola R 125
MANN, Arthur Arvid 265 Embie 184
    John 184 Louis 30
MANNAS, John 125
MANNERS, John 214
MANNING, Thomas 125
MANNON, C M 30 Charles M 30 125
    Elizabeth 125
MANSS, F H 214 Paul M 214
MANTELI, John William 210 214 265

MANTELL, John 210
MANTELLI, J W 30
MANTILA, Dan 265
MANTILI, Saund Maia 211
MANNUS, John 214
MARANDO, Giacomo 265
MARBLE, Mrs F C 125
MARCH, Ed 30 J E 214 James 125
    Sarah 186
MARCO, Marchesi 265 Siri 265
MARDERS, C H 125
MARIA, Togana 180
MARIANI, Romilda 229
MARIAUI, John 30
MARIN Mrs 107
MARINO, Antone 125 Charles 125
MARION, Harry 214 Mrs W M 125
MARISA, John 265
MARKHAM, Mrs Susan 221
MARKKULA, A 195 Emanuel 265 Isaac 125
    Matt 30 Mrs Matt 104
MARKS, A I 30 Adolph I 125 215
    Caroline 125 Henry 125 Seymour 125
    Solomon 126
MARON, F 126
MARQUES, Sebastio 265
MARRIS, Mrs E A 80
MARSH, Harry 126 John S 126
    Mrs R B 126
MARSHALL, Asa 126 Asa Jr 126 C H 30
    C L 126 Clifton 126 J H 126 Jay 126
    John 149 May 180 Mrs Sarah 126
MARTELLA, Peter 215
MARTELLE, Pete 30 Mrs Peter 126
    Pietro 215
MARTIN 215
MARTIN Mrs 73 92 Alfred W 215
    Mrs Beth 103 C B 265 Charles 30 215
    Clifford A 215 Frank Everett 265
    Hattie 198 J W 126 Jesse Elmer 265
    Karl A 265 Lois J 237 Rachel B 223
    Sibyl 201 Stephen Byron 126
MARTINAZZI, Henrietta M 192
MARTINDALE, C G 215
MARTINELLI, Carmelino 227 Ottavio 265
MARTINEN, John 215
MARTINETTI, Gabriel 126
MARTINEZ, Mrs Katherine 126 M 126
    Ray E 215
MARTINI, Anastasia 182 Domenico 215
    Guido 126
MARTINO, Spirito 126
MARTINS, John 30
MARTONOVICH, M 30
MARVIN, Harvey A 208 Mrs Lizzie 126
    Marian 208
MASOLINI 127 George 127
MASON, B D 30 Bessie 225 Florence 206
    Florence May 215 Guy 215 H H 127
    Vera 193 Mrs Zella 220
MASOTTI, Frank 215
MASSAVELLI, Pete 265
MASSIMO, Bello 265
MASSOLETTI, Stephen 265
MAST, Blanche 187 George 187
MASTAMAKI, Lusa 211
MASTERS, C L 215
MATANA, John 265
MATERNE, Mrs E 59
MATHER, Edward R 265
MATHEWS 31 Mrs 68 87 Albert 127
    Bessie 127 Charles W 127 Charles
    William 127 Mrs Charles William 127
    Charlie 127 Mrs Clyde 127 Ed 215
    Ernest J 127 F S 215 Genevieve 211
    George 31 Inez 127 J 31 J J 68 127
    J R 211 J W 127 James 127 James R
    127 Leonard 127 Leta 127 Mabel 127

MATHEWS (Continued)
 Obediah 127 Mrs Obediah 127
 Paul 127 Rodney 127 William 127
 William Charles 215 265
MATHISON, Charles 215 George 31
 Robert 265
MATSON, Walter 127
MATTHEWS, Sam 127
MATTILA, Charles 127 Isaac 128
 Victor 128
MATTINZZO, Giovanni 265
MATTOCKS, George 215
MATTSON, Andrew 128 H 31 Mrs M 166
MAUHA, Andrew 128
MAUNA, Anna S 207
MAXIN, Betsey Perkins 72
MAXWELL, P 31
MAY, Franklin P 128 William A 265
MAYALA, Waino 265
MAYESTRIS, Geovanina 201
MAZE, Dave 265 George A 265
MAZZANTI, Charles 128
MAZZETTA, Jarvcis 31 Madalene 192
 N 199 Pietro 265
MAZZINA, Battisa 266 Vittorio 266
MAZZINI, B 266 Rosa 197
McABEE, Mrs Alice 85
McAINICK, Harry 215
McARTHUR, Atalkia 220 David 128
McCABE, Albert 75 128 William C 266
McCALLUM, Daisy 115 Dan 128 Gwen
 20 Gwenlian 202 John 31 128
 Xarrissa 122
McCAMMON, Robert 215
McCANDLESS, Elsie Alice 181
McCANSE, Ed 31 Mrs Eva McAbee 128
 George 128 Marguerite 128
McCARREN, Rita H 188
McCARTHY, Lloyd Farrer 216 Mrs Signa
 202 Mrs Thomas 128 William Jr 128
McCLAIN, George 128
McCLARY, F May 226
McCLELLAN, Mrs John W 128 Freta L 194
 Urith 210
McCLELLAND, George 128 George Jr 128
 Mrs J G 31 James 128 Theresa F 128
McCLENDON, Frank 216 George W 216
 Walter 97 Mrs Zila Elizabeth 128
McCLINTOCK, B S 31 Hazel 229
 Norma 227 P S 112 W 112
McCLURE Mrs 63 Alice 183 Elmer H 216
 Lillian Harper 236 N T 129
 Nelson 183 W 216
McCOMBS, Ralph Vernon 216
McCORMICK, Grace 215 William 215
McCORNACK, Alex 129 Alexander 216
 Edith Forrest 183 Emily B 202
 John 129 Roy 129 Dr William Andrew
 129 183 202
McCOSKER, Mrs James 156
McCOWEN, Mrs Fannie 165 George 74
 Hale 74 Hale Jr 216 Helen 74
McCOWN, A E 216
McCOY, Charles 216
McCREARY, B 216
McCULLOUGH, Mrs Lillian 132
McCUTCHEON, Mrs R 163
McDONALD Mrs 68 168 A A 31 A C 72
 Alexander 216 Alexander J 216
 Angus A 216 Charles 129 Ed 31
 Edward 129 Edward 217 Florence M 218
 Forrest 129 George H 216 Glen 31
 James 72 John 31 129 216 Mrs John
 129 John Jr 129 John Daniel 216
 Josephine 226 Josephine Jean 129
 Lorne 129 Malcolm 216 Richard 72
 Rose 129
McDONNEL, John Andrew 216

McDOUGALL, James 129 John 129
 Mrs Peter 129 W S 129
McDOWELL, Asa R 266 James 129
McELROY, Floyd L 266
McEWEN, Mrs Pearl 129
McFARLAND, Mrs Ann 107 James 31
 Mrs James 106 Mrs Sarah 129
McFAUL, Arthur P 129 216 Charles A
 129 Mrs Charles A 129 Charles W 129
 Mrs Ed 107 194 Edson Jasper 31 129
 L R 129 Mrs Mary Elizabeth 129
 Wilson E 129
McGAHAN, C H 216
McGARVEY, Taylor 31 W T 216
McGARY, Mrs Walter M 130
McGEE, Mrs Catherine 121
McGHANEY, Edward Jasper 266 Edward
 Jersey 216
McGILL, Archie 130 James 266
McGILVRAY, J A 130
McGIMSEY, Alva P 266 Charles L 217
 Helen 224 Jack A 266 Phocian 130
 266 Mrs T J 130
McGINTY, Eva 213
McGLASHAN, Jennie W 203
McGOUGH Mrs 130 Mrs John 130 T M 130
McGOWAN, Frances 230
McGOWEN, Eugene 130
McGUINESS, Joe 266
McGUIRE, Cecil 266 Ruby 130
McILREE, Alexander 130
McINTYRE, Henry J 130 Mrs M S 130
 Mrs Mary 75 Mrs Mary E 130
McKAY, Andrew 180 Della 180 Jim 130
McKEAN, Andrew L 217
McKEE, Mrs Ellen 130 Frank H 130
 Mrs J S 163 Nettie 213
McKELVE, William 56
McKENZIE, Harry 103 Lillian 215
 Thomas 217
McKIBBON Dr 130
McKILVA, William 56 130
McKINDLEY, Mrs Robert 130
McKINLEY Mrs 131 Daisy 204 Duncan 130
 Edwin Lawrence 217 Ethel 192 J W 31
McKINNA, Charity Eliza 130
McKINNEY, Belle 131 C E 217
McKINZIE, Robert 131
McKNIGHT, Edward 217
McLAUGHLIN, Earl E 266
McLEAN, Dan 31 Daniel 131 217
 Mrs Ethel 202
McLEOD, Irene 200 Oliver 131
 Mrs Oliver 131
McLINTOCK, Pamelia 197
McMAHON, James 131 Margaret T 224
McMANNIS, D F 266
McMANUS, Alice 179 Catherine L 180
 J 31 J P 86 Mrs Leona 152
 Mrs Lenora 152 Patrick Sr 131
McMASTER, Mrs Charles 85 George 131
McMILLEN, A L 32 Alfred W 215 C A 32
 Lee 211
McMULLEN, George 217 Russell 217
 Mrs Victoria 217
McMURCHY, Robert 32 217
McMURPHY, David T 217
McMURRAY, V C 131
McMURRY, Ella 202
McNAB, A V 206 Edna 206
McNAMARA, Mrs Alice 131 Emma E 194
 Florence 217 Mary 131 Patrick 131
McNAMER 217
McNARY, Oscar 217
McNEIL, Allie 131 J 131 Mrs Justin
 131 Ollie 131
McOMBER, E R 217
McPEAK, Hattie 55 J H 131 Mrs J H 131

McPHERSON, C 217 Gertrude H 217
   J L 131 Martin 131
McPHILLIPS, Pat 32
McRAE, Inez J 233
McRAY, Bertha J 206 Mrs Mary J 131
McSWEGAN, Addie 156
McWATERS, Emma 238
McWHINNEY, Archie 266
MEAD, Albert 131 Mrs Anna 63
   Clark 217 Cora M 221
MEADOR, Mrs I 132
MEANS, Millard E 167 217
MECHAM, Alice 185
MECUM, J D 132 Mrs J D 132
   Stephen 132
MEDCALF, Leila Alice 209 Lurena
   Margaret 206
MEDEIROS, John 266
MEDERS, Foster S 217
MEDICAS, Argie 266 Lucius O 266
   Sidney Clarence 266
MEDITZ, George 132
MEECH, Elizabeth 132 Ervin 132
   Mae 154
MEEHAN, Eugene 132 John J 266
MEEK, Edward 217
MEESE, Warren L 266
MEHTLAN, Aner 132 Aner Jack 266
   Ben 132 Charles 132 Lempie 132
   Mamie 132 Mary 132 Millie 132
   Nan 132 Otto 132 266 Mrs R 104
   Richard 132
MEIKLEJOHN, Ellen 116
MEISTER, Al 217 Mrs Amy 61
MELLON, F 32
MELO, E 184
MELTON, Ben 132 Robert 132
   William 132
MELVILLE, William 32
MELTON, Mrs Eva 85
MELVILLE, Mrs C B 119
MELVIS, Joseph 132
MEMINEN, Emil Edward 266
MENDEL, Ethel 232
MENDOSA, Antone J 266 Frank Joseph
   266 John Sylvester 266 Joseph
   Albert 266 Jose J 266 Mayme 212
   William Arthur 267
MENAFEE, W A 32 Mrs W A 178
MENCUCCI, Peter 217
MENEFEL, V 32
MENKKINEN, Tilda 180
MEREDITH, Mildred Leila 204
MERGA, D 132
MERINI, Eliza 188
MERO, Hazel M 230 Kathleen 37 38
   M Lovetto 217
MERRILL, Charles 132 Ruth E 184
MERRITT, Howard M 32 217
MERROW, Henry 217
MERRY, Agnes 205
MESSENGER, Rev Richard 132
METHALA, Hinni 210
METZLER, Alba 231
MEYERS, Fred 177 Mary 233 Oliver 132
   S L 78
MEYSER, G C 132
MICHAELSON, John 132
MICHEL, Lucy 128
MICHELETTI, Joseph 267
MICHETTI, Francisco 132
MIDDLETON 32 Frank J 267
MILINE, Edna Jean 196
MILLAR, Dave 132 George 132 James 132
   Mary A 132
MILLARD, J E 267

MILLER 32 Albert 132 Annie 212 Arthur
   N 217 Mrs Bert 68 Mrs Carrie 133
   Curtis A 218 Elisha 133 Elisha B
   Elizabeth 204 Esther 225 Mrs G B 59
   G Whitmore 218 George 133 218
   Herman 218 J J 32 Mrs J M 133 Jack
   133 John 133 John F 267 Joseph 267
   Kittie 190 Lena 55 Maud E 222 R 133
   R A 32 Mrs Rose A 133 Wallace 32
MILLIKEN, Alden J 218 Charles Morton
   218 Edna 217 Elizabeth 189 H F 218
   Mrs H F 68 Dr J W 184 Leland 32
   Lizzie 184 Newell 133 Sadie 184
MILLS, Benjamin 133 S D 133
MILRICK M 32
MINNEHAN, Dan 32
MINTON, J W Jr 32 Mrs John 133
MISH, Gerald 218
MITCHELL, Alma 201 Claude H 218
   Ebenezar 133 Fred 32 Luella May 229
   Peter 176 Rhoda 234 Shelby 218
MOCKLER, T R 133
MOE, Albert 32
MOFFINI, Maria 213
MOFFINO, Ansfgelo 218
MOFFIT, Howard 267 Ruth 211
MOGLE, Mrs L 99
MOHN, Newton Charles 267
MOILNEN, Matt 32
MOISALA, Jack 218
MOKKA, Leonard 267
MOLDOVEAN, Nicholas 88
MOLISE, Emma 204 Frank 218
MOLSBERGER, Richard 218
MONISE, Manuel 267
MONNA, Anna S 207
MONROE, Ethel 199 George 133 Mrs
   George 133 John 133 Mrs Kate 159
MONSEN, Carl W 267
MONSON, Pauline 193 Peter 133
MONTAGUE, Josephine A 207 Kittie 112
   Susie 112
MONTEDONICO, A 32
MONTGOMERY, Bessie 241 C C 33
   Clarence C 267 Clarence E 218
   Elbert P 267 Mrs Emily 67 J E 267
   J P 267 James 33 Thelma A 227
   W D 267
MONTINI, C 33 Camillo 218 Vinenzo 133
MOODY, L A 133 Mrs L A 76
MOORE Mrs 152 Alexander 218 Bernard
   Dudley 218 Bonnie 180 C E 33
   Clarence 134 J E 180 John 218
   Leonora 200 Marthena 206 Nathan A
   134 Mrs Reuben 134 Thomas 33
   Walter H 267
MOOREHEAD, A E 134 Thomas 134
MORAN, Edna 240 Lewis 134
MORAND, Alice 232 Charles 134
   Elizabeth 134
MORANDA, Sodorico 218
MORANI, G 33
MORBY, Los A 267
MOREHEAD, Hugh 134
MORETTA, A 33
MORETTI, A 197 Leta 197
MORES, Jose J 134
MORGAN, Edna K 184 Hale C 218 Ora 65
MORIARTY, Daniel 134 Mrs Mary J 134
MORIEL, John 218
MORLEY, Albert 134 Bert 33 Christian
   H W 33 John C 134
MORONI, Antone 218 Mike 33
MORRIS, J M 218 John Wesley 134
   Mrs Mary Florence 224 Mrs Minnie
   158 Richard 218

MORRISON, Canideva 230 E L 134 Ed 134
    Eva Mary 192 Frank 134 Ida J 194
    Lulu 218 Mrs Mattie 134 Milton 267
    William 218
MORRONE, Mike 33
MORROW, H L 219 Howard 219
MORSBERGER, Lee 219
MORSE, J B 134
MORTON, Frank W 134 Mrs Frank W 134
    Mrs Iley 87 Jessie 33 Stewart 219
    Stuart 219
MOSEBERGER, Dick 134
MOSHER, Tom 134
MOSIER, F M 33
MOSS, Mrs Catherine M 134
MOSTACHETTI, Antone 143
MOTT, Roy 219
MOUNGOVAN, Mrs Anna 135 Mrs P 174
    Thomas O 219
MOWREY, Ed 84
MOYLES, James L 267 Milton J 33 219
MUIR, Guy E 267 H B 47 235 Hattie J
    207 Leta 217 Ora 235 Ray 219
MULLIS, Walter 267
MUMMEL, Henry 219
MUNK, William 219
MUNROE, Andrew 135 J R 219
MUNSON 200
MURCHISON, Flora Margaret 216
MURK, Fred 267
MURKALA, Anna 210
MURPHY, Jerry 135 John 135 Mary 234
    P 135 Patrick S 135 R P 135
    Mrs T F 135 Tim 135
MURRAY, Carl 135 Charles 135
    Mrs Charles 135 Dayton 135 Gertrude
    185 Mrs Isaac 135 J C 219 J P 135
    John 135 L P 33 Timothy 135
MUSSETTI, Antonio 267
MUSTER, Al Jr 217
MYERS, D 135 Edwin P 135 Elmer A 219
    Mrs Elmer 135
MYRING, John B 135 Laura Ivy 135

N

NABB, Erich 135 Isaac 267
NADAL, Joe 267
NAGAMURA, Shix 208
NAIDUCCI, Frederick 219
NANNI, E 135
NASH, Frank C 219
NEAL, Isabelle 136 Sam 136 Zoe A 179
NEALY, Julius 33
NEARY, Mary A 232
NECKRITZ, Adolph Emil 267 Richard 136
NEECE, George 88 Hala 88
NEEDHAM 33
NEFF, J E 219
NEIGHBOR 136 Juanita 230
NEIGHBORS, Blanch N 192 Iris 202
    Kenneth 267
NEILSEN, Lauretz Carl C 219
NEILSON, Peter W 219
NELLEST, William 219
NELSON 136 A T 33 Alfred 136 Amelia
    136 Arthur 267 Arthur C 267 Arvid
    33 Charles Theodore 267 Christopher
    136 Enoch M 268 Erick 136 Gus 67
    185 H F 219 Hilda O 201 Mrs Jack A
    85 Jacob Arvid 268 John 136 219
    Mrs John 143 Justin 136 Leroy 219
    Mamie 220 Marie 228 Nellie 185
    Nels 219 Norman 219 Peter Emil 136
    R F 136 Rea Alvin 268 Robert 268
NENICCO, Frank 136
NESBIT, Sam 219
NESBITT, Samuel 33 136

NESS Mrs 138 Annie 198 Arthur 136
    Carl Walfred 268 Edwin 220 John 136
    John A 220 Oscar Irwin 267
NESTELL Mrs 136
NETO, Dr J R 33 136 J S 136
    Maria S 237
NEUHAUS, Irma J 210
NEVIN, H L 137 J 268
NEWBERG, George B 268
NEWBERRY, Helen 187
NEWBURY, George Burnhart 268
NEWGARD, J 33 Mary 205
NEWMAN, Elizabeth 137 Jacob Andrew
    268 Mrs John 137 Marie 189 Matt 137
    Otto 137
NEWTON, Mrs D O 58 H 137 William 33
    William N 137 William Niel 220
NICHOLS, Edith 137 Edith Naomi 236
    Georgia W 205 Harry V 220 Helene
    233 Herbert 34 137 J H 34 James
    Albert 137 Joseph 34 137 Mrs Joseph
    136 Joseph Frances 137 268
    Mrs Margaret 215
NICHOLSON, Alfred 34 268 J W 137
    Mrs J W 137 William 137
    Mrs William 61
NICKS, Conrad 137
NICOLAI, Alfred 220
NICOLS, Alfred 137 Ardelle 137
    George 137 Grace 137 Jesse 137
    Joseph Frances 137 282 Laura 137
    Naomi 137
NICOMEDA, Pinoli 268
NIEBARGER, Ed 170
NIEGHBORS, Blanch N 192
NIELSEN, Elmer Lawrence 34 220 268
NIELY, Julius 34
NIEMA, Jenny 240
NIEMELA, Earl E 220 Jennie 237
NIEMI, Issac 137 Manuel 137
    Oscar 137 268
NIEMLA, Jack 268
NIEMINEN, Emil E 268
NIKULA, Juhan Eelis 268
NIMELA, Earl E 268
NIMELE, Emil Edward 268
NISSEN, Roy 220 William 137
NOBLE, Mrs L L 137
NOBLES, Adeline May 185 Hattie 187
    Iva M 212 Mrs M M 138 Marion M 138
    Yell 138
NOHF, Herman 268
NOILANDER, Olaf 34
NOLA, Manuel G 268
NOLAN, M 220 Mrs M 68 M A 220
    Millard 138 Mrs Millard 138
NOLTE, Mrs Alma 154
NONCENTELLI, L 34
NONIS, Mrs Nancy Jane 138
NORBACK, John 268
NORBECK, Mrs John 138
NORBERRY, Charles 138 Charles Jr 138
    J E 138 John 138
NORDWALL, Carla 204
NOREIL, Ralph 220
NORGARD, Chris 34
NORRGARD, Selma 207
NORRIS, Clarence A 220 Ida 192
NORTHLAND, Ericka 232
NORTON, Charles R 220 James E 220
NORWALL, Charla 204
NOWLIN, A M 234
NOYER, Joseph G 138 Joseph J 220
NOYO, Joseph G 138
NUNN, Alda 205 Ellen 85
NUNON, Comrado 268
NURNBERGER, Evelyn Ruth 138
NUTTER, Audelaide A 204

PECK, Joe 141 Mrs Mary H 72
   Philander W 141
PEDDICORD, Dr Harper 36 222
PEDRATTI, Lemuel Raymond 270
PEDRETTI 222 Louis 270
PEDRO, Mrs Joe 36 William J 222 270
   Mrs William J 123
PEDROTTI, Mrs C 141 Charles 141
   L R 222 Ray 36
PEERS, Albert 36
PEGG, Mrs Rose 59
PEIRSOL, Mrs H J 141
PELASCINI, P 222
PELETTI, Joe 141
PELLETTI, Alcide 270
PELLIEI, Angelo 222
PELLIGRINI, J 222
PELLO, Joseph E 270
PELTOMA, John 141
PEMBERTON, Bennett Edward 222 270
PENCETTA, Thomas 270
PENLAN, Dick George 270
PENLAND Mrs 174
PENDLETON, O F 36
PENNCHE, Pete 141
PENNELL, Mrs Minerva 141
PENNINGTON, Albert E 141 Alfred 141
   William Higham 141
PENTILA, Annie 141
PENTILLA, Oscar 142
PENWELL, Aron 152 Ben 142 Johanna 152
   Mrs Lena 166
PEPPER, L H 270
PERA, Guido 270 Michele 270
PERCY 142
PEREIRA, Avelino 270 John 270
   Jose 223 Mary 195 Thomas 270
PERES, Antonio 270
PERKINS, Arthur Stanley 223 Blanche
   179 Charles Roy 36 223 David 223
   Hillman 142 Mrs Imogene 142 145
   Mrs N E 162 Victoria E 205
PERRERIA, Eleanor 225 Emily Agnes 220
   Mrs Joe 142 Manuel 138
PERONETTE, Casimir 142
PEROTTI, Della 224
PERRY, Mrs Alice 176 Amelia 180
   Antone 36 E B 142 Mrs Effie 142
   Ernest 142 Ethyle 228 Frank 142
   J D 231 Lester 223 Mabel 195
   Margaret 231 Mrs Mary C 142 Rube
   228 Walter 142 223 Walter B 36
   William 142 Willis 223
PERSHBAKER, Adam 142
PERSICO, Louisa 237
PESSERI 36
PETERS, C J 36 Goldie M 204
   Robert S 223
PETERSEN, Amy 142 D H 270 Louis 142
   Minnie M 215
PETERSON, Al 142 Andrew 142
   Mrs Andrew 143 Andrew P 142
   Annetta 207 August 36 C 36 Carl 36
   143 Elsie 240 Elva 217 Eric 160
   George 223 Gus 143 223 Gust 143
   Ida Mary 241 John 143 217 223
   Julius 223 Mrs Kate 162 L 143
   Louis 223 Oscar 143 223 Preston 143
   R 142 Thomas H 143 W 143
   William H Mrs William H 143
PLOWMAN, George 37 Mrs George 144
PLUMB, Louisa 144
PLUMMER, Albert 144 C B 144 224
   Charlie 37 H 37 Harold 144 224
   W P 144 224
POCAI, Harry Americo 270
POE, David 224 Jim 37 Philip Oscar
   224 Robert 224

POGGIE, Mrs N G 144
POLE, Frances 220
POLIN, Oscar M 224
POLK, Charlotte 239
POLLOCK, William A 271
POLLARD Mrs 144
POLLY, A 224
POLONELLE, Italo 144
POMON, Denie 224 Elias 271 Poll 271
POMONON, P 271
PONCE, Pedro 271
POND, Will 144
PONTANE, Peter 144
PONY, Mamie 184
POOL, H F 224 Lloyd B 230
   William L 224
POOLE, Clarence E 224
POPE, Sarah Ann 132
POPOFF, Fred J 270
POROTI 37
PORRO, Michael 270
PORTER, Mrs 206 Burton Claude 224
   J R 144 224 Rex 37 Thomas H 145
PORTERFIELD, George 37 George Harold
   145 271 282 James 145 Mrs James 124
POSTI, Nicholas 224
POTT, Erick 145
POTTER, Eber W Sr 145 Mrs George 145
POWELL, Alexander 145 E W 224
   Hattie 139
POZZI, A 37
PRATE, Mrs C 145
PRATHER, Mrs Ella 204 Hale 37 Harvey
   D 224 Lloyd W 224 Maurice R7 145
PRATOLO, Guido 224
PRATT, C A 37 Mary A 225
PREIRTALI, Clementine 215
PRENTIOUS, Cecil G 224
PRENTON, T L 37
PRESLEY C M 224 Vernon 37
PRESSY Dr 134
PREST 37 John 225
PRESTON, Charles 145 George W 37 38
   H L 145 225 H P 38 225 Howard 145
   Hugh 145 John 145
PREVITALI, Geni 126 215
PREVOSTINI, Pit 271
PRICE, Belle 185 Gilbert 38
   Mrs Harrison 145 Herbert 145
   Leila 196
PRICHARD, Fred R 271
PRITCHARD, Arthur A 271 Bertrim 145
   James W 271 282 Robert 145
   Mrs Robert 124
PROBST, Thomas 145
PROSSER, Mrs M F 165
PROTHERO, Clarence J 271
PRUITT, J C 38 James Calvin 271
   John Anderson 271 Robert 38
   William Franklin 271
PRYOR, Mrs Ida 68
PUCCINELLI, Angelina 182
PUCK, Herman 145
PUDAS, Lizzie 221
PUGH, John Dee 271
PULLEN Mrs 79 Anna 58 Mrs Elizabeth
   145 Frank 225 Steven E 107
   Mrs Wilder 107 William Harrison 271
PULOLA, Matt 271
PULSE, J J 78
PURCELL, Hattie 208 Howard 145
PURDY, Carl 214 Elmer C 38 225
   John H 271 Mabel 214
PURIONA, Pucetti 215
PUSCA, Luigi 145
PUSCONI, Guiseppe 273
PYHALNOTO, Mrs Anna W 145
PYORRE, Sadie 225

Q

QUADRIO, Joseph 271
QUAILL, Antone J 90 225 Arthur 38
   Frank 146 271 Joe 38 Joseph J 38
QUAINI, Martin 271 Martini 271
QUASS, Emil 146
QUEEN, Christopher 146 Mrs D 146
   Lucinda D 146
QUEENS, Mrs C 86
QUESENBERRY 102
QUINLIVEN, Bessie M 202 E W 225
   Margaret Williams 80 Rosella 194
   Mrs T 146
QUINN, Charles 146 Charles Jerome 271
   Charles Joseph 271
QUOI, Leung Yong 146
QUONG, Don 271
Quoon, Ah 271

R

RAAB, Nellie F 186
RACINE, Paul 38 Mrs Paul 176
RADEMAKER, M J 225
RADER, Mrs Mary Hazel 210
RADNICK, Frank 38 146
RADOKOMIE, M 146
RADOSEVIC, Nikola 271
RAFFETY 146 A L 146 Mrs Elizabeth 146
   Keene 146 William 146
RAFTER, C 38 Mrs C F 63 Charles 146
   225 Felecitas 146 Fred E 146
   J H 146 Jerome 146 Mrs Jerome 68
   Jerome H 146 Romie 146
RAININEN, Jack 225
RAINES, Bolivar 38 C H 28 Frank 225
RALSTRON, Charles P 225
RAMIEZ, Martin A 225
RAMSDELL, Irene 188
RAMUS, Conceicco Madira 237 J T 38
   Joseph Vincent 271 Mary 157
   Victor Frederick 271 William 146
RANDALL Mrs 129 Bernice 193 E J 193
   Grace D 193 H J 146
RANDELL, Mrs H J 106 W 38
RANDIS, J E 38
RANDOLPH, J W 216 Kathleen 223
   Mollie 216
RANG, Albert Edward 271 Emma 233
RANI, Maria 146
RANSDELL, Wade 225
RANTA, August 225
RANTALA, August 146 Mrs August 146
   Axel 146 Blanche 146 Everett 146
RANTANEN, Isak 271
RASMUSSEN, Allen 225 Esther 5 Luella
   M 213 Mrs N P 86 Natalie Elizabeth
   227 Pete 207 213 Violet 207
RASPI, Frank 272
RAUDIO, Annie 204 Mrs August 147
   Charles 38 147 204 206 225 227 272
   Charles Jr 147 Charlotte Lucele 147
   Hilda 227 Ida 206 Mrs Juliette 186
   Sophia 179
RAUSE, George 225
RAWLES, Austin N 272 Earnest Everett
   272 Lenore 180 McDonald 272
   Thomas E 147 Vernon R 225 272
   Zelphia R 186
RAY, Avon C 225 Charles Quincy 225
   Effie 240 Gus 272 J L 38 John 272
   Maude 217 Paul 38 Sam M 225 272
RAYMOND, Edna 240 Mrs Elvira 120
   Joe 225
RAYMONDA, Manuel 225

REA, J N 147 Mrs J N 97 S 38
REDEMEYER, Otis 38
REDMAYNE, Mrs Carrie 70
REDMOND, Sam 272
REDWINE, Guy 226 Marie 181
   Sanford 147
REED, Mrs Alice 133 Bessie 204 E 231
   George C 226 I C 147 Lilford
   Warren 226
REESE Dr 147 Charles D 226 Lewis B
   226 Mrs R E 144 147
REEVES, Mrs C A 147 Mrs J R 87
   Warren 147
REID, Mrs Anna Morrison 134 Mumm 226
REIDI, Serafini 226
REIDMILLER, George Patrick 226 272
REILINGER, Samuel 147
REILLY, Clara Theresa 218 J W 226
   Joe 38 Mrs Katheryn 147 Mary 84
REINKE, G 38 Gustave A 226
   Mrs Therese 147
REINKING, Mrs C W 156 Grace 184
   Mrs Ruth 147
REMMER, Victor 226
REMSTED, Fred 38
REMSTEDT, R 39 Robert E 226
   Sam 39 226
RENCKLY, E 147
RENICK, Gladys Rae 192
RENNER, Harold G 226
RENNICK, Carl 226 272
REQUA, Abe 39
RESCADA, Katrina 147
RESTOLIA, Oscar 226
REUCK, Theodore 39
REVIS, M 147
REYES, Mrs Fabian 65 170 Flora 65 170
   Raymond 272
REYNAUD, Juliette 225
REYNOLDS, Mrs Dora 147 J A 147 Myrtle
   228 Robert 147 Mrs S 175
RHEINHART, George 226
RHINEHART, Grace 191
RIANOLDA, A 39
RICARDO, Pinocchi 272
RICE, Charles 39 Charles Lewis 226
   J C 39 Louis 161 Ludy May 182
   Lydia 161 233 Stephen 148
   William Isaac 148
RICETTI, Pete 148 Teresa 212
RICH, Chester 148 Mrs E F 189
   Gertrude 237 J 226
RICHARDS, Elizabeth 184 George 39 226
   George 39 226 272
RICHETTI, L 39
RICHEY, C A 272 Eva 203
RICHMOND, Alice Amelia 193
   Walter 226
RICHTER, Olga 233 Theodore J 272
RICKS, Mrs Cora 76 Dr T B
RICNEY, G 272
RIDGWAY, Arnold 226
RIDLEY 39 E 39 148 Edward 226
   Mrs Jessie Fee 148
RIEFF, Lester 39
RIELLI, Agnes L 199
RIELLO, Agnes L 199
RIES, W H 39
RIFFE, Bertha 241 Edward 148 L L 39
   Lester 226
RIGBY, B H 272
RIGDEN, Ben 148
RIGDON, Ben 148
RIGGS, Artie E 216 I S 238 M M 39
   Minnie 148
RILEY, Electa 148
RIMMER, Bert 227

RINALDI, Andrew 39
RINALDO, Andrew 39 227 Guiseppe 272
RINALDSON, Mrs E 158
RINARDO, Pinocchi 272
RINKE, George 148
RINNE, Sakari A 272
RIRA, P 272
RISCO, William 148
RISKEE, Emil 272
RISKY, Lauri 272
RIST, Mary 207
RITCHER, Theodore J 272
RITONIENI, Hilya 240
RITSCHEL, Raymond 229
RIVETT, Mrs A 148 Benjamin 148
   Charles 148 Henry 148
RIVETTI, Alfredo 148
RIVINGTON, Hattie 148
RIZZI, John 39
RIZZOLI, Enrichetti 188
ROACH, G M 39 George 39 Patrick 148
ROBAK, Mathust 272
ROBBINS, E H 272 E P 40
ROBEJOHANNES, C 272
ROBERTS Mrs 148 A 236 Amilcar 272
   Harold 227 J 227 J C 75 John 40
   Max 227
ROBERTSON, Lulu 241
ROBILLIARD, Louis 142
ROBINSON, Clarence A 227 Clarence E
   272 Elmer E 227 Mrs Elmer E 148
   Mrs Emma 148 Isabelle 201 J W 227
   Mrs Julia 189 Margaret 189
   Myrtle 183
ROCCA, Mario J 227
ROCHELLE, Terisa 175
ROCHETTI, Frank 272
RODDA, A G 148 Mrs Anna F 148
   Edith 148
RODENBURG, C F 40
RODERIGEZ, Pascal 40
RODGER, Agnes 149 186 Andrew 149
   David 149 Henry 149 James 149
   Lizzie 85 Mrs Margaret 149
   William 149
RODGERS, Charles 227 Mrs Emily 130
   J S 40 John 40
RODRIGUER, Antonia 272
RODRIGUES, Manoel 273 Manuel John 273
RODRIQUEZ, Enrique 273 T 149
ROEBKE, M 227
ROELKE, George H 149
ROESMAN, Mary A 149 Thomas 149
   Walter 40
ROGERS, Mrs A T 149 Mrs Addie H 207
   Charles Myron 273 E J 40
   Mrs L C 163 Nellie 189
ROHRBOUGH, Carter W 149 Evan F 273
   John S 149
ROLAND, Mrs Al 149
ROLF, Vina E 149
ROMER, Arthur 227 Bertha Louise 202
   L J 227
ROMERI, Giacinto 273
RONEY, Edward T 227
RONN, Mary 186
ROPER, C H 149 Edgar A 149 Irma 186
ROPLA, Andrew 149
ROSA, Emil 273
ROSE, Anna Josephine 237 Clara 232
   Estella Edith 212 Gus 149 Mrs J W
   76 Leila 227 Mrs M 149 S I 204
ROSELLE, Phil 136
ROSENBLATT, Otto M 40
ROSEWARN, Ray 149
ROSEWARNE, W J 227
ROSITTI, Constanti 227

ROSS 40 Abram 227 Alice R 234 Beryl
   214 Mrs Dave 81 David 227 Eugene
   149 273 I W 150 Mrs J O 78 175 J S
   179 Lorin B 273 Mamie 78 Mary 227
   R A 227 R R 227 Robert 40 214 227
   Robert Ralston 40 Mrs S 176
   Vaglini 223 William 150
ROSSETTI, C 227
ROSSI 40
ROSSINI, P 150
ROSSITER, Delbert S 40 227
ROSSKOFF, Agnes M 203
ROSSOLTI 150
ROTH 40
ROTLUFF, Julius 273
ROUSE, Mrs Dortha Enola 181 Eugene
   150 Mrs G N 140
ROUSSAN, Eugene 150
ROUX, J W 40
ROWAN, Richard W 227
ROWE, B G 40 Ciussius M 150 Frank 40
   George 40 Gus 40 Hattie E 224
   Mrs T F 177
ROWLAND, Mrs A 120 Mrs F 132
ROYMAN, Joel E 227
ROYSTER, R 40 Walter S 227
RUCHETTI, John B 273
RUCKER, Addison 150 Clara 150 Earl 41
   Miles 150 W E 41 William 228
RUCKSTILL, G E 228
RUDD, Joseph 228 Paul 41 228
   Mrs Paul 150
RUDDICK, Ernest V 273 Herbert 228
   L M 150 Lewis S 150
RUDDOCK, C J 228 Calvin 87 Florence
   225 J C 150 Mrs Mary 105 Mrs Maude
   Hayter 150 Vernon 273
RUDERICK, Andrew David 150
RUDOLPH, Fred 228
RUDRISK, Adam 273
RUFF, Elsie Caroline 212
RUKKA, Adeli L 180
RUNK, Willard E 273
RUONAVAARA, J 41 John 41 228 Matt 41
RUPE, Alva 182 Ernest 228 John 182
RUPOLA, Matt 273
RUSCA, G 273
RUSCHETTI, Mary 213 P B 273
RUSCOE, Mrs W C 150
RUSCONI, A Guiseppe 273
RUSH, Anna K 191
RUSHING, Mrs E J 114
RUSS, Kenneth 150 William 150 228
RUSSE, Emma 225
RUSSELL, Dave 41 J E 228 L 273
   R D 41 Robert 41
RUTTIKAINEN, John 151
RUUSKA, Matt 41 228 Mrs Matt 151
RYAN, Ed 41 Edgar B 228 George 151
   Lottie 46 William 151
RYERSON, Adrian 151
RYNEARSON 41 C E 228

S

SAAIJARVI 151
SAARI, John 151
SACKS, Mrs John 151
SAGEHORN, Annie M 193 Lottie 228
ST.CLAIRE, Richard 41
ST.JOHN, W 273
ST.LOUIS, Effie 236
SAIVA, Ellis 273
SAKETT, Mrs A A 151
SALA, Aurelia 237 E 222
   Thomas William 273
SALAMEDA, Frank 151

SALANAVE 41 Edward 228
SALEMAN, Mrs Rose 117
SALINES, F 41
SALING, A 205
SALIR, Guilio 273
SALLA, Louise 234
SALLADAY, Rose Etta 228
SALLINEN 41 Charles A 273
  Christopher L 228 Ed 41 F 41
  Frank 41 Mrs Frank 211 John 211
  Mrs John 151 Josephine 222
  Mary J 211 Peter 151
  Robert Arthur 273 282
SALMELA 41 Matt 151 Walter 151
SALMEN, Ellis 228 273
SALMI, William 151 273
SALO, Thomas W 228
SALOMON, J L 228 Louisa 218 Mabel 218
SALSBURY, Oliver 151
SALVADOR, Annie 213 Charles 41 228
  Mrs J 140 John 42 228 Mrs John 114
SAME, P G 273
SAMPSON, Donald 229 Gus Myer 42 229
  May 151 Mrs Rachael Francana 151
SAMUELSON, A 87 Alan 229 Allen 87
  Alan 229 Allen 87 Ileen 219 Ilie
  219 J G 274 John 87 151 229 274
  Mrs John 151 Sophie 184
SANBORN, Dr Franklin H 151 229
SAND, Evelyn 229 Walter 229
SANDELIN, Frank W 274
SANDERS, Mrs Carrie 96 John 152
SANDERSON, Alexander 152
  Mrs Alexander 152 David Alexander
  152 Lorraine 239 Tom 152 Wilma 152
  Wilma Mae 196
SANDKULA, Elvira S 241 Walter
  Leander 274
SANDRONI, Gio 274 Joe 274
SANDS, Esther 194
SANEL, Earl 229
SANFORD 42 E J 42 J B 42
SANINI, Rose 222   222
SANKOVICH, Antone 152 Matt 42 229 274
  Michael 152
SANTALA, Selima 240
SANZONI, N 152
SAPP, A 42 Goldie 208
SARGENT, Lulu Pardee 241
SARGENTINE, J 42
SARGENTINI, R F 152
SARINA, Mary 232
SARJA, Andrey 274
SAROWSKI, J C 152 229 Mrs J C 152
SATCHELL Dr 152
SATNDADS, Joseph M 229
SAUDADE, John M 229
SAUERS, Carl 42
SAUKKAR, Herman 229
SAUKKO, W O 229
SAUNDERS, Albert L 76 274 D H 42
  Eugene W 229 Ida 187 J H 152
  Joe 140 152 Mrs L 152 Lawrence R
  229 Mrs Scott 163 T R 42 Tom R 42
  W S 62 187 Mrs W S 68 Walter 42 65
SAUSO, Jack 274
SAUZA, Antonio 274 Joe 274
SAVER, C W 42
SAVO, Carl 229 274
SAWYERS, Goldie 42
  H C 229 Mrs Hal F Hazel M 183
  Louis D 229 Rev M K 153 Millie 42
  Murvin Lee 42
SAXON, Hazel G 218 Laurence 229
  Lawrence 153 Mable Juanita 217
  W T 134 153 Mrs W T 153
SAYE Mrs 139
SBRANA, Bruno 153 274

SBREGIA, Settimo 274
SBROGGIA, Settino 274
SCAMMON, P F 42
SCAMPINI, R 274
SCARONA, Domingo 42
SCARRY, Mrs Ed 153
SCESCO, Amelio 153
SCHAAF, Golda 202 John 42
SCHAEFFER, Charles 153 Charles
  Christian 153 Charles F 274
  David 153 Hattie 236
SCHAMBER, Kuno 274 Matilda 236
SCHAMP, Gus 153
SCHANDRI, Albert 229
SCHAPP, Mrs Emma 153
SCHEELE, Dr F M 229
SCHEPER, Mrs Jack 112 Mrs John 207
SCHERINI, Antonio 153
SCHIBI, J B 229
SCHILLER, Mrs A W 153
SCHLACTER, Charles Percival 153
SCHMIDT, E 274 Elizabeth 215
  Herman 229 Julius 229
SCHNEIDER, Charles 89
SCHNITKER, Francis 153 George 153
SCHNOOR, Henry S 153
SCHOLL, Fred 154 Mrs Mary 153
SCHONBECK, Fred 230
SCHRANDT, Joseph 229
SCHREIBER, Henry 154
SCHROEDER, Ed 42
SCHROOF Mrs 175
SCHROTER, M 236
SCHUHL, Leon 230
SCHULTIZE, Hazel 199
SCHULTZ, Mrs Cora 109 Edna 154 G W 42
  Henry 154 Mrs Johanna 154 Otto 154
  Paul 154 Ray J 274
SCHUTZ, Luzanne H 214
SCHWANDT, William 42
SCHWANTNER, August 154
SCHWARTZ, Charles J 230
SCOBLE, William 230
SCOGGEN, James W 230
SCOOFY, L J 78
SCOTT 43 154 Mrs 132 154 Abbe P 43
  Adeline 181 Alice Myrtle 188
  Benjamin 154 274 Mrs C A 105 222
  Mrs C C 218 Chester 43 Chester A 43
  Mrs Delia 172 E S 230 Edna M 227
  Frank O 43 154 G H 181 George A 154
  George H 154 George R 230 George
  Wiley 230 H B 230 Mrs Helen 193
  Hiram 154 Mrs Joe 154 John 154
  Lloyd B 230 Mrs M S 179 Martin L
  154 Mrs Myrtle 195 Otto 43 Otto
  Harrison 230 274 Ralph M 274
  Mrs Sarah 154 Dr Saxon 43 154 230
  Will 230 William 43
SCOTTEN, Steve 154
SCRADER, George C 274
SEAHOLM, Otto 43
SEAMAN, Lena 182
SEAMMON, Paul 230
SEATON, Mrs Mabel 154
SEAWELL, Volney R 230
SEERY, John James 154
SEIDNER, Abbie 189
SELLERS, Mable 240
SEMAN, Sene 192
SEMPLE Mrs 126 Edith 188 H F 274
SENDERS, W 43
SENE, Mrs Jacob 154
SENINI, Guiseppe 230 Maddalena 230
SENTENEY, Nellie 235 S A 230
SEPANTALO, Viljo 88 154
SEPPA, Mrs Ella 155
SEPPALA, Agusti 274 August 274

SERI, Emelio 274
SERLIJA, Matt 155
SERTORI, James 274
SERVATY, A 215
SEVA, Mauriel 274
SEVERANCE, Fred A 155
SEVERIAN, Giossa 182
SEWARD, Edna 206 H T 274
SEYMORE, R 230
SEYMOUR, Albert Charles 274 Mrs Fred
    155 Frederick 155 Irene 226
    John 155 Lena 228 Ronald 275
SHAFFER, Clee 43
SHAFSKY, Mrs Albert 160 Harry 43 230
    Sam 94 Mrs Sam 93
SHANDRY, A 43
SHANE, C Donald 155 Mrs C Donald 155
SHARP, Fred 230 275 Fred Franklin 230
SHARRATT, Frank G 230 Mrs F 163
SHARROCK, George 231
SHATTUCK, W J 231 Will 43
SHAVER, Georgia 46 234
SHAW, Henry 67 Joseph 155
    Palmer H 155 William 231
    William T 231
SHE, Dong 275
SHEAN, Ed 43 Robert Edward 231
SHELTON, Birdie 205 C 43 Charles 43
    Mrs Charles 162 Clarence 155
    Eugene 43 Jerry 43 Laura E 239
    T 155 Thomas 231
SHEPHERD, Masse 111
SHER, Dong 275
SHERBORN, K J 43
SHERIDAN, Michael 155
SHERMAN, Mrs Edward 176 James
    Schoolcraft 155 John J 175
SHERRICK, C 44
SHERWOOD, Alfred 155 Mrs Andrew 155
    Charles E 44 Charles Henry 156
    Mrs Foster Elijah 156 Harry 275
    Henry 155 Homer 155 231 Mrs Ida 63
    Joe 155 Joseph Addison 156
    Lawrence T 275 Nellie 161
    Robert Foster 156
SHIBLEY, J H 44 231 L A 44 231
    Maretta O 237
SHIELDS 156 Harry LeValley 275
    Nelson 156 Rena May 237
    Willaim E 231
SHIMINOWSKY, M 275
SHIMMIN, B 44 Della 44 Estelle 212
    Robert Larue 156
SHIMONWSKY, B 275
SHINN, Frank 156 George 156
    Mrs Harriet A 156 Ruth 208 S D 156
SHIPLEY, Claude A 275
SHIRE, J B 275
SHOEMAKE, Earnest 231
SHOEMAKER, Mrs Elizabeth 156
SHOLTZ, Paul 231
SHORE, Inez 210 Sam 231
SHORES, John G 156
SHORT, Myrtle Agnes 213
SHRINGHELLI, Serefino 275
SHUDY, Janet Louise 186
SHULAR, C H 275
SHULL, D E 156
SHUSTER, C L 44 Evelyn R 187
SIALDINI, Piacentini 275
SIALVIANI, Paicentini 275
SIBBIS, Alfred 156
SIBLEY, David 156
SICHI, Lena 193 Narcisa 223
SIERCK, Russell 231
SIFTON, A W 156
SIIPOLA, Hilja 156 John 156
SILBERHORN, Mrs Anna K 156

SILL, Fred 231 William James 231
SILTANEN, Leander 231 275
SILVA, Anna F 231 Antone 156 231
    Belle 231 Casimiro 231 Cecilia 231
    Elizabeth M 219 Joe King 44 156
    L 156 Mrs Maria 44 156 Sebastian
    156 Tony L 275 William 156
SILVERA, Tonie 157
SILVERIA, Amelia 233 Antone V 44 C A
    157 Helen 206 John M 231 Joseph M
    231 Manuel 231 Theodore 157
SILVERSTINE, Henry 157
SILVERTHORN, James L 157
    Mrs James L 157
SILVERTHORNE, Mabel 18
SILVERTHRONE, Milo 44 231
SILVIA, Mrs Barbara 157 J G 157
    John 63 157
SIMEASSON, Hilda 201
SIMILA, Ella 210
SIMKINS, Charles A 231
SIMMERLY, Frank O 44 Mrs G 157
    Gary S 232 Grace 220
SIMMONDS, Seth 275
SIMMONS, Ernest 275 Johnnie 275 282
    L G 157 Seth 275
SIMMS, Pat 157
SIMON, Julius 157
SIMONA, Jennie 179
SIMONDS, Evelyn F 207 John 157
SIMONI, Alfred 275
SIMONIN, Annie 237 J 231
SIMONINI, Battista 157
SIMONS, Lois 203
SIMONSON, Ida 61 O M 44 Zacharias 157
SIMPSON, Arthur 232 Mrs H B 132
    Henry 44 157 232 275 Stella 214
    Thomas B 44 157 232 William 44 157
    William Henry 157
SINCLAIR, Ernest A 232 275 J A 232
SING, Lee 44
SINGLETON, Mike 157
SINGLEY, Carrie 130 Mrs Sarah 157
SIPE, Walter J 275
SIPILA, Elmi 201 John 228 Matt E 275
    Ninnie 228
SIPPALA, Agusta 275
SIPPOLA, Sauna Maria 225
SIRIZZOTTI, Angelo 232
SIVERTS, Sigue 218
SJOLUND, Eskil E 157 Vendel 239
SJOSTROM, Mary A 183
SKELETON, James 275
SKIFFINGTON Mrs 157 John 158
    Mrs May 96
SKIRK, William E 44
SKROZA, Emanuel 275
SLACK, F M 232 William 232
SLATTERY, John J 44
SLEEPER, Julian 232
SLOAN, Bud M 275 Ernest 158
    George 44 158 Grace T 188
SLOPER, Harold C 275
SLOTTE, Andrew 158
SLYE, Irvine Erving 275 Preston 232
SMART, Ora 141 Una 209
SMEDLEY, Joseph 158
SMIDT, Albert 158
SMILEY, Mrs J J 59
SMITH 44 Mrs 44 158 Rev 158 A 45
    Albert 158 Alex 158 Alice 192
    Ana J 158 Andrew J B F 158
    Benjamin 159 C A 45 C P 159 C W 158
    Carolino 232 Carrie 159 Charles 158
    Charles F 158 Charles H 158
    Charles L 232 Charles M 276
    Charles P 158 Mrs Charles P 158
    Clair 232 Daisy Hill 159 Dorothy G

SMITH *(Continued)*
   198 Mrs E 123 E L 45 Edna I 186
   Mrs Elizabeth Brooks 159 Emil 159
   Emily 236 Emma 228 Mrs Emma 159
   Enex F 239 Etta 240 F C 159 F J 159
   Mrs F J 159 Frank 232 Frank M 159
   Fred 45 Fred H 159 Frederick Hale
   159 George 276 Mrs George 159
   George A 232 George M 232 Gordon A
   232 H B 159 Helen 159 Henry 159 232
   J C 45 158 J J 232 J M 45 J P 45
   159 J R 182 Mrs J W 159 Jennie 159
   John 159 276 John F 276 John Henry
   276 John Jacob 276 John S 232 L S
   232 Lena E 220 Link 105 Mrs Lucy 55
   Lulu 221 Luther 276 Mrs M B 159
   Mart T 159 Mary 70 Mary Hartin 159
   May I 69 Mildred R 227 Nancy A 159
   Otto 159 P H 276 P W 227 Mrs P W 40
   149 158 Perry M 159 Peter 159
   Phoebe May 192 R E 45 232 Robert
   160 Roy 45 Ruth 159 Mrs Theora 160
   Vera 3 182 W W 159 Wallace 160
   Warner C 160
SMYRLE, Mrs Nellie 86
SNELL, Albert 160
   Mrs Emilia Peterson 160
SNICKERS, Albert 276 Mrs Ed 160
   Hulda 204
SNIDER, Abe 187 Mrs D 160 J 45
   Mamie C 187 Mattie 235
SNODGRASS, David M 232 276
SNOOK, L M 45 Lloyd Melvin 160 276
   T L 160
SNOW, Charles 160 Hazel Oletha 160
   W Clyde 160
SNUFFIN, Mrs Phoebe 222
SNUFFION, Amos 160
SNUGG, Emil 160 Erich 160 Esther 160
   Mrs Lena 160
SNYDER, Bert 232
SOANES, J L 45
SOBEY, Percey A 232
SODERLAND, John Victor 276
SODINI, Joseph 160
SOFFIA, Marian 241
SOLD, Toivo 233
SOLDANI, A 222 Joe 45 Mary 215
SOLDINA, Julia 227
SOLOLA, Ida 221
SOMERSEL, James 233
SORENSEN, S M 233
SOROLA, Khristian 161
SOSICH, Matt 276
SOSIE, Michael 276
SOUSA, J 45 John 276
SOUSI, Peter 233
SOUTHARD, Bert 203 C E 233 Carrie 229
   Mrs Fannie 161 Juanita 203
SOUZA, John 233 Manuel Carreia C 276
SPADONI, Nello 276
SPARKS, Mrs Olive 125
SPEER, Mrs J F 161
SPELLMAN, Ora 186
SPENCER, Emmett 276 H A 161
SPENSER, L D 45
SPINI, Bob 161
SPITTLER, George 45 126
SPOONEMORE, Homer C 233
SPRADLEY, J 45
SPEAR, Ed 45
SPOTSWOOD, Gus 233 J W 161 Mabel 239
SPOTTSWOOD, Joseph 121
SPOZIA, Mrs E A 54
SPRAGUE, Mrs Clair 161
SPRINGER, E C 233 Ellis 161 233
   Mrs Ellis 161

SPRINKLE, Bessie 186
SQUIRES, George E 233 Roscoe 233
   Sidna 218
SRACK, Emmet G 276
STAFFLER, Mable 191
STAGER, Mrs C 161
STAHL, Eillen 226 J 45
STAMPE, Hendrix 233
STANDLEY, Alma 241 Amos 233 Bertha M
   200 Hale 161 J M 161 Mrs J M 161
   Jack 45 Jesse 204 Ruby 195
   Mrs Sarah Charity 161 Mrs William
   161 William Raymond 233 276
STANLEY, Dick 161 Mrs Florence 226
   Geraldine 238 J 45 O L 161 Perry 61
   W 238
STARK, Felix 161 John T 161
STARKEY Mrs 161 Charles 161
STARR, Belle V 231
STAUER, Dave 162 David 161 H 46
   H J 162 Jacob H 161 Mrs Nellie 161
   162 Rose 161 162
STAYTON, Archie C 162 233 Charles 162
   Charles R 276 Inez 232 John D 162
   233 Robert 162 Mrs Sarah C 162
   Mrs Will 162
STEBI, Mrs C 162
STEDHAM, Perry 162
STEEL, Donald 233
STEELE, Miss B 49 Bert 233 Bertha L
   236 Clifford A 233 Mrs F W 62
   Fred William 233 Mary 232
   Winifred 233
STEFFANETTI, Bob 276
STEIMLE, Henry 233 Louise 186
STEMILE, William 276
STENBERG, Alex 234 P Alex 46
STEPNEY, Henry 85
STERNBERG, Charles 162 L L 162
STEUDEMAN, Eileen 162 Grace 162 H 162
STEUMBEE, Henry 276
STEVENS Mrs 79 Clara B 227 E C 276
   Edward J 46 Ella 213 Emily H 187
   Frank 162 Herman A 276 Isaac 162
   Mary 197 Mrs Mary O 98 S B 98
   Steve 276
STEVENSON, Archie 276 Charles 46
   Charles Thomas 276 George 162 204
   Hazel M 204 J O 162 James 162 Joe
   46 162 234 LeRoy 162 William 162
STEWART, Mrs C C 54 Calvin 234
   Mrs Calvin 172 Calvin C 179 234
   Ella 179 Frances Mary 241
   Mrs George 87 Mrs Guy R 146 Isaac
   162 T J 162 Mrs T J 162 W P 162
   William A 162
STICKNEY, Mrs A T 162 F W 162 Dr F W
   162 Ruel 79
STILLWELL, C W 163 Mrs C W 163 H
   Charles 276 Mrs J 163 Samuel M 277
STILWELL, John 163 Perley 277
   Robert 277
STIMLEY, Louise 186
STINSON, Lillie G 205
STIPP, A B 46 Allen George 233
   Arthur 233 Mrs C 90
STITER, Harold Harrison 277
STITT, James 232 Mabel 232
STOCK, G L 234
STODDARD E T 130 163 Ed 46
   Mrs M B 130 Mark B 163 Mrs Minnie
   Hall 163 Susie 130
STODULSK, Michael 163
   Mrs Victoria 163
STOKES, Joe 163 Vera 45 Verna 163
STOLPE, Alex 277 Carl 277 Isaac 163
   John 234

312

STONE, A G 234 Mrs A G 70 Betty 5 66
    Charles B 163 Elizabeth 5 66 Helen
    5 66 L G 234 Leonard 5 66 Lola Etta
    209 R M 234 William 234
STOPPA, Giovana 222
STORER, Mrs A C 163
STORNER, James L 163
STORNETTA, A 46 163 234 A O 163 Fred
    163 J O 46 163 234 John 234 Leslie
    163 Mary 214 Mrs Pauline 163
    Philip 46 Raymond 163
STORY, Mrs Jessie 229
STOSCHKE, Fred A 234
STOVER, Fannie May 205
STOWE, William O 277
STRAIGHT, F 46
STRAIT, Charles 277 Edgar Ernest 277
STRAND, Tom I 234
STRANSBERRY, Lizzy 211
STRAW, Edna 223
STRAWN Mrs 152
STREET, C V 163 Mrs E B 163 Will 163
STRIDER, Pearl May 190
STROM, Ada 209 John 120 Lenna 120
STROND, Mrs Hilda 163 Ray J 163
STRONG, George 46 Homer 277
    Hugo W 277
STROUD, Raymond J 234
STRUBY, Carl 46
STRUSS, William P 277
STRUZ, J G 277
STRUZZ, William P 277
STUART, Mrs Edna 164
STUDDERT, Cora M 226
STUDEBAKER, Alvin L 277 Irvin E 277
    Loretta 196
STUMP, Benjamin 277 Emil 277
    Hilda 218
STURN, Dora M 216
STURTEVANT, Rev A J 234 Arthur 234
    Crystal 65 Mrs G 90
STUTSMAN, Margaret G 226
SUCCETI, J 234
SUFFREGINI, Alberto 277
SULLIVAN, Thomas 277
SUMMERVILLE, Arthur 234
SUMNER, Charles L 234
SUNFARI, Selmia A 164
SURANTO, Matt 164
SURRYHNE, William J 144
SUTHERLAND, Arthur R 277 Eva 201
    John 164 L H 164 Robert L 164 T 46
    T W 277
SUTTA, Eli 144
SUTTON, David 164 Me 200 Peter 164
SVENDSEN, Gerhard 277
SVERKO, John 277 Joseph 46 234 277
    Matt 164
SWAIN, Geneva 184
SWALES Mrs 134 R D 46
SWAN, Eugenia Josephine 179 F P 234
    Mrs Georgia 46 William Wallace 46
SWANSON, Mrs A 120 Alfred 234 Alfred
    Donald 277 Anna M 233 August 221
    234 Carl 46 Carl Emil 235 Edith 221
    Erick 148 Gustaf 235 Henry 46 T 46
    Thomas 164 Walter 277
SWARTZ, Peter 164
SWEDEBERG, Emma 212
SWEENEY, H O 277 Lawrence 235
    Mabel 40
SWEET, Benjamin 164 Edna 238
    Reva D 185
SWEETSER, Archie Lee 235 277 Emery C
    278 282 Emory H 235 Mary M 185
    Myrtle Winifred 183
SWENEY, Mabel Harriet 227

SWITZER, A J 46 Albert 64 164 Bud 46
    Mrs Clara Moore 164 Emily Ada 102
    George 46 47 164 Mrs George 117
    George H 235 Harold Harrison 278
    John R 235 Peter 164
SYMES, Frank 278
SYPRIANO, John C 235
SYRES, William 165

T

TABOAS, Frank C 278
TABOR, Mrs E F 75
TAFT, Mrs Susie
TALBOT, Clara 80 191 Clare 191
    Eva D 187 Lillian 190
TALERI, Corinna 219
TALKINGTON, Charles 47
TALLINAN, Elva 205
TALLMAN, Elva 205 Henrietta 181
    J J 47 Jesse James 165 278
    Lilly B 213
TALUS, Andrew 165
TAMAGINI, Ernest 165
TAMBORINI, Mary 183
TANNER, George 165
TANNEY, Mrs Annie 165
TAPPINES, Martin 165
TARAMONTANAS, Kiriatos 278
TARI, Olevi 212
TARRO, Giaccomo 165
TARWATER, C A 235 Mary Ann 176
TAYLOR, Anderson 235 Austin 235
    Bertha 158 C P 278 Ernest M 47 235
    George 196 Harris 187 Hazel 196
    J T 47 John 165 Lee 47 Mrs Mary 165
    Mervin Earl 235 Nat Milton 278
    T Effie 228 Vivian 187 W R 235
    Wharton Shields 235 278
TAYLOS, H A 235
TAZZARI, Guido 278
TEALE, G F 165
TELEN, Carina 228
TENCHIO, Guiseppe 165
TENNY, Frank R 278
TERIN, John S 278
TERRY, Helen 226 L C 235 Myrtle 217
THATCHER, A 165 W W 165
THELEN, Max 47 235
THERRIEN, Eugene Clifford 235
THOM, Faith 213
THOMAS, Mrs Ariana L 165 C R 47 165
    Eva 194 Frank 235 H P 165 J G 165
    Rev J P 165 J R 165 Marguerite 190
    Mrs Phronia English 88 T F 47
    W A 165 W P 190
THOMASON, J S 165
THOMPSON 47 Mrs 132 165 A 278 A D 47
    166 August 47 165 Bernt 166 Bert
    192 Mrs Bert 162 Chris 166 Edith R
    216 Florence 101 Mrs Fred 165
    George 166 Hilda 210 Isom 235
    John 166 Mrs John 166 John S 166
    Joseph 166 L F 47 Maybelle 191
    Peter 166 Robert D 166 S R 166
    Thomas Ernest 278 W 47
THOMSON, D E 47
THORN, John Clayton Larkin 278
THORNTON, A R 166 Albert 47 Albert
    Ross 278 Ross 166
THORPE, Mayme E 233
THORSTROM, Hilia 234 J 234
THRAILKILL, Goldie 180
THRUSH, DeForrest 166 Mrs Martha A
    166 William 166 Winnie 166
THURLOW, Edwin 166
THURMAN, H A 47 Henry 235 John 47
    John Edward 236

VOLFI, Frank 237
VON EMMEL, H 49
VON HERMAN, Otto 49
VON KRUSZE, Harold Erick 279
VON KRUZE, Harold Erick 279
VOREIS, Eugene 237
VOSBRINK, Herman 279
VOSS, Henry 49

W

WAARA, Charles R 237 Charles Robert
  279 Eddie Oscar 279 Elizabeth 169
  John 169 Oscar John 169
  Mrs Oscar 169
WADE, Mrs Ada 102 Charles Henry 88
  169 Edward H 237 Gladys M 238
  Lem 169 S R 169
WAGENSELLER, N 169
WAGES, Ida Bell 190 Lena 49
WAGGONER, O F 237 Mrs O F 169
WAGNER, Carl 170 Grant 237
  Theresa 219 W 279
WAH, Jeow You 279
WAHLBERG, Mrs E J 234
  Isabelle Elvira 234
WAHLSTROM, Olga 220
WAIDI, Alma T 237
WAILES, Ruth A 95
WAINIE, Imer W 237
WAINO, Kark Hjalmar 279
WAINWRIGHT, Edward 59 Harry 59 Isaac
  59 Minnie 181 Samuel 59
WAIT, Thomas A 237
WAITE, George W 237
WAKELEY, Beth 240
WALBRIDGE, Charles 237
WALCOTT, Elmer 170
WALDNER, Ida 182 Ben 170 Bert 170
  H R 170 Walter 49 170
WALDO, Ben 237 Walter W 238
WALDSEN, Thorn 279
WALDTEUFEL, E L 49
WALDRON, Emerson 170
WALGREN, Jennie M 202
WALKER, Aaron 170 238 C M 238 Cecil E
  238 Charles 49 David 170 Elmer L
  238 Raymond H 238 279 Roy 238
  W A 238 Will 170 William 50 238
  William Earle 279 William R 170
WALL, Alex 238
WALLACE, E J 50 Elmer 50 Grace 192
  Jacob 238 Mrs Leona 186 Thomas S
  50 238 W T 170 238 William 50 238
WALLACH, Charles 50 228
  Mrs William 170
WALLEN, E W 50
WALLER, Ray W 50 238
WALLEY, Ida A 210 214
WALLGER, Ross Wessley 279
WALLI, Sophie 230
WALLONIUS, Eino 279
WALSH, Clara 220 Frank 170 George 170
  Mrs J 109 J A 55 John 140 170
  Louis 238 Patrick 170
WALSKY, Walter 279
WALTERS, Harvey J 170 Nina E 226
  Raymond 279 Roland 170 Rowland 170
  Theresa 170
WALTON, Ben 170
WALTRIP, Mrs Mary E 170
WARD, C M 238 Cleone 206 Edna
  Lorine 237 Engelena 227 Ernest 279
  Esther 87 G E 238 G K 238 George 50
  65 170 Hannah 87 Nellie 185
  Mrs Nora 170 Pearl 87 Raleigh J 280
  Mrs S 170 Mrs W B 227 Walter 50
  William W 50

WARE, Clyde 238 E W 149 Elmer J 238
  Leiland P 238 Raymond E 280 W W 238
  Mrs W W 146
WARNELL, Amanda C 229
WARNER, Erick 171 George E 50
WARRE, John 280
WARREN, B H 171 C L 171 Mrs Frankie
  88 Fred H 171 John 50 S L 171
  Samuel 280
WARTEN, James 238
WASHBURN, Cecil 171 M T 171 Mack 50
WASHINGTON, Minerva 199
WATENBERG, Myrtle 208
WATERS Mrs 101
WATKINS, Ethel May 194
WATSON, Alice 223 Crystal Delia 223
  Henry 171 John 171 Mary 171
  Mrs Rachel 171 Sadie Marguerite 180
WATTENBERG, Mrs C S 107
WAUGH, Dorothy 239 Elmer 50 171
  Fred 50
WAYLAND, Charlotte 238
WAYMIRE, Claude 238 J A 171
  Rudolph 238
WEAVER, Isaac E 239
WEBB, Mrs Martha A 171 S W 171
WEBSTER, G C 239 William 171
WEED, Gust 280
WEEKS, George F 239 William 171
WEGAR, Frank 50
WEGER, Francis M 171 Oscar 171
  Viola 179
WEGNER, F J 50 Frank 135
WEIMER, Orpha V 181
WEIR, Laura 194 Leyland P 280
WEISS, Mrs Christy 171 Frederick 171
WEISSE, John 50 239 Walter Howard 280
WELCH Mrs 241 Albert 171 Fred 176
  Mrs Lorraine 152 Mrs T 152
  Thomas 176 239
WELDON, Dayton E 172 Mrs Harry 172
  Mrs T J 172
WELLER, Alice 92 C H 172 239 Mrs C H
  172 Mrs C R 80 Charles R 172 191
  Delia 172 Elisha B 280 Flossie 172
  Mrs H A 54 Helen 189 Horace A 172
  239 Horace A Jr 50 172 James 239
  Lucile 172 M J 201 239 Marguerite
  172 Martha 201 Mattie 172 Maude 172
  Minnie 172 T O 280
WELLINGTON, Mrs E 94
WELLMAN, Blanche 225 David C 239
  Mrs E A 97 E D 172 Sam J 280
WELLS, Edward N 172 Eli Henry 172
  Fred 172 Lillie 73 J 92 Minnie 92
  Naomi 172 O P 50 Rose 73 92 Roy
  Elsworth 280 Mrs Viola 172 Walter
  Walter 239 Mrs William 73 92
  William Bennett 172
WEMPLE, L A 239
WENKE, George 172
WERENER, May 217
WERNER, Mrs F 99 Mae 29
WERTNEN, Olga 224
WESALA, Gust 55 172
WEST, Mrs E 158 Mrs Erich 173 Erick
  50 Mrs Frank 186 Gus 198 Minnie 201
  Ned 239 Sifla 195 Sophia 195
  Sylvester P 173 Walter R 280
WESTBERG, Hilda 173
WESTERBERG, Annie 173 C A 280
WESTERGART, Laura 229
WESTERLUND, J V 239 Victor 51
WESTERMAN, P B 70
WESTFALL, Fred J 280 W 51
WESTFELT, Mrs Mary E 173
WESTPHALEN, Joseph F 51 239
WETHERBY, Jack 51

Y

Z

NOTE: Officials and clergy performing
      ceremonies and services are not
      included in the Index because
      of numerous citations.